Prostitution, Sexuality, and the Law in Ancient Rome

Prostitution, Sexuality, and the Law in Ancient Rome

Thomas A. J. McGinn

New York   Oxford
Oxford University Press
1998

Oxford University Press

Oxford   New York
Athens   Auckland   Bangkok   Bogotá   Buenos Aires   Calcutta
Cape Town   Chennai   Dar es Salaam   Delhi   Florence   Hong Kong   Istanbul
Karachi   Kuala Lumpur   Madrid   Melbourne   Mexico City   Mumbai
Nairobi   Paris   São Paulo   Singapore   Taipei   Tokyo   Toronto   Warsaw

and associated companies in

Berlin   Ibadan

Copyright © 1998 by Thomas A. J. McGinn

Published by Oxford University Press, Inc.,
198 Madison Avenue, New York, New York 10016

Oxford is a registered trademark of Oxford University Press

Library of Congress Cataloging-in-Publication Data
McGinn, Thomas A.
Prostitution, sexuality, and the law in ancient Rome /
by Thomas A. J. McGinn.
p.   cm.
Includes bibliographical references and index.
ISBN 0-19-508785-2
1. Prostitution (Roman law)   2. Prostitution—Rome.
3. Prostitutes—Rome—Social conditions.   I. Title.
KJA3468.P76M39   1998
306.74'0937'6—dc21   97-17435

1 3 5 7 9 8 6 4 2

Printed in the United States of America
on acid-free paper

For Eileen

Preface

Despite the development in recent years of intense scholarly interest in the institutions of marriage and the family and the status of women in Greco-Roman antiquity and despite the survival of a great number of sources relevant to the topic (the sources are literary, legal, epigraphical, and archeological in nature), no serious and detailed study of prostitution in classical Rome has ever been attempted.[1] This situation contrasts sharply with patterns of research in other historical periods, such as the Middle Ages and nineteenth-and twentieth-century Europe and the United States, where historians have made a substantial contribution to our knowledge about prostitution. An important example is the work of American feminist historians, who have examined in detail such questions as the formation of policy and why and how women become prostitutes.

This work fills part of the gap in our knowledge about prostitution in antiquity. It originated with my doctoral dissertation, entitled *Prostitution and Julio-Claudian Legislation: The Formation of Social Policy in Early Imperial Rome,* written under the supervision of Bruce W. Frier at the University of Michigan and completed in

---

[1] The need for such a study is acknowledged by Stroh, "Liebeskunst" (1979) 335; Finley, *Slavery* (1980) 96, with n. 14. Apart from some popular surveys made by nonspecialists, one can cite two articles by Herter, listed as Herter 1 (1957) and 2 (1960) in the Bibliography, that are essentially collections of sources. An article by Adams, "Words" (1983), is an isolated example of an analytical approach and invaluable for its presentation of Latin terminology relating to prostitutes and prostitution. For late antiquity, see the study by Leontsini, *Prostitution* (1989). I am gratified by the engagement with elements of my dissertation and other published work shown by Sicari, *Prostituzione* (1991), and by Riggsby, "Lenocinium" (1995).

1986. The dissertation has been partly reelaborated and supplemented through a series of specialized studies that have appeared in the form of articles over the last decade.[2]

I am grateful for the opportunity to have presented elements of this work in a series of public lectures over the years. I have discussed my findings on the manipulation of women's status and its symbolic associations by the Augustan adultery law at the American Academy in Rome (AAR) in 1985; subsequently at the 1987 annual meetings of the American Philological Association (APA); and at the 1988 summer seminar, sponsored by the National Endowment for the Humanities, on women's dress in ancient Rome held at the AAR (in this latter regard, I would like to thank in particular Professor Norma Goldman). I spoke on the rate of taxation imposed on prostitutes at the annual meetings of the APA in 1986, on the restrictive covenant in the sale of slaves *ne serva prostituatur* at the spring meetings of the Classical Association of the Middle West and South (CAMWS) in 1988, and on the text of Ulpian dealing with the subrubric (under the delict of *iniuria*) *de adtemptata pudicitia* and women's clothing at the spring meetings of CAMWS in 1990. Various aspects of the legal definition of "prostitute" were the subject of invited lectures given at Duke University in 1990, the University of Tennessee at Knoxville in 1991, and Wesleyan University in 1993. I presented diverse elements of my treatment of criminal *lenocinium* at invited lectures at Sweet Briar College in 1995; at Indiana University in 1996; as part of the series of Parthenon Symposia in Nashville in 1996; as well as at the annual meetings of the APA in 1996.

Since this study is devoted to female prostitution, I expressly qualify all specific mentions of male prostitutes as such. When the context permits, however, "prostitute" can notionally refer to male and female. The same is true for the term "pimp": I refer specifically to the *leno* as a pimp and the *lena* as a procuress, but some contexts allow "pimp" to refer to male and female. The phrase "practitioners of prostitution" encompasses pimps and prostitutes of both genders. Text within angled brackets, $< >$, contains conjectural restorations, that within square brackets, [ ], interpolations.[3] All translations not expressly attributed are my own. The nature and scope of this work has not permitted me to add new bibliography, after it went to press in January 1997, apart from rare exceptions.

In the course of writing this book I have accumulated professional debts too great, I fear, to repay with a mere expression of gratitude in this place. My deepest sense of obligation is for the advice and encouragement I have received from Bruce Frier over the years. I must also offer heartfelt thanks to Dennis Kehoe and Susan Treggiari, who read nearly the entire manuscript different and offered many corrections and suggestions. Ernst Badian, Robert Drews, James Ely, Judith Evans Grubbs, Ludwig Koenen, Wolfgang Lebek, Barbara Levick, Jerzy Linderski, Sarah Pomeroy, William Race, Giunio Rizzelli, and Alan Watson read drafts of significant portions of the manuscript and/or of one or more of the preparatory studies, con-

---

[2] See the Bibliography for the dissertation *(Social Policy)* and subsequent studies.
[3] See Schiller, *Roman Law* (1978) xxxvii.

tributing vast improvements. Bruce Frier, Judith Evans Grubbs, Cynthia Patterson, Andrew Riggsby, and Giunio Rizzelli have shared with me portions of their work prior to publication. My Vanderbilt colleagues Joyce Chaplin and Samuel Mc-Seveney provided welcome assistance with bibliography on the problem of American slavery. I offer my profound thanks to all.

Writing this book would not have been possible without generous financial assistance from a number of institutions. These include the American Academy in Rome and the Fulbright Commission, both of which supported my dissertation research in Rome; the National Endowment for the Humanities, which enabled me to return to Rome with a Summer Stipend and a grant to attend a Summer Seminar; and the Vanderbilt University Research Council, which has provided me with ample support for leave time and travel over the years.

I could not have written this work without the unfailing assistance of librarians. During my time in Rome I was very fortunate to have the help of Floriana Bettini of the Istituto di Diritto Romano of the Università di Roma (La Sapienza) and Lucilla Marino of the American Academy in Rome, as well as their staffs. The Interlibrary Loan service of Vanderbilt University has been an indispensable resource for me for over a decade. I cannot adequately thank James Toplon and his colleagues, Marilyn Pilley and Matthew Stoeffler, for the patience, zeal, and good humor they have shown in tracking down a small mountain of requests.

Even by the exemplary standards of the American South, the hospitality afforded me over the years by the Istituto di Diritto Romano in Rome must be counted as extraordinary. It has been a great privilege and pleasure to be able to conduct research using the superb resources of the Istituto, generously placed at my disposal through the kindness of faculty and staff.

I want to thank the editors, readers, and assistants at Oxford University Press for their expert guidance in helping me prepare this manuscript for publication, in particular, Angela Blackburn, who saw it through its acceptance by the Press, and Susan Chang, Paula Wald, and Will Moore, who saw it through to publication.

Finally, I owe a special debt of gratitude to my family for their encouragement and support, especially my wife, Eileen, and my son, Thomas Albert.

Nashville, Tennessee   T. A. J. M
January 1997

Contents

Abbreviations

For the abbreviations of philological, historical, and legal literature, see the bibliography. The abbreviations for jurists' names generally follow those listed in the preface of the *Oxford Latin Dictionary* (Oxford 1982). This list refers chiefly to standard works of reference. For abbreviations of collections of papyri and related works, see J. F. Oates et al., *Checklist of Editions of Greek and Latin Papyri, Ostraca and Tablets*[4] (Atlanta 1992) (*BASP* Supp. 7).

ANRW	H. Temporini ed., *Aufstieg und Niedergang der römischen Welt: Geschichte und Kultur Roms im Spiegel der neueren Forschung* (Berlin 1972–).
CIL	*Corpus inscriptionum latinarum* (Berlin 1863–).
CIS	*Corpus inscriptionum semiticarum* 3.2 (Paris 1926).
ED	*Enciclopedia del diritto* (Milan 1958–1997).
FIRA	S. Riccobono et al., eds., *Fontes iuris romani antejustiniani*[2] (3 vols.) (Florence 1940/1969).
Heumann-Seckel	H. Heumann and E. Seckel, *Handlexikon zu den Quellen des römischen Rechts*[11] (Jena 1907; repr. Graz 1971).
ICret.	M. Guarducci ed., *Inscriptiones Creticae* (4 vols.) (Rome 1935–1950).
IG	*Inscriptiones Graecae* (Berlin 1873–)
IGR	R. Cagnat et al. eds., *Inscriptiones graecae ad res romanas pertinentes* (4 vols.) (Paris 1911–1927; repr. Chicago 1975).

ILS	H. Dessau, ed., *Inscriptiones latinae selectae* (3 vols.) (Berlin 1892–1916).
Index Itp.	E. Levy and E. Rabel, eds., *Index Interpolationum quae in Iustiniani Digestis inesse dicuntur* (3 vols. and suppl.) (Weimar 1929–1935).
Inscr. Ital.	*Inscriptiones Italiae* (Rome 1931–)
IPortes	A. Bernand ed., *Les Portes du désert: Recueil des inscriptiones grecques d'Antinooupolis, Tentyris, Koptos, Apollonopolis Parva et Apollonopolis Magna* (Paris 1984).
L & S	C. T. Lewis and C. Short eds., *A Latin Dictionary* (Oxford 1879).
LSJ	H. G. Liddell, R. Scott, H. Stuart Jones et al. eds, *Greek-English Lexicon*[9] (with Suppl.) (Oxford 1940–1996).
Mommsen and Krüger —	T. Mommsen and P. Krüger et al. eds., *Corpus Iuris Civilis* 1: *Institutiones* (P. Krüger, ed.), *Digesta* (T. Mommsen and P. Krüger eds.)[17] (Berlin 1963).
NNDI	*Novissimo Digesto Italiano* (Turin 1957–1975).
OGIS	W. Dittenberger ed., *Orientis graecae inscriptiones selectae* (2 vols.) (Leipzig 1903–1905).
OLD	*Oxford Latin Dictionary* (Oxford 1968–1982).
Philadelphia *Digest*	A. Watson ed., *The Digest of Justinian* (4 vols.) (Philadelphia 1985) [English translation with Latin text edited by Mommsen and Krüger].
PIR²	*Prosopographia imperii romani*[2] (3 vols.) (Berlin 1933–).
RAC	*Reallexikon für Antike und Christentum* (Stuttgart 1941–)
RE	A. F. von Pauly ed. (rev. G. Wissowa et al.), *Real-Encyclopädie der classischen Altertumswissenschaft* (Stuttgart 1894–1980).
SIG³	W. Dittenberger ed., *Sylloge inscriptionum graecarum*[3] (4 vols.) (Leipzig 1915–1924).
TLL	*Thesaurus linguae latinae* (Leipzig 1900–).
VIR	O. Gradenwitz et al. eds., *Vocabularium iurisprudentiae romanae* (Berlin 1894–1987).

Prostitution, Sexuality, and the Law in Ancient Rome

1

Introduction
Law in Society

1. Design of the Book

This book is a study of the legal rules affecting the practice of female prostitution at Rome during the central part of its history, a period extending from approximately 200 B.C. to A.D. 250. The focus is on the formation and precise content of the legal norms developed for prostitution and those engaged in this profession. My intention is to examine these norms in relation to their social context. The goal is not only to evaluate the extent to which the legal and political authorities were able to adapt this aspect of their law system to the needs of contemporary society but also to shed light on important questions concerning marginal groups, marriage, sexual behavior, the family, slavery, and citizen status, especially the status of women. Prostitution, for years a marginal theme in historiography,[1] stands at the center of some fundamental modern concerns with past societies.[2]

The legal sources themselves largely determine the chronological limitations of this study. The vast majority of professional interpreters of law, known as jurists, worked during this period. Its span embraces the preclassical jurists (100 B.C.–30 B.C.) and their classical successors (30 B.C.–A.D. 235).

Given the important changes in the Roman political, social, and especially legal systems in the third century A.D., and the fact that no major enactments of positive law affecting prostitution derive from before 200 B.C., the period I have selected

---

[1] See, e.g., Otis, "Prostitution" (1985) 137–138; Leontsini, *Prostitution* (1989) 12.
[2] Rath, "Prostitution" (1986) 553.

3

is a convenient frame for the study of other, non-juristic, sources of law as well. I do not hesitate, however, to adduce evidence from outside the prescribed time limits when it sheds important light on the period of study. An example is the discussion of the late antique evidence for the collection of the tax on prostitutes, which appears in Chapter 7.

The emphasis on law means that the evidence presented for analysis is Rome-centered. Nearly all of the jurists whose work is preserved in the *Digest* or other postclassical compilations lived and worked in Rome. The capital is where assembly, Senate, and—most often—emperor made law.[3] It is no mere chance that most of the nonlegal evidence derives from the center as well. The same spirit of pragmatism that informs my approach to chronological limits operates here as well. When important evidence leads out of Rome, I pursue it to the fringes of the empire. Study of the tax on prostitutes in Chapter 7, for example, takes us to such far-flung corners of the Roman world as North Africa, Egypt, Palmyra, and the Crimean Bosporus.

2. Law in Society

Throughout the book, and especially in its final chapter, my intention is to explore the "fit" between the law system and the socioeconomic reality. I conclude that the closeness of this fit is best grasped when the policies adopted by the Romans toward prostitution are measured, not against abstract and artificial criteria of success or failure, but by the standard of social adequacy.[4] My interest, then, is not precisely law, or legal history, but what might better be described as law in society.

Prostitution provides an excellent field of study for this approach, since, perceived as a social problem, it often encourages the formation of policy not only in the area of public law but also in that of private law. Sexuality is a field in which social values are often translated into legal norms in a direct, relatively uncomplicated fashion. For these reasons, the subject affords a good opportunity to understand how the Romans made social policy.

What this book offers is only part of a larger story. The reason dictating a narrow focus on law and its immediate sociological context is largely one of convenience. The economic and social factors that shaped the broader matrix in which the law existed must be reserved for separate treatment.[5] Male same-sex prostitution, an important but largely independent object of study, also merits discrete analysis, though some aspects of the status of male prostitutes are essential for understanding that of females and so are treated in Chapter 2.

Again, my method is twofold. One part is simply to discover what the law says. For all of their importance, the rules are often given in the sources in an

---

[3] This is not to deny that a number of the questions raised in the writings of the high and late classical jurists, as well as those that are answered in imperial rescripts, originated in the provinces. On petition and response as a basis for Roman policy formation, see Millar, *Emperor* (1992).

[4] On social adequacy in law, see Luhmann, *Rechtssystem* (1974) 49–54. For a recent application to Roman law, see Frier, "Bees 2" (1994) esp. 136–137, 144–145.

[5] This background is discussed in McGinn, *PRS* (forthcoming).

obscure and ambiguous way. An example is Domitian's denial of privileges to *feminae probrosae,* a group often assumed to include prostitutes but who are better identified as adulteresses.[6] Once the content of a rule is discovered, its larger meaning can be explored with reference to the social context in which it operates. So it is possible, for example, to understand better the difference between the marriage prohibitions designed for members of the senatorial order and those for other freeborn Romans.[7]

Concentration on the legal sources has its advantages but hardly enables us to escape all difficulties. Some of these are tied to traditional approaches in the interpretation of the classical juristic evidence known broadly as interpolation criticism. This source criticism, which tended to assign large portions of this evidence to the postclassical period, no longer enjoys the popularity it held earlier this century. It repays study, however, for two main reasons. First, although one may disagree with an argument that a passage is not classical, the critics' profound knowledge of the juristic sources and the Latin language makes it useful to consider their reasoning even where their conclusions cannot be accepted. Second, the interpretation of the texts in general is inevitably bound up with the challenge of source criticism.

It is consistent with current trends in source criticism to view the bulk of interventions in the juristic texts attempted by Justinian's compilers as abbreviations, as opposed to positive rewriting of law.[8] To argue for an instance of the latter, one has to be ready to provide a coherent rationale for it, that is, one that makes sense in terms of Byzantine law.[9] Nevertheless, it may be helpful to remind nonspecialists that we cannot simply assume the entire contents of the *Digest* to be classical, that the texts were also vulnerable to alteration in pre-Justinianic late antiquity, and that non-Justinianic juristic collections have their own history and thus their own problems of textual transmission.

Another difficulty is that it is never easy to take the measure of the law's effects.[10] The problem extends beyond the familiar lack of adequate sources: even with much better evidence, the counterfactual question of what society would have been like without a particular norm would pose a serious challenge.[11] All the same, it is the business of an approach attentive to law's place in society to raise this question and attempt an answer, where one seems possible.[12]

Still one more problem lies in the attempt to assess the derivation of legal norms from moral prescription and social practice. A popular, though not universal,

---

[6] See the discussion in Chapter 4.
[7] See Chapter 3.
[8] A statement of current thinking on source criticism is found in Kaser, "Jahrhundert" (1979/1986). Cf. Wieacker, *RRG* (1988) 154–182; Lokin, "End" (1995).
[9] For explicit recognition of this fact, see Beaucamp, *Statut* 1 (1990) 13.
[10] See Rath, "Prostitution" 558; Leontsini, *Prostitution* 172. For a general discussion, see Friedman, *System* (1975) chs. 3–5.
[11] See Nörr, *Rechtskritik* (1974) 146, who makes a similar point about the Augustan marriage legislation. Universal knowledge of the law cannot be assumed: Clark, *Women* (1993) 13.
[12] See, e.g., Gaudemet, "Tendances" (1978) 187; Beaucamp, *Statut* 2 (1992) 272, 337, 350–352, 368; Crook, *Advocacy* (1995) 5.

contemporary approach to explaining this aspect of the relationship between society and law contemplates a process whereby changes in social values and practices are followed, often at a distance of decades, by corresponding adjustments in legal rules. The premise is that law adapts itself to changes in practice in a gradual evolution that proceeds almost inexorably in one direction. This "evolutionary hypothesis" has been advanced in various forms with subtlety and skill by a number of social historians.[13] My purpose is not to offer a full critique of this hypothesis but to attempt an alternative explanation that I regard as a more satisfactory account of the relation between law and society.

The evolutionary paradigm is of course an important intellectual legacy of the nineteenth century.[14] Its usefulness for explaining change in ancient society is due in large part to a capacity for nuanced analysis that avoids assuming what it attempts to prove. Reliance on older versions of evolutionary theory has encouraged description of social change in broadly teleological terms, degenerating at worst into a form of presentism.

Awareness of this problem appears to be on the rise among historians of classical antiquity. In recent years, we have been liberated from the notion that the history of Roman women shows a gradual progression toward "emancipation."[15] Attempts to describe the history of the elite Roman family in terms of a long-term shift from an agnatic to a looser cognatic form may now be tending toward a recognition that these two models existed side by side in a manner that resists the conclusion that development occurred in a straight line.[16]

I agree with those who view the "evolutionary hypothesis" as particularly unsuited to describing change in law.[17] Not every social norm is translated into a legal rule. Evolution by itself cannot account for this selection, nor does it adequately describe the mechanism by which such a translation occurs.[18] It tends to assume a simple correspondence between the legal norm and its supposed prelegal version, as if legal culture were simply an extension of social culture.[19] Nor does it have much regard for the manner of application of a rule and how this may affect our understanding of its meaning.[20] It is not well suited for drawing a dis-

---

[13] See Dixon, *Mother* (1988) esp. ch. 3; Marshall, "Civil Courts" (1989) 38; Beaucamp, *Statut* 1.5, 2.368–369; Boatwright, "Imperial Women" (1991) 538; Evans-Grubbs, "Constantine" (1993) 137, 141; Bagnall (rev. Beaucamp) (1995) 84. A line may be traced from these works back through those of Paul Veyne and Michel Foucault and from there to the work of historians of sex, gender, and the family who study more recent periods.

[14] For a thorough critique, see Giddens, *Constitution* (1984) ch. 5; Humphreys, "Law as Discourse" (1985) esp. 248–250; Patterson, *Family* (forthcoming) ch. 1.

[15] See the criticism of this idea in Cameron, "Women" (1989) 17; Marshall, "Maesia" (1990) 49.

[16] This is to judge from the remarks of Shaw, "Meaning" (1991) esp. 69–70; Cantarella, "Famiglia" (1992); Bradley (rev. Evans) (1993) 239.

[17] Friedman, *System* (1975) ch. 10; Humphreys, "Law as Discourse"; Cohen, "Greek Law" (1989). See also Sawer, *Law* (1965) ch. 4. In its cruder applications, evolutionism appears to be a means of avoiding hard thinking about law. This is certainly not true of Niklas Luhmann, whose version of evolutionism is, to be sure, highly nuanced. See, e.g., his *Theory* (1985) 227–230.

[18] See Friedman, *System* 288.

[19] On the relationship, see Friedman, *System* 15–16, 168–69, chs. 8–9. Note also the argument of Luhmann, *Theory* 283, that a legal order is a normatively closed system.

[20] For critical reflections on this idea, see Summers, *Instrumentalism* (1982) 53–56, chs. 11–12.

tinction between the status of a rule upon its introduction and its subsequent role as part of a working system of legal norms, though this process itself appears broadly "evolutionary" at first glance.[21] Most telling of all, it views the formation of legal rules as an uncomplicated, linear process transforming the social norm into the legal rule, where no other interests are in play to promote, hinder, or modify the result.[22]

We require a model that explains, first, the social and legal forces that contribute to lawfinding; second, the structures and rules that make up the "law"; and, third, the impact the law has on behavior in society.[23] While the difficulties— and the importance—of understanding the effects of the law tend to receive a merited attention, the evidence from Rome for the other two elements is not appreciably better. For legal structures and rules, the problem is not only that we depend so heavily on what Justinian's compilers have left us of the juristic sources but also that the classical statutes themselves (as well as their application in the courts) have largely to be reconstructed from the same evidence, insofar as this is possible. Understanding the forces at work behind the creation of the law is complicated by gaps in the record that have helped set the teleological trap of evolutionism described above. In sum, we are not well placed to grasp the "absorption of smaller pushes" that Luhmann regards as essential for explaining the relationship between society and law.[24]

My contention, simply put, is that a study of law's social adequacy promises a better understanding of these problems than the evolutionary paradigm can offer by itself. At stake is our understanding of a basic function of a legal system, that of social control.[25] I hope to be able to contribute to the debate over the role of the Roman jurists and the relationship of their work to society at large[26] through an examination of their contribution to lawfinding in a field that they share with the policymaking of statute and emperor. We want to know whether it is possible to justify a model that reconciles the particular culture of Roman jurisprudence with the external demands placed upon it. What was the relevance of the work of the jurists to the political elite and society at large?

It is too easy to replace the evolutionist hypothesis with a static model of input/processing/output.[27] This reduces the role of the state, in its legal system, to that of an arbiter of claims made from the outside and an enforcer of the rules laid down as the product of arbitration. One might argue, for example, that Augustus was simply responding to social pressures when he promulgated his marriage legislation. A model of this kind ignores the fact that the state has interests of its own

---

[21] See Sawer, *Law* ch. 8, on the distinction between social control and social order.

[22] For critical assessment of such factors, see Summers, *Instrumentalism* 34–35, 45, 275–277. This is not to say that instances of this phenomenon are impossible. For an example that appears to come close, see what Friedman, *System* 273, describes as "hidden ratification." See also Sawer, *Law* 132.

[23] For this threefold division, see Friedman, *System* 2.

[24] Luhmann, *Rechtssystem* 51. For an illustration from American law, see Friedman, *System* 171.

[25] Friedman, *System* 18.

[26] For a recent statement of positions in this debate, see Frier, "Bees 2" esp. 144–145.

[27] What follows owes a particular debt to the work of Bruce Frier. See, above all, "Bees 1," (1982/3), *Rise* (1985), "Bees 2."

to safeguard in certain areas of legal policy; foremost among these are maintenance of social order[28] and the defense of the legal system's legitimacy.[29]

The role of organized government extends beyond that of adapting the law to social change or balancing competing interests: aspects of this role include deterrence,[30] coercion,[31] as well as the practice of persuasion, in the form of the education of all of society in the norms and values of the lawmaking elite.[32] Examples of deterrence and coercion are found in the criminal sanctions of the Augustan adultery statute, as well as in the system of rewards and penalties advanced by the marriage law and in the regulations enforcing the restrictive covenant on sale that prohibited the prostitution of slaves. Allied with these strictures is the law's educative purpose, as seen in the adultery law's manipulation of the statuses of respectable and nonrespectable women, as well as that of the husband-pimp, and in the marriage prohibitions of the *lex Iulia et Papia*. Even the pedagogic function of the covenant *ne serva prostituatur* looms large.[33]

This is not to say that such factors as competing social interests are ignored in the process of making policy. At the margins of the law, for example, in the juristic treatment of key elements of the Augustan laws on marriage and adultery, it is possible to perceive a clash of competing social viewpoints and interests. Such a struggle is especially vital when the state has not fully staked out its position or has attempted to do so without complete consideration of social usage, as seen in the tension between the rules of the *lex Iulia* on adultery and the practice of concubinage.[34]

Most important, law is an ongoing and recursive process,[35] operating at a fairly high symbolic level[36] and at the same time producing real and tangible effects on the society around it. It also deploys receptors for evaluating those effects and is prepared to make adjustments in light of this information.[37] There is good reason to think that this complex legal apparatus does not always work that well. When the Romans attempted to regulate especially delicate matters such as sexual conduct, the results were often inadequate, self-contradictory, or just bad law.[38]

To an extent, I am loading the dice by selecting a problem for examination in which concerns of public policy are paramount. Much of the Roman law regarding

---

[28] See the discussion in Cotterrell, *SOL²* (1992) 95–98.

[29] This is far from exhaustive: see the discussion of social postulates of legal systems, the distinction between public interests (those of the state or organized government) and social interests (of which the state may serve as guardian), and, last, "legal institutions," which regulate some of the basic circumstances in life, in Sawer, *Law* ch. 9.

[30] See Cotterrell, *SOL²* esp. 142–145.

[31] See Summers, *Instrumentalism* ch. 10.

[32] On the constitutive rhetoric of the law, see White, *Heracles' Bow* (1985) ch. 2.

[33] See the conclusion to Chapter 8.

[34] See McGinn, "Concubinage" (1991).

[35] For a general description of the role of communication in the making of policy, see Deutsch, *Nerves* (1966).

[36] Cotterrell, *SOL²* 102–106. Cf. Friedman, *System* 50–51, 98.

[37] As a system of communication, the legal order is cognitively open but normatively closed, in the famous statement of Luhmann, *Theory* 283.

[38] For an illustration, see the discussion in Treggiari, *RM* (1991).

prostitution is generated, not through the work of the jurists at first instance, but through legislation of one form or another. I do not, therefore, argue that the results should be generalized without qualification to the entire Roman system of law. I argue instead that this area forms part of a complex and difficult whole, and that the overall social adequacy of this system can only be the object of speculation at this point. If an improved understanding of the work of the jurists on matters related to prostitution makes it easier to concede that they were not isolated members of the policymaking establishment, more or less insensitive to various demands for social change, that will be a satisfactory result.

3. Problems with Nonlegal Evidence

Any approach to the legal sources that aims at more than an exegesis of the rules themselves introduces of necessity much nonlegal evidence, and with this arise fresh challenges to our understanding. The nonlegal sources on matters of sex and gender in ancient Rome are scattered and composite.[39] Like the legal sources, they are the product of a male elite.[40] To put the matter another way, prostitutes from ancient Rome cannot tell us their story, a traditional problem in the historiography of prostitution.[41]

The sources are, above all in the area of sex and gender, difficult to trust because they exaggerate, misrepresent through omission of facts, and prescribe instead of describe. A great deal of moralizing distortion must be expected as a matter of routine from the historical evidence on prostitution.[42] As one scholar writes, "in the realm of sex and gender the norms of practice and the norms of ideology typically operate in a state of conflict, ambiguity, and tension."[43]

A study of such evidence must present its own justification. The importance of prostitution in ancient Rome, insofar as the sources allow us to understand it, lies chiefly in its symbolic significance. Discourse on prostitution reads as a kind of shorthand for a prescriptive ordering of society on the basis of sexual behavior, or at least reputation. It is inextricably linked to a larger discourse on sex, gender, and reproduction, both biological and social.[44] In an ideal sense, social status was tied directly to sexual honor, more acutely and directly for women. The role prostitution played in the thinking of male members of the elite was a fundamental aspect of the Roman *mentalité* on patriarchy, or social hierarchy based on gender.

[39] For discussion of similar difficulties in the study of actors at Rome, see Ducos, "Acteurs" (1990) 19; Leppin, *Histrionen* (1992) 6, 71. For sexuality in ancient Greece, see Halperin, *Hundred Years* (1990) 5.

[40] For the peculiar distortions this fact tends to introduce in sexual matters, see Corbin, *Women for Hire* (1990) 203.

[41] See Villa, "Prostituzione" (1981) 307; Rath, "Prostitution," 558.

[42] See Corbin, *Women for Hire* 322, 328, 334.

[43] Cohen, "Augustan Law" (1991) 112 (cf. 119). See also Marshall, "Women on Trial" (1990) 340. For a parallel from slavery, see Bellen, "Sklaverei" (1989) esp. 208.

[44] For a recent exploration of this theme, see Edwards, *Politics* (1993) 76.

The task of interpretation is not always easy, not only owing to the inadequacies of the evidence already mentioned but also because of profound Roman ambivalence on this subject. Prostitution was both socially approved and suspect for moral reasons. This ambiguity is of crucial importance for our understanding, and an exploration of its nuances can offer a valuable insight into the interaction between morality and law.

There are, to be sure, two problems of a more general nature that it is preferable to address in this place because of their intimate connection with the formation of social policy through law, but to whose resolution this book can make at best only a partial contribution. These problems are the honor-shame syndrome and the status of prostitutes and pimps as a marginal group.

4. Honor and Shame

It is inevitable, in a book on sexuality in ancient Rome, for the issue of the honor-shame syndrome to be raised.[45] As the discussion that follows suggests, this syndrome plays an important role above all with regard to some essential features of the Augustan adultery law, such as the sexual double standard, the *ius occidendi,* and *lenocinium,* as well as other aspects of the legal regulation of sexuality, such as the restrictive covenant on slave sale that prohibited prostitution and certain of the juristic texts examined in Chapter 9. The concept of the honor-shame syndrome derives from the work of anthropologists observing traditional Mediterranean societies in the generation following the Second World War. They locate the syndrome at the level of the individual household and describe it in terms of a gender-based division of labor. The roles of men and women show fundamental differences in such societies but are also conceived of as complementary: the man protects the family's (sexual) honor; the woman conserves her (sexual) purity. The honor of the family pertains to everyone; it is collective in nature.

Any individual in the family group may compromise this honor, but women are regarded as especially vulnerable because of certain assumptions about their sexual nature. The link between personal and familial honor extends beyond the family unit, to the extent that female chastity tends to serve as a prime indicator of social worth. As such, it assumes an aspect that is almost material, something to be counted among a family's assets or liabilities as viewed by the community.

Because of the restraints on role and deportment that this value complex imposes, a woman's honor depends to an important degree on her sexual conduct or, more exactly, on the community's estimation of this. Since feminine honor defines not only a woman's social personality but also the honor of the group she represents, the integrity and solidarity of the family are threatened or even destroyed when a female member compromises her honor. For this reason, the family ideally retains exclusive control over the sexual behavior of its female members. The

---

[45] This should be distinguished from the contrast between shame-culture and guilt-culture, which was articulated by an earlier generation of American anthropologists. See Wlosok, "Scham" (1980) esp. 158, for an application to Roman evidence.

responsibility for defending the women's honor, or for avenging any breaches or affronts, devolves upon the male members of the group.

This syndrome is argued to constitute a Mediterranean-wide pattern, appearing in the basic form just described in all traditional societies of this area that have been studied, without significant differences produced by geographical situation, religious affiliation, or historical development.

The honor-shame syndrome has met with its share of controversy. Criticism arose first from anthropologists themselves, who challenged the alleged unity of the syndrome, asserting that assumptions of its historical continuity in the Mediterranean basin were far from proven. They also raised questions about its specifically Mediterranean character, demonstrating that some of its fundamental aspects are found in non-Mediterranean societies as well. This critique provoked a response that, while admitting the danger of overgeneralization, reasserted the syndrome as a unifying feature of Mediterranean cultures.[46]

Classicists, in my view, are able to avoid the weight of these critical objections by using the modern evidence as comparative data, which most seem inclined to do,[47] and by recognizing that some elements are a regional manifestation of wider phenomena associated with the sexual double standard[48] or, more broadly speaking, patriarchy.

More difficult are the objections raised in recent years by classicists themselves, above all, by Susan Treggiari,[49] to using the syndrome to explain the evidence from ancient Rome. This criticism has two main elements. One is positive, in that it associates the honor-shame syndrome with Islam. The other, negative element in summary form is that the evidence, especially that of the first centuries B.C. and A.D., does not support the presence of the syndrome.

The positive criticism is at first glance devastating. No modern traditional society studied by the anthropologists who describe the syndrome—at least none known to me—has escaped the influence of Islam at some point in its history. This includes such areas as Portugal, Spain (Andalusia and Aragon), Cyprus, northeast and northwest Greece, and Sicily, to say nothing, of course, of North Africa, Turkey, and Egypt. The only possible exception is a town in southern Italy studied by Davis,[50] though this inevitably raises a quibble about how one defines influence. To counter Treggiari's objection, we need a clear example from a society on the northern rim of the Mediterranean basin far from the reach of Islam.

A historian, Guido Ruggiero,[51] has supplied such an example with his study of sexual norms in Renaissance Venice. What he describes is consistent overall with the general features of the syndrome. It is unlikely that the Venetians imported

[46] See Gilmore, *Honor and Shame* (1987), esp. the introductory essay. The most compelling critic had been Michael Herzfeld. A survey of criticism is in Golden, "Uses" (1992).

[47] An exception is Cantarella, "Homicides" (1991), who traces developments in the law of adultery in Italy over two millennia. Cf. Hobson, "Context" (1988), who assumes continuity between ancient and modern Egypt.

[48] See, e.g., Thomas, "Double Standard" (1959) 210–213.

[49] Treggiari, *RM* 311–313.

[50] Davis, *Pisticci* (1973).

[51] Ruggiero, *Eros* (1985).

this value complex from their deadly enemies, the Turks. Moreover, Ruggiero suggests that the syndrome is perfectly compatible at root with a Christian culture.

The second element of Treggiari's critique is even more difficult to challenge.[52] Recently it has been argued that the late Republic and early Principate witnessed "a decline of the ancient 'code based on honour,' " at least among core elements of the urban elite.[53] In other words, Treggiari is correct for this sector of society and for this period of time, but her argument cannot be generalized further.

Although I am inclined to agree, I am not confident this criticism can be proved, at least not in the terms stated. What is required first is a frank statement of the strength of Treggiari's objection, followed by an examination of some of the premises of her argument. It is only by testing these, I believe, that real progress can be made.

Supporting Treggiari is the simple and obvious fact that the Mediterranean anthropologists studied simple village cultures. Roman society, as it is known to us, is a nexus of urban centers[54] with a complex high culture, not a collection of villages. The vast bulk of our evidence derives from the city of Rome, but what we can know of life lived in the towns of the Roman world suggests a complex sociopolitical structure, which is very different from the societies that the anthropologists have studied.[55]

Is it really necessary to emphasize the difference in sexual norms between a backwater Andalusian village and a metropolis with a sophisticated elite culture? A crucial distinction is the presence or absence of social differentiation itself. It is difficult to assume a homogeneity of values across a modern polity marked by a high degree of socioeconomic stratification. While one would look in vain for this phenomenon in a hamlet of the Sarakatsani, the elaborate social hierarchy of ancient Rome should alert us to the possibility, if not the actual presence, of such differentiation. The only Mediterraneanist known to me to display an awareness of this problem is Pitt-Rivers, who discusses the difference in attitudes toward honor-shame between the aristocracy and the people of the *pueblo,* or small town.[56]

Romans—for example, Tacitus and Pliny—like to emphasize the moral solidity of the towns of Italy in contrast with the corruption of the capital. The sources are not always reliable, to be sure, when they draw broad moralizing generalizations.[57] We no longer trust them on the subject of the well-worn theme of decline in morals (*Sittenverfall*). Cicero's depiction of life at Larinum in the mid–first century suggests that a lively social pathology might be found in such places.[58]

---

[52] See, however, the skepticism of Bradley (rev. Evans) 243. On Treggiari's assertion that the Romans had no word for "cuckold," see Chapter 5.

[53] Evans Grubbs, *Law* (1995) 212–215, cf. 321–325.

[54] See, e.g., Shaw, "Epigraphy" (1984) 489.

[55] So Dyson, "Rotary Club" (1992) 384.

[56] Pitt-Rivers, "Honour" (1966) 65, cited by Evans-Grubbs, *Law* 212, in support of her argument. See also Pitt-Rivers, *Shechem* (1977), e.g., 27–30, where he recognizes a further distinction between aristocratic attitudes in small towns and in large cities.

[57] In fact, a close examination of this subject shows a complexity of attitudes. See Wallace-Hadrill, "Elites" (1991) 244–249, who concludes that the Roman elite had "its ideology rooted simultaneously in town and country."

[58] Cic. *Clu.*

Moral behavior or ideals cannot automatically be predicted from an individual's social or geographical origin.

One example will perhaps suggest that, even on the level of the urban elite, we can easily misread behavior. Julius Caesar was criticized for his behavior in connection with Clodius, alleged lover of his wife Pompeia.[59] We cannot know his motives; that is, we cannot be certain if he truly believed her to be unfaithful and, if so, with whom. He divorced Pompeia for mere suspicion of adultery, which the later Augustan law would not have required of him.[60] If Caesar's personal standard was higher than that of a criminal law with which Augustus, as is commonly supposed, was trying to reform the morals and marital behavior of the Rome-centered aristocracy, where can we locate the breakdown in the ancient code of honor?

Still another problem emerges in the attempt to make a facile leap from the modern village to the capital of the Mediterranean world in antiquity. The Mediterraneanists are almost totally unconcerned with law. For them it is public opinion, operating on a very particularized local level, that makes the rules and enforces them.

It seems absurd to compare this mechanism to a comitial law, promulgated by the emperor, that laid down criminal penalties for adultery enforced through a system of standing courts employing some of the finest rhetorical talent ever assembled. At first glance it seems easy to explain aspects of the *lex Iulia de adulteriis coercendis* in terms of the honor-shame syndrome, like the *ius occidendi,* or "right of slaying," conditionally allowed by the statute to the father and husband of the offending woman. Closer examination suggests, however, that it is at times difficult to link specific details of the statute to the syndrome.[61] Even a feature of the statute as archaic and extralegal in appearance as the *ius occidendi* is too complex and sophisticated to be easily explained by the syndrome without reductionism.

These objections do not, however, prove that the Romans did not know a version of the honor-shame syndrome. At most they caution against its crude application to the Roman evidence. The question of the role of the syndrome in the formation of policy must be examined strictly on its merits. The demonstration of a Roman version of honor-shame and an explanation of its significance depend on the presentation of evidence accompanied by close argument. It is important to remain alert to differences, sometimes merely of nuance, often of substance, between the modern syndrome and its ancient Roman counterpart. But I believe that the syndrome is useful in understanding certain aspects of Roman sexual ideals and—where it is possible to discover this—behavior, especially where important distinctions based on gender are at work.[62]

This study aims, not to prove the existence of the modern syndrome at Rome, but to suggest that a Roman variant of the honor-shame syndrome helps explain

---

[59] See the discussion of the evidence in Moreau, *Clodiana Religio* (1982) ch. 1.

[60] The rules are given in Chapter 5.

[61] See Russo Ruggeri, "*Ius occidendi*" (1989–1990) 107–108, for what I view as a forced attempt to explain some details with reference to the syndrome. See Chapter 5 for discussion of the *ius.*

[62] For illustration of this point, see the discussion of *lenocinium* in Chapter 5 and that concerning the restrictive covenant in slave sale *ne serva prostituatur* in Chapter 8.

some essential features of the legal regulation of sexuality in that society. Much work remains to be done. It would be good to test the notion that different sectors of the elite exhibited different attitudes (and practices, as far as they can be recovered) regarding sexual morals. Another element of the hypothesis worth further examination is the question of change over time. The most prominent elements of the elite under the late Republic appear to have had more in common with the prevailing influences at the court of Nero, whereas the regimes of Augustus (particularly after the first decade) and Tiberius might well be compared with the ethos of the men of the political elite under the Flavian emperors.[63]

If it is indeed true that there is an elementary distinction to be drawn between the older elite of the capital and their social replacements from the urban centers of Italy and the provinces, this is a valuable insight. It helps explain, for example, the roots of the Augustan moral reform in a way that the sources by themselves cannot. The picture they paint of the late Republic as a sinkhole of moral corruption seems, to say the least, incomplete. At the same time, we are able to take seriously the content of the demands put forward by the victorious side in the Roman revolution, that is, Augustus's political power base in the Italian towns.[64] Such a model allows for at least two competing contemporary visions of Roman society. I believe it may explain the value of the Augustan social legislation to the Romans. This book can hope to contribute only in small measure to an understanding of the social matrix that lay behind the law. At any rate, a more nuanced view seems desirable if we are to understand the complex dynamics of sexuality, political life, and elite culture at Rome.

5. Marginal Status

The "marginality" of prostitutes, the legal contours of which are the essence of this book, merits a brief discussion of fundamental points. Recent years have witnessed increased attention among ancient historians to the subject of marginal types. What is new is not so much the unearthing of evidence, most of which has long been available, though not always easily accessible, in the works of antiquarians but the sophistication of method and the vigor of approach spurred by developments in the social history of more recent periods. An incomplete notice might include the studies devoted to members of despised professions, such as gladiators (Wiedemann) and actors (Leppin, Ducos), those belonging to an inferior legal status, such as Roman slaves (Bradley) and persons often inaccurately lumped together as *humiliores* (Rilinger), and the physically deformed and disabled, such as the left-handed, ugly, and obese (and many others) in Greece and Rome (Garland).

Defining a category of persons as marginal is a delicate enterprise, in part because there is no acceptable diachronic concept of "marginal group."[65] It is nec-

---

[63] For the latter, see Grelle, "*Correctio morum*" (1980).

[64] What precedes suggests an accommodation between Syme, *RR* (1939), and the famous criticism by Momigliano (rev. Syme) (1940).

[65] Graßl, "Grundsätzliches" (1988) 42; Mrozek, "Randgruppen" (1988) 253.

essary to adopt a definition appropriate to the society under study.[66] What matters most of all are those persons and groups who are stigmatized by the center, which in the Roman Empire consisted of the official social hierarchy of urban elites.

Marginal groups are not as a rule utterly excluded from a society, in the sense of being branded as absolute outcasts,[67] though some are treated worse than others.[68] One purpose of this study is to attempt to determine, through an examination chiefly of the legal evidence, where prostitutes and pimps stood on the margin at Rome. The mapping of a group's position on the fringes of Roman society is complicated by the gap that existed between the elite, whose own margin I would describe as the lower ranks of the decurionate, and the mass, or the top echelons of the *plebs*.[69]

In a sense, the lower side of that divide is where the margins of Roman society begin. This is not to deny that, ideally, marginality should be evaluated along a horizontal, as well as a vertical, axis.[70] The Roman elite, however, tended to conflate low social status with marginal status (this is especially true in the matter of sexual status), and it is difficult to escape the circle drawn by this evidence. We have here an instance of what sociologists call "social reaction," the idea that stigmatization by the center defines the category of "marginal."[71] The precise function of social reaction is linked to control, which is designed to keep the marginal on the margin.[72] The result for the historian is that the frontiers of the marginal world are not easy to locate or define.[73]

An ideal distinction might also be drawn between the conceptual categories of marginality and deviance, so that persons, like prostitutes, defined as deviant on the basis of their behavior constitute a subset of the marginal.[74] The notion of deviance helps correct a perceptible distortion in the scheme that marginality imposes on ancient societies, where the "center," identified as the sociopolitical elite, is typically rather small, much smaller perhaps than the marginal categories that encompass it.[75] It seems easier to conceive of an elite-derived norm contrasted with a deviant group (or a number of deviant groups).[76] Through the process of "labeling," deviants are rewarded for behavior that conforms to their deviant role and punished for behavior that does not, encouraging the formation of persons whom specialists term "career deviants."[77] Whether one prefers to focus on the deviant

---

[66] Geremek, *Margins* (1987) 3.

[67] See Germani, *Marginality* (1980) 8, 23, 63; Geremek, *Margins* 2–3, 8.

[68] The status of absolute outcasts is argued for the deformed and disabled in Greece and Rome by Garland, *Eye* (1995) 28.

[69] See Pleket, "Labor" (1988) 267.

[70] See the discussion in Weiler, "Randgruppen" (1988) 18, 20. Cf. Germani, *Marginality* 7, 23, 26–27, 46–48.

[71] See Bellebaum, "Randgruppen" (1988) 54; Palmer and Humphrey, *Deviant Behavior* (1990) 21, 45, 49–55, 165.

[72] Palmer and Humphrey, *Deviant Behavior* 16.

[73] Geremek, *Margins* 2–3.

[74] Students of marginality tend to overlook this distinction. See, e.g., Bellebaum, "Randgruppen" 50; cf. Palmer and Humphrey, *Deviant Behavior* 1, 8–10.

[75] For this problem, see Bellebaum, "Randgruppen" 53; Weiler, "Randgruppen" 14–15, 19.

[76] See Palmer and Humphrey, *Deviant Behavior* 3–5.

[77] Palmer and Humphrey, *Deviant Behavior* 50–52.

or the marginal as object, their study has important lessons for our understanding of the norm or center of a society.[78]

Any attempt to define an individual's status with reference to marginality is inevitably complicated by the factors of wealth and legal status, that is, whether someone is freeborn, freed, slave, or peregrine.[79] One might hazard the guess that most Roman prostitutes and pimps fell into one of the latter three categories.[80] Speculation is unlikely to be profitable, however, and thus agnosticism is to be preferred. It is simply worth pointing out the obvious, that most of the legal rules for practitioners are irrelevant for slaves and peregrines.[81] Freed status imposes its own limits on the privileges of citizenship, though these are generally not relevant to prostitutes and pimps, because they suffered from more serious disabilities than did freedpersons, as we shall see in Chapter 2.[82]

A further potentially complicating factor for the marginal status of female prostitutes and procuresses is their gender. Despite the patriarchal nature of Roman society, however, women cannot be identified as a marginal group.[83] This is partly because gender was not a unitary social category but also because Rome was not characterized by as extreme a degree of misogyny as is sometimes assumed. In fact, Roman society was not remarkably misogynist, unless one regards misogyny to be an intrinsic feature of patriarchy.[84]

The unity of the legal status of prostitutes and pimps is also undermined by the way in which it came to be defined, not through a series of related, systematic measures but in a haphazard manner in a variety of different areas of the law. These include the law of persons, criminal and constitutional law, the law of procedure, property law, and marriage law. It would not be easy to predict in advance the pattern of application of law to the status of practitioners.

Uniting these disparate strands was a double concern to protect the prestige and patrimony of the elite. The conventional construction of morality defined the elite, both by keeping out undesirables and by regulating the conduct of members who might threaten to undermine the moral hierarchy through behaving like undesirables themselves. In an important sense the elite was defined, at least ideally, in the negative by reference to those who most emphatically did not belong.[85] The classical Roman "label" promoted a relatively restrictive but absolute (as well as

---

[78] See, e.g., Geremek, *Margins* 5.

[79] For a similar point about actors, see Ducos, "Acteurs" 19, 26.

[80] Freeborn were not numerous among actors: Ducos, "Acteurs" 26. It is safe to say that most prostitutes in the provinces were peregrines or slaves before A.D. 212.

[81] In other words, the categories of moral and legal censure appropriate for members of the citizen community have no content for them. See Ducos, "Acteurs" 26, on the exclusive applicability of terms like *infames, turpes,* and *famosi* to free persons; see also Chapters 2 and 8.

[82] The status of freedpersons as a marginal group is open to question: Weber, "Freigelassene" (1988) 257.

[83] See Chapter 2.

[84] For explicit recognition of Roman society as a particular type of patriarchy, see Hallett, *Fathers and Daughters* (1984) ch. 1.

[85] It has been recognized for a long time that political and moral categories overlapped; see Earl, *Tradition* (1967) esp. ch. 1. For a pessimistic assessment of Roman ability to distinguish moral from immoral on the elite level, see Edwards, *Politics* 57–58.

permanent, for the individual) conception of ''prostitute.'' The mechanisms for determining who qualified for membership in the upper orders, as well as the principles that animated them, are essential to this study.

Uncontrolled sexuality, represented above all by adultery, posed a threat to the moral and political order. Prostitution played an important role in safeguarding this order. Though part of a disgraced milieu that embraced the lowest orders of society, it complemented the respectable aspect, which in sexual and reproductive terms meant marriage and the rearing of children. It functioned in this way for males by distracting potential predators from women whose honor was deemed worth preserving and for females by serving as a warning of the consequences should sexual honor be lost. Prostitution—disgraced but tolerated—formed a licit area of Roman sexuality and enjoyed an ambivalent status rendered the more nuanced after the introduction of the Augustan legislation on sex and marriage and the Caligulan tax on prostitution, the latter of which contributed a certain degree of legitimacy to its practice.[86]

This introduction is in part meant to adumbrate the difficulties confronting explorers in this territory. It is too much to hope that the following chapters will provide a definitive resolution to all of the many problems inherent in such an enterprise. The documentation and analysis provide a basis of study for anyone interested in the broad problem of sexuality and the law in ancient Rome. If it encourages more, and better, writing on the subject of prostitution in ancient Rome, this book will have achieved its purpose.

Another way of stating this purpose is to express the firm hope that this book communicates a sense of the subject's vast importance. A deconstructionist might argue of Augustus's legislation on sexual matters that in order to clarify and centralize the ideal, which was procreative sex within marriage, he felt it necessary to develop the margin, that is, prostitution and adultery. So on a different scale this book explores the idea that a complete understanding of the center of Roman society is not possible without a sense of how that center develops its own fringe. Prostitution is only one segment of the margin, but it is one that repays investigation with matter of central importance for the social historian of Rome.

6. Defining Prostitution

The notorious difficulty of the task of defining prostitution has probably encouraged the multiplication of definitions.[87] The German sociologist Iwan Bloch, writing in 1912, knew of hundreds of such attempts.[88] One principle is paramount: definitions of prostitution tend to be functional in nature. The specific motive for constructing

[86] For a very different assessment of the role of prostitution in Renaissance Venice, identifying it as an illicit milieu of sexuality, see Ruggiero, *Eros* 10–11.

[87] What follows is of necessity summary in form. A fuller discussion of the problem of defining prostitution will be found in McGinn, *PRS*.

[88] Bloch, *Prostitution* 1 (1912) 7.

a definition inevitably affects its content, and this is especially true of moral, legal, and medical definitions of "prostitute."

The task of definition is of enormous importance because prostitution must be distinguished from other forms of nonmarital sexual relations, including adultery and concubinage. All of these types will assume different forms in different societies. A definition of prostitution that includes the three criteria of promiscuity, payment, and emotional indifference between the partners seems best suited to this distinction and flexible enough to allow for the great variety these forms of sexuality exhibit in different societies, both present and past.[89] An objective definition of this sort helps guard against casual generalizations from present-day prostitution to that in Roman culture. It also provides a useful measure to evaluate Roman legal definitions of "prostitute," a central subject of this book.

The challenge of defining prostitution points to a deeper issue. Even armed with an adequate definition, one finds it difficult to isolate prostitution as either a legal or a sociological phenomenon. Nor would it be useful to attempt to do so, since such an exercise, conducted a priori, precludes real analysis of the content and meaning of the norms regarding prostitution.[90]

The legal rules directed at prostitution and its practitioners are rarely if ever developed without reference to the other types of nonmarital sexual relations mentioned above or indeed to the institution of marriage itself or to a range of issues intimately connected with sex and status in the broadest sense. Without full consideration of the matrix of sexuality and social structure, it is impossible to understand these rules in any significant way. A glance at any of the traditional handbooks that set forth the law of prostitution in past societies may suggest the limitations inherent in an approach that neglects the broader historical context.

7. Prostitution, Sexuality, and the Law

Ancient Rome, to be sure, knew no "law of prostitution." Such an acknowledgment betrays a central conclusion of this book, but it should surprise few of my readers, and perhaps no one who has taken a hard look at the Table of Contents. The book is organized in terms of the several areas of the law in which rules concerning prostitution manifest themselves. One encounters mention of prostitutes among the disqualifications for town councillors and in other provisions affecting one's status as a citizen, in the law of marriage, criminal law (adultery), tax law, the law of slave sale, and a wide range of juristic passages dealing with various unrelated aspects of Roman private law. Far from suggesting a unified, coherent line in the policies adopted by emperors and jurists, these areas show a diversity of approach that extends into incongruency and even contradiction.

[89] I take this definition from the work of sociologists: Flexner, *Prostitution* (1914) 11; Davis, "Sociology" (1937) esp. 748–749; Palmer and Humphrey, *Deviant Behavior* 150.

[90] The need for a broader perspective is generally accepted in the historiography of prostitution. See, e.g., Goldman, *Gold Diggers* (1981) 9.

Chapter 2 contains a comprehensive discussion of the civil status of pimps and prostitutes. By what means, and under what rationale, did the Romans exclude these persons from the enjoyment of political rights? What was the nature of various legal disabilities imposed on them? I propose a synthetic explanation of how the Romans' conception of sexual and social honor influenced their perception of the ideal distribution of rights within the citizen community (See the section "The Core of *Infamia* and the Community of Honor"). They attempted to put this ideal into practice in a manner that is imperfectly articulated in positive law but that deeply influenced its application.

Separate chapters (3 and 5) discuss the Augustan laws on marriage and adultery, which deal extensively with prostitution and its practitioners. In fine, this legislation aimed to keep pimps and prostitutes out of the upper classes and to prevent members of those classes from behaving, in effect, like pimps and prostitutes. It attempted this through a manipulation of social status, insofar as received opinion linked social status to sexual behavior. For example, the adultery law punished female offenders by relegating them to a class of "prostitutes," and it punished their complaisant husbands by creating a new criminal offense, that of the husband-pimp. Two more chapters (4 and 6) treat subsequent legislative amendment and juristic interpretation of these laws and show how an attempt was made to reconcile the laws with each other and with the existing social reality.

Chapter 7 examines the tax on prostitutes imposed by Caligula and its subsequent history.[91] The primary, if not exclusive, motive for introducing the tax was to increase state revenue. The evidence suggests the immense profitability of prostitution in most of the Roman world. More interesting perhaps are the implications of the tax for legitimizing the practice of prostitution. Whether deliberately intended or not, this tendency toward legitimizing represents an important current in public policy toward prostitution, one that runs counter to other trends.

In Chapter 8, I treat a special category of imperial legislation that dealt with contracts for the sale of slave women under a covenant that they not be prostituted by the buyer.[92] Its importance lies principally in the fact that it represents the limit of Roman official intervention for the amelioration of conditions affecting the practice of prostitution. Here we can trace the intrusion of public policy considerations in the field of private law, a central concern of the Conclusion.

Chapter 9 reviews a diverse assortment of legal sources directly linking prostitution and the private law. One of these suggests how the value complex known as honor-shame explains the decrease in value of a slave given as "real" security (*fiducia*/pledge) after she has been prostituted. A series of passages dealing with inheritance, mandate, and *usucapio* in sale show a concern with wasteful expenditure connected with prostitution. On the other hand, the prostitute was not denied her fee, as a text on *condictio* shows. A similar respect for the rights of prostitutes (and their owners, in the case of slaves) is not displayed by juristic discussions of problems arising under theft and wrongful appropriation. The competing claims of

---

[91] This is a revised version of McGinn, "Taxation" (1989).
[92] This is a revised version of McGinn, "*NSP*" (1990).

honor and economics are seen to intersect in a series of texts treating inheritance, arbitration, and *operae*. Finally, the conduct of respectable women is at issue in a passage concerning the delict of *iniuria* (outrage), and a passage dealing with gift raises interesting questions about the nexus linking sexual behavior with social status.

The evidence from the jurists is so varied in fact that comprehensive discussion of all the issues they raise is not possible in this book. Instead, I offer a summary of my conclusions, reserving more detailed treatment for specialized publications.

The Conclusion (Chapter 10) contains a brief synthesis of the arguments presented in preceding chapters. I identify the main trends in Roman policy, which are strikingly diverse in character, and suggest the approaches of policy that tie these trends together.

2

Civic Disabilities

The Status of Prostitutes and Pimps as Roman Citizens

1. Women and Citizenship

> There are many points in [Roman] law where the condition of females is inferior to that of males.
>
> —Papinian (31 *quaest.*) D 1.5.9

> All men rule over women, we rule over all men, but women rule over us.
> —Cato the Elder *apud* Plut. *Cato M.* 8.2

The disabilities imposed on prostitutes and pimps constitute a broad range of infringements on their rights and standing as Roman citizens. This chapter examines only a segment of these: disabilities relating to political and social life, on the one hand, and to the operation of the courts, on the other. The imposition of certain disabilities in other areas, such as marriage, taxation, and private law, forms the subject of later chapters.

Citizenship is an ambiguous institution, one of whose basic functions is to discriminate.[1] Like many such definitions ancient and modern, that of Roman citizen was informed by certain criteria that excluded individuals from the category that it defined. The definition is of necessity complicated by the fact that, once the dividing line between citizen and noncitizen was drawn, the definition did not stop there but articulated a range of differences on the citizen side of the line.[2] A further

---

[1] For what follows, see Riesenberg, *Citizenship* (1992) esp. xvii.

[2] The distinction between citizens and noncitizens is not always as simple as it might seem, to judge

complication arises in the historical evolution of the definition and its components. A concrete example is the development in the early Empire of the distinction drawn, with resonance mostly for public, especially criminal, law, between *honestiores* and *humiliores,*[3] which is not an isolated instance.[4]

The phenomenon I describe is recognized and, in its most important aspects, well understood in the standard works on the subject of Roman status.[5] Little attention has been paid, however, to the role of honor, particularly sexual honor, in this system of status differentiation.[6] The problem of charting the influence exerted by questions of sexual honor is a delicate one, especially because women in antiquity were routinely excluded from many of the privileges and responsibilities of citizenship, to the point where their very status as citizens might be questioned.[7]

Aristotle defines the citizen as someone with the right to participate in judicial functions and in office.[8] It has been argued persuasively (against a widely held modern view) that this exclusion from the public sphere did not prejudice the citizen status of Athenian women by relegating them to a second-class or partial citizenship.[9] The definition of the status of Roman women, who were commonly described as *cives,* is perhaps less problematic. To be sure, they were routinely excluded from the public sphere, often with the justification that they were the "weaker sex."[10] But many criteria have an equal, if not better, claim than gender

---

from the treatment of *peregrini* as "pretend-citizens" for certain purposes: Gardner, *Being* (1993) 187–191. The situation of marginal groups such as *incolae* shows interesting complications on the municipal level: Millar, "Empire" (1983) 81; Mrozek, "Randgruppen" (1988).

[3] It is generally accepted by specialists that no strict dichotomy existed, certainly in the classical period, which of course hardly means that social status was an irrelevant factor before the law. See Garnsey, *Status* (1970) esp. 234, 278–280; Rilinger, *Humiliores* (1988).

[4] For example, Link, "Bürgerrecht" (1995), argues for the development in the very early Principate of a differentiation in the content of grants of citizenship to provincials. See also the roughly contemporary institution of Junian Latinity.

[5] The bibliography is enormous, and only some of the more important contributors can be listed here (more literature is found in the notes to this chapter and in the Bibliography): Garnsey, *Status*; Sherwin-White, *Citizenship*[2] (1973); Nicolet, *World* (1980); Alföldy, *Social History* (1988); Rilinger, *Humiliores*; Gardner, *Being.*

[6] An exception worth noting is Gardner, *Being* esp. ch. 5.

[7] Another enormous bibliography looms here, but a short list should include Pomeroy, *Goddesses* (1975) chs. 8–10; Waldstein, "Stellung" (1983); Peppe, *Posizione* (1984); Gardner, *Women* (1986); Dixon, "*Infirmitas*" (1984); Beaucamp, *Statut* 1 (1990), 2 (1992); Bauman, *Women* (1992); Gardner, *Being* ch. 4.

[8] Arist. *Pol.* 3.4 (1275 A 22).

[9] See Patterson, "*Attikai*" (1987). For what I take to be a restatement of the older, male-oriented, view of citizenship, here regarding the role of women in the Greek East during the Roman period, see Van Bremen, *Limits* (1996) e.g., 85.

[10] See Dixon, "*Infirmitas.*" I am not persuaded by her thesis that this notion was a Greek import: Colum. 12 pr. 4–5 opines that it is women's physical weakness, and its psychological consequences, that render them unfit for the male pursuits of agriculture and warfare. The Romans hardly needed the Greeks to arrive at this conclusion, whatever one thinks of it. See also Beaucamp, *Statut* 1 esp. 11–16, *Statut* 2.49, 266, 273, 282, 292, 368; Marshall, "Maesia" (1990); Bauman, *Women* esp. 232 n. 30; Clark, *Women* (1993) 56–62, 139.

to establish a ranking of citizens, such as social and economic status, kinship, and community.

On balance, there is no serious case to make that Roman women were not citizens. The question of whether they were second-class or partial citizens is trickier and depends to a great extent on what criteria one selects for a definition of "citizen." This is all the more difficult because modern debates on women's status inevitably intrude and threaten to distort the argument, so that Roman women may be held up as an example to follow or avoid by anyone with a case to make. It is preferable in my view to avoid the wholesale assigning of Roman women to the ranks of a second-class status, above all, on the basis of a male-oriented definition of citizenship. More important, it is not the best way of understanding their position in Roman society.

Patriarchy, of course, implies a hierarchy of gender. There is no cause to assert that Roman society formed some odd exception to this principle or that it was simply not a patriarchy. Above all, the point I want to make is that women were not consigned to the margins of society because of their gender.[11] This is important for understanding the situation of prostitutes, who really did suffer an inferior status.

A disability that applies to more than one category of person does not always have the same rationale in each case.[12] A denial of a privilege, for example, to the deaf, may be intended neither to punish nor to express moral disapprobation. This is true even for those categories lumped together as "*infames*" (see below). The distribution of privilege in Roman society is a tangled affair, and it is hoped that tracing the thread of disabilities imposed on prostitutes and pimps may assist others interested in taking apart for examination this complex fabric.

2. Religious, Political, and Civic Disabilities Imposed on Prostitutes and Pimps

Under the Republic, prostitutes and pimps were burdened with a bundle of restrictions that were apparently discrete and unrelated.[13] They were kept from public office, and limits were placed on their access to the private law system. These disabilities varied greatly in terms of their rationale, mechanism, and effects. By the late second century A.D. at the latest, they had become part of a much tighter, more coherent set of restrictions, which were imposed in predictable circumstances, largely by the legal system itself, and which gave rise to uniform results. They amounted to a prescribed set of exclusions from the responsibilities and privileges of a full Roman citizen, disabilities that pimps and prostitutes shared with other socially marginal types, like actors and gladiators. We begin with religious worship

---

[11] Contra Weiler, "Randgruppen" (1988) 20, citing De Ste. Croix.

[12] See Gardner, *Being* 110.

[13] For the historical development described here, see Nicolet, *World* (1980) 9.

and then proceed to the arena of political and civic life,[14] from which women were formally excluded.

Cult

The participation of Roman women in religion was structured in a manner that reflects deeply embedded notions about the connection between social status and sexual behavior. On the most elementary level, the organization of religious experience for females shows a reverence for hierarchy that finds easy parallels in other spheres of social and political life. Limitations of space forbid a complete survey of Roman women's participation in cult. This would include consideration of Vestals, the cult of Isis, and household rites. The Vestals straddle conventional gender classifications, whereas the cult of Isis, who was herself said to have been a prostitute, tends to obliterate them.[15] Not all the cults surveyed here qualify as state observances,[16] a distinction that is not crucial for this discussion.

Cults were identified as suitable for women of high or low status (e.g., patrician or plebeian), women who were old or young, married or unmarried, respectable or nonrespectable.[17] The relationship between some of these categories is of particular interest, especially those that intersect conceptions of sex and status.

The estrangement of practitioners of prostitution from the life of the community is informed in several respects by their part in cult. Prostitutes did play an important role in religious celebrations, above all in the Floralia.[18] This participation is significant because it guarantees the integration, however qualified, of the prostitute into the citizen body. Utter outcasts would not have been granted as much. Indeed, it is no small measure of the different valuation placed on pimps that they are not known to have played any explicit role in public cult.

All the same, the analogy between status and role in cult of respectable women and prostitutes can be taken only so far. Participation in cult by respectable women is convincing evidence that they were not second-class or partial citizens.[19] The same is not precisely true for prostitutes. In their case, it is fair to say that the articulation of religious ceremony may have excluded as much as integrated. Prostitutes were by implication banished from certain cults celebrated by respectable women, such as the rituals for the Bona Dea performed by the wife of

---

[14] For the distinction, see Nicolet, *World* 8.

[15] For the Vestals, see Beard, "Status" (1980); Beard "Re-reading" (1995). For Isis, see Pomeroy *Goddesses* 217–226; Kraemer, *Her Share* (1992) ch. 6.

[16] See Palmer, "Shrines" (1974) 122–123.

[17] Palmer, "Shrines" (1974); Pomeroy, *Goddesses* 206; Sensi, "Ornatus" (1980/1981) esp. 66, 76; Kraemer, *Her Share* 50; Bauman, *Women* 15–18, 23–24.

[18] Herter 1.1178, 1203; Herter 2.98; Wissowa, *RE* Floralia (1909); Scullard, *Festivals* (1981) 110–111 (Apr. 27). On the connection of the Floralia with the mime, see now Leppin, *Histrionen* (1992) 28. Compare the Vinalia (below) and the Larentalia, which honored Acca Larentia, the prostitute-benefactor of Rome: Herter, 1.1178; Scullard, *Festivals* 210 (Dec. 23).

[19] Convincingly argued by Peppe, *Posizione* esp. 14–16, 144–147. Kraemer, *Her Share* 64–65, equivocates.

the *pontifex maximus* and the rites of the goddess Ceres.[20] The formulation of a rhetorical *lex* by Seneca the Elder that forbade unchaste women to serve as priest-esses[21] suggests a fundamental exclusion of prostitutes from any role as official celebrants in cult.

More significant is the positive aspect, the relegation of prostitutes to a separate cult either by themselves or among a group of nonrespectable women. *Meretrices* were banished to the rites of *Venus Erycina extra portam Collinam,* while respect-able women worshiped the goddess on the Capitoline in connection with the festival of the Vinalia Priora.[22] The cult had been imported from Sicily and "cleaned up" in its manifestation on the Capitoline.[23] The other version of the cult was set up outside the *pomerium,* as was the rule for *peregrina sancta,* and perhaps retained something of its non-Roman flavor.[24]

Mulieres humiliores, a category that must have included prostitutes, were as-signed to the cult of Fortuna Virilis, *honestiores* to that of Venus Verticordia, celebrated on the Kalends of April.[25] The Nonae Capratinae were celebrated on July 7 by the *feriarum ancillae,* a group considered by moderns to include both slaves and women of servile origin (compare the ritual physical abuse of a slave woman by matrons at the Matralia, the feast of Mater Matuta held on June 11).[26] Both categories will have included prostitutes. The rites, sexually explicit in con-tent, parodied or paralleled the cults observed by respectable women.[27] Sacral pros-

[20] Prostitutes and pimps were routinely excluded from temples, according to Sen. *Contr.* 1.2.2, 4, 10. For cult worship by *matronae,* see Gagé, *Matronalia* (1963); Bauman, *Women* 240 n. 13; and, specifically on the cult of Ceres, Pomeroy, *Goddesses* 216–217. *Paelices,* a category that probably included prostitutes, were explicitly forbidden the worship of Juno Lucina: Gell. 4.3.3; Festus 248L. The epigraphical record shows that worship of the Bona Dea was not limited to aristocratic women: Kraemer, *Her Share* 53. According to Ovid. *Fasti* 6.473–568, only *matronae* were admitted to the Matralia (the rites of Mater Matuta), while slaves were specifically excluded (except one, evidently admitted for purposes of ritual abuse; see below).

[21] Sen. *Contr.* 1.2 *thema:* "sacerdos casta e castis, pura e puris sit."

[22] Apr. 23. See *Fasti Praenestini;* Ovid. *Fasti* 4.863–900; Wissowa, *Religion*² (1912) 290–291; Schilling, *RR* (1982) 258–259; Latte, *RR* (1960) 85–86; Eisenhut, *RE* Vinalia (1965); Humbert, *Re-mariage* (1972) 51; Scullard, *Festivals* 106–108.

[23] Schilling, *RR* 237–239, 249–250. Palmer, "Shrines" 136, relates the introduction of worship of Venus Verticordia (see below) to a desire to counter "any unwholesome influences" from Venus Erycina. On the cult in Sicily, see below and Eppers and Heinen, "*Servi Venerii*" (1984) 228 with n. 17.

[24] Schilling, *RR* 262. Cf. Wissowa, *Religion*² 291; Latte, *RR* 185 n. 4. Schilling, "Vénus" (1980), finds a similar phenomenon outside Casinum: a temple of Venus that attracted a number of freedwomen, some bearing names reminiscent of famous Greek prostitutes; the whole context is redolent of Greek influence. Zucca, "*Venus*" (1989), illustrates the ties that link worship of Venus Erycina in Sicily, Sardinia, and Africa.

[25] See Pomeroy, *Goddesses* 208–209, and Kraemer, *Her Share* 57–58, who assume "courtesans and prostitutes" to have exhausted the category of *humiliores,* but there is no evidence to support this: *humiliores* means "lower-status women" and has a social, as well as sexual, component. Kraemer, *Her Share* 60–61, makes the interesting suggestion that Ovid's conflation of the cults of Fortuna Virilis and Venus Verticordia (*Fasti* 4.133–164) was intended to elide the distinction between respectable and nonrespectable women.

[26] Plut. *Quaest. Rom.* 16. On the festival, see Scullard, *Festivals* 161–162.

[27] On this festival, see Gagé, *Matronalia* 17–18.

titution, which was not a Roman tradition, may be understood to have functioned in a similar way, admitting a role for prostitutes in cult while at the same time marking them apart from the rest of the community.[28]

Prostitutes were regarded as so impure that a priestess could not even encounter one without dishonor.[29] Typically, festivals gave prostitutes an opportunity to ply their trade, and little more.[30] Where they were admitted, this was done in a manner that emphasized their isolation from the rest of the community. The magnitude of the divide that separated them from respectable women is perhaps represented best by a standard feature of their own festival, the Floralia, where (we are told) prostitutes stripped themselves naked at the urging of the public. Nothing can testify more decisively to their total lack of honor.

In sum, the status and role of female prostitutes in cult testifies eloquently to their ambiguous position as members of the citizen community. Participation by matrons in religious matters highlighted and even guaranteed their status as full citizens, but the same is not true for prostitutes. Although their inclusion in cult is important in itself,[31] their relegation to separate rituals and institutions emphasized the gulf that existed between them and their respectable counterparts, defining their status as citizens in a manner that suggests that it was sexual honor more than gender itself that was decisive in articulating differences of standing among citizens. Women's status depended in part on their chastity, or perceptions of it. A firmly established principle of Greek and Roman thought identified as one "the virtue of women and the welfare of the state."[32] This formed part of a broader notion that privilege and moral worth should go hand in hand. This conclusion is borne out by an examination of other aspects of the status and role of male and female practitioners of prostitution in the Roman community.

Office-Holding and Public Life

We begin with a brief look at the exclusion of prostitutes and pimps from the senatorial order, the equestrian order, the roll of judges *(album iudicum),* the decurionate, and the army. The treatment will of necessity be summary in nature, relying heavily on the detailed studies of others. This approach is partly predicated on the curious fact that, although direct information on the status of practitioners in these areas is extremely limited, the overall picture drawn of their situation is noncontroversial. It must be stressed that, since women were routinely barred from participation in most facets of public life, the following discussion concerns only male pimps and prostitutes, apart from explicit indications to the contrary.

[28] See Herter 2.72–73.

[29] Sen. *Contr.* 1.2.3, 5, 7; cf. 2, 4, 10, for the implication that they were barred from temples.

[30] See Chapter 7, below; Herter 2.86. Perhaps this is how some of the Christian evidence on the involvement of prostitutes in cult should be understood. See, e.g., Tert. *Apol.* 15.7; Min. Fel. 25.11.

[31] Participation of prostitutes in festivals and other public occasions can be understood as a sign of their integration into the community: Rath, "Prostitution" (1986) 569; Geremek, *Margins* (1987) 241.

[32] Pomeroy, *Goddesses* 211.

The Senatorial and Equestrian Orders

If we imagine a pimp with political ambitions at Rome, it is difficult to avoid a sense of the ludicrous. The barriers to entry into public life were high enough without this burden.[33] In all periods, the qualifications for advancement were social and economic more than legal: prestige, wealth, education, and political support.[34] Even if narrowly construed, the barriers were insuperable for such persons. Let us suppose that a pimp possessed, besides free birth, an adequate census.[35] How would the man find himself in a position to fulfill the 10 years of military service required until Sulla's day,[36] and how could he muster the political support necessary to be elected to an entry-level political office, even if he avoided the oversight of the censors (or, later, those with censorial authority), whose approval was—before Sulla—necessary for gaining admission to the Senate, and was, even afterward, necessary to remain there?[37]

A tenuous, unstable unity within this system of disbarment may be discerned in the operation of the *regimen morum,* the routine by which the censors advanced appropriate men to and removed dishonored men from positions of social prominence and political responsibility.[38] Their most effective weapon was at one time perhaps the sheer inculcation of shame,[39] but our evidence attests to a more concrete means of repression at their disposal. These magistrates reviewed all the necessary qualifications for high rank, including birth, property, physical ability, and professional behavior, as well as moral character.[40] This moral oversight was exercised every five years at the census, when the *lectio senatus* and *recognitio equitum* took

[33] The official and unofficial requirements are explored by Wiseman, *New Men* (1971); Nicolet, "Classes" (1977); Nicolet *World* introduction, esp. 6; Raepsaet-Charlier, "Egalité" (1982); Hopkins, *Death* (1983) chs. 2–3.

[34] Syme, *Tacitus* 2 (1958) ch. 43. Compare the four criteria for membership in the elite offered by Alföldy, *Social History* 106: wealth, office, social prestige, membership in an *ordo.*

[35] Free birth was required of senators, equestrians, and *equites* who sat on the jury panels: *Tabula Bembina* (lex Acilia repetundarum [?], 123–122 B.C. [?]) = *FIRA* 1² 7.13–14, 17. See Lintott, *Reform* (1992) 90–93, 116–118. Augustus set the minimum census for senators at HS 1,000,000 probably in 18 B.C. or soon after; see Talbert, *Senate* (1984) 10; Chastagnol, *Sénat* (1992) ch. 3. Before then, the HS 400,000 required of equestrians since the early second century seems to have held for them as well; see Nicolet, "Cens" (1976/1984). On Guarino's criticism of this argument for the period preceding the first century B.C., see Nicolet, "Augustus" (1984) 91, also 98.

[36] Polyb. 6.19.1–5. As *equites equo publico,* young aristocrats would fall directly under the purview of the censors: Nicolet, "Cens" esp. 146–152. (On pimps, prostitutes, and army service, see below.)

[37] I can find no evidence for the advancement of practitioners of prostitution even at much lower levels, for example, in that nursery of social climbers known as the apparitorial *decuriae:* Purcell, "Apparitores" (1983); Badian, "Scribae" (1989). The Sullan *lex de XX quaestoribus* ordained that *viatores, praecones,* and (a fortiori) *scribae* should be *eo ordine digni: FIRA* 1² 10.1.32–37, with Cic. *Clu.* 126; Cohen, "Ordines" (1984) 38–41.

[38] See Nowak, *Censoren* (1909); Schmähling, *Censoren* (1938); Suolahti, *Censors* (1963) 47–52; Pieri, *Cens* (1968) 99–122; and more recently, the surveys of Astin, "*RM*" (1988), and Baltrusch, *RM* (1989) 5–30; cf. the comments of Schrage, "Infamie" (1990) 391.

[39] See Wlosok, "Scham" (1980) 158.

[40] For the composite nature of *dignitas,* see esp. Nicolet, "Augustus" 91, 92–93, 95.

place.[41] The censors enjoyed a broad discretion but tended to respect certain principles, for example, in the certification of qualified ex-magistrates as senators.[42] Dionysius of Halicarnassus found the *regimen morum* remarkable because it extended into the Romans' bedrooms.[43] In other words, it respected no distinction between public and private realms.[44]

Moreover, although there were no strictly defined categories of offenses, several areas consistently formed the focus of the censors' attentions:[45] military indiscipline, religious offenses, dereliction of public duty or abuse of magisterial power, conduct detrimental to the censorial authority, and waste or mismanagement of patrimony, especially ostentatious consumption.[46] Pimps and prostitutes did not stand a chance of admission to the higher orders of Roman society,[47] where, both ideally and, to a great extent, in practice,[48] position was correlative with moral worth, as defined by the political community.

The censors' purview might extend over areas where legal liability arose, under both the law of delict and the criminal law.[49] The consequences of their intervention, however, lay essentially outside the legal realm, producing, overall, no negative impact on the exercise of private or even public rights beyond those occasioned by diminution of status brought about by the *nota,* and this required confirmation by successive censors in order to last.[50]

Under the Empire, the responsibility for moral oversight of society passed to the emperors,[51] who by legislating created a number of automatic exclusions from high rank.[52] A Republican precedent is the *lex Roscia* (67 B.C.), which excluded

---

[41] Suolahti, *Censors* 41–43, 53–56; Wiseman, "Definition" (1970) 68 (arguing persuasively that the *recognitio* took place before the closing of the *lustrum*); Astin, "*RM*" 26–32.

[42] Nicolet, "Classes" 730; Astin, "*RM*" 19–26.

[43] Dion. Hal. 20.13.2–3.

[44] Gizewski, "Mores" (1989) 87, 89–90.

[45] See the discussion in Astin, "*RM*" 20–26.

[46] Excessive spending on prostitutes was, not surprisingly, a target of censorial reproof. This to judge from Scipio Aemilianus's attack on Claudius Asellus, shortly after the former's censorship (Gell. 6.11.9 = fr. 19M): "si tu in uno scorto maiorem pecuniam absumpsisti, quam quanti omne instrumentum fundi Sabini in censum dedicavisti . . . si tu plus tertia parte pecuniae paternae perdidisti atque absumpsisti in flagitiis. . . ." See Astin, "*RM*" 24.

[47] Also excluded were public performers, who were denied all political rights. Nicolet, *Ordre* 1 (1966) 87–88, admits the exclusion of actors from the *ordo equester* but not that of gladiators, a distinction that does not convince.

[48] This is not to deny the arbitrary behavior of some censors, which, I believe, receives fairly full attention from the sources. The qualified optimism of Astin, "*RM*," on the efficacy of the *regimen morum* is most welcome. Of course, there were periods in which the system experienced great strain, above all, in the late Republic.

[49] Kaser, "Infamia" (1956) 225–226.

[50] Kaser, "Infamia" 226.

[51] See Greenidge, *Infamia* (1894) 82–87, 96–105; a thorough study of the imperial censorship is needed. Baltrusch, *RM* 133–189, analyzes the role of imperial legislation, especially the Augustan social legislation, in the regulation of morals. On the politicization of and consequent loss of legitimacy by the censorship in the late Republic, see Baltrusch, *RM* 27–30.

[52] At the time of the last civil wars of the Republic, when the normal mechanism of censorial approval ceased to operate, an anticipation of the later imperial system of promotion can be seen in

from the XIV Rows it reserved for equestrians in the theater[53] *decoctores* (this is consistent with the requirement of an equestrian census), gladiators (i.e., *auctorati*),[54] freedmen,[55] and actors,[56] defining, at least indirectly, the membership requirements for the equestrian order.[57] In the late Republic, individual criminal statutes included loss of *dignitas* and ineligibility for office as penalties; a summary of relevant offenses perhaps appeared in the Augustan *lex Iulia iudiciorum publicorum*.[58]

Law obviated the need for authoritative intervention in individual cases, the political costs of which might be rather high, as the delicacy of the approach taken by Augustus and Claudius to the *regimen morum* suggests.[59] Imperial legislation assisted in the creation of a mechanism that placed tight controls on access by newcomers.[60] Augustus restricted the wearing of the *latus clavus,* a status signifier consisting of a broad purple stripe on the tunic, to the sons of senators, which made the order, in a very broad sense, hereditary;[61] entry into the minor offices that enabled young equestrians to embark on a senatorial career depended, of course, on imperial favor.[62] He liberalized, in one respect, the *lex Roscia,* which had excluded bankrupts, by allowing anyone who had possessed, or whose family had possessed, the equestrian census, to sit in the favored XIV Rows.[63]

---

nomination to the post of military tribune, the path to the equestrian order in those years, a procedure entirely in the hands of the triumvirs. See Demougin, ''Notables'' (1983).

[53] This is the definitive regulation of a privilege similar to that granted senators in 194 B.C. See Bollinger, *TL* (1969) 2–8; Alföldy, *Social History* 45; Demougin, *Ordre* (1988) 797–799; Baltrusch, *RM* 137–144. The seating privilege for equestrians has been argued to originate with C. Gracchus: Nicolet, *World* 365. For conditions outside Rome, see ''*lex Ursonensis*'' (*FIRA* 1² 21) ch. 125, 127; *Lex Civ. Narb.* (*FIRA* 1² 22) 5–9; Suet. *Aug.* 44.1–3. For extension of the rules to amphitheater and circus, see Bollinger, *TL* 10–11. On seating arrangements for women, see Schnurr, ''*Lex Julia*'' (1992).

[54] Scamuzzi, ''*Lex Roscia*'' (1969) 269–270, (1970) 47–57, distinguishes gladiators and *auctorati*.

[55] Nicolet, ''Augustus'' 97.

[56] This is to judge from the experience of Laberius (see below) and from Quint. *IO* 3.6.18–19. The latter strictly speaking must refer to the *lex Iulia theatralis,* a law that presumably took up this provision (and much else) from the *lex Roscia.* See Bollinger, *TL* 11–12; Rawson, ''*Discrimina*'' (1987/1991) 535; Baltrusch, *RM* 139; Leppin, *Histrionen* 77.

[57] On the general problem of the definition of *eques* under this law, see Demougin, *Ordre* 799–801; Schnurr, ''*Lex Julia*'' 158.

[58] Mazzacane, *ED* infamia (1971). Macer D. 48.1.7 implies as much. On ''*infamia*'' as a penalty in the imperial criminal law, see Levy, ''Infamie'' (1932/1963), who is, by today's standards, too ready to admit postclassical interpolation. I place *infamia* and its cognates in quotation marks to signal the fact that no unitary conception of *infamia* has been proved for the classical period.

[59] For Augustus, see Chapter 3. For Claudius, see Tac. *Ann.* 11.25; Suet. *Claud.* 16.1–4, with Alföldy, *Social History* 100, 102, 110, 119.

[60] Emperors now performed the *lectio* and *recognitio,* usually, if not always, qua censors: Wiseman, *New Men* 70.

[61] To say that the order was now ''virtually hereditary'' goes too far: Nicolet, *World* 4; cf. Nicolet, ''Augustus'' 93.

[62] Chastagnol, ''*Ordo*'' (1973/1984); Talbert, *Senate* 9–16.

[63] Nicolet, ''Augustus'' 97. In other respects, the *lex Iulia theatralis* simply ratified the requirements laid down by the *lex Roscia,* see above.

An adjustment was made to the system by Caligula, who began permitting certain *equites* the *latus clavus*.[64] Claudius initiated the practice of *adlectio*, by which more senior men were brought into the Senate; like the grant of the *latus clavus*, this device was entirely in the hands of the emperor.[65] There was similar regulation of the *ordo equester*. A *senatus consultum (SC)* in A.D. 22, followed by the *lex Visellia* a year later, stipulated as requirements three generations of free birth, a census of HS 400,000, and possession of the right to sit in the XIV Rows of the theater.[66]

While some think all imperial *equites* received the *equus publicus*,[67] which would mean that promotion to and demotion from this status remained firmly within the emperor's grasp, the question remains controversial, with others insisting on a greater status differentiation within the *ordo* in the imperial period.[68] Under Augustus, the annual parade *(transvectio)* of the *equites* was transformed into a censorial-style review (at least of the young equestrians and sons of senators),[69] albeit Augustus also held the *recognitio* at other times.[70] His successors moved between *transvectio, recognitio,* and full-blown exercise of the censorship until responsibility for the moral oversight of the equestrian order was transferred to the imperial bureaucracy, perhaps before the end of the first century A.D.[71]

In fact, it was impossible to improve one's status without a legal decision or official authorization that allowed entrance into an *ordo*.[72] For this purpose very precise juridical and moral conditions had to be satisfied: free birth, honorable conduct, and the proper census were necessary components of *dignitas*.[73] The accent was placed firmly on merit and morals, insofar as subventions were occasionally made to those thought deserving.[74]

[64] Chastagnol, *"Latus Clavus"* (1975/1984); Talbert, *Senate* 11–12. See now Chastagnol, *Sénat* chs. 5–8.

[65] Chastagnol, *"Latus Clavus"*; Talbert, *Senate* 15–16; Chastagnol, *Sénat* ch. 8.

[66] This legislation unified the equestrian order: Plin. *NH* 33.29–36. Henderson, *"Ordo"* (1963) 67–68, and Rawson, *"Discrimina"* 532, propose jury service as an additional qualification, in the sense that the seating privilege had previously been granted to those among the *iudices* who possessed the equestrian census. Dobson, "Centurionate" (1970) esp. 106, argues that *primipilares* enjoyed equestrian status under the Empire, but Demougin, *Ordre* 359–385, holds that they were not automatically granted this status. See also on this law, Wiseman, "Definition" 81–82; Reinhold, "Usurpation" (1971) 286; Levick, *Tiberius* (1976) 116–117; Baltrusch, *RM* 114.

[67] Stein, *RR* (1927) 54–57; Nicolet, *Ordre* 1. 177–188; Duncan-Jones, "Rank" (1967) 149–151; Kolb, "Symbolik" (1977) 251 [252] n. 54, 255; Alföldy, "Stellung" (1981) esp. 173 n. 26, with further literature; Demougin, *Ordre* ch. 4 (a full discussion).

[68] Jones, "Elections" (1955/1960) 39–45; Brunt, "Lex" (1961) 77; Henderson, *"Ordo"* 65–70; Sherwin-White, *Pliny* (1985) 130–131; Birley, "Notes" (1970) 75–77; Wiseman, "Definition" 82, with n. 88; Reinhold, "Usurpation" 280; Millar, *Emperor* (1992) 280. Wiseman, "Definition" 82, taking up an idea of Mommsen's, proposes a historical evolution. On the parallel controversy over the definition of equestrians under the Republic, see also Hackl, "Eques" (1989).

[69] Nicolet, "Augustus" 99.

[70] Demougin, *Ordre* 135–175.

[71] Demougin, *Ordre* 175–188. On the role of the *ordo equester* under the Principate, see Alföldy, "Stellung"; Brunt, "Princeps" (1983); Demougin, *Ordre* chs. 5–6.

[72] See Reinhold, "Usurpation" esp. 280, 285–286.

[73] Kolb, "Symbolik" 251; Nicolet, "Augustus" 92–93, 95; Demougin, *Ordre* 367.

[74] Nicolet, "Augustus" 94, cf. 96. See the evidence presented in Chapter 4, below.

All of this suggests a tidier, tighter arrangement than that which prevailed during the Republic, especially its turbulent last century.[75] From the beginning of the Principate, equestrians, as well as senators, were more closely integrated into the structure of state and society.[76] Augustus regularized and refined the Republican machinery for encouraging responsible behavior on the part of members of the elite: a series of status (re)definitions grounded in legislation and guaranteed by imperial oversight aimed to close loopholes, discourage abuses, and promote coherence and stability in the design and application of the rules.[77]

Jurors and the Album Iudicum

The same principles apply generally to the men serving as jurors *(iudices)* in the criminal and civil courts. Ordinary Roman citizens were excluded from the judiciary. Before the passage of the *lex Aurelia iudiciaria* in 70 B.C., the only persons ever entitled to this privilege were senators and equestrians.[78] This law added a third group, the *tribuni aerarii,* who, it is commonly believed, shared the census, but not the status, of the senators and *equites equo publico,* who composed the other two decuries. Nevertheless, they were often described as equestrians in common speech.[79] There is agreement that the *tribuni aerarii* were, both in their old role as paymasters and in their rejuvenated status as *iudices,* confirmed in this rank by the censors.[80]

This third decury was dropped by Caesar and reintroduced later (whether it was again composed of *tribuni aerarii* is controversial). Under the Principate, jury service was shared by senators and equestrians, with the latter forming the vast majority of jurors. Augustus added a fourth panel (which had a lower census rating of HS 200,000), and Caligula a fifth.[81]

Upon the constitution of a new *quaestio,* or in the intervals between censorial reviews, the magistrate in charge of the standing court was responsible for moral oversight of the jurors; presumably he was expected to apply the same standards as the censors themselves. So the *praetor peregrinus* was instructed, according to the *Tabula Bembina,* not to choose as juror someone convicted of an offense "with the consequence that it is not permitted to enroll him in the Senate.''[82] This mag-

[75] See Reinhold, "Usurpation" 278–281.

[76] See Baltrusch, *RM* 184; also Chapter 5 below.

[77] On its limitations, see above all Reinhold, "Usurpation."

[78] Before 123 B.C., jurors were chosen exclusively from the Senate. See Nicolet, *World* 374; Baltrusch, *RM* 193. On the inadequately documented and much-disputed history of the jury rosters in the late Republic, see Parks, *Schools* (1945) 43, 45; Stavely, "Iudex" (1953); Brunt, "Judiciary Rights" (1988); Santalucia, *DPR* (1989) 67, 75, 80, 92; Cloud, "Constitution" (1994) 509, 527. Like the *lex Roscia,* the *lex Aurelia* was pitched to equestrians: Griffin, "Tribune" (1973) 205–208.

[79] Henderson, "*Ordo*" 63–64; Wiseman, "Definition" 79; Bruhns, "Kompromiß" (1980); Cloud, "Constitution" 509. The amounts of the senatorial and equestrian censuses in the Republic were identical; see above.

[80] Henderson, "*Ordo*" 63–64; Nicolet, *Ordre* 1.598–613; Brunt, "Judiciary Rights" 210.

[81] Stavely, "Iudex" 205–213; Jones, *Courts* (1972) 88–89; Birks, "New Light" (1988) 52–53.

[82] *Tabula Bembina (lex Acilia repetundarum* [?], 123–122 B.C. [?]: *FIRA* 1² 7.13; see Lintott, *Reform* 90, 116–117): "quod circa eum in senatum legei non liceat." There is a gap in the text here, where

istrate was also asked not to appoint as *patronus* or juror anyone condemned in a *quaestio* or *iudicium publicum*.[83] Possibly, there is also an instruction to reject as *patronus* anyone whose mores were found to be objectionable.[84] These regulations suggest that no great divide existed between the *mores* of the censorial regimen and the legal concept of *boni mores*.[85] At minimum, the standard of the praetorian edict on *postulare* applied.[86]

This method of selecting *iudices* held true under the Principate, with the emperor filling the role of the censors.[87] Recruitment of jurors was accomplished with an inquiry *(inquisitio)*.[88] With the lapse of the exercise of the censorship after Domitian, the task passed to the imperial bureaucracy, which assumed its definitive form for this purpose under Hadrian.[89] Social degradation was accomplished by removal from the *album*.[90] Under the Principate, the roll of jurors contained senators, equestrians, and municipal notables.[91]

Municipal Honors

Practitioners were also excluded from municipal magistracies and the decurionate. We owe this information to the *Tabula Heracleensis*,[92] where, in a section of the law dating to 45 B.C.,[93] pimps and prostitutes, among dozens of others, are visited with this disability.

---

the editors place gladiators, a reading of Mommsen's; cf. 16. At 23 a reference to those condemned for *pecunia capta* is all reconstruction.

[83] At 11, 13, 16 (the latter two instances, dealing with the appointment of jurors, depend on restorations).

[84] This is partially restored as well: 11. See Nicolet, *Ordre* 1.491–511 (criticism of the suggestions put forward by Mommsen and others; Nicolet suggests reading a reference to bribery); Albanese, *Persone* (1979) 409; Venturini, *Crimen* (1979) 199 n. 167; Lintott, *Reform* 115–116 (who sees a reference to obstruction of justice); Lebek, "*Lex Lati*" (1993) 176–177. Cf. also the instruction to choose *recuperatores* from among the *prima classis* in the *lex agraria* of 111 B.C. (*FIRA* 1² 8.37).

[85] On the latter, see Mayer-Maly, "*CBM*" (1986).

[86] To judge from the remarks of Cicero, *Clu.* 121; see Greenidge, *Infamia* 155–156, cf. 188–192.

[87] On this aspect, see Plin. *NH* 29.18; with Stavely, "Iudex"; Kunkel, "Quaestio" (1963/1974) 96–97; Bringmann, "Reform" (1973) 243; Demougin, "Juges" (1975) 188–189. Qualifications for municipal *iudices* are discussed in the next section.

[88] Plin. *NH* 29.18.

[89] Demougin, "Juges" 189.

[90] Suet. *Dom.* 8.3. Jurors not on the *album* were subject to less rigorous rules, overseen by the praetor: Lanza, "Impedimenti" (1987) esp. 506–508, 536–539. The *ignominiosus* might qualify as an *arbiter* in the informal adjudication known as *compromissum*: Lab.-Ped.-Pomp.-Ulp. D. 4.8.7 pr. Ulp. D. *eod.* 9.3 implies a limit in case of the man's *manifesta turpitudo*. This would appear to exclude pimps and prostitutes. The best discussion of this evidence known to me is Talamanca, *Compromissum* (1958) 134 (135) n. 214.

[91] Demougin, "Juges."

[92] The bibliography is extensive; only a selection is offered here: Legras, *Table* (1907), with Kübler's review (1907); Hardy, *Laws* (1911–1912) 136–163; Gradenwitz, "Tafel" (1916); Premerstein, "Tafel" (1922); Hardy, *Problems* (1924) ch. 8; De Martino, "Nota" (1956); Frederiksen, "Municipal Laws" (1965); Laffi, "Senati" (1983) 70–74; Brunt, *IM* (1987) 519–523; Galsterer, "Loi" (1987).

[93] The date, sometimes challenged, is secured by Cic. *Fam.* 6.18.1. Not all of this section originates with Julius Caesar, however; see below.

The other professionals laboring under a permanent disability[94] were actors, gladiators *(auctorati),*[95] and gladiatorial trainers. With the addition of *bestiarii,* these are the same professions penalized under the praetor's edict (as supplemented below). The edict is not irrelevant here, since the denial of lesser privileges tends to imply the denial of greater ones. The jurists were reluctant to extend the field of excluded persons, especially in the case of a shortage of qualified candidates.[96] *Navicularii* were also barred, probably for reasons of public policy, not because they were dishonored.[97]

Such persons were excluded from magistracies and council membership, as well as marks of honorary membership, such as sitting with decurions at games, gladiatorial contests, and public meals (the latter exclusion appears to have been total, though this is perhaps an error):[98]

> *TH* 122–123: . . . queive corpore quaestum / fecit fecerit . . . queive lenocinium faciet.
>
> . . . or he who has made or will have made a living with his body . . . or he who will practice pimping.

The phrase on prostitutes is unremarkable but for the fact that it is taken up by the Augustan legislation on marriage and morals, with the feminine pronoun added or, at least in the case of the adultery law, substituted for the male.[99] The phrase on pimps is problematic,[100] because here, instead of the "fecit fecerit" that occurs with the other professions named at this place in the document,[101] we have simply "faciet." Mommsen sees here a departure from the legislative prototype, which had "fecit fecerit," a departure perhaps motivated "out of personal considerations," by which he presumably means that there were pimps (or ex-pimps) with enough political muscle to get the law changed.[102] The result is that the status of pimps was made equal to that of criers/auctioneers, ushers/referees, and funeral directors.

This argument is not compelling. There is no evidence that pimps ever enjoyed the kind of ascendancy that would enable them to influence legislation, at Rome

---

[94] *Praecones* (criers/auctioneers), *dissignatores* (ushers [e.g., at public games]/referees), and *libitinarii* (funeral directors) were excluded only as long as they practiced their professions. See the discussion in Lo Cascio, *"Praeconium"* (1975/1976). On *praecones,* see also Hinard, *"Praecones"* (1976); Rauh, "Auctioneers" (1989).

[95] That is, persons who were not prisoners of war, criminals, or slaves. For the distinction, see Aigner, "Stellung" (1988) 207.

[96] Call. D. 50.2.12.

[97] Paul. D. 50.2.9.1.

[98] See *TH* 133–134, 138–139.

[99] See Chapter 5.

[100] "Eine crux," according to Gradenwitz, "Tafel" 18.

[101] Pimps and prostitutes are grouped with actors and *lanistae (auctorati)* occur at *TH* 112–113). On the phrase "fecit fecerit," see Chapter 4.

[102] Mommsen, "Stadtrechte" (1855/1905) 310 n. 70: "Es unterliegt wohl keinem Zweifel, dass auch hier im Entwurf stand: 'queive lenocinium fecit fecerit,' und nachher, wahrscheinlich aus persönlichen Rücksichten, dies geändert ward; sehr ungeschickt, denn es war dann nötig, das *lenocinium* zu dem *praeconium* stellen."

or anywhere else. Male pimps in particular were thoroughly despised, held in greater disrepute than procuresses and female prostitutes.[103] We would expect their legal position at all times to be at least as low as that of actors and gladiatorial trainers.[104]

Furthermore, it is remarkable that the alleged equivalence of *lenocinium* and *praeconium* is faulty. In the latter case the document reads "whoever practices the trade of auctioneering, ushering at public games, or acting as a funeral director, as long as he practices any of these."[105] The section on pimps lacks the final qualifying phrase, which means that even on Mommsen's theory we have to accept the fact of an engraving error.[106]

The idea that an engraving error is present in itself suggests a solution to the main problem. Thanks to Martin Frederiksen, we are well-informed about the problems that arose in the transmission of Republican laws. Frederiksen points to the "singular incompetence" of the engraver of the *TH,* to whom he ascribes many of the peculiarities of style and sense found in this document.[107] We might very well add one more and attribute the idiosyncratic "faciet" to this hapless fellow. It is the most economical explanation. The text should read "queive lenocinium fecit fecerit."[108]

Although the list of exclusions given by the *TH* is known to date from 45 B.C., it must be mostly tralaticious in character, depending on earlier, largely similar versions.[109] The existence of such models is suggested by Cicero when he remarks that C. Claudius Pulcher drew up such regulations for Halaesus, "in which he ordained many rules, [for example,] concerning the minimum age for men [eligible for public office], so that no one is chosen who is less than thirty years old; concerning their professions; concerning their level of wealth, and other matters."[110]

---

[103] See Chapter 4. An exception is, to be sure, male prostitutes.

[104] Cf. Formigoni Candini, *"Lenones"* (1990) 106, whose acceptance of the text as it stands leads her to speculate about the "very gradual" translation of social prejudice into legal disability for pimps. Most scholars accept the provision as written: Legras, *Table* 129; Gardner, *Being* 151 (who argues [130–134] that the auctioneers et al. were excluded not because their professions were despised but out of conflicts of interest); and below.

[105] *TH* 94, 104–105: "quei praeconium dissignationem libitinamve faciet, dum eorum quid faciet."

[106] Mommsen himself recognizes that problems arose in the preparation of the text, caused in part "a scriptore incurioso sane nec fortasse Latini sermonis satis gnaro" (*CIL* 1² p. 486). Premerstein supposes that the notice was originally meant to appear with the other three professions just mentioned: the editor, observing that insertion at these places in the text would render pimps eligible for membership in *fora* and *conciliabula,* placed them in the margin at 123, from where the notice crept into the text itself (Premerstein, "Tafel" 103; cf. *TH* 90, 98–99, with Premerstein, "Tafel" 97).

[107] Frederiksen, "Municipal Laws" 188 (cf. 195), with choice illustrations.

[108] For a similar conclusion, see Daube, "Marriage" (1967) 382 n. 11.

[109] Laffi, "Senati" 74 n. 95.

[110] Cic. *Verr.* 2.2.122: "in quibus multa sanxit de aetate hominum, ne qui minor triginta annis natus; de quaestu, quem qui fecisset ne legeretur; de censu, de ceteris rebus." The date is 95 B.C. Cicero writes "de quaestu," which refers to professions that render candidates ineligible. Lo Cascio, *"Praeconium"* 365, with n. 40, rightly criticizes Gabba, "Senati" (1959) 312 n. 15, who sees in *quaestus* a reference to the practice of prostitution. Lo Cascio, however, generalizes Cicero's meaning too far and would exclude the practitioners of any profession; in other words, only landed proprietors would be eligible for the town council.

Cicero adds that L. Cornelius Scipio Asiagenus had long ago done the same for Agrigentum: "in these laws those same things were laid down."[111] P. Rupilius instituted similar rules for council elections at Heraclea.[112] Also relevant are the regulations given by the *lex Pompeia* for Bithynia.[113] Cicero assumes that such regulations are the norm,[114] and his words should be taken to reflect the existence of a standard, predictable set of exclusions subject to minor change over time and to adjustment to local circumstances.[115] Condemnation in a *iudicium de dolo* probably was inserted after 66,[116] status as informant in proscriptions after 64,[117] and the situation of *praecones* corresponds to the innovation mentioned by Cicero in 45.[118] The adjustment to local traditions described by Cicero[119] in the context of Sicily may be at least partly explained by the status of the locals as *peregrini,* whereas the regulations in the *TH* were designed for Roman citizens.[120]

It is uncertain if this set of exclusions ever formed part of a general municipal law.[121] Several scholars adopt the view that such a law existed, attributing this legislation variously to Sulla, Cinna, Caesar, and Augustus.[122] Frederiksen's notion of a "matrix-law" is similar, though he insists on a comitial law as the antecedent of every municipal charter.[123] This view receives support from Lebek's thesis that in 82 or 83 Domitian promulgated a comitial *lex Lati* that formed the basis for the *leges datae* whose extensive fragments constitute our evidence for the Flavian Municipal Law (see below).[124] Frederiksen seems correct in arguing that the list found on the *TH* is part of the raw material for a town charter. The rules, which correspond to censorial practice at Rome, are intended to standardize the practices of communities of varying status.[125] In any case, this list, as it evolved, will have served as a model for town charters into the Principate.[126]

---

[111] Cic. *Verr.* 2.2.123: "in quibus [sc., legibus] illa eadem sancta sunt." The date is presumably 193 B.C., when Asiagenus was praetor for the island of Sicily: Broughton, *MRR* 1 (1951) 347.

[112] Cic. *Verr.* 2.2.125. Rupilius was consul in 132 B.C.: Broughton, *MRR* 1.497.

[113] Plin. *Ep.* 10.79.1.

[114] Flamininus presumably used similar standards for Thessalian councillors and jurors in 194: Liv. 34.51.6. See also Jones, "Rome" (1971) 524, 539.

[115] Gradenwitz ("Tafel" 18), Frederiksen ("Municipal Laws" 196), and Galsterer ("Loi" 192) all stress the tralaticious quality of these rules.

[116] Cic. *Off.* 3.60–61; Cic. *Nat. Deorum* 3.74.

[117] Suet. *Iul.* 11.

[118] Cic. *Fam.* 6.18.1.

[119] Cic. *Verr.* 2.2.123–124.

[120] Cf. Gabba, "Senati" 318.

[121] This much-debated topic is treated by Galsterer, "Loi"; Galsterer, "Municipium" (1988) 89–90; and Lamberti, *Tabulae* (1993) 201–208, who argue that such a law never existed.

[122] See Johnston, "Three Thoughts" (1987) 66, esp. n. 18, for literature. Galsterer himself ("Loi" 193, 197, 203) allows for a "regulatory model" ("règlement-modèle") whose exact nature remains unclear.

[123] Frederiksen, "Municipal Laws" 191–192.

[124] Lebek, "*Lex Lati*" 161; Lebek, "Curien" (1995) 136–139. Cf. Lamberti, *Tabulae* 233–238.

[125] Laffi, "Senati."

[126] On moral character as a qualification for the decurionate under the Empire, see also Jacques, *Privilège* (1984) 333–337.

The relevant parts of the Flavian Municipal Law (FML) have not been recovered.[127] The rules on magistrates' qualifications, which receive two references in the surviving part of the law[128] are thought to have come at some point before a fragmentary chapter that dealt with the functions and privileges of *duumviri*.[129] The part of the law dealing with requirements for decurions perhaps came soon after chapter 31.[130] The requirements for magistrates were possibly similar to those given for decurions. An independent list was necessary, if it was true that membership in the *ordo* was not a prerequisite for election to office.[131]

The FML (ch. 54) forbids anyone from holding office who would be ineligible for the *ordo decurionum* if he were a Roman citizen. This may be taken to suggest that the requirements were not identical and that the Roman qualifications were more stringent (all the same, the differences may have been fairly trivial); the stipulation is best viewed in light of similar features of the FML that impose Roman regulations on the Latin *municipia*.[132]

The chief magistrates of the town were responsible for applying these regulations upon the election or co-optation of new members to the *ordo*.[133] Points of law were naturally referred to the governor, sometimes even to the emperor.[134] Presumably, the magistrates performed the same function for honorary decurions, for whom the rules of admission were evidently less stringent. Nicols identifies four types of "decurions": actual decurions, patrons of the municipality, *praetextati,* and a fourth group, who did not sit in the *curia,* were not listed in the *album,* but did enjoy many of the same privileges accorded regular members of the *ordo*.[135] In this last category he places centurions, veterans, freedmen, and actors. Given

[127] On the FML, see D'Ors, *Ley* (1986) (text and commentary); González, "*Lex Irnitana*" (1986) (text, translation, and commentary); Lamberti, *Tabulae* (text, translation, and commentary). For a possible fragment of the section in question, see Fernández Gómez and Del Amo y de la Hera, *Lex* (1990) 35.

[128] FML chs. 51 and 54.

[129] Ch. 18; see D'Ors, *Ley* 98, 129; González, "*Lex Irnitana*" 200, 215; Galsterer, "Municipium" 79. for a partial reconstruction, see Fernández Gómez and Del Amo y de la Hera, *Lex* 37; Lamberti, *Tabulae* 269; Lebek, "Duumvirn" (1994) esp. 270–271.

[130] A reference occurs in ch. 30, and another occurs just at the point where ch. 31 breaks off: González, "*Lex Irnitana*" 207, 208; Galsterer, "Loi" 190; Galsterer, "Municipium" 82; cf. the "*lex Ursonensis*" ch. 101.

[131] See FML ch. 21, with Lamberti, *Tabulae* 33; against González, "*Lex Irnitana*" 215; Galsterer, "Municipium" 86, 90.

[132] González, "*Lex Irnitana*" 149.

[133] *TH* 83–88, 98–107; FML ch. 31. On procedures of the Sicilian cities of the late Republic, see Gabba, "Senati"; Nicols, "Size" (1988) 715. The "*lex Ursonensis*" (chs. 105, 123, 124, with Mommsen, *Strafrecht* [1899] 998) provides a judicial procedure to deal with decurions accused of unworthiness. Neither this statute nor the *TH* excludes freedmen, a state of affairs that changes under Augustus: Treggiari, *Freedmen* (1969) 63–64; Lo Cascio, "Praeconium" 369–370. (Some argue that the change originates with the Tiberian *lex Visellia*; see Abramenko, "Liberti" [1992].) Sons of freedmen were routinely admitted into the *ordo:* Garnsey, "Descendants" (1975); López Barja de Quiroga, "Mobility" (1995).

[134] Plin. *Ep.* 10.79.

[135] Nicols, "Size" 717–718. Patrons and *praetextati* received the *ornamenta* but did not vote: Nicols, "Size" 716.

the exclusion of actors and others from marks of honor under the *TH*, it is difficult to say if this amounts to a change, a violation of a norm, or the exploitation of a loophole.[136] Until an inscription is found relating the award of the *ornamenta decurionatus* to a prostitute or pimp, I would prefer to think that such persons were excluded even from these lesser honors.

Even for "ordinary" decurions, the rules could have been tighter. Elite social prejudice embraced a wider range of professions, to judge from a famous passage of Cicero,[137] than we know to have been excluded from the town councils. The reason for this disjuncture, in my view, lies not so much in the fact that Cicero's senatorial perspective is too lofty for this social level but that the councils themselves varied greatly in terms of their social composition, depending on the size and prosperity of each town.[138]

The FML provides new information on the qualifications for municipal *iudices*.[139] Some were chosen from among the decurions. For the rest, specific requirements of free birth, age (not younger than 25 years), and census (HS 5,000 minimum at Irni for the subject or his holder of *potestas*), as well as excuses (bad health, old age, official responsibilities, legitimate absence, lack of property qualification),[140] are given, but the issue of moral qualifications is left to the appointing magistrate(s), who must swear an oath on the suitability of the appointees before no fewer than 10 decurions (litigants were also allowed to choose judges themselves).[141]

The list of exclusions contained on the *TH* is generally recognized as bearing some relationship to the praetorian regime on *postulare*;[142] it is simply fuller.[143] There is also a clear connection with the censorial *regimen morum*.[144] It is natural for Cicero to draw a comparison between the two, when he complains of the

[136] *TH* 135–142. See the discussion in Ducos, "Acteurs" 21–22, 27–28; Leppin, *Histrionen* 105–106 (among others, an actor as decurion and Roscius as *eques*). Aigner, "Stellung," treats the social mobility of gladiators (210) and athletes (215).

[137] Cic. *Off.* 1.150, with Lo Cascio, "*Praeconium*" 370–371.

[138] Jacques, *Privilège* 527–537, 562–570.

[139] FML ch. 86. See the discussion in Birks, "New Light" Lamberti, *Tabulae* 167–177 (with literature). An improved reading is offered by Lebek, "*Lex Lati*" 172–176.

[140] Of course, the excuses would also apply to those decurions who served as judges.

[141] Compare the fragmentary ch. 114 of the "*lex Ursonensis*," which, as reconstructed, mentions at least one concrete ethical disqualification: "[. . . qui iud(icio) publico praevaricationi]s causa / [condemnatus erit . . .]" (in Girard and Senn, *Lois*[7] [1977] 31). Cf. ch. 123.

[142] Greenidge, *Infamia* 116; Gradenwitz, "Tafel" 16; Hardy, *Problems* 291; Frederiksen, "Municipal Laws" 195. A connection is doubted by Kaser, "Infamia" 241; see next note.

[143] The *TH* denied a greater privilege; see below. Some minor differences may be explained in terms of historical development (our legal sources yield a more mature classical version of the edict), to say nothing of the interventions of the *Digest*'s compilers or the faults of the inscription's copyist (see above).

[144] Greenidge, *Infamia* 72, 114; Hardy, *Problems* 256, 306; Laffi, "Senati" 72–73; cf. Nicols, "Size" 715, who describes the duumviral duty to keep up the numbers of the decurionate in terms of "censorial power." Plin. *Ep.* 10.79.3 refers to the magistrates responsible for keeping the rolls of the Bithynian *senatus* as *censores*. On these magistrates, see Sherwin-White, *Pliny* 672–673. Cf. also the *lex Osca Tab. Bant.* (FIRA 1[2] 16) 18–23, 27–29; *TH* 139–141, 144.

unfairness (only contemplated, not in the law) of barring former *praecones* from serving as decurions when practicing *haruspices* were admitted to the Roman Senate.[145]

    There is a principle implicit in Cicero's comment that is worth expanding on. Obviously, he assumes that the standards for membership in the Senate are higher than those for the municipal councils: an ex-*praeco* would have no chance in the former case. But the comparison makes clear the relationship between, and the rationale behind, the different sets of exclusions. As one moves up the ladder, from praetorian *postulare* to the list on the *TH,* from this to the censorial regime for the senatorial and equestrian orders, the exclusions become more detailed. But a core set of exclusions, roughly identifiable with the praetor's list, can be discerned.

    The existence of such a core formed the bedrock of the *regimen morum,*[146] largely invisible to us because it involved, in the majority of cases, persons of status too low for our literary and legal sources to take an interest in. Besides this, the privilege in question was almost always far less important than membership in the Senate. The censors increased the strictness of their *regimen* as they moved up the ladder. Again, this principle can be grasped by comparing the *TH*'s list with that of the praetor: the greater the privilege, the more extensive the set of exclusions.

    By the same token, ineligibility for lesser honors spelled disqualification for greater ones, a principle granted explicit recognition by the jurist Pomponius.[147] This practice is consistent with the principle that political authority, indeed legitimacy, was ideally grounded in correct moral behavior.[148] The exemplary nature of the censors' proceedings was fundamental, since it advertised the unity between principle and practice.[149]

    It may help to visualize this arrangement with an image often invoked to explain the air-traffic control system at major airports: the upside-down wedding cake. With tier upon tier, each one larger than the one beneath, this system incorporates the substance of the lowest level into each higher one. It is an unusual way of imagining Roman society, because it fastens on those marginalized, in different degrees, for reasons of dishonor. It hardly excludes more familiar devices for understanding social structure, for example, the pyramid, which, logically enough, places the elite on top.[150] It simply attempts to explain, in part, how that structure is constituted, using a vertical stratigraphy in place of a horizontal one.[151]

    It is interesting to observe that the upside-down wedding cake of dishonor itself has a respectable counterpart. A large slice of this cake may be envisioned

[145] Cic. *Fam.* 6.18.1.

[146] Its usefulness is guaranteed by the fact that both the classical jurists and Justinian's compilers took it as a foundation stone for the construction of more comprehensive concepts of *infamia*; below.

[147] Pomp. D. 1.9.4.

[148] Pólay, "*RM*" (1971) 269–270 (cf. 317).

[149] Pólay, "*RM*" 270, 290.

[150] A useful illustration is in Alföldy, *Social History* 146.

[151] On the importance of both perspectives for understanding marginal status, see Weiler, "Randgruppen" 18.

in the image of the social stratification presented by the Augustan regulations for seating at the theater: senators occupied the most honored seats in the orchestra, followed by the XIV Rows reserved for equestrians, then free Roman citizens arranged by tribe, with those in compliance with the marriage law given preference, and noncitizens, women, and slaves up at the back.[152]

This three-dimensional perspective helps explain both the variety of controls and the degree of discretion permitted those officials with the most delicate responsibilities of all, the censors. Mommsen fully recognizes the anecdotal quality of the evidence for the *regimen morum* and its tendency to highlight the unusual.[153] Those who have followed in his train have sometimes overstated his case, pressing the distinction between censorial *ignominia* and praetorian *infamia* too hard.[154] The censors were followed by the emperors, whose control of access to the different grades of the Republican hierarchy was, if anything, even more complete and consistent.[155]

Unlike the principles of the *regimen morum,* the rules for *postulare* and the decurionate receive positive expression. The design of the praetorian regime can be explained in terms of expediency: this constituted a small set of exclusions, but one that was potentially applied more often, and in a broader range of circumstances, than the rules enforced by the censors. The need for legal certainty was balanced against the opportunity for making changes when necessary. The fact that the qualifications for decurions were enshrined in legislation[156] has been explained as a consequence of the moral lassitude thought to prevail in the municipalities of Italy in the first century B.C.[157] or as predicated by the lack of local officials with *imperium* or censorial authority.[158] It seems more likely to have resulted from a concern of the central authority to see Rome's moral ideology become standard everywhere in its dominion, above all, in those areas of Italy that received citizenship after the Social War, if the new citizens were to prove worthy of their increased *dignitas.*

This objective was perhaps more than matched by a desire on the part of the municipalities to discover these standards and apply them faithfully.[159] In principle, they probably did not deviate widely from previous local usage, certainly not, I believe, from local practice regarding the treatment of pimps and prostitutes.

[152] In the theater, the Roman was confronted with the whole of social and political organization, and not least the crucial fact of his own place in this scheme: Zanker, *Power of Images* (1988) 149–151; André, "Zuschauerschaft" (1990) 166–167.

[153] Mommsen, *Staatsrecht* 2³ (1887/1969) 375–388.

[154] So Kübler (rev. Pommeray) (1938) 300, when he views the distinction between the two as lying in "die Unterscheidung von *mos* und *ius,* Sittlichkeit und Recht, von Subjektivismus und Objektivität."

[155] See Wallace-Hadrill, "Civilis Princeps" (1982) 47.

[156] Cic. *Fam.* 6.18.1 speaks of a *lex*; see Galsterer, "Loi" 190.

[157] De Martino, "Nota" 229.

[158] Hardy, *Problems* 306. His argument from lack of *imperium* is odd, since the Roman censors themselves had none.

[159] This idea owes much to Frederiksen's argument in "Municipal Laws" that the drive for Romanization, at least on the level of municipal regulations, is perhaps better explained as a pull from the fringe more than as a push from the center. On regional conservatism toward legal norms, see Dixon, "Infirmitas" 348, 355.

The Army

The evidence for the exclusion of pimps and prostitutes from the military is again indirect. Good morals were a quality of the ideal soldier.[160] Convicted adulterers were not permitted to enlist and, if already soldiers, were dishonorably discharged.[161] Homosexual behavior among the troops was severely repressed.[162] By the late classical period, at least, praetorian *infamia* (see below) barred a number of types from the service.[163] Prostitutes and pimps might not even be tolerated in camp by a strict commander.[164]

Censorial Oversight of Lower-Status Romans

Lower-status citizens did not escape the attention of the censors. Under the *regimen morum,* they could be demoted to one of the four urban tribes and placed in the class of the *aerarii* and/or that of the Caerites.

The evidence is ambiguous and has been variously interpreted.[165] No attempt at resolving the general difficulties will be attempted in this place. For Mommsen, demotion to a city tribe, relegation to the *aerarii,* and assignment to the Caerites are the same after 312 B.C., since censors no longer had the authority to exclude citizens from all tribes.[166] For Greenidge, removal to one of the four urban tribes was less serious than demotion to the ranks of the *aerarii,* since in the former instance the right to vote was retained.[167] Pieri, building on the work of Fraccaro and Nicolet, argues that tribal demotion and relegation to the *aerarii* were two separate penalties, the latter a fine imposed through multiplication of liability for *tributum* (only this could be imposed independently).[168] An older, harsher punishment was demotion to the Caerites, outside any tribe: this deprived its object of the right to vote and to hold office.[169]

---

[160] Nicolet, *World* 96.

[161] Ulp. D. 3.2.2.3; Arr. Men. D. 49.16.4.7; Plin. *Ep.* 6.31.5.

[162] Polyb. 6.37.9; Dion. Hal. 16.4.1–3; Val. Max. 6.1.10, 11, 12. Effeminacy itself was considered a disqualification from service, to judge from Liv. 39.15.9, 13–14. See MacMullen, "Love" (1982/1990) 181; Dalla, *Venus* (1987) 55–62.

[163] Argued from Arr. Men. D. 49.16.4.4. On this text, see Levy, "Infamie" 523–524; his criticism does not affect my argument. For a possible exception to the principle argued for, observe the case of the actor P. Valerius Comazon, who served (it is uncertain whether as a regular legionary or as an auxiliary soldier) in Thrace in the late second century. Comazon's later career (following demotion to the fleet, he became praetorian prefect, consul, and city prefect, holding the last office three times) was exceptional: Dio (in Xiph., *Exc. Val.*) 80.4.2, with Watson, *Soldier* (1969) 125.

[164] On Scipio Aemilianus's ejection of undesirables from the camp at Numantia, see the sources given by Schmähling, *Censoren* 123. Cf. C. Gracchus's report in Gell. 15.12.1–4.

[165] See, e.g., Cic. *Off.* 1.40; Cic. *De Or.* 2.260 (with Gell. 4.20); Liv. 24.18.7–9, 29.37.12–16, 42.10.4, 44.16.8, 45.15.1–8.

[166] Mommsen, *Staatsrecht* 2³ 392–394, 402–405 (with 404 n. 2).

[167] Greenidge, *Infamia* 105–112.

[168] Pieri, *Cens* 115–122. Cf. Siber, *RV* (1952) 222–223; Fantham, "Censorship" (1977) 45; Astin, "*RM*" 17.

[169] See Siber, *RV* 223; Nicolet, *World* 27, 86. For a different view, see Grieve, "*TC*" (1983).

What is most significant is the evidence that this declassing was routinely applied to actors, gladiators, and other public performers:[170]

> Since they considered the dramatic art and the theater in general to be disgraceful, they desired such persons not only to do without the privileges of other citizens but also to be demoted from their tribes through censorial *nota*.[171]

> On this account the practice remains that the actors of Atellan farces are not demoted from their tribe and they serve in the army, as though they had nothing to do with the dramatic art.[172]

> Moreover, the Atellan farces were taken from the Samnites. This sort of entertainment has been tempered by Italian moral conservatism and so is not inflicted with the *nota:* the Atellan actor therefore neither suffers demotion from his tribe nor is rendered ineligible for service in the army.[173]

> Take the fact that they themselves cast aside and demote those who produce and supervise the games, not to speak of the very popular charioteers, actors, athletes, gladiators . . . better yet, they openly condemn them to social disgrace and legal degradation, keeping them from the Senate house, speakers' platform, senatorial order, equestrian order, and all other offices as well as certain distinctions.[174]

> The Romans . . . do not permit even a plebeian tribe to be disgraced by the inclusion of actors, let alone the Senate.[175]

> The censors Lucius Metellus and Gnaeus Domitius expelled all theater professionals from Rome except for Latin flute players, along with the singers who accompany them, and those engaged in the private nightclub [*ludus talarius*].[176]

The first four passages mention *tribu movere,* which is consistent with demotion to an urban tribe or worse, if one takes the view that transfer to the *aerarii* and/or Caerites was a distinguishable penalty (see above). Tertullian emphasizes the paradox in Roman attitudes toward performers, who are wildly popular yet discriminated against. Ulpian's declaration that the juristic consensus holds that

---

[170]For similar, though not as routine, treatment of freedmen, see Nicolet, *World* 227–229; Masi Doria, "Bürgerrecht" (1993).

[171]Cic. *Rep.* 4.10 (from Aug. *Civ. Dei* 2.13): "Cum artem ludicram scaenamque totam in probro ducerent, genus id hominum non modo honore civium reliquorum carere, sed etiam tribu moveri notatione censoria voluerunt."

[172]Liv. 7.2.12: "Eo institutum manet, ut actores Atellanarum nec tribu moveantur, et stipendia, tamquam expertes artis ludicrae, faciant."

[173]Val. Max. 2.4.4: ". . . Atellani autem ab Oscis acciti sunt. Quod genus delectationis Italica severitate temperatum ideoque vacuum nota est: nam neque tribu actor nec a militaribus stipendiis repellitur." By implication, other actors were normally punished. On the exemption accorded Atellan players, see Gardner, *Being* 139–140.

[174]Tert. *Spect.* 22.2: "Etenim ipsi auctores et administratores spectaculorum quadrigarios, scaenicos, xysticos, arenarios illos amantissimos . . . deponunt et deminuunt, immo manifeste damnant ignominia et capitis minutione, arcentes curia rostris senatu equite ceterisque honoribus omnibus simul et ornamentis quibusdam." On the text, see Turcan, *Tertullien* (1986) 269–272.

[175]Aug. *Civ. Dei* 2.13: "Romani . . . hominibus scaenicis nec plebeiam tribum, quanto minus senatoriam curiam dehonestari sinunt."

[176]Cassiod. *Chron.* (under cos. for 115 B.C.): "L. Metellus et Cn. Domitius censores artem ludicram ex urbe removerunt praeter Latinum tibicinem cum cantore et ludum talarium."

xystici and others are not *ignominiosi* may convict Tertullian of rhetorical exaggeration.[177] Or the jurist may be writing of the effects of *ignominia* only with regard to the right of *postulare* (see below) and not eligibility for higher privileges.[178] Only two late sources, Augustine and Cassiodorus, state or imply more punitive measures than demotion to an urban tribe.

The action taken by the censors of 115 B.C., recorded by Cassiodorus, is the most drastic of all. All public performers are removed except for the Latin flute players and singers used in religious rites and performers in "the equivalent of private nightclubs: the *ludus talarius*."[179] The language, if it can be relied upon, perhaps suggests a ban on performances proper as opposed to expulsion of persons;[180] all the same, expulsion of actors occurred periodically under the Principate, with the goal of maintaining public order.[181] In any case, expulsion from Rome is a harsh penalty, affecting a broader range of persons than just those listed above, since presumably peregrines and slaves were included (they may have been the chief target). These censors had a reputation for severity.[182]

One caveat must be set forth. Generalizations about the treatment of public performers do not mean that exceptions did not exist, for various reasons. One of these is known, from Crete in the first century B.C.[183] It is easy to imagine how this man escaped the clutches of the censors, especially in that period.

The exception does not overturn the rule. According to Macrobius, Laberius claimed to have lost his equestrian status the instant he appeared onstage.[184] This implies a firm principle of degradation. Censorial concern with actors and the theater in the Republic was long-standing and consistently severe in its approach.[185] The repressive actions of Vitellius and Domitian as censors fit the pattern.[186]

The numerous enactments under Augustus and Tiberius designed to repress public performances by members of the upper orders are an unsurprising reaction to the deterioration of a moral convention, not proof that a censorial ban did not exist; the censorship itself was by now in crisis. The principle of social exclusion, like other aspects of the censorial regime, was taken up by the *lex Iulia et Papia*. As with freedmen, however, this was softened, so that acting was forbidden only to those who married members of the senatorial order, not equestrians as well.[187]

---

[178] See the discussion in Greenidge, *Infamia* 26, 112; Ducos, "Acteurs" (1990) 21; Leppin, *Histrionen* 78, with n. 37; Pennitz, "Athleten" (1995). Cf. Tert. *Apol.* 15.3; Tert. *Nat.* 1.10.45.

[177] Sab.-Cass.-Ulp. D. 3.2.4 pr.

[179] Fantham, "Censorship" 44.

[180] Cf. Gizewski, "Mores" (1989) 96.

[181] Gardner, *Being* 144.

[182] Nowak, *Censoren* 44–45; Schmähling, *Censoren* 93.

[183] Leppin, *Histrionen* 73, cites four examples of actors belonging to rural tribes. Three of these date from the Principate (late first to third century) and so say nothing about Republican practice. The fourth is attested by an inscription from Crete dated to the first century B.C.: *ICret.* 4.222 A (= *IGR* 1.975).

[184] Macrob. *Sat.* 2.7.2–3 (cf. 2.3.10, 2.7.7; Suet. *Iul.* 39.2; cf. Cic. *Fam.* 10.32.2; Quint. *IO* 3.6.18–19). See Jory, "Syrus" (1988).

[185] See Schmähling, *Censoren* 42–44, 90–96, 146–151; Baltrusch, *RM* 20–21, 27, with n. 134.

[186] Tac. *Hist.* 2.62; Suet. *Dom.* 8.3; Dio (in Zon.) 64.6.3.

[187] See Chapter 3.

All the same, the language the jurists use is significant,[188] and even more important is the manner in which they apply the law. A senator's wife who takes up acting should be divorced.[189] A senator's daughter who prostituted herself, took up acting, or suffered condemnation in a *iudicium publicum* was free to marry a freedman with impunity.[190] The effect of the disgraceful action or event was understood to be declassing.

It is reasonable to suppose that the same oversight was exercised to the detriment of prostitutes and pimps. The low regard in which such persons were held by censors is indirectly illustrated by Cato's expulsion of the ex-consul Flamininus from the Senate in 184. The ground alleged was Flamininus's execution of a man during his campaign in Cisalpine Gaul in 192, at a dinner party and at the behest of a prostitute.[191] One may compare the excessive spending on prostitutes criticized by the ex-censor Scipio Aemilianus mentioned above. The positive translation of censorial practice into the rules defining eligibility for decurions and magistrates in the *TH* suggests that repression of pimps and prostitutes, though hardly necessary for the upper orders, formed a routine feature of censorial activity at Rome. The actions of the censors of 179 B.C., who constituted the tribes on the basis of professions (*quaestus*) and other factors,[192] while unusual in their wholesale approach, may be taken to betray a more consistent concern with the professions of individuals, or even certain individual professions en bloc.

The argument has been advanced, to be sure, that the censors focused on lower-class citizens only irregularly or hardly at all.[193] Without doubt, the upper orders, above all senators and equestrians, absorbed the lion's share of censorial time and energy in the *regimen:* in their case, an investigation might be conducted, questions asked, nuances weighed.[194] But there is no good reason to think that men who were known, or generally thought, to be pimps and prostitutes were not routinely branded with the *nota.* The censors determined military and fiscal obligations, as well as political privileges, for all citizens.[195] Although the censors were concerned with promoting "the sense of identity, the social values, and the coherence"[196] of the aristocracy, the overall goal of the *regimen morum* was to extend these traits in a differentiated way to all of Roman society.[197]

---

[188] On *nota* and its cognates, see Chapter 4.

[189] Paul. D. 23.2.44.7.

[190] Paul. D. 23.2.47.

[191] See Schmähling, *Censoren* 97, and Astin, "*RM*" 21, with n. 37, for evidence of the different versions of this story.

[192] Liv. 40.51.9.

[193] Pólay, "*RM*" 296; Astin, "*RM*" 17–19, 23. Cf. the more extreme position of Baltrusch, *RM* 24–25, 28, 47–8 (and 192, for a similar argument about Republican sumptuary legislation, which in his view was only formally directed at the entire body of citizens), with the criticism of Chaniotis (rev. Baltrusch) (1991) esp. 69, 72, 82, 84. In principle, I agree with Greenidge, *Infamia* 34–40.

[194] Astin, "*RM*" 19–26.

[195] Nicolet, *World* 52. They took account of degrading occupations, certainly, when practiced by members of the higher orders: Nicolet, *World* 80.

[196] Astin, "*RM*" 34.

[197] Chaniotis (rev. Baltrusch) 73; see also Suolahti, *Censors* 49; Gizewski, "Mores" 89; Nicolet,

Their transfer to the ranks of the Caerites and/or *aerarii* would have denied practitioners the right to hold office or to vote. The first never existed for them in any real sense, but the loss of the second was perhaps felt more keenly, as by any lower-status citizen. It eliminated any motive for a candidate for office to court them, thus cutting prostitutes and pimps out of the Roman system of patronage at a very basic level.[198] "Mere" demotion to an urban tribe would have had almost the same effect.[199] At the same time, Caerites were liable to military and fiscal obligations imposed by the state. Practitioners were barred from the army, often a vehicle for social mobility. They were excluded, one may state with confidence, from all of the Roman *ordines,* that is, all ranks of society with any claim to true respectability.[200] This left only payment of taxes as a form of participation in government. Such men were Roman citizens only in a partial sense.

3. Disabilities at Law

The distinction assumed here between political and juridical rights is a traditional one and has its own justification.[201] And although this distinction is not entirely defensible, insofar as the latter set of rights can reasonably be viewed as a subset of the former, nonetheless it is convenient to focus on the rules governing the participation of pimps and prostitutes that were developed by and for the legal system itself. One special justification for this procedure is that at this juncture a new axis of analysis opens up: the role of women. First we examine the privilege of requesting a private law remedy before the praetor, then that of making accusations in the criminal courts, and finally that of acting as a witness in both venues.

The Praetor's Court

Handbooks on Roman law prefer to emphasize that private law offers citizens not so much rights as remedies. These were guaranteed by the *praetor urbanus,* the supreme judicial magistrate at Rome, through the edict he issued at the outset of his yearlong tenure. By and large this document was tralaticious in nature, with

---

World 317. The interest taken in defining social distinctions in colonies both citizen and Latin as well as Sicilian towns is instructive: Gabba, "Strutture" (1983) 41; Laffi, "Senati" 59–60, 64–65. For the situation prevailing under the Principate, see Nicolet, *World* 75.

[198] On patronage as an institution that connected the center of power to the margins and provided access to resources to those situated on the periphery of society, see Wallace-Hadrill, *Patronage* (1989) 71–81, 85. On the inappropriateness of friendship with (male) prostitutes, see Sen. *Ben.* 2.21.1–2.

[199] Contra Leppin, *Histrionen* 73, who argues that the aim of demoting performers was to dilute the impact of their votes. I doubt we can be sure that actors voted as a bloc or, even if we assume they did, that their numbers or electoral influence were significant enough to matter.

[200] See the discussion in Cohen, "Ordo" (1975).

[201] There is reason to distinguish political from procedural rights and disabilities, public law from private law. But the way in which such distinctions are applied is often influenced more by modern legal thinking than by the categories employed by the Romans themselves. Note, for example, the reasoning of Karlowa, "Geschichte" (1870) 209, cf. 223. Compare the comments of Mazzacane, *ED* infamia 384, and the sources given by Kaser, "Rechtswidrigkeit" (1940) 136 n. 5, 137 n. 1.

individual praetors making few innovations, even in periods of relatively pro-nounced judicial activism.[202] The praetor was not free from constraints, among which are to be counted the possibility of intervention by magistrates with equal or greater *imperium,* the threat of prosecution at the end of his tenure, and the less acute but more broadly influential weight of tradition and public opinion.[203] All the same, he enjoyed considerable discretion in the exercise of his official respon-sibilities. It was left to him to determine whether a particular remedy should be granted or not. For the prospective litigant, denial of a remedy was tantamount to loss of a legal right.

Postulare

A litigant might direct a request *(postulatio/postulare)* at any remedy offered under the edict: *actio, interdictum, restituere in integrum.*[204] Both plaintiff and defendant were entitled to make such requests; for example, the latter might *postulare ex-ceptionem,* that is, raise an affirmative defense. The litigants might turn over re-sponsibility for *postulare* to an assistant *(advocatus).*[205] Or they might choose a "substitute" to represent them at law, a *cognitor* or *procurator.*

"Advocacy" in this sense is best construed broadly.[206] The praetor could de-cide to take into account the requests of one or both parties in his construction of the *formula,* the stereotyped set of instructions to the finder of fact *(iudex)* that defined the issue to be decided.[207]

The right to make such requests, *postulare,* was not equally available to all Roman citizens. The praetor issued a series of three rubrics restricting this privilege. The first imposed an absolute prohibition, which applied to those who had not yet completed their seventeenth year and to deaf persons. If necessary, the praetor granted a legal assistant *(advocatus)* to act on their behalf.[208] The praetor could also prohibit certain persons from acting in this general capacity: a man might be banned generally from acting as an *advocatus,* either permanently or for a fixed term.[209]

---

[202] For a treatment of the praetor's conservatism in the face of legal change, see Pugliese, "Pretori" (1989).

[203] Urban praetors were further constrained by the passage of the *lex Cornelia* in 67 B.C., whose exact significance is controversial: Kaser, *RP* 1² (1971) 206, with n. 6.

[204] Ulpian's definition is general. Ulp. (6 *ad edictum*) D. 3.1.1.2: "Postulare autem est desiderium suum vel amici sui in iure apud eum, qui iurisdictioni praeest, exponere: vel alterius desiderio contra-dicere." On *postulare,* see Leifer, *RE* postulatio (1953); Pugliese, *Processo* 2.1 (1963) 304–310; Kaser, *RZ* (1966) 150–151, 171–172.

[205] The *advocatus* was not a full representative in law in the sense of *cognitor* or *procurator;* see below.

[206] See Crook, *Advocacy* 146–163, cf. 46–57. In the criminal proceedings of the *quaestio* system, the main request made to the magistrate *(nomen deferre)* was to accept the formal accusation: Crook, *Advocacy* 159. I take up this issue below.

[207] The requests might be numerous and varied, as the parties and their legal counsel jockeyed for an advantageous position going into the second stage of the suit: Leifer, *RE* postulatio 877–880.

[208] Ulp. D. 3.1.1.4: see Pugliese, *Processo* 2.1.306; Kaser, *RZ* 150.

[209] Ulp. D. 3.1.6.1; Pap. D. *eod.* 8; Ulp. D. 48.19.9 pr.-8.

The next two rubrics on *postulare* restricted the right to act on behalf of others before the praetor. Those who were not permitted to make requests *pro aliis* included women,[210] blind men, any man "qui corpore suo muliebria passus erit" ("who will have suffered womanly things with his body"),[211] men condemned on a capital charge, and men who had hired out their services to fight with wild beasts.[212]

The third rubric, which restricted the right of *postulare* to close relations, patrons, their parents and children, and a small group of others, fell into two parts. One justified the exclusion of certain persons on the ground that positive legislation, whether comitial law, *SC*, magisterial edict, or imperial court decision *(decretum)*, had remanded them to this category.[213]

The second part of the third rubric, which came to form the cornerstone of Byzantine *infamia*,[214] gave a list of certain types who fell under the restriction. These were the recipient of a dishonorable discharge from the army; the actor;[215] the pimp ("qui lenocinium fecerit"),[216] the man convicted of malicious or collusive prosecution in a *iudicium publicum*; the man condemned for armed robbery *(vi bona rapta)*, theft *(furtum)*, outrage *(iniuria)*,[217] fraud *(dolus malus/fraus)* in his own name, or who had settled such a suit out of court; and the man condemned in his own name, and not in a cross-action, in a suit on partnership, mandate,[218] guardianship *(tutela)*, or deposit. Also included were the man who, after the death of a son-in-law, knowingly gave in marriage a woman he had in his power before the traditional period of mourning had elapsed; he who married such a woman without being ordered to do so by him in whose power he stood; he who allowed a man in his power to marry such a person; he who, in his own name and not on the order of someone in whose power he stood, or in the name of him or her whom he had in power, simultaneously entered into two agreements for betrothal or marriage.

The praetor qualified these restrictions by noting that they applied only where the subject had not benefited from *in integrum restituere*, meaning here the can-

---

[210] See Lab.-Ulp. D. 3.1.1.5 for women and the blind.

[211] For this type and the two that follow, see Pomp.-Ulp. D. 3.1.1.6.

[212] The last three groups are identified by the jurist as *in turpitudine notabiles:* Lab.-Ulp. D. 3.1.1.5. Pace Greenidge, *Infamia* 117–118, the expression cannot be praetorian: see Kaser, "Infamia" 246 n. 118; Gardner, *Being* 114, 117.

[213] See Karlowa, "Geschichte" 207–209. On the relationship of the two parts of this rubric, see Krüger, "Verweisungsedikte" (1916) 257–265.

[214] [Iul. (1 *ad edictum*)] D. 3.2.1. Lenel, "Kunde" (1881) 56–62; Lenel, *Pal.* (1889/1960) 1 col. 484 n. 4, 2 col. 441 n. 3; Lenel, *EP³* (1923/1974) 77; Kaser, "Infamia" 245, with n. 111 ("kaum eine Interpolation ist so gut gesichert wie diese"; see 273); Beaucamp, *Statut* 1.122; Formigoni Candini, "*Lenones*" 107 n. 47. The text is accepted as it stands by Gardner, *Being* 126, 128, 143.

[215] On the wide range of persons embraced by this provision, see Pennitz, "Athleten."

[216] Krüger, "Verweisungsedikte" 266–267, errs in conflating this commercial pimp with the *maritus-leno* of the Augustan law on adultery.

[217] FML ch. 84 specifies that the defendant in theft and *iniuria* must be free or, in the case of theft, the liability of the master must be at stake.

[218] Conviction under the *actio pro socio* or *mandati* produced "*infamia*" only if the finder of fact specified that the act was done *dolo malo:* FML ch. 84. The same is true of the *actio fiduciae*, reported in the FML and by Gaius but not in the Justinianic *Corpus*. Cf. the extraordinary action on *stellionatus:* Ulp. D. 3.2.13.8, D. 47.20.2.

cellation of the disability, so that the previous legal status of the *"infamis"* was restored.[219] Because by the second century this privilege was typically granted by emperor and Senate, the question was raised as to the precise nature of the praetor's competence: Pomponius and Ulpian limited this to the removal of the exclusion from *postulare*.[220] The praetor himself could *in integrum restituere* only in matters consistent with his own jurisdiction.[221] Anyone condemned in a *iudicium famosum* might be later *restitutus* by the magistrate, that is, freed from the effects of praetorian *"infamia"*.[222]

Ulpian comments that *restituere* was rather unlikely to be granted in the more serious cases given under the second rubric, that is, persons described by the phrase "in turpitudine notabiles."[223] Of course, *restituere* of this type was possible where *"infamia"* was produced by a court sentence,[224] and so, of those types given under the second rubric, only those condemned under a capital charge were really eligible.[225]

The information preserved by the compilers in the second two rubrics has for some time been recognized to be incomplete. *Lanistae* (i.e., trainers) and gladiators are notable by their absence, which is explained by the disappearance of gladiatorial shows by Justinian's day.[226] Trainers perhaps appeared under the third rubric, while gladiators, qua *auctorati*, fell along with *bestiarii* under the second, but we cannot be sure.[227] Other omissions have been detected. These include conviction under the *lex Laetoria*, bankruptcy, *tutor curatorve suspectus*, marriage with a ward (or with father's ward), failed accusation to the *fiscus*, usury, conviction on the *actio sepulchri violati* or *actio expilatae hereditatis*, and *stellionatus*.[228] A definitive list may not be possible.[229]

---

[219] Ulp. D. 3.1.1.9. Provisions for *in integrum restituere* are found in the *TH* (118), the *lex Iulia et Papia* (Mod. D. 37.14.9.1), and in criminal statutes, such as the *lex Iulia repetundarum* (Cass.-Marcel. D. 1.9.2) and the *lex Iulia de vi* (Call. D. 22.5.3.5; Ulp. *Coll*. 9.2.2). See Mommsen, *Strafrecht* 481–487; Waldstein, *Begnadigungsrecht* (1964) esp. 131–136, 217–218; Zilletti, "Note" (1968) 46–51; Kaser, "Restitutio" (1978) 181–182; Selb, "Edikt" (1986) 270–271.

[220] Pomp.-Ulp. D. 3.1.1.10.

[221] As with the protection of minors: Pomp.-Ulp. D. 3.1.1.10. Senate and emperor had authority *restituere* in matters of criminal law: Zilletti, "Note" 52.

[222] On the effect of *in integrum restituere* in providing a clean slate, see Ulp. D. 50.4.3.2. Macer D. 47.2.64(63) shows that release from *"infamia"* could not accompany the original sentence; *in integrum restituere* had to be a separate act.

[223] I agree with Zilletti, "Note" 47, against Lenel, "Kunde" 61, who had argued for a restriction of the *restitutus* phrase to the third rubric.

[224] Greenidge, *Infamia* 179. Although Severus's rescript on ex-slave prostitutes (see below in the text) is a kind of *in integrum restituere*, it is significant that this action relies on imperial authority.

[225] In fact, the nonlegal evidence seems to concern criminal cases (which fell under the second rubric): Cic. *Verr*. 2.2.109 (argument by analogy); Quint. *IO* 5.10.108; cf. the grounds for removal of the disability given in Cic. *Phil*. 2.56. See below on *turpitudo*.

[226] Greenidge, *Infamia* 121; MacMullen, "Difference" (1986/1990) 148; Gardner, *Being* 129.

[227] Lenel, *EP*³ 79; Greenidge, *Infamia* 121; Kaser, "Infamia" 237 n. 85, 239 n. 94; Pugliese, *Processo* 2.1.310; Albanese, *Persone* 410.

[228] Greenidge, *Infamia* 134–143.

[229] Pugliese, *Processo* 2.1.309–310, includes bankruptcy and conviction under the *lex Laetoria*. Albanese, *Persone* 409 n. 289, 414, has bankruptcy and conviction on the *actio fiduciae*. D'Ors, "Lista" (1984), agrees with false accusation to the *fiscus* (Call. D. 49.14.2 pr.; Marci. D. *eod*. 18.7), conviction

More striking than the absence of gladiators and trainers is the absence of a clear reference to prostitutes. Insofar as women are categorically excluded under the second rubric, only male prostitutes are eligible for the disability. The relevant phrase is "qui corpore suo muliebria passus erit," which is found in the same rubric as women. The reference is broad enough to include all passive male homosexuals, and there can be little doubt that prostitutes are also meant.[230] The possibility that some male prostitutes consistently played the active role in sexual relations is simply ignored by the edict.[231] The moralizing, emotive tone of the phrase is striking, especially when compared with the neutral language typically employed by the legal sources when speaking of (female) prostitutes. The extraordinary tone encourages a departure from the general principle I have followed in analyzing these disabilities, so that I would argue that the lumping of women and passive homosexuals under the same rubric is no coincidence.

The praetor had no list of individuals to be excluded on the basis of these disqualifications, so that as a practical matter it depended on an adversary, if he had knowledge of the fact, to raise an objection.[232]

Legal Representatives/Substitutes

Other praetorian edicts restricted the ability of certain persons to act as legal representatives of other persons, that is, as *cognitores* and as *procuratores*.[233] Legal representatives or, better, substitutes are to be distinguished from *advocati*, who rendered legal advice and assistance.[234] The *cognitor* was formally appointed by a litigant before his adversary.[235] The figure of the *procurator* is both complex and controversial. There is now general agreement that the so-called *procurator ad litem* existed in classical times.[236] This figure evolved out of the figure of *procurator*

---

under the *lex Laetoria* (Gaius 4.182 is not exhaustive; the point is now confirmed by FML ch. 84), and conviction for *sponsio in probrum* (FML ch. 84), interpreted by D'Ors as a procedural *sponsio* made *calumniae causa* (this might rather refer to an ordinary wager, as prohibited by statute: Paul. D. 11.5.2.1; Marci. D. eod. 3). Discrepancies among lists have various explanations, chief among them purpose (that of the *TH* is markedly different from that of the edict, for example) and chronology: Kaser, "Infamia"; D'Ors, "Lista"; González, *"Lex Irnitana"* 228.

[230] Despite Gardner, *Being* 128, who sees an omission of prostitutes here. Kaser, "Infamia" 239 n. 93 (perhaps after Lenel, *EP*³ 76 esp. n. 8), holds that the phrase referred exclusively to male prostitutes, but he broadens this in *RZ* 151: "der Mann, der sich von einem anderen geschlechtlich hat mißbrauchen lassen."

[231] Cf. Sen. *Contr.* 5.6 and Firm. Mat. *Math.* 8.19.7 ("Cinaedus publica damnatus infamia"; see also 7.25 passim, 8.25.4, 8.27.8) and the discussion in Gleason, "Semiotics" (1990) 397–398. The jurists Pomponius and Ulpian (Pomp.-Ulp. D. 3.1.1.6) held the view, evidently controversial, that those raped by bandits or enemy soldiers fall outside the scope of this provision: Dalla, *Venus* 52–55.

[232] Gardner, *Being* 112–113.

[233] Lenel, *EP*³ 91–93 (for *cognitores*), 96–97 (for *procuratores*; here the praetor simply refers back to the list for *cognitores*). Those forbidden to act as *cognitores* were effectively barred from serving as any type of legal representative: see below and Pugliese, *Processo* 2.1.334.

[234] Rasi, *NNDI* avvocati (1957); Crook, *Advocacy* 158–163.

[235] See Zablocka, "Costituzione" (1984/1985).

[236] Solazzi, "Definizione" (1923/1957); Solazzi, "Note" (1937/1960) 601–635; Solazzi, *"Procurator ad litem"* (1949/1972).

omnium rerum, himself capable of serving as a legal substitute.[237] Substitutes were regularly appointed in case of the principal's age, illness, or absence.[238] It was also possible to employ substitutes in the arbitration process known as *compromissum.*[239]

Cognitores had gone out of fashion by Justinian's day, so that the compilers have not preserved the list of exclusions. This list seems to have encompassed soldiers, women,[240] and all *"infames"* banned from *postulare* under rubrics 2 and 3.[241] Lenel declares, with logic, that all those prohibited, qua *"infames"* or not, from *postulare* were barred here too. We do not know if the ban was absolute or mimicked the threefold articulation of the *postulare* rubrics. Perhaps the latter held true,[242] with exclusion possible, upon application of the opponent, for those who were *"infames."*

We now know that all persons forbidden to act as *actores* or *cognitores* under the provincial edict were also barred from appointment as municipal legal representative *(actor).*[243] The rules of the provincial governor's edict were presumably modeled on the urban praetor's edict (the regulations on *actores* may have referred to the edict on *postulare*).[244] González thinks the governor's edict contained regulations specifically devoted to municipal representatives,[245] but in the absence of evidence it is hard to discern types that would fall under one rubric but not under the other, and so this might be an unnecessary duplication. The disability is related to that which prevented *"infames"* from bringing an *actio popularis,* where the accuser appeared as the legal substitute for the community.[246]

Yet another set of praetorian regulations prohibited certain persons from appointing a *cognitor* or *procurator* to conduct a suit on their behalf.[247] This list too

---

[237]Pugliese, *Processo* 2.1.331; Kaser, *RZ* 156; Kaser, *RP* 1² 266; Angelini, *Procurator* (1971) 175–192; Burdese (rev. Angelini) (1971) 325; cf. Behrends, "Prokuratur" (1971) 217, 245, 247–274.

[238]*Rhet. Her.* 2.20; Inst. 4.10 pr., on which see Behrends, "Prokuratur" 244–245.

[239]Bonifacio, *NNDI* compromesso (1959) 785.

[240]Soldiers and women were excluded for reasons of public policy: Lenel, *EP*³ 92. On soldiers, see now De Pascale, "Divieto" (1987). Alex. Sev. C. 2.12(13).9 *(anno incerto)* suggests a generous interpretation was the norm: see Mayer-Maly, *"Verecundia"* (1988) 387. In the later Empire, soldiers were forbidden the practice of certain professions on similar grounds: *HA Duo Maxim.* 8.4; Leo C. 12.35(36).15 (a. 458).

[241]So Lenel, *EP*³ 80, 89–93; Kaser, "Infamia" 247; Kaser, *RZ* 154–155. See PS 1.2.1: "Omnes infames, qui postulare prohibentur, cognitores fieri non posse etiam volentibus adversariis." Lenel, *EP*³ 92–93, accepts—and Levy, *PS* 66–75 (joined by Kaser, "Infamia" 248 n. 1, *RZ* 155 n. 22), rejects—the general expression "omnes infames." I use the term *infames* advisedly; a comprehensive conception of *infamia* for the classical period remains to be proved.

[242]So Karlowa, "Geschichte" 221 n. 28.

[243]FML ch. 70.

[244]See Johnston, "Three Thoughts" 65.

[245]González, "Lex Irnitana" 222.

[246]Paul. D. 47.23.4, with Greenidge, *Infamia* 8 n. 1. Casavola, *Azioni* (1958) esp. 120–124, emphasizes the fact that the accuser is deemed to pursue his own interest; this cannot, in the case of pimps and prostitutes, be identified with that of the community.

[247]Lenel, *EP*³ 89–91 *(cognitores),* 96–97 *(procuratores;* again the praetor simply refers back to the previous list). Effectively, the right to name any type of representative (including, e.g., *defensores*) was precluded: FV 322, 323, with Pugliese, *Processo* 2.1.324–334.

has disappeared, aside from a fragment,[248] but Lenel argues that it would have comprised all the *"infames"* given under the *postulare* rubrics. At the same time a new element was added: female *"infames,"* since women were not categorically excluded here, a new listing was necessary. The incorporation of female *"infames"* explains their presence in the fragment, as well as how they come to be mentioned in the juristic commentaries on this part of the praetor's edict.[249] It can be asserted with confidence that female prostitutes and procuresses were named in this place.[250]

The precise date of these provisions is unknown. Most scholars date the regulations concerning *postulare* and *cognitores* to the final decades of the second century B.C. at the latest.[251] A passage of Plautus, which is recognized to be a parody of a praetorian edict and which among other things forbids prostitutes from being seated onstage, is suggestive but ultimately inconclusive evidence.[252] At any rate, the regulations probably predate the main period for the development of the urban praetor's edict, which occurred in the decades following 100 B.C.[253]

Against this view is the argument of Krüger, who claims that a number of the specific provisions in the third rubric were the product of comitial legislation.[254] There is no evidence that this was so even where we might have good reason to expect it, for example, with those convicted under the *lex Laetoria*.[255] But to make the praetor's provision on pimps depend on the *TH* and to assert that the *lex Iulia* on adultery placed convicted adulterers in the third rubric, only to be deleted by the Byzantines, forces the evidence; there is no reason to assume a unitary, positive source for all of these disabilities.[256]

The regulations for *procuratores,* insofar as they are explicitly modeled on those for *cognitores,* are somewhat later in origin than the latter, though once again certainty is elusive. Watson argues for the existence of the so-called *procurator ad litem* in the first century B.C.[257] To be sure, a *procurator* with a general mandate might also act in court, and the edictal terms would have applied to him at a relatively early date. For what it is worth, Ulpian, citing Labeo, holds that a *slave's*

[248] *FV* 320.

[249] Karlowa, "Geschichte" 212–229, was the first to identify *FV* 320 as part of the edict *ne dent cognitorem* and justify the inclusion of female *infames* under this heading. He has been widely followed: Greenidge, *Infamia* 173; Lenel, *EP*[3] 89–91.

[250] Karlowa, "Geschichte" 225 n. 36, argues for the presence of prostitutes.

[251] See Leifer, *RE* postulatio 874, who describes these provisions as "sicher alte." See Kelly, "Edict" (1966) esp. 351, whose argument is not, I believe, inconsistent with what is argued here; Leppin, *Histrionen* 161. Schrage, "Infamie" 393, links the prohibitions on *postulare* to a provision of the XII Tables (8.22W = Gell. 15.13.11); the connection is unproven, in my view.

[252] Plaut. *Poen.* 16–45. Watson, *LM* (1974) 49–50, understands the passage as an indication that the praetor issued regulations on behavior at festivals he oversaw. Or Plautus may be taking a swipe at the regulations that governed the magistrate's own court.

[253] Watson, *LM* 35.

[254] Krüger, "Verweisungsedikte" 237–238, 257–270.

[255] Di Salvo, *Lex Laetoria* (1979) 199–215.

[256] Krüger's argument in "Verweisungsedikte" 266–267 that *lenocinium* served as a bridge assisting the incorporation of *adulterium* into the edict after the passage of the adultery statute is founded on a conflation of commercial *lenocinium,* as in the edict and *TH,* and the criminal kind, as in the adultery law. I know of no evidence to support the assertion of Dixon that the exclusion of women dates "probably from the early Empire": Dixon *"Infirmitas"* 359.

[257] Watson, *Obligations* (1965) 198–203. This is contested by Angelini, *Procurator* 182–186.

general *procurator* could not act on his behalf in court, which suggests, *ex contrario*, that in Labeo's day such *procuratores* routinely acted as legal substitutes.[258]

Although changes were introduced from time to time, the professional exclusions on these lists were probably original.[259] Changes occurred as late as the middle of the first century B.C., when women and the blind were excluded. The latter disability was introduced during (or just after) Brutus's tenure as urban praetor in 44 B.C.[260] The former is associated with the activity of the advocate Afrania (or Carfania),[261] who dates to the Sullan period.[262] Before women's categorical exclusion, it is quite likely that the original *postulare* edict specifically mentioned procuresses and female prostitutes. This would make the list of exclusions given under the edict *ne dent cognitorem* identical, save for minor subsequent alterations, with the portion of the original *postulare* edict that dealt with "*infames.*"

The purpose behind the imposition of these disabilities has been explained as a concern with the maintenance of decorum in the praetor's court.[263] The evidence for the *postulare* edict, which also suggests other reasons for the introduction of particular provisions, supports this rationale. Obviously, the same holds true for the edict *ne dentur cognitores* and the analogous rules on *procuratores,* at least where the appointment of a representative was not intended as a means to effect the transfer of a claim.[264]

These reasons do not, however, explain the prohibitions against assigning a *cognitor* or *procurator.* If the presence of a postulating pimp was irksome, why not allow the man to appoint a legal substitute? Lenel suggests that the point was to make the pursuit of civil litigation difficult for such persons. This is persuasive, especially since it captures the punitive intent behind the denial of these privileges.[265] But it raises a further question: why make this difficult? Why not allow a pimp to act as a *cognitor* or *procurator in rem suam*? Other suggestions have been put forward: the appearance in court of an "*infamis*" gave his or her opponent an edge; the ability to engage a legal substitute was understood as a mark of honor and so was stripped from disgraced persons; the point was to deny the "*infamis*" the opportunity to avoid exposure to public humiliation through appearance in court.[266]

The notion of honor offers a unitary solution to the question of what purpose these restrictions served. "*Infames*", who were by definition men and women who had lost their honor, were denied certain privileges reserved for those whose dignity

[258] Lab.-Ulp. D. 3.3.33 pr. On the text, see Behrends, "Prokuratur" 248–249.

[259] They then serve as early examples of the importation of moral/social values into the edict: Wieacker, "OW" (1977/1983) 185.

[260] Lab.-Ulp. D. 3.1.1.5.

[261] Lab.-Ulp. D. 3.1.1.5.

[262] Val. Max. 8.3.2. See Chapter 5. Ideally, if not always in practice, a woman would be represented by a male, often a close relation: Anagnostou-Cañas, "Femme" (1984); Marshall, "Civil Courts" (1989) 51, with n. 46.

[263] Greenidge, *Infamia* 114; Pugliese, *Processo* 2.1.304.

[264] See Gehrich, *Kognitur* (1963) esp. 1, 49.

[265] The praetor might refuse to let anyone *postulare* on behalf of a litigant: Leifer, *RE* postulatio 876, on Cic. *Red. Sen.* 22. This was tantamount to *denegare actionem,* on which see the literature given below.

[266] Karlowa, "Geschichte" 222–224; Greenidge, *Infamia* 159–160.

was unimpaired. Concern with public order and decorum was one motive;[267] punishment was another. The dishonored were cut off from the community at large
both by the blight on reputation that the praetor's list entailed and by the practical
consequence that they were denied the power to assist all but a very small circle
of friends and relations before the bar of private law. Provision of legal assistance
played an important role in political and personal friendship at Rome.[268] Nor could
pimps and the others hide behind the mask of a legal representative; that too was
a preserve of the dignified.[269]

By forcing *"infames"* to come to court in their own cause, the praetor was
better able to discriminate against them by excluding them from a range of legal
remedies/rights available to respectable litigants. Of course, it is likely that pimps
were aware of popular prejudices against them,[270] that is, the humiliating treatment
they received and could expect to receive in court. A pimp who was a prospective
litigant might therefore find it inconvenient to appear before the praetor even in
pursuit of a just claim. Any pimp who did dare to make an appearance offered the
magistrate an opportunity to demonstrate firmness on the issue of where those
without honor stood in his court.[271]

The praetorian phrase concerning pimps deserves brief comment. The quotation from the edict offered in our principal source gives a single verb form here
as in the other cases it lists.[272] That is, it reads "qui lenocinium fecerit" instead
of "fecit fecerit."[273] This phrasing may be explained as a compilatorial abbreviation, or it may in fact be original to the edict, which is typically more abstract and
less prone to enumerate every possible circumstance of application than other types
of Roman legislation.[274] In either case, this is a typical legal formulation in that it

[267] The centrality of this rationale is shown by the reasons given for the exclusion of non-*"infames,"*
which are also subsumable under the notion of honor: Lab.-Ulp. D. 3.1.1.5 (*pudicitia,* not *pudor:* the
legal construction of chastity). Cf. Ant. C. 2.11(12).8 (a. 205) and the reasons offered for women's
exclusion from public office: Paul. D. 5.1.12.2, Paul D. 16.1.1 (the justification is *mores*); Ulp. D.
50.17.2 pr. See Dixon, *"Infirmitas"* 360, 367.

[268] Pugliese, *Processo* 2.1.308 (apropos of the limits placed on the right *postulare pro aliis*): ". . .
questa limitazione era sentita dai Romani, per cui l'esercizio del patrocinio costituiva un po'' una
piattaforma politica, come una grave umiliazione morale." See, in general, Crook, *Advocacy.*

[269] The principle is illustrated by the fact that condemnation in a *iudicium famosum* did not confer
"infamia" on a defendant if his case was conducted from the beginning by a legal substitute: Ulp. D.
3.2.6.2. The privilege of appointing a substitute was inappropriate for those already dishonored. Note
the argument of Mattingly, "Naevius" (1960) 428 n. 65, and of Leppin, *Histrionen* 74, which connects
ignominia of actors with the requirement to remove their masks onstage after a performance.

[270] Pimps were perhaps familiar with the rough justice served up to (or simply anticipated by) their
bretheren in Plautine comedy, a fairly reliable indicator of popular attitudes: e.g., *Pers.* 745–746; *Poen.*
1342–1343; *Rud.* 860–866. See the list in Kelly, *Litigation* (1966) 62–64. Declamatory evidence is
another good source: Calp. Fl. 5. Cf. Herodas *Mim.* 2 for a send-up of a pimp's attempt to vindicate
his rights in court in a Greek context.

[271] That the *"infamis"* did not as a rule venture into court, especially to assert a right not absolutely
his own, is perhaps suggested by an observation of Justinian justifying the abolition of the rules governing persons who appoint or act as *procuratores* in court: Inst. 4.13.11(10).

[272] [Iul. (1 *ad edictum*)] D. 3.2.1.

[273] Cf. also Ulp. (6 *ad edictum*) D. 3.2.4.2 (see the next section).

[274] See Vonglis, *Loi* (1968) 65–69. Cf. the discussion of the statutory phrasing in Chapter 3, including
the evidence of Cicero against "fecit, fecerit" in the edict of his day.

describes what the actor does rather than characterize the actor himself. Outside the legal sources *leno* is the rule.

Ulpian and the Postulating Pimp

The treatment pimps receive from the jurists sheds further light on the content and purpose of these provisions. As so often, we have only Ulpian's commentary to guide us, but this may be taken as representative of the classical juristic position:

> Ulp. (6 *ad edictum*) D. 3.2.4.2: Ait praetor: "qui lenocinium fecerit." lenocinium facit qui quaestuaria mancipia habuerit: sed et qui in liberis hunc quaestum exercet, in eadem causa est. sive autem principaliter hoc negotium gerat sive alterius negotiationis accessione utatur (ut puta si caupo fuit vel stabularius et mancipia talia habuit ministrantia et occasione ministerii quaestum facientia: sive balneator fuerit, velut in quibusdam provinciis fit, in balineis ad custodienda vestimenta conducta habens mancipia hoc genus observantia in officina), lenocinii poena tenebitur.

> The praetor says, "One who will have acted as a pimp." He acts as a pimp who will have kept slave prostitutes, though the man who carries on this trade with free prostitutes[275] is in the same position. Moreover, he will be liable to the penalty whether he conducts this as his main line of business or whether he adopts this as a sideline to another type of business (for example, if he was the manager of a tavern or inn and he kept, as part of his staff, such slaves, who, in the course of their duties, prostituted themselves; or if he will have been a bath manager who, as is the practice in certain provinces, keeps in his baths slaves hired to watch over clothing and they plied this sort of trade in the workplace).

The phrase "ut puta . . . in officina" is attacked as an interpolation by Eisele and others.[276] Eisele views the phrase "ut puta" with suspicion, but this is now accepted as typical of Ulpian.[277] He also rejects "talia" as "entirely unconnected," but this is true of neither grammar nor sense. The "mancipia talia" are the same as the "quaestuaria mancipia" mentioned at the beginning of the text: Ulpian has declined to repeat "quaestuaria," presumably for reasons of style. Several details of Eisele's criticism are extreme by today's standards.[278] This is true for his claim that the words "hoc genus observantia" are "comic." The resort to euphemism is unusual, but the motive might have been the avoidance of unnecessary repetition.[279] Similarly,

[275] Sicari, *Prostituzione* (1991) 32 n. 11, takes *in liberis* to refer to the prostitution of children by their fathers, but this seems impossible, especially given the contrast with *mancipia* in the preceding phrase.
[276] Eisele, "Beiträge" 14 (1890) 13–14, followed by H. Krüger, "Bemerkungen" (1900) 459; P. Krüger and Mommsen in the *Digest*; Schulz, *Studium* (1916) 26–27.
[277] See Honoré, *Ulpian* (1982) 71.
[278] These tend to be subjective. His substitution of "occasione" for "accessione" is otiose. Eisele, "Beiträge," condemns "si caupo . . . habuit" as "breitspurige." One can, I think, question whether this phrase can seriously be attributed to Tribonian and his colleagues. Eisele, to be sure, does not provide a date or a justification for the interpolation.
[279] H. Krüger, "Bemerkungen" 459, claims that *observare* possessed the special meaning of slaves performing services for their masters only for the Byzantines. This criticism relies on an uncertain foundation, insofar as it is supported by only one instance of usage, and is also irrelevant because that is not what the word means here.

the condemnation of "velut" and the tense of "fuit" and "habuit" is unjustified.[280]

The basic genuineness of the passage is suggested by the introductory "ut puta," the pairing of *caupo* and *stabularius*,[281] and the content of the examples given, which are drawn from the social and economic life of the classical period.[282] (Schulz accepts the content of the text as classical.)

Ulpian asks what the edict means by "qui lenocinium fecerit." He then sets forth two different kinds of distinction. After defining a pimp as a man who keeps slave prostitutes, the jurist qualifies this with the remark that someone who keeps free prostitutes also counts as a pimp.[283] Given its formulation, the distinction may be taken to mean one of two things. The pimp who keeps slave prostitutes is emphasized either because this type was more significant as a socioeconomic phenomenon or because a special legal reason (not evident to us) required this.[284] Whatever the rationale, Ulpian's phrasing signals the beginning of a discussion devoted principally to the subject of pimps with slave prostitutes.

Ulpian then makes another distinction, which applies to both types of pimps: whoever keeps prostitutes as a main line of business or as a sideline in connection with some other pursuit is liable to the *poena lenocinii*. The examples he gives, however, all concern slave prostitutes, whether under the direction of a *caupo*, *stabularius*, or *balneator*. Leaving aside the problem of slave prostitutes for a moment, we can say that this information is valuable for two reasons. On a sociological level, it supplements the evidence drawn from other sources on the close association of prostitution with a number of service industries. Legally, it shows that the jurists construed the edict extensively.

Just how extensively the jurists understood these rules is suggested by an examination of Ulpian's phrasing. A progression is traceable from the first sentence, which contains a clear implication that the pimp not only manages but profits directly from his prostitutes: "quaestuaria," "hunc quaestum exercet." This is precisely what one envisages where the type of business is chiefly ("principaliter") devoted to prostitution.

But the text suggests that more than one type of setup was possible and that the pimp did not always profit directly from the practice of prostitution on his premises, that is when this was just a sideline, incidental to another business. The description of prostitutes on the staff of the *caupo* or *stabularius* ("mancipia . . . facientia") is broad enough to embrace both those prostituting themselves at the behest of management and those simply freelancing. The description of slaves working for bathkeepers seems only to include the latter. They are, it seems, hired to watch the clients' clothing, not to perform sexual services. They presumably

---

[280] Schulz's protest, *Studium* 26–27, against the switch in tenses from "fuit" and "habuit" to "fuerit" and the number of participles has some weight, but these features are better understood as signs of editing, not wholesale invention.

[281] The two are often found together, especially in commentaries on the two edictal rubrics that name them both: Lenel, *EP³* 131, 333. Cf. Gaius D. 44.7.5.6.

[282] Ulpian's mention of provincial practice with regard to the bathkeeper is one of the sporadic juristic references to social usages: Wacke, "*Potentiores*" (1980) 568–569.

[283] The gender of the prostitutes is left indeterminate and must be regarded as irrelevant to the discussion.

[284] The former seems more likely: see the comments of Formigoni Candini, "*Lenones*" 116.

might engage in the latter on their own initiative and for their own or their masters' benefit. Legally, their earnings belonged to their owners and not to the bath manager who hired them, barring prior agreement to the contrary. Various informal arrangements were no doubt worked out, however, with the bathkeeper acting *in loco lenonis.* The important point is that the *balneator* is branded as a pimp under the edict, which suggests that he, like the *caupo* and *stabularius,* played a role in the selling of sex in his establishment. The prostitutes must in some sense be under his control or supervision, and/or he must profit from their exchange of sex for money.

Ulpian's discussion does not, at first glance, seem capable of resolving all potential cases. Suppose a man owns a brothel where he employs, or owns as slaves, intermediaries who qualify under the edict as pimps. Is this man himself a pimp, on Ulpian's analysis? Suppose that a man operates a tavern, inn, or bath staffed or simply frequented by free prostitutes. Is he too a pimp in the sense of the edict?

The extensive slant taken by the jurist suggests an answer to the second question. The first sentence of the text shows that anyone who makes money from prostitutes, slave or free, is identifiable as a pimp. The examples given at the end of the passage suggest that the same is true of anyone who employs persons who act as prostitutes in his place of business, whether or not he himself directly profits from this sideline.

There are then two tests for the pimps as defined under the edict: direct profit and direct control. Either criterion by itself is sufficient, as suggested by the case of the *balneator,* though in most cases they probably would have coincided. It does not matter what role is played by prostitution or what percentage of the business is devoted to this. Free prostitutes who solicit customers in a man's place of business do not make him a *leno,* unless he takes all or part of their earnings and/or supervises them at their jobs. Slave prostitutes, in most circumstances, fulfilled both criteria, which perhaps partly explains the emphasis accorded them.

Yet another part of the solution to this problem of definition, and an answer to the first question posed above, is suggested by the following texts:

> Pomp.-Ulp. (6 *ad edictum*) D. 3.2.4.3: Pomponius et eum, qui in servitute peculiaria mancipia prostituta habuit, notari post libertatem ait.

> Pomponius says that even he who as a slave had slave prostitutes belonging to his *peculium* is marked by the *nota* after manumission.

> Ulp. (6 *ad edictum*) D. 3.2.24: Imperator Severus rescripsit non offuisse mulieris famae quaestum eius in servitute factum.

> Emperor Severus said in a rescript that a woman's standing was not compromised by the profession she practiced while a slave.

The two passages are rightly compared by the editors of the *Digest.*[285] Because it deals with female "*infames,*" the second passage must directly concern, not the edict on *postulare,* but that on *ne dent cognitorem* (see above). There is a problem

---

[285] Mommsen and Krüger ad loc. Lenel, *Pal.* 2 Ulp. #280, places both passages together, along with D. 3.2.4.2.

in that it derives from the sixth book of Ulpian's commentary on the edict, which dealt with the former, instead of book 8, which discussed the latter. Karlowa observes that this is not the only juristic passage that, although evidently treating women's *"infamia,"* derives from a commentary on *postulare.*[286] Kaser sees no clear connection.[287] Might this not be taken as a subtle indication that the late classical jurists themselves took this edict as a foundation for their discussions of praetorian *"infamia,"* so that women came into consideration here? Since the rescript addresses the situation of a woman, it is open to question whether the holding applies to males as well. This may be doubted, since, as we have seen, male prostitutes are assimilated to pathics under the second rubric on *postulare,* so that their position is even less privileged.[288]

Two points about the first passage deserve particular notice. Pomponius and Ulpian do not proceed up the chain of command in their definition of a pimp, as they make no mention of the slave pimp's master, who might fairly be described as a pimp himself. This omission implicitly exonerates anyone not directly involved in the operation of the brothel or other business where prostitutes worked. Presumably, this was equally true where the master owned the pimp (and therefore also the *peculiaria mancipia* themselves) and where the pimp was a free employee and/ or the prostitutes were of free status. This had the effect of insulating upper-class investors from the consequences of praetorian dishonor.[289] The jurists construed the definition of *leno* extensively in a horizontal direction but restrictively on the vertical plane. They insisted narrowly on the principles of direct profit and direct control.

The second point is that Pomponius and Ulpian want to make liable to the disability, after manumission, of course, the ex-slave pimp who had prostituted slaves in his own *peculium.* Ulpian's citation of his predecessor and his phrasing (*"et eum"*) suggest that the point was controversial, but this should not be pressed too far. It is almost certainly true that pimps remained *"infames"* even after retirement. Perhaps other jurists, however, were persuaded that a pimp's condition of slavery was a mitigating circumstance, whereas Pomponius and Ulpian at first sight appear to have looked to the fact that the edictal stipulation was phrased objectively, without regard to fault on the part of the subject.

This renders the companion passage all the more remarkable. The legal rule in this case was produced by a rescript of Septimius Severus, a fact suggesting that former slave prostitutes had previously been subject to the same rule as freedwomen who had acted as pimps while still slaves, which is to say they suffered from the disability after manumission. This was perhaps the law for most of the classical

---

[286] Karlowa, "Geschichte" 225 n. 6.

[287] Kaser, "Infamia" 225 n. 6.

[288] Contra, Dalla, *Venus* 55 (implying that Severus improved matters for prostitutes of both sexes); Gardner, *Being* 223 n. 80 (suggesting that the woman in question was not necessarily a prostitute: "the kind of *quaestus* is not specified and need not have been *corpore*"). As noted above, Ulpian remarks that *restituere* was rather unlikely to be granted in the more serious cases given under the second rubric, which cautions against extending the scope of Severus's ruling here.

[289] On this phenomenon, see McGinn, *Social Policy* (1986) 13–19; and now Riggsby, "Lenocinium" (1995). This subject is discussed further in Chapter 9.

period.[290] The passage reproduces, not a juristic hypothetical, but an actual case where a woman appears to have appealed her status as an "*infamis*" under the edict.[291] This conclusion supports the observation made elsewhere that the tendency of the legal sources to speak of female, as opposed to male, prostitutes is grounded in the reality that the law both reflects and attempts to regulate.

The content of Severus's ruling can be contrasted with Ulpian's holding, apropos of the *lex Iulia et Papia,* that a prostitute's *turpitudo* did not abate after she leaves the profession.[292] Of course, permitting an ex-prostitute to appoint a *cognitor* is not a concession equivalent to approving her as a potential marriage partner for an *ingenuus*.[293] And the rule applies only to former slave prostitutes, not to anyone who has given up the trade.[294] It falls in with the classical regime on *operae,* which could not be required of a former slave prostitute after manumission, and with the rules developed for the restrictive covenant on sale, *ne serva prostituatur,*[295] in the sense that it provided relief for exploited (or exploitable) women only by exception.

At any rate, Severus's ruling is a concession, no matter how attenuated, and one that is thrown into relief by the parallel passage on freed pimps. A comparison of the two holdings suggests how the imposition of praetorian dishonor might be associated with the notion of fault. Pomponius and Ulpian inflict the disability on the man who has slave prostitutes in his *peculium*. His case is more difficult than that of the free pimp, because he presumably acted at the behest of his master. The stipulation that the slave prostitutes form part of a *peculium* is important, however. They were under the slave pimp's direct control; indeed, the *peculium* was typically left to the independent management of the slave, and its exploitation might benefit him directly.[296] The holding also has import for the first point raised above, in that by assigning the ex-slave responsibility it eliminates any sense that this resides with his former master, effectively insulating the latter from the taint of *lenocinium*. In contrast to this treatment of the exploiter, a remission is granted the exploited woman herself.

The notion of punishment administered for reprehensible conduct is reinforced by the description of the pimp's disability as a *poena*—*poena lenocinii,* to be exact. The same idea is found elsewhere in the juristic commentaries on this edict.[297] The emphasis given pimps with slave prostitutes in Ulp. D. 3.2.4.2 is perhaps now clear. They were deemed more worthy of the disability imposed by the edict.

This instance demonstrates that, at Rome, legal categories of analysis are not neutral descriptions of reality, meant to be applied indifferently to individual cases

---

[290] The notion of temporary *infamia,* imposed by court sentence, goes back to Hadrian: Greenidge, *Infamia* 184–185.

[291] It can be assumed that she wished to appoint a legal substitute; see above.

[292] Ulp. D. 23.2.43.4: see Chapter 4.

[293] Similarly, Karlowa, "Geschichte" 225 (226) n. 36.

[294] This fact receives emphasis from the Byzantine commentator: Beaucamp, *Statut* 1.204.

[295] For the first, see Call. D. 38.1.38 pr. (discussed in Chapter 9); for the second, see Chapter 8.

[296] On the management of the *peculium,* see Chapter 8.

[297] Gaius D. 3.2.3; Ulp. D. *eod.* 8, Ulp. D. *eod.* 13.3, Ulp. D. *eod.* 13.7. Cf. the use of *delinquere* in Ulp. D. 3.1.1.7 and the frequent appearance of *nota* and its cognates in *Digest* Titles 3.1 and 3.2.

as they arise.[298] Instead, they are informed by the meaning they receive from the legal rules they are intended to help implement. In turn, the rules depend upon the foundation of public policy. Those pimps singled out by the jurists were not simply more numerous or visible but those who met the tests of profit or control. Pimps who prostituted slaves were pimps in the truest sense, when considered in light of the ideology of honor and shame that influenced policy in this field. They were men who sold the honor of "their" women for money, presenting the reverse image of honorable men who protected the honor of their women.

The notion of fault represents something of a departure from the original thrust of the edict, which defined the circumstances of its application in an objective manner. Of course, given the content of these provisions, all of which, under the third rubric, describe instances of reprehensible conduct, this was a small step to take. The change in focus that characterizes the classical juristic conception of these disabilities has more to do with the overall design of the edict on *postulare* than with the meaning of individual provisions. It is important to note however that the different weight of the disabilities imposed on male prostitutes, male pimps, and female prostitutes reflects the varying intensity of popular hostility toward each type.

Criminal Accusations

The right to make criminal accusations, in most cases theoretically open to *quivis ex populo,* was in reality restricted in a manner analogous to the right of *postulare.*[299] Women and *pupilli* were barred, unless they were pursuing a wrong done to themselves or a family member.[300] Exceptions were made for the former in matters of pressing public interest, such as *maiestas* or malversation of the public grain supply.[301] Soldiers were admitted to the latter type of prosecution but otherwise barred.[302] Magistrates could not bring prosecutions.[303] *Filii familias* were barred without permission of *pater,* except where they prosecuted their own wives for adultery.[304] Freedmen were forbidden to prosecute for adultery unless they had a son or a minimum patrimony of 30,000 sesterces; an exception was made where

[298] For a statement on this point, see Frier, "Bees 1" (1982/1983) 106; cf. Frier, "Bees 2" (1994) 138, 142, 144.

[299] In general, see Mommsen, *Strafrecht* 368–372. A more recent review of the evidence is in Rilinger, *Humiliores* ch. 6.

[300] Ulp. (71 *ad edictum*) D. 43.29.3.11: "... mulier vel pupillus ... et publico iudicio reos facere possunt, dum suas suorumque iniurias exsequuntur." Pap. D. 48.2.2.1; Macer D. *eod.* 8, Macer D. *eod.* 11 pr.; Alex. Sev. C. 9.1.5 (a. 222). Men less than 25 years old faced statutory restrictions on their right to prosecute for adultery: Ulp. D. 48.5.16(15).6; Pap.-Paul. *Coll.* 4.4.2.

[301] Marci. D. 48.2.13 (citing a rescript of Severus and Caracalla); Pap. D. 48.4.8 (citing the role of a woman—evidently Fulvia—in the toppling of the Catilinarian conspiracy); Papir. Iustus D. 48.12.3.1 (citing a rescript of the *divi fratres*).

[302] Macer D. 48.2.8; Marci. D. *eod.* 13.

[303] Macer D. 48.2.8.

[304] Pap. D. 48.5.38(37); cf. Iul.-Paul. D. 44.7.9.

they avenged their own wrongs.[305] They could not prosecute their patrons at all,[306] except for adultery[307] and *maiestas*.[308]

Mommsen identifies a further set of exclusions with praetorian *"infamia."*[309] This extension applies without reserve to the *actiones populares*.[310] Several criminal statutes prohibited certain persons from bringing prosecutions on the ground of their own wrongdoing.[311] The *Tabula Bembina*[312] bars the man convicted in a *quaestio* or *iudicium publicum* from acting as a *patronus*; other, evidently similar, prohibitions are lost in the lacunae.

Despite Cicero, one may identify the common thread of motivation for such exclusions, which was nowhere stated explicitly, as the imposition of *ignominia,* that is, a loss of reputation amounting to a diminution of status.[313] These sanctions were, it appears, given general application to the criminal court system through the *lex Iulia iudiciorum publicorum* of 17 B.C. The most complete list of disabilities is given by Ulpian in a passage taken from his commentary on the adultery law.[314] That the adultery law is not the actual source of the list is suggested by the stipulation that those condemned in a *iudicium publicum,* otherwise excluded, are allowed to avenge at law the death of children, parents, and patrons or pursue their own interest (''vel rem suam exsequatur'').[315] The adultery law, passed at about the same time, perhaps itself contained a list similar to that under discussion; it forbade *"infames"* to prosecute except where the adultery of their own wives was concerned,[316] although the jurists allowed a father *integrae famae* to take precedence over an *"infamis"* husband as privileged prosecutor.[317]

Other evidence suggests that the Augustan law on the criminal courts contained such a list of exclusions.[318] This list includes those condemned in a *iudicium publicum,* those guilty of malicious prosecution, those who have been sent into the arena to fight wild beasts, performers and pimps (''quive artem ludicram vel lenocinium fecerint''), and those who have been adjudged in criminal proceedings to have done anything by way of collusive or malicious prosecution or have been found to have accepted money for the purpose of bringing an accusation or of

---

[305] Pap. *Coll.* 4.5. Mommsen, *Strafrecht* 370, is wrong to generalize the patrimony/progeny requirement given in this passage: it applies only under the adultery statute.

[306] Macer D. 48.2.8.

[307] Macer D. 48.2.8; Pap. D. 48.5.39(38).9; Pap.-Paul. *Coll.* 4.4.2; Pap. *Coll.* 4.5.

[308] Mod. D. 48.4.7.2.

[309] Mommsen, *Strafrecht* 370–371.

[310] Paul. (3 *ad edictum*) D. 47.23.4: ''Popularis actio integrae personae permittitur, hoc est cui per edictum postulare licet.''

[311] Cic. *Clu.* 120; Cic. *Rosc. Am.* 57.

[312] *FIRA* 1² 7.11.

[313] Cic. *Clu.* 120. Cf. Dioclet., Maxim. C. 9.1.15 (a. 294), where *existimatio integra* is required of the criminal accuser.

[314] Ulp. (2 *de adult.*) D. 48.2.4.

[315] Levy, ''Anklägervergehen'' (1933/1963) 384, 402, 408; Kaser, ''Infamia'' 259 n. 181.

[316] Paul. *Coll.* 4.4; Pap. *Coll.* 4.5.

[317] Ulp. D. 48.5.3.

[318] Ven. Sat. D. 47.15.5; Macer D. 48.1.7, Macer D. 48.2.8, Macer D. *eod.* 11 pr.; Marci. D. *eod.* 13; Mod. D. 48.4.7 pr.

causing (legal) trouble for someone. This sort of grouping perhaps encouraged the jurists to employ generalized expressions when speaking of such persons, such as *infames, famosi, turpitudo status.*[319]

It is almost certain that Ulpian's text does not give the full range of exclusions laid down by the Augustan statute on the criminal courts. *Auctorati, lanistae,* and (male) prostitutes are three notable omissions. The first two were probably left out by the compilers as irrelevant in their day (see above). The third omission is difficult to attribute to them; since it is consonant with the lack of attention given male prostitutes by the classical jurists in general, Ulpian himself may have neglected to mention this type, although it was perhaps in the law. Macer adds condemnation in a *iudicium famosum,* naming *furtum, bona rapta vi,* and *iniuria,* as well as *sepulchrum violatum* and (at least under certain circumstances) *praevaricatio.*[320]

As persuasive as these proposed supplements may be, it is difficult to proceed further and argue for the incorporation of all of the praetorian exclusions. A different order of public policy concerns pervades the regime on criminal prosecution, as is evident from the fact that all of the exclusions given are riddled with exceptions.[321] *"Infames"* were admitted to prosecution when the charge was *maiestas* or malversation of the grain supply.[322] A pimp or prostitute who stepped forward in the public interest could therefore expect to be heard. Even where a *res sua* was at stake, a hearing, even a favorable hearing, was not entirely out of the question, above all where a public interest, such as the maintenance of public order, was concerned.[323]

The outcome of *il caso* Manilia, where a prostitute wronged by a public official successfully sought redress, demonstrates this point vividly. The aedile Hostilius Mancinus charged Manilia with assault, claiming he had been struck with a rock hurled from her residence. The prostitute appealed to the tribunes, asserting that Mancinus had approached her house not in an official capacity but as a reveler. When refused admission, he attempted entry by force and was repulsed by a shower of stones. The tribunes found Manilia's actions to be justified and blocked Mancinus's prosecution of her.[324]

[319] Macer D. 48.2.8, Macer D. *eod.* 11 pr.; Marci. D. *eod.* 13; Mod. D. 48.4.7 pr.; Ulp. D. 48.5.3; Pap.-Marci. D. 48.16.1.10; Paul. *Coll.* 4.4; Pap. *Coll.* 4.5.

[320] Macer D. 48.1.7 (cf. Macer D. 47.2.64[63]), as well as Macer D. 47.12.9, Macer 47.15.4, with Kaser, "Infamia" 260.

[321] Kaser, "Infamia" 259, rightly points to the vagueness of Macer (2 *de iud. publ.*) D. 48.2.8: ". . . alii propter delictum proprium, ut infames. . . ." What follows (". . . alii propter turpem quaestum . . .") seems at first glance more pertinent, except that the jurist goes on to give two examples that involve prosecutorial misconduct and not a socially despised profession.

[322] Marci. D. 48.2.13; Mod. D. 48.4.7 pr.

[323] The freedom of discretion allowed the presiding magistrate must not be underestimated, since *mores* was one criterion for deciding among rival prosecutors: Ulp. D. 48.2.16. Of course, Ulpian uses this term to cover a wider range of persons than *"infames."*

[324] Gell. 4.14. On Mancinus's career, see Broughton, *MRR* 1.455, 460 n. 5, who tentatively dates this affair to 151 B.C. Discussion of the episode is in Mommsen, *Strafrecht* 465 n. 1; Jones, *Courts* 15; Peppe, *Posizione* 114–117; Garofalo, "Competenza" (1986) 454–455. See Santalucia, "Edili" (1989/1994) 73 n. 30, against the view that Manilia's alleged offense was "political."

This incident may be compared with the premise of a rhetorical exercise in which the inmate of a brothel kills a soldier who attempts to rape her.[325] She is acquitted of the charge of homicide.

These two accounts, one historical, one fictional, are remarkable for two reasons. It is true that the privilege conceded to the prostitute in each case is formally minimal. The two are, after all, cast as defendants in a criminal proceeding. At the same time, both stories suggest the existence of a certain sympathy for prostitutes, as well as a recognition of the violent and oppressive atmosphere in which they carried on their trade. They were not such outcasts as to be denied every protection or redress under the law.[326] This sympathy rides on the perception of their status as innocent victims, though one quickly discovers its limits, for example, in the *controversia* when the woman who killed the soldier in the brothel applies to become a priestess and is excoriated.

As for the overall status of prostitutes at criminal law, it is possible to say that honor ranked high among public policy concerns but was not granted an absolute preference.

Testimonium

The Romans employed witnesses in their criminal courts, in private suits *(causae pecuniariae),* and in a number of acts-in-the-law, such as *mancipatio* and making a will.[327] One consistent demand made of witnesses was that they be of good character: a number of sources stress the importance of witnesses' *dignitas, fides, mores,* and *gravitas.*[328] Women were taken at their word, at least if they were able to muster a showing of conventional modesty.[329] As with ineligible accusers, criminal statutes contained lists of persons excluded from the right of giving testimony. Two of our most detailed sources on the subject are passages by Ulpian and Callistratus that report the exclusions of certain types of witnesses for the prosecution given by the *lex Iulia de vi.*[330] Freedmen are forbidden to testify against their patrons or patrons' parents, *impuberes* are flatly prohibited, as are those condemned in a *iudicium publicum*[331] (unless granted *in integrum restituere*), those who have

---

[325] Sen. *Contr.* 1.2.

[326] See the court minutes of the trial of a prostitute's murderer from late antique Egypt preserved on papyrus (*BGU* 1024: Chapter 4); see also [Quint.] 297.

[327] Arc. Char. D. 22.5.1.1; Mommsen, *Strafrecht* 401–418, 990–993; Kaser, *RZ* 281–283, 493–495; Kaser, *RP* 1² 42–43, 274–275; Rilinger, *Humiliores* (1988) 132–136; Vincenti, *Genera* (1989) 54–63, 92–95, 108–116.

[328] See, e.g., Arc. Char. D. 22.5.1 pr.; Mod. D. *eod.* 2. The theme pervades *Digest* Title 22.5. Cf. C. 4.20 and Quint. *IO* 5.7 (esp. 30) with Garnsey, *Status* 211–212. For the literary evidence, see Lévy, "*Dignitas*" (1965); Schmitz, *Zeugen* (1985); Carvarzere, "*Fufio*" (1988); Crook, *Advocacy* 144–145.

[329] Marshall, "Civil Courts" 51.

[330] Call. (4 *de cogn.*) D. 22.5.3.5; Ulp. (9 *de off. proc.*) *Coll.* 9.2.2. Callistratus paraphrases the statute; Ulpian purports to quote it.

[331] This feature, lacking in the *Collatio* text, is an editorial supplement. See Cloud, "*Lex Iulia* 2" (1989) 460–461. We know for certain that some persons were excluded from giving testimony as a consequence of condemnation under a specific *lex,* such as those punishing adultery and *repetundae:* Ulp. D. 28.1.20.6; Ven. Sat. D. 48.11.6.1.

been chained or placed in public custody, those *depugnandi causa auctorati*,[332] those who have hired themselves out to fight wild beasts,[333] prostitutes, and those convicted of having accepted money in exchange for giving or not giving[334] evidence. Other persons were released from the obligation of providing testimony if they were related to the defendant.[335]

For prostitutes, Callistratus has "quaeve palam quaestum faciet feceritve," and Ulpian has "palamve corpore quaestum faciet feceritve." Ulpian's omission of the pronoun, if it correctly reflects the wording of the statute, means that the masculine pronoun should be read from the item immediately preceding in the text. But it is more likely that the law had either the masculine pronoun *(quive)* or both masculine and feminine *(quive quaeve)*.[336] Callistratus's insertion or retention of "quae" is significant because it registers the juristic tendency to discuss female, rather than male, prostitutes. Another possible solution to the dilemma is raised in a passage of Juvenal,[337] which implies that a passive homosexual *(mollis)* was unsuitable as a *testis* or *iudex*. Perhaps the *lex Iulia de vi* (or, at any rate, the *lex Iulia iudiciorum publicorum*) contained a prohibition that, like that of the praetorian edict examined above, was directed at pathics and thus included male prostitutes.

Both texts have "faciet" where we would expect to find "fecit." Elsewhere Ulpian, evidently faithful to the law's wording, retains the proper perfect, future perfect sequence ("locavit, locaverit," "missus est erit").[338] All of this suggests that the odd tense in the phrase regarding prostitutes may derive ultimately from the statute itself, perhaps inscribed in error. Finally, "corpore" is found in the generally more accurate Ulpianic text, which, when corrected, gives the Augustan statutory description of prostitute.[339]

The *lex Iulia de vi* that established these exclusions was an Augustan statute.[340] Most or all of these provisions were perhaps taken over from earlier laws on *vis*,[341] and there is a strong likelihood that at least several of them were adopted by the *lex Iulia iudiciorum publicorum*.[342]

---

[332] Significantly, this item does not appear in the *Digest* passage; see above. It is dropped as a gloss by Cloud, "*Lex Iulia* 2" 461–462.

[333] The *Collatio* makes an exception for those who have been sent to Rome for the purpose of hurling javelins. This qualification is omitted in Callistratus's text.

[334] Ulpian's text omits "vel non dicendum."

[335] Ulp. *Coll.* 9.2.3.

[336] Cloud, "*Lex Iulia* 2" 460.

[337] Iuv. 2.75–76.

[338] For problems with the verb tenses in the Ulpianic text, see Cloud, "*Lex Iulia* 2" 459.

[339] See Chapters 3 and 5.

[340] Cloud, "*Lex Iulia* 1" (1988) (against Mommsen, who held for a Caesarian statute). Cloud accepts (against Kunkel) the existence of a predecessor generated by Caesar and argues for a single Augustan law, which made no clear distinction between the two categories of *vis* named in the sources (*publica* and *privata*). See also Cloud, "*Lex Iulia* 2" 455.

[341] For the tralaticious element in Roman *leges de vi*, see Cloud, "*Lex Iulia* 2" 435. The possibility is overlooked by Vincenti, *Genera* 59.

[342] This law did discuss qualifications for witnesses: Paul. D. 22.5.4. For one apparent difference from the list in the *lex Iulia de vi*, see Vincenti, *Genera* 57 n. 33. Others were excluded from giving testimony as a consequence of condemnation under a specific *lex*; see above.

It is strange that pimps are not included. The fact that they appear on neither list[343] argues against casual omission either by the jurists or by the compilers. All the same, given the routine rejection of testimony offered by persons regarded as suspect because of their social rank, lifestyle, or morals,[344] it is difficult to believe that they were not excluded, with prostitutes, from giving testimony in *iudicia publica* as a matter of law.[345]

The legal implications of this characterization were potentially far-reaching for pimps and prostitutes. Both were perhaps routinely excluded from giving testimony in the regular criminal courts (aside from exceptional circumstances like trials for *maiestas*), as well as in the praetor's court, at least in matters where they had no interest, and from acting as witnesses in private legal transactions that required the presence of honorable persons.[346] Is it possible to go further and deny them all testamentary capacity? This extension is simply not attested for pimps and prostitutes. They could both make wills and receive under them.

Again, the motive for these exclusions is not simply the preservation of court-room decorum. Both pimps and prostitutes, defined as persons without honor, could not be trusted to tell the truth in court.[347] Cicero's characterization of Clodia as a *meretrix* in the *Caeliana* is relevant here; his aim was to prejudice her standing as a witness.[348] Moreover, when an honorless person testified against someone of relatively high social status, insult was added to injury:

> Suet. *Claud.* 15.4: Equitem quidem Romanum obscaenitatis in feminas reum, sed falso et ab impotentibus inimicis conficto crimine, satis constat, cum scorta meritoria citari adversus se et audiri pro testimonio videret, graphium et libellos, quos tenebat in manu, ita cum magna stultitiae et saevitiae exprobratione, iecisse in faciem eius, ut genam non leviter perstrinxerit.

To be sure, there was a widely reported incident in which an *eques Romanus,* charged with lewd behavior toward women, but on a false charge fabricated by unscrupulous enemies, who, when he saw common harlots called as witnesses

---

[343] Kaser, "Infamia" 261, accepts the double tradition as authoritative.

[344] Callistratus does give, as justification for exclusion, *nota et infamia vitae suae,* which can certainly embrace pimps. Cf. Call. D. 22.5.3 pr.

[345] Sen. *Contr.* 1.2.6 implies that a pimp gave testimony in a trial for murder. If at all trustworthy, this suggests at most a possible admission of practitioners of prostitution as defense witnesses or as witnesses in trials featuring another practitioner as defendant.

[346] Ulp. D. 16.3.1.36; Gaius D. 29.3.7; Leo C. 8.17(18).11.1 (a. 472). They were thus incapable of witnessing wills; some sources suggest status as an *intestabilis* also prejudiced the ability to make a will: Gaius D. 28.1.26 (evidently a minority opinion); cf. Ulp. D. *eod.* 18 pr. and Inst. 2.10.6 with Mommsen, *Strafrecht* 990–993.

[347] Cf. Cic. *Flacco* 51, where it is implied that a witness's lack of sexual restraint *(libido)* renders his testimony unreliable. An interesting case from nineteenth-century Nevada shows the testimony of a madam in a trial for murder was accepted both by the court of first instance and on appeal. The state supreme court ruled for acceptance of such evidence as a matter of law, in the face of the defendant's claim that the woman's lack of chastity vitiated the value of that evidence: Goldman, *Gold Diggers* (1981) 78.

[348] See Carvarzere, "*Fufio*" 122–129; Craig, *Form* (1993) 113; Swarney, "Status" (1993) 150–153.

against him and their testimony admitted into evidence, hurled the stylus and tablets that he had been holding in his hand into the emperor's face with such force as to graze his cheek badly, at the same time complaining loudly of his stupidity and cruelty.

This comes at the end of a series of anecdotes retailing instances of Claudius's behavior as judge that inspired ridicule and contempt.[349] It is intended as a shocker. We do not have to accept the point about the man's innocence at face value, but, given Suetonius's sympathy for his fellow equestrians,[350] it is fair to say that he would have found this procedure irregular even in a case of manifest guilt. Although it is not surprising to discover that the rules in the so-called *cognitio extra ordinem* were freer than in a regular *quaestio*,[351] it is clear that the admission of prostitutes' testimony was felt to be unusual, to say the least. The move is in fact taken as a sign of Claudius's *stultitia et saevitia*. It is correct to identify the defendant's expressed attitude with the author's in this context, which indicates just how deeply this prejudice was felt.

The rules excluding prostitutes and (presumably) pimps were extended to the *cognitio* procedure by the Severan period at the latest. This is shown by the inclusion of the list in Ulpian's monograph *De Officio Proconsulis* and in Callistratus's *De Cognitionibus*. Further, the passage of Suetonius deals with a charge of *obscaenitas*, not *vis*. Where prostitutes and pimps were not excluded by statute, they were probably barred in practice or their testimony discounted as a matter of routine.[352]

The evidence suggests the existence of a court practice that was older and more stringent than the positive rules developed by statute and emperor. It is interesting to note that in fact the interventions of Senate and emperor tended to be expansive rather than restrictive.[353] This tendency renders Claudius's false step less extreme and also explains why it was important to maintain a small number of exclusions. This core functioned as a control, that is, as a safeguard against the tendency of emperors, at least some emperors, of treating their subjects as equal to each other.

If not for this, formal exclusions might, in a very strict practical sense, seem redundant. It surely did not require the efforts of a second-rate trial lawyer to tear to shreds a pimp who appeared for the defense in a trial *de vi*.[354] The constitution of a small group of exclusions from the right to bear witness, even if inconsistently applied, was an advertisement that the court system was prepared to operate on the basis of principles that most Romans considered just.

[349] Suet. *Claud.* 15.1–4. See Levick, *Claudius* (1990) 115–120.

[350] Wallace-Hadrill, *Suetonius* (1983) esp. 100–110.

[351] Suetonius does not say that Claudius violated a procedural norm in admitting prostitutes as witnesses: Carvarzere, "*Fufio*" 126.

[352] So the evidence of Sen. *Contr.* 1.2.1 ("absint ex hoc foro lenones, absint meretrices . . ."), 9 (pimps as sureties of chastity!), 10 (the credibility of prostitutes and pimps as witnesses is attacked); cf. 6.

[353] Vincenti, *Genera* 114.

[354] For this reason, I am inclined to view with skepticism the relevance for the Roman courtroom of the distinction developed, on the basis of legislative exclusions from offering testimony, by Vincenti, *Genera* 63, between "la verità processuale e la verità reale."

4. The Core of *Infamia* and the Community of Honor

A commonplace holds that not all Roman citizens were juridically equal. It is obvious that freedmen, sons-in-power, *cives sine suffragio,* and women serve as examples of those who did not enjoy the full complement of (male) citizen privileges. Those stamped by magistrate or statute with dishonor—*infamia* or *ignominia*—compose yet another category of citizens with a "special" status.

Max Kaser has shown that dishonor never existed as a positive legal concept at Rome.[355] *Infamia/ignominia* was not, for him, a unitary notion, either in origin or for much of its life in classical law. Kaser argues that the reasons why dishonor was imposed by the legal and political authorities vary, as do the mechanisms employed and the results, that is, precisely what privileges were removed.[356] But some consistency of principle can be discerned, at least where *infamia/ignominia* was routinely inflicted.

Kaser recognizes a "core" to this disability, which is a valuable idea specifically because it enables us to evaluate the precise position of pimps and prostitutes with respect to other "*infames*" and to the community of honorable citizens. Pimps and prostitutes stand at the center of this core notion of dishonor. With a small group of professions, including *auctorati, bestiarii,* gladiatorial trainers, and actors, they suffer virtually every form of legal disability the Romans devised. From the standpoint of such persons, *infamia* must have seemed a fairly unitary system at all times.

Indeed, when we turn away from the praetorian scheme and its implications, the position of prostitutes and pimps may be distinguished even from these other types. They were the only professionals forbidden to marry all *ingenui* under the Augustan law. Actors were forbidden only to senatorials. The others receive no mention, although the condition of the sources allows no firm conclusions to be drawn.[357]

Legal inequality is typically reinforced by social convention, so that the position of persons whose status is compromised by legal disabilities may be in reality considerably lower than the positive law by itself can suggest. Under convention, one may distinguish discrimination by mere social practice from that translated into a de facto legal sanction. An example of the former is found in the famous inscription from Sarsina that prohibits burial to suicides by hanging, gladiators *(auctorati),* and "quei quaestum spurcum professi essent."[358] The last phrase is variously interpreted[359] but may well embrace both prostitutes and pimps.

If the broader social prejudice that envelops and informs positive legal sanctions is imagined as casting a penumbra beyond the black letter of the law, this penumbra was especially wide and dark for Roman prostitutes and pimps. Where the shadow

[355] Kaser, "Infamia." His position is now the *communis opinio*; see, e.g., Mazzacane, *ED* infamia 383.

[356] This variety has received increasing attention in recent years: Rilinger, *Humiliores.*

[357] See Chapter 3.

[358] *CIL* 1² 2123 = 11.6528 = *ILS* 7846.

[359] See Aigner, "Stellung" 207–209, who understands it as a reference to pimps; McGinn, "*SC*" (1992) 278.

is most opaque, social discrimination is transformed into de facto legal inequality, often coterminous with and at times virtually indistinguishable from the dark circle of disability *de iure*. Two concrete examples for pimps demonstrate the effect of this discrimination. One involves the exclusion of their sons from the upper orders; the other the point-blank denial to pimps of their rights at private law.

Juvenal[360] complains that the sons of pimps, of *praecones,* of gladiators,[361] and of gladiatorial trainers took seats in the XIV Rows of the theater reserved for equestrians. The poet implies that the behavior he describes is consonant with the letter of the law, with reference to the *lex Roscia theatralis* of 67 B.C.[362] The recently discovered Larinum *SC* of A.D. 19, which repressed public performances by members of the upper orders, mentions the sons and daughters of actors, of gladiators, of trainers, and of pimps. Because of gaps in the text, the connection is not clear, but on the best reconstruction,[363] these types, along with those members of *uterque ordo* who had already performed onstage or in the arena (and so disgraced themselves), are exempted from the sanction "ne . . . libitinam haberet," the denial of the right to proper burial.[364]

The inscription from Sarsina denying certain types of person burial is at first sight puzzling since it already seems to bar such persons from *libitinam habere.* But there are reasons why this contradiction is illusory. First, this inscription, unlike the *Tabula Larinas,* is vague in its formulation and does not qualify as a legal prescription: it is better understood as the expression of social prejudice. Further, at issue in the *Tabula Larinas* are not professionals but their offspring. Some scholars write as if the professions themselves, and not the disability, were hereditary,[365] but if so the text would simply have, for example, *leno lenave.* It is strange that a penalty is given at this point and not in a *sanctio* at the end of the *SC* and not together with the penalty of *exilium,* which was also inflicted by the *SC*.[366]

The penalty applied to all those who were, or rather had been, members of *uterque ordo* as defined by the *SC*.[367] The *SC* addressed the behavior of those who in order to circumvent previous bans on public performances by members of the senatorial and equestrian orders had deliberately declassed themselves. By implication, those who had performed previously, and therefore qualified for the exemption, no longer belonged to *uterque ordo*[368] either objectively (a point they

---

[360] Iuv. 3.153–159.

[361] The word is *pinnirapus,* which is understood as a type of gladiator or gladiator-in-training: Courtney, *Juvenal* (1980) 176–177; Levick, "*SC*" (1983) 102.

[362] The relevant provisions of the *lex Roscia* were evidently taken up by the Augustan *lex Iulia theatralis:* Plin. *NH* 33.32; Brunt, "Lex" 76; Rawson, "*Discrimina*" 531.

[363] Levick, "*SC*" 98–99, cf. 103.

[364] Baltrusch, *RM* 198.

[365] See Demougin, *Ordre* 575, 577.

[366] On this point, see McGinn, "*SC*" 286–288. Lintott, *apud* Levick, "*SC*" 103, takes the phrase to refer to the profession of a funeral director, that is, another exemption. This interpretation has its difficulties: Levick, "*SC*" 103. I am not persuaded by the attempt of Formigoni Candini, "*Lenones*" 115, to rewrite the Latin.

[367] See *Tab. Lar.* 7–9.

[368] See *Tab. Lar.* 11–15. Appearing on stage or in the arena by this time automatically had the effect of removing a person from *uterque ordo:* see above.

shared with the group just mentioned) or in the sense of the statute (which in this regard distinguished them from the first group). They might well have continued to fall under the scope of the *SC* in other respects, however. This legislation, in an effort to combat deliberate declassing in defiance of the ban on performances, defined its field of application in terms not of personal status but of relation to those possessing the rank in question.[369]

The same point might be made concerning children of professionals: it was not in theory impossible that they had equestrian relations. More than this, if the argument advanced above is correct, they themselves might enjoy the legal right to sit in the XIV Rows, the definition of equestrian status on which this pre-Visellian statute found at Larinum relies.[370] But by lumping them together with disgraced former members of the *ordo equester,* the *SC* served notice that they were not, in the full sense, equestrians.

The provision in the Larinum *SC* concerning the children of professionals is consonant with the spirit of the Augustan social legislation. The former statute contains a more objective, rigid statement of the principle: no verbal phrase is employed that might permit a restrictive interpretation. The children are in a sense marked for life, almost as if by caste. Of the four professions given for their parents, two—actors and pimps—are found among the marriage law prohibitions, which suggests that children of pimps were forbidden to marry *ingenui.* If so, the same held for children of prostitutes.[371]

The Larinum *SC* does not mention children of prostitutes, which is explained perhaps by the greater likelihood that the children of the exploiters (pimps) would enjoy the economic status (patrimony of HS 400,000) necessary to qualify for a seat in the XIV Rows. A rhetorical *lex,* given by Seneca,[372] by implication[373] forbids children of prostitutes from priesthoods. It is difficult to believe that any challenge to the assumptions regarding children of practitioners embedded in the *SC* would have been sustained.

The Larinum *SC* enforced a disability that, even after its incorporation into positive law, retained its basis in social prejudice.[374] The same can be said of the second example drawn from the penumbra of disabilities imposed on pimps, where we move from legislation to the sphere of procedural law, as reflected in actual court practice. Our information is an anecdote from the late Republic recounted by Valerius Maximus[375] in which Metellus Creticus, as urban praetor,[376] denied a pimp

[369] Previous offenders against the spirit of the ban were let off the hook in a strict sense, but being grouped with the sons and daughters of the professionals was perhaps conceived as a penalty in itself.

[370] See *Tab. Lar.* 7–9. This point is overlooked by Baltrusch, *RM* 198 n. 22, who views the inclusion of these types as superfluous. On the use of this and similar phrases to describe equestrian status in the early Principate, see Demougin, *Ordre* 577.

[371] On the lack of direct evidence for the application of the Augustan marriage prohibitions to children of prostitutes and pimps, see Chapter 3.

[372] Sen. *Contr.* 1.2.

[373] See Sen. *Contr.* 1.2.1, 12, 13, 15.

[374] Again worth emphasizing is that Sen. *Contr.* 1.2.1 implies that the daughter of a prostitute was ineligible for a priesthood. On prejudice against the children of prostitutes in late antiquity, see Leon-tsini, *Prostitution* 191–192. See also Proc. *Anec.* 1.11.

[375] Val. Max. 7.7.7.

[376] Most likely in 73: Broughton, *MRR* 3.37–38.

bonorum possessio of a testamentary bequest. No mention is made of a legal justification, and we should assume the pimp to be objectively entitled to the legal
remedy. Metellus did not wish to treat the pimp as if he were a citizen in good
standing *(integer civis)*.

Those who stand at the core of the Roman concept of *"infamia"* I identify as
prostitutes, pimps, gladiators, trainers, beast-fighters, and actors. Social prejudice
helped create and reinforce this disability at law.[377] To view this "core" from the
center of Roman society is to see it placed on the very margin.

This conclusion will surprise no one, and yet it raises another series of questions about the precise position of these types on the margin. Comparison with
other cultures suggests their position might be highly nuanced. Prostitutes might
lack citizen rights in large part, or even totally. Marked as outsiders to the extent
that the only disagreement arising among the legal authorities concerns how few
rights they might still be granted, they might still be allowed to prosecute and
punish in matters affecting them or, in an extreme opinion, might not be held bound
to obey the law themselves.[378] Not only the articulation of the range of disabilities
but the definition of the type subject to them raises instructive contrasts. No matter
how severe the disability, the question must be put as to its real impact on the
daily lives of ordinary citizens, including practitioners of prostitution.[379]

Neither prostitutes nor pimps were *cives integri*. The equality of Roman citizens at private law was attenuated in ways that reflected their inequality in public
law. Both prostitutes and pimps labored under a set of black-letter disabilities that
were elaborated to their disadvantage. Beyond this, a penumbra of social prejudices
hardened into a denial of legal rights theoretically assured them.[380] Their position
within the Roman regime on dishonor can be analyzed on two planes. One is
vertical, where practitioners form part of a core group of *"infames"* who suffer
disabilities imposed at the very lowest level and find themselves incorporated into
each succeeding tier of disabilities as one moves up the scale. The other is horizontal, where pimps and prostitutes labor under disabilities imposed by both the
positive law and the time-hallowed usage of the *regimen morum* and were at the
same time liable to a practically boundless set of "legal" impairments that went
beyond the letter of the law or the routine official administration of moral oversight.
In these two senses a limit can be set to Kaser's analytical conception of Roman
infamia, which is at the same time confirmed in its main lines.

True, there is an important differentiation even within the narrow field under
study. The disabilities imposed on male prostitutes, male pimps, female prostitutes, and procuresses receive a varied articulation both in positive law and
within the penumbra. But all of these types, together with a small group of other

[377] See, e.g., Sen. *Ben.* 2.21.1–2, who maintains that it is inappropriate to establish friendship with
a male prostitute, even when a heavy obligation existed, as when the man saved one's life.

[378] See Brundage, "Prostitution" (1975/1976) 837; Rath, "Prostitution" (1986) 570; Guy, *Sex*
(1991) 80.

[379] Gardner, *Being* 111–117, 154.

[380] Compare the contrast drawn between juridical equality and *"de facto* inequality of different
individuals and groups" by Nicolet, *World* 384.

professionals, form a core group of "*infames*" set off from the community of respectable citizens. By denying dishonored persons legal rights, the community not only asserted a material interest, that of preserving economic resources, but sought to shape the contours of a society that was more honorable, on its own terms, and so more just.

3

The *Lex Iulia et Papia*

1. The Statute

Augustus employed his *tribunicia potestas* in introducing a marriage law, the *lex Iulia de maritandis ordinibus,* before the *concilium plebis* in 18 B.C.[1] This legislation was followed by the *lex Papia Poppaea,* a comitial statute that Augustus encouraged the suffect consuls for A.D. 9, M. Papius Mutilus and Q. Poppaeus Secundus, to sponsor.[2] The two enactments are usually distinguished in the sense that the first encouraged marriage; the second, the bearing of children.[3] In fact, the *lex Iulia* itself rewarded parents.[4] The second statute both supplemented and partly recast the first, eliminating loopholes[5] and relaxing some of the rules.[6] Thus the jurists and modern commentators can refer to the two laws as one: the *lex Iulia et*

---

[1] The date is suggested by Dio 54.16.1 and confirmed by the *SC de ludis saecularibus* passed the following year: Jörs, *E.* (1893/4) 28–34; Rotondi, *Leges* (1912/1962) 444. On the dating of the Augustan *leges Iuliae,* see Arangio-Ruiz, "Legislazione" (1938/1977) 250–251. On Augustus's use of the *tribunicia potestas,* see Jörs, *E.* 29, 36; Rotondi, *Leges* 444; Mette-Dittmann, *Ehegesetze* (1991) 19.

[2] Jörs, *E.* 49. Many modern works confuse the names of these consuls: Spagnuolo Vigorita, "Nota" (1985) xix with n. 19.

[3] See below and, e.g., Astolfi, *LIP²* (1986) 314.

[4] The *lex Iulia de maritandis ordinibus* first instituted the *ius liberorum:* Jörs, *V.* (1882) 33–34.

[5] The *lex Papia Poppaea* accomplished this primarily by specifically requiring children and penalizing the childless: Jörs, *V.* 29–32. This law introduced *delatores:* Jörs, *V.* 8 with n. 2.

[6] Such as those for the *vacationes,* or grace periods allowed widows and divorced women; see below.

Papia.[7] For convenience, I use this title for both laws and generally treat them as a single statute in what follows.[8]

To understand better the connection between the two statutes one might invoke the jurist Papinian's famous observation on the relationship between the *ius civile* and the *ius honorarium:*[9] the *lex Papia Poppaea* functioned "to support, supplement, and correct" the *lex Iulia de maritandis ordinibus.* The two were not completely integrated; for example, the minimum age for bearing children under the *lex Papia Poppaea* was lower than the minimum age for marriage demanded by the *lex Iulia de maritandis ordinibus,* an anomaly not formally eliminated until Septimius Severus.[10]

The summary just given takes into account only the legislation enacted (albeit with modifications of detail) permanently. Scholars have seen, on the basis of a vague passage from Propertius,[11] a vaguer one from Tacitus,[12] and other, even less satisfactory evidence, a prototype of the marriage law dating to c. 28 B.C., but whether this measure in fact anticipated the Augustan marriage legislation, the adultery law, both, or neither is uncertain.[13] If enacted, it did not last long.[14] In A.D. 4 Augustus promulgated a statute that evidently would have sharpened considerably the *lex Iulia de maritandis ordinibus,* but this was suspended twice, first for a period of three years[15] and then for another two, until it was finally abandoned in favor of the *lex Papia Poppaea.*[16]

This summary ignores the legislative activity of the Senate, which devoted much attention to the marriage law during Augustus's reign.[17] It is unlikely that the *lex Iulia de adulteriis coercendis* closed the loophole under the *lex Iulia et Papia* whereby, at first, betrothal counted, without reservation, as marriage, which encouraged fraudulent behavior, such as arranging engagements with infants.[18] Either an *SC* or even, in spite of the obvious implication of the context of Dio's report,[19] the *lex Papia Poppaea* may have remedied the problem.[20]

---

[7] The jurists use *lex Iulia et Papia (Poppaea)* in the titles of their commentaries: Jörs, *V.* 57, 65. For criticism of the modern habit of treating the laws as one, see Spagnuolo Vigorita, "Nota" xviii–xx. I make no apology for referring to this *lex* through the singular law and plural laws, when the context demands.

[8] It may be noted that the marriage prohibitions, which form the focus of our attention, must derive originally from the *lex Iulia de maritandis ordinibus* but were evidently repeated (with or without changes, we cannot know) in the *lex Papia Poppaea:* Jörs, *V.* 9–10.

[9] Pap. D. 1.1.7.1.

[10] Tert. *Apol.* 4.8.

[11] Prop. 2.7.

[12] Tac. *Ann.* 3.28.2.

[13] See Jörs, *E.* 3–28, with Spagnuolo Vigorita, "Nota" xi, xiv n. 11, xxi, and the skeptical Badian, "Marriage Law" (1985). Not everyone is persuaded by Badian's argument: Williams, "Maecenas" (1990) 267 n. 19; Moles, "Livy's Preface" (1993) 151.

[14] Jörs, *E.* 5.

[15] This *vacatio triennii* (Suet. *Aug.* 34.1) does not refer to a grace period following the death of a spouse, as claimed by Mette-Dittmann, *Ehegesetze* 132 (cf. 162).

[16] This is a rough summary of the reconstruction by Jörs, *E.* 49–63. Del Castillo, "Fecha" (1974), argues unpersuasively for the identity of the statutes of A.D. 4 and 9.

[17] Hor. *Saec.* 17–20 *(decreta patrum);* see also below.

[18] For another view, see Jörs, *V.* 17; Jörs, *E.* 36–39.

[19] 18 B.C.: Dio 54.16.1.

[20] See Dio 56.7.2.

The *lex Iulia et Papia* established two categories of marriage prohibitions. Members of the senatorial order, which included senators and their sons, daughters, and, in the male line, grandsons, granddaughters, great-grandsons, and great-granddaughters, were forbidden to marry or to betroth themselves to freedmen, freedwomen, actors, actresses, and anyone whose father or mother was an actor or actress; later legislation added persons condemned in a standing criminal court, a category to which jurists (perhaps) appended those condemned by the Senate.[21] All other freeborn persons were forbidden prostitutes, pimps, procuresses, and persons condemned for adultery or caught in the act.[22] Senatorials of course could not marry such persons either.[23] Freedmen and freedwomen could presumably marry anyone they pleased, aside from members of the senatorial order.[24] The prohibitions are an illustration of the Roman tendency to merge categories of the social (freedpersons) and moral (prostitutes).

Spouses in marriages that violated the terms of the law were immune to its privileges and liable to its penalties.[25] That is, they counted as *caelibes,* even if their marriages were completely valid under the *ius civile.* The statute itself did not render such unions invalid.[26] Because it lays down a penalty without voiding acts in contravention, the law qualifies as a *lex minus quam perfecta.*[27] This state of affairs remained true until an *SC* passed under Marcus Aurelius and Commodus rendered void those unions that violated the prohibitions designed for the senatorial order (i.e., all unions forbidden senatorials).[28]

The most important of the law's *praemia et poenae* involved the law of succession. As such they had resonance mainly for the political and economic elite, a point consistent with Roman notions of moral responsibility, which viewed the upper orders ideally as models of behavior for the lower.[29] The rules for intestacy were unaffected,[30] but persons who were unmarried or whose union violated the

[21] Paul. D. 23.2.44 pr. This passage quotes the law, providing the first comprehensive definition we have of the senatorial order and coming not by coincidence a year after Augustus's second review-cum-purge of the Senate: Talbert, *Senate* (1984) 39–47. For later legislation, see Ulp. D. 23.2.43.10–11; *Tit.* 13.1–2, with the discussion below.

[22] Ulp. D. 23.2.43 pr.–9, 12–13; *Tit.* 13.2; and the discussion below. Convicted adulteresses were forbidden to remarry by the statute on adultery: see Chapter 5.

[23] This is made explicit not by the law but by the jurists: Paul. D. 23.2.44.8; Marcel. D. *eod.* 49.

[24] Compare Edwards, *Politics* (1993) 42, who would rank freedpersons among the *ceteri ingenui.*

[25] Indirect proof of this is offered by the *SC de ludis saecularibus* of 17 B.C., which offers a dispensation to those "qui lege de marita[ndis ordinibus tenentur]"; they are described in the *relatio* of the decree as those "qui nondum sunt maritati." See *FIRA* 1² 40.1; Jörs, *E.* 31.

[26] Savigny, *System* 2 (1840) App. 7; Jörs, *V.* 24 n. 3, 58 n. 1; Jörs *E.* 21–22; Corbett, *Marriage* (1930) 35–39; Gaudemet, *"Matrimonium"* (1950/1979) esp. 124–140; Astolfi, *LIP²* 108; Baltrusch, *RM* (1989) 164; Treggiari, *RM* (1991) 64 (cf. 44, 50). Children born to marriages that violated the law were legitimate: Ulp. *FV* 168, with Astolfi, *LIP²* 109.

[27] The sources are far from lucid on this issue, so that the opposing view, that the law invalidated marriages that violated its prohibitions, has received strong support: Nardi, "Divieti" (1941); Weaver, *FC* (1972) 171; Volterra, *"IM"* (1972) 459–465; Raepsaet-Charlier, *"Clarissima femina"* (1981) 193.

[28] Astolfi, *LIP²* 117.

[29] On this attitude, see Cic. *Leg.* 3.30–32 and the remarks of Astolfi, *LIP²* 318–321. The law's reach was nonetheless fairly broad: see below and Astolfi, *LIP²* 323.

[30] Interference here would have contradicted the goal of safeguarding and promoting the interests

law could receive nothing under a will unless they fell within the sixth degree of blood relationship (seventh, in the case of children of second cousins). That such a broad range of relations was exempted is nowhere attested explicitly by the sources, owing to later changes made in the law.[31] Spouses with no children could receive only a tenth of each other's estate upon death, with an additional tenth for each child from a previous marriage.[32] Even without mutual children, the partners might receive the usufruct of one-third of the other's estate, and the wife could receive her dowry as a legacy.[33] Spouses (as well as betrothed couples), their parents, and sons-and daughters-in-law were excused from the obligation to give testimony against each other in cases arising under the *lex Iulia et Papia*.[34]

Children conceived in the marriage itself gave parents full capacity with respect to each other if one child survived past puberty, if two lived more than three years, or if three survived to their "naming day" (nine days past birth for males, eight for females).[35] Apart from this, the *orbus* was granted half capacity, that is, the right to one-half of every individual bequest,[36] but only one child was sufficient for both men and women to receive[37] bequests from others, in their entirety,[38] and to become eligible for *bona caduca*, or bequests whose intended recipients, named under the same will, could not take under the law. *Patres* were eligible for those bequests that were assigned to others in the same will but that they could not claim because they were *caelibes* or *orbi*, as well as any bequests that failed because of the death of the intended recipient or the nonfulfillment of a condition.[39] If there were no such persons eligible, the property in question went to the state treasury,[40] originally the *aerarium*, later the *fiscus*.

---

of the Roman family: Astolfi, *LIP*² 311. For the evidence, see Voci, *DER* 1² (1967) 436–437; Astolfi, *LIP*² 11–13. An exception has been argued for the praetorian regime on succession between husband and wife: Astolfi, *LIP*² 121–123. See also Treggiari, *RM* 381.

[31] See, however, the convincing demonstration by Wallace-Hadrill, "Family and Inheritance" (1981) 73–76; see also Astolfi, *LIP*² 69–72. Upon the death of a woman married in contravention of the law, her dowry was confiscated: *Gnom. Id.* 24–26; *Tit.* 16.4. It is worth noting that the Augustan tax on inheritances exempted close relatives: Dio 55.25.5, with the remarks of Nicolet, "Augustus" (1984) 110.

[32] *Tit.* 15.1; *Gnom. Id.* 31 (it is clear that a tenth of all property, not of a given bequest, is meant; cf. *Tit.* 15.3), with Riccobono, *Gnomon* (1950) 157. A Severan reform opened a loophole through resort to gift: Treggiari, *RM* 371–374.

[33] *Tit.* 15.3–4. Full ownership of the one-third was possible if the spouse remarried and produced children: Humbert, *Remariage* (1972) 151; Astolfi, *LIP*² 17, 36.

[34] Argued from Gaius D. 22.5.5.

[35] *Tit.* 16.1a; Macrob. *Sat.* 1.16.36. If only one or two survived to the naming day but did not make it to puberty, an extra tenth was awarded for each: *Tit.* 15.2. The law recognizes a high rate of infant and child mortality. On the naming day and its rituals, see Rawson, "Relationships" (1991) 14.

[36] Gaius 2.111 (as supplemented) and 286a show that this was the basis for the calculation, not one-half the estate, as with spousal *decimae*.

[37] Some have claimed the *ius liberorum* (see below) to be necessary for women, at least in some circumstances, but note Astolfi, *LIP*² 24 n. 5.

[38] Iuv. 9.87–88.

[39] Jörs, *V.* 28–29, 46–52. Astolfi, *LIP*² 307, argues that, among equally qualified recipients, preference was given to those with the greatest number of children.

[40] Gaius 2.206–208; *Tit.* 1.21.

The law allowed *caelibes* 100 days to comply by marrying before their portion went to the *patres* named in the will.[41] Women whose marriages had terminated through death or divorce enjoyed grace periods of 2 years and 18 months, respectively.[42] The *lex Papia Poppaea* increased the limits imposed by the *lex Iulia* of 1 year for death and 6 months for divorce.[43] The demands of the law thus conflicted with an ideal of loyalty to a deceased spouse represented by the *univira*.[44]

The law granted a dispensation for marriage to males younger than 25 and females younger than 20. It did the same for men 60 or older and women 50 or older.[45] This was amended by the *SC Persicianum* passed under Tiberius, which stipulated that those who had not married in compliance with the law before reaching the maximum age limits could no longer benefit from the dispensation.[46] The *SC Claudianum* permitted such men to marry women younger than 50 and still reap the rewards, while a further enactment, the *SC Calvisianum,* expressly removed this possibility for women over the maximum age.[47] Another dodge was met with the *SC Gaetulicianum,* of uncertain date,[48] which closed the loophole that permitted childless wives *in manu* to receive more from their husbands either on intestacy or under a will than they were strictly permitted by the statute.

Yet another statute, passed in the reign of Vespasian, extended the regime created by the marriage law to *fideicommissa*[49] and one more *SC* included *donationes mortis causa*.[50] Of course, legislation did not address every dodge, nor was it always successful where it attempted to do so.[51]

Caracalla, in designating the *fiscus* as the destination of *caduca,* imposed severe restrictions on the regime for this type of property: only ascendants and descendants up to the third degree remained eligible for it.[52] This change enhanced considerably the tendency of the statute itself to serve as a mechanism for supple-

---

[41] *Tit.* 17.1; *Frag. de iure fisci* 3; cf. Gaius 2.144.

[42] *Tit.* 14.

[43] For a speculative discussion of the reasons for the change, see Geiger, "Tiberius" (1975).

[44] Treggiari, *RM* 235. For a different view of the *univira,* see Krause, *Witwen* 1 (1994) 105–106, 157, 171. For discussion of the reasons why the law allowed these grace periods only to women, see Jörs, *V.* 44.

[45] On the age limits, see *Gnom. Id.* 24–28, with Riccobono, *Gnomon* 149–155; Tert. *Apol.* 4.8; *Tit.* 16.1, 3.

[46] *Gnom. Id.* 27–28; *Tit.* 16.3. The statute evidently provided for the confiscation of dowry in such circumstances: *Gnom. Id.* 24–26.

[47] *Tit.* 17.3–4. On these statutes, see Astolfi, *LIP*² 46–48; Zablocka, "Modifiche" (1986).

[48] Volterra, "*Conventio*" (1966) 351–353, dates this to the period after the passage of the *SC Orphitianum* in A.D. 177. Noy, "*SC*" (1988), more persuasively places it in the first century.

[49] This is the *SC Pegasianum* (ca. A.D. 73): Gaius 2.286, 286a. See Manthe, *SC* (1988) 18–19, 43; Johnston, *Trusts* (1989) 34, 38, 42, 45–46.

[50] Paul. D. 39.6.35 pr. (other texts are given by Astolfi, *LIP*² 13–14). Its exact date is unknown; it probably falls subsequent to the *SC Pegasianum* but not later than the mid–second century.

[51] Treggiari, *RM* 388, 396.

[52] *Tit.* 17.2 (cf. 1.21). The two views taken of this passage can, I think, be reconciled as in the text: Spagnuolo Vigorita, "*Bona Caduca*" (1978) 145 n. 71; Astolfi, *LIP*² 252–255. A change in the rules for *exceptae personae* has also been attributed to this emperor: Wallace-Hadrill, "Family and Inheritance" 74.

menting state revenues, a tendency that may fairly be regarded as the hallmark of the postclassical regime.[53]

The testamentary provisions aimed exclusively at the rich. The *Gnomon of the Idios Logos* applies the law only to men with property valued at 100,000 sesterces or more and to women with a census of 50,000 sesterces or more.[54] This feature is generally understood to have been empirewide, a conclusion suggested by the law's provisions for freedmen with patrimonies valued at 100,000 or more.[55] These freedmen were required, whether they died leaving a valid will or intestate, to leave a *pars virilis* to their patrons if they had fewer than three children.[56] Informers received perhaps one-half of the amount in question;[57] this was reduced to one-fourth by Nero.[58]

Only the elite would have been interested in the law's stipulation that the consul with wife and children had precedence in assuming the *fasces*.[59] The statute removed one year for each child from the minimum age requirements for political office[60] and favored fathers in the replacement of magistrates who had died in office and in the distribution of provincial governorships.[61]

The Flavian Municipal Law (FML) stipulates that when candidates for municipal office have the same number of votes, those who are married or count as married[62] and/or have children shall receive preference, and that when the members of the town council cast their votes, priority is accorded to those with the most children born in *iustae nuptiae* (and to those who would so qualify if they were Roman citizens).[63] *Patronae* with two or three children were given special rights over the wills of their (wealthy) freedmen.[64] The exemption afforded by the *ius liberorum* from *munera civilia* (at the start, perhaps only *tutela* and *cura*) would have interested only the wealthy.[65]

---

[53] See Spagnuolo Vigorita, *Pernicies* (1984).

[54] *Gnom. Id.* 30, 32.

[55] Gaius 3.42; see Riccobono, *Gnomon* 156–158. Contra Mette-Dittmann, *Ehegesetze* 160; however, the Augustan tax on inheritances instituted in A.D. 6 excepted very close relatives and the poor: Dio 55.25.5.

[56] Gaius 3.42.

[57] So Nörr, "Ethik" (1972) 17–18; Astolfi, *LIP*² 271 n. 103.

[58] Suet. *Nero* 10.1.

[59] Gell. 2.15.3–8; Ulp. *FV* 197.

[60] Tac. *Ann.* 15.19; Plin. *Ep.* 7.16.2; Ulp. D. 4.4.2, with Astolfi, *LIP*² 299–300. On the age requirements, see Talbert, *Senate* 16–27.

[61] For replacing magistrates, see Tac. *Ann.* 2.51.1; for provincial assignments, Tac. *Ann.* 15.19; Fronto *Ep. ad Ant. Pium* 8.1; Dio 53.13.2 (before the law), with Astolfi, *LIP*² 300.

[62] Among these who "count as married" are persons engaged two years or less (the maximum allowed by Augustus) and soldiers, since Claudius (see below).

[63] See the FML ch. 56 for the first provision, ch. 40(?) (= B) for the second (cf. Pap. D. 50.2.6.5), with the remarks of González, "*Lex Irnitana*" (1986) 209–210, 216.

[64] These rights are structured according to the facts of birth and gender in interesting and complex ways: Gaius 3.49–54; *Tit.* 29.6–7; Mette-Dittmann, *Ehegesetze* 154–156.

[65] Three children were required at Rome, four elsewhere in Italy, five in the provinces: *FV* 168, 197, 198, 247. It is not certain, however, that this provision derives from the statute itself: Jörs, *V.* 23, 55 n. 4; see also Sirks, "*Munera*" (1989) 91; Parkin, *Demography* (1992) 116–119; Mette-Dittmann,

Other provisions of the law aimed at a broader range of persons. A woman with the *ius liberorum* was freed from the *tutela muliebris*.[66] Freedmen with two children *in potestate* or one child at least five years of age were released from *operae* if they were not actors or beast-fighters.[67] *Caelibes* were forbidden to attend public spectacles and banquets, a prohibition inferred from two remissions, one that allowed the unmarried to attend the Ludi Saeculares of 17 B.C. *(SC de ludis saecularibus)*[68] and one that permitted them to join in the celebrations for Augustus's birthday in 12 B.C.[69] *Caelibes* enjoyed less desirable seats in the theater, which perhaps suggests a later relaxation of an absolute ban.[70]

Although in practice only the rich were subject to the testamentary *poenae,* the *praemia* were evidently open to *patres* of all classes.[71] Literary evidence suggests that Augustus intended the law effectively to embrace the citizen body as a whole.[72] If it is true, as scholars have argued in recent years,[73] that elements of the Roman political elite experienced difficulty in replacing themselves politically, if not biologically and socially, it was crucial for Augustus to reach below the senatorial order. To be sure, he had uses for the equestrian order in its own right,[74] as well as for other groups among the non-senatorial *ingenui*.[75]

The term *ius liberorum* signifies the right to enjoy the entire bloc of privileges allowed under the marriage law.[76] Exceptions are those political benefits mentioned above that do not depend on an absolute number of children, but one usually relative to the number possessed by rivals, and the arrangements for release from

---

Ehegesetze 148. Exemption from serving as a juror evidently originated with the Augustan legislation on the civil and criminal courts: Suet. *Claud.* 15.1; *FV* 197–198.

[66] See the discussion below. Three children were enough for an *ingenua,* but freedwomen needed four to qualify, with the stipulation that a *pars virilis* be left to the patron, who otherwise would, as *tutor,* exercise authority over the will: Gaius 3.47; *Tit.* 29.3.

[67] Paul. D. 38.1.37 pr.-1; Alex. Sev. C. 6.3.7 (a. 224). See Astolfi, *LIP*² 309.

[68] *FIRA* 1² 40.1.50–57.

[69] Dio 54.30.5. See Jörs, *E.* 30–32.

[70] Suet. *Aug.* 44.2; Mart. 5.41.8. See Rawson, "*Discrimina*" (1987/1991) 525–527.

[71] So Humbert, *Remariage* 145 n. 15.

[72] So Brunt, *IM* (1987) 562. See Calderini, "Riforme" (1939) 132. Mette-Dittman, *Ehegesetze* 20 (cf. 30), cites precedents from the Republic. For another opinion, see Gardner, *Being* (1993) 126: "in practice, little concern was taken over the marriages of the lower orders, since neither politically nor privately, for such matters as property rights, was their married status particularly important." Similarly, Fehrle, "Ehegesetze" (1984) 22; Bagnall, "Divorce" (1987) 51–52. Generalizations about the *ceteri ingenui* should acknowledge that this category extended to those with equestrian and decurional status.

[73] Hopkins, *Death* (1983) ch. 3; Dixon, *TRF* (1992) 123. Note the criticism of Shaw, "Believers" (1984); Jacques, "Sénat" (1990). On recruitment of municipals into the equestrian order, see Demougin, "Notables" (1983) 283.

[74] See, e.g., Kienast, *Augustus* (1982) 151–162; Demougin, *Ordre* (1988) 135–175, 286–293.

[75] For example, Augustus established a fourth decury of *iudices* whose members had a minimum census of HS 200,000: Suet. *Aug.* 32.3. A patrimony of HS 100,000 or less did not necessarily spell poverty: Humbert, *Remariage* 143–144.

[76] Jörs, *V.* 35, 55, 59. On the *ius liberorum,* see Jörs, *V.* 33–35, 54–56, 59–66; Kübler, "Ius 1" (1909); Kübler, "Ius 2" (1910); Steinwenter, *RE* ius (1919); Astolfi, *LIP*² 78–86; Zablocka, "*Ius*" (1988). The honorific designation *matrona/femina stolata* dates from the late second century at the earliest, more probably from the beginning of the third, and has no connection with the marriage law, as once thought: Holtheide, "Matrona" (1980).

munera.[77] The most important of these privileges were, for women, freedom from *tutela*;[78] for men and women, enhanced patronal rights in the succession to his or her freedmen and full *capacitas* (which meant eligibility for *caduca*).[79] Three children secured the *ius* for males and freeborn women; freedwomen needed four.[80] Those who did not earn the privilege through having the requisite number of children might receive it as a special grant from Senate or emperor. Dio records a grant of the *ius liberorum* to Livia in 9 B.C.[81] Claudius is the first emperor we know to have usurped the Senate's role in granting the *ius*,[82] but his concession of the privilege to groups, such as soldiers[83] and those who financed the building of merchant ships,[84] suggests that grants to individuals had by now become routine; in fact, the statute itself evidently provided for a dispensation for those whom nature had denied.[85] Vestals received the privilege early, and thereafter automatically,[86] as did emperors from Antoninus Pius on.[87]

The *ius liberorum* exempted a woman from the strictures of the *lex Voconia*.[88] The privilege also released its bearers from the obligation to remarry imposed by the law.[89] Mere eligibility for the *ius* was itself a mark of honor, so that we find it invoked even in situations where it was technically unnecessary.[90] This privilege

---

[77] If the latter are original to the law (see above). According to Jörs, *V*. 41–42, only the *ius liberorum* granted by the emperor or the *ius communium liberorum* (the privilege awarded to spouses who had children in common) gave *libera testamenti factio*, that is, freedom from the strictures of the *lex Voconia*. For another view, see Wallace-Hadrill, ''Family and Inheritance'' 165.

[78] It is hardly coincidental that the XII Tables freed Vestals from *tutela*: Gaius 1.145. On the XII Tables as a model for Augustan legislation, see Bellen, ''Status'' (1987) 309, 323, 334. On the ideal identification of Vestals with *matronae*, see Purcell, ''Livia'' (1986) 84.

[79] Gaius 3.39–54 summarizes the rules governing patrons, their children, and freedmen where the *ius* was involved. One was not penalized qua *caelebs* when a marriage ended: Steinwenter, *RE* ius 1281 (cf. Jörs, *V*. 44). The *ius* exempted one's daughter from service as a Vestal: Capito *apud* Gell. 1.12.8.

[80] *Gnom. Id*. 28. It is not known for certain if four were also required of freedmen: the particular application given in Gaius 3.42 mentions only three. The requirement of three for *ingenuae* and four for *libertinae* was restated by the *SC Tertullianum*: *PS* 4.9.1, 7.

[81] Dio 55.2.5–6.

[82] See Dio 59.15.1 for Caligula's award by the Senate.

[83] The *iura maritorum*: Dio 60.24.3; see also Chapter 4. *Caelibes* and *orbi* could evidently receive under a soldier's will: Gaius 2.111 (as supplemented).

[84] According to Suet. *Claud*. 19, (male) citizens received a *vacatio* from the *lex Papia Poppaea*, females the *ius liberorum*. Sirks, ''Favour'' (1980), argues that the latter privilege was addressed only to freedwomen.

[85] Mart. 2.91.5, 92, 8.31; Plin. *Ep*. 2.13.8, 10.2, 94, 95; Suet. *Galba* 14.3; Jörs, *V*. 54–56; Daube, ''Martial'' (1976/1991); Besnier, ''Pline'' (1979) (Calestrius Tiro's tribunate should be that of the *plebs*). Cf. the ways in which Junian Latins might achieve full citizenship status: Mette-Dittmann, *Ehegesetze* 194–195. On empresses, see Beaucamp, *Statut* 1 (1990) 274.

[86] Dio 56.10.2; cf. Plut. *Numa* 10.3.

[87] Astolfi, *LIP*[2] 86–87.

[88] Augustus, evidently in the *lex Papia*, allowed some women to escape the strictures of the *lex Voconia*, which forbade persons worth the equivalent of HS 100,000 or more to institute women as heirs: Dio 56.10.2. Despite the hesitations of some (Astolfi, *LIP*[2] 301–302; Mette-Dittmann, *Ehegesetze* 153), these women were almost certainly endowed with the *ius liberorum*: Zablocka, ''Ius'' 376.

[89] Seckel/Meyer, ''Gnomon'' (1928) 438–439; Humbert, *Remariage* 147 n. 5, 153–154; Rawson, *FAR* (1986) 53 n. 94; Zablocka, ''Ius'' 376.

[90] See Sijpesteijn, ''Papyri'' (1965) esp. 187–188.

was abolished in 410.[91] Constantine had already eliminated the *incapacitas* of *caelibes* and *orbi,* leaving only the rules governing bequests between spouses.[92] The same emperor imposed a new set of marriage prohibitions.[93]

The purpose of the *lex Iulia et Papia* has been hotly debated. Earlier generations of scholars adopted a moralizing approach, pessimistic about what the need for the legislation signified and, typically, about its effects.[94] Much work has been motivated, as well as characterized, by contemporary concerns.[95] There has been an inevitable tendency to view the law through the ideological prism of the author's own time.[96] More recently, discussion has centered on the question of whether Augustus's purpose was essentially moral or demographic.[97] Especially worthy of note are those contributions that attempt a close examination of the details of the legislation in order to assess its purpose and putative effects.[98]

A full interpretation of this statute can hardly be attempted here, but a few central points should be raised. First is the law's purpose. The distinction between morality and demographics is a false one to draw for the Romans. The very existence of the marriage prohibitions shows how demographic ends might be pursued within a framework determined by considerations of rank and gender.[99] Concern with the reproduction of the body of Roman citizens goes back to the second Punic War and, like other public issues of any importance, was conceived and presented in moral terms.

Augustus was hardly the first to attempt a solution; the policies espoused by

---

[91] Hon., Theod. CTh. 8.17.2 (a. 410) (= C. 8.57[58].2). The emperors effectively granted the *ius* to everyone: Hon., Theod. CTh. 8.17.3 (a. 410) (= C. 8.58[59].1); cf. Arc., Hon. CTh. 8.17.1 (a. 396). Iustinianus C. 6.51.1 (a. 534) abolished the regime for *caduca.*

[92] Constantinus CTh. 8.16.1 (a. 320) (= C. 8.57[58].1). See Evans Grubbs, ''Constantine'' (1993) 123; Evans Grubbs, *Law* (1995) 119–139.

[93] Constantinus CTh. 4.6.3 (a. 336).

[94] See Gardthausen, *Augustus* 1.2 (1896/1964) 897–906; Ferrero, *Grandezza* 4 (1906/1914) ch. 7 (cf. 21–27); Rice Holmes, *Architect* 2 (1931) 41–46, 151–152. A refreshing exception, certainly in his assessment of the law's effects, is Last, ''Social Policy.'' The moralizing approach has its latter-day analogues: Csillag, *Augustan Laws* (1976); Raditsa, ''Legislation'' (1980). Scholarly pessimism continues as well: Fehrle, ''Ehegesetze''; Dixon, *TRF* 80, 121, 123, 132; Evans Grubbs, ''Constantine'' 123. A notable exception is Eck, ''Sozialstruktur'' (1973) 383.

[95] Bouché-Leclercq, ''Lois'' (1895), wrote against the backdrop of a debate over France's demographic policies at the end of the last century.

[96] Siber, ''Ehegesetzgebung'' (1939) 156, 158, 159. Siber's discussion is rich in detail and valuable for its commentary on individual provisions of the law. More obviously ideological are Oppermann, ''Bevölkerungspolitik'' (1936), and Riccobono, ''Politica'' (1937), ''Opera'' (1939).

[97] Field, ''Purpose'' (1945), and Jonkers, ''Reflections'' (1946) hold for demography, especially upper-class demography; Frank, ''Legislation'' (1975), and Galinsky, ''Legislation'' (1981), for moral ideology, though conceding the two issues to be inseparable. Des Bouvrie, ''Legislation'' (1984), criticizes Galinsky, arguing that the purpose was limited to a restoration of civic morals. Brunt, *IM* 562, 565, emphasizes the demographic motive. Krenkel, ''Familienplanung'' (1978/1988), holds for an attempt to increase the birthrate prompted by an economic crisis. A balanced view of the legislative intent is given by Spagnuolo Vigorita, *Pernicies* 124–125. See also Villers, ''Mariage'' (1982) 294–299.

[98] Nörr, ''Legislation'' (1981); Wallace-Hadrill, ''Family and Inheritance.''

[99] Cf. Gaudemet, ''*Matrimonium*'' 124; Baltrusch, *RM* 178.

the Gracchi are perhaps familiar enough. Many individual aspects of the law derived in fact from earlier approaches to similar problems.[100] The most dramatic
example is the speech promoting marriage and child-rearing by Metellus Macedonicus, censor in 131–130, which Augustus read to the Senate to justify his own
policy.[101] Freedmen with children were allowed in the army in 217 B.C. and were
later permitted to retain the privilege of enrollment in the rural tribes.[102] Caesar's
assignation, in 59, of the remainder of the *ager Campanus* to citizens with three
or more children is another example.[103] Octavian awarded his wife and sister release
from *tutela* in 35 B.C.[104] Married men and fathers of children enjoyed preference
in the allotment of provinces beginning in 27 B.C.[105] Equally important is Cicero's
call for moral reform and demographic increase in 46.[106] Pompey and Caesar both
wielded extraordinary authority with regard to supervision of morals.[107]

The censors had for centuries been responsible for moral oversight, a field that
included the promotion of marriage, with the particular aim of raising children.[108]
In the year preceding the introduction, on his tribunician authority, of the *lex Iulia
de maritandis ordinibus,* Augustus assumed the functions, if not the title with full
authority, of a *cura morum et legum.*[109] Significant in this connection is the story
of how Augustus, qua ''censor,'' castigated an *eques*—wrongly, as it turned out—
for noncompliance with his marriage legislation.[110]

Resort to a positive act of legislation was something new[111] and entailed obvious inconveniences, as well as certain advantages. The difficulty of designing a
system of rewards and punishments that had any chance of influencing the behavior
of the lower orders is noteworthy. Those who would argue that the law had no
concerns of this sort should first look at the system it was designed to replace.
Moreover, some of the individual provisions contained in the *lex Iulia* itself are
telling. The penalties regarding public entertainments were broadly conceived and
were perhaps more keenly felt than we tend to imagine. The law evidently imposed
a tax on celibate women with fortunes of 20,000 sesterces or more, a measure that

[100] Nörr, ''Legislation'' 358, makes this point.

[101] Liv. *Per.* 59; Suet. *Aug.* 89.2; Gell. 1.6 (who mistakenly names Metellus Numidicus, who was
a censor in 102, as the author of the speech).

[102] Liv. 22.11.8, 45.15.1; cf. Gell. 5.19.11–15 and also the *lex Terentia de libertinorum liberis,* Plut.
Flam. 18.1, with Rotondi, *Leges* 274.

[103] Suet. *Iul.* 20.3; App. *BC* 2.10; Dio 38.1.1–3, 38.7.3, cf. 43.25.1–2.

[104] Dio 49.38.1.

[105] Dio 53.13.2.

[106] Cic. *Marc.* 23; cf. *Leg.* 3.7.

[107] See Mette-Dittmann, *Ehegesetze* 19.

[108] Baltrusch, *RM* 14.

[109] The subject is much debated, but most accept that Augustus exercised the *censoria potestas,* not
the censorship: Parsi-Magdelain, ''Cura'' (1964); Volkmann, *Augustus*² (1969) 194–198; Pieri, *Cens*
(1968) 183–201; Demougin, *Ordre* 142–150; Baltrusch, *RM* 172–173. He almost perfectly observed
the traditional five-year intervals between censuses: Nicolet, ''Augustus'' (1984) 91.

[110] Macrob. *Sat.* 2.4.25; cf. Suet. *Aug.* 39; Dio 54.16.6.

[111] As such, it serves as another reflection of what Baltrusch, *RM* 3 (see also 13–14), describes as
''die Jurifizierung des *mos maiorum.*'' Compare the remarks of Kaser, ''Rechtswidrigkeit'' (1940) 117.
139; Nörr, ''Legislation'' 359; Bellen, ''Status''; Mette-Dittmann, *Ehegesetze* 13, 14, 192–193.

reached fairly far down the social scale.[112] With perhaps a better chance of success, Augustus developed a means, outside the legislation, of communicating "his" values to a broader audience.[113] Still, it is important to try to understand the legislation in the broader context of public opinion and social practice: it too bore a "message" that could resonate beyond the scope of the law in its direct, technical application.

What is most striking is the law's attempt to create a meritocracy of virtue. This is hardly limited to the preferential treatment accorded upper-class office seekers married with children. The behavior rewarded by the law was truly a "*carrière ouverte aux talents,*" and anyone with material assets worth transmitting to the next generation could find a motive for respecting the statute here. Wealthier freedmen were disadvantaged by the law with respect to their testamentary duties to *patroni* unless they had three children.[114] As noted, just two children held *in potestate* were enough for an exemption from *operae* unless the freedman was disgraced by his profession, and a freedwoman who married with patronal approval was delivered of this responsibility.[115] A freedwoman with four children could escape *tutela* and write her will without interference, obligated to leave not more than a fifth of her estate to the *patronus,*[116] whereas a freeborn woman needed only three children to be independent of a tutor.

The requirements for lower-status persons are consistently higher than those established for others. For example, the number of children required of a patron to become eligible for succession to his freedman is less than that which the latter needed to limit or exclude such rights.[117] The real difference here resides not in the absolute number but in the whole sociolegal context. Freedwomen manumitted after the legally prescribed age of 30 might have found it something of a challenge to produce four children, though more for reasons of fertility rather than of mortality, as is sometimes assumed.[118] In this regard, the law favored those freed early "*matrimonii causa,*" and we find that the wives of imperial *liberti* were especially privileged.[119] *Ingenuae* who married in their late teens or earlier enjoyed a head start of just over a decade at minimum, in order to produce one less child than freedwomen. Bearing three children was evidently not a heroic achievement in Augustine's world at any rate; instead, such a family was

---

[112] Argued from *Gnom. Id.* 29 (which, like some other provisions of the *Gnomon,* I assume to be empirewide in application). See Riccobono, *Gnomon* 155–156.

[113] Flory, "Exempla" (1984); Zanker, *Power of Images* (1988).

[114] See above. Other freedmen were unaffected.

[115] The law cited *bestiarii* and actors as ineligible; see above and Astolfi, *LIP*[2] 309.

[116] *Gnom. Id.* 28; *Tit.* 29.2–3 (cf. 7); Astolfi, *LIP*[2] 78. For many women, *tutela* was no real disadvantage: Dixon, "Finances" (1986). But the justification for this institution, the *infirmitas sexus,* was taken quite seriously: Dixon, "*Infirmitas*" (1984). Under the law, a woman might demonstrate her sense of responsibility by having the requisite number of children, thus proving the supervision of a tutor to be superfluous for her. This does not, from a Roman point of view, necessarily render the justification for *tutela* specious for other women, as has been argued.

[117] Astolfi, *LIP*[2] 312.

[118] See discussion in Wacke, "Manumissio" (1989) 419; Robinson, "Status" (1987) 160; Weaver, "Children" (1991).

[119] Weaver, *FC* 99.

considered optimal in size and was maintained through recourse to exposure of unwanted infants.[120]

Aside from the encouragement the law offered to nonsenatorial freeborn Romans to marry freedpersons (see below), various hindrances to marriage were removed. Children *in potestate* could buck the wishes of their *pater familias* when he placed unjustified obstacles in the way of their marriage.[121] So Julian allowed marriage for the *filius familias* of a father held as a prisoner of war or who was simply absent for three years, provided the partner was appropriate.[122] Marcus conceded marriage for the son of a *furiosus*.[123]

The law provided that the urban praetor appoint a tutor to approve a dowry if a woman had a tutor who was underage and so unable to lend his *auctoritas*.[124] It protected dowry, essential for remarriage, by placing restrictions on the husband's ability to profit from the manumission of a dotal slave.[125] It also liberated freedpersons from an oath imposed on them, presumably by their patrons, not to marry, provided that they wished to contract a marriage "properly" ("recte").[126]

Entirely in keeping with the spirit of the marriage law is the provision of the *lex Aelia Sentia* that enabled a Junian Latin to obtain full citizenship for himself and his wife and children if a child of the marriage lived a year.[127] The law not only recognized and rewarded a best-case scenario of the maximum number of children but established modest levels of achievement, tailored to a range of individual circumstances, and so united the spirit of the ideal with a sense of the practical and possible.[128]

In sum, obeying the law was an exercise in virtue that liberated one from other social responsibilities. As one scholar has remarked, apropos of the exemption from curatorship furnished by the *ius liberorum,* raising one's own children was a means of escaping the responsibility of raising the children of others.[129] For example, the position of the *pater familias* who fulfills his social responsibilities is not weakened but enhanced.[130]

[120] Shaw, "Family" (1987) 11. Compare the incentives granted to slaves: Colum. 1.8.19; Iul.-Ulp. D. 40.7.3.16 (evidently founded on a real case), with Scheidel, "Ius" (1994).

[121] Marci. D. 23.2.19; see Mette-Dittmann, *Ehegesetze* 133–134.

[122] Iul. D. 23.2.11; cf. Iul. D. 49.15.23.

[123] Iustinianus C. 5.4.25 (a. 530); cf. Inst. 1.10 pr.

[124] *Tit.* 11.20, with Mette-Dittmann, *Ehegesetze* 135.

[125] See Ulp. D. 24.3.64 pr.-10.

[126] Paul. (2 *ad legem Aeliam Sentiam*) D. 37.14.6.4 (cf. Paul. D. *eod.* 15); Ter. Clem. D. 40.9.31, 32 pr. (the prohibition was taken up by the *lex Aelia Sentia*). It is unclear exactly what Paul, who may be quoting the statute, means by "recte," since we know of no marriage prohibitions that applied to freedpersons independent of the ones designed for senatorials. Paul may refer to these, or perhaps he means that freedpersons are eligible for this benefit only if they respect those prohibitions laid down for the *ceteri ingenui.* If so, this would be another instance of the law's creation of a meritocracy of virtue.

[127] Gaius 1.29–30, 71–72, 80.

[128] See Mette-Dittmann, *Ehegesetze* 179.

[129] Bouché-Leclercq, "Lois" 275. For a similar argument, re sumptuary legislation, see Baltrusch, *RM* 129; re manumission laws, Mette-Dittmann, *Ehegesetze* 191 (cf. 194–195).

[130] Compare Mette-Dittmann, *Ehegesetze* 185 (also 29, 205), who overemphasizes the law's penalties and their implications.

Augustus's interest in reinvigorating the upper orders, such as it was,[131] is at best only a partial explanation of his motives. If members of the upper classes were unwilling to shoulder their part of the burden, the law was prepared to reward those who were.[132] The emperor's intent was in part the creation of a new, moral elite.[133] The overture can only have been greeted with support, even enthusiasm,[134] from broad sectors of Roman or, better, Italian society,[135] despite the opposition it encountered in some quarters.[136]

Augustus did not attempt to create a social order *ex novo* but granted legal recognition to developments already under way.[137] Over time, as the law's reach over the lower orders was extended further and its goals came increasingly to be conceived as fiscal rather than demographic, there was a tendency to level the social hierarchy, a process that allowed the authority of the *princeps* to emerge enhanced, by contrast. On an institutional level, the emperor's purpose was to raise the dignity of marriage. *Matrimonium iustum* was the form preferred above all others, which is not to say that other types of union were utterly ignored.

Legislation had another advantage, in that it abstracted the norms it established, made for uniform application (at least in theory), and avoided direct reliance on the personal authority of Augustus or a potential rival for its enforcement.[138] Augustus could not, for obvious reasons, serve as anyone's model in this area, and yet it was hardly opportune for him to turn over the supervision of morals to others. This was not only politically risky but even impossible, given the moral climate prevailing among the upper orders at the time.[139] Neither Augustus, with one child, nor Livia, with two, was in full compliance with the statute: most important, they

---

[131] Salutary is the skepticism expressed by Siber, "Ehegesetzgebung" 165, and Syme, *RR* (1939) 445, over whether Augustus seriously believed it possible to renew the old aristocracy or win them to his side. Augustus's intentions in this regard have been too often simply assumed.

[132] Wallace-Hadrill, "Family and Inheritance," shows how the law was designed to cut the unmarried and childless out of the advantage they had enjoyed in Roman society and transfer this to the *patres*. This affected not just the recipients but the person making the will. A good example is the construction of the regime on the property of freedmen (especially Junian Latins); see above and Bouché-Leclercq, "Lois" 271.

[133] One notes in this connection the relatively relaxed demographic standard laid down by the law. If Augustus had wanted to guarantee full replacement at the core of the elite, say a consul in one generation followed by another in the next, he might have required twice the number of children demanded for the *ius liberorum*: Hopkins, *Death* ch. 3, Shaw, "Believers"; Jacques, "Sénat."

[134] Vell. Pat 2.89.4: "leges emendatae utiliter, latae salubriter."

[135] Syme, *RR* 453–458; cf. Ferrero, *Grandezza* 4.285.

[136] For hostility to the law, see the evidence surveyed by Spagnuolo Vigorita, *Pernicies* 150–152. For contemporary opposition, particularly from elements of the equestrian order, see Mette-Dittmann, *Ehegesetze* 203.

[137] See Raaflaub and Samons, "Opposition" (1990) 434–435; Mette-Dittmann, *Ehegesetze* 185.

[138] The loss of authority experienced by the censorship in the late Republic is well recognized: Fantham, "Censorship" (1977) 50. The sensitivity over exercise of censorial duties that Dio puts in the mouth of Maecenas is not wholly anachronistic: Dio 52.21.3–7; cf. 40.57.3. Note that Augustus used the marriage law to create the first legal definition of the *ordo senatorius:* Talbert, *Senate* 39–47.

[139] The point is perhaps illustrated by the emperor's reliance on two unmarried, childless sponsors for the second law: Dio 56.10.3.

had no children in common.[140] Especially telling is a famous exchange between emperor and Senate in prelude to the marriage legislation.[141]

It is difficult to take the measure of the law's effects. We lack much useful demographic information. Some recent assessments have tended toward the guardedly optimistic, citing as justification a robust increase in the census returns in the period following its passage.[142] It is impossible to be certain that this phenomenon was produced by the law,[143] though the result hardly justifies pessimism.

The ancients engaged in a ferocious polemic on the law, a discourse that addressed its operation or side effects but avoided criticizing its fundamental aims, as if these were beyond discussion.[144] Through careful selection of socially despised types for the marriage prohibitions (while omitting to invalidate unions that contravened them), Augustus seems to have avoided the pitfall of comparison with another, much-maligned prohibition of marriage, the provision of the XII Tables that forbade matrimony between patricians and plebeians. Though it was of short duration, soon repealed by the *lex Canuleia,* this measure offered an inauspicious and potentially embarrassing precedent for his program, which in important respects relied on this statute as a model for the transformation of *mores* into law. There is, to be sure, no certain example known to me of criticism of the marriage prohibitions.[145] This success may reflect an aspect of the marriage law often neglected by moderns: Augustus perceived a reluctance to marry and responded with a liberalization, especially remarkable in the matter of unions between freed and freeborn outside the senatorial order, as we will see below.

One source, Pliny in his *Panegyricus,*[146] implies that the law was demographically effective for the upper classes only. His point is well taken: direct economic assistance was more likely to yield results, at least as far as the poor were concerned. But it should not be pressed, since the remark falls in the context of flattery of Trajan, whose aim was, not merely to emulate, but to outdo Augustus, precisely by offering a form of direct economic assistance, the *alimenta,* to the poor.

Nörr has shrewdly observed how the law set up a mechanism that was almost fail-safe.[147] The state could not lose between the motives of revenue and repro-

[140] The gap between policy, especially as represented by the law on adultery, and personal history of the *princeps* was obvious to contemporaries. See Suet. *Aug.* 69.

[141] The scene is described by Dio 54.16.3–5. Jörs, *E.* 35, captures perfectly the atmosphere and significance of this episode. See also Syme, *RR* 452, and the reference to Augustus at Ovid. *Met.* 15.832–839: a dubious compliment, if it is meant as one.

[142] Humbert, *Remariage* 177; Nörr, "Legislation" 354; Zablocka, "*Ius*" 381; Seiler, "Ehe" (1990) 85. See now, in general, Astolfi, *LIP*² 330–331; Treggiari, *RM* 77–80. Brunt, *IM* 565 (cf. 561), is pessimistic.

[143] Nörr, *Rechtskritik* (1974) 146.

[144] Humbert, *Remariage* 170–173; Nörr, *Rechtskritik* 76–78, 104–106, 146; Humbert, "Individu" (1990) 180–182; Seiler, "Ehe" 82–83.

[145] Prop. 2.7 cannot in my view be relied on with certainty for evidence of such criticism. For outrage over the famous proviso of the XII Tables, see Cic. *Rep.* 2.63.

[146] Plin. *Pan.* 26.5.

[147] Nörr, "Legislation" 354. A different emphasis is offered by Siber, "Ehegesetzgebung" 163,

duction: the more disappointing the results in one field, the better they were in the other. Wallace-Hadrill takes the redistributive analysis one step further, observing how the state's income from *bona caduca* and *vacantia* strengthened its ability to provide subventions for the fruitful but needy, for example, Hortensius Hortalus.[148]

Arguments about the the the law's effects should not be confused with impressions of Augustus's intentions. Scholars are divided on the issue of whether the emperor fully intended the fiscal dynamics of the legislation.[149]

Finally, whatever the demographic or fiscal benefits, the law made a fundamental contribution to the construction of a moral ideology.[150] The lineaments of responsible behavior were laid down with solemnity and rigor for the contemplation and improvement of the entire community. Those whose values and preferences were incorporated into the new legislation were well placed to receive its benefits; of course, anyone seriously interested in a political career had to reckon with the new rules of the game.[151] The emperor was confirmed in his place at the apex of the social and political pyramid.[152] Armed with the privilege of granting exemptions, he was able to oversee the working of the mechanism and to sort out any contingent conflicts between moral and political worth. An explanation of the law's centuries-long popularity with the policymaking establishment has to be sought to a large extent in its ideological implications.[153]

Despite the hostility of some authors, ancient and modern, the law actually interfered rather little with one's freedom to write a will or marry.[154] The scope of those relations who qualified as *exceptae personae* is impressive; significantly, they were the same persons who might expect to receive most testamentary bequests. Any male with less than 100,000 sesterces or female with less than 50,000 sesterces could marry whom they chose or not marry with impunity as far as the testamentary *poenae* were concerned. Until Vespasian, will-makers liable to the law could circumvent the whole regime through resort to *fideicommissa.*

The same point holds for the marriage prohibitions themselves. They limited one's choice of partner only in a very few situations, all of which concern persons against whom a deeply felt social prejudice is either attested or fairly presumed, a prejudice that was weighted even more heavily against them as potential spouses of respectable, socially prominent persons. Since these prohibitions embraced prostitutes and pimps, it is the law's treatment of these types that will form the focal point of the following discussion.

---

who identifies the law's provisions as "Finanzmaßnahmen mit starkem sozialem Einschlag." See also Wacke, "Manumissio" 414.

[148] Wallace-Hadrill, "Family and Inheritance" 72.

[149] See Spagnuolo Vigorita, "Nota" xiii n. 10; Astolfi, *LIP*² 331.

[150] See Spagnuolo Vigorita, *Pernicies* 126–127. I find unpersuasive the suggestion of Bénabou, "Pratique" (1990), that the law encouraged materialistic cynicism about marriage. See just Sen. *Ben.* 3.33.4.

[151] Eck, "Sozialstruktur" 383.

[152] See, e.g., Wallace-Hadrill, "Civilis Princeps" (1982) 46–48.

[153] On this popularity, see Chapter 4.

[154] Wallace-Hadrill, "Family and Inheritance" 62; Nörr, "Legislation" 358.

2. Marriage with Prostitutes before Augustus

The question of whether, during the Republic, freeborn Romans were able to contract marriages with prostitutes and pimps is a difficult one, inextricably bound up with the debate over the rule on marriage of freeborn with freedpersons in this period. This is because our principal piece of evidence concerns a woman who was both a *libertina* and a prostitute. I will review the debate over the latter issue of freed-freeborn marriage, which has received more attention, and then draw a conclusion about the marriage status of prostitutes and pimps under the Republic.

The modern debate over the status of marriage between freed and *ingenui* began with Mommsen, who claimed that such unions were prohibited by law under the Republic and so void (he concedes a laxer practice for the late Republic, when the evidence for such marriages is better).[155] Karlowa argued that they were not subject to a legal ban and were valid under the law but were morally and socially disapproved and even liable to censorial punishment[156].

Both positions have been criticized by Humbert, who proposes a third alternative, whereby the unions in question are visited with a sanction that renders them less than fully valid.[157] It is not clear what Humbert means by this.[158] The idea that the censors would exercise such a power is unsupported by any evidence. Moreover, Humbert's argument runs to a paradox: since the primary censorial sanction would be the declassing of the male upper-class partner (practitioners themselves had little to lose, if my argument about routine censorial declassing of them in Chapter 2 is correct) and since there was unlikely to be much interest in punishing such unions between lower-class partners, it is difficult to see the point behind the penalty he proposes.

Karlowa's view is the dominant one and is the more convincing, as strengthened by the arguments of Watson and Treggiari, who show that in the Republic such marriages were completely valid, not punished by any law,[159] though socially

[155] Mommsen, *Staatsrecht* 3.1³ (1887/1969) 429–431. He is followed by (among others) Csillag, *Augustan Laws* 236 n. 281; Villers, ''Mariage'' 295.

[156] Karlowa, *RR* 2 (1901) 172 (doubt had already been expressed by Jörs, *E.* 20, with n. 2), followed by (among others) Corbett, *Marriage* 30–34; Watson, *Persons* (1967) 32–38; Treggiari, *Freedmen* (1969) 82–86 (and now *RM* 64); Kaser *RP* 1² (1971) 315; Baltrusch, *RM* 164. Astolfi, ''Endogamia'' (1994) 80–81, argues a strange hybrid of the positions of Mommsen and Karlowa by supposing that invalidity at law of marriage between freeborn and freed was somehow transformed by the first century B.C. into *disprezzo* for the male partner when he was a member of the upper classes. This view finds no support in evidence or—in my view—compelling logic.

[157] Humbert, ''Hispala'' (1987).

[158] He is evidently prepared to concede them full legal effect; moreover, the descriptive terminology he employs is vague (*matrimonium iniustum, illegitimum, illecitum* are not necessarily synonyms): Humbert, ''Hispala'' 136.

[159] Liv. 39.19.5–6 (see below); Cic. *Sest.* 110, where Cicero attacks the credibility of a witness, L. Gellius Poplicola, who married a freedwoman. Gellius was an *eques* who had been stripped of the *ornamenta* of this order. We would expect Cicero to tax his victim with the invalidity of the marriage if this were the case: Treggiari, *Freedmen* 84. See also Cic. *Phil.* 2.3, 3.17, 13.23, and Cic. *Att.* 16.11.2, where Cicero denounces the marriage of Antony with Fadia, the daughter of a freedman: testimony a fortiori to the prejudice against unions with freedpersons themselves.

despised, and that in this sense Augustus actually introduced a liberalization by prohibiting only marriages between freed persons and members of the senatorial order.[160] Watson is right to argue that Augustus was the first to introduce a statutory prohibition of marriage with freedpersons—obviously this held only for members of the senatorial order, whereas the Republican censorial sanction applied to all marriages with *ingenui*.[161]

All the same, I believe that the permission granted the *ceteri ingenui* was not simply implied (or granted "non-technically" as Watson has it) by the prohibition contained in the law. The language of Dio and Celsus (the latter is especially important because he seems to cite the law: "*cavetur*") suggests that there was some form of explicit encouragement, although this may have been hedged about by an acknowledgment that concubinage was a more acceptable arrangement. In a similar way, the *lex Aelia Sentia* of A.D. 4 allowed early manumission for slave women whose masters wished to marry them.[162]

The text that is of central importance to us concerns the granting of privileges to Faecenia Hispala, a freed *meretrix* and the heroine of the crisis caused by the Bacchanalian conspiracy in 186 B.C.:[163]

> Liv. 39.19.4–6: 4. Senatus consultum factum est . . . utique consul cum tribunis plebis ageret, ut ad plebem primo quoque tempore ferrent . . . 5. utique Faeceniae Hispalae datio, deminutio, gentis enuptio, tutoris optio item esset, quasi ei vir testamento dedisset; utique ei ingenuo nubere liceret, neu quid ei qui eam duxisset ob id fraudi ignominiaeve esset; 6. utique consules praetoresque qui nunc essent quive postea futuri essent, curarent ne quid ei mulieri iniuriae fieret; utique tuto esset. id senatum velle et aequum censere ut ita fieret.

> (4) A decree of the Senate was passed . . . to the effect that the consul should encourage the tribunes of the *plebs* to promulgate, at the earliest opportunity, a plebiscite . . . (5) to the effect that Faecenia be granted the power of alienating property, changing her legal status, marriage outside her (i.e., her patron's) *gens,* and likewise choice of a tutor, as if a husband had allowed this to her in his will, and to the effect that it be permitted for her to marry a freeborn male, and that neither *fraus* nor *ignominia* be imputed to him who marries her, (6) and to the effect that the consuls and praetors, both those in office at present and those elected in future, should see to it that no harm befall this woman, and to the effect that [all of this] be guaranteed. The Senate declared this as its will and granted consent for it to be carried out.

The technical precision of Livy's language is obvious: "there is little doubt that Livy is doing nothing more than put into indirect speech the direct wording of the decree."[164]

The first four privileges concern Faecenia's status as a woman and/or as a

---

[160] Dio 54.16.1–2, 56.7.2; Celsus D. 23.2.23; Paul. D. *eod.* 44 pr.; *Tit.* 13.1.

[161] Watson, *Persons* 37.

[162] Gaius 1.18–19; *Tit.* 1.12–13a, with Wacke, "Manumissio"; Treggiari, *RM* 120.

[163] There is a huge bibliography on this topic. See Pailler, *Bacchanalia* (1988).

[164] Watson, "Enuptio" (1974) 332. The actual grant of the provisions was made by a plebiscite: Watson, "Enuptio" *LM* (1974) 7, 334.

freedperson and so are not of direct concern.[165] It has been doubted whether the permission to marry a freeborn male is related to her status as a prostitute. Mommsen argues that there was no connection, because the prohibition contained in the *lex Iulia et Papia* would be otiose if one already existed and because such a bar, if it did exist, would have been total, rendering a concession covering only *ingenui* without sense.[166]

Karlowa insists that the concession rested not only upon Faecenia's freed status but upon her profession.[167] Watson views the concession as primarily concerned with the woman's status as *libertina* but points out that censorial *ignominia* was a prospect for any *ingenuus* who married a prostitute.[168] Treggiari dismisses the possibility that the permission concerned her status as a prostitute,[169] citing the emphasis laid by the passage on the freeborn status of the putative marriage partner and the fact that even freedmen might suffer disgrace in marrying such women.[170]

There is plenty of room for disagreement,[171] but some weakness is discernible in the arguments of those who reject the idea that the concession is in any way tied to Faecenia's profession. For example, they must explain the evidence of Cicero[172] as reflecting a change in the rule, a change that is unattested, or treat it as the product of a degeneration of morals in the late Republic.[173] Mommsen's argument cannot stand, since the Augustan law, which in many instances translated social values into positive law, in fact allowed marriages between freedmen and prostitutes. Treggiari's observation is valid as far as it goes and suggests another way of looking at the question.

Unions with prostitutes, if shameful for freedmen, would be even more so for *ingenui*. The Senate's permission for Faecenia to marry an *ingenuus* embraced freedmen, a fortiori. The fact that Augustus allowed unions between freedmen and prostitutes implies no more than the concession granted to marriages between freed and nonsenatorial freeborn. Previously, such unions were socially and morally objectionable and at least theoretically liable to censorial sanction (which may not have been a deterrent to many *libertini*). If before the *lex Iulia* marriages between

[165] On *gentis enuptio,* see Watson, "Enuptio"; cf. Thomas, "Mariages" (1980) 374; Astolfi, "Endogamia." There is disagreement as to whether the point about the husband's testament applies to all of the preceding privileges: Watson, "Enuptio" 333; Humbert, "Hispala" 140–143. On *deminutio,* see Peppe, *Posizione* (1984) 63–69. Like her lover, Faecenia was also given a large cash award: Liv. 39.19.3.
[166] Mommsen, *Staatsrecht* 3.1³.430 n. 2.
[167] Karlowa, *RR* 2.172 n. 2; cf. Karlowa, "Geschichte" (1870) 214 (215) n. 18. His conclusion is adopted by Corbett, *Marriage* 31–34, and, generally, by Dixon, *TRF* 209 n. 84. See also the "analytical" approach favored by Astolfi, "Endogamia," 79–80.
[168] Watson, *Persons* 33 n. 3, followed by Villers, "Mariage" 295.
[169] Treggiari, *Freedmen* 85, followed by Pailler, *Bacchanalia* 375–376.
[170] On the evidence for marriage between freed and freeborn, see Treggiari, *Freedmen* 213.
[171] Contra Franciosi, *Clan*⁴ (1989) 64, for whom the evidence "clearly" presupposes a prohibition of *conubium* between freeborn and freed. A similar confidence is shown by Del Castillo, "Conubium" (1994).
[172] Cic. *Sest.* 110.
[173] See Corbett, *Marriage* 32; Villers, "Mariage" 295.

freeborn and freed were so objectionable, unions between freed and prostitutes may have been less so, though if so this does not mean they were entirely immune from censure. These considerations generally support the view of Karlowa and Watson. Admittedly, however, the burden of proof rests squarely with those who wish to argue that the practice of prostitution is relevant to the Senate's concession.[174]

So far, so good. A solution to the problem may be discovered in Livy's description of Faecenia's relationship with P. Aebutius, a young aristocrat:[175]

> Liv. 39.9.5–7: Scortum nobile libertina Hispala Faecenia, non digna quaestu cui ancillula adsuerat, etiam postquam manumissa erat, eodem se genere tuebatur. huic consuetudo iuxta vicinitatem cum Aebutio fuit, minime adulescentis aut rei aut famae damnosa: ultro enim amatus appetitusque erat et maligne omnia praebentibus suis meretriculae munificentia sustinebatur. quin eo processerat consuetudine capta ut post patroni mortem, quia in nullius manu erat, tutore ab tribunis et praetore petito, cum testamentum faceret, unum Aebutium instituerat heredem.

> A prostitute of sterling character, the freedwoman Faecenia Hispala, unworthy of the means of making a living she had grown accustomed to while still a slave, sustained herself in the same way even after she had been freed. She maintained a sexual relationship with Aebutius, a young man of the neighborhood, which was in no way harmful to his patrimony or reputation. This was because she had taken the initiative and sought him out, and since the provisions his family had made were utterly insufficient to meet his needs, he was supported through his dear lover's generosity. Why, matters even reached the point where, smitten with the relationship, she, finding herself *sui iuris* after her patron's death, having applied for and received a tutor from the magistrates, in writing her will made Aebutius sole heir.

It is clear that Livy emphasizes Faecenia's profession, not her status as a *libertina,* when he describes her relationship with Aebutius. The apologetic tone is remarkable.[176] She is described with the oxymoron *scortum nobile*[177] as unworthy of her profession and merits a series of diminutives *(ancillula, meretricula)* that sound patronizing but that are evidently intended as compliments. Livy perhaps imagines

---

[174] The marriage between the freedman Pompeius Demetrius and the prostitute Flora advanced by Treggiari, *Freedmen* 214, cannot support a conclusion. Flora's status is unknown (Treggiari conjectures "probably a freedwoman"). It is not clear to me from the source (Plut. *Pomp.* 2.2–4) that Flora and the wife of Demetrius are the same person.

[175] His father was an *eques equo publico* (Liv. 39.9.2), that is, a member of the 18 equestrian centuries in the *comitia centuriata,* which at this time included senators; see the discussion in Wiseman, "Definition" (1970). For Aebutius's background, see Pailler, *Bacchanalia* 355–361.

[176] Livy's description of the two protagonists has aroused a well-founded suspicion: Watson, "Enuptio" 332, cf. 338–339. This difficulty does not affect my argument, which depends on the social prejudice reflected in Livy's account, not the literal truth of every detail it contains. For a defense of its reliability, see Rousselle, *Persecution* (1982) esp. 9, 19.

[177] The adjective obviously concerns her character, not birth: *OLD* s.h.v. 6, 7b. Compare Velleius's phrase (describing Cicero): "vir novitatis nobilissimae" (2.34.3). *Nobilis* was often used to describe prostitutes, and not necessarily as a compliment: Austin, *Caelio*³ (1960) 89. The sense may be generalized as "above the common run of prostitutes." Note Tacitus's transformation of the phrase into "principale scortum" (*Hist.* 1.13.3), more akin to the rather different type of oxymoron "meretrix Augusta" (see Chapter 5). For a different view, see Hillard, "Stage" (1992) 45, with n. 22, with whom I agree that "noble whore" is an inadequate translation of the phrase.

Faecenia as a character type, the whore with a heart of gold familiar from Roman Comedy.[178] The two great dangers recognized by the Romans in such affairs are deprecated by Livy: harm to reputation and loss of patrimony.

The first of these threats is softened, if not obviated entirely, by the fact, as Livy presents the situation, that it was Faecenia who approached Aebutius in the first place (not surprising behavior for a prostitute)[179] and she alone who made an emotional investment in the union. The second pitfall is avoided to the extent that Aebutius actually benefits financially from the relationship.[180]

Faecenia's profession was decisive for Livy's presentation of the relationship and explains why he displays such sensitivity about it. The historian's remarks in this context are equally important for understanding the contents of the *SC,* since what was true of attitudes about love affairs[181] was even truer for marriage.

Aebutius's status as the son of an *eques equo publico* was no doubt an aggravating factor, but marriage between a prostitute and any *ingenuus* would still have been a matter of some delicacy, as the decree of the Senate, which clearly does not contemplate Aebutius as the sole prospect,[182] suggests. Nor need we presume that Livy's emphasis on the profession stems from a contemporary perspective at odds with the historical reality of the early second century, whereby the objections to marriage between *ingenui* and freedpersons had softened while the social prejudice against marriage with prostitutes remained strong.[183]

The evidence supports the conclusion that it was both Faecenia's status as freedwoman and her profession as prostitute that would ordinarily have barred her marriage with freeborn males. In other words, in the time of the Republic, marriage of freeborn with freedwomen was punishable in exactly the same way as marriage with prostitutes. The terms *fraus* and *ignominia* employed by the *SC* do not suit the argument for nullity but suggest the violation of a purely social norm, punished

---

[178] Pailler, *Bacchanalia* 368 (cf. 372), argues that the sympathy for Faecenia derives at minimum from the consul Postumius, who as the chief suppressor of the conspiracy had every motive to present his informant in a good light. This seems quite possible but has no consequences for my argument.

[179] I understand Faecenia to continue as a prostitute after linking up with Aebutius; otherwise, one would expect Livy to praise her explicitly for ceasing prostitution.

[180] To this extent he acted as her pimp, a role he may have pursued more actively, as Watson, "Enuptio" 338–339, suggests. The young Sulla received an opportune bequest from a prostitute: Plut. *Sulla* 2.4 ("a whore, but wealthy").

[181] Humbert claims that the relationship between Aebutius and Faecenia was concubinage: "Hispala" 132 n. 9. It is difficult to argue the point from the word *concubitus* (Liv. 39.11.2), which typically denotes "sexual act" or at most "sexual relationship," nothing more, or from Livy's description of the testamentary arrangements, which is tendentious.

[182] Livy's apologetic presentation of the relationship between Faecenia and Aebutius is suited for the affair of a young man with a prostitute: the "rules" (whatever the Senate might decree) change for marriage. Given that fact, the lack of evidence for such a "happy ending" (though Faecenia did make Aebutius her heir), and the rarity of extremely status-dissonant unions over the history of Roman matrimony, I am inclined to view the idea that Aebutius married Faecenia as a romantic fantasy. See notably Pailler, *Bacchanalia* 367, 369, 377–380.

[183] See the evidence reviewed above, which dates to the late Republic and the time of the marriage law itself. Livy's conservatism guarantees that his views do not simply reflect the innovations of the *lex Iulia,* which was almost certainly passed before he wrote book 39 of his history; for the putative date of composition, see Luce, *Livy* (1977) 5 n. 5.

with the sanction of the censors.[184] This was directed at the male partner and meant removal from the Senate or from the ranks of equestrians for members of either order and demotion from one's *tribus* and assignment to the *aerarii* for all other *ingenui*. A fine might complement social degradation.[185] If anything, attitudes were perhaps more liberal regarding marriage between freedmen and non-elite *ingenui*; at any rate, by the time of the late Republic it is difficult to imagine routine censorial intervention in such cases.[186] The same regime, with similar qualifications, perhaps held true for those who concluded marriage with any of the women who fell in the categories proscribed by Augustus in the *lex Iulia et Papia*. Admittedly, direct evidence is lacking, though it may be significant that Augustus was called upon to consider the case of a man who had married his former partner in adultery in his exercise of the *cura morum*,[187] and Domitian as censor removed a man from the equestrian order who had remarried, without first obtaining an *abolitio*, a woman he had accused of adultery.[188]

Whatever view one takes of the last point, a broad continuity emerges in the treatment of prostitutes both before and after the Augustan law. This point can be pressed further. As noted, the *lex Iulia et Papia* punished offenders against its marriage prohibitions as *caelibes*. The Republican censors were entrusted with the responsibility of ensuring that Romans married and that these marriages produced children.[189] Augustus can be regarded as having done no more than codify an aspect of the *regimen morum*,[190] with, one might argue, some attenuation of the penalties, since those who violated his marriage prohibitions would not be subject to *ignominia* but only to the financial disabilities visited upon the unmarried both before and after the reform.

At the same time it is obvious that Augustus went beyond the practice current in the Republic. The law applied to all *ingenui*; indeed, it lumped all nonsenatorial *ingenui* together in a way that was unlikely if not impossible for the censorial *nota*. Women were included, a novelty.[191] Beforehand a woman who entered into a dis-

---

[184] On *fraus*, see Krüger and Kaser, "Fraus" (1943) esp. 117–120, 134, 173–174. Greenidge, *Infamia* (1894) 66 n. 1, views *fraus* as a reference to violation of a legal norm. Cf. Humbert, "Hispala" 132–133; Humbert, "Individu" 186, who is ambivalent over whether the norm was legal or social. On *ignominia*, see Kaser, "Infamia" (1956) 229.

[185] So Humbert, "Hispala" 134.

[186] See Treggiari, "Ladies" (1970/1971) 198.

[187] Dio 54.16.6.

[188] Suet. *Dom.* 8.3.

[189] On marriage, see Val. Max. 2.9.1 (*aes uxorium*; cf. Plut. *Camil.* 2.2; Festus 519L); Cic. *Leg.* 3.7; Plut. *Cato M.* 16.1; Gell. 1.6.1–6, 4.20.3–6. On children, see Dio 43.25.2; Dion. Hal. 2.25.7; Plut. *Cato M.* 16.1; Gell. 4.3.2 (5.19.15: *praemia patrum*); Liv. *Per.* 59; Suet. *Aug.* 89.2.

[190] The language of the censors' oath was taken up by legislation pursuant to the marriage law and by private documents drawn up in connection with marriage under the Empire: Daube, *Duty* (1977) 24–25. Such phrasing may have been in the law itself: Ter. Clem. D. 35.1.64.1. Compare Augustus's act of reading Metellus Macedonicus's speech as the signal that a traditional line was to be pursued: Liv. *Per.* 59; Suet. *Aug.* 89.2; Gell. 1.6.1.

[191] Women were exempt from the direct moral oversight of the censors. In the phrase of Suolahti, *Censors* (1963) 49, "they were neither taxpayers, nor soldiers, nor voters" (a principle evidently not injured by an irregular levy: Peppe, *Posizione* 138–147; Dixon, "Breaking" [1985] 520); cf. Gell. 10.23.4; Schmähling, *Censoren* (1938) 27; Siber, *RV* (1952) 222; Pólay, "*RM*" (1971) 309–310, 315.

graceful union would have been chastised by her relations, not by censors. The senatorial order itself was given more precise definition. Presumably there had been little prospect of censorial interference for a fourth-generation descendant of a senator living in relative obscurity. This was now no longer true. The new law was uniform for all and inexorable, deaf to entreaty and incapable of making the fine (or arbitrary, depending on one's point of view) distinctions that the old aristocracy had been accustomed to draw. It was a suitable foundation for a new moral order constructed from the materials of the old.

3. The Terms of the *Lex Iulia et Papia* regarding Marriage with Practitioners of Prostitution

Problems with Evidence

Aside from the prohibitions against marriage with *ingenui,* prostitutes and pimps were placed under the same regime as everyone else, with one important exception. My aim is to survey briefly the evidence directly relevant to these prohibitions and to discuss some of their effects. A more detailed treatment is reserved for a special feature of the law affecting prostitutes, the so-called *quarta.* Finally, the phrasing of the legislative prohibition and its implications are examined.

It is widely recognized that our most important source, a passage from the so-called *Tituli ex corpore Ulpiani,* is deeply flawed:

> *Tituli* 13: De cael<ib>e orbo et solitario patre.
>
>   1. Lege Iulia prohibentur uxores ducere senatores quidem liberique eorum libertinas et quae ipsae quarumve pater materve artem ludicram fecerit, item corpore quaestum facientem.
>
>   2. Ceteri autem ingenui prohibentur ducere lenam et a lenone len<a>ve manumissam et in adulteri<o> deprehensa<m> et iudicio public<o> damnata<m> et quae arte<m> ludicram fecerit: adicit Mauricianus et a senat<u> damnatam.

> On the unmarried man, childless man, and unmarried man with children.
>
>   1. By the *lex Iulia,* senators and their sons are indeed forbidden to marry freedwomen and those who themselves or whose father or mother have been actors or actresses, likewise, a woman making money with her body.
>
>   2. Moreover, all other freeborn men are forbidden to marry a procuress and a woman manumitted by a male or female pimp and a woman caught in the act of adultery and her who has been an actress: Mauricianus adds also a woman condemned by the Senate.

It is obvious that the heading does not accurately describe what follows in the text. The text was all but gutted by an unknown editor following the reforms enacted by Constantine, who rescinded the disabilities imposed by the classical law on the three types named in the heading.[192] The authorship and early history of the *Tituli*

---

[192] Constantinus CTh. 8.16.1 (a. 320) (= C. 8.57[58].1); Schulz, *Epitome* (1926) 39; Astolfi, *LIP*[2] 43–45.

ex corpore Ulpiani have been much debated; a recent examination argues that its genesis lies with a colleague/student of Ulpian who edited the master's material and dates the revised version we possess to 320–342.[193]

A glance at the text betrays a number of purely formal problems.[194] The difficulties do not stop there. There is no reference to a prohibition on betrothals, which must have been in the *lex Iulia et Papia,* or to women belonging to either the senatorial order or the *ceteri* category or to the requirements of wrongful intent and knowledge (i.e., of partner's status) for the commission of an offense.[195] While the law evidently defined the senatorial order down to the fourth generation in the male line,[196] this text gives only sons of senators.

More serious is the conflict with the information given in the *Digest* regarding some of the types of women prohibited. There it says that those condemned in a criminal court are forbidden senators by an *SC;* their status is then compared to that of women caught in the act of adultery.[197] In this case the evidence of the *Digest* should perhaps be preferred, at least for the first group,[198] which suggests that the remark concerning the woman condemned by the Senate belongs in this category of prohibitions, too. This means that women condemned in any criminal court are forbidden under the *SC* to marry senatorials, whereas the law itself forbade only those condemned for adultery (or caught in the act) to all freeborn persons.

What precedes is the solution elaborated by Riccardo Astolfi.[199] His preference for the evidence of the *Digest* is the line taken by Mommsen and most scholars with respect to two other, similar conflicts.[200] One involves actors, actresses, and their progeny, all of whom the *Digest* places among the senatorial prohibitions.[201]

---

[193] Mercogliano, *"Tituli"* (1990) esp. 194–195 (the article also contains a useful discussion of modern scholarly opinion).

[194] Astolfi, *LIP*[2] 106, notices "eas" missing before "quae" in the first paragraph, as well as "fecerit" for "fecerint" (the *lex Iulia et Papia* had "facit fecerit"). Add "eam" before "quae" in the second paragraph.

[195] Astolfi, *LIP*[2] 106, on the basis of Paul. D. 23.2.44 pr.

[196] Paul. D. 23.2.44 pr.; on the problem in general, see Astolfi, *LIP*[2] 98–102. Chastagnol, *Sénat* (1992) 175, argues despite this evidence that the marriage prohibitions did not apply to female members of the senatorial order until the reign of Marcus Aurelius.

[197] Ulp. D. 23.2.43.10–13. Talbert, *Senate* 450, tentatively identifies this *SC* as the Larinum *SC,* which at the time he wrote had been wrongly conflated with the Vistilia *SC:* McGinn, *"SC"* (1992). All the same, an early date, especially in Tiberius's reign, seems likely. Biondi, "SCC" (1946/1965) 318, posits an Augustan date.

[198] For a detailed discussion, see Astolfi, *LIP*[2] 103–108, who concludes that both the *deprehensa* and the woman condemned for adultery were forbidden to all *ingenui* by the Augustan law itself.

[199] Lenel, *Pal.* (1889/1960) 2 col. 940 n. 4, followed, for example, by Falcão, *Prohibiciones* (1973) 16, prefers to emend the *Digest* passage to reconcile it with *Tit.* 13.2, so that actors and actresses are forbidden to all freeborn Romans. Cf. Mette-Dittmann, *Ehegesetze* 146 (cf. 167, 185), who accepts a broad ban on marriage with actresses out of an assumption that the marriage prohibitions coincided with exemptions provided under the Augustan adultery statute. She describes the exempted women as *feminae probrosae*; see Chapter 4.

[200] Astolfi, *LIP*[2] 106–108.

[201] Paul. D. 23.2.44 pr. Gaudemet, *"Matrimonium"* 126, (citing Iustinus C. 5.4.23 [a. 520–523]), argues that the compilers suppressed a prohibition against the marriage of actresses and *ingenui*; cf. Karlowa, "Geschichte" 214–215; Castelli, "Concubinato" (1914/1923) 151; De Robertis, "Condizione" (1939/1987) 185 (cf. 181–182); Falcão, *Prohibiciones* 21–22. This theory explains neither why

The other concerns prostitutes, whom the jurist Paul,[202] who gives only the senatorial prohibitions and who purports to quote the law, omits.[203] The discordant participial construction "item . . . facientem" and the fact that Ulpian[204] in his commentary mentions pimps and prostitutes together have persuaded Mommsen and others[205] to place the latter among those women forbidden to marry *ingenui.*[206]

It is possible, though unprovable, that progeny of prostitutes and pimps, like those of actors and actresses under the senatorial prohibitions, were embraced by the law.[207] They are not mentioned in the juristic commentaries as we have them, which give plenty of space to problems concerning the status of actors' children. It is conceivable, however, that the types forbidden senators and their kin received more careful definition. By the same token, senators were forbidden to marry those persons prohibited to *ingenui,* and children of pimps, gladiators, and trainers are grouped together in an *SC* of A.D. 19.[208]

Women manumitted by pimps also receive no mention by the jurists and are best regarded as a postclassical insertion, placed here as compensation for the transposition of true prostitutes to the senatorial paragraph: it is interesting that these women should be regarded as in some sense equivalent to prostitutes.[209]

In sum, the law instituted two categories of marriage prohibitions. Members of the senatorial order, which included senators, their sons, daughters, grandsons, granddaughters, great-grandsons, and great-granddaughters in the male line, were forbidden to marry or to betroth themselves to freedmen, freedwomen, actors, actresses, and anyone whose father or mother was an actor or actress. Later legislation added persons condemned in a standing criminal court, to which the jurists (perhaps) appended those condemned by the Senate. All other freeborn persons were forbidden prostitutes,[210] pimps, procuresses, and persons convicted of adultery or caught in the act.

By implication, there were three possible courses of action open to prostitutes and pimps under the law. Either they obeyed it, by marrying freedmen and bearing

---

the prohibition to senatorials remains in the *Digest* nor why it alone is repeated in both categories in the text of the *Tituli.*

[202] Paul. D. 23.2.44 pr.

[203] On this text, see Chastagnol, "Femmes" (1979) 10–11; Raepsaet-Charlier, "*Clarissima femina*" 192–194; Astolfi, *LIP*² 98–102. Raepsaet-Charlier and Astolfi (contra Chastagnol) take the entire fragment as deriving from the *lex Iulia et Papia*—rightly, in my view.

[204] Ulp. D. 23.2.43 pr.-9.

[205] Mommsen *apud* Karlowa, "Geschichte" 216–217; Greenidge, *Infamia* 171 n. 1. Nardi, *Posizione* (1938) 21 with n. 1, improves the phrase on the basis of Ulp. D. 23.2.43 pr.-5. Solazzi, "Glossemi" (1939/1963) 183, and Astolfi, *LIP*² 107, accept Mommsen's more conservative version "item . . . facientem <et>" (after "ducere"). Given the state of the text there is little to choose. Schulz, *Epitome* 39, holds the phrase to be a postclassical gloss, but Nardi, *Posizione* 20 n. 2 (following Corbett) points out that the section of Marcellus's commentary devoted to the *lex Iulia* and Ulpian's commentary on the same both connect prostitutes with the statute (see Chapter 4).

[206] For a dissent, see De Robertis, "Condizione" 182 n.1.

[207] See Astolfi, *LIP*² 57.

[208] *Tab. Lar.* 16, on which see Chapter 2.

[209] The item is evidence for the expansion, in postclassical times, of the legal conception of "prostitute." See McGinn, "Definition" (forthcoming).

[210] For a medieval echo of the ban on marrying prostitutes, see Otis, *Prostitution* (1985) 16.

children, or married *ingenui* in defiance of it or simply did not marry at all. Marriages with prostitutes and pimps in violation of the statute were punished the same way as any other such union:

> *Tituli* 16.2: Aliquando nihil inter se capiunt, id est si contra legem Iuliam Papiamque Poppaeam contraxerint matrimonium, verbi gratia si famosa<m> quis[211] uxorem duxerit, aut libertinam senat<or>.

> Under certain circumstances [spouses] receive nothing from each other, that is, if they have married contrary to the terms of the *lex Iulia et Papia,* for example, if someone [i.e., an *ingenuus*] marries a woman stigmatized by the statute, or a senator marries a freedwoman.

The *famosa* at minimum is a prostitute,[212] but I see no reason why the term should not refer to procuress and adulteress as well: so also for *ignominiosa* below.

Such spouses, if married with *manus,* would have been prevented by the *SC Gaetulicianum* from inheriting upon intestacy,[213] and in all other respects counted as *caelibes.* It is important to note that persons married *contra legem* were deprived of any benefits accorded by the legislation. The *lex Iulia et Papia* did not permit a freedwoman married to her patron to divorce him without his consent.[214] But if the woman was, for example, a prostitute, the (freeborn) patron could not claim this privilege:[215]

> Ter. Clem. (8 *ad legem Iuliam et Papiam*) D. 23.2.48.1: Si ignominiosam libertam suam patronus uxorem duxerit, placet, quia contra legem maritus sit, non habere eum hoc legis beneficium.

> If a patron marries his own freedwoman even though she is disgraced, it is the prevailing view that, because he is her husband in violation of the statute, he does not enjoy the benefit conferred by the statute.

Similarly, although the law provided that if a woman had a minor for a tutor, she might ask the urban praetor to grant one for the purpose of constituting her dowry, he was obligated to refuse her request if the ensuing marriage would violate the law.[216]

The *Quarta*

One would tend to assume that prostitutes and pimps who did not marry would, as *caelibes,* be rendered completely *incapaces,* but one source introduces a wrinkle of sorts:

[211] Some follow Huschke and insert "ingenuus" for this word (Nardi, *Posizione* 25; Solazzi, "Glossemi" 183 n. 5), a reasonable emendation.

[212] So Astolfi, *LIP*² 120.

[213] See above.

[214] See esp. Astolfi, *LIP*² 164–186.

[215] Technically, this point is the fruit of interpretation, not established by the law itself ("placet"). But the principle that those who violate the statute should not enjoy its benefits is established by the law itself, so that it seems opportune to include it here. "Quae specialiter prohibentur" in Dioclet., Maxim. C. 5.4.15 *(anno incerto)* refers to the *manumissor,* not the *liberta,* so that this text has nothing to say on the prohibition against marrying prostitutes (contra Astolfi, *LIP*² 131).

[216] *Tit.* 11.20.

Quint. *IO* 8.5.17: Pro Spatale Crispus, quam qui heredem amator instituerat decessit, cum haberet annos duodeviginti: "hominem divinum, qui sibi indulsit."

19: Trachalus contra Spatalen: "placet hoc ergo, leges, diligentissimae pudoris custodes, decimas uxoribus dari, quartas meretricibus?"

For Spatale,[217] whom a certain lover had made heir, and died when he was eighteen years old, spoke Crispus: "O lucky man, who knew how to be good to himself!"

Against Spatale, Trachalus: "O laws, the most unrelenting guardians of sexual honor, is this then pleasing, that wives be given only tenths of an inheritance, but prostitutes a quarter?"

The two advocates are L. Iunius Q. Vibius Crispus (cos. I suff. before 60) and P. Galerius Trachalus (cos. ord. in 68). The evident longevity of both men makes the encounter difficult to date, but a time early in Domitian's reign seems probable.[218] The *leges* are without doubt the *lex Iulia et Papia*.[219] The *decimae* refer to the amounts for which a married person who had no children in common with his or her spouse was eligible to take from a decedent spouse's estate.[220]

The significance of the provision regarding *meretrices* is, however, less clear. Hartmann argues that although Trachalus must refer to statutory provisions relating to *capacitas,* these cannot concern prostitutes, who were, in Hartmann's view, not allowed to receive bequests qua *caelibes*.[221] Trachalus, when he says "prostitutes," really means "concubines" (Hartmann appeals to the notion of rhetorical hyperbole), to whom the law would have granted one-fourth capacity; Trachalus contrasts their situation with that of wives, to whom the same statute allowed a minimum of one-tenth.

Solazzi approves Hartmann's idea that the *lex Iulia et Papia* did not grant the *quarta* to prostitutes, on the ground that such a measure would have contradicted the moral aims of the legislation.[222] On the other hand, he argues, the law did not deprive these women of all capacity to receive bequests. This enabled the jurists to make allowance for prostitutes, who were effectively barred from marriage by the law (unlike Hartmann, Solazzi acknowledges that the law entitled them to marry freedmen but doubts that any self-respecting *libertinus* would have wanted a prostitute as a wife), and to grant them complete capacity. Since the law was designed to encourage matrimony and the raising of children, he concludes that the provision mentioned by Quintilian concerned neither prostitutes nor concubines but the *mater solitaria*.[223]

[217] As often, the prostitute bears a "significant" name: "lascivious" (*LSJ* s.h.v.).

[218] Both are spoken of as deceased by Quintilian elsewhere (*IO* 10.1.119). The *Institutio Oratoria* dates from the mid-90s: Conte, *LL* (1994) 759. Other evidence suggests that both men lived on well into the reign of Domitian: Jones, *DSO* (1979) index s.h.v. Spatale herself is the subject of an epigram by Martial (2.52). This tribute to the size of her breasts was published c. 86: Conte, *LL* 759. A date between 85 and 90 for the lawsuit cannot be ruled out; see Chapter 4.

[219] So Astolfi, *LIP*² 66, following Hartmann, "Incapacität" (1866) 221–222; Jörs, *V.* 64; Solazzi, "*Caduca*" (1942/1963) 334.

[220] *Tit.* 15.1. The spouse was eligible for other benefits too; see below.

[221] Hartmann, "Incapacität" 222.

[222] Solazzi, "*Caduca*" 334–351.

[223] Wallace-Hadrill, "Family and Inheritance" 75, has a hybrid version, identifying Spatale as "a mistress with children of her own."

Astolfi[224] suggests simply that before Domitian's move against the *feminae probrosae,* those women (among whom he includes prostitutes, procuresses, actresses, adulteresses convicted or caught in the act, women condemned in any *iudicium publicum,* as well as former prostitutes, procuresses, and actresses)[225] were allowed to receive one-fourth, without defining the circumstances under which this was possible.

Hartmann assumes that prostitutes were perforce *caelibes* and thus by operation of law incapable of accepting testamentary bequests. As noted, however, they might marry freedmen and, despite Solazzi, we cannot be sure that such a match would have been undesirable for all lower-class males. There is no evidence that Spatale was her benefactor's concubine. Certainly, the mere fact of the bequest suggests their relationship was more than casual, but this hardly proves it amounted to the institution of concubinage recognized by the jurists.[226] At any rate, nothing in the text uses their relationship as a way of justifying or explaining the bequest: Spatale is simply identified as a prostitute.

The same reasoning holds against Solazzi's claim about the *mater solitaria:* there is not a word about children. The arguments of both Hartmann and Solazzi depend on taking *meretrix* as a term of abuse for another type of woman, but this is unlikely.[227] When Trachalus speaks of "prostitutes," he must mean "prostitutes." The same criticism can be made of Astolfi's introduction of the category of *feminae probrosae.*

Furthermore, if we accept Solazzi's view on the *solidi capacitas* of prostitutes, Trachalus's point becomes unintelligible. Why would he identify the opposing litigant with a group whose capacity was greater than that of the group to which she actually belonged? The lawyer's artifice seems to lie simply in the contrast of the best possible situation of an unmarried prostitute under the law with the worst possible situation of a wife (i.e., he assumes her to be childless).

Trachalus, to be sure, neglects to mention some of the other benefits that the law granted the childless wife, such as the capacity to take a third of the spouse's patrimony in usufruct, her dowry in a legacy, a *pars virilis* on intestacy if married with *manus* (before the *SC Gaetulicianum,* which, however, probably preceded this case), and the rule for *exceptae personae,* or that granting half capacity for bequests made by persons other than the spouse. We have here a useful showing of how unreliable the remarks of a trial lawyer can be as a source of information about the law. At all events, it is difficult to agree with Solazzi that the jurists, otherwise so sensitive to the moral aims of the legislation,[228] would have flouted them so extravagantly here.

---

[224] Astolfi, *LIP²* 66.

[225] In Astolfi's view, these women were deprived by Domitian of complete capacity. See Chapter 4 for a full discussion.

[226] The word *amator* is used of a prostitute's clients: Plaut. *Most.* 286; Cic. *Cael.* 49. On "respectable" concubinage, see Treggiari, *"Concubinae"* (1981); McGinn, "Concubinage" (1991).

[227] *Meretrix* is possible as a term of abuse, but *scortum* and other terms were favored: Adams, "Words" (1983). Moreover, the word, when employed as a term of abuse, typically means "woman of loose morals" or the like, without a specific referent such as "concubine."

[228] On this, see Spagnuolo Vigorita, *Pernicies* 126–127; Astolfi, *LIP²* 338–343.

Astolfi's view must be modified in two respects. As already seen, there is no justification for extending the application of the regime for the *quarta* to the *feminae probrosae*, however these women are defined. Beyond this, an overall limit of one-fourth on the testamentary eligibility of prostitutes seems harsh, even punitive, and at odds with the spirit of the law, which permitted them to marry freedmen and adopted a neutral, at times even benevolent approach toward the lower classes. Prostitution was widely tolerated at Rome and was given an explicit sanction of sorts by the adultery law of Augustus, to say nothing of Caligula's tax.

In sum, it would be strange to find such a draconian measure here. It also seems to run against the grain of one of the more obvious aims of the legislation. The *lex Iulia et Papia* was built on a series of rewards and penalties. A woman whose capacity was limited to one-fourth at best might not consider that she had much to lose by violating its terms. Above all, why should she be punished for obeying them? In other words, why should she be limited to one-fourth capacity if she married a freedman and bore children?

It is admittedly difficult to determine the precise nature of this *quarta*. Whether or not Trachalus is contrasting the best possible situation for a prostitute with the worst for a wife, it is true that he contrasts *meretrices* with *uxores*. In other words, it appears that he was thinking, not of married prostitutes, but of unmarried ones. If the *quarta* applied only to the latter, who were of course *caelibes,* then it may be understood as a mild form of encouragement for prostitutes not to marry. On this hypothesis, their situation would have been better if they married within the law (and had children) but worse if they married against it.

This measure provided a comfortable middle ground, which enabled prostitutes to carry on their trade without contracting unions that, although legal, were ipso facto dishonorable and without compromising the goals of the legislation by unduly rewarding any group for not observing it. In sum, wives of freedmen (without a child by their current husbands) were entitled to the *decimae* whether they were prostitutes or not, but the unmarried prostitute could claim a *quarta* from a generous lover.

Astolfi views this as being one-fourth of the actual bequest.[229] He rightly takes the *decima* as one-tenth of the patrimony, so that this would represent a ceiling on the share of the total inheritance that the woman might receive.[230] Although Trachalus may be comparing apples and oranges, the better view is that the *quarta* represents one-fourth of the patrimony.[231] The disposition bears witness more to the testamentary freedom enjoyed by Romans, a freedom that the *lex Iulia* restricted only modestly, than to favoritism toward prostitutes. The idea was to discourage marriage: a prostitute stood to gain far more from a lover by not marrying him (if he were not a *libertinus* and the pair did not have children).

---

[229] Astolfi, *LIP*[2] 66.

[230] Astolfi, *LIP*[2] 34.

[231] So Nörr, "Legislation" 358. Alternatively, we may suppose that the *quarta* was regulated in a manner similar to the one-half capacity of *orbi,* so that one-fourth of an estate might be left them as a *licita quantitas:* Astolfi, *LIP*[2] 29–30.

All the same, Augustus wanted to avoid giving prostitutes a motive to marry even those whom the law permitted them to marry, a motive that might indeed have strongly influenced them if they otherwise faced the complete loss of *capacitas*. Overall, this is a milder and more balanced approach than simply forbidding them to marry at all and then subjecting them to the full range of penalties imposed on those who did not marry in accordance with the law. Such a course might be expected from policymakers much more hostile to prostitution than Augustus and his successors appear to have been.

At the same time we are entitled to ask: just how relevant was all of this for most Roman prostitutes? The obvious answer is not very much. It would apply only to those who, like Spatale, posed a threat to elite patrimonies and to those who were egregiously successful at plying their trade and aimed at securing their retirement with a marriage match well up the social scale. These are the prostitutes who threatened to blur the distinctions in society Augustus and his collaborators considered so important.

Given that repression of prostitutes or prostitution was not one of the law's purposes, this provision fits in well with the other exemptions prostitutes might enjoy under it, such as those associated with age, wealth, and status as *exceptae personae*. It may be compared with the *quarta* guaranteed heirs under the *lex Falcidia,* though this was a minimum figure, not a maximum as we have here.[232] A better analogy might be the *quarta* that was the maximum amount an Alexandrian citizen might leave to his wife when they had no children in common (otherwise, the wife received a *pars virilis* of the estate).[233] Besnier argues that this would have discouraged the peregrine woman from having children: childless, she was better off than a Roman wife without children.[234] His explanation is that the Roman state had no interest in the reproduction of the peregrine population. A similar point can be made about Roman prostitutes. They too were considered irrelevant for the demographic concerns of state and society. Thus their position in the law of succession was more advantageous than that of other Roman *caelibes*.

One other advantage to the *quarta* is that, for all its generosity, it cut prostitutes out, to a large extent, from the considerable rewards of Roman testamentary bequests. I emphasize the three-fourths of an estate for which the unmarried prostitute was not eligible. The squandering of wealth on prostitutes was a perennial concern in antiquity. Most of the expenditure seems to have taken place *inter vivos,* but, as the evidence of Quintilian suggests, some prostitutes could expect a healthy remuneration from clients upon their demise. The law limited such generosity, in the same way that it cut *caelibes* and *orbi* out of the considerable social and financial benefits that accrued to their status.[235] It is well known that inheritance was the chief way of acquiring wealth in the ancient world. The provision for the *quarta*

---

[232] Even so, the equation with the minimum laid down for the Falcidian heir shows that the *quarta* was far from being considered a trivial amount. On this law and its *quarta,* see Voci, *DER* 2² (1963) 755–789.

[233] *Gnom. Id.* 6. See Reinach, "Code 1" (1919) 590–591; Riccobono, *Gnomon* 118–119.

[234] Besnier, "Lois" (1949) 114.

[235] See Wallace-Hadrill, "Family and Inheritance."

complemented the prohibition of marriage with *ingenui,* in the sense that they blocked two paths by which prostitutes might ascend to the upper orders, through marriage and accumulation of wealth.

There is no evidence that the *quarta* was permitted to any of the other types that fell within the marriage prohibitions of the *lex Iulia.* As already noted, Trachalus mentions only prostitutes. Since freedpersons were allowed to marry all nonsenatorial *ingenui,* it is hard to see what role the *quarta* might have played here. It was hardly Augustus's aim to make celibacy attractive to such a broad segment of the population. Actors, actresses, and those condemned in a criminal court, although hardly so numerous, must fall under the same assumption, since they too were permitted to the *ceteri ingenui.* If scruples existed about such persons marrying outside the senatorial order, one would expect to see broader prohibitions, not compensating benefits.

As for adulteresses caught in the act, although technically they did not fall under the absolute prohibition against marriage enacted by the adultery law for convicted adulteresses,[236] there was a motive to punish at work here that was not present in the case of prostitutes, so that it is very unlikely that the *quarta* pertained to them. This leaves only pimps and procuresses, about whom nothing firm can be said either way, although it is quite possible that they were treated by the law in the same way as prostitutes.

Characterization of Practitioners by the Statute

One matter remains to be discussed, and that is the precise way in which the law phrased the provisions on pimps and prostitutes. The latter can be determined fairly easily from the commentaries of the jurists:[237] "qui quaeve palam corpore quaestum facit fecerit."[238] The insertion of the male pronoun is justified by the inclusion of women in the class of *ceteri ingenui.*[239] The usage of the double verb is suggested by the fragment of the law quoted at Paul. (1 *ad legem Iuliam et Papiam*) D. 23.2.44 pr.: ". . . quae ipsa cuiusve pater materve artem ludicram facit fecerit . . ." (the phrase is repeated with the male pronoun later in the passage). The use of the present tense, "facit," instead of the more common "fecit,"[240] is guaranteed not only by its twofold appearance here but by Ulpian's remark that not only she who prostitutes herself ("facit") but she who has done so ("fecit") is liable under the

<hr>

[236] Ulp. D. 25.7.1.2, Ulp D. 48.5.30(29).1. See Chapter 5.

[237] See Ulp. (1 *ad legem Iuliam et Papiam*) D. 23.2.43 pr.: "palam quaestum facere", 2: ". . . palam corpore quaestum facere." Paul. (2 *ad legem Iulia et Papiam*) D. *eod.* 47: "quae corpore quaestum . . . fecerit." *Tit.* 13.1: "corpore quaestum facientem." *PS* 2.26.4 (= *Coll.* 4.12.3): ". . . qui corpore quaestum faciunt." See also the phrase of the *Tabula Heracleensis (TH),* given below. Ovid may poke fun at the phrase with his description of the soldier at *Am.* 3.8.20.

[238] Astolfi, *LIP*[2] 103, prefers the order "mulier quae palam quaestum corpore fecit," but this is found in only one legal passage, whose text is disturbed: Marci. (12 *inst.*) D. 25.7.3 pr. (Given the wording of Paul. D. 23.2.44 pr., it is also doubtful that *mulier* appeared in the law.)

[239] See above. The jurists make no mention of male prostitutes and pimps in the context of the *lex Iulia et Papia,* for reasons that are discussed in Chapter 4.

[240] See, for example, the phrase from the *TH* quoted below in the text.

law.[241] If "fecit" was the word used by the law, this observation would seem gratuitous.[242]

The phrase finds a parallel in earlier legislation. The *Tabula Heracleensis (TH)*, when listing those persons ineligible to belong to the town council and to hold a magistracy, contains the expression "queive corpore quaestum fecit fecerit."[243]

Why was this rather ponderous expression preferred by legislators to such commonly used terms as *meretrix* and *scortum*? The answer is perhaps that descriptive phrases were typically used in place of nouns to describe persons liable to the law, a usage grounded in the meticulous, even fussy, concern with precision characteristic of Roman legislation, particularly under the Republic.[244] In some cases the words used in everyday speech might carry unwanted connotations or be too highly charged. This was true both of *scortum* and (to a lesser extent) *meretrix* (see above).

One notes minor differences in phrasing between the late Republican version and the Augustan law. The change in verb tense from "fecit" to "facit" is difficult to account for. There is a chance it may reflect a dispensation for those who practiced prostitution before the law was introduced.[245]

The same change occurs with the expression for actors and actresses in the two statutes: *TH* 123 and Paul. D. 23.2.44 pr. The reading *facit* is guaranteed by the reasoning of Pomp.-Paul. D. 23.2.44.5, where in commenting on this provision, the jurists except the woman whose parent was engaged in the acting profession before her birth or adoption or whose adoptive father has emancipated her or whose birth father has passed away before the marriage. They justify these exceptions with reference to the *sententia legis,* which must, I think, be understood from the phrase "facit fecerit." The rule that emerges is that the father has to be alive and, if an adoptive father, have the daughter *in potestate* at the time of marriage.

This suggests that ex-prostitutes would be exempted at the time the law took effect, but not those who left the profession afterward.[246] A general grace period was granted, according to one source, at the introduction of the *lex Papia Poppaea*.[247] The *lex Iulia de maritandis ordinibus* laid down a grace period of one

---

[241] Ulp. (1 *ad legem Iuliam et Papiam*) D. 23.2.43.4.

[242] It is worth noting that the jurists restricted the application of the provision concerning, not actors, but their children, despite the less generous wording of the law: Pomp.-Paul. D. 23.2.44.5. See the acute observations of Vonglis, *Loi* (1968) 124–126, on this passage.

[243] *TH* 122–123. See Chapter 2. The phrase *quaestum facere* had long been associated with prostitutes: Plaut. *Poen.* 1140; Ter. *Heaut.* 640 (cf. *Andria* 79).

[244] Compare the usage in the edict discussed in Chapter 2. The aim, not always realized, was to avoid equivocation, confusion, and undesirable interpretations; for a good discussion, see Daube, *Forms* (1956) esp. 6, 45–46; Vonglis, *Loi* 61–63; also Bauman, *"Leges"* (1980). The circumlocution may also have been considered more dignified. Compare *bestiarius,* which never appears (in Latin) in the *Digest*. In its place appear phrases such as "qui operas suas ut cum bestiis pugnaret locaverit."

[245] Compare the situation of *praecones* discussed in Cic. *Fam.* 6.18.1 for an imperfect, yet suggestive, parallel; see Chapter 2.

[246] The use of the future tense by the *lex Iulia de vi,* though itself perhaps an error, may signal a similar purpose; see Chapter 2.

[247] Dio 56.10.1, whose account is muddled, registers a grace period of one year in connection with this statute.

year during which spouses who were left bequests by decedent spouses under the condition of not marrying could do so, offering an oath that the marriage was intended to produce children, without penalty.[248] *Caelibes* had one hundred days to marry after a decedent's will was opened.[249] They also enjoyed a remission for the Ludi Saeculares of 17 B.C.[250] Another kind of grace period is found in the fact that the immediate forerunner of the *lex Papia Poppaea* was promulgated in A.D. 4 and was suspended twice, once for three years, then for another two, before it was withdrawn permanently.[251] Both the *lex Iulia de maritandis ordinibus* and the *lex Papia Poppaea* granted *vacationes* to women whose marriages ended in death and divorce (see above).

Against this argument is the doctrine, championed by Ulpian,[252] that the *turpitudo* of prostitutes was permanent. It is unlikely, however, that the original dispensation can have held much meaning for a jurist writing two centuries after it became irrelevant.

Further support for this interpretation of "facit fecerit" is perhaps to be found in a diatribe Cicero directed against a portion of Verres's edict as urban praetor.[253] Verres framed a provision that closed a loophole in the regime of the *lex Voconia* and made the new rule retroactive with the phrase "fecit fecerit." His motives were corrupt, argued Cicero. Moreover, such language was without parallel in the edict ("Fecit, fecerit? Quis umquam edixit isto modo?": "Fecit Fecerit? Who ever framed the edict in this way?").

The Voconian law itself was not retroactive. The same was true for a number of criminal statutes, but this principle is especially worth observing in private law, from which Cicero cited specific examples, besides the Voconian law itself. The only exception he was willing to concede concerned those matters that by their very nature were so terrible, so awful, that even if there had been no law against them, they merited prevention at all costs.

Prostitution and pimping surely fall within this special category of matters "terrible and awful" ("scelerata ac nefaria"). It is not surprising to find that in the public law provisions of the *TH*, prostitutes are excluded from participation in municipal honors even if they had abandoned their profession before the enactment of the rule. The phrase used is "fecit fecerit."[254]

The *lex Iulia et Papia*, to be sure, is a private-law statute that dealt in part with the delicate matter of selecting an appropriate spouse. In doing so, it touched upon the category of matters terrible and awful. In light of Cicero's reasoning Augustus might have proceeded in either direction but evidently chose to grant a dispensation to those practitioners who had retired at the time of the law's passage. In this way he exempted already existing marriages between such persons and *ingenui*—we can be fairly sure that there were no such unions with members of

[248] Astolfi, *LIP*² 157–163.
[249] *Tit.* 17.1, with Jörs, *V.* 48.
[250] *FIRA* 1² 40.1.
[251] Jörs, *E.* 57–60.
[252] See Chapter 4.
[253] Cic. *Verr.* 2.1.107–108.
[254] See Chapter 2.

the elite (see below)—while condemning existing marriages with still-practicing prostitutes and pimps. This minor concession perhaps allowed the statute to appear somewhat less intrusive into the lives of its objects.

The use of "palam" by the law created a different problem.[255] The jurists offered differing interpretations of this word, as we shall see. Insofar as we can divine the legislative intent, this qualifier was not meant to exclude prostitutes who did not practice their trade "openly," or "publicly," but rather to specify more exactly the kind of behavior targeted by the law. More than a description of the soliciting practice of prostitutes, it has a moralizing ring, and in this sense resembles the English phrase "common prostitute."[256]

The exact wording of the phrase regarding pimps is less clear. That this was a short, simple expression is suggested by the commentaries on the law[257] and the precedents that survive, from the praetor's edict and again from the *TH*. The latter strangely adopts the future tense (123): "queive lenocinium faciet." This may be the result of an error;[258] in any case we should prefer the wording of the edict, at least as a foundation.[259] Thus the phrase of the *lex Iulia* would run "qui quaeve lenocinium facit fecerit," if we assume a dispensation of the kind for which I argue.

4. Marriage Practice and Possibilities

"The real test of social acceptability is marriage."[260] The criteria of acceptability set by statute are clear enough: prostitutes and pimps are situated beyond the pale of freeborn Roman society, eligible only for unions with freedpersons. It is awkward to speak of the law's effects, since we cannot be sure what these were. The counterfactual experiment of imagining away its existence will yield no certain results. All the same, an interesting and perhaps answerable question remains. To what extent did the law's strictures resonate in social practice?

There is, to be sure, no satisfactory evidence on actual unions with practitioners of prostitution that violated the Augustan prohibitions. As far as we know, the law was broadly successful on the senatorial level. The explanation lies in the fact that this prohibition rested on a bedrock of social practice that was even more strict. It is interesting that with the possible exception of a passage of Propertius,[261] the exact significance of which is far from certain, I can find no negative reaction to

---

[255] Its association with prostitutes predates Augustus. Cato employs it in his speech *De Re Floria* (Gell. 9.12.7): "qui palam corpore pecuniam quaereret." The meaning approximates that in the *lex Iulia*. The same is true of its use by Cicero at *Red. Sen.* 11 and *Cael.* 38, 49.

[256] See the *OLD* s.h.v. 1a and 1c: "explicitly, openly."

[257] See Ulp. (1 *ad legem Iuliam et Papiam*) D. 23.2.43.6.

[258] See Chapter 2.

[259] [Iul. (1 *ad edictum*)] D. 3.2.1.

[260] Wiseman, *New Men* (1971) 53.

[261] Prop. 2.7 *may* complain of the attempted establishment of a set of marriage prohibitions in a measure that preceded the *lex Iulia de maritandis ordinibus* by approximately a decade, but this is not certain; see above.

the marriage prohibitions themselves. That is, no one complains that a freeborn Roman cannot marry a prostitute or a senator a *libertina*.[262] Moralists in general show a higher standard for the character of marriage partners than that embodied in positive law, at least for the classical period.[263]

A quantitative study performed by Raepsaet-Charlier on known senatorial marriages in the first three centuries shows that in 67% of the certain cases members of this order married each other.[264] Of the remaining 33%,[265] the overwhelming majority of unions were contracted by senatorials with members of the equestrian order or local aristocracies.[266] Marriage in this sector of society is strictly ''endogamous'' in the terms of the Augustan law.

There is only one certain example known to me of a union between a member of the *ordo senatorius* and a freedman, and this particular marriage must have been accomplished with imperial permission.[267] The widow of the senator Annius Libo married Agaclytus, a freedman of L. Verus.[268] Moreover, Raepsaet-Charlier finds that only one uncertain example of this type exists.[269] The traces of another may be detected in a text of Marcian,[270] which relates a rescript of Antoninus Pius. The circumstances, including the enactment by rescript of the rule and the situation of fact itself, suggests a real case; it is significant, however, that the existence of this union depended on a fraud. Overall, given the high profile of the senatorial order in our sources, as well as Roman sensitivity over such unions, the lack of evidence is telling.[271] Raepsaet-Charlier cites no examples of unions between members of this *ordo* and actors, actresses, et al., and I know of none.

It is, of course, impossible to state the case in such categorical terms for the *ceteri ingenui*.[272] Among non-senatorial elements of the elite, one would expect to find a similar pattern. It is not surprising to learn that in Byzantine Egypt, all daughters of *bouleutai* whose husbands are known married other *bouleutai*.[273] The record of the *ordo equester* in the Julio-Claudian period suggests that for all its

[262] I find no evidence to support the assertion that many senators were disposed to make marriage alliances with wealthy freedpersons: Weber, ''Freigelassene'' (1988) 259–260.

[263] Humbert, *Remariage* 60.

[264] For these results, see Raepsaet-Charlier, ''Vie'' (1994) 179: ''on peut donc parler d'une certaine 'endogamie sénatoriale.' '' Raepsaet-Charlier, ''Vie'' 181, reveals interesting differences occurring over time, with a relatively more endogamous pattern shown in the very early Principate. See 187–188 for the distinction in practice between descendants of senators and *novi*.

[265] If one classifies as ''senatorial'' those women with a brother who is a new senator, the percentages change to 73% and 27% respectively: Raepsaet-Charlier, ''Vie'' 179.

[266] Raepsaet-Charlier, ''Vie'' 179 n. 80, cites only three examples of marriage between members of the senatorial order and persons of very low status. Only one of these involves a freedperson (see below).

[267] See Ulp. D. 23.2.31.

[268] Raepsaet-Charlier, ''Egalité'' 463; Raepsaet-Charlier, ''Vie'' 192. Cf. Chastagnol, *Sénat* 176.

[269] So Raepsaet-Charlier, *Clarissima femina* 192 (193) n. 23. See Weaver, *FC* 171, for other dubious cases.

[270] Marci. (4 *regul.*) D. 23.2.58: ''A divo Pio rescriptum est, si libertina senatorem deceperit quasi ingenua et ei nupta est. . . .''

[271] See Dixon, *TRF* 82, with 91, 93.

[272] On marriages with prostitutes, see below and Chapter 4.

[273] Beaucamp, *Statut* 2 (1992) 20.

heterogeneous composition, a similar pattern held, with persons at the top of the order marrying senatorials and those at the bottom marrying municipal aristocrats;[274] only a handful of unions with freedwomen are known.[275]

As for the rest, a passing remark of Quintilian should prompt caution, suggesting as it does that our lack of evidence may mask an important truth. In the context of a discussion over what technique to adopt when criticizing an opponent for a fault shared with the speaker, the author cites the example of a father who disinherits his son, born of a prostitute mother, because that son has also married a prostitute. Quintilian remarks that, although this type of case is based on a theme in school exercises, it is "not out of the question in actual court practice."[276] Would that we were better informed on the nature and frequency of such unions.[277]

[274] Demougin, *Ordre* 657–676.

[275] See Demougin, *Ordre* 668–669.

[276] Quint. *IO* 11.1.82: "sed non quae in foro non possit accidere." Quintilian is of course good evidence for trial practice: Crook, *Advocacy* (1995) 166, 169–171.

[277] Compare the theme of Sen. *Contr.* 2.4, and see Gell. 2.7.18–20.

4

Emperors, Jurists, and the *Lex Iulia et Papia*

1. History of the Statute

The lack of independent evidence for the Augustan law and the cause of convenience have already made necessary the introduction, in the preceding chapter on
the *lex Iulia et Papia*, of much matter derived from the works of the jurists or from
subsequent legislation. This chapter offers an analysis of similar material, but with
a different purpose. In place of an effort to isolate and explain the terms of the
original legislation, the intent is to show how these were developed and applied
over time. The focus of this chapter is twofold, concentrating on both the refinements and supplements introduced by Augustus's successors and the interpretative
work of the jurists, as they elaborated the law.

Most of the new legislation did not concern prostitutes and pimps directly.
Our attention will be concentrated on two measures, one of Domitian and one of
Hadrian.[1] The preponderance of the juristic evidence dates from the late classical
period. Over the span of two centuries there was inevitably change in the way the
statute was interpreted and applied. The task of the jurists was to construe the law
in light of the evolution of Roman society and the judicial system. But the significance of these changes should not be exaggerated. The social and economic con-

---

[1] The most important enactments pursuant to the Augustan statute are surveyed at the beginning of
Chapter 3. The best treatment of the historical development of this law is in Astolfi, *LIP*[2] (1986) 304–
353.

text of Roman prostitution was not drastically altered during the classical age, nor did the institution of marriage undergo profound transformation.[2] The gradual change in the law of procedure[3] perhaps gave the jurists greater flexibility but made no fundamental difference in the way these laws were interpreted and applied.

2. Subsequent Legislation

Domitian's *Correctio Morum* and the *Feminae Probrosae*

A reformist impulse similar to that which shook the Rome of Augustus and created a demand for moral legislation emerged after the dynasty he founded ceased to exist. For a decade or so, reformers grappled for supremacy with the rear guard of a political ascendancy that traced its roots to the reign of Nero, until the moralists finally triumphed under Domitian, who was the last emperor to assume the censorship, and who enacted a host of measures aimed at improving the moral condition of Rome.[4]

Modern scholars have inclined to number among these reforms what they regard as one of the most severe rules ever directed against prostitutes. Our only source is a passage from Suetonius, in which the biographer offers various details of Domitian's *correctio morum*. Because the context of the detail of direct interest to us is essential for its understanding, I give the entire passage with translation:

> Suet. *Dom.* 8.3: Suscepta correctione morum licentiam theatralem promiscue in equite spectandi inhibuit; scripta famosa vulgoque edita, quibus primores viri ac feminae notabantur, abolevit non sine auctorum ignominia; quaestorium virum, quod gesticulandi saltandique studio teneretur, movit senatu; *probrosis feminis lecticae usum ademit iusque capiendi legata hereditatesque*; equitem Romanum ob reductam in matrimonium uxorem, cui dimissae adulterii crimen intenderat, erasit iudicum albo; quosdam ex utroque ordine lege Scantinia condemnavit; incesta Vestalium virginum, a patre quoque suo et fratre neglecta, varie ac severe coercuit, priora capitali supplicio, posteriora more veteri.

> Having undertaken the correction of morals, he [sc., Domitian] repressed unruly conduct at the theater, where unqualified persons had been sitting in the seats reserved for equestrians. He destroyed a series of insulting writings that had been broadly disseminated and in which prominent men and woman were criticized for their behavior; the authors he punished with social degradation. He banished from the Senate a man obsessed with acting and dancing. *He took away from disgraced women the use of litters, as well as the right of receiving inheritances and legacies.*

---

[2] The point is well made by Vonglis, *Loi* (1968) 194, with respect to imperial legislation, above all the Augustan marriage law. In his view, the conservative approach adopted by the jurists in interpreting this legislation is explained by the permanence of values regarding sexuality and the family in the first three centuries.

[3] With respect to the marriage law itself, the most significant change affected the mechanism through which *bona caduca* fell to the state treasury: Spagnuolo Vigorita, *"Bona Caduca"* (1978); Spagnuolo Vigorita, *Pernicies* (1984). For relevant changes to the adultery law, see Chapter 6.

[4] In general, see the superb essay by Grelle, *"Correctio morum"* (1980).

He removed the name of a Roman *eques* from the jury rolls, because the man had remarried his ex-wife, whom he had divorced and then begun to prosecute for adultery. He judged certain individuals from the senatorial and equestrian orders guilty under the *lex Scantinia*. He punished the sexual misbehavior of Vestals, which had been overlooked even by his father and brother, with measures that were different in content but alike in their severity: the first cases were visited with mere execution; the later ones with the old-fashioned means of punishment.

The crucial part of the text is italicized for the reader's convenience. The text is difficult and, not surprisingly, controversial. There are essentially two questions. Who are the *feminae probrosae* and why did Domitian choose to punish them?

Suetonius identifies these women with only two words: *feminae probrosae*. We do not know if Domitian himself used the term. It appears in no legal source, so that it cannot be assumed to have a technical significance. It is rather a moral epithet, like *feminae famosae*.[5] While *probrum* and its cognates may have more than one meaning when used of women, the overwhelming number of such usages refer to sexual misbehavior, above all, to adultery.[6] Without further qualification, the reader of Suetonius would understand only "sexually disgraced women."

Taking sexual incontinence as our point of departure, we may better define the possible meanings of the phrase. Actresses must be excluded from consideration.[7] They were often regarded as women of easy virtue, and a number of them may qualify as prostitutes under a sociological definition,[8] but their degradation qua actresses had only to do with their appearance on stage, which was regarded by the Romans as shameful in itself.[9] The fact that they were permitted as approved marriage partners to the *ceteri* (nonsenatorial freeborn) is firm evidence that their behavior was not identified with that of prostitutes and procuresses. In sum, we are left with, as candidates for Domitian's targets, these two latter types, plus adulteresses, whether convicted or caught in the act.[10] I will show first why Domitian's measure could not have concerned prostitutes or procuresses, and then why it must have been directed at adulteresses.

There is no question that, as it is used in the legal sources, *probrum* had a special resonance for prostitutes, for reasons already given.[11] But at issue here is the meaning of the moral epithet *probrosae* as used by a nonlegal source. Most of

---

[5] Suet. *Tib.* 35.2 For a survey of the long history of scholarship on *famosae* and *probrosae,* see McGinn, "*Feminae Probrosae*" (1997/8).

[6] See Ulpian's definition of *probrum:* Ulp. D. 50.16.42. The same tendency is found in the nonlegal sources: Plaut. *Amph.* 882; Cato *apud* Gell. 10.23.4; Cic. *Phil.* 2.99; Liv. 25.2.9; Suet. *Iul.* 43.1; Suet. *Titus* 10.2. Cf. Festus s.h.v. 277L (sexual offense of a Vestal). On *probrum* and its range of meaning, see Adams, *LSV* (1982) 207.

[7] I follow the reasoning, though not the conclusion, of Astolfi, *LIP*[2] 54–55.

[8] To be precise, a definition that includes the three criteria of payment, promiscuity, and emotional indifference between sexual partners; see below.

[9] The position was similar for those upper-class Romans who took to the stage and the arena: Levick, "*SC*" (1983); Lebek, "*SC*" (1990) esp. 43–58.

[10] See Schneider, *RE* meretrix 1026, for a similar conception of *feminae probrosae.*

[11] The same point is conceded for terms that can be considered broadly as synonyms, such as *famosa, ignominiosa, turpis,* all of which qualify prostitutes in the legal sources.

the uses of *probrum* and its cognates, when they concern the sexual behavior of women, concern adultery. The reasons for this are close to hand. A prostitute was a woman without honor by definition. Whereas a respectable woman might be insulted or degraded by being called a prostitute, especially a slang equivalent, the same cannot be maintained for prostitutes themselves. They already lay outside the community of honor, and because they were considered "shameless," they were in a sense beyond reproach. It makes little sense for Suetonius to describe them as *probrosae,* a term better suited for "respectable" women who had abandoned their sexual honor.

My argument, which in its negative form is that Domitian did *not* deprive prostitutes of the right to receive bequests, encounters a more serious obstacle in the form of a legal text that at first glance suggests that the opposite was true:

> Pac.-Paul. (8 *ad Plautium*) D. 37.12.3 pr.: Paconius ait, si turpes personas, veluti meretricem, a parente emancipatus et manumissus heredes fecisset, totorum bonorum contra tabulas possessio parenti datur: aut constitutae partis, si non turpis heres esset institutus.

> Paconius says that if a son, emancipated and manumitted by his father, had instituted as heirs base persons, such as a prostitute, *bonorum possessio* of the whole inheritance contrary to the terms of a will is to be granted to the father, or only [*bonorum possessio*] of the legally prescribed share, if a base person had not been instituted heir.

Apart from "constitutae," which should refer to "one-half" under classical law, there are no serious problems with the text.[12] According to Astolfi, the text assumes that the prostitute (whom he describes as *femina probrosa*) is made sole heir.[13] On her taking up the inheritance depend the rights of the *parens manumissor*. Since she cannot, qua *incapax,* enter, the praetor probably invoked the fiction that she had entered upon the estate, and gave the *parens* his *bonorum possessio*.

The text however says nothing about the prostitute being made sole heir. Though this is possible in the abstract, it seems unlikely. The prostitute was allowed a maximum of one-fourth of the estate under the *lex Iulia et Papia* (a rule that, as seen, Astolfi rejects for the period after Domitian). More important, the *parens manumissor* could expect at least one-half, no matter who else was instituted heir. Paconius states his holding abstractly and does not give details of a specific case. Absolute certainty is impossible, but we should not hasten to suppose that even if the *parens* had been awarded his half under a will, and the prostitute's share was limited to one-fourth, the former could not claim *totorum bonorum possessio,* under the principle given here.

---

[12] Since Faber, scholars have accepted that the classical text read "dimidiae" instead of "constitutae" largely because Justinian limited the father's share to one-third: *Index Itp.* ad loc. Lenel, *Pal.* (1889/1900) 1 col. 1160 n. 2, wanted to eliminate the phrase "aut . . . institutus" as a superfluous gloss, but neither this suggestion, nor the doubts of the editors of the *VIR* about the part of the phrase "non . . . institutus" can carry conviction. Solazzi, "*Manumissio*" (1927/1960) 202 n. 16, observes that a Vulgate manuscript of the *Digest* erases "emancipatus." None of this affects the status of the part of the text that concerns us.

[13] Astolfi, *LIP²* 59 n. 11.

Nor is there any reason to believe that the heir had to enter in order for the praetor to assign the property to the *parens*.[14] Even apart from this point, Astolfi's interpretation forces the sense of the passage. The text does in fact suggest that in ordinary circumstances a prostitute might be made heir. The sensitivity over testamentary bequests made by emancipated children is grounded in the belief that the former *pater familias* retained a legitimate interest in their property. Without the release from *patria potestas,* all such property would vest in this man, whose interest, after emancipation, is compared to that of a patron in the will of a freedman.[15] It is arguably even greater, since both before and after the *lex Iulia* a freedman could cut the patron out through having an appropriate number of children, whereas this does not seem to have been possible for the *emancipatus.* Such claims were felt to be more pressing when the patrimony was in danger. According to the rhetor Cornelius Hispanus,[16] an affair with a prostitute might be grounds for disherison.

Under the circumstances, it is not surprising that such an exemplary squandering of patrimony as that described here provoked the intervention of the praetor. If prostitutes were completely incapable of receiving bequests, it would have been easy enough for Paul and Paconius to say so; the problem would not have been defined as it is here. My conclusion is that the testamentary regime for prostitutes was the same before and after Domitian. It receives support from the argument of Berger[17] that Paul took this opinion from Plautius's work: Paconius must therefore precede him and date to the mid–first century. Plautius was a contemporary of Caelius Sabinus, cos. suff. in 69.[18]

Another text has been adduced to support the case, unintentionally rich in paradox, for the broad definition of *feminae probrosae.* This one actually grants the prostitute rights to succession, though admittedly on intestacy:

> Ulp. (13 *ad Sabinum*) D. 38.17.2.4: Et[19] si mulier sit famosa, ad legitimam[20] hereditatem liberorum admittetur.[21]

---

[14] As in all cases of *bonorum possessio contra tabulas,* the praetor held the will to be invalid, then made the appropriate dispositions of property: Voci, *DER* 1² (1967) 178–179, 183–184.

[15] Ulp. 37.12.1 pr. See Dixon, "*Infirmitas*" (1984) 349; Dixon, *TRF* (1992) 48; Gardner, *Being* (1993) 47, 67, for legal and social parallels between the rights of a patron over a freedman's inheritance and those of a father over that of an emancipated child. Emancipation did not sever the bonds of *pietas:* Saller, "Punishment" (1991) 149–150.

[16] *Apud* Sen. *Contr.* 2.1.14.

[17] Berger, *RE* Paconius (2) (1942) 2124–2125.

[18] Kunkel, *Herkunft*² (1967) 131, 134.

[19] The inclusion of this word is argued for by Nardi, "Incapacitas" (1938) 169 n. 66, 171, and by Astolfi in his first edition (*LIP*¹ 152 n. 45). Mommsen does not print it, but I include it here for argument's sake. Ulpian favored the use of this conjunction: Honoré, *Ulpian* (1982) 52. Joined with *si,* it parallels in meaning *etiamsi,* which also occurs frequently in his work: Honoré, *Ulpian* 55.

[20] The objections of Solazzi, "Glosse" (1936/1972) 162–163, to this word where it means "conforming to the *ius civile*" are unfounded. It is very commonly used, especially in the law of succession and above all with regard to the *SC Tertullianum,* where it was perhaps mentioned in the statute: *Tit.* 26.8; Ulp. D. 29.6.1 pr., Ulp. D. 38.17.2.14 (three times); and the other texts at D. 38.17 cited by Solazzi himself. See also the abundant literary parallels in *TLL* s.h.v., especially I and II.

[21] The suggestion of Bonfante, *Corso* 6 (1930) 330 n. 6, that *non* be inserted before this word has been roundly decried: Nardi, "Incapacitas" 169 n. 66; Solazzi, "Divieti" (1939/1963) 93; Astolfi, *LIP*² 59 n. 11.

Even a woman of notorious reputation will be admitted to the intestate succession of her children.

The jurist is commenting on a statute, the Hadrianic *SC Tertullianum,* which under certain conditions improved a mother's position in the intestate succession to her own children.[22] Previously, she had, under the *ius civile,* no claim; though the praetor admitted her among the *cognati,* she was outranked by her children's agnatic relatives, who qualified as *legitimi.* The *SC* gave her superior standing under the civil law, so that henceforth she enjoyed priority over *cognati* if the decedent was legitimate; if illegitimate,[23] she came second only to a son's *sui heredes,* to no one in the case of a daughter. Only women with the *ius liberorum*[24] were eligible.[25]

The *SC Tertullianum* has been convincingly explained as an effort to keep property within a child's family of origin and prevent its dispersal either among more distant relatives (favored under both the traditional civil and the praetorian succession) or to a patron (if the woman were freed).[26] The ultimate end was not so much to benefit the woman as to preserve the property for her surviving children, to whom the estate (it was assumed) would be left when she died.

This assumption appears to have been a very strong one.[27] From the time of the late Republic at the latest women are seen to protect the economic interest of their children and are praised for it.[28] In classical times these expectations were safeguarded at law, to an extent, by the praetor under the *querela inofficiosi testamenti,* and later on intestacy were protected by the *SC Orphitianum* of A.D. 178.

The interests of children were also protected by individual parents whose spouses survived them, through resort to such legal devices as *fideicommissa,* conditions directed at emancipation, and legacies of usufruct or *usus.*[29] It seems that in the majority of cases the transmission of a decedent's property to the children of a union was simply entrusted to the surviving spouse.[30] The most practical course was to leave, for example, the mother a high degree of flexibility.[31]

---

[22] D. 38.17; *Inst.* 3.3; *Tit.* 26.8; *PS* 4.9. See Voci, *DER* 2² (1963) 18–21; Meinhart, *SCC* (1967); Gardner, *Women* (1986) 196–198. Meinhart, "Datierung" (1966), defends the Hadrianic date of the *SC.*

[23] A juristic extension; see below.

[24] Three children were required of an *ingenua,* four of a freedwoman; see Chapter 3.

[25] The rationale behind this requirement is explored by Meinhart, *SCC* 24–27; see below in the text.

[26] Here I follow Gardner, *Women* 197–198, and above all Dixon, *Mother* (1988) 51–60. I question Gardner's inference that a woman's tutor would have effectively exercised pressure in favor of her family as opposed to that of her husband (and so her children's) in the making of a will when agnatic tutelage had already been abolished by Claudius.

[27] On this assumption, see Cic. *Att.* 11.16, 23 (cf. 12.18a); Val. Max. 7.7.4, 7.8.2; Plin. *Ep.* 4.2.2, 5.1, 7.24.2; and the other evidence discussed by Dixon, *Mother* 51–60. Justinian's attitude is especially pronounced: Beaucamp, *Statut* 1 (1990) 24; Treggiari, *RM* (1991) 358.

[28] Dixon, *TRF* 77.

[29] Humbert, *Remariage* (1972) 181–300; Champlin, *FJ* (1991) ch. 6, esp. 120–126. For an interesting variation, see Marcel. D. 24.1.49.

[30] So Humbert, *Remariage* 251.

[31] Treggiari, *RM* 383 (cf. 384–387, 391). Note Dixon's conclusion (*Mother* 59): "the general expectation was . . . that mothers, like fathers, would and ought to pass their estates on to children unless the children had behaved so disgracefully as to forfeit their birthright"; cf. Dixon, "*Infirmitas*" 354.

It is legitimate to interpret those measures that allowed women freedom to dispose of their property by will as at least partly motivated by these considerations.[32] The force of the bias regarding mothers is thrown into relief by the odium felt for stepmothers.[33]

These assumptions were built into the *SC Tertullianum,* which thus assured the mother, upon the death of her child, a life interest in what had been her deceased husband's property.[34] It was expected that she would then pass on to the surviving children what had been their father's property.

All of this explains why only women with the *ius liberorum* were granted this privilege: the point was not simply to avoid the interference of a tutor but to ensure as far as possible that there be surviving children to benefit from the statute's largesse.

The jurists lost little time in extending the privilege to mothers with illegitimate children.[35] This is entirely consistent with the aim of the *SC,* which was to benefit ultimately the surviving children.[36] Indeed, the mother had to be "unmarried," that is, a widow, to receive the benefit of the *SC.* The *SC* did not displace the father in favor of the mother even when the former had emancipated the child. Thus, in order for the *SC* to have effect, the father had to be dead.[37] The child would presumably have received a share of the paternal estate, and it is essentially the disposition of this property that the statute seeks to regulate. Given the fact that the *SC* assumes dissolution of the marriage by death, the extension to illegitimate unions is a logical one: unless the widow remarries, no marriage (i.e., no *matrimonium iustum*) exists in either case.[38]

The *SC* then was designed to help the children more than the mother. This explains an apparent contradiction between this statute and the *SC Orphitianum,* which explicitly excluded at least two types of *"infames"*, the *rei capitalis damnatus* and the *bestiarius.*[39] Perhaps prostitutes and pimps were excluded as well. The recognition that the heirs assisted by the later *SC* were the ultimate beneficiaries of the property transmitted, whereas the mother aided by the *SC Tertullianum*

---

[32] See Dixon, *"Infirmitas"* 348, 355, 368–369.

[33] See Treggiari, *RM* 392–394.

[34] On this, see Dixon, *Mother* 47–51.

[35] Iul.-Ulp. D. 38.17.2.1 (Ulpian credits Julian with the move). Meinhart, *SCC* 32–48; Gardner, *Women* 198. Astolfi, *LIP*² 31–32, 61–62, 301–302, thinks illegitimate children counted under the *lex Iulia et Papia* itself only from Hadrian's day on (see below).

[36] Julian's interpretation may have been purely declaratory, insofar as the *SC* may not have specified legitimate children.

[37] So Meinhart, *SCC* 24, 132; Humbert, *Remariage* 147 (148) n. 5.

[38] The notion of material support for demographic purposes has a long history, for example, in the alimentary programs roughly contemporary with the *SC,* and had been taken up with vigor by Augustus himself, in a subvention to Hortensius Hortalus (Tac. *Ann.* 2.37–38; Suet. *Tib.* 47), as well as to others (Dio 55.13.6), including lower-status parents (Suet. *Aug.* 46; cf. Gell. 10.2.2). His successors are known to have followed his example. For evidence, see Baltrusch, *RM* (1989) 142; Lebek, "SC" 55, and add Sen. *Ben.* 2.7.2–3; Tac. *Ann.* 2.37.1, 48.1; Suet. *Vesp.* 17; (for what it is worth) *HA Hadr.* 7.9, 11, 22.9. Widow's remarriage was thought to prejudice her willingness to hand over property to the children of her previous marriage. See Krause, *Witwen* 3 (1995) esp. Ch. 6, who, to be sure, discounts the remarriage chances of most widows.

[39] Ulp. D. 38.17.1.6.

functioned simply as an intermediary who could be trusted to pass it on to them, would justify the difference in treatment.

It is important to emphasize the complexity of the Augustan law, which did indeed favor certain unions above others but which was also broadly interested in encouraging child-rearing. Producing three children (or four, in the case of freed-women) was remarkable, and perhaps extraordinary, for a prostitute, so that rec-ognition of this achievement—provided, we must stipulate, that the union that produced them did not violate the statute—is consistent with the law's overall aim to construct a meritocracy of virtue. Making such an allowance for dishonored women (for whom the Augustan statute itself provided with its *quarta*) taught a lesson intended for others. There is no obvious motive for the jurists to treat the *ius liberorum* independently of the law. By extending its scope as widely as they did they were expressing their sympathy for the statute and its goals.

Because the *SC* ultimately aimed to provide for the woman's surviving chil-dren, and because under the Augustan statute itself prostitutes were not treated with undue harshness, it would be surprising if the jurist excluded these women from the benefit mentioned in the principal text. This is especially so once the jurists made the quite natural extension given in this text: a *mulier famosa* is not an unlikely candidate for the figure of a mother with illegitimate children. The prin-cipal text assumes that prostitutes were already eligible for the *ius liberorum*.

The passage by itself says nothing outright to define the *famosa*, a term that must, however, refer in this context to women forbidden by the *lex Iulia et Papia* to marry the *ceteri ingenui*.[40] Nardi is right to reject the view held by Scialoia and others that this text shows, *ex contrario,* that such women were excluded from intestate succession in general.[41] There is simply no evidence for this.

In my view, it is just as wrong to argue, *ex contrario,* that the text suggests that such women were unable to receive under a will.[42] This interpretation is forced—as if one were to argue, for example, from Ulpian's mention of the eli-gibility of freedwomen[43] that they could not otherwise take under a will. If there is any contrast implied here, it is not with the disgraced woman's (alleged) lack of testamentary rights but with her ineligibility for this form of relief before the ju-ristic extension of the scope of the *SC*.[44] In other words, the language reflects the natural assumption that this is a more difficult case than that of the respectable woman.

This introduces the fundamental issue raised in the principal text. Were some dissolute women to be entrusted with a patrimony and therefore granted a privilege

[40] The arguments of Meinhart, *SCC* 116–119, 130, with n. 71, taking up a suggestion of Kaser, "Infamia" (1956) 263–264, strike me as correct. The only other characterization made by a jurist of a woman as *famosa* is at *Tit.* 16.2, a coincidence that argues well for the conclusion that the principal text speaks of women denied as marriage partners to the *ceteri ingenui.* Beaucamp, *Statut* 1.204–205, who argues that prostitutes lacked *capacitas,* does not mention the principal text.

[41] Nardi, "Incapacitas" 169–170.

[42] Both Nardi and Astolfi have stressed the significance of the *et si* construction. See now Astolfi, *LIP*[2] 59–60.

[43] At Ulp. D. 38.17.2 pr.

[44] This is the proper interpretation of the *et si* constructions that appear in the texts flanking our passage: Ulp. (13 *ad Sabinum*) D. 38.17.2.3, 5; cf. Lenel, *Pal.* 2 col. 1046. It is of course easier to follow Mommsen and omit the *et* in the text under discussion.

not expressly laid down in the legislation? In most cases of this type the answer was surely negative. With the *SC,* however, Roman assumptions about the strength of the bond between mother and child overcame the suspicion that the *famosa* was not to be trusted with property, above all other people's property, and superseded the principle that disgraced women were not to be admitted to the privileges accorded the community of honor.[45]

Two more pieces of evidence support the argument that Domitian did not strip prostitutes of their *capacitas.* The lawsuit over Spatale's bequest reported by Quintilian may have taken place as late as 85–90.[46] This makes it possible that the suit followed the move against the *feminae probrosae,* which most likely falls into the same period. Domitian became censor in 85 and *censor perpetuus* later that same year.[47] Grelle attributes the degradation of both the dancing senator and the uxorious *eques* to Domitian's activity as censor.[48] Not all of the items listed in *Dom.* 8.3 are directly linked to the censorship—Suetonius is simply interested in the emperor's overall program of moral reform.[49] The new campaign against adultery came at the same time or later, in the form of imperial legislation (Grelle suggests an edict), but before 90, the date of Martial's sixth book.[50] Grelle connects the move against the *probrosae* with this measure, while adhering to Astolfi's definition of the category of *feminae probrosae.*[51]

A priori assumptions about the content of Domitian's measure have traditionally been used to date it earlier. Certainty is impossible, but enough has perhaps been said to clear Quintilian of the charge—in this case, at any rate—of a gross legal anachronism.[52] Whether Spatale's *quarta* was challenged before or after Domitian punished the *probrosae,* the regime for prostitutes under the *lex Iulia et Papia* was not altered by this emperor.

Next, there is another juristic text, overlooked by Astolfi:

Maec. (6 *fideicomm.*) D. 36.1.5: Sed et qui magna praeditus est dignitate vel auctoritate, harenarii vel eius mulieris, quae corpore quaestum fecerit, hereditatem restituere cogetur.

But even a man of high rank or great influence will be compelled to turn over the inheritance of a gladiator or of a woman who has earned money with her body.

---

[45] Cf. Meinhart, *SCC* 122–124, who in my view exaggerates the hostility of jurists to the marriage law (Paul. D. 23.2.44.6, though genuine, is no proof of such hostility; cf. Ter. Clem. D. 35.1.64.1, with Bouché-Leclercq, ''Lois'' [1895] 283, and below) and the scope of the *SC* of Marcus and Commodus pursuant to this law, which voided only marriages that violated the prohibitions imposed on members of the senatorial order. In practical terms, this would have had little impact on *famosae.*

[46] Quint. *IO* 8.5.19; see Chapter 3.

[47] Buttrey, *Chronology* (1980) 31, 39.

[48] Grelle, ''*Correctio Morum*'' 346, with n. 25.

[49] Bauman, ''Resumé, Suetonius'' (1982) 121–124; Jones, *Domitian* (1992) 106–107.

[50] Mart. 6.2, 4, 7; cf. Dio (in Xiph., Zon.) 67.12.1.

[51] Only Janssen, *Vita* (1919) 43, and Mooney, *Vita* (1930) 546, think that the measure punishes adultery and nothing else.

[52] For the charge, see Grelle, ''*Correctio Morum*'' 352, with n. 40; Astolfi, *LIP*² 67. The assumption has been that Quintilian, writing in the early 90s, had information about a court case that, on the best evidence, took place in the previous decade but had no knowledge—or simply forgot—that a general enactment had, in the meantime, drastically altered the law.

Maecianus is concerned with the regime established by the *SC Pegasianum* of ca. A.D. 73.[53] Under this statute, a person who thought herself entitled to a *fideicommissum* could approach the *praetor fideicommissarius* in order to compel the reluctant heir to comply.[54] The extreme case put by the jurist—that of a socially prominent or politically influential heir and a socially despised and powerless beneficiary of a trust—is clearly intended to drive home the theoretically unfettered force of the *Antrittszwang,* or compulsory entry on the inheritance.

The text has an obvious importance for my argument. Perhaps a half-century or more after Domitian's measure,[55] Maecianus writes as if prostitutes were fully entitled to *fideicommissa.*[56] The *SC Pegasianum* had applied the regime of the *lex Iulia et Papia* to trusts, in that the capacity of *caelibes* and *orbi* to take these bequests was limited in the same way as with inheritances and legacies. This must also mean that persons married contrary to the law were also treated as *caelibes* with regard to trusts from this point on. In other words, the rules on marriage prohibitions were extended as well. A further implication, not alluded to in the principal text,[57] can be drawn, namely, that unmarried prostitutes were now eligible for a *quarta* with regard to *fideicommissa* as well.[58]

In order to share the opinion of Astolfi and the others, one has to suppose that Domitian himself overlooked the possibility that his measure could be circumvented through recourse to *fideicommissa.* True, Suetonius mentions only inheritances and legacies. But his account cannot reasonably be regarded as exhaustive. Indeed, one might credit the omission of trusts to the policymaker only—perhaps— if it is accepted that Domitian's measure was in no way pursuant to the marriage law, whose regime was now fully extended to trusts, thanks to the *SC Pegasianum.* But whatever the nature of the new rule, whoever its targets, it is difficult to believe that Vespasian's son could have allowed *fideicommissa* to slip through his fingers. Maecianus's assertion of prostitutes' eligibility for these bequests is best understood to mean that they continued to receive inheritances and legacies, within the limits imposed by the *lex Iulia* itself.

This is perhaps enough to demolish the notion that prostitutes (and procuresses)[59] were denied the *ius capiendi* as well as the use of litters.[60] We are not,

---

[53] On the *SC,* see Manthe, *SC* (1988); on *fideicommissa,* see Johnston, *Trusts* (1989).

[54] See Manthe, *SC* 85–92.

[55] The career of L. Volusius Maecianus, who served on the *consilia* of Pius and the *divi fratres,* spanned the mid–second century: Kunkel, *Herkunft*[2] 174–176.

[56] Earlier, though later than Domitian, Juvenal does the same: 10.236–239. Cf. Hieron. *Ep.* 52.6.

[57] The jurist simply ignores this issue: note also his mention of the *harenarius,* on whom the *lex Iulia et Papia* places no limits. The context of the passage is significant: Book 6 of Maecianus's *Fideicommissa* deals exclusively with the *Antrittszwang* and its implications.

[58] Coincidentally, this is the amount stipulated by the *SC* for the testamentary heir burdened by *fideicommissa:* Manthe, *SC* 76–78.

[59] I note in passing Dioclet., Maxim. C. 3.28.19 (a. 293), which allows a daughter who lives "turpiter et cum flagitiosa foeditate" to be excluded from her father's will. Such conduct may amount to prostitution or *adulterium/stuprum,* more likely the latter.

[60] Although it is not utterly inconceivable that the latter penalty was aimed at prostitutes, the likelihood is that upper-class adulteresses were denied the privilege of using a litter. Along with loss of *capacitas,* this denial was a means of social degradation. Like ordinary prostitutes (with whom, thanks to Augustus, they shared a mode of dress), henceforth they would go on foot: see McGinn, "*Feminae Probrosae.*"

however, left with the only true alternative, adulteresses, by default. A positive case can be made that they formed the object of Domitian's measure. The context of the report gives the first clue. The very next item deals with an offense against the adultery law, which may be considered a type of *lenocinium*.[61] Two other examples of sexual offense follow, behavior that violates the *lex Scantinia* and sex with Vestals.[62] A pattern emerges: *adulterium, lenocinium, stuprum cum masculo, incestum.*

Another pattern can be discerned in Suetonius's account. Conviction on a charge of adultery meant social degradation for women. They were forbidden marriage and reduced to the status of a prostitute. In this text, the disabilities imposed on them proceed a step further and cut them out of inheritances and legacies, a loss, generally speaking, far more likely to have been felt by upper-class adulteresses than by lower-class prostitutes. The item falls neatly into place with those that immediately precede and follow it, revealing a second pattern: male removed from senatorial order, woman or women removed from upper-class status, male removed from equestrian order.

The nature of the penalty imposed by Domitian also deserves inspection. Unlike prostitutes, adulteresses labored under a severe testamentary regime, at least in later law. The rules for *indignitas* specified that bequests from one partner in adultery to the other were invalid and forfeit to the state.[63] This was the result of a positive legislative enactment, whose date we do not know. It is not strictly relevant to Domitian's measure, which inflicts *incapacitas,* not *indignitas,*[64] and was more broadly conceived (at least in the form in which it is reported to us), since it struck at inheritances and legacies no matter what their source, not just at those from a lover. But I think it correct to see it either as a sharpening of the regime for adulterous *indignitas,* if this existed already, or a harbinger of the same, if it did not. The latter, more plausible view is argued below.

Domitian punished certain individual adulteresses as part of his *correctio morum.* Though Republican censors did not punish women directly, he may have acted in his capacity as censor.[65] This punishment was followed by a renewal, to all appearances a sharpening, of the *lex Iulia* on adultery. Domitian promulgated this renewal while he was a censor but not qua censor (the censors did not enact laws), following a specific act or series of acts that punished adulteresses, depriving them of the use of litters as well as the right to testamentary bequests.[66] Another possibility is that Domitian issued an imperial edict.[67] The point is that two

---

[61] See Chapter 6.

[62] The cases involving Vestals preceded Domitian's assumption of the censorship and were dealt with by him in his capacity as *pontifex maximus:* Grelle, ''*Correctio Morum*'' 345.

[63] Voci, *DER* 1² 478. See Pap. D. 34.9.13, 14.

[64] There is no reason to question Suetonius's terminology on this point. Generally he can be held to a high standard of technically precise language: Wallace-Hadrill, *Suetonius* (1983) 20, 90. Presumably, bequests in contravention of Domitian's ruling went first to the *patres* in the will as *caduca* and not directly to the state.

[65] This is perhaps reflected in Dio's account (Dio [in Xiph., Zon.] 67.12.1) of the punishment of both women and men for adultery in A.D. 91.

[66] This perhaps explains the language of Mart. 6.2, 6.4, 91 (cf. Statius *Silvae* 4.3.10, 14, with its mention of censor and *leges*—the latter apparently did not embrace the adultery law itself).

[67] As Grelle, ''*Correctio Morum*'' 346, 350, suggests.

separate actions were taken.[68] The initiative regarding the adultery law receives no mention from the biographer, any more than he treats at *Tib.* 35.2 the generalized norm that followed the punishment of Vistilia. The purpose and pattern of repression in both cases were the same, even if the form taken was different.

Was the disposition denying *capacitas* to adulteresses taken up in the sequel? About this we have no unambiguous information, but the following suggests that this is precisely what happened.

A Hadrianic Extension

Tryph. (18 *disp.*) D. 29.1.41.1: Mulier, in qua turpis suspicio cadere potest, nec ex testamento militis aliquid capere potest, ut divus Hadrianus rescripsit.

A woman on whom a disgraceful suspicion falls cannot take anything under the will of a soldier, as the deified Hadrian stated in a rescript.

The idea that Hadrian's ruling is tied to Domitian's measure is widely accepted but has caused difficulties for those who adopt a broad definition of *feminae probrosae*. These difficulties center on the phrase *turpis suspicio*, used to identify the type of woman denied *capacitas*. Its vagueness and the fact that it does not correspond to the language used by Suetonius have occasioned disquiet. Some see a generalization, advanced by either emperor or jurist, of a preexisting norm.[69] The meaning of *turpis* is hotly disputed.[70]

Suspicio has also caused problems for those who favor a broad definition of *feminae probrosae*. How can somebody be "suspected" of being an actress?[71] What could have been the point of forbidding actresses to receive under a soldier's will, when under the *lex Iulia* soldiers were allowed to marry actresses, at least after discharge?[72] Worse, how can mere suspicion justify a denial of *capacitas*?[73]

It will not come as a surprise to learn that, for this reason, the phrase has been condemned as interpolated.[74] Astolfi defends the text, suggesting that *turpis suspicio* is a euphemism for a woman who has a notorious reputation for one of those acts that rank her as a *probrosa*.[75] Euphemism it may be, but it is hard to see how someone may be "suspected" of having been convicted of murder in a criminal court, for example.

---

[68] On the date, see Mart. 6.7 and above in the notes.

[69] Nardi, "Incapacitas" 166–169; Astolfi, *LIP*[2] 65 (Astolfi admits, however, that the generalization may be nonclassical).

[70] Nardi, "Incapacitas" 167–168, maintains that sexual disgrace, above all of prostitutes and procuresses, is meant; Solazzi, "*Caduca*" (1942/1963) 339, denies this.

[71] See Nardi, "Incapacitas" 167–168. He attempts to resolve the dilemma by arguing that if suspicion determined liability, a fortiori certainty must have, so that actresses were included (Nardi, "Incapacitas" 168 n. 62).

[72] After Severus, soldiers, like all nonsenatorial *ingenui*, could marry actresses and the daughters of actors and actresses even before discharge: below.

[73] Nardi, "Incapacitas" 167.

[74] By Solazzi, "*Caduca*" 339.

[75] Astolfi, *LIP*[2] 65.

Without further qualification, *turpis* (and its cognates), employed as a moral epithet, all but certainly refers to sexual disgrace when used of a woman.[76] As with *probrum* (and its cognates), it describes prostitutes (and possibly procuresses) and/or violators of the adultery statute. *Suspicio* permits us to decide in favor of the latter. In the classical period, women were prosecuted for adultery (or *stuprum*)[77] either because they had been caught in the act *(deprehensae)* or on suspicion of the crime *(ex suspicione)*.[78] The vast majority of adultery cases probably fell in the latter category,[79] for which *suspicio* comes to represent a term of art as early as the elder Seneca.[80] As such it was taken up by Hadrian himself as a familiar and reasonably precise term when he extended Domitian's measure to military wills.[81] Military wills were less subject to restriction than others, so that it is more likely that a regulation of this kind originated with nonmilitary wills. Hadrian had a particular interest in soldiers' wills. Both considerations strengthen the argument that Hadrian is extending Domitian's measure.

The text does not specify if the criminal act is supposed to have taken place between the woman and the soldier himself. This seems likely to have been true in the case that provoked the rescript, though it cannot be proven.[82] Presumably, the soldier was already dead at the time his will was contested, so that the question of his guilt or innocence was regarded by both the trial court and the emperor as an issue of secondary importance. Another reason for the lack of emphasis accorded this point is that by Tryphoninus's day bequests between lovers fell under the regime of *indignitas* (see below). This does not prejudice the thesis that benefactor and recipient were suspected of being joint offenders against the adultery law: this was a culture where a bequest to a married woman from a male "friend" itself provided grounds for suspicion of adultery.[83]

---

[76] Solazzi, "*Caduca*" 339 n. 118, is right to point out that the word has other meanings, but he overlooks the context. See Ter. *Heaut.* 1042; Catull. 42.8; Ovid. *Am.* 1.6.72, *Her.* 13.133; Ulp. D. 48.5.24(23) pr.; cf. the entries in *L & S* and *OLD* s.v. *turpis, turpiter, turpitudo.*

[77] The distinction is usually made with respect to adultery, but it must have held for *stuprum* as well.

[78] On the distinction and its widespread acceptance during the classical period, see Venturini, "*Accusatio*" (1988) esp. 92–98. Naturally the suspicion had to be justified to the finder of fact: there is no conflict here with Trajan's famous "presumption of innocence doctrine" (Ulp. D. 48.19.5 pr.). Nardi's objection that mere suspicion is insufficient in criminal matters misses the point.

[79] So Venturini, "*Accusatio*" 92–98. The distinction also operated in the law of theft: Lab.-Proc.-Pomp. D. 12.4.15.

[80] What follows cannot be exhaustive. Literary sources: Sen. *Contr.* 2.7 *thema,* 3, 6, 8; Val. Max. 6.3.10; cf. Quint. *IO* 5.9.14; Suet. *Iul.* 43.1 (it was a ground for divorce before the passage of the adultery law). Legal sources: Afric.-Ulp. D. 40.9.12.6; Iustinus C. 5.4.23.7 (a. 520–523) (incest); Sev., Ant. C. 9.9.2 (a. 199); Iustinian. C. 9.9.35(36) pr. (a. 532). A late legal text sets out the fundamentals: Theod., Valent. C. 5.17.8.3 (a. 449).

[81] So Astolfi, *LIP*² 58: "poiché Adriano la dà come presupposta." He evidently bases this conclusion on the word *nec,* which he translates as "nulla neppure." But because the word can mean simply "not," it is an extremely small peg on which to hang this hypothesis.

[82] Nardi, "Incapacitas" 167, argues that there is no indication that the soldier is implicated in the offense.

[83] See Chapter 5.

The text concerns the *ius capiendi*. A general denial of *capacitas* may be posited, again on the model of Domitian's measure.[84] This is an important difference from the regime of *indignitas,* which, in the matter of adultery, is limited in its application to the denial of bequests between the two guilty parties. If the point about the relationship between the *mulier* and the *miles* is correct, this would date the rule making lovers *indigni* to receive bequests from each other to a time later than Hadrian. A similar case, reported by Papinian,[85] of a woman found guilty of criminal fornication with a soldier demonstrates this point: she cannot benefit under his will, as a consequence of *indignitas.*[86] At all events, the woman's guilt would be determined by the court hearing the challenge to the will, no doubt with evidence provided by the parties who stood to gain from her exclusion, which is apparently what happened in the case of the woman whose case Papinian relates.[87]

From the beginning of the Principate until the reign of Septimius Severus, Roman legionaries were forbidden to marry, a ban that, unlike the *lex Iulia et Papia,* rendered attempts at evasion invalid under the *ius civile.*[88] The "marital" unions of soldiers (the evidence shows such relationships were common) were thus void in all their effects.

The aim was to maintain discipline, but, paradoxically, informal unions were tolerated, apparently for much the same reason.[89] At bottom, the claims of morale and discipline were thought to be served by banning marriage but allowing informal unions. Growing recognition at law of these relationships was perhaps partly motivated by the fact that the Roman army in the second century became increasingly dependent on soldiers' sons as recruits, though this is not guaranteed as a motive.

Decisive for my argument is the fact that Hadrian's measure is reported by Claudius Tryphoninus, who wrote after Severus had granted permission for soldiers

---

[84] Even so, the broad phrasing of the principal text seems to embrace more than inheritance and legacy: Astolfi, *LIP*² 58. There is, however, no suggestion that the rules on intestate succession were altered.

[85] Pap. (8 *resp.*) D. 34.9.14: "mulierem, quae stupro cognita in contubernio militis fuit. . . ."

[86] So Astolfi, *LIP*² 65–66 (following Biondi and Voci), against Nardi and Solazzi, who hold for *incapacitas.* Cf. Astolfi, *LIP*² 124–129.

[87] Astolfi, *LIP*² 66, strains the meaning of the text when he claims that her *indignitas* resulted from her status as a person *iudicio publico damnata.* Pap. D. 34.9.13 and Pap. D. *eod.* 16.1 suggest that an actual conviction was not needed for the rule on *indignitas* to be invoked (so Astolfi, *LIP*² 124). Cf. Dioclet., Maxim. C. 9.9.22 (a. 290), where a woman *stupro cognita* is not liable to a charge of adultery because she is a prostitute: the language suggests that a finding of fact by a trial court could be and was distinguished from conviction. So a conviction of one lover would suffice for the exclusion of the other.

[88] Severus lifted the ban relatively early in his reign, c. 197 (Herod. 3.8.5). Herodian's statement has generated debate as to the exact nature of this concession and therefore as to the legal situation that preceded it. Most scholars agree that Severus permitted lawful marriage for the first time: Meyer, "P. Cattaoui" (1906) 68–69; Sander, "Recht" (1958) 152–163; Watson, *Soldier* (1969) 137; Smith, "Reforms" (1972) 493, with n. 71; Campbell, "Marriage" (1978), with Whitehorne, "Ovid" (1979); Wolff, "Wirksamkeit" (1984); Behrends, "Eheverbot" (1986). For different views, see Castello, "Soldati" (1940) (Augustus did not ban marriage); Garnsey, "Severus" (1970) (Severus permitted concubinage, not marriage); Jung, "Eherecht" (1982) (Augustus forbade both marriage and concubinage; Severus certainly allowed concubinage and, at least by implication, marriage).

[89] The tension over conflicting policies and the rationale underlying them are explored by Watson, *Soldier* 135. Cf. 136 for Hadrian's interest in soldiers' wills and their families.

to marry.[90] It is unlikely that military consorts in respectable unions, whether *matrimonium iustum* or not, continued to be penalized after this.

These considerations support the explanation I have been developing about the nature of the *mulier* mentioned in the text of Claudius Tryphoninus. Hadrian took aim at a relationship not at all like the serious, stable union that could be counted on to produce children and become a *matrimonium iustum* upon the "husband's" discharge.[91] Some of these children might fill the shoes of their fathers as legionary recruits, though it is difficult to say whether this was a motive for Hadrian's measure.[92] The important point is that adultery and criminal fornication presented a threat to discipline without any of the corresponding benefits attaching to other "irregular" relationships.

Some idea of the undesirable consequences of adultery and *stuprum* when committed by soldiers may be derived from an actual case, reported by Pliny,[93] involving a centurion and the wife of a military tribune. This matter was regarded as delicate enough to be referred to Trajan and his *consilium*. Significantly, in rendering judgment, the emperor added a general statement on the subject of *disciplina militaris,* "ne omnes eius modi causas revocare ad se videretur" ("to make clear he did not wish all cases of this kind to be referred to him").

Besides the disciplinary motive for Hadrian when he determined the content of the rescript mentioned in the principal text, there was perhaps the idea of preventing such women from profiting unreasonably from their illegal behavior, especially to the detriment of a soldier's "wife" and children, where these existed. Even when the soldier did not have a family, the measure may stand as an attempt to inhibit the formation of attachments with undesirable women, since such affairs would discourage the type of union permitted and, to an extent, encouraged by the authorities. Seen in this light, the rescript is perfectly consistent with other provisions made by Hadrian for the benefit of soldiers' families.

This logic does not apply as neatly to soldiers' bequests left to prostitutes. Sexual relations with prostitutes were not illegal or contrary to public policy, and the interests of soldiers' families were already protected by the *quarta* rule. Until Severus "normalized" the domestic life of soldiers, that rule may have seemed adequate protection for an institution that itself violated the law.

Adulteresses and the *Ius Capiendi*

The traditional, broad construction of the category of *feminae probrosae* is untenable. The rules on bequests to prostitutes established by the *lex Iulia et Papia* remained unchanged by statute law throughout the classical period of Roman law,

---

[90] On Tryphoninus's life and background, see Kunkel, *Herkunft*[2] 231–233. Book 18 of the *Disputationes* was written in 213 or shortly thereafter: Fitting, *Alter*[2] (1908) 81.

[91] Tomulescu, "Justinien" (1972) 318–319.

[92] On the controversial subject of the recruitment of soldiers' sons and especially of the nature and extent of the privileges granted to soldiers' sons recruited into the military, see Watson, *Soldier* 37, 134–135, 148; Campbell, "Marriage" 157, 165; Mirkovic, "Soldatenehe" (1980); Saller and Shaw, "Tombstones" (1984) 142–145; Schiemann, "Soldatenkinder" (1986); Cherry, "Recruitment" (1989).

[93] Plin. *Ep.* 6.31.4–6.

except insofar as new rules affected the situation of all women.[94] *Feminae prob-rosae* were adulteresses, and Domitian punished them as part of, or prologue to, his renewal of the *lex Iulia de adulteriis coercendis*.[95] The removal of the *ius capiendi* represented a blow to their economic and social status, and the denial of the use of litters compromised their public dignity. Both measures were consistent with Augustus's adultery law, which imposed penalties on adulteresses' patrimony and lowered their social standing by rendering them the symbolic equivalent of prostitutes.

3. Juristic Interpretation

The Marriage Prohibitions and the Law of the Jurists

The primary concern of the jurists was to ascertain exactly who came within the terms of the *lex Iulia et Papia*. In other words, just who was embraced by its marriage prohibitions?

The three sections that follow examine various approaches taken to this problem by the interpreters of the statute. The first centers around a text from the jurist Paul that shows how certain behaviors linked to the marriage prohibitions themselves might lead to a declassing of a member of the senatorial order, through the imposition of a permanent social disgrace. The second section treats the juristic definitions of "prostitute" and "procuress" under the law, which are the only major legal definitions of these types that have survived. The third places the work of the jurists in perspective by looking at the evidence for their overall attitude toward the Augustan law, which emerges as distinctly favorable.

Declassing a Senator's Daughter

One way to take on the problem of identifying who fell under the marriage prohibition was to define circumstances in which the law did not apply:

> Paul. (2 *ad legem Iuliam et Papiam*) D. 23.2.47: Senatoris filia, quae corpore quaestum vel artem ludicram fecerit aut iudicio publico damnata fuerit, impune libertino nubit: nec enim honos ei servatur, quae se in tantum foedus deduxit.
>
> A senator's daughter who has been a prostitute or an actress or has been convicted of a criminal offense can marry a freedman without penalty, because a woman who has behaved so disgracefully is left without honor.

---

[94] The rule found in the Syro-Roman Lawbook at L. 9, P. 4, cannot be classical, for reasons of both content and context. See Vööbus, *SRL* 1 (1982) esp. xix–xxiv, *SRL* 2 (1983) esp. 5–6.

[95] The story of Acca Larentia merits brief mention. According to one version, she was a prominent prostitute who left a significant amount of property either to Romulus or to the Roman people: sources and discussion in Voci, *DER* 1² (1967) 417–419.

The last phrase presents a problem. Koehler suggested *dedecus* instead of *foedus,*[96] a substitution that gives good sense but is paleographically difficult. Perhaps a word has dropped out, so that the text originally read *tantum foedum dedecus.* It is, however, more probable that *tantum* did indeed modify *foedus* in the original. Regardless of whether *dedecus* or a synonym is preferred, this solution yields a tone of middle-brow moralizing that is thrown into relief by the jurist's sharp-edged sarcasm: "quae se in tantum foedus deduxit" describes a sexual union of which Paul does not at all approve.[97]

To what sort of union does the phrase refer? The most likely answer is marriage with a *libertinus,* though this raises an obvious problem. *Nec enim* introduces a justification for the view that a *filia senatoris* who prostitutes herself or becomes an actress or is condemned in a criminal court can marry a freedman without violating the regime of the marriage law.[98] The marriage itself cannot be the justification. Otherwise, anyone could free themselves from the strictures of the law simply by violating it.

Perhaps the compilers have shortened considerably a text that explicitly made the point, easily deducible from the text as it stands, that a *filia senatoris* who engaged in any of the three named activities declassed herself. As a result, her marriage to a *libertinus* did not violate the *lex Iulia et Papia.*[99] Paul then went on to say that such a woman, by marrying a freedman, declassed herself anyway, with the obvious difference that her marriage was not immune from the penalties of the law.

Such reconstructions are speculative, but, without something of the kind, we are left with a vague reference to sexual unions that takes a swipe at both *filia*'s marriage with a freedman and her behavior as a prostitute, the first example of declassé behavior given by Paul.

The jurist's main point, then, is somewhat at odds with the spirit of an element of Augustus's social legislation and the early imperial enactments pursuant to this. In general, these laws sought to prevent members of the upper orders from declassing themselves in order to engage in activity, such as appearing onstage or in the arena, forbidden to persons of their status. In response to attempts to dodge the ban, status was defined not absolutely but in terms of relationship to someone possessing the status. This approach was of course adopted by the marriage law itself. The result was the creation of a senatorial order that extended beyond the members of the Senate to embrace some descendants.

---

[96] His suggestion is recorded by Mommsen and Krüger, ad loc.

[97] *Tantum* signifies quality: *L & S* s.v. *tantus* I; *OLD* s.h.v. 1 (a negative judgment is implied). *Foedus* refers to the union itself: *L & S* s.h.v. IIa; *OLD* s.h.v. 3. This may be marriage or something like marriage. *Se deducere* is unusual, rather paradoxical. *Deducere* has the special meaning "to escort," as in to escort a bride to or from a wedding ceremony: *L & S* s.v. *deduco* I B5c; *OLD* s.h.v. 10b; Treggiari, *RM* 439. One cannot escort oneself, unless perhaps one is a headstrong, determined *filia senatoris* bent on marrying whom she wishes. This appears to be the gravamen of the jurist's attitude to the problem raised in the text.

[98] So Rilinger, *Humiliores* (1988) 162.

[99] Compare the *patrona* deemed so *ignobilis* she may marry her freedman: Ulp. 23.2.13. Cf. Mod. D. 23.2.42 pr. (= D. 50.17.197).

The activities mentioned in the text—prostitution, acting, condemnation on a criminal charge—all fell within the scope of the marriage prohibitions. By engaging in any of these a *filia senatoris* rendered herself unfit for marriage with other members of the *ordo senatorius*; one such behavior (prostitution) made her ineligible for marriage with any *ingenuus*. Nevertheless, Paul permits her to evade the statute and marry a freedman with impunity.

The explanation of this difficulty is that the jurist is writing with two later regulations in mind.[100] One declared, in part, that the daughter of a senator, when she married a man of lower rank, lost her status as a *femina clarissima*,[101] a late classical term for adult female member of the senatorial order.[102] The other statute at the root of the holding is the decree of Marcus and Commodus invalidating marriages that violated the senatorial prohibitions of the marriage law.[103] Whatever their chronological and substantive relationship to each other, both these measures were almost certainly in force at the time Paul wrote his commentary on the marriage law.[104]

With this, we can better grasp the meaning of *impune* in the principal text. Because the *filia senatoris* has forfeited senatorial status, the union does not violate the *lex Iulia* and so is not rendered void by the *oratio Marci*.[105] Freedmen were permitted to marry any of the types given. The measure on marriage and status as a *clarissima* was, strictly speaking, rendered irrelevant by operation of the *oratio*, although the former must be the source of the notion, central to Paul's reasoning, that one could remove oneself from the *ordo* through one's own behavior.[106]

The disgraced *filia* found herself in an unenviable position. She could never regain her senatorial status, which was generally permitted under the *clarissima* rule, because she was now denied marriage with members of that *ordo*. Any attempt to escape in this way the consequences of her behavior was automatically invalidated by the *oratio*. Though, in a sense, Paul's decision is in line with the thrust of the marriage law, since he permits the woman to marry, his true purpose is to ensure the permanent social disgrace of the offending woman.

---

[100] Cf. Wesel, *Statuslehre* (1967) 116–117, who sees the holding as consistent with the *sententia* of the marriage law itself.

[101] See Ulp. D. 1.9.8 (cf. 10); Pap. D. *eod.* 9.

[102] On this subject, see Chastagnol, "Femmes" (1979); Chastagnol, "Dioclétien" (1982) 65–67; Chastagnol "Clarissimat" (1983); Raepsaet-Charlier, "*Clarissima femina*" (1981); Alföldy, "Stellung" (1981) 194–198; Chastagnol, *Sénat* (1992) ch. 12. For the rules on how emancipation and adoption affected senatorial status, see Paul. D. 1.9.6 pr.-1.

[103] See Chapter 3. This meant all marriages explicity or implicity prohibited to members of the *ordo*, including those prohibited to the *ceteri ingenui*, not just those specifically denied to senatorials: Astolfi, *LIP²* 117. The jurists regarded such relationships with hostility. For example, *donationes* between partners were void: Ulp. D. 24.1.3.1. The marriage itself remained void even when a senator father lost his status: Pap. D. 1.9.9.

[104] Sometime after the death of Marcus in A.D. 180: Fitting, *Alter²* 91–92.

[105] According to Solazzi, "Glossemi" (1939/1963) 181, with n. 2, *impune* suggests that the marriage liberates the woman from the penalties for celibacy but that the union was still "invalid" in light of the *oratio* with its *SC*. This seems impossible to me. See Nardi, "Divieti" (1941) 128.

[106] As noted, Paul may be suggesting that a *filia* who marries a freedman is thereby rendered ineligible for marriage within the *ordo*, regardless of whether the offending union is void or not.

The real prospect of marriage between daughters of senators and freedmen was slim.[107] As for the hypothetical situations offered by Paul, although acting and condemnation in a criminal court[108] are not at all far-fetched, the possibility that a woman of this status would actually prostitute herself is much less likely.[109] If anything, the fragment shows how far the jurists were prepared to follow the logic of the *lex Iulia* in keeping prostitutes out of the upper orders.

The Juristic Definition of "Prostitute" and "Procuress" under the *Lex Iulia et Papia*

The conclusion just reached is of broad significance. In the interpretation of the *lex Iulia et Papia,* the primary concern of the jurists with regard to the prostitute and the procuress was to ascertain precisely who came within the law's terms, that is, to define these types in a way that made sense of the law. Their understanding of the aims of the statute was supremely important for this task. Relevant here was the goal of keeping such persons out of the upper classes, which they might aspire to reach through marriage or a testamentary windfall. The law did not intend the repression of prostitutes (for whom its moral and demographic aims were irrelevant), as can be deduced from its provision for the *quarta.*

There is a tension between these two points. The first encouraged a broad application, so as to embrace a range of women whose social circumstances and sexual behavior rendered them objectionable as marriage partners and characterized them as threats to family estates. The second suggested some limits should be imposed, since the *quarta* might have encouraged women who should have been liable to the full rigor of the law to claim this privilege, just as the prospect of exemption from the penalties of the adultery law provoked, albeit on only one occasion known to us,[110] similar behavior.

In defining a prostitute, the jurists took as their point of departure the legislative phrase I have reconstructed as "qui quaeve palam corpore quaestum facit fecerit."[111] It is worthy of note that the jurists never mention male prostitutes in their commentaries on the law as extant;[112] in other words, they do not discuss the marriage prohibitions for female *ceterae ingenuae.* Three explanations for this are possible. Such prohibitions never existed. They existed and were discussed by the jurists but did not survive the compilers. They existed but were never given much, if any, attention by the jurists.

[107] See Chapter 3.

[108] Astolfi, *LIP*[2] 55–66, generalizes from the text to place all such women on the level of the prostitute, but this holds true only in the sense that these women are forbidden to marry members of the senatorial order under the statute.

[109] Contrast Evans, *War* (1991) 164, who takes the hypothetical as evidence that some women of senatorial rank prostituted themselves.

[110] Vistilia; see Chapter 6.

[111] See Chapter 3.

[112] We do not possess a version of the marriage prohibitions for the *ceteri* that actually quotes the law, as Paul. D. 23.2.44 pr. does for the senatorial order. Cf. *Tit.* 13.2 and the discussion in Chapter 3.

The first alternative has had its supporters[113] but seems unlikely, for two reasons. The technique of Roman legislators is known to have been specific and inclusive,[114] and we know that Augustus did include male freedmen and actors among the prohibitions he imposed on the senatorial order. There is no reason easily imagined that would have permitted marriages between *ingenuae* and pimps (or, a fortiori, between daughters of senators and pimps) while outlawing unions between freeborn males and procuresses.

No certain choice lies between the latter two alternatives. But even if we admit some amount of compilatorial intervention, it is difficult to believe that the focus on women is purely fortuitous, an accident of transmission.[115] Female prostitutes appear to have been more numerous and, in terms of the way their social role was understood, more important.

This was not necessarily true of procuresses, as opposed to male pimps, but there is another reason that explains their prominence, as well as the concern with female prostitutes, in these legal sources. Men, not women, tended to marry their social inferiors. This held from the time of the law's passage, when men outnumbered women among the upper orders.[116] The true emphasis of the commentaries, visible only in the negative, is placed on upper-class males, whose potential marriage partners are the subject of discussion. Although one cannot rule out discussion of male marriage partners—a discussion that would have been cut by the compilers—we are entitled to assume at least that this was less prominent, less extensive. The very structure of their analysis betrays the way in which the jurists reconciled a perceived social reality with their understanding of the law's purpose.

This concern is also evident when the jurists come to expound the meaning of the statutory wording. A difficulty is caused by a change from the late Republican legal formula for prostitute:[117] the apparent insertion of the adverb *palam*. The phrase now read ''qui quaeve palam corpore quaestum facit fecerit.'' With this addition the legislator meant to specify more precisely the sort of behavior characteristic of those persons liable to the law. More than neutral description, it is a form of moral censure.[118]

The idea that prostitutes sell themselves ''openly'' is obviously not an invention of the legislator. Commercial sex, that is, everything but the act of intercourse itself, was a public business at Rome, as demonstrated by the remarks of the rhetor Porcius Latro regarding a woman who claimed to have preserved her virginity in a brothel: ''you were escorted into a brothel, you took up your spot, a price was

---

[113] Evidently something like this is assumed by Corbett, *Marriage* (1930) 37, who suggests the senatorial females of Paul. D. 23.2.44 pr. are a later insertion. See also Daube, ''Marriage'' (1967) 384, 389; Chastagnol, *Sénat* 173–176; Raepsaet-Charlier, ''Vie'' (1994) 189.

[114] This holds for the classical period. In late antiquity the male perspective tends to win out in legislative texts on marriage partners: Beaucamp, *Statut* 1.267.

[115] The same reasons given above preclude the possibility that the compilers eliminated a lengthy discourse on male pimps and prostitutes. The jurists rarely discuss male prostitutes.

[116] Dio 54.16.2.

[117] Given the state of the text of the *Tabula Heracleensis,* it is possible that *palam* has dropped out by accident. At any rate, we have no evidence that this document or any like it exercised an influence upon the jurists, so that the interpretative history of the legislative definition of ''prostitute'' begins with the Augustan law.

[118] See Chapter 3.

set, a notice written up: up to that point information is available about your situation; about the rest, I know nothing.''[119]

One assumes that jurists, in accord with the legislative phrasing, would demand proof of intercourse and payment, which implies in turn a potential for tension between the juristic definition and the popular one.[120] The possibility that such tension existed has important implications that cannot be explored further in the absence of evidence; one concerns how the jurists' definition might have fared when applied in the courts.

Palam, to be sure, challenged the jurists, since, if taken in a literal sense, it seems to make the marriage prohibitions apply only to those who prostitute themselves "openly" or "publicly." In this way, clandestine prostitutes would not be embraced by the legal definition and would be able to marry not just nonsenatorial *ingenui* but even members of the senatorial order.[121]

Despite modern assumptions to the contrary, there is no evidence that any jurist understood the law in this way. In fact, this interpretation contains a double flaw. It is at odds with what can reasonably be deduced about the legislative intent. The prohibition is overlimited, or, to put it another way, the group of women deemed worthy of marriage with *ingenui* is expanded too much.[122] Why should the secret or open nature of the business be decisive, when at issue is the definition of suitable marriage partners and not the preservation of public order?[123] Moralists tended to be more alarmed by the former type of vice.[124]

The distinction also ignores the reality of Roman prostitution. Prostitution in many societies, including Rome, is generally characterized by the notoriety of its practice.[125] Many women rather easily definable as prostitutes did not practice their trade "openly" or "publicly," however. The contexts in which they worked varied greatly, with prostitutes known for example to have solicited customers in every venue associated with public entertainment. Further, if this interpretation were ever accepted, it should have been relatively easy for those prostitutes whose method of solicitation made them liable to this interpretation of the law to alter their activity so as to escape the strictures imposed by the prohibition of marriage. In other words, adoption of this view would have invited attempts to dodge the law.

That *palam* can mean something more than "openly" when used of prostitution is suggested by a phrase of Valerius Maximus: "as to the fact that that young man had made a practice of flagrantly and openly selling his body.''[126] I argue that the phrase "palam atque aperte" is no mere pleonasm but a moral

---

[119] *Apud* Sen. *Contr.* 1.2.1: "Deducta es in lupanar, accepisti locum, pretium constitutum est, titulus inscriptus est: hactenus in te inquiri potest; cetera nescio."

[120] Cf. Hobson, *Virtue* (1990) 129, on the question of whether a girl who worked in a brothel as a domestic without servicing customers qualified as a prostitute.

[121] That this was the law is argued by Astolfi, *LIP*² 55.

[122] One notes the tension over the desired scope of the law: a restrictive interpretation would go too far, however, and reverse the relative importance of the two aims.

[123] See the working definition of "prostitute" offered in Chapter 1.

[124] Aurelius Victor *Caes.* 28.6–7; cf. Nov. 14 (a. 535). For concern with hidden deviance, see also Herter 1 (1957) 1163; Grodzynski, "Tortures" (1984) 389; Gleason, "Semiotics" (1990) 394–399.

[125] See Herter 1.1167.

[126] Val. Max. 6.1.10: "... quod adulescens ille palam atque aperte corpore quaestum factitassent. ..."

condemnation of the prostitute's behavior, meaning something like "flagrantly and openly." The use of a frequentative verb accomplishes the same moralizing end, this time by emphasizing the habitual, repetitive nature of the behavior. In other respects, Valerius's language echoes the legislative phrase itself.

In short, the jurists encountered wording that, if understood literally, would quickly lead to results that were undesirable or impractical, especially when viewed in light of the law's purpose.[127] Their predicament is a good illustration of Nörr's point that the legislator's concern with completeness caused problems in application and posed an obstacle to really comprehensive planning.[128] One man's approach comes close to outright rejection of the troublesome word:

> Marcel. (26 *digest.*) D. 23.2.41 pr.: Probrum intellegitur etiam in his mulieribus esse, quae turpiter viverent vulgoque quaestum facerent, etiamsi non palam.

> Disgrace is understood to be incurred also by those women who lived shamefully and made a living from promiscuous sexual relations even if this was not done "openly."

This text, like most others discussed in this section, is free from suspicion of interpolation. Ulpius Marcellus wrote his *Digesta* in the mid-160s.[129] Book 26 is one of five that were devoted to the *lex Iulia et Papia*.[130]

The language used by the jurist as he seeks to unburden himself of *palam* is of interest. *Probrum* can be taken in its general meaning of "disgrace," "ignominy," "shame."[131] There is also a more specialized sense, for the word served as a technical expression for the offenses that once provoked censorial punishment.[132] The jurists evidently understood the law to exercise a quasi-censorial function, as can be gathered from their use of the word *nota* and its cognates in the context of the marriage prohibitions.[133] The Republican censors punished prostitutes no more than any other women, but here it is precisely the theme of social degradation that resonates. Just as these magistrates were responsible for maintaining the rolls of the senatorial and equestrian orders and might penalize any freeborn male citizen by removing him to an inferior tribe, so this law worked to keep prostitutes and pimps out of unions with freeborn men, above all, upper-class men.[134] At the same time, an even narrower sense can be teased out of Marcellus's

---

[127] Vonglis, *Loi* ch. 3, has a fine analysis of this problem. It is rather less common than its opposite, where a restriction not found in a law is required in order to avoid unwanted results in application.

[128] Nörr, "Legislation" (1981) 360.

[129] Fitting, *Alter*² 60–62. See also Kunkel, *Herkunft*² 213–214.

[130] Lenel, *Pal.* 1 cols. 630–632.

[131] *OLD* s.h.v. 2a.

[132] See Greenidge, *Infamia* (1894) 4 n. 1; Kaser, "Infamia" 225. Note the range of moral offenses punished by these magistrates: Mommsen, *Staatsrecht* 2³ (1887/1969) 377–382.

[133] Ulp. D. 23.2.43.4, 12, 13; Paul. D. *eod.* 44.5.

[134] The marriage prohibitions were valid for all, although the testamentary penalties were evidently not enforced below the level of men with a patrimony of HS 100,000, of women with HS 50,000; see Chapter 3. Note the somewhat transferred sense of *probrum* here and the more literal use of *probrosae* in the passage of Suetonius discussed above (*Dom.* 8.3), where Domitian acts as a censor in declassing adulteresses.

usage, one associated closely, though not exclusively, with prostitutes and pimps, namely, "sexual shame."[135]

Two descriptive phrases contribute something to Marcellus's definition of "prostitute." "Quae turpiter viverent" means "who lived[136] shamefully": the reference to lack of sexual shame is obvious. "Vulgoque quaestum facerent" means "and who made a living through promiscuous sexual relations."[137] The jurist felt that *vulgo* was a more appropriate expression. This word was far more widely used than *palam* in nonlegal descriptions of prostitutes.[138]

Marcellus is, on the one hand, balancing awkward statutory phrasing against his perception of the legislative intent; his method is revealed as interpretation *ex voluntate*. On the other hand, he is attempting to incorporate a social ethic directly into his understanding of the law. Not surprisingly, the notion of "common" is preferred to that of "open." But the consequences of this approach for the text of the statute are rather dramatic: Marcellus all but substitutes *vulgo* for legislative *palam*.

Others felt it was not absolutely necessary to discard the wording of the statute in order to arrive at a more satisfactory accommodation between its goals and the social reality in which it must operate. So Ulpian, writing in Caracalla's reign,[139] begins his extended definition of a prostitute with an observation drawn from this context:

> Ulp. (1 *ad legem Iuliam et Papiam*) D. 23.2.43 pr.: Palam quaestum facere dicemus non tantum eam, quae in lupanario se prostituit, verum etiam si qua (ut adsolet) in taberna cauponia vel qua alia pudori suo non parcit.

> We will say that not only does the woman who prostitutes herself in a brothel make a living "openly" but also any woman in a tavern or inn (a common practice) or any other woman who[140] does not spare her sense of shame.

It has already been suggested to what extent prostitution was associated with inns, taverns, and other places of public entertainment.[141] The jurist does not simply describe the economic context,[142] but seeks to integrate this with his understanding of the law's purpose. The law evidently aimed at all prostitutes.[143] Even if taken

---

[135] In this meaning, the word can also refer to adulteresses. See, e.g., Catull. 61.99; Cic. *Phil.* 2.99; Suet. *Iul.* 43.1; and the discussion above.

[136] Or "used to live." The imperfect tense may imply the same point made by Ulpian at D. 23.2.43.4 (see below); it also conveys the sense of repeated, habitual behavior.

[137] The ellipsis of "corpore" is without importance. I give prominence to the notion of promiscuity in the translation of *vulgo* but do not exclude another meaning suggested by the *OLD* s.h.v. 1a: "in a way common to all, publicly." Both are certainly present. A narrow emphasis on the latter leads to the curious conclusion that the law excluded clandestine prostitutes; see above.

[138] See Adams, "Words" (1983) 344.

[139] Fitting, *Alter*[2] 117–118; Kunkel, *Herkunft*[2] 245–254. See also Honoré, *Ulpian* 157–158, 183, 188, who specifies A.D. 216–217 as the period in which this commentary was composed.

[140] The Philadelphia *Digest* takes *qua alia* to be the object of the implied preposition *in:* "in taverns or in other places." Cf. Castello, *Matrimonio* (1940) 123.

[141] See Chapter 2. The phrase *taberna cauponia* also appears at Paul. D. 33.7.13 pr.

[142] His knowledge, which seems casual, is illustrated by the striking parenthesis "ut adsolet."

[143] It does not embrace, nor does Ulpian understand it to embrace, women who work in taverns who are not prostitutes (whether as *ministrae, cauponae,* or *tabernariae*). Contra Herter 2 (1960) 74; Bas-

literally,[144] *palam* would not restrict its application to brothel prostitutes, since women who worked in taverns, for example, could hardly be said to ply their trade in secret.[145]

It is remarkable that Ulpian does not content himself with vague generalizations like "quae viverent turpiter" but instead describes, in part, what a prostitute does.[146] At the same time a thread of moralizing runs through his commentary, as the words "pudori suo non parcit" demonstrate.[147] The language is also broad, as the last phrase shows. In both respects, he is true to the spirit of the law, insofar as the import of *palam* is concerned.

Ulpian takes his definition a step further:

> Ulp. (1 *ad legem Iuliam et Papiam*) D. 23.2.43.1: Palam autem sic accipimus passim, hoc est sine dilectu: non si qua adulteris vel stupratoribus se committit, sed quae vicem prostitutae sustinet.

> "Openly" we then take to mean "everywhere," that is, "without discrimination": not anyone who gives herself to adulterers or partners in *stuprum* but one who plays the part of a prostitute.

Passim is the ideal transition. In its meaning "everywhere, in every place," it looks back to the content of the preceding fragment, while under another meaning "indiscriminately, at random," it stands at the center of the passage.[148] At the same time, *palam* and *passim* are hardly equivalent. The logic that connects them is that of a jurist attempting to reconcile the wording of the *lex Iulia et Papia* with its intent. Next, Ulpian glosses *passim* with "hoc est sine dilectu."[149] Sexual indiscriminateness emerges as fundamental to the legal definition of a prostitute.[150]

---

sanelli Sommariva, "Considerazioni" (1988) 312–313; see also below and Manfredini, "Costantino" (1988) 332.

[144] Note the definition Ulpian gives regarding the declaration of heirs, where *palam* means "non utique in publicum sed ut exaudiri possit . . .": Ulp. (2 *ad Sab.*) D. 28.1.21 pr. Cf. Ulp. D. 50.16.33 (see below).

[145] All the same, this was potentially less obvious than brothel prostitution, so that employment in a tavern might provide a cover for slaves prostituted in violation of a *ne serva* covenant on sale: Alex. Sev. C. 4.56.3 (a. 225).

[146] The distinction is fundamental between a definition that describes what a prostitute does and one that defines who a prostitute is. The approach is typical of Ulpian: note his famous distinction at D. 12.5.4.3.

[147] A variation on the rhetorical *color* for sexually dissolute males, "pudori neque suo neque alieno pepercit": Cic. *Rab. Perd.* 8; Suet. *Cal.* 36.1 (with *pudicitia* substituted for *pudor*). See Edwards, *Politics* (1993) 81–84. Bloch, *Prostitution* 1 (1912) 34, sees a reference to the variety of sexual services offered by the prostitute.

[148] Contrast *OLD* s.h.v. 2a with 3.

[149] This has been taken to signify lack of emotional content: Bloch, *Prostitution* 1.32. It hardly means sex without payment by itself, as Herter 2.80 assumes.

[150] I believe that the exegesis given here is how the passage must hold together, but it does not exclude the possibility that Ulpian's treatment is the fruit of a historical development whereby *palam* was first understood as *passim* and later interpreted as *sine dilectu*. A comparison may be drawn with Ulpian's definition of *iniuria* under the *lex Aquilia*, which is often understood in much the same way. First *iniuria* = *non iure*, then = *contra ius*, finally = *culpa*: Ulp. (18 *ad edictum*) D. 9.2.5.1.

As it stands, the construction is broad, leaving the jurist with a twofold problem. He must discover the intent of the statute and reconcile this to the *lex Iulia de adulteriis coercendis*. He handles this in both a negative and a positive way. First the former: the essential quality of promiscuity is limited so that sex that violates the adultery law is excluded. The problem illustrates a consequence of the polarized classification of sexual relations, fostered by the adultery statute, into what is permissible and what is not. For men, this means, in stark logic, that outside marriage, one has sex with a prostitute, procuress, or slave or one violates the law. For a woman, sex within marriage is the only sex permitted, unless she is a prostitute, procuress, or slave.

Consider the implication: if a woman is not married to her partner, she must have many of them in order to meet the definition of a prostitute and escape the penalties of the law. But sheer numbers are not enough, since the mere multiplication of the offense will not protect her. Ulpian introduces the positive element at the end of the fragment, specifying that she must "play the part of," "live," or "act like a prostitute."[151] Behavior defines a prostitute. This returns us to the core problem of definition: how does one play the part of a prostitute?

Ultimately of course the question had to be decided by a court. Social class and lifestyle might be taken into account. In other words, Ulpian has opened the door to a purely descriptive, morally neutral approach.[152] This would serve the purpose of isolating and defining different types of unacceptable sexual behaviors, especially among the lower classes. That is, it would tend to facilitate the imposition of a certain control, through classification of sexual behavior, of the lower orders.[153] At Rome the point of this exercise was more ideological than sociological: the idea was to distinguish professionals from respectable women, not to establish a complex system of controls over the behavior of poor women.[154]

No account is taken of the possibility that such categories corresponded little to the experience of poor women.[155] The absence of such classification spelled a lack of fixed boundaries between respectable and nonrespectable spheres.[156] The adoption of plain neutral language describing prostitutes can actually foster the institutionalization of the profession and their isolation from the mass of the poor.[157]

[151] Compare the phrase "meretricio more"; see Chapter 6.

[152] Otis, *Prostitution* (1985) 2, suggests the truth of this argument when she uses Ulpian as a basis for constructing her own definition of prostitution: "a socially identifiable group of women earn their living principally or exclusively from the commerce of their bodies."

[153] Cf. Hobson, *Virtue* 213: "Essentially, the terms *public* and *visible,* when translated into actual policies, were gender and status classifications" (her emphasis).

[154] For a similar development of an "ideological" classification among twelfth-and thirteenth-century canonists and civilians, see Brundage, "Prostitution" (1975/1976) 827; Otis, *Prostitution* 16. Contrast Hobson, *Virtue* 106, who describes attempts to implement just such a system as mentioned above in the mid-nineteenth century United States.

[155] The Victorian Contagious Diseases Acts were accused by critics of operating precisely in this way. The reply was that "immoral or adulterous intercourse, if confined to one man at a time, was not illegal": Walkowitz, *Prostitution* (1980) 185.

[156] See Hobson, *Virtue* 106, 180, on the reality of prostitution in the nineteenth-century United States.

[157] Otis, *Prostitution* 50, describes a similar development in Languedoc at the end of the fourteenth

By this logic, the problem of defining a prostitute is simple: either a woman is a prostitute or she is not. The method may be contrasted with the sort of broad moralizing that defines many, or all, forms of objectionable sexual behavior— especially female sexual behavior—as prostitution.[158]

Even so, Ulpian is not about to throw out the moralizing framework already established by his predecessors. The jurist acknowledges as much when he asserts the repeated, habitual practice of indiscriminate sexual relations as central to the legal definition:

> Ulp. (1 *ad legem Iuliam et Papiam*) D. 23.2.43.2: Item quod cum uno et altero pecunia accepta commiscuit, non videtur palam corpore quaestum facere.

> Likewise, because a woman has intercourse with one or two men after accepting money from them,[159] she is not held to have made a living with her body "openly."

In this text, the emphasis accorded promiscuity reduces the criterion of payment to a secondary concern. Compare Valerius Maximus's use of the frequentative verb "factitasset" to describe the behavior of a prostitute.[160]

Given the law's wording, this interpretation is quite extensive, almost ignoring the presence of *quaestum facere*. Accepting money for sex is not enough for a woman to qualify as a prostitute: indiscriminate sexual activity is what distinguishes the true professionals.[161] The jurist perhaps wishes to discourage unworthy applicants for the *quarta*. Persons who stood to lose under the testamentary regime of the *lex Iulia et Papia* should not seek partial relief by pretending to be prostitutes. The adultery law also determines the outcome: no one may claim exemption as a prostitute simply on a showing that money or other consideration had changed hands.[162]

For these reasons, I am not certain that the aim was to let upmarket prostitutes, or courtesans, off the hook.[163] Such women would either have been identified as "common prostitutes" or exposed to the rigors of the adultery law.

Ulpian then takes a further step, which all but eclipses completely the notion of payment:

> Oct.-Ulp. (1 *ad legem Iuliam et Papiam*) D. 23.2.43.3: Octavenus tamen rectissime ait etiam eam, quae sine quaestu palam se prostituerit, debuisse his connumerari.

---

century, where prostitutes came to be designated officially as "public women" in contrast with the moralizing epithets of an earlier period. In this case, the adoption of a more neutral vocabulary was tied to "the increasing institutionalization of prostitution, which transformed the public woman from a free-lance worker to an agent of positive public policy on prostitution and sexual morality, enjoying certain privileges as well as obligations" (Otis, *Prostitution* 70).

[158] An example is the 1911 Chicago Vice Commission report, which embraced potentially all sexual activity outside marriage; as a result, prostitution seemed rampant: Connelly, *Response* (1980) 17–20.

[159] Ulpian assumes that in the normal course of events, payment precedes performance.

[160] Val. Max. 6.1.10.

[161] Compare the distinction implicitly made at Ter. *Andria* 74–79. For an interesting comparison from nineteenth-century Buenos Aires, see Guy, *Sex* (1991) 50, 79.

[162] It is common, even expected, that adulterers shower their partners with gifts (Chapter 5), a fact that Ulpian may have in mind here.

[163] See Treggiari, *RM* 302.

Octavenus nevertheless says, quite correctly, that even she who has prostituted herself without payment ought to be included in this category.

Ulpian's citation of Octavenus suggests that this point was controversial.[164] Beyond dispute, it shows that discussion occurred fairly early: Octavenus wrote a century earlier at minimum.[165] In this text, the word *palam* reappears, this time with a nontechnical expression for prostitution ("se prostituerit"). True, the jurist avoids the absurdity of a formulation such as "quae sine quaestu palam corpore quaestum fecerit." But it is precisely the legislative phrasing that he implicitly criticizes. In the passage of Marcellus we saw how *palam* was downplayed and the rest of the phrase retained and amplified. Here a similar operation has been performed on another part of the formula.

Octavenus and Ulpian do appear to draw back from an outright rejection of the statute's wording. There is a suggestion that the legislation might have been more expertly constructed,[166] but the jurist will not go so far as to rewrite it.[167]

In one respect, this point may not have mattered much in practice. The evidence suggests that the overwhelming majority of prostitutes accepted payment in exchange for their services. Octavenus and Ulpian are here interested in hard cases for which a straightforward application of the legislation will not suffice. One example might be ex-slaves who had been made to service their masters and others without payment. Again, leeway is conceded to the finder of fact. If a court had its reasons, the issue of payment might be ignored.[168] The law aimed at keeping sexually promiscuous women out of the upper classes, which explains why Octavenus and Ulpian were willing to go this far. Promiscuity emerges as an almost absolute requirement of this definition, which does not differ much in substance from that offered by Marcellus, although the method of interpretation he employs is not at all the same.[169]

Ulpian then takes up another, less important change made by the *lex Iulia et Papia* in the legal formula for "prostitute":

Ulp. (1 *ad legem Iulia et Papia*) D. 23.2.43.4: Non solum autem ea quae facit, verum ea quoque quae fecit, etsi facere desiit, lege notatur: neque enim aboletur turpitudo, quae postea intermissa est.

Not only she, moreover, who practices prostitution is subject to degradation [the *nota*] according to the statute, but also she who has done so in the past, even if she has ceased to practice this profession. The reason is that sexual disgrace is not effaced by ceasing the behavior that led to it.

The Augustan law altered the Republican double verb from "fecit, fecerit" to "facit, fecerit," perhaps providing a dispensation to prostitutes practicing before

---

[164] The "tamen" also points to a (suppressed?) controversy.
[165] Octavenus lived in the late first to early second century: Kunkel, *Herkunft*[2] 150–151.
[166] So the perfect tense of "debuisse" is perhaps significant.
[167] See Wesel, *Statuslehre* 112.
[168] The holding suggests one should hesitate before generalizing "payment" as the fundamental criterion for "*infamia*" incurred as the consequence of exercising a dishonorable profession: see Gardner, *Being* 145–152.
[169] Note how Ulpian's treatment of *palam* here contrasts with the definition of the word he gives in his commentary on the edict: Ulp. (21 *ad edictum*) D. 50.16.33: "Palam est coram pluribus."

the time the law was passed.[170] In Ulpian's day at any rate, prostitutes who were reformed or retired did not benefit from this exemption.

Sexual *turpitudo* is not removed by a cessation of the behavior that produced it in the first place, a principle consistent with the regime of the *Tabula Heracleensis*. In expounding this doctrine, the jurists resolved an important aspect of the dilemma of defining "prostitute" versus "prostitution" and, in so doing, made application of the definition easier. Sexual disgrace is conceived as something staining and corrosive. The thought is the same as that which lay behind the prohibition against remarriage imposed on convicted adulteresses.[171]

Not all forms of *turpitudo* were indelible.[172] Ex-actresses could escape it by the sixth century.[173] Inherited *turpitudo* might be attenuated: if a parent ended his or her acting career before a child was adopted, that child was released from the prohibition.[174] Not even the *turpitudo* of prostitutes was in every respect permanent, as illustrated by the rescript of Severus removing the restrictions on legal representation placed on female prostitutes when the latter had practiced the profession as slaves.[175] This took away a disability in the law of civil procedure; marriage was another question entirely.

We may smile (or frown) at the calculations of medieval theologians as to the number of partners that defines a woman as a prostitute,[176] but their approach throws into relief the harshness of Ulpian's method and its result: "once a prostitute, always a prostitute."[177] In this way prostitutes were effectively marginalized once and for all.

Ulpian's position suggests a sharp demarcation with mainstream Christian attitudes on prostitutes. As far as I am able to tell, the idea that prostitutes might be rescued, reformed, and redeemed is entirely new and originates in Christian doctrine.[178]

By this stage in his commentary, Ulpian has developed the core of his definition. *Turpitudo* has the sense, for prostitutes, of both "indiscriminate sexual behavior"[179] and the "social/sexual disgrace" that results from it.

The jurist continues in the same vein:

[170] See Chapter 3.

[171] See the remarks of Esmein, "Délit" (1886) 109.

[172] See Greenidge, *Infamia* 189–190. Nor was all *turpitudo* (directly or indirectly) sexual: Kaser, "Rechtswidrigkeit" (1940) 135; Kaser, *Verbotsgesetze* (1977) 71–72.

[173] Iustinus C. 5.4.23 (a. 520–523).

[174] Pomp.-Paul. D. 23.2.44.5, with Vonglis, *Loi* 124–126.

[175] Ulp. D. 3.2.24, discussed in Chapter 2.

[176] Some attempted to define a prostitute in terms of the number of partners a woman has had; estimates ranged from a low minimum of 40 to a high minimum of 23,000: Bloch, *Prostitution* 1.18.

[177] For a parallel from nineteenth-century France, where prostitutes were written off as if afflicted with disease or madness, see Corbin, *Women for Hire* (1990) 298.

[178] See Proc. *Aed.* 1.9.1–10 and Nov. 14 (a. 535) for Justinian's views. Cf. Herter, 1.1207; Rossiaud, *Prostitution* (1988) 84; Hobson, *Virtue* 54–55. The example of prostitute saints is most striking: Ward, *Harlots* (1987).

[179] The context speaks for the *lex Iulia et Papia,* but the same is true for the adultery law. Marcellus means much the same thing when he writes "quae turpiter viverent" in D. 23.2.41 pr. (see above).

Ulp. (1 *ad legem Iuliam et Papiam*) D. 23.2.43.5: Non est ignoscendum ei, quae obtentu paupertatis turpissimam vitam egit.[180]

She is not to be excused who, on the plea of poverty, has led a very disgraceful life.

One might suppose that the plea of poverty came up in practice frequently enough for the jurist to take note of it. The notion of a plea, phrased here as a pretext or excuse, and the idea of pardon (denied) suggest Ulpian imagines an actual hearing granted an offender before a court. The language is moralizing, but the legal basis of the claim would have been lack of intent to commit the "offense," on the theory that economic circumstances forced the woman to take up the profession.

In fact, we have a transcript of a trial of a man for the murder of a prostitute in which the "plea of poverty" meets with sympathy.[181] I think it obvious that this difference is explained by the circumstances: there is a wide gulf between the marriage prohibition and murder.[182] At any rate, this text too highlights Ulpian's familiarity with the real-life circumstances of prostitution. Conditions of poverty and limited employment opportunities for women drove many to prostitution as a means of making a living.

Ulpian's approach is, once more, moralizing rather than sociological. He uses the epithet "turpissimam" to describe the prostitute's behavior. *Turpitudo* cannot be removed either by giving up the profession or by claiming that it was exercised because of compelling economic circumstances, a point that confirms the importance of sexual indiscriminateness as a defining element.[183] Ulpian is speaking of free women, obviously, with perhaps a trace of the idea (especially credible perhaps to the mind of an upper-class male) that such women were morally to blame because they had "chosen" this profession. On the other hand, Ulpian may well have regarded the subjective element as irrelevant, so that if a woman had been a prostitute as a slave through the compulsion of her master, she might remain an unfit marriage partner for *ingenui* even upon manumission and abandonment of this line. For this reason, the editorial suggestion "elegit" for "egit" must be left in the air.

Ulpian, to be sure, asserts an upper-class standard of morality and applies this to a foreign context. The stringency of his method is softened by the consideration that, in practice, the law would have had a serious impact only in situations where one of the marriage partners came from the higher end of the social scale. It is submitted that the jurist is aware of this. His remark is not a case of moralizing for its own sake but is grounded in an appreciation of the law's purpose and scope of application. Some *ceteri ingenui* were rated "more equal" than others: one thinks especially of the decurionate and the equestrian order.

---

[180] Mommsen and Krüger propose "elegit," which is more pointed.

[181] *BGU* 3.1024.6–8 (later-fourth-century Hermopolis). On this text, see Bagnall, *Egypt* (1993) 196–198, who rightly defends it against critics; see, e.g., Beaucamp, *Statut* 2 (1992) 56.

[182] In other words, I see no reason to ascribe the sympathy accorded this argument in the murder trial to the influence of Christianity, though it is true that Christian ideology tends to view the "plea of poverty" as a mitigating factor. See Otis, *Prostitution* 86; Rossiaud, *Prostitution* 84.

[183] For a classical Athenian parallel, see Aesch. 1.160.

Writing a juristic commentary on this part of the marriage law was not as straightforward a task as it might at first seem. The jurist had first to resolve the problems raised by the wording in a manner consistent with his understanding of the law's purpose. Next, the social reality of his own time, with its widespread practice of prostitution, had to be accommodated. There was then the challenge of reconciling one's approach to another important legislative act, the *lex Iulia de adulteriis coercendis*. Ulpian, at least, had the benefit of relying on two centuries' worth of trial experience and juristic elaboration. We do not know that the structure and function of prostitution in Roman society had changed very much during this time, at least in ways that would have influenced the application of the law.[184] The application of both the marriage and the adultery statutes remained essentially unchanged, at least insofar as prostitutes and pimps were concerned.[185]

To an extent, this conservatism tied the jurists' hands by limiting the opportunity for freer interpretation of the law. But it also promoted the development of a juristic consensus. One result of this is the extensive definition given prostitutes. All who prostitute themselves, whatever their venue or methods of solicitation, are liable to the law. Ulpian and Marcellus differ greatly in technique, and I think it possible to contemplate a difference in the effectiveness of their approaches, but the direction they take is essentially the same.

Central to the juristic consensus is the focus on indiscriminate sexual activity as a basis for defining a prostitute. The emphasis on the criterion of promiscuity is at the root of Marcellus's remarks and dates back to Octavenus in the late first century, going back perhaps to Labeo.[186] Both Marcellus and Ulpian place great weight on the word *palam,* viewing it as closely connected with the notion of *turpitudo,* or promiscuous sexual behavior. There is an important restriction, in the sense that adulteresses and amateurs are excluded.[187] But not much space is devoted to this issue, which appears to be uncontroversial as a point of law and which the jurists conceive to be a question to be left routinely to the finder of fact to decide. The extensive aspect is the more remarkable by far, with Octavenus and Ulpian hinting that some women who do not ask for money for their services, and who are not therefore commercial prostitutes in any real sense, are included in the definition.[188]

This solution may be criticized with reference to the three criteria—payment, promiscuity, and emotional indifference—set forth in Chapter 1. It is plain that Ulpian's definition has emphasized the second criterion, promiscuity, to the complete exclusion of the other two, payment and emotional indifference between sexual partners. This legal definition is dominated by moral considerations, to the extent that it is little more in substance than a conventional moral definition cast in a legal form.

---

[184] An increase in slave prostitutes would have been irrelevant; see Chapter 3.

[185] For an overview of the historical development of aspects of the latter statute, see Chapter 6.

[186] Argued from Lab.-Marcel.-Ulp. D. 12.5.4.3.

[187] For a later example of moralizing legislative language encouraging restrictive interpretation, see Goria, *Studi* (1975) 156 n. 171.

[188] On the ability of the jurists to interpret different elements of the same law extensively and restrictively in pursuit of a consistent policy overall, see Bauman, "*Leges*" (1980) 140–141, 173.

The implications of this conclusion are limited, however. To the modern mind, the moral content of Ulpian's definition is accentuated by our own tendency to qualify the other two criteria as nonmoral, "payment" being identified as "commercial" in nature and "lack of affection" as "psychological."[189] Both are thereby rendered morally neutral, with promiscuity isolated as *the* moral criterion.

For the Romans, however, all three criteria were moral in nature. The acceptance of payment for any service was regarded as degrading and morally doubtful.[190] Cicero says, in a famous passage of the *De Officiis:* "illiberal too and mean are the wages of all who work for payment, whose services, not talents, are purchased, for in their case the very wages are the warrant of slavery."[191] Seneca echoes this sentiment with the phrase *meritoria artificia.*[192]

The same can be said of the affective criterion. Dio Chrysostom in his Euboean Oration decries the lack of emotional content in relationships between prostitutes and their customers.[193] The tone and substance of his remarks show that this aspect too was understood entirely in moral terms.

The motive for the exclusive emphasis placed by the jurists on the criterion of promiscuity can be sought in its practical effects. A broad range of women was embraced by their definition, including many who would have been excluded by a straightforward application of all three criteria. The purpose behind this part of the law, namely, the identification of proper marriage partners for freeborn Romans, was of crucial importance for their approach. A secondary influence was grounded in the desire to retain the fruits of testamentary succession for members of the community of honor, especially those who obeyed the law by marrying and rearing children. This double motivation explains the jurists' concern with *turpitudo.* Sensitivity over female promiscuity was the underlying issue. An extensive interpretation of the statute addressed this concern and reconciled the solution to the regime imposed by the adultery law.

If prostitutes made the least desirable marriage prospects, *lenae* were not far behind. Many of these women were former prostitutes. Also, their disgrace qua procuresses was tied to that of prostitutes, in that they made the sexual honor of their charges the object of commerce. Ulpian's exegesis of the part of the *lex Iulia et Papia* dealing with (female) pimps begins with an apparently banal remark:

Ulp. (1 *ad legem Iuliam et Papiam*) D. 23.2.43.6: Lenocinium facere non minus est quam corpore quaestum exercere.

To practice the profession of a procuress/pimp is nothing less than to earn money through the sale of sexual services.

[189] See Brundage, "Prostitution" 826.

[190] There is plenty of evidence for moral condemnation of the acceptance of payment by prostitutes. See just *CIL* 4.1860 Add. p. 464 (= *Eph. Ep.* 1 p. 53, *CE* 942): "quae pretium dixit, non mea (puella) sed populi est"; Phaedrus App. 4.4: "quaestus placebat . . . meretricius."

[191] Cic. *Off.* 1.150: "inliberales autem et sordidi quaestus mercennariorum omnium, quorum operae—non, quorum artes!—emuntur; est enim in illis ipsa merces auctoramentum servitutis."

[192] Sen. *Ep.* 88.1.

[193] Dio Chrys. 7.133.

This is usually understood to mean something like "to procure/pimp is nothing less than to prostitute oneself for money."[194] In other words, the status of procuresses and the status of prostitutes are equated. Sometimes the phrase is interpreted to make the status of both types equal not just before the marriage law but in all of Roman private and public law, a practice that goes back to the Byzantine commentators on the *Digest*.[195] One instance is enough to disprove the validity of the assumption: the different treatment accorded pimps and prostitutes in the context of the praetor's edict.[196] Ulpian's remarks apply strictly to the *lex Iulia et Papia*.[197]

The equality before the law of pimps and prostitutes lay, then, in the sense that the law forbade both groups to marry *ingenui,* but this would have been perfectly obvious from the statute itself and suggests that the comment is gratuitous.[198] A better interpretation is suggested by expanding the translation given above to read "to pimp is nothing less than to earn money through the sale of (someone else's) sexual services." Ulpian provides a succinct definition of pimping, which is exactly what one would expect to find at this point in his commentary, where the section on pimps is introduced. This meaning is suggested by the usage "hunc quaestum exercet" in another *Digest* passage dealing with pimps[199] and easily derived from the sense of *exercere,* "to operate, run a business."[200] The statement is not without a moralizing hue, implied by the *non minus.*

All the same, I do not think prostitutes and pimps are equated morally or that the phrase should be understood as "pimping is no less (wrong) than prostitution." Moral opprobrium tended to weigh more heavily on pimps, so that they, especially male pimps, were more despised than prostitutes.[201] Both pimps and procuresses were viewed as exploiters of the weak and merchants of dishonor.

The breadth of the definition is of interest. As Ulpian's commentary develops, an implied preference emerges for the noun *lena* over the more cumbersome legislative phrase taken as a point of departure in the fragment just examined:

> Ulp. (1 *ad legem Iuliam et Papiam*) D. 23.2.43.7: Lenas autem eas dicimus, quae mulieres quaestuarias prostituunt.

> Furthermore, we describe those who prostitute women for money as "procuresses."

Ulpian makes a distinction here and in the next fragment similar to the one he draws for prostitutes: between *lenae* who only manage prostitutes and those who

---

[194] See, e.g., De Robertis, "Condizione" (1939/1987) 190 n. 3 (with literature); cf. 193 n. 1.

[195] Beaucamp, *Statut* 1.122 n. 1.

[196] See Chapter 2.

[197] As noted in Chapter 3, pimps were perhaps eligible for the *quarta.* If they were not, however, this would circumscribe even further the scope of Ulpian's comment, because it would be limited to the marriage prohibitions themselves.

[198] The point is of course not so obvious from the legal sources themselves: Karlowa, "Geschichte" (1870) 215–217.

[199] Ulp. (6 *ad edictum*) D. 3.2.4.2. Cf. *Ulp.* D. 23.2.43.8–9 in the text below.

[200] *OLD* s.v. *exerceo* 7b.

[201] Dio Chrys. 7.133; Herter 1.1170. Note the odium expressed at Dioclet., Maxim. C. 8.50(51).7 (a. 291); NTh. 18 (a. 439); Nov. 14 (a. 535). For the idea of increments of *turpitudo,* see Quint. *IO* 11.1.83.

do so while operating some other business.[202] The expression "mulieres quaestu-arias" abbreviates the phrase "quae palam corpore quaestum facit fecerit": when describing prostitutes it was difficult to avoid expressions that emphasized in some way the taking of money, which points up the artificiality of Ulpian's comment in fragment 3.[203]

Ulpian proceeds to the other half of the distinction:

> Ulp. (1 *ad legem Iuliam et Papiam*) D. 23.2.43.8–9: 8. Lenam accipiemus et eam, quae alterius nomine hoc vitae genus exercet. 9. Si qua cauponam exercens in ea corpora quaestuaria habeat (ut multae adsolent sub praetextu instrumenti cauponii prostitutas mulieres habere), dicendum hanc quoque lenae appellatione contineri.

> (8) We will understand "procuress" to include even the woman who practices this way of making a living under another name.[204] (9) If any woman operating an inn should have prostitutes working there (as many are accustomed to do on the pretext that they are part of the service staff), it must be said that she too is classified as a "procuress."

There is again a reference to widespread practice ("ut adsolent") coupled with a specific example (the staff of an inn). The passage complements the comment on prostitutes discussed above (in the *principium*) and should be compared with the oft-cited fragment from Ulpian's commentary on the praetor's edict, with its more detailed set of examples. All three texts are not merely neutral descriptions but attempt to reconcile social reality with the goals of public policy as reflected in the edict and the *lex Iulia et Papia,* respectively. All procuresses and pimps are em-braced by the statute, whatever the actual circumstances in which they practice their profession.[205]

The word *instrumentum* is interesting, insofar as it suggests that the prostitutes were slaves.[206] Since the status of the prostitutes is irrelevant to the application of the law, this may be taken as evidence that, in Ulpian's day, prostitutes were typically slaves.

Expressions like "hoc vitae genus" and "sub praetextu" continue the mor-alizing strain visible throughout Ulpian's commentary. It is tempting to take the latter phrase as a sign that attempts were made to avoid identification as procur-esses. At least two motives can be postulated for this behavior: to escape the penalties of the *lex Iulia et Papia* and to avoid paying the tax on prostitutes. Most procuresses and pimps would have had little motive to avoid the former and would

---

[202] The distinction he draws between those who manage slave prostitutes and those who manage free prostitutes (Ulp. D. 3.2.4.2) is relevant for the edict but not here.

[203] See "quaestuaria mancipia" in Ulp. (6 *ad edictum*) D. 3.2.4.2 and "corpora quaestuaria" in Ulp. D. 23.2.43.9, given in the text below.

[204] I.e., "under the name of another (way of making a living)." Similarly, Riggsby, "Lenocinium" (1995) 424. I do not understand the preference of the Philadelphia *Digest* for "under the name of someone else." For *vita* as "means, way of making a living," see Ulp. D. 1.18.6.5 and *OLD* s.h.v. 7b.

[205] This passage, as well as the others given by Manfredini, "Costantino" 332, with n. 31, do not identify the prostitute or the *lena* with the *tabernaria* in classical law (see above).

[206] It is often used to denote equipment or chattels of various kinds: *OLD* s.h.v. 2. The same point is suggested by "corpora quaestuaria."

have been unable to escape the latter, given the way in which it was collected.[207] Of course, Ulpian, as an upper-class male, may simply take for granted a routine effort on the part of procuresses to conceal their true profession because he assumed it to be shameful for them.

We seem to have all of Ulpian's commentary on the legislative phrase for procuresses, and yet there is no mention of *turpitudo*. Perhaps the sexual disgrace associated with these women was, under the law, qualitatively different, less or more damaging than that of prostitutes, or it was simply assumed that most procuresses were former prostitutes, so that the point had no independent value. There is no question that these were women considered to be without sexual honor.

For a full understanding of the juristic treatment of these definitions, it is necessary to keep in mind the purpose behind the law itself, namely, the identification and ranking of proper marriage partners for freeborn Romans, especially upper-class Romans, and the desire to retain the fruits of testamentary succession for the community of honor, especially that part which obeyed the marriage law and reproduced itself. This principle explains the juristic concern with *turpitudo*. Sensitivity over female promiscuity made prostitutes the least desirable prospects for the law's purpose. Procuresses came next, many of whom were former prostitutes. Their disgrace qua pimps was tied to that of prostitutes in that they made the honor of such women an object of commerce. Like actresses, both types belong to socially despised professions. At the same time, prostitutes and procuresses are classed apart in the marriage prohibitions, for the reason that the profession of acting was not by itself *sexually* disgraceful, although suspicions were often entertained about the chastity of such women.

Whether or not the sexual *turpitudo* of procuresses and, by implication, pimps is to be understood as direct, secondhand, or a combination of the two, the rationale behind the extensive interpretation of both phrases in the law is clear.[208] The treatment of the definition of "prostitute" is especially striking. Ulpian comments on wording that is unsatisfactory to the point of being defective, investing it with a series of meanings that add up to a brilliant interpretation of the legislative intent *ex verbis*. He moves between the techniques of restrictive and extensive interpretation in accordance with the particular claims of social policy in each separate context. His predecessor Marcellus had preferred an approach that was more radical in terms of method, if not result: interpretation *ex voluntate*.

Of course, Ulpian's own method was informed by his appreciation of the law's purpose and potential application. The overall thrust is extensive precisely for this reason. Ulpian pushes the interpretation *ex verbis* as far as he can make it go, until in agreement with Octavenus he comes to recognize a type of "prostitute" found nowhere in the legislation itself.

---

[207] I refer to the collection of the tax by the military. See Chapter 7.

[208] Note, for the sake of contrast, the restrictive interpretation preferred by Ulpian in his commentary on the edict with regard to another profession: Pomp.-Ulp. (14 *ad edictum*) D. 4.9.1.2. For discussion and literature, see Vonglis, *Loi* 168, with n. 4.

Jurists and the *Lex Iulia et Papia*

To read the works of many modern scholars, one would never guess the extent of the popularity the *lex Iulia et Papia* enjoyed among the Roman jurists.[209] The clearest statement of this is given by Terentius Clemens: ". . . the statute was enacted for the common good, namely, to promote the procreation of children, [and so] is to be furthered through interpretation."[210] One might infer the same both from the sheer size and number of juristic commentaries on this law and above all from the favorable treatment it generally receives at the hands of these men.[211] The law's continued vitality in the eyes of the legal professionals is guaranteed not only by the number of other enactments it tied in with or directly inspired but also by the repeated efforts of the jurists to keep the regime of the *lex Iulia et Papia* in line with the changing needs of society and public policy.[212]

[209] The great exception is Riccardo Astolfi, to whom the following paragraph owes a huge debt.

[210] Ter. Clem. (5 *ad legem Iuliam et Papiam*) D. 35.1.64.1: ". . . legem enim utilem rei publicae, subolis scilicet procreandae causa latam, adiuvandam interpretatione." See Astolfi, *LIP*² 330.

[211] For both points, see Astolfi, *LIP*² 341.

[212] See Astolfi, *LIP*² 344.

5

The *Lex Iulia de Adulteriis Coercendis*

1. The Statute

A few months after the passage of the *lex Iulia de maritandis ordinibus,* a companion statute was brought before the *concilium plebis* by Augustus, who was acting once more on the authority of his *tribunicia potestas*.[1] The *lex Iulia de adulteriis coercendis* had as its principal aim the repression of those forms of nonmarital sexual relations considered unacceptable by Roman society, particularly adultery.

Aside from adultery and criminal fornication *(stuprum),* there is disagreement as to what the adultery law punished. There is controversy over whether it punished incest,[2] but even the late classical jurists treat this as a separate crime,[3] to the extent that even incestuous marriages might in some cases receive protection under the adultery statute.[4] *Stuprum* with (male) *ingenui* was punished by the Republican *lex*

---

[1] Dio 54.16.3–6. Better evidence on the date is lacking: Rotondi, *Leges* (1912/1962) 445–447. It falls in with the series of *leges Iuliae* passed at this time: Arangio-Ruiz, ''Legislazione'' (1938/1977) 250–251. The two fundamental modern studies remain Esmein, ''Délit'' (1886), and Mommsen, *Strafrecht* (1899) 688–701.

[2] Guarino, ''*Incestum*'' (1943), argues against Lotmar, ''Incestum'' (1912), and others that the law punished incest. Opinion remains divided: Kaser, *Verbotsgesetze* (1977) 80 n. 15; Santalucia, *DPR* (1989) 94; Guareschi, ''Note'' (1993) 455–456.

[3] See, above all, Pap. D. 48.5.39(38) pr.-7.

[4] Ulp. D. 48.5.14(13).4.

Scantinia (c. 149 B.C.), though the details are obscure.[5] The adultery statute almost certainly did not punish this offense.[6] By the late classical period this crime may have been brought within the ambit of the *lex Iulia* (through the work of the jurists or, more likely, legislative act).[7] It has also been argued that the statute repressed rape.[8] Though this is untenable,[9] the offense was punishable qua adultery/*stuprum*. Adultery was incontestably the main offense, overshadowing even *stuprum*.[10]

Such acts were punished for the first time by trial in a standing criminal court, the *quaestio perpetua de adulteriis*.[11] Before the passage of the *lex Iulia,* the repression of sexual misbehavior was generally conceded to the private sphere. Most of our information concerns adultery, especially the offense of the married woman and her lover. If the husband caught an adulterous pair in the act, he might kill both parties on the spot.[12] Other cases were dealt with by a *iudicium domesticum* conducted by the father of the offending woman if she were still *in potestate,* and by the husband if she were married with *manus* or (perhaps) if she were *sui iuris.*[13] Divorce was an easy recourse, at least for members of the upper classes.[14] A woman guilty of adultery might lose a portion (if not all) of her dowry in the *iudicium de moribus* (or through *retentio* in connection with the *actio rei uxoriae*).[15] The aediles prosecuted, in the *iudicia populi,* cases that were especially notorious, or

[5] Mommsen, *Strafrecht* 703–704; Pfaff, *RE* stuprum (1931); Berger, *Dictionary* (1953) s.v. *lex Scantinia, stuprum cum masculo*; Fantham, "*Stuprum*" (1991) 279–281; Ryan, "*Lex Scantinia*" (1994).

[6] Molé, *NNDI* stuprum 587; Rizzelli, "*Stuprum*" (1987) 385 n. 7; Cantarella, *SN* (1988) 184.

[7] So two texts from Papinian and Modestinus (barring interpolation): Pap. D. 48.5.9(8) pr.; Mod. D. *eod.* 35(34).1.

[8] Coroï, *Violence* (1915) 207–216; Flore, "*Vis*" (1930) 348–352.

[9] Dalla, *Venus* (1987) 121; Goria *ED* ratto (1987) 710.

[10] See Corbett, *Marriage* (1930) 139; Guarino, "*Incestum*" 185–186; Thomas, "Accusatio" (1961) 65; Rizzelli, "*Stuprum*"; Beaucamp, *Statut* 1 (1990) 178–181.

[11] On the situation prevailing before the passage of the *lex Iulia,* see Esmein, "Délit" 73–74; Kunkel, *Untersuchungen* (1962) 121–123 (who refutes Mommsen's extreme pessimism over the supposed "inadequacy" of the pre-Augustan regime); Pólay, "*RM*" (1971) 280–282; Jones, *Courts* (1972) 15, 30; Pugliese, "Linee" (1982) 731–732 n. 17 (who holds that Sulla's legislation, see below, never became law); Garofalo, "Competenza" (1986) esp. 455–475 (who argues that the competency of the aediles in all criminal matters involving women defendants derived from their responsibility for prosecuting sexual offenses); Balzarini, "*Lex Cornelia*" (1988) 589 with n. 76; Marshall, "Maesia" (1990) n. 26; Treggiari, *RM* (1991) esp. 268–269; Bauman, *Women* (1992) 107 with nn. 23, 24; Dixon, *TRF* (1992) 78; Bauman "*Metus*" (1993); Robinson, *CLAR* (1995) 58. On the rules repressing adultery attributed to Romulus, see Giunti, *Adulterio* (1990); with Astolfi, "Aspetti" (1992).

[12] For killing the wife, see Gell. 10.23.5. A variety of insults might be visited upon the lover: Plaut. *Curc.* 30, *Miles* 1394–1426, *Poen.* 862–863; Ter. *Eun.* 957; Catull. 15.19, 21.7–13; Hor. *Serm.* 1.2.37–46, 64–79, 127–134; Verg. *Aen.* 6.612; Val. Max. 6.1.13 (cf. 5.9.1); [Acro.] *ad Hor. Serm. 1.2.46.* Guarino, "Lui" (1993) 418, argues for a lack of sanctions against the lover in early law, but see Dignös, *Aedilen* (1962) 34; Treggiari, *RM* 293.

[13] Punishment of women convicted for offenses in the Bacchanalian scandal of 186 B.C. was left to kinsmen, except for those married with *manus,* who were remanded to their husbands, by the *SC de Bacchanalibus:* Liv. 39.18.6. For two women found guilty of poisoning their husbands and punished "propinquorum decreto," see Val. Max. 6.3.8. Discussion in Pólay, "*RM*" 303; Evans, *War* (1991) 10–13; Guarino, "Lui" 419.

[14] Treggiari, *RM* 211, 275.

[15] See Val. Max. 8.2.3 and below for literature.

(perhaps) where a domestic tribunal could not be constituted.[16] Some legislation existed on the subject, to judge from the statement by Paul[17] that the first chapter of the Augustan statute abrogated many laws and the report attributed to Sallust by Plutarch[18] that Sulla introduced legislation on marriage and *"sōphrosunē."* If so, its content remains unclear: at all events, the thin evidence inclines most scholars to view the regulation of women's sexual behavior under the Republic as left largely to the family.[19]

The Augustan *quaestio* continued to function throughout the classical period of Roman law, until as late as the early third century,[20] though the change evidently came earlier in the provinces.[21] Afterward, offenses were addressed exclusively through a procedure that modern scholars style the *cognitio extra ordinem.*[22]

Criminal penalties were ordained for the adulterous female spouse and her lover. These were chiefly patrimonial in nature, dictating the confiscation of one-half of the lover's property and one-third of the adulteress's, as well as one-half her dowry.[23] The incidence on the dowry was far more severe than the one-sixth taken under the *retentio propter mores.*[24] Most scholars attribute this fixed portion along with the others just named to the *lex Iulia de adulteriis coercendis* itself.[25]

After conviction, neither party could ever give oral or written testimony before a court, nor could the man witness a will (women were categorically excluded from this function). The latter is apparently a juristic extension.[26] As with other criminal statutes, violation spelled loss of civic privileges, including that of serving in the army.[27] Such disabilities are in later classical law described en bloc as *infamia.*[28]

---

[16]Cic. *Rab. Perd.* 8; Liv. 8.22.2–4, 10.31.9, 25.2.9; Val. Max. 8.1 *absol.* 7. Cf. Plut. *Marc.* 2.3–4 and Val. Max. 6.1.7 for offenses against males.

[17]Paul. *Coll.* 4.2.2.

[18]Plut. *Comp. Lys. et Sullae* 3.2. The reliability of the report has often been doubted: Marshall, "Maesia" 51 n. 16. Santalucia, *DPR* 73, proposes to view this rule as a chapter of the *lex Cornelia sumptuaria.*

[19]See above in the notes for a survey of opinion. Val. Max. 8.1 *absol.* 8 is not convincing evidence on pre-Augustan legislation, but note the reference at Hor. *Serm.* 1.3.105–106. Moreau, *Clodiana Religio* (1982) 28–32, and Robinson, *CLAR* 58, argue that adultery might qualify as *iniuria* (the delict of outrage) in this period.

[20]That the *quaestio* persisted this long is the dominant thesis, represented by Kunkel, "Quaestio" (1963/1974) 74, and defended by Bauman, "*Quaestio*" (1968), against Garnsey, "Adultery Trials" (1967); see also Brasiello, "Desuetudine" (1962/1963).

[21]Liebs, "Provinzialjurisprudenz" (1976) 312 n. 167, cf. 341.

[22]On the *cognitio* procedure, see Buti, "*Cognitio*" (1982).

[23]*PS* 2.26.14. Though the source is postclassical, the penalties it gives are widely accepted as deriving from the Augustan statute. (Cf. Paul. *Coll.* 5.2.2.)

[24]*Tit.* 6.12 (of course, the dowry was rendered useless for remarriage by the stipulation that prevented the woman from remarrying).

[25]On the *iudicium de moribus* and the *retentio propter mores,* see Corbett, *Marriage* 130–150; Cremades and Paricio, *Dos et Virtus* (1983) esp. 49; Venturini, "Matrimonio" (1988) 176–181; Venturini, "Ripudianda" (1988) 259, 260 n. 12, 272; Beaucamp, *Statut* 1.171; Treggiari, *RM* 360–361. Husband's rights were protected against the *fiscus:* Pap. D. 48.20.4.

[26]See Pap. D. 22.5.14; Paul. D. *eod.* 18; Ulp. D. 28.1.20.6.

[27]Ulp. D. 3.2.2.3; Arr. Men. D. 49.16.4.7; Plin. *Ep.* 6.31.5.

[28]Kaser, "Infamia" (1956) 259–260; cf. Mette-Dittmann, *Ehegesetze* (1991) 130. (See in general Chapter 2 above.)

In addition, there was *relegatio in insulam,* separate islands, for both parties.[29] We do not know if the *relegatio* was permanent or for a set period of time.[30] The evidence on this point is of such a quality that some have questioned whether any form of *relegatio* was imposed by the law itself.[31] The contrary view is more convincing, however.[32] The provision stipulating separate islands appears legislative in origin. More important, the early cases where *exilium* (a harsher punishment than *relegatio*) is meted out as an aggravated penalty suggest the *relegatio* was in fact the statutory penalty.[33] *Deportatio* (a later term for *exilium*) is given as a penalty where adultery is combined with incest.[34]

A woman convicted under the Augustan adultery statute was forbidden to remarry.[35] If she did, her new husband was guilty of *lenocinium,* and where adulterous lovers married each other their union was void.[36] The *lex Iulia et Papia* forbade persons caught in the act, as well as those convicted of adultery, to marry the freeborn.[37] Marriage contracted in violation of this ban rendered the spouses *caelibes* under the marriage statute; an *SC* passed under Marcus and Commodus went further and declared totally void unions that violated the prohibitions imposed on the *ordo senatorius.*[38] Women were also compelled to wear the toga as a symbol of their shame.[39]

Later law established the death penalty. The references to this penalty in sources from before the death of Constantine[40] have been convincingly shown to be interpolated.[41] Aside from a special case involving slaves convicted of adultery, the death penalty makes its first legitimate appearance in a law of Constantine's sons.[42] The postclassical development itself is disputed.[43]

Those guilty of a type of complicity identified by the law as *lenocinium* were subjected to the same penalties as adulterers; in fact, all accessories to the main

---

[29] The sole explicit legal source is the postclassical *PS* 2.26.14, which insists on separation of the guilty couple: "dummodo in diversas insulas relegentur."

[30] Sehling, "Strafsystem" (1883) 162, holds for the latter, basing his conclusion on the provisions against remarriage and giving testimony.

[31] Brasiello, *Repressione* (1937) 93–96; Branca, *ED* adulterio (1958) 621; Bauman, "*Quaestio*" 80 n. 95; Rilinger, *Humiliores* (1988) 177; Venturini, "*Accusatio*" (1988) 88 n. 61.

[32] See also Biondi, "Poena" (1938/1965) 50–57; Garnsey, *Status* (1970) 116.

[33] Tac. *Ann.* 2.85.1–3, with Suet. *Tib.* 35.2; Tac. *Ann.* 3.24.

[34] Marci. D. 48.18.5: "duplex crimen."

[35] For the prohibition against remarriage, see Ulp. D. 48.5.30(29).1 (more evidence in Beaucamp, *Statut* 1.165 n. 150, cf. 169 n. 176).

[36] Pap. D. 34.9.13.

[37] Ulp. D. 23.2.43.12–13 (*Tit.* 13.2 shows a later extension of the principle). See Chapter 3.

[38] Astolfi, *LIP²* (1986) 114–119.

[39] On the penalty of the toga, see below.

[40] Alex. Sev. C. 9.9.9 (a. 224); Diocl., Max. C. 2.4.18 (a. 293); and Constantin. C. 9.9.29(30).4 (a. 326). Inst. 4.18.4 falsely claims to derive this penalty from the statute itself.

[41] Esmein, "Délit" 111–112; Biondi, "Poena"; against the view of Mommsen, *Strafrecht* 699, who argued for introduction in the third century. See now Beaucamp, *Statut* 1.166, with n. 157.

[42] Constantius, Constans CTh. 11.36.4 (a. 339).

[43] Biondi rather improbably attempts to derive it from the *ius occidendi* (on this right of self-help recognized by the law, see the discussion below). Better are Venturini, "*Accusatio*" 68; Bonini, *RDG²* (1990) 109–112, 151–153; Beaucamp, *Statut* 1.168.

crime were punished, by the late classical period at least, in the same way as the principals.[44] In time, most accessory crimes under the statute came to be identified as *lenocinium*.[45] We are not informed as to the statutory penalties for *stuprum*.[46]

The law did not, to all appearances, offer a definition of the acts it outlawed. There was a simple prohibition of *stuprum* and *adulterium,* qualified by the requirement of a *mens rea*.[47] The jurists complain that the law did not distinguish adequately between the two principal crimes but used the words *stuprum* and *a-dulterium* indiscriminately.[48] Properly speaking, *stuprum,* although in a generic sense it might refer to any type of illicit sexual activity (even adultery), meant, under this law, fornication with an unmarried woman who was not exempt from the statutory penalties, whereas *adulterium* was the sexual offense committed with a nonexempt married woman.[49]

This point is of crucial importance. The question of liability under the law always depended, as we have seen, on the status of the female partner to the sexual act, a status that the law defined only (aside from scattered references to the *mater familias*) in the negative. This was accomplished by setting forth, expressly or by implication, certain categories of women with whom sexual relations might be enjoyed without fear of prosecution. In this way, Augustus drastically curtailed the range of possible sexual partners for Roman males outside marriage, at least insofar as this range was defined at law. Exempt women eventually included prostitutes, procuresses, slaves, convicted adulteresses, and peregrines not wed to Roman citizens.[50]

The status of the male partner was thus immaterial to the definition of a sexual act as *adulterium* or *stuprum* under the law. He might be slave or free, married or unmarried, citizen or peregrine. A married man who had sexual relations with a woman not his wife did not commit *adulterium* unless the woman was married to another man and was not exempt. A wife could not charge her own husband with adultery, although the mere fact that this question was raised should caution us against accepting that the Romans held a husband to have no moral duty of fidelity to his wife. A declaratory rescript, addressed to a woman, of Severus and Caracalla states unambiguously that the statute expressly denied women the right to bring accusations, "although they might wish to lodge a complaint about an outrage to their own marriage."[51] Women were generally excluded from bringing accusations in the criminal courts unless they themselves or a member of their household were

[44] For *lenocinium,* see Pap. D. 48.5.9(8) pr.: "quasi adulter."

[45] See the discussion below. Note that the wife who accepts money "ex adulterio viri" is punished "quasi adultera": Marci. D. 48.5.34(33).2.

[46] Sehling, "Strafsystem" 160, argues that they were identical to those laid down for adultery. I agree, though it is difficult to see how the financial penalties can have held much weight for, say, an unmarried daughter-in-power.

[47] Ulp. (1 *de adult.*) D. 48.5.13(12): "Haec verba legis ''ne quis posthac stuprum adulterium facito sciens dolo malo'' et ad eum, qui suasit, et ad eum, qui stuprum vel adulterium intulit, pertinent."

[48] See Pap. D. 48.5.6.1 (cf. Ulp. D. *eod.* 14[13].2); Mod. D. *eod.* 35(34) pr.; *Mod.* D. 50.16.101 pr.

[49] For a careful study of the terminology see Rizzelli, "*Stuprum.*" The statute's inexactness reflects usage: see Cic. *Cael.* 49, 50, and the other examples collected by Rizzelli.

[50] The question of the exempt categories is explored below, in the section on exemptions.

[51] Sev., Ant. C. 9.9.1 (a. 197): "quamvis de matrimonio suo violato queri velint."

victims.[52] So a woman prosecuting her husband for adultery would only be pursuing a wrong done by him and his partner to her husband, in the conception of the law.[53]

At the very least, the husband was expected to set a good example. Ulpian instructs the judge trying an adultery case to inquire into the morals of the husband.[54] A misbehaving husband might be penalized with respect to the dowry upon dissolution of marriage.[55] Wives' tolerance of unfaithful husbands should not be exaggerated.[56] But the law, by defining fault in terms of the gender of each party, remains "asymmetrical."[57]

The *lex Iulia de adulteriis coercendis,* like most other criminal statutes, allowed anyone "*quivis ex populo*" to launch an accusation, aside from a few stated exceptions. These were the "*infames,*" who were individually identified in the law itself, as with other statutes inaugurating a *quaestio perpetua*. Peregrines, *pupilli* (where their own interests were not concerned and the permission of their guardian was lacking), and freedmen with a patrimony of less than HS 30,000 or without a son were excluded, as were women, men younger than 25 years old (under this law), and sons-in-power without the permission of their *pater familias*.[58]

Unlike other criminal laws, this statute created a special right of accusation, the *ius mariti vel patris,* accorded to the husband and father of the woman accused of adultery. The right of the father is correctly described as accessory to that of the husband, in the sense that it depended on an act of the latter (divorce) to be legitimized and that where both raised an accusation the husband was to be preferred.[59] There was no privileged accusation for the father in case of *stuprum*.[60] Another unusual feature of the law is its rule that accusations could not be brought after five years had passed from the date of the commission of the offense.[61] Later law restricted the right of prosecution to close kin, placing primary responsibility on the husband.[62]

The privileged accusation had six major benefits.[63] These were (1) exclusive rights of prosecution for 60 *dies utiles* (counting only the days when accusations could actually be brought) after divorce;[64] (2) admission as prosecutors of those otherwise excluded by the statute, such as "*infames,*" minors, freedmen insuffi-

---

[52] Gardner, *Women* (1986) 127, with Pap. D. 48.2.2 pr.

[53] Beaucamp, *Statut* 1.140 n. 6. For an explanation of the relative rarity of accusations of adultery launched against men, see Golden (rev. Rawson) (1988) 79.

[54] Ulp. D. 48.5.14(13).5 (based on a *constitutio* of Caracalla reported by Augustine: *Con. Ad.* 2.8); see De Churruca, "Rescrit" (1995) Cf. Sen. *Ep.* 94.26; Iuv. 6.41–47; [Quint.] *Decl. fr.* 3.

[55] *Tit.* 6.13.

[56] See Schmähling, *Censoren* (1938) 35 n. 73, on Val. Max. 6.7.1.

[57] See Beaucamp, *Statut* 1.139–140, 170, 178 *(stuprum).* Compare Treggiari, *RM* 264, who defines the structure of the offense as triangular rather than bilateral.

[58] See Mommsen, *Strafrecht* 368–372.

[59] Rizzelli, "Accusa" (1986) 422–423.

[60] Pap. D. 48.5.23(22).1.

[61] See Thomas, "Prescription" (1962).

[62] Constantinus CTh. 9.7.2 (a. 326). See Evans Grubbs, *Law* (1995) 208–215.

[63] I rely principally on two articles by Ankum: "*Captiva*" (1985) and "*Sponsa*" (1987).

[64] If this period passed without action by husband or father, other prosecutors *(extranei)* were admitted over a four-month period: Ulp. D. 48.5.30(29).5–8; other sources in Mommsen, *Strafrecht* 698 nn. 2, 3, 4.

ciently wealthy or fertile, sons-in-power without permission of *pater familias*; (3) admission of those who were already conducting two simultaneous prosecutions in the *iudicia publica* (the limit imposed by the *lex Iulia iudiciorum publicorum* of 17 B.C.); (4) eligibility for simplified procedural formalities; (5) exemption from *calumnia* (although this was controversial for a time); (6) the right to submit the slaves belonging to the married couple and accused lover to the torture, as well as any slaves placed at their disposition by their parents.[65]

Husbands were also admitted to an adultery prosecution where the marriage was not valid because *conubium* was lacking, as were the male partners in concubinage where the relationship was defined as serious and stable. In such cases, the prosecutor was entitled only to the unprivileged *ius extranei,* but in the late classical law he could still avail himself of several of the benefits associated with the privileged accusation. He could, upon showing good cause for his delay, displace a third-party prosecutor even after the 60-day delay or raise an accusation after a trial conducted by an *extraneus* had resulted in acquittal.[66] All of the status exemptions listed above were eventually carried over to the "husband" prosecuting *iure extranei.*[67] Freedom from *calumnia* was guaranteed by a constitution of Alexander Severus.[68] The right to the *quaestio servorum* was granted by Marcus Aurelius and confirmed by subsequent emperors, a privilege apparently permitted to all *extranei,* not just the offended "husband." In this way sexual infidelity was punished where the wife was a peregrine, younger than the legal age for marriage (12 years for females), related closely enough to the husband so that the relationship was itself incest, or in some limited situations where marriage was not intended (or not yet intended), as with *sponsae* and certain types of concubines.[69]

Another important feature of the law was the so-called *ius occidendi.*[70] This granted the offended husband and father the right to kill the guilty party or parties on the spot. Here the respective positions of the privileged pair were the reverse of what we find with the *ius accusandi:* the father was given pride of place. He might kill both daughter and lover but under no circumstances might the husband kill his wife. Failure to observe this rule resulted in liability for murder under the *lex Cornelia,* although the penalty might be mitigated upon appeal to the emperor. The husband was permitted to exercise his right upon the lover only if the man fell within a special category of persons defined by the law: slaves, freedmen of family members, or certain disreputable types.

Upon closer inspection, the *ius occidendi* turns out to have been hedged about with restrictions. The father could only kill the lover if he also dispatched his daughter. Both father and husband might exercise their right only if they discovered the guilty pair in the house of father or husband, if the discovery was made while

[65] On this unusual privilege, see Liebs, "Schutz" (1980) esp. 151–152, 168–169; Schumacher, *Servus Index* (1982) esp. 119.
[66] Ulp. D. 48.5.4.2.
[67] Ankum, "*Captiva*" 172, argues that the prohibition against more than two simultaneous criminal prosecutions was relaxed in this case too.
[68] Alex. Sev. C. 9.9.6.1 (a. 223).
[69] Ankum, "*Sponsa*" esp. 178–182, 188–198.
[70] On this see the discussion below.

the lovers were engaged in sexual intercourse, and if the remedy was applied *sua manu*. These requirements were interpreted in a restrictive manner by the jurists. The idea was obviously to discourage self-help, especially abuses of self-help, and to move the entire matter before a court, where the titularies to the *ius occidendi* could exercise their right to the privileged accusation. The role that the adultery statute designs for these male members of the family reflects the mixture of innovation and tradition characteristic of the law overall.[71] Another aim was to create a subsidiary deterrent to the commission of adultery, at least of a particularly flagrant or objectionable kind.[72]

The *lex Iulia* lowered the status of the wife found guilty of adultery to that of the prostitute and correspondingly defined the actions of the complaisant husband as *lenocinium*. At the same time it exempted true prostitutes and (probably) procuresses from its sanctions.[73] They were able to practice their professions without fear of prosecution for adultery, *stuprum*, or *lenocinium*. In short, the law created certain statuses for women, statuses that were defined in terms of a traditional complex of values that established a firm connection between social rank and acceptable sexual behavior.

2. The Status of the *Mater Familias*

The definition of an extramarital sexual act as a crime, and its further classification as *adulterium* or *stuprum,* always depended on the female partner. That is, it only mattered whether she was married or single, free or slave, a member of an exempted profession or not. The status of the male partner was irrelevant to this end. The *lex Iulia* created a broad category in order to indicate what women were liable for either offense. It did not, however, define this category explicitly or give any details that might suggest a definition. The evidence shows that the status of *mater familias* or *matrona* was the sole positive criterion for establishing a woman's liability under the law. This point is deducible from the meager evidence for the statute itself. Fortunately, it is possible to obtain a better understanding of what this standard meant in practice by supplementing this evidence with the commentary of the late classical jurists, together with literary texts much closer in date to the law's passage.

Papinian's definition of *mater familias* suggests that this term was used in the law to refer to those women potentially liable to its sanctions:

Pap. (2 *de adult.*) D. 48.5.11(10) pr.: Mater autem familias significatur non tantum nupta, sed etiam vidua.

Moreover, *mater familias* means not only a married woman but also an unmarried woman.[74]

<hr>

[71] See Mette-Dittmann, *Ehegesetze* 207.
[72] See the discussion below.
[73] Since the definition of the sexual act as a crime was linked to the status of the female partner, male prostitutes and pimps were not exempt from the law.
[74] The unusually broad phrasing for the translation of *vidua* receives justification below.

No reference to *mater familias* occurred in the context of the statute's description of the two principal crimes. To judge from Ulpian's quotation of this part of the law, the text was rather vague:[75]

> Ulp. (1 *de adult.*) D. 48.5.13(12): Haec verba legis "ne quis posthac stuprum adulterium facito sciens dolo malo" et ad eum, qui suasit, et ad eum, qui stuprum vel adulterium intulit, pertinent.
>
> The words of the statute "let no one hereafter knowingly and with wrongful intention commit criminal fornication or adultery" apply both to him who counsels either crime and to him who (forcibly)[76] performs the act.

It is possible that a phrase like "cum matre familias" has dropped out of the text owing to an abbreviation made by the jurist or the compilers, but the greater likelihood is that the law was no more explicit than this evidence suggests.[77] This means in effect that the legislator failed to define precisely a standard of liability. Reference to this was made only in indirect fashion. One of these references occurs in the context of the prohibition of providing a venue for lovers' trysts:

> Paul. (3 *de adult.*) D. 48.2.3.3: . . . quod domum suam praebuit, ut stuprum mater familias pateretur . . .
>
> . . . that someone made his house available for an act of *stuprum* to be committed with a *mater familias* . . .
>
> Pap. (2 *de adult.*) D. 48.5.9(8) pr.: Qui domum suam, ut stuprum adulteriumve cum aliena matre familias vel cum masculo fieret, sciens praebuerit vel quaestum ex adulterio uxoris suae fecerit: cuiuscumque sit condicionis, quasi adulter punitur.
>
> He who knowingly provides his own house so that an act of *stuprum* or adultery be committed with another's *mater familias* or with a male, or makes a profit from the adultery of his own wife, is punished as an adulterer, whatever his status.[78]

Tryphoninus, in the context of a discussion of the inadequacy of actor's mental state alone for the definition of an offense, makes the point in the negative:

---

[75] I argue elsewhere that this vagueness was deliberate. The offense was certainly stated in more concise fashion than one finds in Republican statutes: Bauman, "*Leges*" (1980) 132.

[76] *Inferre stuprum* and *inferre adulterium*, in my view, signify forcible rape: *L & S* s.v. *infero* II A; *OLD* s.h.v. 9a. Liability under the adultery law held only for the rapist: Ulp. D. 48.5.14(13).7.

[77] One might read "-ve" as in Tryph. D. 4.4.37.1 and Pap. D. 48.5.9(8) pr. rather than take the two key words as a catachresis, as does Rizzelli, "*Stuprum*" 384, with n. 102. Daube, "Lex Julia" (1972) 378, asserts of this passage "here is the main crime of the *lex Julia*." On the phrase *sciens dolo malo*, see MacCormack, "*Sciens*" (1984), who asserts that the inclusion of the phrase in the adultery law is superfluous. But the requirement for an act to be accomplished *sciens dolo malo* was of crucial importance for liability in cases of rape (Ulp. D. 48.5.14[13].7), deception (Pap. D. *eod.* 12[11].12), and simple ignorance of a situation of fact (Iul.-Gaius D. *eod.* 44[43]).

[78] On this final phrase, see Rilinger, *Humiliores* 177 n. 129.

Tryph. (1 *disp.*) D. 50.16.225: ... nam et furem adulterum aleatorem quamquam aliqua significatione ex animi propositione cuiusque sola quis dicere posset, ut etiam is, qui numquam alienam rem invito domino subtraxerit, numquam alienam matrem familias corruperit, <numquam alea luserit,>[79] si modo eius mentis sit, ut occasione data id commissurus sit, tamen oportere eadem haec crimina adsumpto actu intellegi ...

... For although someone might describe a person as a thief, adulterer, or gambler to some effect solely on the basis of the man's mental state, so that even he (might be thought to qualify) who never made off with another's property without permission of the owner, never seduced another's *mater familias,* <or never gambled>, provided he possesses the intent to carry out the act if the opportunity presents itself; nonetheless, one must realize that these offenses are committed only when the act itself is carried out. ...

The law may similarly have referred to the *matrona* as a woman potentially liable to it.[80] This emerges from a text of Ulpian that discusses the question of liability in terms of the *nomen matronae.*[81] It is easy to imagine places in the statute where the term *matrona* may have appeared. One possible context is the law's stipulation of proper dress for matrons: "They generally used to call those women who had the right to wear the stola matrons."[82]

At one point the law may refer to a *femina,*[83] which would be evidence of a certain inconsistency in terminology, especially credible given the law's confusion of *stuprum* and *adulterium.* The fact that, in contemporary official usage, the terms *matrona* and *mater familias* were used interchangeably supports this view. The inscription recording the Ludi Saeculares of 17 B.C. gives both terms, and while one might expect a document of this kind to preserve an archaic distinction, they are given apparently with indifference as to meaning.[84] The commentators treat the terms as equivalents.[85] It is interesting that in the inscription *matres familias* is qualified by *nuptae.* This usage, which suggests a deliberate qualification of a *mater familias* as a married woman,[86] is remarkable.[87] Of course, *mater familias* might bear this meaning by itself (see below), but the combination is plausibly explained by the contemporary appearance in the *lex Iulia* of *mater familias* without qualification to mean both married and unmarried women.

[79] Mommsen and Krüger ad loc.
[80] McGinn, *Social Policy* (1986) 188–201; cf. Bassanelli Sommariva, "Considerazioni" (1988) 318; Beaucamp, *Statut* 1.202–203; Treggiari, *RM* 279.
[81] Ulp. (2 *de adult.*) D. 48.5.14(13) pr. Cf. below and Tert. *Uxorem* 2.18.3.
[82] Fest. 112L: "matronas appellabant eas fere, quibus stolas habendi ius erat."
[83] Scaev. D. 48.5.15(14) pr. See Chapter 6 on this text.
[84] *CIL* 6.4.2.32323 (78, 80, 101, 109, 112, 123, 125–126, 130–131, 138; cf. *feminae* at 73 and 114, *mulieres* at 71). The same holds for the Severan *Commentaria* of A.D. 204.
[85] Mommsen, "Commentaria" (1913) 600–601, 613–614; Gagé, *Jeux* (1934) 61–64; Pighi, *Ludis²* (1965) 264–265.
[86] So Humbert, *Remariage* (1972) 55 n. 26.
[87] Cf. Tac. *Ann.* 15.44.1.

A number of sources point to an identical meaning for *mater familias* and *matrona*.[88] Both are often applied to *viduae* and *virgines*.[89] This relatively extensive meaning predates the *lex Iulia*.[90] Much of the literary evidence, from the period subsequent to the law's passage and examined below, shows that both terms were used rather frequently to refer to woman potentially liable under the adultery statute.

It is not absolutely necessary to assume that the word *matrona* was found in the law. The expression *nomen matronae* predates the *lex Iulia,* occurring as early as the comic poet Afranius a century before.[91] It is an obvious truth that if both *matrona* and *mater familias* were used as early as Cicero in the extended sense of "respectable woman," the former term did not have to appear in the law in order to be employed, even in legal sources, with the same meaning afterward. The statute also inspired usages that can be understood as equivalents of *nomen matronae,* such as *honestas matris familias*[92] and *nomen matris familias.*[93]

This assessment of the contemporary meaning of *mater familias* does not, however, provide a certain answer to the question of what role the term played under the regime established by the *lex Iulia.* Two questions may be raised. What did the law itself intend by the phrase? What did the jurists understand it to mean? The second is by far the easier to answer. In Papinian's definition of *mater familias,* the inclusion of *viduae* shows that by the Severan period the term embraced widows and divorced women, a conclusion supported by a similar definition from Ulpian.[94] Contemporary evidence shows that *mater familias* could also mean a woman never married, that is, a *virgo.*[95] That Papinian certainly did not mean to exclude such women is suggested by the fact that in juristic usage the term *vidua* itself might signify "woman never married"[96] and is confirmed by the following two passages, which treat the issue of liability relatively fully:[97]

> Pap. (1 *de adult.*) D. 48.5.6.1: Lex stuprum et adulterium promiscue et *katach-rēstikōteron* appellat. sed proprie adulterium in nupta committitur, propter partum

[88] See Kunkel, *RE* mater familias (1930) 2184 (section 3); Schroff, *RE* matrona (1930) 2300–2301 (Schroff's definition of *matrona* is too narrow); Fuchs, "Frau" (1960) 36. Treggiari, *RM* 414, makes an interesting distinction: after marriage, a woman was "a man's wife and *mater familias,* and to the outside world a *matrona.*" On the interchangeable usage of these terms, see also *TLL* s.v. *matrona* 486.40–49.

[89] *TLL* s.v. *matrona* 484.15–27, 486.26–39, 50–57; s.v. *mater familias* 440.

[90] See above all Cic. *Cael.* 32, 57, where both terms appear as equivalents for "respectable unmarried woman." At Nepos *praef.* 6, *mater familias* appears with the sense of "respectable woman." See the nearly contemporary Liv. 8.22.3: *stuprata mater familias.*

[91] Daviault, *Comoedia* (1981) 227 (*apud* Non. Marc. 225L).

[92] Marcel. D. 23.2.41.1

[93] Constantinus C. 9.9.28(29) (a. 326) (= CTh. 9.7.1, which lacks the phrase in question).

[94] Ulp. D. 50.16.46.1; see below.

[95] Tert. *Virg. Vel.* 11.6: "mater familiae vocatur, licet virgo, et pater familiae, licet investis." The text suggests a parallel meaning of "respectable man" for *pater familias,* which finds a juristic parallel: Ulp. D. 34.2.23.2. See also the use of the term in Petron. 8.

[96] Lab.-Iav. (2 *ex post. Lab.*) D. 50.16.242.3. See Penta, "Viduitas" (1980) 343–345; Peppe, *Posizione* (1984) 49, 140–142. Similarly, for *vacans,* see Beaucamp, *Statut* 1.107 n. 1.

[97] The passages given in the text raise problems that cannot be dealt with here; see the recent treatment by Rizzelli, "Stuprum" 375–388. On liability under the law for sex with males, see above. It is possible to identify at least one section of the law that did not distinguish *adulterium* and *stuprum*; see below.

ex altero conceptum composito nomine: stuprum vero in virginem viduamve committitur, quod Graeci *phthoran* appellant.

The law refers to *stuprum* and adultery indiscriminately and rather contrary to the true sense of these terms. But, properly speaking, adultery is committed with a married woman, the term being derived from the begetting of children by another man; *stuprum,* however, is committed against a woman never married or a widow; the Greeks call it "corruption."

Mod. (1 *reg.*) D. 48.5.35(34).1: Adulterium in nupta admittitur: stuprum in vidua vel virgine vel puero committitur.

Adultery is committed with a married woman; *stuprum* is committed with a widow or divorced woman, a woman never married, or a boy.

In the following text, Modestinus speaks only of *viduae* being liable for *stuprum:*

Mod. (9 *diff.*) D. 50.16.101 pr.: Inter "stuprum" et "adulterium" hoc interesse quidam putant, quod adulterium in nuptam, stuprum in viduam committitur. sed lex Iulia de adulteriis hoc verbo indifferenter utitur.

Some people think that there is this difference between *stuprum* and adultery, that adultery is committed against a married woman, *stuprum* against a widow or divorced woman, but the *lex Iulia* on adultery uses this word indifferently.

The same contradiction emerges with Modestinus as with Papinian. In two texts the jurists give *viduae* and *virgines* as potentially liable to *stuprum*; in another only *viduae*. One might argue for abbreviation by the compilers as an explanation for the latter, but it seems easier to conclude that the jurists use the word *vidua* in two different senses, the usual meaning of "widow" or "divorced woman" and the more extensive meaning developed by Labeo, which includes women never before married.[98]

At all events, the late classical jurists accepted that the standard of liability laid down by the statute embraced women regardless of marital status. The exempt categories examined below instruct us that not just any woman qualified, however. A *mater familias* was a woman of respectable moral and social status, at least according to the mature juristic definition of the term.

The same can be said for the meaning of *mater familias* in the law itself. There is no satisfactory text of the legislation, and we have no juristic testimony from the early Principate on this point, but there is an abundance of literary evidence. Just before and just after the passage of the *lex Iulia, mater familias* was used as the *mot juste* for a woman with whom adultery or *stuprum* is committed.[99] It thereby functions as a prestige term, one that conveys a certain sense of social rank

---

[98] I believe that the latter meaning appears, again with reference to the adultery law, at Pap. D. 48.5.23(22).1. On the extensive interpretation of this term by the jurists, see Mayer-Maly, *RE* vidua (1958) 2098, 2104–2105.

[99] Liv. 8.22.3 (cf. 10.31.9, 25.2.9 [*matronae*]); Val. Max. 6.1.8 and 8 *absol.* 12; cf. Sen. *Ep.* 97.5. *Rhet. Her.* 4.8.12 may refer to rape.

and appropriate sexual responsibility. Perhaps for this reason it was preferred by the legislator, even at the cost of some obscurity over precisely who was subject to the law. This cost should not be exaggerated, however. As argued below, the obscurity in meaning was entirely deliberate and consistent with the law's purpose.

It is well known that *mater familias* enjoyed a wide range of meaning in the classical period.[100] Kunkel has shown that the term had four different meanings: originally wife *in manu*, then by extension a wife in any legitimate marriage, then a woman of good morals whether married or not, and, finally, a specialized usage, a woman *sui iuris*. Kunkel argues that the *lex Iulia* adopted the second sense given, noting that widows were embraced by the statute. This makes sense in chronological terms, since he is able to demonstrate that *mater familias* is used to denote "wife" in Caesar, Cicero, and Livy.[101]

Kunkel's third category, however, is more appropriate for the *lex Iulia*.[102] In connection with this category, he notes the transition from the meaning of "wife" to that of "woman of good morals" by remarking that "the *mater familias,* as lawful wife, stands in a moral contrast to the *meretrix* and to the *concubina.*"[103] The *lex Iulia* recognized the first of these two contrasts and elevated it to the level of a sociolegal paradigm. The contrast itself was hardly an invention of the law but was deeply rooted in Roman ideas about social status and sexual morality.[104] This is why the law punished sexual relations with unmarried respectable women *(stuprum).*[105]

A favorite device of Plautus and Terence,[106] this juxtaposition was so familiar that the two statuses could be introduced as easily understood opposites for even a mundane point of comparison (again, *matrona* was a synonym for *mater familias*). So Laberius has a woman express regret at her fall from grace by invoking the pair.[107] Cicero uses it in an especially apt manner, given that the context is a discussion of Epicurean ethics.[108] Another example is from Horace, writing shortly before the passage of the *lex Iulia.*[109]

---

[100] I follow the reconstruction of Kunkel, *RE mater familias* 2183–2184. See also Wolodkiewicz, "*Mater familias*" (1983). Wolodkiewicz has three definitions to Kunkel's four, omitting (respectable) married women as a separate category. But this definition almost certainly had a historical importance as the meaning of the term evolved. The archaizing definitions found in Cic. *Top.* 14 and Gell. 18.6.9 are properly viewed with skepticism.

[101] Treggiari, *RM* 34–35, traces the meaning of "honorable wife" to Plautus and Terence.

[102] Similarly, Wolodkiewicz, "*Mater familias*" 751.

[103] Similarly, Kaser, "Rechtswidrigkeit" (1940) 133–134.

[104] Grimal, "Matrona" (1985) 199, speculates that it dates back to the very early Republic.

[105] Concern with the sexual behavior of widows predates the law: Treggiari, *RM* 500.

[106] There are no fewer than four explicit examples from Plautus: *Cas.* 585; *Cist.* 78–80; *Miles* 789–793; *Most.* 190. See the discussion in Schuhmann, "Charakteristik" (1983). See also Ter. *Ad.* 746–747.

[107] Non. Marc. 89L (= Lab. 33–35R): "Quo quidem me a matronali pudore prolubium meretricie [R. has "meretricium"] progredi coegit." On the adultery mime, see Reynolds, "Mime" (1945); McKeown, "Elegy" (1979); Kehoe, "Mime" (1984); Leppin, *Histrionen* (1992) 26.

[108] Cic. *Fin.* 2.12: "Quid enim necesse est, tamquam meretricem in matronarum coetum, sic voluptatem in virtutum concilium adducere?" Cf. *Phil.* 2.105.

[109] Hor. *Ep.* 1.18.3–4: "Ut matrona meretrici dispar erit atque/discolor infido scurrae distabit amicus." The first book of the *Epistles* was published about 20 B.C.: Conte, *LL* (1994) 753.

The contrast between respectable women and prostitutes was, if anything, strengthened by the law. In an important passage Ovid contrasts prostitutes first with *matronae,* then with Vestals.[110] The law's creation of the sociolegal status of *mater familias* also guaranteed a broad field of application. From the beginning, unmarried women were liable as well. *Mater familias* no longer simply meant "wife"; the application of the term now endowed a woman with a certain moral status.[111]

Besides the moral element, properly emphasized by Kunkel, we should add another factor, which is social status. The law, of course, made neither of these explicit, but its use of *mater familias* was clearly understood in this way and probably thus intended. The criteria of moral and social standing were crucial; marital status itself was nonessential, as Kunkel himself has shown. Confirmation comes from the following passage, though this is drawn from another context:[112]

> Ulp. (59 *ad edictum*) D. 50.16.46.1: "Matrem familias" accipere debemus eam, quae non inhoneste vixit: matrem enim familias a ceteris feminis mores discernunt atque separant. proinde nihil intererit, nupta sit an vidua, ingenua sit an libertina: nam neque nuptiae neque natales faciunt matrem familias, sed boni mores.

> We ought to define as *mater familias* a woman who has not lived dishonorably; for it is moral character that separates and distinguishes her from other women. So it will make no difference if she is married or unmarried, freeborn or freed, for neither marital status nor status at birth makes a *mater familias,* but proper behavior.

Strictly speaking, Ulpian emphasizes only the moral criterion, but I think that the social element is not far out of the picture. The jurist in essence concedes that there is more than one way to classify women. More important than marital status or birth, for the definition of *mater familias,* is moral character.[113] One finds the social aspect implied in the following:[114]

> Ulp. (71 *ad edictum*) D. 43.30.3.6: . . . cum audis matrem familias, accipe notae auctoritatis feminam.

> . . . by *mater familias* you must understand a woman of known reputation.

A number of passages that refer to a special and distinct costume for the *mater familias* (or *matrona*) in the period following the law's passing support the argu-

---

[110] Ovid. *Tr.* 2.309–312: "Saepe supercilii nudas matrona severi/et veneris stantis ad genus omne videt./corpora Vestales oculi meretricia cernunt,/nec domino poenae res ea causa fuit."

[111] For this reason the prostitute ideally enjoyed greater physical freedom with her partner than the married woman: Dixon, *TRF* 87.

[112] Lenel, *Pal.* (1889/1960) 2 col. 779; Lenel, *EP*[3] (1923/1974) 411–412. The text is a comment on the edictal rubric "qui neque sequantur neque ducantur," which deals with personal execution. See further Kaser, *RZ* (1966) 300, 406–407.

[113] See Penta, "Viduitas" 349–351.

[114] This passage is drawn from Ulpian's commentary on the praetorian interdicts *de liberis exhibendis et ducendis,* which provided for the producing of children in court for the purposes of identification and safe return to their proper home: Lenel, *EP*[3] 488; Kaser, *RP* 1[2] (1971) 342–343. Cf. *honesta matrona* at Ulp. D. 25.4.1.6.

ment that the *lex Iulia* itself took up the already existing paradigm of "respectable woman" and strengthened, broadened, and clarified it through the creation of a new sociolegal status. Clothing's role as a status marker receives repeated recognition from the jurists.[115] I reserve for discussion in the next section the evidence that draws a contrast between matrons' dress and that of prostitutes.

Decisive for my present purpose is Ovid's frequent mention of certain garments typically associated with matrons, such as the stola, a long dress with embroidered hem, and the *vittae*, fillets worn in the hair.[116] Especially noteworthy are those places in the amatory poems where the poet purports to exclude certain women from his putative audience, defining them precisely in terms of such articles of clothing.[117] In other words, Ovid describes women liable to the *lex Iulia* in terms of their distinctive dress. The chronology of his work makes him a crucial witness, but of course he is not the only one to make the point.[118]

The legislation did not invent this association: important social distinctions had long been manifested in the style and color of garments,[119] and the stola in particular was already considered a garment characteristic of married women.[120] We know that the question of appropriate dress for women was thought to be a problem of some urgency in the Augustan period. It was one of the topics treated by the emperor in a discourse he held before the Senate on the general theme of control of female sexual behavior just before the adultery statute was passed.[121]

Augustus's interventions in the field of clothing merit brief review.[122] He enjoined the aediles to enforce public wearing of the toga in the center of Rome and forbade wearers of dark-colored garments (i.e., not the toga)[123] to sit in the *media cavea* of the theater.[124] He renewed the annual equestrian *transvectio*, whose participants wore a new uniform of *trabea* and crown of olive leaves.[125] Members of the Senate and their sons were allowed the privilege of the *latus clavus*, the broad purple stripe on the tunic that signified membership in that order.[126] Cassius Dio

---

[115] Ulpian has a well-known discussion of what clothing is appropriate for the status, gender, and age of the wearer. Ulp. (44 *ad Sabinum*) D. 34.2.23.2: "muliebria . . . penulae" (cf. Ulp. D. *eod.* 25.10).

[116] *Ars* 1.31–34 (= *Tr.* 2.247–250) (*vittae tenues, instita longa:* the latter was the embroidered hem of the stola), 2.600 *(instita)*, 3.483–484 *(vitta); RA* 386 *(vitta); Tr.* 2.251–252 *(stola, vitta); Ep. ex Pont.* 3.3.49–58 *(vitta, stola longa).*

[117] *Ars* 1.31–34 (with *Tr.* 247–250), 2.600, 3.483–484; *RA* 386. In a passage written in exile he contends that the *Ars Amatoria* was written only for prostitutes: *Tr.* 2.303–304.

[118] See, e.g., Sen. *NQ* 7.31.2; Mart. 1.35.8–9.

[119] See, e.g., Culham, "Colour" (1986) 239; Weiler, "Verhalten" (1988) 179–180.

[120] Bieber, *RE* stola (1931) esp. 58–60; Wilson, *Clothing* (1938) 155–156. Note in particular *CIL* 1² 1570 (= 10.6009): "hic me decoraat stola" (of a freedwoman married to her patrons' son). See Varro *LL* 8.28, 9.48, 10.27, on the stola as signifier of gender.

[121] Dio 54.16.3–5.

[122] I know of no comprehensive treatment of this important subject and I do not attempt one here. See the comments of Sensi, "Ornatus" (1980/1981) esp. 78; Zanker, *Power of Images* (1988) 162–166; Goette, *Toga* (1990) esp. 8.

[123] Rawson, "Discrimina" (1987/1991) esp. 510–511.

[124] Suet. *Aug.* 44.2 (cf. 40.5). The strictures on the toga seem to have run against the grain of contemporary practice and had little lasting effect: Talbert, *Senate* (1984) 216.

[125] See Henderson, "Ordo" (1963) 66.

[126] Talbert, *Senate* 216.

tells us that Augustus allowed only senatorial magistrates to wear purple garments.[127]

The legislative résumé given by Suetonius describes the adultery statute as "[sc. legem] de adulteriis et de pudicitia."[128] That the proper dress of matrons played a role is supported by Valerius Maximus's invocation of Pudicitia: "te custode matronalis stola censetur."[129] The language, particularly "custode," may be taken to suggest a law.[130]

The law emphasized the connection between respectability and the stola[131] and broadened its scope by including unmarried, as well as married, women.[132] Similarly, it reinforced the association of the prostitute with the toga. The purpose of this manipulation of symbol and status was to guarantee the dignity of the former group and the disgrace of the latter.[133]

Characteristically for the Augustan social legislation, the *lex Iulia* combined a reassertion of a conservative tradition with an innovative approach, which in this connection was the enforced wearing of the prostitute's toga by the convicted adulteress, the fallen *mater familias*.[134] On a more general level, by casting the traditional elements in the form of positive law, Augustus changed forever their nature and function in society.

Although the law did not say what women were to be included in the category of *mater familias,* it did specify or imply certain exemptions. These were four in number; a fifth was added by the jurists. Few though these were, their very existence meant that *mater familias* could be defined, to an extent, in the negative. Theoretically, a *mater familias* might be any woman not a slave, prostitute, procuress, peregrine, or convicted adulteress. But these exemptions turned out to be less than completely helpful when it came to resolving problems raised by the law's lack of clarity. This point is demonstrated by the number of juristic passages that attempt to address the thorny issue of applicability of the status of *mater familias* and thus the question of potential liability under the law.[135]

To sum up, Augustus, at the same time he exempted prostitutes (and probably procuresses), established a potential liability under the law for the *mater familias*.

[127] Dio 49.16.1.

[128] Suet. *Aug.* 34.1.

[129] "With you as guardian, the matron's stola is given its [moral] rating": Val. Max. 6.1 pr. Prop. 4.11.61 (16 B.C.) suggests the wearing of the stola was an honor to be earned (cf. the *vitta* at 34). Tert. *Apol.* 6.2, though broadly phrased, may embrace this statute's ordinances regarding clothing.

[130] For the hypothesis that the rules concerning clothing formed a separate legislative act, see Badian, "Marriage Law" (1985) 83 n. 3. If so, this law must have been closely tied to the adultery statute. It is less likely that the rules were associated with Augustus's revival of the cult of Pudicitia in 28–27 B.C. (see Palmer, "Shrines" [1974] 137–139) or the marriage law (Biondi, "Leges" [1946/1965] 260).

[131] Unconnected with the law is the much later title *matrona/femina stolata*; see Chapter 3. Fest. 112L (quoted above) does, however, seem to refer to the adultery law.

[132] The law itself apparently did not require outright that these women wear the stola; see the discussion of the evidence from Tertullian below.

[133] Augustus, in the *lex Iulia theatralis,* established special seating in the theater for stola-clad *matronae:* Rawson, "*Discrimina*" 516; Schnurr, "*Lex Julia*" (1992) 151, 160.

[134] His actions find an interesting counterpoint in those of Justinian, for which see below.

[135] Typically, the jurists try to rely on the exemptions, not always a satisfactory approach; see below.

In this way he recast and gave legal force to a social and moral paradigm. At one end was the despised prostitute, sexually promiscuous but exempt from the law's penalties; at the other was the exalted *mater familias,* for whom expectations of sexual conduct as well as penalties for failure to meet them were both very high. The two groups were distinguished by dress; more important, those among the latter group who failed to maintain the standard of sexual conduct defined for them by the law were relegated to the status of the former. This aspect of the *lex Iulia* is discussed more fully in the following section.

One should hesitate before concluding that the vagueness of the law in establishing criteria for liability was the product of carelessness or indeliberateness on the part of the lawmaker. As noted, the law was, like all of the enabling statutes for standing *quaestiones,* designed chiefly with the upper classes in mind. But the standard of liability was evidently intended to apply to a very broad range of Roman women.[136] The few exemptions allowed were narrowly framed in a deliberate manner and not to be freely extended. The emphasis in the above discussion on the role played by the status of *mater familias* as a basis for liability may be a bit misleading.

Indeed, the legislation had a "positive" side, which would have been more visible to the Romans than it is to us. This may fairly be described as the creation of a status to which it should have been the ambition of every free Roman woman to aspire. The *lex Iulia* was an important element in a self-conscious effort to reconstruct a private standard of sexual morality within a new public framework. For the future, the share in honor and the heightened social status that went with it, guaranteed by compliance with the statute, exalted not only individual and household, but the entire citizen community. This satisfaction was now in theory placed within the reach of every woman not relegated to the exempt category. The legislator did not displace the older morality, crystallized in a tradition represented by the myths of Lucretia and Verginia, but gave it a new life, extending the scope of the values it taught beyond the upper reaches of society and linking it more than ever before explicitly to the interest of the state.

3. The *Adultera* as Prostitute

> La pureté est le pouvoir de contempler la souillure.
> —Simone Weil, *La pesanteur et la grâce*

The status of *mater familias* was not the only one to be created by the *lex Iulia.* As part of the established penalty,[137] a woman convicted of adultery was to be publicly humiliated through open identification as a prostitute. This was mainly achieved by stipulating that the *adultera damnata* should wear the toga,[138] which

---

[136] McGinn, *Social Policy* 203; similarly, Treggari, *RM* 298.

[137] On the penalty system, see above.

[138] Divorce, with the attendant prohibition against remarriage, also spelled loss of status: Gardner, *Being* (1993) 148. As did the financial penalties: see above.

heretofore only prostitutes among women had been accustomed to wear. The imposition of this "scarlet letter" seems largely to have escaped the attention of legal scholars, for the reason, perhaps, that there is no legal evidence for it,[139] and it has been misunderstood by many students of *Sittengeschichte,* who make a generalized extension to various types of women.[140]

The literary evidence is abundant enough. First, that regarding prostitutes. There are some early indications that prostitutes wore clothing distinct from that of *matronae.* We begin, however, with the information that at some point in the distant past both men and women wore the toga:[141]

> Non. Marc. 867–868L:[142] Not only men, but even women used to wear the toga. Afranius in his *Fratriae:* "Now, really, the idea of her standing there eating lunch with us dressed in her toga!" Varro, in book 1 of his *De Vita Populi Romani:* "Aside from this fact, they previously used to wear togas while reclining on the dinner couch. For once long ago the toga was the all-purpose garment, worn day and night by women and men."

> Serv. *ad Aen. 1.282:*[143] GENTEMQUE TOGATAM: "Gentem" is nicely put, since both sexes and all social strata used to wear the toga.... moreover, the use of *cyclades* and the *ricinium* [two types of bordered mantles] shows that women too had the toga.

The evidence is inconclusive for regular wearing of the toga by adult Roman women in the early period: it cannot be excluded that Nonius, Servius, and perhaps Varro are generalizing from, or confused by, the wearing of the toga by prostitutes, the use of the *toga praetexta* by respectable girls, or both.[144] If such women did

---

[139] See Esmein, "Délit" 110–117; Mommsen, *Strafrecht* 698–699; Biondi, "Poena"; Branca, *ED* adulterio 621. Gardner, *Women* 252, explicity rejects it, offering instead (see 129) the theory that convicted adulteresses tended to take up the practice of prostitution.

[140] See, e.g., Marquardt, *Privatleben* 1² (1886/1990) 44 n. 1: "die toga [war] aber das Kleid der *meretrices* und aller bescholtenen Frauen, namentlich *iudicio publico damnatae, in adulterio deprehensae....*" Marquardt and Mau cite Heinecke, *Commentarius³* (1747) 130–131, as an authority, although he says nothing of the kind. Many others adopt their conclusion: Wilson, *Toga* (1924) 124; Goethert, *RE* toga (1937) 1652–1653. Others, correctly, have only prostitutes and (after the law) adulteresses wear the toga: Becker, *Gallus²* (1920) 435, 438; Bömer, *Fasten* 2 (1958) 215–216; Courtney, *Juvenal* (1980) 133; Richlin, "Approaches" (1981) 394. I am grateful for the opportunity to have addressed the 1988 NEH summer seminar on Roman dress, whose participants were evidently persuaded by my argument; see, e.g., Goldman, "Clothing" (1994) 228, with n. 7, who alone acknowledges this fact.

[141] The evidence from Afranius in this passage must be discounted, because the woman in question is almost certainly a prostitute: Daviault, *Comoedia* 188 n. 21.

[142] "TOGA non solum viri sed etiam feminae utebantur. Afranius Fratriis: "et quidem prandere stantem nobiscum, incinctam toga." Varro de vita populi Romani lib. 1: "praeterea quod in lecto togas ante habebant. ante enim olim toga fuit commune vestimentum et diurnum et nocturnum et muliebre et virile." "

[143] "GENTEMQUE TOGATAM: Bene *gentem,* quia et sexus omnis et condicio toga utebatur ... togas autem etiam feminas habuisse cycladum et ricini usus ostendit."

[144] There is, I believe, a chance that the sources speak of the *toga praetexta,* a garment worn by Roman girls before puberty in an early period, though the contrast drawn between males and females does not support this. For an instance of an adult woman wearing a toga that is clearly exceptional, see Plin. *NH* 34.28 (Cloelia's equestrian statue). For Afranius, see just above.

so, at some later time respectable women took up other forms of clothing and the toga was retained only by prostitutes:

> Plaut. *Miles* 791–793:[145] . . . and so bring her here, all decked out like a *matrona*, with her hair done right, wearing *vittae*, and have her pretend she's your wife. . . .

Vittae, hair-ribbons, are characteristic of the matron's costume (see below). The plan under discussion is to have a prostitute pose as a respectable woman; a similar operation may be under contemplation in the comedy of Afranius quoted by Nonius:

> Non. Marc. 868L:[146] Prostitutes, according to the works of ancient writers, used to wear a garment that was tucked up rather tightly. Afranius in his *Exceptus:* "A prostitute in a stola?" "When they find themselves in a strange place, they tend to wear it for self-protection."

The *vestis longa* is not a tunic but the matron's stola.[147] Too much weight cannot be placed on *subcinctior vestis,* since Nonius is evidently inferring this directly out of *vestis longa,* but the proper garment for a prostitute can reasonably be identified as the toga.[148]

Nonius quotes a double entendre of the comic writer Titinius:

> Non. Narc. 653L:[149] Even "shelter" can be described as a toga. Titinius in his *Gemina:* "if he decides to head out of town with the whore, I want the keys hidden immediately, so that there be no chance for him of any undercover business in the country"; that is, [no chance] of shelter.

Toga means both "roof" and "prostitute's garment" and then by synecdoche "house (to have sex in)" and "prostitute (to have sex with)."

Finally, Nonius defines *lupari,* using the work of the comic writer Atta:

> Non. Marc. 193L:[150] LUPARI, that is, to act as a whore or be prostituted. Atta in his *Aquae Caldae:* "when like prostitutes they whore their way through the streets dressed like us."

The author evidently criticizes female behavior in connection with a resort, perhaps, like Baiae, in the neighborhood of the Bay of Naples. Without a context, it is impossible to make much sense out of the fragment. The speaker might be a matron indignant at the behavior of prostitutes usurping matronly garb or a prostitute in-

---

[145] ". . . itaque eam huc ornatam adducas ex matronarum modo,/capite compto, crinis vittasque habeat adsimuletque se tuam esse uxorem. . . ."

[146] "MERETRICES apud veteres subcinctiore veste utebantur. Afranius Excepto: "meretrix cum veste longa?" "peregrino in loco solent tutandi causa sese sumere."

[147] Daviault, *Comoedia* 180 n. 12.

[148] See note 141 above for the evidence of Afranius's *Fratriae.*

[149] "Dicitur et tectum [sc., toga]. Titinius Gemina: "si rus cum scorto constituit ire, clavis ilico abstrudi iubeo rusticae togai ne sit copia"; id est, tecti."

[150] "LUPARI, ut scortari vel prostitui. Atta Aquis Caldis: "cum meretricie nostro ornatu per vias lupantur." "

dignant at matrons adopting her mode of dress.[151] The passage does confirm, however, that prostitutes and matrons had different, and quite distinct, modes of dress
in the late Republic. With the other evidence just examined, it allows us to conclude
that as a matter of custom, not law, matrons wore the stola and prostitutes—alone
among adult women, before the *lex Iulia,* aside from perhaps the rogue matron—
wore the toga.

What to make of the origins of this "symbolic transvestism"?[152] Was it simply
a matter of comic usage, at least originally? Quintilian, in a discussion of facial
expressions, mentions the importance of methods used in Comedy to distinguish
prostitutes from *matronae* and other characters, but this need not mean a garment
type.[153] Donatus mentions a saffron-colored *pallium* (the color to denote greed) as
the prostitute's distinguishing garment in Comedy.[154] It is difficult, however, to
imagine Augustus taking over a status indicator that had a recognizable pedigree
in the theater. Or was the gender inversion implied by the wearing of this garment
a product of a religious ordinance, a curiously variant image of the rite by which
humiliores donned the stola to worship Fortuna Virilis?[155] The idea is suggestive,
but the parallel is inexact, and satisfactory evidence is lacking.[156] Neither hypothesis
can be proven.[157]

The earliest clear and explicit testimony that the prostitute's hallmark was a
toga is given by Cicero, as part of his famous diatribe directed against Antony:

> Cic. *Phil.* 2.44–45:[158] You took up the toga for males, which you immediately
> converted into that of a woman. At first you were a common whore: there was a
> fixed price for the dirty deed and not a small one at that; but soon Curio came on
> the scene and took you away from your harlot's way of making a living and, as
> though he had given you a stola, placed you in firm and lasting wedlock. No slave
> boy bought in order to serve as an object of lust was ever in his master's grip as
> much as you were under Curio's spell.

The point of the remark concerning the *muliebris toga* assumes the exclusive identification of the wearing of the "female" toga with prostitutes. It was Curio who
"made an honest woman" out of Antony, "tamquam stolam dedisset." Of course,
this marriage was anything but respectable, as the comparison with the master-
slave relationship goes on to stress. Given Cicero's masterful use of Roman

---

[151] Or a matron indignant at other matrons acting like prostitutes while dressed in the stola or a
husband indignant at matrons wearing the toga. For the first, see Daviault, *Comoedia* 255–256; for the
second, see Gardner, *Women* 252.

[152] For official concern with another kind of transvestism, see below at n. 499.

[153] Quint. *IO* 11.3.74.

[154] Ev. *Com.* 8.6.

[155] So Gagé, *Matronalia* (1963) 119. See Chapter 2.

[156] Note the late antique trend that had holy women (among them repentant prostitutes) adopting the
garb of monks as a denial of their sex: Patlagean, "Moine" (1976/1981).

[157] For further discussion of this symbolic transvestism, see below.

[158] "Sumpsisti virilem, quam statim muliebrem togam reddidisti. primo volgare scortum; certa flagitii
merces nec ea parva; sed cito Curio intervenit qui te a meretricio quaestu abduxit et, tamquam stolam
dedisset, in matrimonio stabili et certo conlocavit. 45. Nemo umquam puer emptus libidinis causa tam
fuit in domini potestate quam tu in Curionis."

Comedy in his rhetoric,[159] his reference to the prostitute's toga does not rule out comic usage as the source of the practice but proves nothing by itself.

Two passages from a satire of Horace and one from a poem in the Tibullan *corpus* attributed to Sulpicia[160] associate the wearing of the toga with prostitutes. Two more sources refer to the distinction between prostitutes' and matrons' garb: it is worth noting that both of these (from Ovid and Martial)[161] postdate the law.

The continued use of the toga is perhaps alluded to in a text taken from Ulpian's commentary on the urban praetor's edict, where he denies liability for *iniuria* when men sexually harass respectable women clothed in the garments of slaves or prostitutes.[162] The passage, although it does not explicitly mention the toga, makes clear that the distinction between the dress of these two categories of women continued to be maintained. It also shows that young unmarried women who were not slaves or prostitutes (two of the categories exempted from the penalties of the *lex Iulia*) were expected to adopt the dress of *matronae* or at least abstain from that characteristic of women exempt under the law.[163] Failure to observe this injunction could lead to undesirable confusion, a point upon which Tertullian insists:[164]

> Tert. *Cultu Fem.* 2.12.1:[165] Let us hope only for this much, that we do not become the cause of true blasphemy. But how much more of an act of blasphemy is it if you, who are said to be the priestesses of chastity, walk about in public adorned and painted up like whores! Or what do those most wretched sacrificial victims of public lust not possess? Even if there are some laws which used to keep them from the garb of respectable women, by now, at any rate, the immorality of this day and age, growing worse every day, has put them on a level with the most respectable women—to the point where you cannot tell them apart.

Tertullian's remarks suggest that the *lex Iulia* (the plural *leges,* as well as the "maritalibus" piled on the "matronalibus," can be read as rhetorical amplification) not only prescribed the toga for prostitutes but actually forbade them to wear the stola. By his day the law was no longer strictly enforced. One may wonder if indeed it ever was. A mechanism for enforcement that would have functioned well

---

[159] See Geffcken, *Comedy* (1973).

[160] Hor. *Serm.* 1.2.62–63, 82–85; [Tib.] 3.16.3–4.

[161] Ovid. *Fasti* 4.133–134; Mart. 1.35.8–9.

[162] Ulp. D. 47.10.15.15. The legal issue falls under a special edict associated with *iniuria*; see Chapter 9.

[163] Some literary and iconographical evidence suggests that respectable young girls wore the *toga praetexta*. See, e.g., Cic. *Verr.* 2.1.133; Prop. 4.11.33–34. If so, it should have been as easy to distinguish this from the prostitute's toga as the latter was from the *toga virilis*. But I doubt the *toga praetexta* was commonly worn by girls.

[164] Cf. Tert. *Apol.* 6.3: "video et inter matronas atque prostibulas nullum de habitu discrimen relictum."

[165] "Optemus tantummodo, ne iustae blasphemationis causa simus. quanto autem blasphemabile, si, quae sacerdotes pudicitiae dicimini, impudicarum ritu procedatis cultae et expictae! aut quid minus habent infelicissimae illae publicarum libidinum victimae? quas etsi quae leges a maritalibus et matronalibus decoramentis coercebant, iam certe saeculi improbitas quotidie insurgens honestissimis quibusque feminis usque ad errorem dinoscendi coaequavit."

in the city of Rome or worked at all outside it is difficult to imagine.[166] Moreover, as Tertullian implies, it was as difficult to keep matrons from adopting the dress of prostitutes as the reverse. Elsewhere, he speaks of a measure dating from the early Principate that aimed at compelling matrons to wear only that sort of clothing appropriate to their status:

> Tert. *Pallio* 4.9:[167] Turn also to the women. You may behold with your own eyes what Caecina Severus sternly pressed upon the attention of the Senate: matrons in public without their stolae. In fact, the penalty inflicted, under the decree of the Senate sponsored by the augur Lentulus, upon any matron who disgraced herself in this way was the same as for *stuprum*. The motivation for this was that certain women had diligently promoted the disuse of garments that serve as the tokens and guardians of social and moral rank, inasmuch as they are a hindrance to promiscuity. But now in prostituting themselves, in order that they may be the more readily approached, they have sworn off their stola, scarf, shoes, and hat, and even the very litters and portable chairs, by means of which they used to be kept aloof, at a discreet distance, even in public. But one man closes his eyes, while another will not open his. Look at the prostitutes, the marketplaces of public lusts, even the very massage-girls, and if it is better to avert your eyes from such shameless spectacles of chastity murdered in public, turn your gaze upward, if you like: at once you will see that they are matrons.

This passage says a good deal about the significance of distinctions of dress with regard to respectable women and prostitutes and about the more general issue of the relationship between clothing and status.[168] Tertullian's rather impressive historical knowledge of the relevant legislation[169] shows that the problem of keeping matrons to their proper dress went back a long way. The remarks of Caecina Severus (cos. suff. in 1 B.C.) on the subject have been plausibly associated by Groag with a speech reported by Tacitus in the context of the year A.D. 21.[170] Since Severus's efforts did not meet with success, Lentulus's proposal must have come at some time later in the reign of Tiberius.[171]

---

[166] Perhaps the aediles were entrusted with responsibility for overseeing this regulation in the city center. On their role in enforcing regulations on clothing, see below.

[167] "Converte et ad feminas. habes spectare, quod Caecina Severus graviter senatui impressit, matronas sine stola in publico. denique, Lentuli auguris consultis, quae ita sese exauctorasset, pro stupro erat poena; quoniam quidem indices custodesque dignitatis habitus, ut lenocinii factitandi impedimenta, sedulo quaedam desuefecerant. at nunc in semetipsas lenocinando, quo planius adeantur, et stolam et supparum et crepidulum et caliendrum, ipsas quoque iam lecticas et sellas, quis in publico quoque domestice ac secrete habebantur, eieravere. sed alius extinguit sua lumina, alius non sua accendit. aspice lupas, popularium libidinum nundinas, ipsas quoque fricatrices, et si praestat oculos abducere ab eiusmodi propudiis occisas in publico castitatis, aspice tamen vel sublimis, iam matronas videbis."

[168] See the remarks of Tibiletti, "Tertulliano" (1981) 76–77.

[169] For discussion of Tertullian's competence in legal matters, and his possible identification with a jurist of the same name (a controversial issue), see most recently Liebs, *Jurisprudenz* (1993) 1–2. At stake here of course is a factual question of legal history, not a technical legal problem.

[170] Tac. *Ann.* 3.33–34; see *PIR²* C 106, and Groag, *RE* Caecina (24) (1897). The purport of the speech, as given by Tacitus, deals with the issue of wives accompanying their husbands to military and administrative posts in the provinces. Severus spoke disparagingly on this occasion of feminine extravagance and public behavior, themes that provide a suitable context for his remarks about the stola.

[171] So *PIR²* C 1379 ("anno incerto Tiberi"), drawing an inference from Tertullian's *denique* and

Given Tertullian's concern with clothing, it must be made plain that there is no connection with sumptuary laws or the social impulses behind such legislation. According to the terms established by Lentulus's successful proposal, a matron who appeared in public without her stola was punished *pro stupro*.[172] That is, she was treated as an adulteress.[173] The rationale behind this severity was the fact that clothing served as the advertisement and guardian of social and moral rank (*dignitas* has both these meanings here).[174] According to Tertullian, and perhaps Lentulus as well, some women had jettisoned the type of clothing proper to their rank in order to facilitate adulterous contacts with men.

The easiest reconstruction of events suggested by these passages is the following. The *lex Iulia* specified certain articles of clothing—such as the stola and *vittae*—as peculiar to *matronae* and forbade these to be worn by prostitutes: thus the *leges* in the passage drawn from the *De Cultu Feminarum* are simply the adultery statute itself.[175] Matrons were not compelled by law to wear the stola and the other "matronal" articles of clothing until Lentulus's measure was passed. Over time this norm ceased to be enforced.[176] Besides the lack of an effective mechanism of enforcement, perhaps the harshness of the sanction, equation of failure to maintain a dress code with *stuprum,* contributed to this. In the meantime, according to Tertullian, matrons had adopted the dress of prostitutes and vice versa, a situation that should have invited the unfriendly attention of public officials. The problem of matronal dress remained acute at the beginning of the third century, to judge from not only Tertullian's polemic but Ulpian's discussion of its implications for Roman delict.

The question of status-appropriate clothing should engage our close attention. In classical antiquity, you were what you wore.[177] The regulation for convicted adulteresses is the first example known to me at Rome of a type of clothing assigned as a punishment.[178] It may not be absurd to view this as a precursor

---

the age of Lentulus (cos. in 14 B.C.) The measure was probably an *SC,* as Groag, *RE* Cornelius (181) (1900), suggests, although it finds no place in the lists given by Volterra, *NNDI* SCC (1969), and Talbert, *Senate* ch. 15. A proposal to forbid, among other things, males from wearing silk garments passed in A.D. 16: Dio 57.15.1; cf. Tac. *Ann.* 2.33.1.

172 The emphasis on public behavior is striking: the phrase "in publico" appears three times in this text. The concern is consistent with the law's aim of manipulating women and their attributes as symbols.

173 This text suggests that Sehling was right to claim the statutory penalties for *stuprum* were the same as those for *adulterium*; see above.

174 Note the phrase "quae ita sese exauctorasset" with its language reminiscent of (dishonorable) discharge from the army. Tertullian plays on the idea of voluntary declassing, as if these women had drummed themselves out of the putative *ordo matronarum.*

175 This would explain the preoccupation of Ovid and Martial with these two articles of clothing; see above. See also Serv. *ad Aen. 7.403:* "CRINALES VITTAS quae solarum matronarum erant: nam meretricibus non dabantur."

176 It may rarely, if ever, have been enforced rigorously at Rome itself, to say nothing of other towns, especially those places where Juvenal says (3.171–172) no one wears a toga until he is dead.

177 Herrin, "Search" (1993) 179: "apparel, far more than physique, identified a person."

178 Note the contrast with the inverse situation of a penalty imposed for failure to wear proper clothing, for example, during a prescribed period of mourning: Greenidge, *Infamia* (1894) 201–206.

of the practice of penal tattooing, whose purpose was similar: social degradation.[179]

Was the toga no longer the badge of dishonor for prostitutes in the Severan period? Neither Tertullian nor Ulpian mentions this as the distinctive *meretricia vestis*.[180] The other evidence suggests that the toga served this function throughout the first century, at least. One token of its currency is its attribution to convicted adulteresses as well as to prostitutes. As suggested above, it was precisely the *lex Iulia* that equated the status of both types.

In Martial we find two certain references to the wearing of the toga by convicted adulteresses. The first runs:

> Mart. 2.39:[181] You give scarlet-and violet-colored clothing to a notorious adulteress. Do you want to give her just what she deserves? Send her a toga.

The toga, not expensive and beautiful garments, is the proper gift for an adulteress. This epigram might be taken, not as a recognition of the fact that adulteresses themselves wore the toga, but as a literary identification of an unchaste woman with a prostitute.[182] Read in this way, the poem would stand as a simple moral condemnation, a theme familiar to readers of Martial:[183] an adulteress is nothing more than a prostitute. But the joke is that such a gift anticipates her conviction under the statute. The following epigram drives this home, removing all doubt about the association of the toga with adulteresses:

> Mart. 10.52:[184] After seeing the eunuch Thelys wearing a toga, Numa said that (s)he was a convicted adulteress.

The joke depends on the understanding that a eunuch is more of a woman than a man, that is, Thelys's wearing of the toga puts him into a class of women who take up this otherwise male garment; the involvement of eunuchs in the practice of adultery is also assumed.[185] The point is emphasized by the name of the eunuch, which is the Greek adjective for "female." The appropriateness of the toga for convicted adulteresses is not demonstrated so much as assumed here. For the assumption to operate, there cannot have been numerous categories of women thus attired. A third passage from Martial mentions the *toga muliebris,* but it is unclear whether the reference is to an adulteress or to a prostitute.[186]

---

[179] Penal tattooing of lawbreakers evidently commences among Romans under the Principate; see Jones, "*Stigma*" (1987) esp. 148–149, where the earliest attestation concerns Caligula.

[180] The same is not true of the stola. Holtheide, "Matrona" (1980), shows that the title *matrona/ femina stolata* attested in the inscriptions and papyri arises in the early third century and is assigned to women married to men in a certain sector of the equestrian aristocracy (130). See Beaucamp, *Statut* 2 (1992) 131, for a possible extension of this range. No connection exists with the Augustan legislation on marriage or adultery.

[181] "Coccina famosae donas et ianthina moechae: / vis dare quae meruit munera? mitte togam."

[182] So Gardner, *Women* 252, understands the poem.

[183] See Sullivan, *Martial* (1991) ch. 5.

[184] "Thelyn viderat in toga spadonem: / damnatam Numa dixit esse moecham."

[185] See Dalla, *Incapacità* (1978) esp. 57–64 (with 58 n. 70), 131 n. 26; Guyot, *Eunuchen* (1980) 37–42, 63–66.

[186] Mart. 6.64.4–5: ". . . sed patris ad speculum tonsi matrisque togatae / filius. . . ."

The evidence of Martial is confirmed by a passage from Juvenal, which is not, however, so readily understood:

> Iuv. 2.68–70:[187] Fabulla is an adulteress; let her be convicted in court, Carfinia too, if you like: upon sentencing she wouldn't take up a toga of that sort.

The passage is introduced by a criticism of the effeminate toga worn by Creticus the trial lawyer. A Carfinia (her name is uncertain)[188] enjoyed a reputation for causing disturbances in court while acting as an advocate. Fabulla was an adulteress. Like a prostitute, she appropriated for herself a male sexual prerogative: promiscuity.

If Fabulla were condemned, or even if Carfinia, a woman who, although not sexually promiscuous, arrogated to herself another male privilege, the right to act as a pleader in a Roman court, were to be convicted of the same crime, neither woman would choose as effeminate a toga as that preferred by Creticus. In other words, either woman can be considered more of a man than Creticus.[189] The point is made both in a direct sexual sense (Fabulla, who is sexually active) and in a broader social sense (Carfinia, acting as a trial lawyer). Not suprisingly, Juvenal assumes that any woman shameless enough to perform the role taken up by Carfinia is capable of committing adultery as well.

This conclusion is supported by Ulpian's explanation of the post-Carfinian prohibition of women acting as pleaders in cases that did not concern themselves, "the reason to be sure for the prohibition against [women] becoming involved with cases not their own, in defiance of the chaste behavior appropriate to their sex, is so that women do not perform functions that are properly those of males."[190] The jurist's remarks make it clear that the sexual shame of women was thought to be compromised in this way: a thin line held for women between impudence and immorality.[191] Of significance is the implication of cross-gender behavior for female chastity. A notable example of masculine character being associated with adulterous conduct is Sallust's portrait of Sempronia.[192] It is a fairly common identification, one that, moreover, is often linked in turn to prostitution, which helps explain the "symbolic transvestism" of the toga. Attributions of adultery, prostitution, and masculinity are all present in Cicero's portrait of Clodia in the *Caeliana*.[193] This association explains, for example, why women with intellectual interests might be characterized as prostitutes.[194]

---

[187] "Est moecha Fabulla, damnetur, si vis etiam Carfinia: / talem non sumet damnata togam."

[188] *PIR²* C 420 lists her as Carfinia, citing only Juvenal. Schulze, *Eigennamen* (1964/1966) 353, defends this version. She appears as Cafrania in Val. Max. 8.3.2 (an editorial suggestion has "C. Afrania"; see Courtney, *Juvenal* [1980] 133: Carfinia is also found in the manuscripts) and as Carfania in Lab.-Ulp. D. 3.1.1.5: Rantz, "Avocates" (1986); Marshall, "Civil Courts" (1989) 44–45; Bauman, *Women* 231 n. 29.

[189] A similar point is made at Iuv. 2.108–109.

[190] Lab.-Ulp. (6 *ad edictum*) D. 3.1.1.5: ". . . et ratio quidem prohibendi, ne contra pudicitiam sexui congruentem alienis causis se immisceant, ne virilibus officiis fungantur mulieres. . . ."

[191] See Marshall, "Maesia" esp. 57.

[192] Sall. *BC* 25. On Sallust's depiction of this woman, see Paul "Sempronia" (1985).

[193] See May, *Trials* (1988) 110.

[194] See Parker, "Body" (1992) 106. It also lies behind Juvenal's criticism of the matron who blows the trumpet at the Floralia: 6.249–250.

Another piece of evidence comes from the scholia to Horace's *Satires*. As noted above, the work commented on predates the law, while the scholia are much later.

> [Acr.] *ad Hor. serm. 1.2.62–63:*[195] *Quid interest:* He says that it makes no difference at all whether someone misbehaves with a matron, a slave, or even an adulteress, having adopted the view of the Stoics, who say that all sins are equal, for they look not to the enormity of the offense but to the intent of the offender. *peccesve togata:* Matronae who were divorced by their husbands because of infidelity used to take up the toga, having put aside the stola because of their disgrace. Indeed, the toga is appropriate for the prostitute. This is because they used to solicit customers like this, dressed only in dark-colored togas, in order to be distinguished from respectable women, and for this reason those women who had been convicted of adultery used to wear this garment. In other words, women who had been convicted of the crime of adultery were said to walk about in public wearing togas. Others say that the woman wearing the toga is a freedwoman, because previously freedwomen wore the toga, but matrons the stola.

The sections "negat . . . spectant" and "togatae . . . <convictae>" are found also in the text of the third-century commentator Porphyrio;[196] how much of the remainder goes back to Acro and the second century is a matter of doubt.[197] There are some problems, which begin with the commentator's understanding of the text. Like some modern readers of Horace, the scholiast misses the irony of the question the poet puts in the verses commented upon:[198] "quid interest in matrona ancilla peccesne togata?" In other words, it is very unlikely that he is representing Stoic doctrine in the straightforward manner claimed here. The curious remark about *libertinae* and the toga is explained as an attempt to relate this passage to the mention of freedwomen as sexual objects a few lines earlier in Horace's poem,[199] where freedwomen prostitutes are meant. This assumes a confusion of *ancilla* and *libertina* on the scholiast's part, a confusion that is also sometimes shared by moderns. Respectable freedwomen wore the stola in the late Republic.[200] To be clear, Horace refers to prostitutes as both slaves and freedwomen. These two status groups may well have formed the majority of prostitutes in Rome throughout the period under study. But they did not wear the toga qua slaves or freedwomen, but qua prostitutes. No other text associates the wearing of the toga with freedwomen: this is a red herring.

[195] "*Quid interest:* Negat interesse quicquam, utrum quis in matrona an in ancilla an etiam in adultera delinquat, secutus opinionem Stoicorum, qui omnia peccata paria esse dicunt: neque enim rei admissae quantitatem, sed admittentis voluntatem spectant. *peccesve togata:* Matronae, quae ob adulterium a maritis repudiabantur, togam accipiebant sublata stola propter ignominiam. toga autem meretrici apta. ita enim solebant prostare cum solis pullis togis, ut discernerentur a matronis; et ideo quae adulterii damnatae fuerant, hac veste utebantur. aliter: togatae dicebantur in publicum procedere feminae adulterii admissi <convictae>. alii togatam dicunt libertinam, quia antea libertinae toga utebantur, stola vero matronae."

[196] His text guarantees the reading of "convictae" in this one.

[197] See Wessner, *RE* Acron (1912) esp. 2842–2843.

[198] Hor. *Serm.* 1.2.62–63.

[199] Hor. *Serm.* 1.2.47–49.

[200] *CIL* 1^2 1570 (= 10.6009).

The text contains an anachronism in that the scholiast implies that the *adultera* would have been made to wear the toga even before the adultery law was passed—so the tricolon "in matrona an in ancilla an etiam in adultera." It is also inexact to say, as he does, that women divorced "ob adulterium" wore the toga. Juvenal and Martial both require a formal conviction for the imposition of this penalty (as does indeed the scholiast himself further on). In other words, the imposition of the toga was part of the sentence meted out under the law. The source of the confusion may lie in the fact that a woman usually had to be divorced even to be prosecuted for adultery in the first place.[201]

There is, despite all this, a bedrock of plausibility to the passage. Respectable women who were convicted of adultery had to abandon the stola in favor of the toga as part of the penalty. Previous to the law's passage, the toga had been associated only with prostitutes among adult women. The purpose of the garment was to provide a means of distinguishing them from respectable women in public. The notion that convicted adulteresses walked about in public clad in the toga may suggest that the *relegatio* imposed as a penalty by the law was only temporary in nature. "In publicum" seems scarcely suited to a small island, and toga wearers were not likely to make the impression desired by the legislator on Pandateria or Seriphos. The loss of the *ius togae* endured by (male) exiles[202] is no help to our understanding, since this seems to rely more on the association between toga and citizen status than on a concern with the exemplary nature of the punishment. All the same, we may ascribe a double purpose to the law's imposition of the garment on convicted adulteresses. It is said that the prostitutes' toga (and presumably that worn by adulteresses) was dark.[203] This would set it apart from the toga worn by males as a badge of citizen status.[204] There is more than a practical aim at work: the toga was to serve as a symbol, perceived and easily understood by the entire community.

Still another qualification must be made. The scholiast's frequent resort to the imperfect tense awakens a suspicion. We might conclude that, at least by Porphyrio's day, both uses of the toga by women had gone out of fashion. Although the nature and purpose of the correct dress for women remained well understood throughout the first two centuries A.D., there is also a suggestion that these regulations were imperfectly observed. In theory, the toga remained the "official" emblem of disgrace, but it was unlikely ever to have been adopted universally. It was probably not intended to be worn in private in the first place, and, again, there

---

[201] Some exceptional circumstances existed where this rule did not hold, such as conviction of the husband on a charge of *lenocinium,* his death, or that of the lover; see below.

[202] Plin. *Ep.* 4.11.3; cf. Suet. *Claud.* 15.2.

[203] Sen. *NQ* 7.31.2 speaks of "colores meretricios." See also Tac. *Dial.* 26.1. If he means clothing and not cosmetics, at any rate he does not mention the toga. For colored garments worn by pimps, see Tert. *Spect.* 23.2; Ev. *Com.* 8.6. The Roman hierarchy of color had white garments ideally reserved for members of the upper orders, dark for the lower: Garrido-Hory, *Martial* (1981) 151.

[204] No source speaks of a special garment for male prostitutes. Even a dark-colored toga might have been thought too close to the honorable version to be satisfactory. Male prostitutes, like most female prostitutes, presumably dressed in the same manner as other lower-class Romans. The reference to assuming the stola in place of the *toga virilis* at Petron. 81 should be understood in a figurative sense.

is not even indirect evidence for official oversight of the practice outside Rome. The conclusion that not all Roman prostitutes wore the toga is supported by the wealth of evidence on the variety of garments worn by prostitutes.[205]

Of interest is a passage from Isidore of Seville:

> Isid. *Orig.* 19.25.5:[206] An *amiculum* is a linen *pallium* worn by prostitutes. In the old days matrons who were caught in the act of adultery used to wear this garment, so that they would soil their chastity in this garment rather than in a stola. For in the old days this was associated with the dress of a prostitute, but now in Spain it is the mark of respectability.

Isidore is inexact about the status of the adulteress ("in adulterio deprehensae" instead of "damnatae"),[207] but the main problem with this text is that the *amiculum,* not the toga, is given as the proper dress for both adulteresses and prostitutes. The author simply has the wrong garment. The *amiculum* was not in fact distinctive: "*amiculum* was a generic name for any mantle that was wrapped or draped about one, as was the *palla.*"[208] The description of this as a *lineum*[209] *pallium* is no more helpful. In origin a Greek item of clothing, the *pallium* was worn fairly frequently by the Romans and was in the end adopted by the Christians as a distinctive form of dress.[210] Isidore's vagueness, together with his concluding remark about contemporary conditions in Spain, may be taken as a sign that the woman's toga had long since disappeared from the scene.[211]

Whatever his inaccuracies of detail, Isidore understands perfectly well the social function of clothing—above all, its role as a status symbol. Like Tertullian, his conception of how this works for women is twofold: certain garments are both indicators of social rank and guarantors of sexual behavior. Isidore makes a particularly telling point about adulteresses. Once they have lost their sexual shame, they are assumed to continue to engage in promiscuous sex, like prostitutes. This makes it all the more important to insist that they give up wearing the stola, so

---

[205] See Marquardt/Mau, *Privatleben* 2² 493, on *vestes Coae,* or see-through silk garments also associated with adulteresses; and Herter 2 (1960) 89–94, 100.

[206] "Amiculum est meretricum pallium lineum. hunc apud veteres matronae in adulterio deprehensae induebantur, ut in tali amiculo potius quam in stola polluerent pudicitiam. erat enim apud veteres hoc signum meretriciae vestis, nunc in Hispania honestatis."

[207] Isidore's confusion springs from an equation of women caught in the act of adultery with those condemned in a *quaestio.* The identification of these two types received legal force in the *lex Iulia et Papia,* which forbade *ingenui* to marry such women (Ulp. D. 23.2.43.12–13) and no doubt was strongly felt in popular opinion. Compare the confusion, noted above, of the scholiast to Horace over women divorced *ob adulterium.*

[208] Wilson, *Clothing* 149.

[209] The idea that the garment of the prostitute and the post-Augustan adulteress was made of linen receives support from Apul. *Apol.* 97, which mentions a bequest of linen garments made to a woman "ad ignominiam." The low value of the bequest, rather than the nature of the fabric, may be the point, but see also Publ. Syrus [?] *apud* Petron. 55.

[210] Wilson, *Clothing* 78–83. To be sure, *pallium* seems to have had for Isidore the general significance of "garment." He places his description of the *toga virilis* under the heading *de palliis virorum (Orig.* 19.24.1). So the stola, like the prostitute's garment, is found under *de palliis feminarum* (19.25.1).

[211] By Isidore's day even the *toga virilis* had disappeared: Wilson, *Toga* 115; Goethert, *RE* toga 1659.

that the polluting consequences of their lack of shame are not communicated to the badge of honor itself.

Uneven in quality and chronologically diffuse as it is, this evidence suggests that the adultery law attributed an elevated sexual and social status to the *matrona* or, more properly, *mater familias*. This was emphasized through the creation of an alternative status, situated at the opposite pole of the sexual and social spectrum. The *mater familias* convicted under the adultery law was forced to shed her status and take up the alternative, that is, she was relegated to the degraded class of prostitutes. The higher her station, the greater her fall. For members of the upper classes, such a punishment would perhaps have been rather effective. The loss of a position in society that such women had been born into, together with most of the advantages associated with it, would have been a devastating blow.

Capping this degradation, the punishment of wearing the toga was a form of public humiliation that contained an element of the ferocious. As outsiders, we can offer the neutral, objective explanation that the award of the toga and the social and moral degradation attendant upon it is consistent with the fears and expectations about gender and sexual behavior characteristic of their society—that, for Romans, the toga served as the public manifestation of the sexual humiliation that these women had already visited upon themselves. For the objects of the adultery regime, the matter may have appeared less neutral. Vistilia's desperate maneuvering in the face of an imminent prosecution for adultery serves as a dramatic example.[212]

The equation of the status of the adulteress with that of the prostitute shows that there were circumstances under which the indiscriminate sexual behavior of prostitutes, something normally taken for granted, could become the object, or, more precisely, the instrument, of moral reproach. If the disapproved sexual behavior (adultery), particularly when attributed to an upper-class woman, transgressed an undefined limit,[213] the accusation of "prostitution" might be raised. The higher the woman's social position, the greater the potential loss in public and private honor. But even a woman of lesser status might have reason to fear public identification as a prostitute.

In this specially determined sense, the line between adultery and prostitution was a thin one. Two moralizing passages show how effectively this identification might work as a weapon of reproach. First, Seneca on Augustus's daughter, Julia:[214]

> Sen. *Ben.* 6.32.1:[215] The deified Augustus relegated his own daughter, who was so promiscuous as to be beyond reproach of promiscuity, and made public the

---

[212] McGinn, "*SC*" (1992) 287.

[213] It is well known that accusations of sexual impropriety are a standard element of invective, especially that directed against women. See Richlin, *Garden* (1992), for the most thorough examination; further, Fisher, "Theodora" (1978/1984) 287; Allen, "Theodora" (1992) esp. 94–96.

[214] Similar details are given in Plin. *NH* 21.9 (cf. 7.45–46); Dio (in Xiph., *Exc. Val.*) 55.10.12–14. Cf. Vell. 2.100.3–5; Sen. *Brev. Vitae* 4.5; Tac. *Ann.* 1.53.1–3, 3.24.2; Suet. *Aug.* 65; Suet. *Tib.* 11.4–5; Macrob. 2.5. Proc. *Anec.* 1.17–19 attributes a similar exhibitionism to Theodora's friend Antonina, the wife of Belisarius.

[215] "Divus Augustus filiam ultra impudicitiae maledictum impudicam relegavit et flagitia principalis domus in publicum emisit: admissos gregatim adulteros, pererratam nocturnis comissationibus civitatem, forum ipsum ac rostra, ex quibus pater legem de adulteriis tulerat, filiae in stupra placuisse, cotidianum

scandals of the imperial household: to wit, that lovers were admitted in droves, that the city was traversed with nightly revels, that the very Forum and speakers' platform, from which her father had proposed his legislation on adultery, received her vote as a venue for fornication, that there was a daily gathering about the statue of Marsyas, when, having turned from an adulteress into a prostitute, she sought the right to every sexual indulgence under a lover who was an utter stranger to her.

The implication that the woman behaved like a prostitute emerges as a bald assertion in the last clause, a rhetorical climax typical of Seneca. He has already prepared us for this finale with his assertion that Julia had passed "ultra impudicitiae maledictum," which is truly characteristic only of a prostitute. Her sexual behavior is then characterized in terms of numbers of lovers and flagrancy, with a few scabrous details thrown in to drive home the point. So we have a brief description of a drinking party, *comissatio,* often associated with visits to a prostitute.[216] Marsyas is close enough to the *rostra* to be associated with the precise spot where the legislation was proposed, a point Seneca has already made. The statue may have been a gathering place for prostitutes in the Forum,[217] but the satyr as a symbol of sexual incontinency is perhaps explanation enough of this detail. The venue has proven fertile ground for the scholarly imagination. Some have argued the statue's symbolic associations with *libertas,* while still another theory stresses the rivalry between Marsyas and (Augustan) Apollo.[218] There are perhaps sufficient layers of meaning to stimulate the palate of the most jaded deconstructionist. Finally, we are led to infer that Julia sought, through her behavior rather than by formal application, the prostitute's exemption ("ius omnis licentiae"). Her promiscuity is then placed well within any definition of the utterly indiscriminate ("sub ignoto adultero").

We learn much the same from the famous passage of Juvenal about the promiscuity of Claudius's wife Messalina, described with the famous oxymoron *meretrix Augusta.*[219] The empress, when she is sure her husband is sleeping, leaves the imperial palace disguised in a blonde wig and a cloak,[220] accompanied by a single attendant. She goes to a brothel, where she behaves like a common prostitute, except that lust, not money, is made out to be her motive. So when the pimp closes down for the night and sends the *puellae* away, Messalina departs relucantly, the last to leave, "adhuc ardens rigidae tentigine volvae, et lassata viris necdum satiata."[221] Filthy from her work, she brings a little of the brothel back to the imperial couch.

---

ad Marsyam concursum, cum ex adultera in quaestuariam versa ius omnis licentiae sub ignoto adultero peteret."

[216] Mau, *RE* comissatio (1901) esp. 618.

[217] Though note the objections of Sattler, "Julia" (1962/1969) 520 n. 86, to this idea.

[218] See Sattler, "Julia" 520–521; Levick, "Rhodes" (1972) 799–800; Bauman, *Women* 246, 247, 249, with literature.

[219] Iuv. 6.115–132. The phrase may owe something to Propertius's description of Cleopatra as "meretrix regina" (3.11.39); cf. Plin. *NH* 9.119.

[220] The garment not only disguises but also declasses her: Hor. *Serm.* 2.7.53–56.

[221] "Still hot from the stretching of her stiffened vulva and worn out from her sexual partners without being satisfied by them."

The implication here of a successful challenge to the professionals on the part of Messalina is anticipated by Pliny the Elder, who gives 25 as the winning number of partners for an *agōn* in which the empress bests a slave prostitute.[222] Dio takes this theme over the top by having Messalina set up a brothel on the Palatine, in the spirit of Caligula, staffed by well-born women, of course (including herself).[223]

In both of these set pieces, female members of the imperial house are described as notorious adulteresses. They represent an extreme of high social position coupled with sexual depravity. It is impossible to accept that either woman was in fact a prostitute or that, in any sense allowed by our definition, either Julia or Messalina behaved like one. Although some have taken the evidence literally,[224] there are skeptics as well.[225]

For an explanation of these presentations of female misconduct, one has resort to the authors' politically motivated hostility, taste for moralizing sensationalism, and literary talent combined with ambition. But there is something of substance beyond mere invention. Social convention unambiguously identified sexual promiscuity with prostitution. It is not difficult to multiply examples. One thinks of Sallust's famous portrait of Sempronia as a *hetaira*,[226] Cicero's casting of Clodia as a well-born *meretrix*,[227] Procopius' demolition of the virtue of Theodora and Antonina.[228] More instructive perhaps than the artifice of Seneca and Juvenal is the offhand way in which Isidore views the adulteress as capable of a promiscuity similar to—or in fact identical with—that of the prostitute.[229] This attitude, which evidently predated the law, formed the basis for one particular feature of the *lex*

---

[222] Plin. *NH* 10.172. Procopius has his champion Theodora take on more than 40 men in a single evening: *Anec.* 9.16.

[223] Dio (in Xiph., *Exc. Val.*, Zon.) 60.31.1; cf. his description of Messalina at 14.3, 18.2, and Aur. Vict. *Caes.* 4.12–15. Dio (in *Exc. Val.*) 26.87 has the Vestals implicated in the 114 B.C. scandal of running a brothel; an accusation accepted by Bauman, *Women* 56–59.

[224] For Julia, see Picard, *Auguste et Néron* (1962) 119–120; Raditsa, "Legislation" (1980) 294 n. 36; Bauman, *Women* 117–118. For Messalina, see Sullivan, *Satyricon* (1968) 101 n. 1; Krenkel, "Pueri" (1979) 183; Longo, "Riflessioni" (1984) 2382–2383; Bauman, *Women* 168. See also Guarino, "Messalina" (1974/1993) esp. 25; Ferrill, "Augustus" (1980). Compare Bauman, *Women* 16, who alleges that the women punished by Fabius Gurges in 295 B.C. for *stuprum* were guilty of "systematic fornication" (i.e., prostitution). Similarly, Fantham, "Stuprum" 282.

[225] Levick, "Rhodes" 795–801 (cf. 792), building on a tradition developed by Groag, Syme, Meise, and others, argues that "the disaster that overtook Julia and her friends in 2 B.C. was due to their political, not merely or at all to their sexual activities. . . ." Cf. for both women Raepsaet-Charlier, "Ordre" (1981/1982) 165. As for Messalina, one notes an observation made by Verdière, "Plaidoyer" (1989) 10: "en tout cas, si l'on pouvait prouver que Messaline s'est relevée sans dommage de la performance sportive que lui prête Pline, il faudrait qu'on lui accordât posthumement la médaille d'or du stakhanovisme de l'amour vénal."

[226] Sall. *BC* 25 (cf. 24). See Paul, "Sempronia"; Edwards, *Politics* (1993) 43. Cf. Plut. *Luc.* 6.2–4 on Praecia.

[227] See, e.g., Cic. *Cael.* 49.

[228] See the recent treatments in Fisher, "Theodora" esp. 300–308; Allen, "Theodora".

[229] Compare *Viris Ill.* 86.2: "Haec [sc., Cleopatra] tantae libidinis fuit, ut saepe prostiterit. . . ." Compare the more analytical, at least in stylistic terms, "et quia meretrix et quae semel fuerat adultera . . ." (Hieron. *Comm. Mat.* 3.777) and "emoicheueto kai eporneueto" (Dio [in Xiph., *Exc. Val.*, Zon.] 60.31.1, on which see Verdière, "Plaidoyer" 8).

Iulia. It illustrates once more the ease with which some types of social values could be translated directly into positive law.

As in the previous section, we have seen here how Augustus in the *lex Iulia* reconciled tradition with an innovative approach. What is new is the use of legislation to impose the toga on adulteresses and, perhaps, to require it formally of prostitutes for the first time. At the least, Augustus capitalized on the long-standing association of this garment with prostitutes in order to define a new degraded status for women convicted of adultery.[230]

An extension of this principle lies in the compelling of adulteresses to work as prostitutes in brothels, a practice abolished by Theodosius I in A.D. 389.[231] But the spirit of the Augustan regime was not extinguished even at this late date, as a law enacted five years later, which prohibited mime actresses and prostitutes from wearing the habit of nuns, attests.[232]

The regime lived on, notionally, at any rate, until Justinian, a conservative innovator worthy of his great predecessor. Justinian made adulteresses take the veil.[233] A similar rule for repentant prostitutes, while not explicitly attested, seems quite possible.[234] One must not exaggerate the departure from the Augustan principle, however. It is fair to view the new treatment of adulteresses simply as a sharpening of the marriage prohibition of the *lex Iulia* to the point of permanent, enforced chastity.[235]

Perhaps the best way to illustrate the balance of continuity and change from classical pagan to Byzantine Christian is to observe that whereas Augustus set out to transform adulteresses into prostitutes, Justinian sought to reconfigure them as nuns. Clothing was a key element in the policy of both emperors.

4. *Lenocinium*

The exclusive focus of the *lex Iulia* on the female partner in constructing a basis for liability meant that there was no reason to invent an elevated status for men parallel to that of *mater familias*. The statute did, however, create a degraded category for men parallel to that of the adulteress/prostitute. A husband regarded as overly complaisant in his own wife's adultery—behavior now classified as a

---

[230] Punishment of adulteresses through prohibition of certain items of clothing is found in a regulation attributed to Solon, which forbade them to wear finery or to appear at public events: Aesch. 1.183. Note also the rules sponsored by Zaleucus at Locri, which allowed only *hetairai* to wear gold ornaments or purple-bordered clothing, a backhanded sumptuary law for respectable women: Treggiari, *RM* 194.

[231] Socr. *HE* 5.18. I know of no earlier evidence of this practice regarding adulteresses.

[232] Theod., Arc., Hon. CTh. 15.7.12 (a. 394) (= C. 1.4.4).

[233] Nov. 134.10 (a. 556), on which see Goria, ''Abito'' (1974) esp. 58–59.

[234] Goria, ''Abito'' 61.

[235] With the important exception of the provision (Nov. 134.10.1) that allowed the woman's husband to take her back, a derogation of *lenocinium mariti*.

criminal offense for the first time—was defined under the statute as a *leno* and his offense as *lenocinium*.[236]

Our first task is to identify the kinds of behavior punished by the *lex Iulia*. How did it define this "husband-pimp"? The sources give a fairly broad picture in answer to this question. By the late classical law, *lenocinium* comprised a variety of behavior accessory to the crime of adultery. This emerges from a list given by the jurist Tryphoninus in the context of a discussion of the eligibility of minors for *restituere in integrum*:[237]

> Tryph. (3 *disp.*) D. 4.4.37.1: . . . si quid eorum commiserit, quae pro adulterio eadem lex punit, veluti si adulterii damnatam sciens uxorem duxerit, aut in adulterio deprehensam uxorem non dimiserit, quaestumve de adulterio uxoris fecerit, pretiumve pro comperto stupro acceperit, aut domum praebuerit ad stuprum adsulteriumve in ea committendum. . . .

> . . . if someone commits any offense which the same law punishes in the same way as adultery, for example, if he knowingly marries a woman convicted of adultery or does not divorce his wife after she has been caught in the act of adultery, or he makes a profit from his wife's adultery, or he accepts payment after discovery of *stuprum*, or if he furnishes a house for the commission of *stuprum* or adultery. . . .

This is the most complete summary of "accessory" offenses under the *lex Iulia*. The five items given in this text are referred to below as *damnatam ducere, deprehensam retinere, quaestum facere, pretium accipere,* and *domum praebere.* On the basis of this and other, less comprehensive texts (see below), Esmein and Mommsen treat all these offenses as instances of *lenocinium*.[238] Although both emphasize specific aspects of *lenocinium,* they do not show how this crime developed over time.[239] Daube made the first solid advance in this area.[240] Alvarez de Cienfuegos argues that only three of these offenses constituted *lenocinium* under the law, and the rest are accessory crimes.[241] In the most sophisticated and detailed treatment of the problem we

---

[236] As seen in Chapter 2, the activity of actual pimps was never in classical law subjected to criminal sanctions per se, although they labored under a number of civic and legal disabilities. This situation was not altered with the introduction of the *lex Iulia*.

[237] Parts of this text have been attacked, though not what is given here: see *Index Itp.* ad loc. and below. The clash of connectives ("aut . . . −ve . . . −ve . . . aut") argues that this list has been stitched together by the compilers, which does not mean that any of the individual items are unclassical in themselves or are unsuited to the context (Tryphoninus himself may have wound up with a general reference to types of *lenocinium*). On the other hand, the text will not stand as evidence that all of these offenses counted as statutory *lenocinium*.

[238] Esmein, "Délit" 101–108; Mommsen, *Strafrecht* 699–701, who adds a sixth, accepting payment in exchange for dropping an adultery prosecution, which is subsumable under the type regarding accepting money after the fact and possibly constitutes a violation of the *SC Turpillianum* as well (see Chapter 6).

[239] Esmein, "Délit" 102–105, singles out the requirement that the husband divorce the wife and take action against the lover in case of flagrant adultery. Mommsen, *Strafrecht* 699–700, regards the husband who sells his wife's services as the most offensive scenario ("dem schlimmsten Einzelfall").

[240] Daube, "Lex Julia". See below.

[241] Alvarez de Cienfuegos, "*Lenocinium*" (1988). The three are the cases where (1) the husband or wife profits from the adultery of the spouse, (2) the husband does not divorce his wife after catching her in the act of adultery, and (3) someone (knowingly) marries a woman convicted of adultery.

have, Rizzelli holds that four of the five were identified by the law as *lenocinium*; the jurists later added the offense characterized below as *domum praebere*.[242]

Two general points may be made. Simply because the jurists classify an offense as *lenocinium,* there is no reason to assume the law did the same. Similarly, it can be shown that if the statute did not regard an offense as *lenocinium,* this says nothing about the late classical law. I argue that the law identified two offenses that it defined as *lenocinium,* while three others, originally conceived of as accessory offenses, were placed under the rubric of *lenocinium* through subsequent legislation and the work of the jurists.[243] Our sources, it is true, do not permit a fully detailed treatment of this problem, but it is possible to isolate the original provisions of the law. This is the aim of this section, while the extensions accomplished by statute and jurisprudence are reserved for the next chapter.

Once again, we must depend on juristic testimony for reconstructing the terms of the statute. One text, however, is remarkably clear on what the law punished as *lenocinium:*

> Ulp. (4 *de adult.*) D. 48.5.2.2: Lenocinii quidem crimen lege Iulia de adulteriis praescriptum[244] est, cum sit in eum maritum poena statuta, qui de adulterio uxoris suae quid ceperit, item in eum qui in adulterio deprehensam retinuerit.

> In fact, the crime of *lenocinium* is established by the *lex Iulia* on adultery, since a statutory penalty is given for the husband who makes a profit by the adultery of his own wife, and also for him who keeps a woman as wife who has been caught in the act of adultery.

The law was directed first against one "qui de adulterio uxoris suae quid ceperit." This is ambiguous, since it can refer to two of the examples mentioned in the Tryphoninus passage: he who "quaestum . . . de adulterio uxoris fecerit" or he who "pretium . . . pro comperto stupro acceperit." The first example was the one identified as *lenocinium* by the law itself, as Esmein[245] and Daube[246] have argued. The wording recalls terms used for prostitutes in other legislation, most importantly the phrase in the *lex Iulia et Papia:* "qui quaeve palam corpore quaestum facit fecerit."[247] Just as, with the adulteress, the *lex Iulia* constructs a new type of prostitute,[248] it now comprehends a new type of pimp. This is the fellow who violates the injunction "ne quis quaestum ex adulterio uxoris suae facito sciens dolo malo."[249]

[242] Rizzelli, "*Crimen*" (1990).

[243] Esmein, "Délit" 107, emphasizes the role of the jurists.

[244] Mommsen ad loc. proposes *expressum.*

[245] Esmein, "Délit" 106 n. 2: "la loi désignait sans doute ce délit par les termes "quaestum facere ex uxoris adulterio"; c'était d'ailleurs une expression consacrée pour désigner la prostitution."

[246] Daube, "Lex Julia" 375: ". . . it appears that this term [*sc. quaestus*] was in the *lex Iulia*." He bases his argument on Ulp. (4 *de adult.*) D. 48.5.30(29).4: "Quaestum autem ex adulterio uxoris facere videtur. . . ."

[247] See Chapter 3.

[248] Note Ulpian's phrase, "meretricio quodam genere," which guarantees the connection with prostitution: Ulp. (4 *de adult.*) D. 48.5.30(29).4. For discussion of the text, see Chapter 6.

[249] I have altered slightly the version Esmein gives of the legislative text in order to conform with such passages as Pap. D. 48.5.9(8) pr. and Ulp. D. *eod.* 30(29).3.

Of course, only the husband of an adulteress was potentially liable for statutory *lenocinium*. This is shown in this instance by Ulpian's language ("in eum maritum," "uxoris suae"). For the other type of statutory *lenocinium* (*deprehensam retinere,* see below), this point is suggested by the fact that the privilege of detaining the *adulter* was not granted to *pater* by the law but was extended to him by the jurists (obviously, only the husband was situated to divorce an adulteress). Also, under the statute, the *praescriptio lenocinii* applied only to the husband.[250]

The fact that this type of *lenocinium* (*quaestum facere*) was defined by the statute itself explains the importance attached to it by the jurists: "he has committed no small offense who has plied the profession of a pimp with regard to his own wife," says Ulpian.[251] Just as the law conceived of adultery as the crime of the woman who had betrayed her honor, so it created *lenocinium* as the offense of the man who had sold not only his wife's honor but his own.[252] The statute demands a high degree of complaisance: to be liable, the husband must do more than turn a blind eye.

It is then possible to exclude, as statutory *lenocinium,* the other possible interpretation of the phrasing given in D. 48.5.2.2, that is, the man who "pretium . . . pro comperto stupro acceperit." This behavior was without doubt punished by the law,[253] but not as *lenocinium.* This conclusion rests upon the fact that Ulpian informs us that this provision might apply to anyone, not just the husband:[254]

> Ulp. (4 *de adult.*) D. 48.5.30(29).2: Plectitur et qui pretium pro comperto stupro acceperit: nec interest, utrum maritus sit qui acceperit an alius quilibet: quicumque enim ob conscientiam stupri accepit aliquid poena erit plectendus. ceterum si gratis quis remisit, ad legem non pertinet.

> He too is punished who takes a bribe upon discovery[255] of *stuprum.* And it does not matter whether he who accepts the payment is the husband or someone else; for whoever takes anything on account of his knowledge that *stuprum* has been committed should be punished. But if anyone lets an offender go without payment, he does not fall within the scope of the statute.

It has been argued that the statute punished only the husband who took money after the fact, and that this was a form of statutory *lenocinium.*[256] In the very next fragment (3), Ulpian discusses *quaestum facere,* an offense of which only the husband of an adulteress could be guilty. He draws an implicit contrast with this

---

[250] Rizzelli, "*Crimen*" 479 n. 45.

[251] Ulp. (4 *de adult.*) D. 48.5.30(29).3: "nec enim mediocriter deliquit, qui lenocinium in uxore exercuit." On the text, see Lenel, *Pal.* 2 col. 938 n. 1. The objections raised by Albertario and Volterra (see *Index Itp.* ad loc.) to such expressions as "mediocriter," "nec enim," and "delinquit" do not convince. Esmein, "Délit" 106–107, misunderstands the text, thinking it to exonerate petty transactions.

[252] The wife who took money for her husband's *adulterium* is assigned a different status; see Chapter 6.

[253] See Chapter 6.

[254] One might propose as the legislative injunction "ne quis pretium pro comperto stupro accipito sciens dolo malo."

[255] On the meaning of *comperire,* see Rizzelli, "*Crimen*" 475.

[256] Rizzelli, "*Crimen*" 473–477.

passage, a contrast that explains the jurist's emphasis that *anyone,* not just the husband, can be liable for *pretium accipere.*

The difference in wording between this provision and that just discussed is significant. Instead of *adulterium,* we find *stuprum* given as the main offense at issue: evidently, this term is meant here to embrace adultery as well as criminal fornication. This may be one of the places in the law where, as the jurists complain, *stuprum* and *adulterium* were used in an unclear and inconsistent manner.[257]

Finally, a text of Papinian places *pretium accipere* in the same chapter of the law as *domum praebere,*[258] an offense that certainly did not originate as *lenocinium* under the statute. This classification makes it more likely that the two enjoyed the same status at the outset. Another passage, by Ulpian, refers to those who are, in contrast to those guilty of *lenocinium* (or *adulterium/stuprum*), liable on a charge of *domum praebere* "et alii similes."[259] The last phrase evidently means offenders against the other two types I identify as juristic *lenocinium,* that is, *damnatam ducere* and *pretium accipere.* The logic of this passage makes it likely that statutory *lenocinium* appeared in a chapter other than that which contained the juristic types. A rescript says that a "certain chapter" of the law has the penalty for *deprehensam retinere* and *damnatam ducere,* not that the same chapter gives the offenses themselves.[260] Of course, even if the two statutory offenses occurred in the same chapter as the three juristic types,[261] this does not mean all were originally *lenocinium.*

Though in cases of adultery husbands were the most likely candidates for a payoff,[262] the concession of a right to prosecute granted by the law to third parties suggests there was no limit to the scope (and thereby the effectiveness) of the statute in this particular.[263] Indeed, the jurists later grouped *pretium accipere* under the rubric of *lenocinium.* This explains the broad phrasing of "qui de adulterio uxoris suae quid ceperit" in D. 48.5.2.2: in Ulpian's day the concept of *lenocinium* was elastic enough to include both this offense and the specific crime of the husband-pimp.

In the same passage Ulpian gives another type of statutory *lenocinium,* the husband "qui in adulterio deprehensam retinuerit." Although this case bears no analogy, in terms of language or the behavior it describes, to the type just discussed, Esmein is correct to argue that the law itself defined this second offense as *lenocinium.*[264] First, this offense too is peculiar to the complaisant husband. Second,

---

[257] Daube, "Lex Julia" 374, while acknowledging this possibility, takes the word *stuprum* to refer exclusively to adultery. It is important to recognize that the lack of clarity is the fault of the legislator, not of the jurists. The latter is assumed by Alvarez de Cienfuegos, "*Lenocinium*" 375–376, who argues that this crime was never considered to be *lenocinium.* On this point, see the criticism of Rizzelli, "*Crimen*" 488.

[258] Pap. D. 48.5.11(10).1. For a very different view of this text, see Rizzelli, "*Crimen*" 488.

[259] Ulp. (4 *de adult.*) D. 48.5.30(29).6.

[260] Val., Gall. C. 9.9.17.1 (a. 257).

[261] See Biondi, "*Leges*" 208–209.

[262] It will be seen in the next chapter how this provision embraced persons other than the husband as potential offenders.

[263] Similarly, Andréev, "Lex Iulia" (1963) 177.

[264] Esmein, "Délit" 102–104.

this provision of the law has special importance because of the rule that no one may undertake a prosecution of the wife unless she has been divorced or her husband has been convicted of *lenocinium*.[265]

The texts mention only an accusation of the husband, not his conviction, for *lenocinium*, but the latter is usually assumed to be necessary.[266] The wife might be accused of adultery if the husband died before divorce, although a careful reading of the evidence shows that there was only a small window of opportunity open here.[267] Failing divorce, or removal of the husband through death or conviction on a charge of *lenocinium*, the only recourse left to a third party was to accuse the lover. We are, to be sure, given contrasting information on this point, a fact that may be explained in terms of a Severan legal innovation.[268]

Volterra's view seems correct that the formal divorce procedure (sometimes referred to as *repudium*) framed by the adultery law was intended to demarcate clearly the beginning of the prescriptive period for prosecution and insulate the husband from a charge of *lenocinium* (strictly necessary only with an *uxor depre-hensa*).[269] Andréev suggests a further aim would have been to discourage spouses, in cases of mutual complicity, from claiming that an informal divorce had occurred prior to the act of adultery;[270] of course, even under this claim the wife would still be liable to a charge of *stuprum*. To be clear, the law laid down a formal procedure of divorce, not to guarantee its validity, but at minimum to publicize it, and so shield the husband from a charge of *lenocinium*.

The law in fact imposed a double duty on the husband, as the following text shows:

> Ulp. (4 *de adult.*) D. 48.5.30(29) pr.: Mariti lenocinium lex coercuit, qui depre-hensam uxorem in adulterio retinuit adulterumque dimisit: debuit enim[271] uxori quoque irasci, quae matrimonium eius violavit. tunc autem puniendus est mari-tus, cum excusare ignorantiam suam non potest vel adumbrare patientiam prae-textu incredibilitatis: idcirco enim lex ita locuta est "adulterum in domo depre-hensum dimiserit," quod voluerit in ipsa turpitudine deprehendentem[272] maritum coercere.

---

[265] Esmein, "Délit" 103. See esp. Ulp. D. 48.5.27(26) pr. This text is criticized (in a manner that does not affect the point made here) by Solazzi, "Storia" (1946/1963) 517–521, and by De' Domenicis, "Origini" (1950), and is defended by Kaser (rev. De' Dominicis) (1951).

[266] Esmein, "Délit" 120; Thomas, "Lex Julia" (1970) 641.

[267] Ulp. D. 48.5.30(29).5 (an imperial rescript).

[268] Pap. *(lib. sing. de adult.)* D. 48.5.12(11).10; Pap. (15 *resp.*) D. *eod.* 40(39).1.

[269] Volterra, "D. 48.5.44(43)" (1965). His view is defended by Thomas, "Lex Julia" 643–644. See also Gardner, *Women* 85–86, and Rizzelli, "*Crimen*" 459–469, who restrict the use of this di-vorce procedure to cases of flagrancy; and Treggiari, "Divorce" (1991) 37, and Treggiari, *RM* 455–458, who adds the motive of insulating the wife who remarries after divorce from a charge that the new relationship was adultery because the prior tie allegedly remained unbroken and the motive of making recovery of the dowry easier. Levy, *Hergang* (1925) 31–43, argues that the pro-cedure was designed to protect the husband by abrogating *manus* where the woman was unwilling to cooperate.

[270] Andréev, "Divorce" (1957), followed by Gomez Ruiz, *Divorcio* (1987) 130–131.

[271] Mommsen suggests inserting "hunc ulcisci"; see below.

[272] For this reading, see Mommsen ad loc.

The statute has punished the *lenocinium* of a husband who has kept his wife and let her lover go; after all, he ought to be angry with his wife as well, since she has committed an outrage upon his marriage. The husband is to be punished when he cannot justify his ignorance or mask his tolerant attitude with the pretext of disbelief: it is for this reason, then, that the law has spoken of the man who "has let go an adulterer caught in his house," because it wanted to compel the husband who catches the lover in the illicit sexual act itself to take action.

The text has been shortened by the compilers.[273] The "quoque" in the phrase "debuit enim uxori quoque irasci" will not bear the weight of the husband's reaction against the lover, as the sense requires. It is also strange that the jurist quotes the legislative provision regarding the *adulter* caught in the act as part of the justification for divorcing the wife. Other evidence suggests that the divorce requirement formed part of the legislation,[274] and Ulpian no doubt discussed it in this place.

The explanation of the divorce requirement is obvious. The *lex Iulia* assigned the husband a pivotal role: he shared the rights of a privileged accuser with the father, but even the latter could not exercise his right to accuse his daughter if the husband did not act first by divorcing her. A measure of the requirement's importance may be seen in the fact that Tiberius released an unnamed equestrian from his oath that he would never divorce his wife, after she was discovered in adultery with her son-in-law.[275] Among other benefits, husband and father were allowed a time period within which they had the exclusive right to prosecute: the 60 *dies utiles* for the *ius mariti vel patris* began to run from the day of the divorce, and only after that was the prosecution opened to *extranei*.[276]

So far we have half of the double duty the law imposed on the husband. He must also not allow her partner to go *(dimittere)*. The husband was punished who "adulterum in domo deprehensum dimiserit."[277] The precise meaning of this second requirement is unclear.[278] One possibility is that either the husband must hold the lover for a period of time (not to exceed 20 hours) after discovery. Another is that he himself is compelled to prosecute the man.

---

[273] Volterra's elimination of "tunc . . . incredibilitatis" does not improve the sense: "Innovazioni" (1930) 11. Rather than introducing new material, the compilers seem to have cut drastically. (See also Chapter 6.)

[274] Note the similar wording in other passages that refer to this requirement: Tryph. (3 *disp.*) D. 4.4.37.1 ("in adulterio deprehensam uxorem non dimiserit"); Ulp. (8 *disp.*) D. 48.5.2.6 ("uxorem in adulterio deprehensam retinuisse").

[275] Suet. *Tib.* 35.1.

[276] On the privileged accusation, see above. The jurists eventually admitted *extranei* before the expiration of the 60-day period when husband and father emphatically denied intent to prosecute: Pomp.-Ulp. D. 48.5.16(15).5.

[277] Ulp. (4 *de adult.*) D. 48.5.30(29) pr., quoting the statute.

[278] Esmein, "Délit" 104–105, connects this duty with the prohibition against accepting compensation. But the evidence does not support this interpretation; the offense he describes is attested as a separate offense under the statute *(pretium)*. If simply letting someone go without payment was no offense, it is hard to see how liability is construed in Marci. D. 48.5.34(33).1.

Recently, Alvarez de Cienfuegos has argued for the first alternative.[279] One might reply that an important text, which perhaps quotes the law, says that the husband "may" ("*liceat*") retain the adulterer for purposes of gathering evidence, not that he "must" ("*debeat*" or an equivalent).[280] In fact, the situation appears to be more complicated. To judge from the way Ulpian's commentary on the adultery statute is written, the dismissal of the wife's lover seems to have been mentioned at two points in the law.

The injunction, which derives from the fifth chapter of the law, is discussed by Ulpian in the second book of his commentary, while *lenocinium* itself is treated in book 4.[281] A repetition of this kind is interesting, because it furnishes an insight into the way the norm itself was articulated. Under the heading of *lenocinium,* the law simply punished the husband who let go the lover *deprehensus* in the married couple's home.[282] In another part of the law, the legislator authorized the husband who, having come upon the *adulter* in the circumstances described, would not or could not avail himself of the *ius occidendi* to detain the man for up to 20 hours for the purpose of gathering evidence.[283]

The jurists extended the privilege to the woman's father and widened it to include cases of *deprehendere* that occurred outside the husband's home.[284] Obviously, the husband was not *required* to detain the man when discovery occurred outside the home, and *pater* was under no such obligation at all. The fact that the same act was articulated both as a duty and as a privilege by the statute suggests that in this instance, at any rate, the jurists did not simply construe a positive right out of an injunction not to do the opposite.[285]

This implies that the husband could escape liability for *lenocinium* by holding the man for much less than 20 hours—perhaps it was enough to hold him only as long as a good faith effort to accumulate evidence required. If witnesses were already on hand, the *adulter* might even be released immediately.

There is no evidence of an obligation to prosecute the lover caught "in domo," nor does the law seem to have imposed a similar duty with regard to the wife. This emerges from a text of Ulpian, where a certain Claudius Gorgus, while conducting a prosecution of his wife before the emperor, "was shown to have remained married to his wife after she had been caught in the act of adultery".[286] He is convicted of *lenocinium,* which suggests that divorce, not prosecution, was what the law required. Since the trial, a "*cognitio,*" did not take place in the standing criminal court, or *quaestio,* for adultery, we cannot be certain that the rules given by the statute apply, but this seems likely.[287]

---

[279] Alvarez de Cienfuegos, "*Lenocinium*" 569–570.

[280] Ulp. (2 *de adult.*) D. 48.5.26(25) pr. Cf. *PS* 2.26.3. See now Rizzelli, "*Crimen*" 468.

[281] See Lenel, *Pal.* 2 cols. 932, 937–938. On the structure and composition of the statute, see Biondi, "*Leges*" 201, 208.

[282] Ulp. D. 48.5.30(29) pr. (quoted above).

[283] Ulp. D. 48.5.26(25) pr.−5. Cf. *PS* 2.26.3.

[284] Ulp. D. 48.5.26(25).1, 2.

[285] As argued by Levy, *Hergang* 10 n. 5.

[286] Ulp. (8 *disp.*) D. 48.5.2.6: "detectus est uxorem in adulterio deprehensam retinuisse."

[287] The case of Appuleia Varilla, for whom no prosecutor could be found, may also be pertinent.

When the husband killed an adulterer caught in the act, the law enjoined immediate divorce but evidently said nothing of prosecuting the wife.[288] That there was some feeling that the husband should, at least under certain circumstances, proceed with prosecution is seen in Pliny's report of a trial held before Trajan and his *consilium*.[289] All the same, this evidence does not permit the firm conclusion that a statutory duty to prosecute existed.[290] We are not told that the lovers tried by the emperor were *deprehensi*. Trajan's insistence that the husband proceed with the prosecution of his wife is motivated by the immediately preceding conviction of his wife's lover. We cannot be absolutely sure that the husband had divorced his wife in accordance with the law and was not instead simply keeping her with him ("domi habuerat"). This trial too was a "*cognitio*," and it is again difficult to be certain that the rules as applied derive from the statute.[291]

The husband was granted 60 days to divorce his wife after discovery.[292] Perhaps Claudius Gorgus's predicament stemmed from the fact that he had let more than 60 days lapse before he divorced his wife. It is more difficult to believe that he sailed into court while still married to the defendant.[293]

One text holds that the spirit, though not the letter, of the law is violated if the husband does not dismiss *(dimittere)* but retains *(retinere)* the offender when he happens to be a member of the household.[294] This would make little sense if the legislative requirement was understood as a duty to prosecute. The law simply said *non dimittere* and might be obeyed through the taking of any appropriate action, such as holding the man while evidence was gathered, prosecuting him, or both: in any case, the duty to divorce the *uxor deprehensa* was clear.[295] The point was to publicize the offense, in order to encourage third parties to step forward in situations where the husband was reluctant to prosecute. Some discretion is allowed the husband, even in very serious cases. Another aim was to punish the husband tainted by overcomplaisance *(patientia)*.[296] The tension between the aim of allowing some discretion and the need to punish raised problems of some delicacy.[297]

There are two other offenses punished by the *lex Iulia* though not originally defined as *lenocinium*. One of these is knowingly to marry a woman convicted of

---

Tac. *Ann.* 2.50; cf. Suet. *Tib.* 35.1, who generalizes from this instance (for another opinion, see Goodyear, *Annals* 2 [1981] 346).

[288] Macer D. 48.5.25(24).1.

[289] Plin. *Ep.* 6.31.4–6, a text discussed further in Chapter 6.

[290] Contra Edwards, *Politics* 39.

[291] For arguments on both sides, see Rizzelli, "*Crimen*" 471 n. 32.

[292] McGinn, "*SC*" 287 n. 73. This period was later shortened, perhaps sometime in the third century: *PS* 2.26.8 (= *Coll.* 4.12.7) punishes the man who does not divorce his *deprehensa uxor* "at once" ("statim"). For the changes wrought by Justinian in this area, see Beaucamp, *Statut* 1.160–165.

[293] The latter is usually assumed: Bauman, "*Leges*" 165; Rilinger, *Humiliores* 173. A similar case may occur at Dioclet., Maxim. C. 9.9.25(26) (a. 293). For the case of a husband whose indictment of his (deceased) wife casts mud on himself, see Quint. *IO* 9.2.79–80.

[294] Marci. D. 48.5.34(33).1.

[295] See Rizzelli, "*Crimen*" 468–469, who points out that a husband's duties to divorce his wife and to detain her lover were "interdependent."

[296] Ovid. *Am.* 2.19.51–52; Plin. *Ep.* 6.31.4–6; Tert. *Patientia* 16.3 (see below).

[297] See Chapter 6.

adultery. The statutory prohibition was extended by the jurists to include women convicted of *stuprum*.[298] The offense itself was at some point redefined as a form of *lenocinium*, as a rescript of Alexander Severus suggests.[299] It has been argued that it originally comprised statutory *lenocinium*, on the basis of language that is inconclusive at best. Alvarez de Cienfuegos[300] takes the phrase in the rescript of Alexander Severus[301] "eadem lege ex causa lenocinii" to mean that the *lex Iulia* itself punished knowingly marrying or remarrying such a woman as *lenocinium*. "Under the same statute as a type of *lenocinium*" may reflect a juristic synthesis. I doubt remarriage was specifically punished by the law, as it was certainly not in the case of the woman *deprehensa*, then divorced.[302] The law hardly needed to spell this out and the detail may have arisen from the situation of fact on which the constitution depends.

Is there an analogy with the *uxor deprehensa*, whose husband was compelled to divorce her?[303] Yes and No: it was strong enough to motivate the jurists to regard *damnatam ducere* as a species of *lenocinium*,[304] but it is doubtful that the same held true for the statute. *Deprehensam retinere* is itself an artificial conception of "pimping" (in marked contrast to *quaestum facere*). This makes a further statutory extension of the *genus* to an even more remote *species* unlikely. While the adultery law denied *damnatae* the right to marry, enforcing the ban by punishing their marriage partners, the main point seems to have been to impose yet another penalty on the women themselves. The same is true of the legislative measure that made the status of the *deprehensa* equal to that of the *damnata* under the Augustan marriage law prohibitions.[305] With statutory *lenocinium*, the complaisant husband stands at the center of the stage.

The final offense in this category is to provide a venue for an act of adultery to take place, *domum praebere*. It is reasonably certain that the law punished such conduct, but no evidence exists that it was defined by the statute as a form of *lenocinium*.[306] Rizzelli[307] argues that *domum praebere* was not actually listed as an offense by the statute but was the product of juristic elaboration. Papinian,[308] however, places it in the same chapter of the law as *pretium accipere*.[309] Tryphoninus[310]

---

[298] Ulp. D. 48.5.30(29).1.

[299] Alex. Sev. C. 9.9.9 (a. 224).

[300] Alvarez de Cienfuegos, "*Lenocinium*" 571–572.

[301] Alex. Sev. C. 9.9.9 (a. 224).

[302] Marci. D. 48.5.34(33).1. See Chapter 6.

[303] Rizzelli, "*Crimen*" 470–473.

[304] See further Chapter 6.

[305] See Chapter 3. It is interesting for this context that the adultery law itself did not make this equation.

[306] See, e.g., Pap. D. 48.5.9(8) pr.–1; Ulp. *eod.* 10(9) pr.–2.

[307] Rizzelli, "*Crimen*" 484–490.

[308] Pap. D. 48.5.11(10).1. I give what I believe to be the plain meaning of the text; cf. Rizzelli, "*Crimen*" 487–490.

[309] The text that immediately precedes, Pap. D. 48.5.9(8) pr., as rightly interpreted by De Robertis, shows how the Augustan statute was understood in the Severan age: it is not necessary to alter its meaning by inserting the word *mulier,* as preferred by Rizzelli, "*Crimen*" 485 n. 60.

[310] Tryph. (3 *disp.*) D. 4.4.37.1: "quae pro adulterio eadem lex [sc. Iulia] punit."

names *domum praebere* among those offenses "which the same law [sc., the *lex Iulia*] punishes in the same way as adultery." Rizzelli[311] argues on the basis of the falsified (by the compilers) reference to the adultery law at Inst. 4.18.4 that the reference to this statute in the Tryphoninus passage is counterfeit. But the two cases are not equivalent. Justinian's *Institutes* present a postclassical norm as classical. There is no obvious reason why the compilers would alter a jurist's reference to an *SC* or imperial constitution as the source of a rule. Such references are retained by the compilers, at least in the *Digest,* where they are relatively common.

A trial of two equestrians before the Senate on a charge of *domum praebere* in A.D. 47 is not absolute proof that the offense was included in the statute.[312] Of course, it hardly proves the opposite, and the incident, above all its early date, is suggestive:[313] the inclusion of charges construed as *maiestas* and the woman's rank motivated trial before the Senate in place of the *quaestio.*[314] The same factors hold true for the men convicted of acting as Albucilla's "stuprorum . . . ministri" in A.D. 37:[315] the language is vague and untechnical as to the charge, but *domum praebere* seems a likely guess. Finally, the prohibition *domum praebere* was written and interpreted in such a manner as to suggest original provenience in the adultery law.[316]

In the following chapter it will be seen how these accessory offenses, *pretium accipere, damnatam ducere,* and *domum praebere,* came to be grouped under the rubric of criminal pimping. Let us turn now to an explanation of the two statutory types, *deprehensam retinere* and especially *quaestum facere.*

The legislator wanted, with *deprehensam retinere,* to compel men with wives whose guilt was manifest to dissolve their marriages and allow the law to run its course. At the same time, they were expected to take some action against their rivals. Failure to act meant possible conviction on a charge that carried a penalty as grave as that of adultery, added to the public stigma of identification as a man who played the role of a pimp for his own wife. The husband's centrality to the operation of the law, and the desire to repress sharply the most notorious, flagrant cases, adequately explain the legislator's interest. The rationale behind *quaestum facere* is not as obvious. Was the law simply concerned to make a statement about the proper role of husbands by constructing a worst case that did not have much chance of practical application? Or was this provision a response to genuine fears about the conduct of some married men? Were these fears in turn grounded in reality?

The evidence does not permit a definitive response. The men who wrote the text of the *lex Iulia* were clearly in the business of manipulating symbols. It is impossible to know the actual frequency of men selling the services of their wives.

---

[311] Rizzelli, "*Crimen*" 484 n. 7.

[312] So Rizzelli, "*Crimen*" 485 n. 59, on Tac. *Ann.* 11.4.1.

[313] For that matter, provision of a venue for a tryst was behavior familiar to Plautus and his audience: *Cas.* 595–598; see also Catull. 68.67–69.

[314] Garnsey, *Status* 18–24; cf. Bauman, *Impietas* (1974) 202–203.

[315] Tac. *Ann.* 6.48.4: the culprits in this case were of senatorial rank, which offers another motive for the Senate's interest.

[316] See the discussion in Chapter 6.

Such behavior appears to be given prominence in the statute at least partly in order to create an egregious specimen of husbandly misbehavior as a counterpart to the infidelity of the wife, whom the law brands not exactly as a whore, but as a prostitute.

There are some instances where men are reluctant to take action against their wives although the women are manifestly guilty. This is true of Titidius Labeo, Claudius Gorgus, and the unnamed military tribune who conducted his case before Trajan.[317] Actual cases of flagrancy, as contemplated by the *lex Iulia,* were perhaps not very common.[318] But it is difficult to find even a single clear-cut case of a man making a profit *(quaestus)* from his wife's adultery. A possible exception, the story of Gabba and Maecenas related by Plutarch,[319] may predate the law or may be pure fiction. The basis for the charge of *lenocinium* leveled at Macro, Caligula's praetorian prefect, is rather opaque, and because of the political motivations behind the charge, it should be regarded as singular.[320]

All the same, the provision does not seem entirely devoid of practical concerns. The legislator anticipated that the law would be abused by those whose behavior it was supposed to modify, and we do hear of such blackmail practiced in the period following its passage. Even more interesting are the signs of a genuine concern about husbandly misbehavior that we find expressed in various quarters. Some of this betrays an upper-class anxiety about the sexual behavior of the lower classes. The law in part responds to a genuine fear, even if it was not a realistic one. A parallel may be sought in the turn-of-the-century concern over "white slavery," a phenomenon that, if it existed, was wildly exaggerated by fears grounded in anxiety over the changing role and status of women, mass immigration, and the consequences of industrialization. This concern was felt in several countries, among them the United States, where it led to the passage of the Mann Act in 1910.[321] Wife sale in early modern England may stand as another example.[322]

The Romans had a proverbial expression, "non omnibus dormio" ("I don't [feign] sleep for everyone"), that was popularized, if not coined, by the satirist Lucilius, writing in the last third of the second century B.C.[323] It derives from a story about one Cipius, surnamed "Pararrhencon," or "the Snorer," who feigned sleep in order to facilitate the adultery of his wife. Cipius tolerated his wife's behavior with an eye to financial gain but was not prepared to put up with interference in his affairs that did not bring a profit, such as a slave stealing silverware

---

[317] For Titidius, see Tac. *Ann.* 2.85.3 and Chapter 6; for the latter two, see above and note the observation of Augustine about the reluctance of husbands to take action at *Ep.* 78.6.

[318] So Venturini, "*Accusatio*" 79.

[319] Plut. *Amat.* 759F–760B.

[320] See Philo *Leg. Gai* 57–61; Tac. *Ann.* 6.45.3; Suet. *Cal.* 12.2, 26.1; Dio 58.28.4, 59.10.6. For the various approaches taken to this problem, see Balsdon, *Gaius* (1934/1964) 21; Bauman, *Impietas* 176; Barrett, *Caligula* (1989) 34; Corbier, "Divorce" (1991) 60; Ferrill, *Caligula* (1991) 88, 107.

[321] Levi, *Introduction* (1949) 33–57; Connelly, *Response* (1980) 58–60, ch. 6; Walkowitz, *Prostitution* (1980) 17, 247; Rosen, *Sisterhood* (1982) ch. 7; Gibson, *Prostitution* (1986) 83; Corbin, *Women for Hire* (1990) 275–298; Hobson, *Virtue* (1990) 61–76, 102, 141–147; Langum, *Crossing* (1994) esp. 26–39. For another view, see Barry, *Slavery* (1979).

[322] Stone, *Road* (1990) 148.

[323] Festus 174–176L.

from the table, thus the point of the proverb.[324] The story perhaps traces its roots to New Comedy;[325] at any rate the nickname suggests a source of Greek literary origin.[326] An important source, an oration of Dio of Prusa, identifies this snoring or snorting with the type of the feminized male, the *kinaidos*.[327]

The theme of the complaisant husband developed into a popular topos in subsequent Latin literature, with several of its occurrences stamped with the influence of Lucilius.[328] This is true of the offhand references to Cipius by Cicero in two letters of 45 B.C. (see above), and of Juvenal, writing satire early in the second century:[329]

> Iuv. 1.55–57:[330] When the "pimp" receives the lover's[331] property (if it happens that the wife cannot receive bequests), he, practiced at gazing at the paneled ceiling, practiced at pretending to snore away at table . . .

By acting as a procurer, the husband renders his marriage invalid with regard to the *lex Iulia et Papia*.[332] The sense is compressed, the thought allusive, and different interpretations are possible. Courtney[333] is right to criticize the older view that the husband receives a *fideicommissum* with the wife as beneficiary.[334] He puts forth two possibilities. One is that the wife was ineligible because of the *lex Voconia,* but this law may have been a dead letter by now.[335] The other is that the wife, not the husband, was unable to receive bequests because of the *lex Iulia et Papia:* "if the husband had children by a previous marriage and the wife had none." But there is no reason to assume that the husband-pimp received a bequest, pace the scholiast, instead of mere payment and no need to posit a previous marriage.

In my view, the force of the joke is perhaps that the wife, presumably freeborn and therefore married to a notional pimp contrary to the prohibitions of the marriage law, is now ineligible for testamentary bequests from her *adulter:* the husband's

[324] See Cic. *Fam.* 7.24.1: "Cipius (opinor) olim, "non omnibus dormio." " Cf. *Att.* 13.49.2, an editorial insertion.

[325] See *Com. Adesp.* fr. 8 (= Plut. *Aud. Poet.* 27C) and Alciphr. 3.62. The theme is employed as a tool of invective by the Attic orators: Aesch. 2.149; [Demosth.] 59.41, 68.

[326] From later Greek literature there is the epigram of Parmenion (*AP* 11.4; see also Callicter at 11.5) about the man who finds "snoring" the path to easy wealth, and the two stories related by Plutarch (*Amat.* 759F–760B), one of which, about Gabba and Maecenas, displays a certain affinity with Lucilius's story.

[327] Dio Chrys. 33, with MacMullen, "Difference" (1986/1990) 145, with n. 25.

[328] Some of these are collected in Tracy, "Leno" (1976/1977).

[329] See Syme, *Tacitus* 2 (1958) 500, who dates all of Juvenal's work to Hadrian's reign; and Courtney, *Juvenal* 1–11, 97–98, who places the first satires in Trajan's. Similarly, Conte, *LL* 760.

[330] "Cum leno accipiat moechi bona, si capiendi / ius nullum uxori, doctus spectare lacunar, / doctus et ad calicem vigilanti stertere naso . . .''

[331] The double meaning of "adulterer" and "prostitute's customer" is especially pointed here: *OLD* s.h.v.; McGinn, *Social Policy* 73 n. 23.

[332] His wife was forbidden to marry a pimp unless she were a freedwoman. See Chapter 3.

[333] Courtney, *Juvenal* 97–98.

[334] No reliance should be placed on the scholiast (fantasy) and Ulp. D. 50.16.71 pr. and [Quint.] *Decl.* 325 (irrelevant).

[335] See Kaser, *RP* 1² 684; Vigneron, "Loi" (1983). For another view, see Dixon, "Breaking" (1985) 530–531.

role as go-between is thereby enhanced (Juvenal does not explicitly say that the husband receives the payoff in the form of a bequest; to insist that he does may press the legal content of the joke too hard). Alternatively, we can take this text as evidence that Domitian's regulation denying *capacitas* to adulteresses is still in force.[336] Under either scenario, we must posit some degree of extralegal collusion between the spouses: in the latter case, Juvenal may be taking a swipe at the ineffectiveness of Domitian's measure.

Less obviously dependent on Lucilius is a satire of Horace devoted to a witty extension of the conversation between Ulysses and Tiresias from book 11 of the *Odyssey*.[337] The seer is lavish with practical advice, chiefly consisting of unseemly ways to acquire wealth. Cadging testamentary bequests looms large, and a surefire way of guaranteeing the goodwill of the will-maker is to hand over Penelope. Horace's treatment betrays a general affinity with the topos developed by Lucilius and Juvenal, and it is sensible simply to view him as playing a variation on it.

In the same way, a woman's generous dowry might raise suspicions about husbandly complaisance.[338] It threatened to render the husband dependent on his wife's wealth, which would make him reluctant or unable to control her behavior.[339] The result was a reversal of the approved hierarchy of gender within the household, and in the end a feminizing of the now subordinate male.[340]

Ovid too exploits this theme.[341] In book 3 of the *Amores* he urges on a husband the material advantages of adopting a tolerant attitude toward his wife's affairs.[342] The tone adopted recalls the cheerfully corrupt advice offered by Tiresias,[343] but the recent passage of the *lex Iulia*[344] may also have influenced Ovid's choice of theme here and at *Amores* 2.19.[345] So Augustus's Golden Age is golden precisely because gold purchased "love."[346]

The association between gifts and a woman's adultery, though of obvious significance for *lenocinium,* enjoys an importance all its own. Here was a touch-

---

[336] See Chapter 4. For the argument that the passage owes more to rhetoric (specifically declamation) than to law, see Cloud, "Satirists" (1989) 55–57.

[337] Hor. *Serm.* 2.5, esp. 75–83.

[338] As, for example, Juvenal does when he attacks (6.136–141) the man who tolerates his wife's infidelities because of her enormous wealth, a distinct, though related, theme. Compare Cato's complaints as registered at Gell. 17.6. See also Iuv. 9.70–80, where the husband's motive in suborning Naevolus is evidently to preserve access to his wife's property.

[339] See, e.g., Plaut. *Aul.* 483; Hor. *Carm.* 3.24.19–20; Mart. 8.12.

[340] Evidence in Treggiari, *RM* 330–331, cf. 97, 104, 106, 198, 218. Mart. 8.12 merits emphasis.

[341] The variations played by the elegists at times blur the distinction between gifts to lover-adulteress and gifts to lover-prostitute: Prop. 2.8.11, 16; 20.25–26; 23.8, 17; 3.12.19; 13; 4.5, esp. 29.

[342] Ovid. *Am.* 3.4. Cf. Martial's salute to the man who has everything: 3.26.

[343] Note the twist put upon Penelope's motives for proposing the test of the bow at *Am.* 1.8.47–48. Odysseus might be similarly impugned: Plut. *Aud. Poet.* 27B–C.

[344] On the disputed chronology of the *Amores,* with its two editions, see Conte, *LL* 340. Of course, we do not know to which edition these poems originally belonged, so that caution is necessary.

[345] Ovid complains that the husband's tolerant attitude is robbing his affair of its joy: "quid mihi cum facili, quid cum lenone marito?" (*Am.* 2.19.57). Cf. *Ars* 2.543–548, esp. 545. For a neat reversal, see Mart. 1.73. The more usual tactic is to complain of the husband's or family's *custodia,* because this separates lovers: André, "Statut" (1980) esp. 57–61.

[346] Ovid. *Ars* 2.277–278; cf. *Her.* 5.143–144 (not universally accepted as genuine).

stone of female vulnerability,[347] which demanded the vigilance of the responsible husband. "What a husband refuses he will see given by other men," cries Cato in the heat of the debate, as Livy presents it, over the repeal of the *lex Oppia*.[348] Gifts were a routine expectation in adulterous affairs,[349] whose discreet delivery was acknowledged as a crack social skill.[350] The mere presence of gifts, without an obvious source, in a woman's house argued the existence of an affair[351] or, at any rate, an attempt at seduction.[352] The association was so familiar it formed the substance of an allusive joke.[353] Adultery was reproved as a source of waste and extravagance, in the same way as gambling.[354]

Whether the wife or the husband (as *leno*)[355] benefited from the lover's largesse, there was an obvious connection with prostitution, that is, the exchange of sex for material gain.[356] The strength of this association helps explain the juristic delicacy exhibited in the following:[357]

Muc.-Pomp. (5 *ad Quintum Mucium*) D. 24.1.51: Quintus Mucius ait, cum in controversiam venit, unde ad mulierem quid pervenerit, et verius et honestius est quod non demonstratur unde habeat existimari a viro aut qui in potestate eius esset ad eam pervenisse. evitandi autem turpis quaestus gratia circa uxorem hoc videtur Quintus Mucius probasse.

Quintus Mucius [Scaevola] is of the opinion that when a dispute arises over the source of property that has passed to a woman, it is better law and more socially acceptable that the property whose provenance is unclear be deemed to have passed to her from her husband or someone in his power. What is more, Quintus Mucius seems to have adopted this position to avoid an inquiry[358] about "ill-gotten gain" with respect to the wife.

In my view,[359] this text makes reasonably clear that when a married woman is found to be in the possession of property whose provenance is unknown, the au-

---

[347] See Apul. *Met.* 9.19.

[348] Liv. 34.4.16–18.

[349] Sen. *Ben.* 1.9.4; Iuv. 1.77. Caesar's presents to his mistresses created quite an impression: Suet. *Iul.* 50.2.

[350] Iuv. 3.45–46.

[351] Quint. *IO* 7.2.52. On testamentary bequests as another means of transferring property to gratify a lover; see Val. Max. 8.2.2 (with Kaser, *Verbotsgesetze* 80–86); Sen. *Contr.* 2.7; Tac. *Ann.* 13.44.1.

[352] See Balzarini, *Iniuria* (1983) 195 on *PS* 5.4.14, and cf. Val. Max. 6.1.8.

[353] Ovid. *Ars* 2.575–576. The *munus* sought by the lover from his *amica* is, of course, sex: Stroh, "Liebeskunst" (1979) 350.

[354] See Sturm, "Weib" (1979).

[355] Juvenal (2.58–61) has a gender reversal, where it is the wife who profits from her tolerance of her husband's affairs with other married women.

[356] Iuv. 3.132–136. Note the horror of Val. Max. 2.6.15 at Carthaginian women at Sicca who prostitute themselves to raise a dowry. The association between gifts and prostitution holds even where the woman's marital status is uncertain: Catull. 110; cf. the evidence of Propertius above, n. 341.

[357] The holding, known to modern scholars as the *praesumptio Muciana*, is restated at Alex. Sev. C. 5.16.6.1 (a. 229).

[358] The editors of the *Digest* suggest reading "evitandae autem turpis quaestus quaestionis gratia" to fill an evident lacuna in the text. My translation reflects this change.

[359] For another view of the rationale behind the holding, see Kaser, "*Praesumptio*" (1956); Kaser,

tomatic assumption in the popular mind is that she must have received it from a secret lover. Mucius Scaevola seals this can of worms with the presumption (presumably rebuttable if evidence is to hand) that the source was respectable. Pomponius's final sentence, though disturbed, preserves enough sense to make the telling identification of the putative adulteress's booty as *turpis quaestus*. The phrase resonates well with her overall assimilation to a prostitute under the *lex Iulia* on adultery.[360]

The topos of the husband-pimp was a popular one, treated with wit and ingenuity by a number of authors and a favorite especially of those working in the satiric tradition. It is difficult to use this evidence as a means of assessing the seriousness, or even the existence, of a contemporary anxiety about such behavior. Purely literary motives influenced the selection of the theme and its treatment. One example of such a motive is the desire to establish a connection with a predecessor working in the same genre. The humor rife in these accounts is another deterrent to reading them as straightforward social commentary. If Ovid was influenced by the passage of the *lex Iulia* in his choice of theme here (and this is far from guaranteed), it would be rash to argue that he viewed the subject with real seriousness.

But it is significant that much of our evidence comes from Satire, a literary genre characterized as much by the aim of moral criticism as by that of entertainment.[361] It does not require an excess of ingenuity or naiveté to resist the conclusion that the fears described are the pure invention of the satirists. Other sources support the view that some genuine concern lay at the heart of this theme. Horace himself, writing not long after the Tiresias poem was published,[362] turned again to the theme of marital collusion, but this time with a very different tone:

> Hor. *Carm.* 3.6.25–32:[363] Then she [sc., the sexually mature young woman] goes after younger lovers while her husband is in his cups. She exercises no discretion over the persons on whom she, on the spur of the moment, in the dark, bestows illicit pleasures, but, when asked, she rises in full view of everyone, her husband in the know, whether it is a traveling salesman who approaches her or the captain of a ship from Spain, the free-spending purchaser of shame.

RP 1² 332. Kaser canvasses, without emphasis, the solution offered here. Similarly, Garcia Garrido, *Ius uxorium* (1958) 119–121. Cf. Pomp. D. 7.8.7 and Paul. D. 28.2.9.1. On the latter text, Kaser, "Rechtswidrigkeit" (1940) 126, is surely right about the rule depending on the anticipation of the husband's death; nevertheless, the notion of adultery persists, in my view.

[360] On prostitutes' *quaestus* and *turpitudo,* see Chapters 3 and 4.

[361] See the treatment by Rudd, *Themes* (1986), esp. ch. 1. Rudd sees a threefold purpose to satire consisting of attack, entertainment, and sermonizing. The relative proportions of this admixture differ from poet to poet and even from poem to poem, with the result that a number of useful distinctions can be drawn. Others lend greater emphasis to the theme of moral exhortation: Witke, *Latin Satire* (1970) 4–15.

[362] Book 2 of the *Satires* dates to 30–29 and *Odes* 1–3 to 23 B.C.: Conte, *LL* 752–753. Past attempts to link this poem with what was widely thought to be a legislative proposal or repealed statute in 28 B.C. founder on Badian's showing that there is no substance to this shadow; See Chapter 3.

[363] "Mox iuniores quaerit [sc., matura virgo] adulteros / inter mariti vina, neque eligit / cui donet impermissa raptim / gaudia luminibus remotis, / sed iussa coram non sine conscio / surgit marito, seu vocat institor / seu navis Hispanae magister, / dedecorum pretiosus emptor.''

The indiscriminate nature of the wife's behavior and the element of payment mark her out as a prostitute;[364] the husband's tolerance (the unmistakable implication is that he is motivated by gain) defines him as a pimp. Horace depicts such behavior as responsible for the ruin of the marriage bond and the Roman family, which in turn has led to a precarious situation for the state. The emergency cannot be remedied by the mere restoration of temples.[365]

We do not have to credit Horace with clairvoyance or with an insider's access to particular details of Augustus's legislative design five years or more before the law's enactment. I think it no exaggeration to regard this passage as a reflection of widespread contemporary concern with the state of Roman society, especially its foundation, the family.[366] It fits into the pattern of a summons to moral regeneration that is characteristic of the age. We cannot hope, of course, to penetrate past the level of public opinion and its formation through prescription and criticism. We do not know if the practice presented by Horace was widespread. He describes a type of behavior that is particularly outrageous and has taken effort to paint it in the darkest colors. But if the scenario is fiction, the fear is real.

The enactment of the *lex Iulia* meant that such behavior was now punishable as a crime. The evidence remains unsatisfactory, but there is more of it. *Lenocinium* appears in the works of the astrologers,[367] becomes a popular subject with the declaimers,[368] and continues to be decried by moralists.[369] It might be fashioned into an effective piece of courtroom rhetoric, even when it did not form the substance of a charge. The last point is illustrated by Apuleius's assault on the character of Herennius Rufinus, whom he arraigns as the chief instigator of the charge of magic laid against him:

[364] The lovers are types who would be expected to frequent a prostitute; cf. the *peregrinus negotiator* of Sen. *Contr.* 2.7.

[365] See *Carm.* 3.6.1–4 and cf. Verg. *Georg.* 1.501–502 with Wallace-Hadrill, ''Golden Age'' (1982) esp. 24–26. This was of course Augustus's great boast: *RG* 20.4; cf. Suet. *Aug.* 29. He revived the cult of Pudicitia in 28–27: Palmer, ''Shrines'' 137–139. This, of course hardly exhausts the range of Augustus's extensive religious program: Kienast, ''Rechtsordnung'' (1984) 137–139; Bowersock, ''Pontificate'' (1990). Galinsky, *Augustan Culture* (1996) ch. 6.

[366] See Hor. *Carm.* 3.6.21–24 and Sall. *BC* esp. 11.6, 12.2, 13.3, 24–25.

[367] Firm. Mat. 6.11.6. More evidence is at Cumont, *Égypt* (1937) 180 n. 1. See Grodzynski, ''Tortures'' (1984) 397–399, and Gleason, ''Semiotics'' (1990) 397–399, against Cumont's view that these sources are irrelevant to the social history of the Empire. *Lenocinium* in the *CGL* often refers to the husband who sells his wife's services: *CGL* 4.106.19; 4.254.29 (''uxoris meretricatio mariti consensu''); 5.112.18; cf. 5.375.1.

[368] For ancient criticism of the declaimers' themes as irrelevant or even fantastic, see Bonner, *Declamation* (1949) ch. 4; Bonner, *Education* (1977) ch. 21. Though even run-of-the-mill material often distorts Roman law, evidently for didactic purposes or by mistake, this material is more reliable than once assumed: Lanfranchi, *Retori* (1938); Parks, *Schools* (1945); Bonner, *Declamation* chs. 4–6; Bonner, *Education* esp. 317–320; Boswell, *Kindness* (1988) 57 n. 6, who rightly asserts its usefulness for ''insights into contemporary moral values and social practice.'' The sources for *lenocinium* include Sen. *Contr.* 1.4 (esp. 2), 2.7, 6.7; [Quint.] *Decl.* 273, 275, 279, 325, 355; cf. Quint. *IO* 5.10.47.

[369] Tert. *Patientia* 16.3. Tertullian compares the Christian ideal of *patientia* with pagan practice. Among examples of the latter figure husbands who tolerate their wives' misbehavior, either because a sizable dowry is at stake or because they are compensated more directly: ''lenociniis negotiantes.'' Cf. *Apol.* 39.12 (''patientissime''), *Nat.* 1.4.12 (''omnem uxori patientiam obtulisse'').

Apul. *Apol.* 75:[370] Even at this very moment—may the gods work his ruin, for I must beg a very great pardon from you for what I am about to say—the man's whole house is a brothel, its inhabitants polluted: the master a pimp, his wife a whore, the kids just like them. Day after day, night after night, the door is battered by kicks, as the young men of the neighborhood have their fun, the windows resound with drunken singing, the dining room is thrown into an uproar by revelers, the bedroom is an expressway for adulterers: after all, no one has to worry about setting foot in there except someone who hasn't paid off the husband. You see, the outrage visited upon his marriage bed was for him a source of profit. There was a time when the crafty fellow earned a common sort of wage with his own body; now he does the same thing with his wife's. He is the one—it's the truth—with whom—I'm telling you—many clients haggle over the price of his wife's services. Here is an example of what we all know as the old spousal "teamwork": no one pays any heed to those who pay a goodly sum to the husband; they can leave when they please. Those who show up short of cash are grabbed, when the signal is given, as if they were committing adultery. And, just as if they had come to a schoolroom, they don't go away before they've signed their names to something.

This piece of mudslinging fits in smoothly with a succession of charges leveled at Apuleius's adversary. First, Herennius Rufinus sold his own body. Then, when he grew too old, that of his wife.[371] Then, when she grew too old, that of his daughter. The last point is crucial to Apuleius's case.[372] The passage is to all appearances a fairly faithful account of the scene one might expect to encounter in a Roman brothel and can take its place beside other such descriptions in Latin literature.[373] The picture given of young men engaged in drunken violence, especially the serenade from the street and the breaking down of doors, communicates the essentials of a drinking party, *comissatio,* while the general atmosphere of fast, indiscriminate sex, money passing hands (here the pimp handles the transaction), and petty criminality all seem taken from life.

The idea that an upper-class male operated such a house with his wife as the principal attraction is more difficult to accept. Apuleius was ostensibly attempting to persuade a provincial governor,[374] and his *consilium.*[375] It may be assumed that these men had heard it all before; on the other hand, that this recital of practices

[370] "In hac etiam aetate qua nunc est—qui istum di perduint! multus honos auribus praefandus est—domus eius tota lenonia, tota familia contaminata: ipse propudiosus, uxor lupa, filii similes: prorsus diebus et noctibus ludibrio iuventutis ianua calcibus propulsata, fenestrae canticis circumstrepitae, triclinium comissatoribus inquietum, cubiculum adulteris pervium; neque enim ulli ad introeundum metus est, nisi qui pretium marito non attulit. ita ei lecti sui contumelia vectigalis est. olim sollers suo, nunc coniugis corpore vulgo meret; cum ipso plerique, nec mentior, cum ipso, inquam, de uxoris noctibus paciscuntur. iam illa inter virum et uxorem nota collusio: qui amplam stipem mulieri detulerunt, nemo eos observat, suo arbitratu discedunt; qui inaniores venere, signo dato pro adulteris deprehenduntur, et quasi ad discendum venerint, non prius abeunt quam aliquid scripserint."

[371] Apul. *Apol.* 60.

[372] *Apol.* 74–80 (esp. 74–76) and 98, where Apuleius explains the true motives behind the indictment: ". . . puellae meretricis blandamentis et lenonis patris illectamentis. . . ."

[373] Sen. *Contr.* 1.2; Petron. 7–8; Iuv. 6.115–132; *Hist. Ap. Tyr.* 33–36.

[374] The governor was Claudius Maximus, whose proconsulship of Africa may be dated to 157/158, 160/161, or (most likely) 158/159: Thomasson, *Laterculi* 1 (1984) 382.

[375] It is widely accepted that Apuleius recast this speech for publication: Conte, *LL* 557–559. Al-

should be dismissed as pure rhetoric or as utterly fantastic is rendered doubtful by the very nature of the task confronting the speaker, for whom plausibility is the touchstone. He does, after all, refer to the racket as "illa inter virum et uxorem nota collusio."

It is no objection to the credibility of this narrative that such activities were illegal under the adultery law. The wrong people sometimes were killed through misuse of the *ius occidendi*.[376] When they were not murdered, adulterers continued to be subjected to varieties of abuse in no way sanctioned by the law.[377] We cannot be sure if the various outrages described by literary sources are lawful.[378] When the matter was regulated by the adultery law, this hardly means abuses ceased. The jurists permitted those adulterers passively eligible for the *ius occidendi* to be mistreated.[379] Quintilian,[380] Martial,[381] Juvenal,[382] Lucian,[383] and Origen[384] suggest that the rights of the outraged husband were limited more in law than in practice.

This was an area where self-help was suggested if not positively invited. The *lex Iulia* allowed an offended husband to hold an adulterer caught in his home for up to 20 hours but had nothing to say on how he should be treated. The man could hardly expect to be handed a cup of tea, and some rough treatment was probably the rule.

Blackmail and extortion are powerful tools, no less so when none of the parties to the transaction has clean hands, or the circumstances render the issue of guilt and innocence murky. A man who had been misled about the status of the woman he was "discovered" with could not theoretically be convicted of adultery given the law's requirement that the act be committed *sciens dolo malo,* but such niceties would have been of small comfort in practical situations of this kind. For the "adulterer" to clear his name, a suspicion that the transfer of money or other property was accomplished after the fact of actual adultery would have to be overcome.[385] As a defendant, he could not plead *lenocinium* in mitigation of his actions, since this plea was inadmissible from anyone already accused of adultery.[386]

---

though there is no guarantee that this section was not added after the trial, its tenor and contents seem broadly consistent with standard treatments of opponents' characters in Roman oratory. A similar difficulty exists for the speeches of Cicero: Stroh, *Taxis* (1975) ch. 2.

[376] For the several cases known to us of abuse of this privilege, see below.

[377] For a famous fictional case of entrapment and mistreatment, see Plaut. *Miles* 1394–1437 (perhaps even better known is a Greek forensic parallel at [Dem.] 59); cf. *Anth. Lat.* 1.1.116.

[378] Evidence from the Republic: Hor. *Serm.* 1.2.37–46, 64–67, 127–134, 2.7.56–71; cf. Plaut. *Curc.* 30, *Miles* 1394–1437, *Poen.* 862–863; Ter. *Eun.* 992–993; Catull. 15.18–19; Varro *apud* Gell. 17.18; Val. Max. 6.1.13.

[379] Pap. D. 48.5.23(22).3.

[380] Quint. *IO* 5.10.88.

[381] Mart. 2.60, 3.85.

[382] Iuv. 6.44, 10.314–317.

[383] Lucian. *Peregr.* 9.

[384] Orig. *Contra Celsum* 7.63.

[385] The jurists treat such deals as something given "pro comperto stupro" by a *deprehensus:* Pomp.-Ulp. D.4.2.7.1; Paul. D. *eod.* 8 pr. Despite the problems of form these texts show, their content is classical: Hartkamp, *Zwang* (1971) 21–23 (contra Kaser, "Rechtswidrigkeit" 109 n. 1, 133 n. 1). Hartkamp's arguments are in my view strengthened by the link I draw with *lenocinium.*

[386] Ulp. D. 48.5.2.4, 7.

Whether or not the man thus compromised was guilty of adultery, he had worse things to fear than prosecution, as the jurists recognized. Physical maltreatment did not exhaust the possibilities. Any sum paid under duress could be recovered through the praetorian *actio de eo quod metus causa factum erit*; the *exceptio* would grant relief to someone sued on a promise made under such circumstances.[387] It was necessary that there be a threat of death or physical force or a threat to pass the information on to someone who might act with violence.[388]

Without such a threat, nothing might be recovered if given *ob stuprum* or to buy oneself out of adultery—that is, a bribe to escape prosecution[389] for criminal fornication or adultery.[390] What a *socius* pays out ''in alea aut adulterio'' cannot be recovered from the common fund.[391]

Despite the broad application of the rule on threats, the remedy was perhaps of limited value. Success with the *actio metus causa* depended on a number of doubtful extralegal factors,[392] and a man fearing an adultery charge, justified or not, might hesitate to oppose the *exceptio* and simply pay up.

The jurists raise an interesting point in this connection.[393] Only a thin line was able to be drawn between statutory *lenocinium,* or profiting from the adultery of one's wife, and the accessory crime of receiving payment *pro comperto stupro.* The activity alleged of Herennius Rufinus demonstrates this. He is really supposed to be hiring out his wife on a regular basis while pretending to catch in the act *(deprehendere)* those unfortunates who have failed to be sufficiently generous as customers. To judge from the legal texts, forcing actual adulterers to pay up was more widespread than running a brothel in one's home; indeed, it was probably a fairly common manner of dealing with adulterers before the law made composition a criminal offense.[394]

This seems sensible from a broader perspective. The legal and literary evidence

---

[387] Pomp.-Ulp. D. 4.2.7.1; Paul. D. *eod.* 8 pr. (who admits the immorality of the transaction); cf. Lenel, *EP*³ 110–114; Kaser, *RP* 1² 244–245. The rule preceded the law on adultery.

[388] Pomp.-Ulp. D. 4.2.7.1.

[389] See Sab.-Peg.-Ulp. D. 12.5.4 pr., on the principle of *turpitudo utriusque.* One notes the number of jurists who concerned themselves with this problem. The phrase *ob stuprum* seems broad enough to cover any sort of payment, even one made to the partner. Cf. Dioclet., Maxim. C. 4.7.5 (a. 294), which applies the rule where a sum is promised through a stipulation (the wording of the text, if genuine, suggests the situation was unusual). Though the text is much criticized, the principle is sound; see, above all, Schwarz, *Condictio* (1952) 183, 185–186.

[390] For Hallebeek, ''Responsum'' (1995), the rationale depends on the prospective squandering of the money paid. No evidence supports this view, which appears to rely on a confusion of criminal fornication with prostitution, which was not punished under this or any statute.

[391] Pomp. (12 *ad Sabinum*) D. 17.2.59.1 (though this may refer to the statutory penalty and not to a bribe). See Sturm, ''Weib.'' Blackmail might also operate with other forms of *lenocinium,* such as *damnatam ducere,* to judge from Dioclet., Maxim. C. 9.9.23.1–2 (a. 290). The text mentions an *SC* that punishes the recipient of the bribe. On the passage, see Wacke, ''*Potentiores*'' (1980) 587, who understands the charge in question to be adultery; cf. Schwarz, *Condictio* 183.

[392] See Kelly, *Litigation* (1966) 14–20, for a realistic treatment of this remedy, despite the criticism of Villers, ''Droit'' (1969) 477.

[393] This receives more attention in Chapter 6.

[394] Varro, *apud* Gell. 17.18; Hor. *Serm.* 1.2.37–46, 133, 2.7.56–71; [Quint.] *Decl.* 279; [Acr.] *ad Hor. Serm. 1.2.133.*

shows that such transactions were considered inadequate to repair the injury to honor wrought by adultery. If anything, composition aggravated the outrage, by transforming the sexual affront into a commercial exchange. Poor men were considered especially prone to such behavior, or at least more exposed to the depredations of the better-off. A poor man with an attractive wife and a wealthy neighbor or patron was considered a prime suspect for the commission of this sort of *lenocinium*. Here is yet another sign that the legislator concerned himself with the moral welfare of society beyond the urban aristocracy. Of course, the law was written by members of an elite who were quite capable of viewing lower-class behavior through the prism of vices exhibited by their fellows: one thinks of how the future emperor Otho used his wife to advance himself while at Nero's court. But it is reasonable to suppose that, in the climate of poverty inhabited by the urban poor, the husband-pimp was not an unheard-of phenomenon.

We are still very far from being able to show that the provision concerning the husband-pimp had much basis in reality. But there is enough to conclude that the scenario described by Apuleius enjoyed at least some plausibility for contemporaries.[395] Everyone knew that women were vulnerable creatures. Worse yet, their male protectors were often all too willing to betray them for easy money or some less tangible advantage. Apuleius's audience, like the men who wrote the adultery law, lived in a society where honor, including sexual honor, might easily form the subject of a transaction. Or so they were willing to believe.[396] In other words, the specter of the husband-pimp was an all-too-familiar fear. The idea of a prominent Roman operating a brothel in his house thus has a certain pedigree.[397]

Apuleius's colorful and detailed account of domestic impropriety may be balanced against the vague generalization made by Pliny in praise of Trajan's wife, Plotina:[398]

> Plin. *Pan.* 83.4:[399] For many prominent men a wife married too recklessly or kept on too tolerantly has been a source of disgrace; so the loss of reputation within the household has contributed to the ruin of those who enjoyed distinction outside it, and what made it impossible for them to be deemed the greatest of citizens was the fact that they were unsuccessful as husbands.

Pliny's apparent reference to *deprehensam retinere* should not be construed in its narrow, legal significance. What Pliny means to decry is the indulgence shown by husbands who "knew" their wives to be unfaithful without having caught them in

---

[395] For a seventeenth-century English parallel, see Stone, *Road* 245; cf. 247, 255, 280–281.

[396] Porcius Latro *apud* Sen. *Contr.* 2.7.1 suggests that self-attribution of fear of a charge of *lenocinium* was a popular ploy when the evidence for adultery was weak. The tactic presupposes the widespread credibility of the charge.

[397] See Chapter 7.

[398] On this passage, see Bradley, "Ideals" (1985) 84–86; Boatwright, "Imperial Women" (1991) 530–540.

[399] "Multis inlustribus dedecori fuit aut inconsultius uxor adsumpta aut retenta patientius; ita foris claros domestica destruebat infamia, et ne maximi cives haberentur, hoc efficiebatur, quod mariti minores erant."

the act itself. Their behavior fell within a gray area, where it might give rise to moral censure but not liability under the law.[400] Pliny is saying that they were condemned only in the court of public opinion.

It seems that popular usage was stricter, less forgiving, than the law itself. Julius Caesar divorced Pompeia for mere suspicion of adultery, which the Augustan law would not have required of him, but did not escape severe criticism of his behavior in the matter, especially that toward the putative adulterer, Clodius.[401] *Patientia* often refers to mere complaisance,[402] as does *facilitas*.[403] As Pliny suggests, ultimately status as a *leno* was a matter of reputation.[404]

The man who sold his wife's honor—or merely overlooked her infidelity—possessed no honor himself. He was not a man. In the bipolar scheme of Roman gender typology, this meant he was a feminized male, a *mollis*.[405] *Pati* and its cognates are strong evidence of this identification.[406] "*Pation* was the technical term of the passive role in intercourse."[407] So it was used, not just of women, but of pathic males: "viri muliebria pati,"[408] *muliebris patientia*.[409] Like Pliny, Ulpian uses such terms while discussing behavior that may or may not give rise to criminal liability.[410] We do well to recall the kinaidic associations of Juvenal's "snoring husband," the figure introduced above. Only a woman might show *patientia* toward a spouse's infidelity and escape censure.[411]

It is possible to view *leno* in this context as a Latin equivalent for "cuckold."[412] Humiliated and emasculated, the betrayed husband was dishonored by his wife's faithlessness.[413] Ulpian, who elsewhere refers to the wife's action as a *con-*

---

[400] The distinction is one we will see the jurists employ (Chapter 6).

[401] Discussion in Moreau, *Clodiana Religio* ch. 1. Cf. the criticism leveled at Pompey for his behavior toward Caesar, whom he suspected of adultery with Mucia: Suet. *Iul.* 50.1.

[402] See Ovid. *Ars* 3.585; Mart. 5.61 (cf. 2.72); Tac. *Ann.* 15.59.5. Compare *nimia patientia* in Sen. *Contr.* 2.7.1: "too much" in this context evidently means the amount that gives rise to criminal liability.

[403] So Livia is *facilis* in the eyes of a tradition that accuses her of supplying her husband with sexual partners: Tac. *Ann.* 5.1.3; Suet. *Aug.* 71.1. Her behavior, as described, is not *lenocinium* under the law; see Chapter 6.

[404] See Plaut. *Merc.* 395–411.

[405] See Ausonius (*Epigr.* 92.3, 94.1), who twice characterizes a complaisant husband as a *semivir*, whereas *mollis* and *kinaidos* describe the husband at Iuv. 9.37–38 (cf. 70–80 for the theme of adultery and 130 for the term *pathicus*). Just before introducing the details of Rufinus's brothel operation (See above), Apuleius refers to the man's *indocta et rudis mollitia*: *Apol.* 74 (cf. "effeminatissime" and "tanta mollitia animi" at 78). On *mollitia*, see the treatment in Edwards, *Politics* ch. 2.

[406] See the evidence of Tertullian given above, n. 369.

[407] Adams, *LSV* (1982) 189.

[408] Sall. *BC* 13.3; cf. Tac. *Ann.* 11.36.4.

[409] Sen. *NQ* 1.16.6; Petron. 9.

[410] Ulp. (8 *disp.*) D. 48.5.2.3; *Ulp.* (4 *adult.*) D. *eod.* 30(29) pr., 4. *Pati* is used of both the prostitute and the adulteress: Sen. *Contr.* 1.2.8; Vell. 2.100.3, respectively. Note that Juvenal condemns not only married women in his sixth satire, but husbands, the latter for their passivity and submissiveness: Smith, "Husband" (1980) esp. 329–330.

[411] To judge from Val. Max. 6.7.1, which may suggest that wives in his own day lacked this tolerance.

[412] Contrast Treggiari, *RM* 312: "there is no classical Latin word for "cuckold," the "word of fear" which terrorized Elizabethan husbands." Similarly, Edwards, *Politics* 54–58. I do not argue that "*leno*" and "cuckold" are identical in every respect, only that "*leno*" is the Roman equivalent for the latter.

[413] Contra Treggiari, *RM* 312: "there is no suggestion that the husband's own honour was ruined."

taminatio that ought to rouse the husband's anger, justifies the outrage against the wife who has defiled her husband's marriage: "quae matrimonium eius violavit."[414] For Velleius, the lovers of Augustus's daughter are thought to have defiled his *domus* when they "debauched" his daughter and Tiberius's wife.[415] Cicero uses the word *contemnere* to express the outrage done to the Lucullus brothers by Memmius, who is supposed to have committed adultery with the wives of both men.[416]

To avoid censure as a *leno,* a husband had to take responsibility for oversight of his wife's morals—which meant punishing her if she erred. In a famous confrontation that took place before the Senate in A.D. 21, Valerius Messalinus was able to defeat Caecina Severus's proposal barring wives from joining their husbands on provincial assignments in no small part by asserting that husbands were the natural guardians of their wives' behavior, which would suffer if the women were left by themselves in Rome.[417] Similar arguments are supposed to have helped clinch a repeal of the *lex Oppia* in 195 B.C.[418]

Sometimes husbands needed assistance—or prodding—from the law, as the adultery statute itself suggests. Another example, which shows how broadly this duty was conceived, is the *SC* passed in A.D. 24 that made administrators liable for the misdeeds of their wives in the provinces even when they were ignorant of them.[419]

As the passage from Pliny's speech shows, the husband's responsibility began with his selection of a partner. Thus Procopius is able to assign blame to Justinian for Theodora's allegedly depraved life before their marriage.[420] Of course, his whole point in attacking Theodora and Antonina, the wife of Belisarius, was to discredit their husbands, a practice with a rich tradition in the genres of rhetoric, biography, and history.[421] There would be no sense in this if husbands were not dishonored by their wives' sexual misbehavior.

An egregious example is that of Messalina and Claudius.[422] This does not necessarily mean of course that the latter qualified as a *leno* under the law, but he certainly does fit the broad social construction of this type. Stupidity was no excuse.[423] Claudius was, in Roman terms, a cuckold.

Once the *impudicitia* of respectable women had been criminalized, it became

[414] Ulp. (4 *de adult.*) D. 48.5.30(29) pr.

[415] Vell. 2.100.4–5: "violator eius [sc., Caesaris] domus," "cum Caesaris filiam et Neronis violassent coniugem"; cf. "uxore violata."

[416] Cic. *Att.* 1.18.3.

[417] Tac. *Ann.* 3.33–34, with Marshall, "Provinces" (1975) 119–120. See above in this chapter.

[418] Liv. 34.7.11–13, with Goria, "Dibattito" (1987) 286–287. For more evidence, see Cohen, "Augustan Law" (1991) 116–118, 121.

[419] Tac. *Ann.* 4.20.4; Ulp. D. 1.16.4.2, with Marshall, "Provinces" 120; "Women on Trial" (1990) 334.

[420] Proc. *Anec.* 10.2–5, with Fisher, "Theodora" 310.

[421] See Fisher, "Theodora" 309, 313 n. 54.

[422] For another view, see Bauman, *Women* 168, who argues that the empress was able to manipulate the criminal sanctions against *lenocinium* to protect her own position in case of disclosure of her adulteries to Claudius.

[423] So the *stultus vir,* the sexually humiliated husband familiar from elegy and mime, qualifies as a *leno*: Ovid. *Am.* 2.19.1; McKeown, "Elegy" esp. 72–76. Cf. Mart. 12.93.7: *morio.*

a political issue as well—standing perhaps as a sort of substitute for *maiestas,* for which charge women were as a rule ineligible.[424] The true significance of the new criminal charge of *lenocinium* is the attempt to make men responsible for the behavior of their wives. This was evidently retrograde, at least for broad segments of the urban aristocracy, which had abandoned this idea in the late Republic.

At issue was not only the loss of sexual honor but the declassing of elite women through such loss. A complaisant husband surrendered both his own honor and that of his wife by treating her—or simply allowing her to act—as a prostitute. Even indifference counted as a fault and might be reduced to the common denominator of exploitation, at least in the popular mind.

The interplay of sex and status was the very essence of such degradation. In another context, it may be read in the anger of Diocletian at a woman who betrayed a well-born captive by prostituting her.[425] The emperor's concern was twofold, in that he lends pointed emphasis to *retinendae pudicitiae cultus* as well as to *servanda natalium honestas.* Or perhaps these expressions are better understood as a hendiadys, given the strength of the connection between sexual and social degradation. The crux lay in the betrayal of a respectable woman's sexual honor by someone in a position of trust. As we have seen, a similar connection between sex and status informs Augustus's construction of the husband-pimp.

5. Exemptions

The fact that exemptions were accorded some women under the adultery law has important implications. As seen at the outset of this chapter, it was precisely the status of the female partner that qualified a sexual act as criminal or not under the law. Even more important, perhaps, the very existence of exemptions shows that the *lex Iulia* was not concerned to safeguard the chastity of all women. Considering the types of women who fell outside the scope of this legislation, I aim to identify the reasons behind each individual exemption and at the same time attempt to relate them to the larger purpose of the law.

Before the law was enacted, a division existed of women or "female types" into permitted and forbidden sexual partners for males.[426] Despite the apparently broad range, it may not be impossible to reconcile these categories with what the law prescribed. The law at minimum introduced a greater degree of clarity to this division, backed up by its sanctions.[427]

Modern students of the adultery law have characterized a number of different types of women as immune to the statutory penalties. Around them has been con-

[424] So Bauman, *Women* 12.

[425] Dioclet., Maxim. C. 8.50(51).7 (a. 291). On the text, see Beaucamp, *Statut* 1.19 n. 22.

[426] Plautus *Curc.* 32–37, with Cantarella, *SN* 155; Ter. *Eun.* 960–961; Cic. *Cael.* 38, 49–50, with Stroh, *Taxis* 274; Hor. *Serm.* 1.2.31–63, 116–126. Note the defense offered by C. Cornelius at Val. Max. 6.1.10 (150 B.C.), which may suggest the *lex Scantinia* contained such an exemption. See the discussion at Fantham, "*Stuprum*" 281.

[427] Instructive is the example of Ovid, who courted trouble by continuing to blur the black-and-white distinctions of status that the law insisted upon: Treggiari, *RM* 306–307.

structed an entire category of women *in quas stuprum non committitur*. This list has its own history in the scholarship, but everyone relies directly or indirectly on the views of the two moderns whose accounts of the regime on adultery have been fundamental for decades, Esmein and Mommsen.

Lack of space forbids anything but a sampling of modern opinion. For example, Bonfante[428] adds to the list, among other refinements, freedwomen. Astolfi[429] rejects freedwomen and is followed (at least for the freedwoman concubine of her *patronus*), by Rizzelli.[430] Nearly everyone has actresses.[431] Beaucamp[432] has ex-procuresses and ex-actresses; Grimal[433] has dancers; Rilinger[434] has "certain concubines." Manfredini[435] includes "persons of very low rank" and so do Rawson[436] ("lower-class") and Dixon[437] ("low birth"). Bassanelli Sommariva[438] merges the categories of women prohibited under the Augustan marriage law with those exempt under the adultery statute.

Esmein[439] begins by taking into account the criterion of social position, which he broadens to include a certain moral element.[440] He lists the women found in both categories of the marriage prohibitions of the *lex Iulia et Papia*[441] (those forbidden to senatorials and those forbidden to the *ceteri ingenui*) and argues that all these women, as well as those from the lower orders who plied low-prestige professions, "seem to have been considered by the ancients as a group abandoned to sexual disgrace."[442] The law did not concern itself with such women, at least if they were unmarried. In fact, every woman not a *matrona,* identified by Esmein as "high-status" ("la femme de la bonne société"), was immune to its penalties: "neither they nor their partners were punished." In this category of exempted women he includes any woman involved in retail trade. Like the others, these women lost their exemption when they married. Slaves were utterly exempt.

Mommsen, after observing that the law applied only to those free women who faced the responsibilities incumbent upon *Ehrbarkeit* (he identifies these persons as *matronae* and *matres familias*), gives a list that consists of slaves and a series of types from whom *Ehrbarkeit* was not expected because of their social position or profession.[443] These include public prostitutes ("öffentliche Dirnen"), only as long as they continued to practice their profession, procuresses, actresses, women

[428] Bonfante, *Corso* 1 (1925/1963) 317.
[429] Astolfi, *LIP*[2] 55.
[430] Rizzelli, "Accusa" 432.
[431] See Mette-Dittmann, *Ehegesetze* 145–146.
[432] Beaucamp, *Statut* 1.203.
[433] Grimal, *Love* (1986) 102.
[434] Rilinger, *Humiliores* 165.
[435] Manfredini, "Vestem" (1985) 261.
[436] Rawson, "*Spurii*" (1989) 38.
[437] Dixon, *TRF* 94.
[438] Bassanelli Sommariva, "Considerazioni" (1988) 312.
[439] Esmein, "Délit" 96–97.
[440] Esmein, "Délit" 96: "... une partie des ces femmes étaient de viles créatures ou des femmes de condition inférieure."
[441] Esmein wrongly includes actresses among those forbidden to the *ceteri ingenui*: Chapter 3.
[442] Esmein, "Délit" 96: "... semblent avoir été considérées par les anciens, comme une part abandonée à la débauche."
[443] Mommsen, *Strafrecht* 691–692 (notes omitted).

who operated public taverns and other businesses, and those who lived in a form of concubinage that was not considered honorable. Mommsen considers marital status as generally irrelevant to the question of exemptions.

Most of the types given by Esmein and Mommsen enjoy textual support of some sort, although the evidence is difficult and its meaning is not always clear. At the outset, an objection can be raised against Esmein's adoption of the prohibited categories of the *lex Iulia et Papia* as a point of departure. These women did not all form "une part abandonée à la débauche." Those forbidden to senators could still marry the *ceteri ingenui,* and all could become the wives of freedmen.[444] This does not mean that certain among them, such as prostitutes and procuresses, were not exempted under the adultery law, but it is an unwarranted assumption that all of them were so exempted.[445]

Mommsen's list may therefore be preferred as a basis for study. First come (female) slaves. The evidence that they were not liable to the law is clear and noncontroversial.[446] It shows that although unauthorized sex with someone else's slaves might be punished under the *lex Aquilia* or the praetorian *actio de servo corrupto,* such activity did not fall within the scope of the *lex Iulia.* A partial explanation for this is that the law was primarily designed to safeguard the chastity of married women. Slaves could not marry, so this protection was pointless for them. Of course, social and legal status determined the design of the law: thus the all-important distinction between free and slave status.[447] Slaves had no sexual honor of their own to safeguard.

On the level of interests, of primary importance is the broad discretion allowed masters over their slaves. The latter were sexually available and completely subject to the will of their owners.[448] An extension of the *lex Iulia*'s exemptions to cover slaves would have been a grave interference in this arrangement. Nor was it thought opportune to afford even a "serious" relationship between master and slave the protection extended, for example, to concubinage between *patronus* and *liberta,* since this would have raised the status of such unions to a level considered socially undesirable.[449] The rules developed in connection with the *lex Aquilia* and the *actio de servo corrupto* avoided this problem while protecting the interests of the master in the sexual integrity of his slave.

---

[444] Marriages prohibited under the *lex Iulia et Papia* were valid (those that violated the rules laid down for the senatorial order were voided only by Marcus and Commodus; see Chapter 3). Prohibited marriages were protected by the adultery statute (Ulp. D. 48.5.14[13] pr.-1), as were certain types of concubinage (see below). Of course, all marriages that complied with the marriage law were protected unless the woman was exempt.

[445] Esmein's assertion that exempt status was lost upon marriage is based upon a doubtful interpretation of a difficult text; see below.

[446] Pap. D. 48.5.6 pr.; Mod. D. 23.2.24; Mod. D. 48.5.35(34) pr.; Dioclet., Maxim. C. 9.9.23 pr. (a. 290); Dioclet., Maxim. C. *eod.* 24 (25) (a. 291); PS 2.26.16; cf. Hieron. *Ep.* 77.3 (with a reference to the jurist Papinian); Paulinus *Euch.* 159–175. *HA Aurel.* 49.4 alleges a change in the law; if true it was temporary.

[447] Consider, for example, the condition of the *statuliber,* whose right to freedom was aggressively protected but who was still left firmly in the power of his master as long as he continued to be a slave.

[448] Slaves might serve as a functional equivalent for prostitutes: McGinn, *PRS* (forthcoming).

[449] Discussion in McGinn, "Concubinage" (1991).

We do not know if the law exempted slaves expressly. It is more likely that the jurists took their cue from the wording (and, arguably, intent) of the law, which referred only to the potential liability of the *mater familias,* or respectable woman.[450] The exemption must have been recognized from the start, although Papinian is our earliest source.[451]

Next are prostitutes. Granted, one text frequently adduced to prove this exemption is of no help,[452] but there is much other evidence.[453] In A.D. 19 a woman named Vistilia attempted to avoid an adultery charge by registering as a prostitute with the aediles.[454] Her action would be unintelligible if no exemption existed. Two juristic sources confirm the immunity of prostitutes, albeit indirectly.[455] Explicit testimony is given by a constitution of Diocletian and by the Christian authors Tertullian, Jerome, and Salvian.[456]

The exemption is undoubtedly classical and just as surely derived from the legislation itself. One clue is the date of the Vistilia affair. This occurred less than 40 years after the passage of the law and 5 years after the death of the legislator, leaving little time for juristic interpretation or legislative modification to create the exemption (there is, of course, no trace of either).[457] Further, the law contrived to equate the status of the convicted adulteress with that of the prostitute while contrasting the prostitute with the eminently liable *mater familias.* The jurists understood the legislative exemption from prosecution to imply immunity from the *ius occidendi* exercised by the offending woman's father.[458] The exemption thus makes sense as an aspect of the original legislation.

It is also significant that in juristic discussions of the problems posed by concubinage in the context of the *lex Iulia* prostitutes are mentioned specifically as eligible concubines (and thus women with whom sexual intercourse was not *stuprum*) even by those jurists who held "minimalist" positions on this issue.[459] This

[450] Treggiari, *RM* 281, makes a distinction between active slave partners (for whom there was liability under the law) and passive slave partners (no liability under the law). Although correct in principle, this formulation overlooks the crucial way in which gender structures liability under the *lex Iulia*. Active slave partners were males, passive ones females, and there was no liability for the male under the adultery law if his partner was a female slave.

[451] Pap. D. 48.5.6 pr.

[452] Ulp. D. 48.5.14(13).2; see below.

[453] Ovid. *Ars* 3.57–58 is usually understood to refer to prostitutes but is too vague to stand as an independent witness.

[454] Tac. *Ann.* 2.85.1–3 is the main source; see the discussion in McGinn, "SC" 280–291.

[455] Mod. D. 23.2.24; Marci. D. 25.7.3 pr. Testimony that is nonlegal, indirect, and late is Ambr. *Abr.* 1.22–26 (see Rizzelli, "*Stuprum*" 374, for a different interpretation). A similar contrast between the *lex divina* and the *iuris publici ratio* is found in Lact. *Inst.* 6.23.

[456] Dioclet., Maxim. C. 9.9.22 (a. 290); for Tertullian and Salvian, see below; for Jerome, *Ep.* 77.3.

[457] Tacitus even claims her behavior violated a *mos inter veteres receptus.* On this assertion, see McGinn, "SC" 281–284.

[458] Marci. (1 <iud.> *publ.*) D. 48.5.25(24).3: "Illud in utroque ex sententia legis quaeritur, an patri magistratum occidere liceat? item si filia ignominiosa sit aut uxor contra leges nupta, an id ius nihilo minus pater maritusve habeat? et quid, si pater maritus leno vel aliqua ignominia notatus est? et rectius dicetur eos ius occidendi habere, qui iure patris maritive accusare possunt." Marcian's answer is thus "it depends," not "yes," as Astolfi, *LIP²* 111, assumes.

[459] See the discussion in McGinn, "Concubinage" 347–354.

can be explained readily as the application of a legislative provision. Finally, there is indirect evidence that the adultery law used a phrase for "prostitute" similar to that employed in its immediate predecessor, the *lex Iulia et Papia*.[460]

Interesting, but perhaps less compelling because of its long pedigree,[461] is the evidence supplied by a favorite theme of declaimers, which suggests that the status of an act of "adultery" committed in a brothel was not, in law, adultery.[462]

For *lenae* and actresses, scholars have relied on the same piece of evidence: a *Digest* passage from Papinian reporting an *SC* issued in connection with the Vistilia affair.[463] This is buttressed for procuresses by a passage of Suetonius that (wrongly) has multiple offenders professing *lenocinium* as a means of escaping the penalties for adultery.[464]

The exemption for actresses is difficult to understand. Unlike prostitutes and *lenae,* who were only allowed to marry freedmen, they were permitted by the *lex Iulia et Papia* to marry anyone, freeborn or freed, outside the senatorial order.[465] The mention of actresses in the text of Papinian may be explained either as a later insertion or as a specific response to problems current when the *SC* was passed (these concerned upper-class performers onstage and in the arena)[466] rather than as a guarantee that actresses were ever exempt from the legislative regime on adultery.

The exemption for *lenae* does not encounter these objections, and the evidence, though garbled (in Suetonius's account), is stronger. There are two possible explanations for their immunity. One is that the *lex Iulia* itself granted an exemption to procuresses, either on the analogy of prostitutes or because, in fact, most procuresses were former prostitutes.[467] The second possibility is that juristic interpretation of the law and/or contemporary court practice had come to regard *lenae* as enjoying the same exemption as prostitutes. Against this latter possibility is, once again, the too brief interval that falls between the law's passage and A.D. 19.

The next category, women engaged in managing taverns or conducting retail trade, depends on two texts that are better explained in light of the postclassical expansion of the legal conception of prostitute.[468]

Mommsen's only remaining category consists of concubines whose relationship with their male partner is considered less than honorable, that is, socially

[460]This consists of variations on "qui quaeve palam corpore quaestum facit fecerit": Mod. D. 23.2.24; Marci. D. 25.7.3 pr.

[461]Ter. *Eun.* 960–961.

[462]Quint. *IO* 5.10.39 (on the exercise of the *ius occidendi* in a brothel), 7.3.6, 9–10. Discussion in Treggiari, *RM* 272–273.

[463]Pap. D. 48.5.11(10).2. See Bonfante, *Corso* 1.317; Astolfi, *LIP*² 56, 64 n. 22.

[464]Suet. *Tib.* 35.2. There was one woman (Vistilia) who registered as a prostitute, not as a *lena:* McGinn, "*SC*" esp. 288–290.

[465]This yields a paradox even for prostitutes and *lenae,* exempt under the adultery law but eligible to marry freedmen under the *lex Iulia et Papia,* but the low social context of such unions must have prevented it from being felt.

[466]See McGinn, "*SC*" 291.

[467]Perhaps the law granted a general dispensation to both male pimps and procuresses that enabled them to carry on their trade.

[468]*PS* 2.26.11; Constantin. C. 9.9.28(29) (= CTh. 9.7.1) (a. 326). These passages are of no significance for the classical regime on exemptions. See McGinn, "Definition" (forthcoming).

acceptable. In his brief mention of this he overlooks a controversy among the classical jurists on this issue.[469] This explains why he mistook the meaning of a passage from Ulpian that refers to certain women as those *in quas stuprum non committitur*.[470] The point is that the relationship itself did not grant them immune status: they had to have this already, so that the relationship itself did not make both parties liable for *stuprum*.[471]

One other passage is directly relevant to the discussion. This too contains a vague and difficult reference to a woman "with whom stuprum is not committed" and has encouraged expansion of the list of exemptions beyond what can reasonably be supported by the evidence:

> Ulp. (2 *de adult.*) D. 48.5.14(13).2: Sed et in ea uxore potest maritus adulterium vindicare, quae volgaris fuerit, quamvis, si vidua esset, impune in ea stuprum committeretur.

> Indeed, a husband can punish adultery in a wife who was promiscuous, although, if she were a divorced woman or a widow, *stuprum* would be committed with her without penalty.

Esmein and Mommsen take *volgaris* to mean prostitute.[472] This is now the standard interpretation.[473] But the word simply means "sexually promiscuous," as the *OLD* defines it.[474] That it cannot mean "prostitute" here is suggested by the consistent usage of the jurists in adopting a variant of the phrase "corpore quaestum fecerit" to describe prostitutes, particularly in the context of the Augustan marriage legislation.[475] It is difficult to see why Ulpian, who used the more familiar legislative term to develop his famous definition of a prostitute,[476] should prefer such a vague and euphemistic expression here. Moreover, if it did mean "prostitute," this would contradict the principle firmly established by other evidence that prostitutes should be immune from the penalties of the law.[477]

Even granted the definition of *volgaris* as "sexually promiscuous," the text remains difficult to interpret. The problem is one of substance: why does Ulpian

---

[469] Mommsen, *Strafrecht* 692 n. 5. The controversy was first noticed a few years after Mommsen wrote by Mitteis, "Papyrusstudien" (1902) 304–314.

[470] Ulp. D. 25.7.1.1.

[471] See McGinn, "Concubinage" 350–351.

[472] Esmein, "Délit" 97; Mommsen, *Strafrecht* 692.

[473] See Nardi, "Divieti" (1941) 130 (with 132 n. 55); Thomas, "Accusatio" (1961) 69; Astolfi, *LIP*² 112; Beaucamp, *Statut* 1.150 n. 68, 203; Treggiari, *RM* 280; Gardner, *Being* 151. So also the Philadelphia *Digest,* ad loc. An interesting exception is Falcão, *Prohibiciones* (1973) 14, who identifies the *volgaris* with the *obscuro loco nata.*

[474] *OLD* s.v. *vulgaris* 5c, citing this passage. Of course, the word can refer to a prostitute: Adams, "Words" 344. The *VIR,* which gives "usitatus, abiectus, communis," does not show any close parallels.

[475] The phrase was found in both the *lex Iulia et Papia* and, as I have argued above, in the adultery statute.

[476] See Chapter 4.

[477] Esmein attempts to explain the contradiction by claiming that prostitutes were exempt until married (an argument contradicted by the maneuver of Vistilia, who was married and yet attempted to claim the exemption). Mommsen believes that the immunity for married prostitutes remained valid only as long as they continued in that profession (an argument that is unsupported by this text, at any rate).

say that (sexually promiscuous) widows and divorced women *(viduae)* are not liable for *stuprum* when other jurists hold them accountable and he himself implies the same in another passage?[478] Society—and beyond it, the state—had as much of an interest in the sexual behavior of such women as it did in that of women who had never been married or who were partners in relationships that were not *matrimonia iusta*. This is particularly true since *viduae* often remarried.[479]

One further problem is that the text seems internally inconsistent because it discusses *stuprum* and *adulterium* with apparent indifference.

The answer to these difficulties is to be found by viewing the text together with that immediately preceding it:

> Afric.-Ulp. (2 *de adult.*) D. 48.5.14(13).1: Plane sive iusta uxor fuit sive iniusta, accusationem instituere vir poterit: nam ut[480] Sextus Caecilius ait, haec lex ad omnia matrimonia pertinet, et illud Homericum adfert: nec enim soli, inquit, Atridae uxores suas amant.
>
> ou monoi phileous' alochous meropōn anthrōpōn Atreidai.

> Clearly, whether his "wife" is a partner in a *matrimonium iustum* or not, the husband will be able to launch a prosecution, for, as Sextus Caecilius said, this statute applies to all marriages, citing that famous line of Homer: "not alone of mortal men do the sons of Atreus love their wives."

The text says that unions without *conubium* (i.e., *matrimonia iniusta*) are protected by the *lex Iulia*. This is true of concubinage (at least, the respectable variety) and marriage between Roman men and peregrine women (Briseis, alluded to in Africanus's citation of Homer, serves as an example of both a concubine and a peregrine woman). A number of other relationships characterized by a defect, such as failure to meet the requirements of minimum age or degree of kinship for a marriage to be valid according to the *ius civile,* were similarly protected, almost all through a grant of the *ius extranei*.[481] In other words, the *volgaris* of our main text is a peregrine woman, whose sexual behavior was of no concern to the Roman state and of no relevance to the *lex Iulia* unless and until she married a Roman citizen.[482]

It is, in my view, easier to accept Mitteis's view that peregrine wives of Roman citizens were not potentially liable under the adultery law itself, at least not until the mid–second century, against Mommsen's view that they were.[483] The general point cannot be argued here, but it makes perfect sense of our passage. At once, the difficulty about prostitutes is removed, proper sense is given to *volgaris,* and we are no longer left in the dark about the exempt/nonexempt status of Roman unmarried women. The apparent confusion over *adulterium* and *stuprum* in this passage is also resolved: the woman is only liable if married (to a Roman citizen), so that she is incapable of committing *stuprum* proper.

---

[478] Ulpian permitted accusations for some classes of concubine: Ulp. D. 48.5.14(13) pr. See the discussion in McGinn, "Concubinage" 348.

[479] See Chapter 4.

[480] The manuscripts give "et," but the editorial conjecture "ut" seems necessary.

[481] On this subject, see Ankum, "*Captiva*"; Ankum, "*Sponsa*".

[482] The word *vidua,* usually translated as "widow," "divorced woman," also embraces "woman never married"; see above.

[483] Mommsen, *Strafrecht* 693 with n. 1, 696 with n. 5; Mitteis, *RP* (1908) 70.

This gives four exempted categories, slaves, prostitutes, *lenae*, and peregrines (at least those not married to Roman citizens). Only two of these at most were defined by the legislation. Peregrines, like slaves, were probably understood to be immune to the penalties of a statute designed to safeguard the chastity of Roman women and passed pursuant to another law, which was designed to encourage marriage and fecundity among Roman citizens. The jurists later added a fifth category, convicted adulteresses, on the analogy of prostitutes.[484]

Another aspect of the exemptions is the register of prostitutes. When were the aediles entrusted with the registration of prostitutes? This responsibility is usually assumed to predate the law. For example, Evans traces it to the mid–second century B.C.[485] The only evidence known to me that seems to support a pre-Augustan date is Tacitus' characterization of the registration as a *mos inter veteres receptus*.[486] I have argued that the *lex Iulia* first gave the aediles the task of registering prostitutes in connection with their exemption under the statute.[487] There was no other practical purpose for registration. The aediles did not function on the model of a nineteenth-century *police des moeurs*. Nor did the *tresviri capitales* play such a role.[488]

Why would the aediles be entrusted with the registration of prostitutes under the adultery law? As noted, they may already have had responsibility for supervision of the brothels themselves, along with other businesses that catered to public amusements,[489] at least from the mid–second century B.C., to judge from the circumstances surrounding the injury visited upon the aedile Hostilius Mancinus when he attempted to enter a brothel.[490] The oversight of brothels continued long after the evidence for the register fades, which is precisely A.D. 19.[491] The abandonment of the aediles' list fits in with the reduction of their duties by the early emperors.[492] Apart from the registration of prostitutes and oversight of clothing regulations, the last new responsibility given these officials concerns the sale of comestibles in *popinae* and *ganeae*,[493] which Claudius removes.[494]

Another aspect of the aediles' magisterial competence was the prosecution, through the *iudicia populi,* of men and women for adultery and other sexual of-

[484] Ulp. D. 25.7.1.2.

[485] Evans, *War* 164 n. 151. Cf. Grimal, "Matrona" 202.

[486] Tac. *Ann.* 2.85.2.

[487] See McGinn, "*SC*" 281–284; cf. Sabbatucci, "Edilità" (1954) 320–327; Nippel, *Order* (1995) 17 n. 13.

[488] Despite Mommsen, *Strafrecht* 159 n. 2. See Kunkel, *Untersuchungen* 71–79; Lintott, *Violence* (1968) 102–106; Garofalo, *Processo* (1989) 78 n. 19, 133 n. 176; Santalucia, "Repressione" (1988/1994); Santalucia, *DPR* 54–55.

[489] Mommsen, *Staatsrecht* 2³ (1887/1969) 510–511; Robinson, *AR* (1992) esp. 136–139, 189. This may explain their competence in maintaining public order, which was not necessarily general or comprehensive: Nippel, *Order* 21.

[490] See Chapter 2.

[491] See McGinn, "*SC*" 281–284. The only evidence I have of a post-Vistilian register of prostitutes that is independent of the tax rolls is that kept by Saint Vitalius in late antique Alexandria: Leontsini, *Prostitution* (1989) 65. For a sixth-century Syracusan inspector of brothels, see Brown, *Body* (1988) 431. For exercise of such oversight (and related responsibilities) in late antique Rome, see Chastagnol, *Préfecture* (1960) 266, 267, 276, 279.

[492] See Dignös, *Aedilen* 95–97.

[493] Suet. *Tib.* 34.1.

[494] Suet. *Claud.* 38.2. See Hermansen, "Inns" (1974) 167–171; Hermansen, *Ostia* (1981) 196–203.

fenses, a practice that extended back into the Republic.[495] This in itself might have suggested to the legislator a role for them in the enforcement of the *lex Iulia*. The irenarchs in some eastern cities had oversight of public order and *mores*,[496] but their role seems broader than that enjoyed by the aediles, who may have intervened only in egregious cases, particularly when the more usual domestic repression was impractical or seemed inadequate.[497]

One aspect of this role is their newly assigned responsibility, noted by Mommsen,[498] of ensuring that persons appearing in and around the Forum wore the toga if that garment was appropriate to their status. It is interesting to find the aediles of A.D. 22 proposing a sumptuary reform that seems to have embraced rules on clothing—specifically, repression of transvestism.[499]

The implications of the legislative provision for registration may now seem clearer. As Tacitus suggests, the maintenance of a register would have acted to discourage any woman with pretensions to respectability from entering prostitution. For those who did become prostitutes, the social stigma was punishment enough, at least from an upper-class perspective. But this was far from being the only or even the major purpose behind this provision. The real intent was to create another objective boundary between respectable women and the outcast class of prostitutes.[500] It fits in well with Augustus's larger purpose of redefining and reinforcing the social and moral boundaries weakened by years of revolution, civil war, and rapid social change.[501]

6. Pimps, Prostitutes, and the *Ius Occidendi*

For prostitutes, the *lex Iulia* was a two-edged sword. On the one hand, they were marked out explicitly, indeed officially, as never before, stigmatized in contradis-

---

[495] Liv. 8.22.3, 10.31.9, 25.2.9; Mommsen, *Staatsrecht* 2³ 494; Jones, Courts 15; Bauman, "Aediles" (1974). They exercised exclusive jurisdiction *apud populum* over offenses committed by women, according to Garofalo, "Competenza" esp. 455 and 475, *Processo* 121–134, an argument challenged by Santalucia, "Edili" (1989/1994) 71–73. Compare Dignös, *Aedilen* 76–80, who prefers to connect this duty not with oversight of brothels but precisely with the keeping of a register. He must therefore date the register as far back as the early fourth century B.C. and assume a steady pace of aedilician prosecutions for sexual misconduct. Evidence on both counts is lacking.

[496] Arc. Char. *(libro sing. de mun. civ.)* D. 50.4.18.7: "... qui disciplinae publicae et corrigendis moribus praeficiuntur." See Hirschfeld, "Polizei" (1913/1975) 605. Republican censors had no direct role in the moral oversight of women: Cic. *Rep.* 4.6; Dignös, *Aedilen* 76. See Chapter 2.

[497] See Kunkel, "Quaestio" 42. The role of *gunaikonomoi* and similar officials also seems to have been broader: Vatin, *Mariage* (1970) 254–261, who cites interesting evidence from the Hellenistic period on their duties regarding women's clothing and registration (of citizens).

[498] Mommsen, *Staatsrecht* 2³ 509, who cites Suet. *Aug.* 40.5: "negotium aedilibus dedit, ne quem posthac paterentur in foro circave nisi positis lacernis togatum consistere." The language has the ring of a legislative enactment.

[499] See Tac. *Ann.* 3.53–54.

[500] Compare the distinguishing form of dress for prostitutes, the toga. On the creation of boundaries between prostitutes and respectable women, see the works of feminist historians and anthropologists cited by Rosen, *Sisterhood* 49.

[501] For more details on the origins, purpose, and operation of the exemption, see McGinn, "*SC*" esp. 280–291.

tinction to a very broad range of women defined as respectable, the *matres familias.* At the same time, the law granted them an official sanction. Without the exemption, they might have found it more difficult to carry on their trade. At all events, the explicit recognition granted by the statute will have meant greater freedom, while the social stigma cannot have had, practically speaking, any great significance for them.[502]

In this respect, the *lex Iulia* is a typical manifestation of Roman official policies toward prostitution. It is broadly tolerant of most conduct, provided certain boundaries of social class and sexual behavior within class are respected. Thus, the purpose of the *lex Iulia et Papia* was to prevent or at least deter prostitutes and pimps from entering the upper classes. By contrast, the normative design of the adultery law cut in the opposite direction and aimed at preventing women of sound social and moral status from behaving, in effect, like prostitutes.

As with prostitutes, the exemption for procuresses was not a straightforward privilege but contained an element of social degradation. This is highlighted by the fact that, in other respects, the status of procuresses and pimps under the law was quite low. The law specifically excluded them from concessions that it granted others and burdened them with special disadvantages. The principle of gender differentiation is especially prominent in this area, since only procuresses enjoyed the benefit of the exemption, and only male pimps labored under the rest of the law's disabilities.

One disadvantage concerned the *ius occidendi,* the right of the husband or father to kill an adulterer caught in the act. Thomas and Rabello[503] have shown that this "right of slaying" was not (despite pre-Augustan evidence that might appear to suggest the contrary) derived from *patria potestas* but was an independent creation of the adultery law,[504] as its attribution to the husband and to some fathers without *potestas* suggests. The father's privilege was relatively unfettered[505] but was compromised by one important requirement: he had to kill his daughter as well as her lover.

The husband was forbidden to kill his wife and might only kill the lover if the man fell in one of the categories established by the law.[506] According to a text of Aemilius Macer,[507] these included pimps, actors, anyone who entered upon a public stage to dance or sing; those condemned in a criminal court but not granted

---

[502] The same was certainly true of another disability imposed on them by other laws and perhaps by the *lex Iulia de adulteriis coercendis.* This concerned the right to give testimony in criminal cases; see Chapter 2.

[503] Thomas, "Lex Julia"; Rabello, "*Ius occidendi*" (1972). On the pre-Augustan regime, see also Treggiari, *RM* 264–275. Russo Ruggeri, "*Ius occidendi*" (1989–1990), holds that the right of the father under the statute reflects Republican practice, a difficult argument in my view. Cantarella, "Homicides" (1991) 232, restates the older view that under the adultery law itself, "if the natural father was to kill with impunity, he had to be a *pater familias.*" Lambertini, "Ancora" (1992), rightly contests the attempt of Lorenzi, "Figlia" (1991), to link father's *ius* with *patria potestas.*

[504] The *ius occidendi* presents an interesting example of the law's mix of old and new elements, a mix characteristic of Augustus's legislation, as argued by Bellen, "Status" (1987) esp. 333–336.

[505] For some of the restrictions, see above and Mette-Dittmann, *Ehegesetze* 35, 62–63.

[506] For limits on the husband's exercise of the *ius,* see above and the sources given by Mette-Dittmann, *Ehegesetze* 36.

[507] Macer (1 *iud. publ.*) D. 48.5.25(24) pr.

in integrum restituere;[508] freedmen belonging to the husband himself or to his wife, father, mother, son, or daughter (we are told that it did not matter if the freedman was shared with another patron); and slaves. A passage from Paul[509] lists slaves, *auctorati, bestiarii,* those condemned in a criminal court, and freedmen, whether they were the husband's own, his father's, mother's, son's, or daughter's (we are assured, at least for the first two, that it does not matter whether the freedmen was a full citizen or a Junian Latin); *dediticii* are added almost as an afterthought.[510] A third text, from the postclassical *Pauli Sententiae,* gives *infames,* male prostitutes, slaves, and, in one version, freedmen.[511]

The reference to *infames* in this last source is a blanket extension in the late law, which may have embraced types not included in the legislation itself. It is strange that the author of this text did not assume that male prostitutes were included in this group. This suggests that the praetorian *postulare* edicts, which did not make specific allusion to male prostitutes, were already used as the central source for defining the category of *infames* in the early fourth century. To be sure, male prostitutes are not mentioned in either of the other two texts. Their presence in this source may then be explained as a postclassical attempt to include all *infames* or as a distant reflection of a classical juristic extension based on the analogy of pimps (so perhaps the "statutory" phrasing "qui corpore quaestum faciunt"). But the omission of male prostitutes by Macer and Paul may be casual, given the evident incompleteness of both lists.

Both Macer and Paul imply that they give the types laid down by the *lex Iulia,* without actually naming the statute.[512] Only family *liberti,* slaves, and convicted criminals appear in both passages, though there can be no doubt that most of the others go back to the statute.[513] Many were already to be found in the praetorian *postulare* edicts, and all are well-known traditional objects of Roman social prejudice.

This does not explain why such persons would be placed on a list of persons liable to be killed by an outraged husband if caught in the act of adultery. Thomas, taking up a suggestion of Corbett, has the most convincing explanation.[514] The *lex Iulia* transformed the older right of a husband—never explicitly recognized by legislation—to avenge affronts to the family honor. Under the adultery law, the husband's *ius* is so qualified as to be ineffectual. Thomas concludes that "Augustus

---

[508] On this privilege, see Chapter 2.

[509] Paul. *Coll.* 4.3.1–4. The text is disturbed, although the content is classical: Cervenca, *"Libri"* (1971) 412.

[510] Paul. *Coll.* 4.3.4: ". . . quo loco et dediticius habetur." Potentially, both provincial *dediticii* and those freedmen defined as *dediticii* by the *lex Aelia Sentia* are meant; the latter are more likely candidates, which suggests that this provision postdates the *lex Iulia* (the *lex Aelia Sentia* was passed in A.D. 4). On the two kinds of *dediticii,* see Sherwin-White, *Citizenship*[2] (1973) ch. 16.

[511] *PS* 2.26.4 (≅ *Coll.* 4.12.3).

[512] Macer (1 *iud. publ.*) D. 48.5.25(24) pr.: "hac lege." Paul. *Coll.* 4.3.2: "secundum leges." The plural may suggest that the list was supplemented by later legislation; see above.

[513] The only obvious exceptions are the *dediticii;* see above.

[514] Thomas, "Lex Julia" 638, citing the remark of Corbett, *Marriage* 136–137: "the liberty to kill certain *adulteri,* a characteristic manifestation of the inequality of Roman Law, would operate as a statutory defence against a charge of murder: but its availability would usually be, from the husband's point of view, a matter of luck."

sought to provide for a reaction compatible with previous practice but, by so restricting the possible validity of its operation, at the same time to ensure so far as practicable that it would not be exercised.''[515] In a similar way, a father's affection for his daughter[516] might well be thought to render the requirement that he kill her, if he killed her lover, an effective deterrent against killing either one.[517] The legislator's principal interest was in provoking a trial, where, interestingly, the relative positions of husband and father were reversed, although both held significant advantages over third-party prosecutors.

This is sensible as far as it touches the offended husband, who might hesitate to kill someone whose death might lead to a murder charge, as well as the father, who might be reluctant to kill his daughter, but it ignores the impact such a rule might have been intended to have on the putative adulterer. Uncertainty about the husband's knowledge of his status might make him pause before committing the offense. A mistaken or rash act would have far more serious consequences for the lover than for the killer. And the prospect of later punishment for the husband was cold comfort at best. The introduction of a long and complicated list of persons eligible for the *ius occidendi* (which the husband might very well choose to ignore), not to mention the chance of an encounter with the women's father (who was entitled to slay any type of adulterer, along with his daughter, and had the right to kill at his son-in-law's house as well as his own), may have been designed to create just enough of an atmosphere of fear and uncertainty to deter the commission of the crime.[518] The occasional exercise of the privilege, even if wrongful, would hardly hurt the law's purpose.[519]

There are a number of attested cases of wrongful killing of adulterers.[520] The tendency was to allow a lighter sentence, although one emperor (Caracalla) granted complete impunity.[521] The threat of unlawful killing was real enough to be taken into account by the jurists in their work on the praetorian edict *quod metus causa*.[522]

I concede that, in cases where the husband's *ius* was restricted or where, in the heat of the moment, there was uncertainty as to whether this applied, a prosecution might be the more likely outcome, as Thomas argues. Even so, uncertainty about the adulterer's status may not have been as characteristic of such encounters as he assumes. Obviously, freedmen of family members would have been easily recognizable, and also slaves, at least those belonging to the family or its immediate

[515] Similarly, Mette-Dittmann, *Ehegesetze* 63.

[516] On the bond between fathers and daughters at Rome, see Hallett, *Fathers and Daughters* (1984).

[517] I am unpersuaded that the law's purpose was to ensure equal treatment for the adulterers, as Lambertini, *DUO* (1992) esp. 33–34, argues. There is no trace of this principle in the husband's *ius*.

[518] McGinn, *Social Policy* 268–279; similarly, Treggiari, *RM* 293.

[519] See above and Richlin, "Approaches" 399 n. 5: ". . . Augustus was trying to legislate shame into the upper orders. . . ." The view of Cantarella, "Homicides" 233, that "Augustus wanted to eliminate adultery as a pretext to justify murders committed for personal or political reasons" has no evidence to support it, to my knowledge.

[520] See, e.g., *CIL* 13.8512.

[521] Pap. D. 48.5.39(38).8 (two cases of a husband killing a wife, one of which was handled by Pius, the other by Marcus Aurelius and Commodus); Alex. Sev. C. 9.9.4 *(a. incerto);* Paul. *Coll.* 4.3.6 (Marcus Aurelius and Commodus, Caracalla).

[522] Ulp. D. 4.2.7.1; Paul. D. *eod.* 8 pr.

neighbors. In fact, it seems quite likely that the identity and therefore status of the adulterer would often have been known to the husband even if he suspected nothing of the affair. If he did suspect something, there was nothing to prevent him from being on the alert or even setting a trap so as to put to use his right of slaying.

The *ius occidendi* was therefore not simply a symbolic concession to previous practice whose main or only purpose was to provoke a prosecution while creating sufficient uncertainty to serve as a deterrent to the commission of the crime in the first place. It was also intended to be used, albeit under certain carefully determined circumstances.[523] Even when it was not, other forms of physical abuse were not out of the question.[524]

What this means, of course, is that the categories of adulterer whom the husband could kill were not determined at random. They represent not so much men whose proclivities or opportunities for adultery tended to be greater than those of other men (although one can concede the latter point for family freedmen and slaves, and literary evidence for affairs of gladiators and actors with married women is, for what it is worth, abundant enough), but those whose sexual relations with another man's wife were considered especially shocking and objectionable.[525] For cases of *stuprum,* the low status of these men perhaps assumed a special significance. Unlike with adultery, many such affairs, if discovered, could be expected to end in a forced marriage, and only the low status of the lover prevented this. The disgrace of a love affair between one's daughter and a pimp was hardly capable of being effaced in that way, which gave sufficient motive to heal the breach of honor with the sword, though, of course, *pater*'s discretion was not so limited.

Valerius Maximus tells how the equestrian Pontius Aufidianus killed his daughter, together with the *paedagogus* who had collaborated with her seducer: "to avoid celebrating a disgraceful wedding he conducted a bitter funeral."[526] I believe this expression refers to the prospect of a "shotgun wedding," perhaps the normal expectation in such circumstances (if so, it might help explain why we hear so little of cases of *stuprum,* compared with adultery).[527] More evidence for the practice may lie in the the rhetoricians' *optio raptae.*[528] The practice of forced marriage following seduction is familiar from modern traditional societies.

A similar principle barred pimps from making accusations under the adultery statute. They were prohibited from instituting all criminal prosecutions, probably

---

[523] On the justification for the privilege defined in terms of the mental state of the outraged husband or father *(iustus dolor),* see Wacke, "Vergehen" (1979) 543; Beaucamp, *Statut* 1. 142–143. Failure to exercise it might be grounds for criticism, if we can trust [Quint.] *Decl.* 279.

[524] Petron. 45 (a slave); Mart. 2.47, 60, 83, 3.81, 85, 92 (6.2 is doubtful evidence); Quint. *IO* 3.6.27; [Quint.] *Decl.* 357; Iuv. 10.310–317; Apul. *Met.* 9.27–29. See Richlin, *"Irrumare"* (1981), and above for evidence of such treatment predating the law.

[525] One text shows that there was a special legally prescribed penalty for family freedmen: Tryph. D. 48.5.43(42) *(poena libertinorum).* The same may have been true of the others passively eligible for the *ius occidendi.* Esmein, "Délit" 116, suggests that this was death.

[526] Val. Max. 6.1.3: "Ita ne turpes eius nuptias celebraret, acerbas exequias duxit."

[527] Linderski, "Pontia" (1990) 90–91, proposes that the seducer was the girl's fiancé, which is consistent with my hypothesis.

[528] E.g., [Quint.] *Decl.* 270.16–18. For a Christian perspective, see Evans Grubbs, *Law* 75: ". . . at Elvira, premarital sex was less harshly punished [than adultery]—provided that it ended in marriage."

under the *lex Iulia iudiciorum publicorum,* although the adultery statute, like most enabling acts for the standing criminal courts, contained a list of persons ineligible for bringing accusations or giving evidence, and it is quite likely that pimps were included on all such lists.[529]

Because criminal laws often made exceptions to such exclusions for those pursuing their own wrongs, we may ask, were pimps permitted to avenge their own dishonor under the *lex Iulia,* either by bringing an accusation[530] or, where appropriate, by resort to the *ius occidendi*?[531] It would indeed be remarkable if, within their own households, those men whom society openly stripped of honor might claim the right to defend what they had left.[532] Women were categorically barred from bringing accusations under this law, and so find no mention in the list that ousts pimps; male prostitutes evidently were not thought worth the trouble of excluding expressly.

The *lex Iulia* thus permitted the outraged husband to kill on the spot a pimp found in the act of adultery in the former's home and prohibited pimps from bringing accusations at minimum where they had no direct interest. Procurers were not the only ones to suffer from such disabilities, but given the sexually explicit nature of their profession and the definition of *lenocinium* in this statute, it is not surprising to find such hostility embedded in the law itself.

7. Social Policy and the *Lex Iulia* on Adultery

The *lex Iulia* on adultery is most often viewed as a companion law to the *lex Iulia et Papia.* The latter statute sought to place the institutions of marriage and the family on a new footing within the context of Roman society. It established a hierarchy of marriages that were endowed with a new kind of legitimacy through being recognized by the law. This legitimacy was fostered by a system of rewards and penalties that were further intended to encourage the raising of children. The

[529] For those typically excluded, see Mommsen, *Strafrecht* 367–362. Levy, "Anklägervergehen" (1933/1963) 384, argues that the list of exclusions from prosecutions given in Ulp. (2 *de adult.*) D. 48.2.4 is taken from the Augustan criminal court statute. On this theory, it overrode one given in the *lex Iulia* on adultery itself. Ulpian's text, whatever its provenance, is adjusted for the purposes of the adultery law, as the absence of prostitutes from this list perhaps suggests.

[530] This can be inferred from such texts as Macer D. 48.2.11 pr., Macer D. 48.5.25(24).3; Paul. *Coll.* 4.4.1–2; Pap. *Coll.* 4.5.1. Note also Pap. (36 *quaest.*) D. 48.5.39(38).9, which allows a freedman to prosecute his patron in such cases "quomodo si atrocem iniuriam passus esset." Daube, "Accuser" (1956) 12–15, argues that all such prosecutors, who were otherwise barred, were allowed to proceed *iure mariti* if the outraged marriage had *conubium*; otherwise, *iure extranei.* Rizzelli, "Accusa" 428–431, holds only the latter to be possible. Note that a respectable father can displace a disgraced husband when both claim the right to the privileged accusation: Ulp. D. 48.5.3.

[531] This can be inferred from Macer D. 48.5.25(24).3 and the other texts cited in the previous note, if one allows a pimp the privilege of *ius mariti.* Against it is the statement at Quint. *IO* 7.1.8 that the *ignominiosus* was ineligible for the *ius occidendi.*

[532] To be sure, the story (and the manner of its telling) of P. Atilius Philiscus, a former prostitute who killed his daughter when he discovered her to be guilty of *stuprum,* is instructive: Val. Max. 6.1.6.

lex Iulia de adulteriis coercendis was designed to protect these institutions by checking the promiscuous sexual behavior that threatened their existence.

Like the *lex Iulia et Papia,* though perhaps even more explicitly, the adultery statute created a hierarchy of status. At one end was the *mater familias*; at the other, the adulteress/prostitute.[533] Linked with the adulteress/prostitute was the corresponding figure of the husband/pimp. In this respect the two laws can be linked to Augustan social policy in its broadest contours.[534] Augustus reorganized the senatorial and equestrian orders, setting new qualifications for entrance and continued membership.[535] The goal was to restore their social dignity and to place their political importance firmly within the context of the new settlement.[536] The same purpose may be assigned to his reorganization of the professional associations, the *collegia,* this time for the benefit of freedmen and freeborn members of the lower classes, and his regulation of membership in the ranks of the *apparitores,* or magistrates' assistants.[537] He attempted to increase the value of Roman citizenship by limiting grants to peregrines.[538]

Limitations placed on manumissions and the creation of the new class of *dediticii* had the deliberate, if indirect, aim of protecting the moral character of the Roman citizenship and raising the status of freedmen.[539] This status was buttressed by the establishment of the *seviri/Augustales,* which permitted freedmen a role in civic and religious life.[540] Finally, the *lex Iulia et Papia* set out a series of marriage qualifications arranged by social rank.

The evident goal of these and similar measures was to create a highly stratified society (notwithstanding some limited and tightly controlled chances for social mobility) and to endow each stratum with its own set of privileges and responsibilities. This was achieved to a significant extent through the use of visible status markers, especially clothing, to identify and separate different statuses.[541] So the overall approach was articulated to define a revitalized hierarchy of status between and within orders, which left the avenues for upward mobility firmly in the hands

---

[533] The division of women into two types is a familiar device, though this procedure is not inevitable. See Rath, "Prostitution" (1986) 553, for a medieval example with five categories.

[534] See, e.g., Reinhold, "Usurpation" (1971) 279–280, with literature; Newbold, "Tension" (1974) 136–137.

[535] See Alföldy, "Stellung" (1981) 211; Kienast, *Augustus* (1982) 126–162; Brunt, "Princeps" (1983) esp. 43–44; Brunt, "Equites" (1988) 192–193; Talbert, *Senate* chs. 1–2; Baltrusch, *RM* (1989) 136.

[536] This meant, inter alia, encouraging members to dedicate themselves to a career of service to the state: Nicolet, "Augustus" (1984) 103–107. On his policy, particularly with jurors, see Bringmann, "Reform" (1973) 242.

[537] Purcell, "*Apparitores*" (1983) 132; cf. 169–170.

[538] See Dio 56.33.3.

[539] See Venturini, "*Manumissiones*" (1984); Gardner, "Purpose" (1991) 23; Gardner, *Being* 18, 41; cf. Mette-Dittmann, *Ehegesetze* 194. On the new hierarchy among slaves and freedmen created through the institution of a new elite, the *familia Caesaris,* see Alföldy, *Social History* (1988) 103.

[540] Treggiari, *Freedmen* (1969) 245; Ostrow, "*Augustales*" (1990); Abramenko, "Liberti" (1992) 96–97.

[541] Kolb, "Symbolik" (1977) 248–250. The regime's purpose was advertised to all social groups through this means and on a grander scale through the Augustan building program: Zanker, *Power of Images*; Mette-Dittmann, *Ehegesetze* 200.

of the regime.[542] As he did to other social groups and statuses, Augustus was responding to the chaos of the late Republic, when the dividing line between respectable and nonrespectable had become blurred.[543] The polarity of *meretrix* and *mater familias* sought to restore a sense of order and clarity to women's status.[544]

The "new" hierarchy of status for women was thus sealed through the manipulation of symbols, as unmistakable badges of honor and shame. The assignation of stola to one group and toga to the other (to take prostitutes and adulteresses together) separated the good from the bad by making a crude distinction that admitted no ambiguity, no degrees of difference, and no possibility of redemption. This stark categorization of women was enforced through the establishment of the register for prostitutes, a device that lent the procedure an objective cast, whatever the actual terms of its application.

Such an approach was by no means inevitable, yet it is striking how many societies have resorted to elements of this strategy over the centuries.[545] Distinctive dress to mark off prostitutes from respectable women was a means preferred by the canon lawyer[546] and was widely implemented throughout the medieval period. Evidence from a series of German towns from the late Middle Ages shows how prostitutes were assigned a distinctive garment (e.g., a municipal decree from Augsburg in 1438 prescribed a veil with a green stripe "two fingers in breadth") and/or forbidden certain types of clothing deemed appropriate for respectable women.[547] A century earlier, a nearly universal feature of the police regulations in the towns of Languedoc was a dress code for prostitutes; in Arles and Avignon they were forbidden to wear veils because this garment was associated with honest women.[548] Throughout southeastern France in this period a typical token assigned them was the *aiguilette,* "a knotted cord falling from the shoulder and of a colour contrasting with that of their dress," or a red armband, the latter justified by a usage of the biblical Rahab, the "harlot of Jericho."[549] Such measures seem all but universal, in principle.[550]

The Roman resort to the toga, a garment in historical times quite distinctively associated with males, finds interesting parallels. As far back as the mid–thirteenth

[542] Mette-Dittmann, *Ehegesetze* 26.

[543] This is argued persuasively by Griffin, *Latin Poets* (1986) 27–28 (in an essay that first appeared in 1976). See, e.g., Varro *Men.* 44 Cèbe.

[544] Note that the Augustan censuses break with tradition by including women and children in the official public totals: Brunt, *IM* (1987) 113–115.

[545] On appearance as a distinguishing characteristic of marginal groups, see Bellebaum, "Randgruppen" (1988) 50.

[546] Brundage, "Prostitution" (1975/1976) 840. A matron who dressed like a prostitute could legally be classed as one: Brundage, "Prostitution" 834.

[547] Rath, "Prostitution" 562–563 (cf. 559); see also Roper, "Discipline" (1985) 8, 20; Geremek, *Margins* (1987) 214, 219, 222. Note the complaints about prostitutes' attire registered in Victorian England: Walkowitz, *Prostitution* 26, 158. For adoption of aspects of their appearance by modern women, see Rosen, *Sisterhood* 107.

[548] Otis, *Prostitution* (1985) 79–80 (cf. 67).

[549] Joshua 2:18. Rossiaud, *Prostitution* (1988) 8, 57, 78.

[550] For late medieval England, see Karras, "Brothels" (1989) 421. For early modern Seville, see Perry, "Lost Women" (1978) 204; Perry, "Insiders" (1985) 140–142 (clothing regulations eliminated visible distinctions between prostitutes and concubines).

century, a number of prostitutes in Florence preferred to dress as men (and were punished for doing so),[551] and in late medieval Venice they adopted men's hairstyles.[552] Reforming preachers from France in this period denounced respectable women who went about town dressed as men in the same breath in which they condemned them for dressing as prostitutes.[553] Men's clothing allowed prostitutes greater freedom of movement and may have suited some customers.[554]

Prostitutes enjoyed notionally the same sexual freedom as men, though in reality a difference existed. Men generally had freedom to choose their sexual partners, whereas women were chosen. This is a reflection of the unequal distribution of power implicit in the exchange of sex for money, an inequality especially notable when the woman is a slave.

The voluntary aspect of this adoption of male dress merits attention. It is reasonably clear why authorities wanted a dress code to distinguish good women from bad. There was a need to isolate—at minimum, symbolically—and so better control unchaste women, to reduce the chance that respectable women (who were assumed to be vulnerable by nature to such temptation) might be lured by the finery of prostitutes into abandoning their husbands and selling themselves to others, in short, to prevent whores from behaving and appearing like respectable women and respectable women from behaving and appearing like whores.[555]

Concern might be especially acute with the upmarket prostitutes, or "courtesans," who were especially thought likely to encourage imitation on the part of respectable women and more than transitory attachments on the part of respectable men.[556] Regulation of dress often formed part of a series of repressive measures that might include prohibition of practice for certain periods of time, especially during Lent, and "zoning" restrictions to a certain area inside a town or away from a church.[557] The purpose was to elide distinctions within the category of prostitute. A similar concern is expressed in various ways by the Augustan adultery law: clothing, register, and verbal description all tended to produce a generic labeling, a leveling effect.[558]

[551] Trexler, "Prostitution" (1981) 995, 996, 998.

[552] Pavan, "Police" (1980) 272–273 (cf. 251, 263). Note the fury of Augustus visited upon an actor attended by a matron with a boy's hairstyle: Suet. *Aug.* 45.4.

[553] Rossiaud, *Prostitution* 149.

[554] See Rossiaud, *Prostitution* 113, 133 n. 7. Prostitutes were punished for wearing men's attire in parts of the United States in the nineteenth century: Goldman, *Gold Diggers* (1981) 120–121. Guy, *Sex* (1991) 155, describes the interesting case of female tango singers in Buenos Aires earlier this century, who donned male formal wear, the tuxedo, in order to claim the right to sing men's songs.

[555] Otis, *Prostitution* 104–105; Rossiaud, *Prostitution* 8, 140–142; cf. Jusek, "Morality" (1989) 126, 134, 141.

[556] Rossiaud, *Prostitution* 131, 134; cf. Corbin, *Women for Hire* 22–24.

[557] Rossiaud, *Prostitution* 8–9; Geremek, *Margins* 214, 219, 222. For an example of promiscuous women being made to live on the street inhabited by prostitutes, see Otis, *Prostitution* 29. For evidence of repression undertaken at the instance of respectable women, see Rossiaud, *Prostitution* 148.

[558] Of reformist preachers in late medieval France, Rossiaud *Prostitution* 164, writes: "they systematically and deliberately confused women in general and whores, applying the same term—*meretrix*—to elegant upper-class women, to lusty women of the people, to courtesans, and to prostitutes in the municipal brothel."

All of this is consistent, I believe, with the motivation of the Augustan law in its regulation of women's clothing. That leaves open the question of why prostitutes were associated with the toga before the law's passing. No evidence provides certainty, but it is possible that prostitutes themselves adopted this garment, for reasons that may coincide with any or all of those given above.[559] This argument is stronger if one accepts my view that the aediles did not register prostitutes before the adultery statute was passed and were entrusted with enforcing the wearing of the toga only at that time; there is in fact no evidence that these magistrates had any responsibilities in the area of clothing regulations before Augustus. In any case, no matter who discovered it at Rome, the sign of the prostitute remained a highly ambivalent symbol,[560] which, as a male garment, put prostitutes quite beyond the pale.[561]

The register has a distinctly modern flavor about it. Indeed, though the usefulness of clothing as a sexual status marker has not been lost on some societies closer to us in time,[562] modern states have tended to prefer registration of prostitutes. The nineteenth and early twentieth centuries saw the heyday of registration, which was the chief instrument of the policy of regulation then in favor. The most overt and urgent reason for adoption of this approach was concern with the spread of sexually transmitted disease, especially syphilis, but the scholarship has been alert to the context in which this policy attempted to serve the interests of public health: an unwillingness and/or inability to address the causes of the extraordinary growth of prostitution in this period and a desire instead to grapple with the effects of this development, namely, a threat to the established social and sexual order.[563] The Romans show no concern with taking measures for public health, and the aediles are no ancient equivalent of the vice squad; at the same time, maintaining the social and sexual order was of paramount importance. The register finds a purpose here.

The register, complemented in many cases by physical segregation, has at different times helped to isolate, supervise, and define a class of women as professional prostitutes.[564] By objectifying the line between good and bad women, the authorities attempted to create a barrier that would ideally prevent prostitutes from penetrating the upper strata of society and discourage women with a claim to high status from risking "declassing" through behavior that might qualify them as prostitutes.[565] Otherwise, it was feared that the (unregistered) prostitute would blend into the community of respectable women, spreading moral and (in the modern

---

[559] It is possible to divine similar motive(s) for their adoption of the stola, of which Tertullian complains vigorously at *Cultu Fem.* 2.12.1; see above.

[560] See Rossiaud, *Prostitution* 160.

[561] "A woman stripped of her honour becomes a man": Pitt-Rivers, *Shechem* (1977) 45 (on early modern Spain). Contrast the idea found among early Christians that "maleness," including the wearing of male attire, was consistent with a woman's holiness: Ward, *Harlots* (1987) 60.

[562] Walkowitz, *Prostitution* 156; Goldman, *Gold Diggers* 43, 120–121; Corbin, *Women for Hire* 20, 85.

[563] Corbin, *Women for Hire* 210–211.

[564] Goldman, *Gold Diggers* 143–144; Walkowitz, *Prostitution* 70, 159. Arrest and conviction had the same effects as registration: Hobson, *Virtue* 19, 104–109, 128–129.

[565] Walkowitz, *Prostitution* 30, 34, 45; Rosen, *Sisterhood* 6, 165–166; Gibson, *Prostitution* 162–165; Corbin, *Women for Hire* 35–36, 87, 135, 336.

period) physical contagion.[566] The status of respectable women was enhanced through the systematic elaboration of an officially recognized category of the debauched and degraded.[567] The latter served as a distraction for energies that might otherwise be directed toward the seduction of the former.[568]

The classification and segregation of women as prostitutes assisted in the formation of a negative stereotype that viewed such women as a relatively homogeneous and thoroughly degraded group.[569] It took no account of differences of status and income among professionals, nor did it distinguish part-timers, clandestine workers, or amateurs.[570] This stereotype might embrace the notions of deviance, criminality, and insanity and foster the idea that the true prostitute was not made but born, though it was admitted that even good women might turn bad if circumstances favored this.[571]

Such consequences were consistent with the aims of the regulationist policy. They may have acted to deter some women, especially lower-class women most vulnerable to the attentions of the police, from promiscuous behavior.[572] Once on the register, it was difficult for women to remove themselves from it.[573] The register stigmatized women, rendering them ineligible for respectable work and isolating them within the context of lower-class society, a sort of marginalization from the marginal:[574] "... the vice squad was in fact the machine for turning temporary prostitutes into permanent ones."[575] For these reasons, a woman of any status might well fear official classification as a prostitute.[576]

Without resorting to a discussion of the successes and failures of the regulationist policy, it is useful to call attention to some of the contradictions under which it labored. The enduring assumption that the honesty of a woman depended on her social status or, to be blunt, the eternal suspicion of the morality of lower-status

[566] Corbin, *Women for Hire* 20–22, 130, 161–162 (cf. 168).

[567] That is to say, the prostitute served as a kind of counterideal that enabled the respectable woman to define herself: Corbin, *Women for Hire* 53 (cf. 331–332); Goldman, *Gold Diggers* 9, 32, 137, 141.

[568] Hobson, *Virtue* 29; Corbin, *Women for Hire* 20. Honest women might be seduced not only into adultery but into prostitution. There was also a concern with abduction for the latter purpose: Corbin, *Women for Hire* 291.

[569] Hobson, *Virtue* 109; Corbin, *Women for Hire* 298.

[570] Barry, *Slavery* 17; Goldman, *Gold Diggers* 143; Walkowitz, *Prostitution* 79, 87, 159, 204; Hobson, *Virtue* 85–87, 106–109; Corbin, *Women for Hire* 22–24. Compare canon law's inclination to equate prostitution with adultery: Brundage, "*Prostitution*" 842–843, with nn. 106 and 112. Cf. Otis, Prostitution 28–29 (adultery is legally impossible in a brothel); Rath, "Prostitution" 560.

[571] Rosen, *Sisterhood* 23–27, 36; Hobson, *Virtue* 24–27; Corbin, *Women for Hire* 300–305.

[572] Though not all the claims of regulationists are to be credited: Walkowitz, *Prostitution* 79, 178. Compare the tactic of inculcating fear in unfaithful wives advocated by reformers in late medieval France: Rossiaud, *Prostitution* 154.

[573] Evans, "Prostitution" (1976) 113; Walkowitz, *Prostitution* 203.

[574] Barry, *Slavery* 25–26; Walkowitz, *Prostitution* 111, 184, 191, 201–203, 209–210; Rosen, *Sisterhood* 5–6; Hobson, *Virtue* 17, 19, 22, 128–129 (arrest had the same effects as registration); Corbin, *Women for Hire* 261, 350–352; Jusek, "Morality" 134. Not everyone shared the assumption that prostitutes were socially and morally beyond redemption: Walkowitz, *Prostitution* 111; Rosen, *Sisterhood* 7–8; Hobson, *Virtue* 151.

[575] Corbin, *Women for Hire* 227 (cf. 327).

[576] Goldman, *Gold Diggers* 142; Gibson, *Prostitution* 164. See Evans, "Prostitution" 114, for successful evasion of the register.

women[577] meant that isolating, supervising, and defining the prostitute were in practice impossible tasks. Though regulationism, certainly in its more extreme forms, sought to control all forms of nonmarital sexual activities,[578] its own inadequacies sometimes fostered the very behaviors it purported to combat.[579]

As with many other aspects of the Augustan program, the *lex Iulia* specified roles (defined in terms of gender and appropriate sexual behavior) and assigned statuses to go with them. Of all Roman social legislation, this law was the one most directly and intimately concerned with women: in the economy of the new order, it was the "women's law."[580] Because society and the state were conscious of an interest in sound marriages, proper sexual behavior was a public concern.[581] The social role and responsibilities of Roman women, which depended, in large measure, on their married state, were recognized and defined in a way that parallels the treatment of the other elements of Roman society under Augustus.[582] The *lex Iulia* enshrined a double standard, in which the appointed role of the male was defender and vindicator of women's chastity.

In this sense, the *lex Iulia de adulteriis coercendis* is more than just a companion piece to the marriage law. It applied to all Roman women, not just to married ones, and certainly not simply to those married in accordance with the *lex Iulia et Papia*. Social dignity was equated with sexual continence, and although expectations with regard to the latter rose or fell depending on the rank of the woman concerned, the law was written in such a way that any woman who was not a member of an exempted category could aspire to the rank of *mater familias*.

Given the traditional link between status and (imputed) virtue,[583] this step may seem revolutionary, but it must be true that this link had been sundered by the behavior of sectors of the elite during the late Republic. Augustus, in a sense, promoted a "*carrière ouverte aux talents.*" Although expectations of behavior remained higher regarding members of the upper orders, the aim was to encourage the lower orders to compete in this field through a meritocracy of virtue.[584]

If what I have written about the law's orientation toward women is correct, then what is truly remarkable about the statute is its manifest concern with the behavior of

---

[577] See, e.g., Rossiaud, *Prostitution* 28; Gibson, *Prostitution* 124–127; Jusek, "Morality" 124–126, 134.

[578] Corbin, *Women for Hire* 27–29.

[579] Corbin, *Women for Hire* 182–185 (cf. 85).

[580] This was not only true in the sense that *pudicitia* was regarded as the "mulieris virtus proprie" (Sen. *apud* Hieron. *adv. Iovin.* 1.49), a point the law makes by linking criminal liability explicitly and exclusively to women's status. On the political significance of the law for women, see Marshall, "Women on Trial" 336–339. Compare, in a similar vein, Ruggiero, *Eros* (1985) 54–55; Purcell, "Livia" (1986) 79, 84, 86.

[581] See, e.g., Quint. *IO* 5.11.9 ("Urbes violata propter matrimonia eversae sunt; quid fieri adultero par est?") and [Quint.] *Decl.* 249.19 ("non estis exhortandi mihi ad tuendam castitatem, civitati ante omnia necessariam").

[582] Now one can perhaps speak with some confidence of an *ordo matronarum*. Compare the anachronistic usage of Val. Max. 8.3.3 with Bauman, *Women* 82.

[583] See, e.g., Pomeroy, *Goddesses* (1975) 211–213; Bauman, *Women* 15–16; Kraemer, *Her Share* (1992) 58. For a different emphasis, see Beaucamp, *Statut* 1.20.

[584] On the importance of proper behavior to non-elite Romans, see the remarks of Dixon, *TRF* 110.

men. This occurs on two levels. Men at their best are regarded as potentially dangerous sexual predators, capable of reducing respectable women to a sexually disgraced,
socially marginal position. The law offered a deterrent, as well as severe punishment
for those who did not heed its strictures. Men's nature required the setting aside of a
class of degraded women to service them. Now for the first time this category is defined crisply, narrowly, legally. Augustus was not such a radical reformer as to revisit
the double standard—instead, he built it into the foundation of the law. This feature
reveals its essentially conservative orientation.

The law did not omit consideration of men at their weakest. The complaisant
husband, unequal to the task of safeguarding his wife's virtue, is punished, as
severely as an adulterer, when he fails to divorce her after catching her in the act
or when he accepts a fee in connection with her infidelity. This refusal to coun-
tenance monetary compensation for adultery represents a major change introduced
by the law; beforehand it had been permitted, though often criticized.[585] The suspicion the statute displays toward husbands and their role is notable.

The exemptions themselves served a number of ends. As noted above, they
threw into relief the dignity of the respectable woman while at the same time—
this is true above all for the prostitute—they acted as a reminder of the degraded
status that awaited the woman who failed to live up to the standard of the *mater
familias*. The exemption of prostitutes may have been conceived more as a punishment than a privilege, as its extension to convicted adulteresses suggests.[586] At
any rate, the degradation it entailed perhaps meant little to prostitutes and procuresses. Finally, the existence of a category of women immune to the law's penalties
allowed Roman males a permissible sexual outlet outside marriage. This is precisely
the social function attributed to prostitution by the Romans, especially important
given the relatively late age at first marriage for males.[587]

A firm principle connected the virtue of women with the welfare of the state.[588]
The availability of venal sex was considered almost as important as the control of female sexual behavior for the protection of marriage and the family: in fact, a direct
relationship was at work.[589] This perceived need for male sexual freedom explains
why the law did not punish men who cheated on their wives.[590] This double standard

---

[585] Sensitivity over the propriety of accepting monetary compensation for adultery is hardly unique
to Rome: Stone, *Road* 92, 94, 237–238, 285–300.

[586] The requirement of conviction for the assignment of this status is worth stressing. There is
palpable tension between the need to punish offenders and the desire to preserve marriages: both were
aims of the law. See Ziegler, *Augustus* (1964) 23–25, for emphasis of the latter aspect.

[587] Saller, ''Slavery'' (1987) 68, makes a similar point about the institution of slavery. Augustus's
approach here is often compared to the establishment of a brothel at Athens attributed to Solon: Leontsini, *Prostitution* 173. The role of the statute in setting aside prostitutes for this purpose is condemned
by Christian writers, who describe these women as expiatory sacrifices to male lust: Tert. *Cultu Fem.*
2.12.1; Hieron. *adv. Helv.* 20; Salv. *Gub. Dei* 7.15. Compare the latter's description of the adultery
law's method and purpose (7.99): ''ut Romana illa decreta, quae scortatores quidem ab alienis uxoribus
removerunt, ad omnes autem solitarias passim admiserunt, adulteria vetantes, lupanaria aedificantes.''

[588] Pomeroy, *Goddesses* 211.

[589] On the relationship between prostitution and the double standard of sexual behavior, see Barry,
Slavery 106.

[590] Though some moral theorists (Pythagoreans and Stoics ranking among the most notable) urged

was not simply sexual, as we tend to think of it, but contained a social dimension as well. The women in the exempt categories, who were in theory permitted the same sexual freedom as men, came by and large from the lower classes.

The *lex Iulia* exploited prostitutes in two distinct ways. As symbols of sexual promiscuity, they were despised and consigned to the bottom rungs of the sexual/social ladder, a *malum exemplum* for decent women to avoid. As recognized sexual objects, they were thought to provide a safety valve for the sexual proclivities of men, directing their attention away from the protected *mater familias*. To this extent they were considered useful. To be sure, the Romans did not want to see pimps and prostitutes joining the ranks of the upper classes; this concern colors much of what they developed by way of official policy regarding prostitution. Above all, it is reflected in the rules laid down by the *lex Iulia et Papia*. But provided this limit was respected, a great deal of tolerance might be extended to this profession. So it is with the *lex Iulia de adulteriis coercendis,* where the positive function of prostitution, at least in the estimation of the Romans themselves, is not to be underestimated.

---

a single standard of sexual behavior both before and after the statute's passage, it is hardly surprising that Augustus and his successors declined to innovate here: Robinson, ''Status'' (1987) 160; Corbier, ''Divorce'' 51; Treggiari, *RM* 191–195, 200, 221–229, 339, 352, 447 n. 59, 463.

6

Emperors, Jurists, and the *Lex Iulia de Adulteriis Coercendis*

1. History of the Statute

The demands of clarity suggest a structure for this chapter that is similar to that of Chapter 4, with a division between imperial law, generated by emperor and Senate, and the law of the jurists. The latter, however, will be seen to be influenced in an especially striking manner by imperial enactments and occasionally by decrees of the Senate as well. The development of *lenocinium* is a good example of the *ius novum* so characteristic of policymaking under the Principate.

2. Subsequent Legislation

The only classical legislation pursuant to the adultery law of any real interest for prostitution is an *SC* passed in A.D. 19. Tacitus provides the fullest information on this measure in his recording of the punishment meted out to a woman who had sought to evade prosecution under the *lex Iulia* as well as an outright ban placed on the practice of prostitution by women of the equestrian and (a fortiori) senatorial[1] orders:

[1] Commentators generally assume this extension, although it is not made explicit, because of Vistilia's senatorial status. Apart from this, there is the principle of interpretation given by the jurist Marcellus, who asserts that the marriage prohibitions of the *lex Iulia et Papia* designed for individuals

Tac. *Ann.* 2.85.1-3:[2] In the same year, women's lust was curbed by tough-minded resolutions of the Senate; and it was laid down that no female should make a living with her body whose grandfather, father, or husband had been an *eques Romanus*. For Vistilia, a woman born from praetorian stock, had made public disclosure of her sexual promiscuity before the aediles, in accordance with the practice of our ancestors, who maintained the belief that adequate punishment of unchaste behavior lay in the very acknowledgment of wrongdoing. The question was also put to Titidius Labeo, Vistilia's husband, as to why, in a situation where his wife's guilt was manifest, he had neglected to pursue the vengeance ordained by the statute. And, insofar as he claimed a 60-day period had been granted for deliberation but had not yet passed, it was deemed sufficient to pass sentence on Vistilia. The woman was thereupon removed to the island of Seriphos.

These events are placed by the historian at the end of his narrative for the year 19.[3] Vistilia, a woman of upper-class lineage,[4] has attempted to escape prosecution for adultery[5] by claiming the exempt status of a prostitute. Her husband is threatened with a charge of *lenocinium* but gets off through an appeal to a statutory time provision.[6] Apart from laying down a penalty for Vistilia, the Senate decides that henceforth no woman whose grandfather, father, or husband had been a Roman *eques* will be permitted to prostitute herself and thus closes the "loophole" in the adultery law that Vistilia had attempted to exploit.

The desperation of Vistilia's ploy is patent: she must have feared imminent prosecution.[7] The words *delicti manifesta*[8] and the fact that her husband was at least conceivably liable to a charge of *lenocinium*[9] indicate that her case was treated

---

of lower social status apply also to those of higher status (D. 23.2.49). The same reasoning applies here. It is therefore not necessary to suppose that Vistilia's husband was an equestrian (see McGinn, "*SC*" [1992] 281 n. 38; the reason equestrian women were included under the ban is explored at 292).

[2] "Eodem anno gravibus senatus decretis libido feminarum coercita cautumque, ne quaestum corpore faceret cui avus aut pater aut maritus eques Romanus fuisset. nam Vistilia, praetoria familia genita, licentiam stupri apud aediles vulgaverat, more inter veteres recepto, qui satis poenarum adversum impudicas in ipsa professione flagitii credebant. exactum et a Titidio Labeone, Vistiliae marito, cur in uxore delicti manifesta ultionem legis omisisset. atque illo praetendente sexaginta dies ad consultandum datos necdum praeterisse, satis visum de Vistilia statuere; eaque in insulam Seriphon abdita est."

[3] Tacitus groups this together with other items of note in standard annalistic practice. Thus the position of the notice does not determine its date within the year.

[4] For her connections, and those of her husband, see McGinn, "*SC*" 281 n. 40.

[5] One notes Tacitus's "untechnical" use of the word *stuprum*.

[6] On the 60-day period granted by the law "for deliberation," see McGinn, "*SC*" 287 n. 83.

[7] For a brief discussion of claims for Vistilia's motives made by Syme and Daube, see McGinn, "*SC*" 287 n. 68.

[8] For the Tacitean use of this construction, see Koestermann, *Annalen* 1 (1963) 410. The use of *delictum* for what was now a *crimen* is interesting (cf. Sen. *Ben.* 3.16.4). If we accept the traditional view of a sharp distinction between *delictum* and *crimen* in classical legal terminology, either Tacitus and Seneca use the word in a nontechnical way or adultery represents a special case. This view has been challenged by Longo, *Delictum* (1976) (see 10–11, 29–30, 40, 107, and 118 for legal passages on adultery that use *delictum* and its cognates). Longo's main argument is persuasive, though his criticism of the texts is too severe: Voci (rev. Longo) (1977).

[9] Thus he was questioned before the Senate as to why he had not divorced his wife and taken action against her lover as the law demanded; see below.

like that of an *uxor in adulterio deprehensa,* though it is not certain whether this resulted from the actual circumstances surrounding the putative act of adultery or was construed through her public registration as a prostitute.[10]

The Senate did not stop with an aggravated penalty for Vistilia.[11] Two more measures, of a general import, can be read in the phrase "libido feminarum coercita cautumque, ne quaestum corpore faceret cui," etc.[12] The "libido feminarum coercita" refers to the first, namely the closing of the apparent loophole in the *lex Iulia* through which women could conceivably escape its penalties by adopting one of the two professions exempted under the law. The scope of this provision went beyond Vistilia's offense, to judge from what follows in the text, in that it anticipated women who would actually practice prostitution, not just register, as Vistilia did, in order to escape liability for adultery. The aim was not simply to punish Vistilia but to discourage any further such attempts at evasion.[13] The principle applied to all women potentially liable under the adultery statute, that is, all free women who were not prostitutes, procuresses, or convicted adulteresses.

A second general measure is the prohibition of the practice of prostitution by women of the senatorial and equestrian orders which, summarized by the phrase "cautumque, ne quaestum corpore faceret cui," etc. obviously does not embrace all women potentially liable to the *lex Iulia,* but is a generalized enactment motivated by the specific instance of Vistilia.[14] The common motivation of the Vistilia affair explains how these different provisions came to be joined in the same decree and why Tacitus places them together the way he does.[15] Vistilia combined a relatively high social position with adulterous behavior—hardly a rare combination, but when she took the further step of registering with the aediles as a prostitute, it was this concurrence of factors that both provoked an immediate reaction from the

[10]Tacitus's language, especially "licentiam stupri . . . vulgaverat," makes the second alternative likelier. This phrase does not prove that "in Rome, women who wanted to engage in prostitution were required to have a license *(licentia stupri . . .)*": so Nelson, "Receipt" (1995) 24, relying on a tradition at least as old as Bloch, *Prostitution* 1 (1912) 447.

[11] *Exilium,* or an early form of what later came to be called "capital exile," was preferred to the statutory *relegatio:* McGinn, *"SC"* 286–288. Outside the *quaestio,* a penalty might be made more severe to set an example: Claud. Sat. D. 48.19.16.10. On the Senate's freedom to act, see Talbert, *Senate* (1984) ch. 16; Vincenti, "Aspetti" (1982). On the Senate as interpreter of the criminal law, see Sherwin-White (rev. Bleicken) (1963) 203.

[12]I do not agree with Koestermann *Annalen* 1.409 that they present an example of "das Allgemeine und das Besondere." Tacitus is evidently quoting the legislative enactment itself. Note the (slightly variant) legislative phrase for "prostitute" (Chapter 3) and the detailed list of (here equestrian) relatives characteristic of statutes: Paul. D. 23.2.44 pr. (senatorial) and *Tab. Lar.* 6–9 (senatorial and equestrian).

[13]The passages of Papinian and Suetonius cited below mention *lenocinium* as the profession in question. This suggests that the *SC* was phrased in broad terms.

[14]Despite the generalization in Suet. *Tib.* 35.2, I argue in *Social Policy* (1986) 284–300 that Vistilia was the only one ever to apply for the exemption. On Suetonius's tendency to generalize, see Nicolet, "Augustus" (1984) 119 n. 18. Most scholars continue to insist on a number of female registrants: Leontsini, *Prostitution* (1989) 175; Formigoni Candini, *"Lenones"* (1990) 111–113; Cohen, "Augustan Law" (1991) 111; Treggiari, *RM* (1991) 297; Gardner, *Being* (1993) 147.

[15]The *SC Macedonianum* is another example of generalized legislation evidently arising from a single outrageous case: Gardner, *Being* 66. The Vistilia decree forms part of a series of *SCC* from the early Principate that elaborated the system of norms that established the criminal court system in the late Republic and under Augustus: Santalucia, *DPR* (1989) 95–97.

Senate and piqued Tacitus's interest.[16] The incident might lie behind Tiberius's complaint four years later (in A.D. 23): "all the laws our ancestors devised, all those enacted by the deified Augustus, are now buried, the former in oblivion, the latter—to our greater shame—in contempt. . . . ''[17]

3. Juristic Interpretation

The Juristic Definition of "Prostitute" under the Adultery Statute

As we have seen in Chapter 4, the jurists accommodated the adultery law in their elaboration of the *lex Iulia et Papia*. This suggests that the same phrasing, and the same definition for "prostitute," served for both laws. No direct evidence supports this conclusion, but an imperial constitution inspires confidence that this was so:[18]

> Dioclet., Maxim. C. 9.9.22 (a. 290): Si ea quae tibi stupro cognita est passim venalem formam exhibuit ac prostituta meretricio more vulgo se praebuit, adulterii crimen in ea cessat.
>
> If a woman who has been found guilty of having committed illicit sexual intercourse [stuprum] with you [or "by you"[19]] on a showing of the facts has everywhere openly offered her body for sale and as a prostitute has made herself available indiscriminately in the manner of a prostitute, the charge of adultery does not lie.

A woman tried for adultery under the "*cognitio extra ordinem*" has been found guilty on the facts of an act of nonmarital sexual intercourse[20] (here *stuprum* bears the general meaning of "illicit sexual intercourse").[21] The *tibi* allows two inter-

---

[16] Levick, "*SC*" (1983) 114, makes a similar point. Scholars emphasize the unevenness of enforcement of the adultery law under Augustus and Tiberius: Treggiari, *RM* 295, quoting Garnsey, *Status* (1970) 24. This impression owes something to the penchant of the sources for the sensational. My account begs a number of important questions raised by such sources as Suet. *Tib.* 35.2; Pap. D. 48.5.11(10).2. More discussion in McGinn, "*SC*" 290–295.

[17] Tac. *Ann.* 3.54.2. The context is sumptuary legislation, but the heft of the complaint obviously ranges beyond this.

[18] The only serious objection to the text is made by Levy, *Hergang* (1925) 63–65, with n. 1, who condemns the phrase "quae tibi stupro cognita est." He understands *cognitus* to have the adjectival sense of *notus* and regards the whole relative clause as superfluous, given the following "si . . . praebuit." Levy follows Heumann-Seckel s.v. *cognoscere* 6 in understanding *stupro cognoscere* to mean "have extramarital sexual intercourse," an unlikely meaning.

[19] If *tibi* is construed with *cognita est* as a dative of agent; see below.

[20] Thus "stupro cognita" refers to a finding of fact by a court: Heumann-Seckel, s.v. *cognoscere* 3. A point of law is then raised and referred to the emperors for disposition. A Similar case is noted in Pap. (33 *quaest.*) 34.9.14, in which a point of law is raised about a woman "quae stupro cognita in contubernio militis fuit" ("who was found guilty, on a showing of the facts, of having committed *stuprum* while engaged in a nonmarital relationship with a soldier"). Contra, *OLD* s.h.v. 5b, which understands "cognita" as a reference to carnal knowledge.

[21] The traditional view is that *stuprum* and *adulterium* are used as synonyms in this text: Levy, *Hergang* 65 n. 1. *Stuprum,* though it can mean "adultery," has a broader significance as well, embracing

pretations. As a dative of agent, it identifies the recipient of the rescript as the provincial official who tried the case. As a dative of reference, it shows up Obrimus, the recipient of the rescript, as the codefendant of the unnamed woman. What concerns us is the application of the exemption for prostitutes and the criteria that the emperors set out in making this evaluation.

The phrasing then constitutes a definition, not a substitution, of the legislative "quae palam corpore quaestum facit, fecerit," a definition that may, despite the fact that it is found in a constitution of Diocletian, derive from juristic discussions pursuant to the *lex Iulia*. The language closely resembles that used in interpretation of the *lex Iulia et Papia*. Again we find the words *passim* and *vulgo* used to gloss *palam*; in fact, the entire phrase "passim . . . exhibuit" explains *palam*. The emphasis is on "open," "public," "indiscriminate" sexual activity. The criterion of payment is downplayed, though not entirely absent. It appears in "venalem," which stands as an equivalent for "quaestuariam" and so glosses statutory "quaestum." The phrase "prostituta meretricio more" is broad enough to cover all important aspects of the juristic definition given for the marriage law.[22] Its broadness recalls Ulpian's language: "quae vicem prostitutae sustinet".[23]

The similarity to the approach taken by the jurists themselves with regard to the interpretation of the phrase for "prostitute" in the *lex Iulia et Papia* is striking.[24] Here too a double constraint is at work. One anticipates a tendency to interpret the adultery law more restrictively in order to prevent unqualified persons from claiming the exemptions, while the marriage law demanded extensive interpretation, so as to discourage unions that were undesirable but marginally acceptable on a strict statutory construction. Because the jurists allowed their understanding of one law to influence their understanding of the other, the result that emerges for the adultery law, at least, is a fairly straightforward piece of declaratory interpretation, to take this imperial text as evidence.

Lenocinium

Criminal Pimping under the Statute

The only other matter directly relevant to prostitution and of any real concern to the jurists is the crime of *lenocinium*. Indeed, this was the only part of the legislation on adultery that underwent profound change at their hands,[25] an observation that should not occasion surprise, given their generally conservative approach to interpreting the Augustan legislation.[26] The atypical attention given to *lenocinium*

---

all varieties of illicit sexual intercourse: Rizzelli, "*Stuprum*" (1987). Given the provisory nature of the trial court's finding, the general meaning seems especially apt.

[22] Compare the phrase "meretricio quodam genere" in Ulp. D. 48.5.30(29).4, discussed below, and "meretricio more" in Cic. *Cael.* 38 (helping to excuse Caelius's affair with Clodia); *HA Elag.* 2.1.

[23] Ulp. (1 *ad legem Iuliam et Papiam*) D. 23.2.43.1.

[24] See Chapter 4.

[25] For another view, see Venturini, "Matrimonio" (1988) 176.

[26] The controversy over concubinage, a field to which the jurists did make a significant contribution,

may be attributed to two factors: the utility of the concept and the unsatisfactory manner in which it was exploited by the statute. This discussion supplements the evidence of the jurists with that provided by imperial constitutions. Partly this is a matter of convenience—making the best of incomplete evidence—but it is more accurate to say that a strict separation of the two is unrealistic.

The original two types of *lenocinium* established by the legislation, *quaestum facere* and *deprehensam retinere,* had a limited field of application. In Chapter 5 we saw how slim the evidence is for the profiteering husband. This suggests something of a gap existed between public concern and the dimensions of the actual problem. The same holds true for the other statutory type. Though *deprehensam retinere* was a crucial feature in the law's design, husbands catching the pair in the act perhaps formed only a small subset of actual adultery cases. At the same time, the concept of *lenocinium* was a forceful one, emotive, with strong ideological overtones, and sufficiently ductile to be manipulated easily by the legal authorities. The jurists enlarged the notion in two ways. They interpreted extensively the statutory types and defined other accessory crimes as species of *lenocinium*.[27] I begin with the most fundamental (because most like commercial prostitution) of the two statutory types *(quaestum facere)* and then examine the accessory crime most like it *(pretium accipere).*

Quaestum Facere

The moral significance that the jurists attributed to the main species of *lenocinium* is clear: "*. . . nec enim mediocriter deliquit, qui lenocinium in uxore exercuit.*"[28] Ulpian gives a strikingly expansive definition of the nature of this offense:

> Ulp. (4 *de adult.*) D. 48.5.30(29).4: Quaestum autem ex adulterio uxoris facere videtur, qui quid accepit, ut adulteretur uxor: sive enim saepius sive semel accepit, non est eximendus: quaestum enim de adulterio uxoris facere proprie ille existimandus est, qui aliquid accepit, ut uxorem pateretur adulterari meretricio quodam genere. quod si patiatur uxorem delinquere non ob quaestum, sed neglegentiam vel culpam vel quandam patientiam vel nimiam credulitatem, extra legem positus videtur.

> He is regarded as having made a profit out of the adultery of his wife who has received something in return for her committing adultery, and, whether he has accepted something rather often or just once, he is not to be let off, since a man is rightly to be regarded as having made a profit from the adultery of his own wife if he has received something in return for allowing his wife to commit adul-

---

is not an exception to this principle, since the adultery statute did not address this problem: McGinn, "Concubinage" (1991).

[27] By identifying two statutory types of *lenocinium,* both of which evidently stipulated the same penalty as the accessory offenses (on the significance of this point see Pap. D. 48.19.41), the law fairly encouraged the classical jurists in this application of a familiar technique, *diairesis.* See the extensive study by Talamanca, "Schema" (1977).

[28] Ulp. (4 *de adult.*) D. 48.5.30(29).3. Similarly, Longo, *Delictum* 30, who defends the text against Volterra's criticism. See Scaev. D. 24.3.47 *(quaestum facere* and *pretium accipere)* and the discussion below.

tery in the manner of a prostitute. But if he tolerates the wrongdoing of his wife, not for profit, but out of negligence or carelessness or a certain kind of tolerance or overcredulousness, he is not regarded as being liable under the statute.

The text has been attacked by Volterra, who condemns "meretricio . . . videtur."[29] But "meretricio quodam genere" is supported by the similar phrases in texts Volterra himself cites.[30] Volterra sees no *meretricium* here, but the identification of the adulteress as a prostitute is fundamental to the adultery law and operates independently of the presence of *lenocinium*.[31] Where both crimes occur, it is entirely natural to find a reference tying them together, above all with this type of *lenocinium*. Volterra's objection to the use of *delictum* for *crimen* is belied by classical usage in literary texts.[32] It seems perfectly appropriate in this context, given the nature of the offense. He also condemns "extra legem positus est" because it finds no classical equivalent, but in fact it is very close to such expressions as "extra legis poenam est"[33] and "qui sunt in aliqua dignitate positi."[34] The objections of Volterra and others to expressions such as *neglegentia, culpa,* etc. are largely subjective and are partly based on the assumption, once widespread, that the compilers were prone to inserting superfluous glosses.[35]

The passage expresses clearly the connection seen between adulteresses and complaisant husbands on the one hand and prostitutes and pimps on the other. The phrase "meretricio quodam genere" makes the identification between prostitution and adultery, typically assumed, explicit. The wife plays the part of the prostitute who offers sex in return for payment; the husband is the pimp who arranges the sexual transaction and himself handles the money.

It is important to note, however, that in the context of the juristic deliberations over the *lex Iulia,* a fundamental distinction emerges between adultery and prostitution. Only one sexual act makes a woman an adulteress, and only one monetary transaction makes her husband a pimp. This gives a broad definition of the term *quaestus* with regard to the *maritus-leno.*[36] Moreover, the consideration does not have to take monetary form, to judge from "quid" and "aliquid."[37] Some sort of transaction is required for there to be liability, as the last sentence makes clear. At this point in the text, the tone of moral condemnation is unmistakable, though liability under the law is denied. A line is drawn, but even as the jurist places limits on this species of *lenocinium,* he leaves open the possibility for liability to

---

[29] Volterra, "Innovazioni" (1930) 9–10, whose criticism is accepted by Longo, *Delictum* 29.

[30] Compare the wording in the constitution of Diocletian cited above and that of Cic. *Cael.* 38 ("meretricio more").

[31] So now Rizzelli, "*Crimen*" (1990) 478 n. 44.

[32] Sen. *Ben.* 3.16.4; Tac. *Ann.* 2.85.3; see above.

[33] Marci. (12 *inst.*) D. 25.7.3.1.

[34] Ulp. (35 *ad edictum*) D. 26.10.3.16.

[35] On this last point, see below.

[36] The word usually refers to "making a living," "earning," in ways that suggest habitualness or repetition; see Chapter 4. This is certainly true of the prostitute's *quaestus,* which is the model for the legislative phrasing.

[37] The same held for *pretium accipere*; see below and Rizzelli, "*Crimen*" 477 n. 42.

be construed under another heading, as the qualification ''quandam patientiam'' suggests.[38]

Pretium Accipere

We saw in the previous chapter that this type was not defined by the statute as a form of *lenocinium,* although it did appear as an accessory crime. We begin with a minor controversy over the the law's articulation of this offense. The most important piece of evidence is a text of Scaevola:[39]

> Scaev. (4 *reg.*) D. 48.5.15(14) pr.: Is, cuius ope consilio dolo malo factum est, ut vir feminave in adulterio deprehensi pecunia aliave qua pactione se redimerent, eadem poena damnatur, quae constituta est in eos, qui lenocinii crimine damnantur.

> He by whose aid and counsel, with malicious intent, it is brought about that a man or woman caught in the act of adultery should buy himself or herself off with money or through any other sort of arrangement, is condemned to the same penalty as the law lays down for those who are found guilty on a charge of *lenocinium.*

Mommsen viewed this holding as a sanction directed at an accomplice who assisted a transaction aimed at heading off an adultery charge.[40] The principal (the leading, but not the only candidate is the husband of the adulteress), the actual recipient of payment, was already to be punished as someone who had received *pretium pro comperto stupro.* Daube,[41] who sees here a partial quotation of the law,[42] wants the fragment to refer not only to the accomplice but to the principal as well. To summarize his argument, Daube questions why there should be a separate legislative provision for accomplices under the *pretium* type of *lenocinium* but not for the *quaestus* type. In fact, he continues, there was none: the law cast its net as wide as possible with a provision that covered both accomplice and principal.[43]

Like Mommsen, Daube makes no clear distinction between the different types of *lenocinium,* or even between the statutory kinds and the broader juristic conception of this offense.[44] Scaevola himself perhaps alludes to the status of *pretium* as ''juristic'' *lenocinium* when he speaks of the penalty: guilty parties are not sentenced on a charge of *lenocinium,* but are given the same penalty as those condemned for *lenocinium.*[45] Since the legislation conceived of *pretium* more broadly than *quaestus,* insofar as it embraced other culprits besides the husband,

---

[38] See the discussion below on the *deprehensa.*

[39] The other evidence cited by the parties to the dispute is Macer D. 48.5.33(32).1, which deals with this offense qua an accessory offense to adultery.

[40] Mommsen, *Strafrecht* (1899) 700.

[41] Daube, ''Lex Julia'' (1972) 377–380.

[42] Daube, ''Lex Julia'' 377, identifies the legislative citation as ''is . . . redimerent.''

[43] Daube, ''Lex Julia'' 378, points out that ''ope consiliove'' can be understood as ''act,'' ''calculation,'' not just ''help,'' ''counsel.''

[44] So Daube, ''Lex Julia'' 373–374, puzzles over why the distinction is maintained concerning whether the money is received before or after the fact, a distinction he regards as a ''quirk.''

[45] The exact phrasing is important: Scaevola is often taken to mean that the legislation embraced this offense as a type of *lenocinium,* but the text does not say this.

there is plenty of room under this heading for a separate offense covering the acts of accomplices. If Scaevola is indeed quoting the statute, as he appears to do, Scaevola's text must concern the offense of the accomplice, since the principal offender, again, perhaps the husband, was already defined by the statute as someone who disobeyed the injunction ''ne quis pretium pro comperto stupro accipito sciens dolo malo.''[46]

The language Scaevola uses is statutory. It is easier to regard this as taken from the Augustan law, but there is a chance that an *SC* pursuant to this is the source. The language is not strictly compatible with the *lex Iulia*. We find *vir* and *femina* instead of *adulter* and *mater familias/adultera, pecunia* instead of *pretium*. In the very next text,[47] Scaevola mentions an *SC* punishing a husband-accomplice.[48]

The problem raised by the text goes deeper. Scaevola, in quoting the legislation, stipulates that the adulterous couple have been caught in the act, ''deprehensi.'' Strictly speaking, this is a different scenario from that envisaged by the provision punishing *pretium accipere*. In the latter case, any knowledge acquired after the fact potentially fell within the scope of the law. The question of language is important, for the law said ''pro comperto stupro,'' not ''pro deprehensis adulteris'' or the like. So the jurists understand the law to punish persons who accept compensation ''ob conscientiam stupri,'' which would certainly include the case of adulterers caught in the act[49] but not necessarily be exhausted thereby.

What this means is that, according to the statute, only those accomplices who intervene in flagrant cases were punished, just as only the husband who catches the guilty pair in the act is compelled to divorce his wife and take action against the lover. Daube's point about the accomplice phrase embracing the principals has merit, insofar as there really is no distinction to be made for this rather particular situation. It is only that, in practical terms, any principal would already fall within the broader rubric of *pretium*. Moreover, the husband who took money in the case of a *deprehensa* would be as much a *leno* for not divorcing her within 60 days.

This leaves us with the somewhat unsettling result that accomplices, though just as guilty, would get off in cases where the lovers were not taken in the act itself.[50] Some amelioration can be sought in the broad construction, discussed below, that the jurists develop for *deprehensam retinere*. Since this would embrace some situations where the lovers were not discovered *in flagrante,* it drives home the possibility that, in all cases where accomplices played a role, they could be punished for their efforts to thwart the operation of the law. The inevitable result

---

[46] See Chapter 5.

[47] Scaev. D. 48.5.15(14).1.

[48] The Augustan statute might seem too early for this idea if we compare the development of the notion of complicity in theft, though in my view the latter notion does not occur as late as MacCormack, ''Ope'' (1983) prefers.

[49] So, for example, money might be given ''pro comperto stupro'' by a man caught in the act (and threatened with death): Paul. D. 4.2.8 pr.

[50] To be clear, this would hold only where the ''accomplice'' had not accepted money or some form of compensation qualifiable as *pretium*. The vagueness of ''aliave qua pactione'' in the principal text opens up a possibility for extensive interpretation, albeit a small one.

would be some confusion between the categories of *pretium accipere* and *depre-hensam retinere*.

It is interesting to note that an *SC* of unknown date punished the husband who connived at his wife's adultery by suborning a lover in order to catch her in the act, not, surprisingly, under a charge of *lenocinium,* but that of adultery itself![51] One may speculate that either this decree came too early to reflect the results of the juristic synthesis that derived so many *species* from the *genus* of *lenocinium* or the husband's behavior was deemed so heinous as to fall beyond the pale even of *lenocinium*. In either case, he was paradoxically guilty of adultery with respect to his own wife—a "constructive" adulterer.[52]

Years of trial experience and learned elaboration broke down the theoretical boundaries between some of the offenses punished by the law itself. In the devel-oped juristic concept of *lenocinium,* accomplices to a payment made after the fact of adultery form, not a separate type, but appendages to one or two of the main types. These are the husband who does not divorce his wife and take action against her lover, a *leno* by statute, and the husband or any person who takes money upon discovery that adultery has been committed, defined as pimps by the jurists.

How did *pretium accipere* come to be viewed as a type of *lenocinium*? There is an obvious analogy between the husband who receives money before the act and the one who does so afterward. The husband, burdened with the duty to maintain the honor of his house, a duty fortified by his status as a privileged accuser un-der the law, was bound to be a central focus of the jurists' attention. He had no obligation to divorce the woman in nonflagrant cases, but this made his position vis-à-vis the law's operation all the more crucial. A refusal to divorce realistically meant no chance at prosecution of the wife by anyone. As a practical matter, the husband was the likeliest candidate for such transactions. So Ulpian places together the husbands who take money before and after the fact:[53] in the abstract, the two could be considered virtually identical.[54]

Of course, the law itself did not regard *quaestum facere* and *pretium accipere* as fungible types. The latter was more broadly conceived. Any person, not just the husband, who took money might be punished, not just for adultery, but for the offense of *stuprum* as well, as Ulpian emphasizes.[55] In one sense, there is an ex-tensive treatment of *pretium* similar to that given *quaestus:* any type of payment ("aliquid") may qualify, not just money. We encounter this extensive interpretation

---

[51] Scaev. D. 48.5.15(14).1.

[52] Presumably the suborned lover was guilty too, so that in this case three persons would be guilty of one act of adultery—a remarkable result. For an identification of the complaisant wife as a construc-tive adulteress on a different but equally striking theory, see below.

[53] Ulp. D. 48.5.2.2; see Chapter 5.

[54] For a concrete illustration, see Dioclet., Maxim. C. 4.7.5 (a. 294), on which see Kaser, *Verbots-gesetze* (1977) 87.

[55] Ulp. (4 *de adult.*) D. 48.5.30(29).2: "Plectitur et qui pretium pro comperto stupro acceperit: nec interest, utrum maritus sit qui acceperit an alius quilibet: quicumque enim ob conscientiam stupri accepit aliquid, poena erit plectendus. ceterum si gratis quis remisit, ad legem non pertinet." (See the translation in Chapter 5).

of the term *pretium* in cases giving rise to the *actio de eo quod metus causa factum erit,* where the idea includes not just what is given by the beleaguered adulterer but what is promised.[56] Again, there must be a transaction, as Ulpian emphasizes. His language points up the fact that *deprehensi* are not exclusively, nor even primarily, concerned.

This fragment contradicts Daube's view that "no passage hints at the receipt of payment simply in order that one may not divulge one's knowledge."[57] He follows Mommsen in making a distinction between a payment to avert a recipient's right to kill or prosecute the culprit(s) and "mere hush money," with the difference that he thinks that the law did not punish the latter. In fact, there is no evidence that the law, or the jurists, recognized this distinction. Why interpret the legislation so narrowly in this instance when the statute itself (if not a later *SC*) specifically punished accomplices to the payoff in cases of *deprehensam retinere*?

Indeed, that the jurists made no such distinction can be inferred from Ulpian's generalizing "ob conscientiam stupri." A further analogy may be sought in the regime of the *actio de eo quod metus causa factum erit,* which covered situations involving payment "pro comperto stupro" where payment was made or promised under duress.[58] With regard to the *lex Iulia,* the legislator was clearly concerned with potential acts of collusion that would thwart the operation of the statute. So, for the recipient to be punished under *pretium,* it would not matter whether he was in a position himself to kill or prosecute the culprits. The suppression of information that might otherwise lead to such outcomes was enough.

Other texts show that *pretium accipere* was understood to embrace any agreement that amounted to an out-of-court settlement in cases of *adulterium* or *stuprum*.[59] Mommsen classified such agreements as a separate category of *lenocinium,* but there is no reason to distinguish this instance from other cases of payment *pro comperto stupro*.[60] Nevertheless, there was a complicating element. The motive for making such payments, even where the lover was not caught in the act and was not threatened with violence, must sometimes have been the avoidance of prosecution.

Agreements to avoid prosecution might run afoul of more than one piece of legislation. The husband who agreed not to prosecute wife or lover violated the injunction, probably laid down by the *lex Iulia iudiciorum publicorum* (whatever its ultimate origins),[61] against making such agreements in criminal cases *(pacisci*

---

[56] Pomp.-Ulp. D. 4.2.7.1; cf. Paul. D. *eod.* 8 pr. and the discussion in Chapter 5.

[57] Daube, "Lex Julia" 374.

[58] See Chapter 5.

[59] Pap. D. 48.5.12(11) pr. (an aggravation of the penalty, perhaps linked to the defendant's status as a soldier); Dioclet., Maxim. C. 2.4.18 (a. 293). See Mommsen, *Strafrecht* 675 n. 7; Berger, *Dictionary* (1953) s.v. *pacisci de crimine, transactio.* Cf. Pap. D. 48.5.12(11).3 (see below). Whatever position one adopts on the genuineness of the phrase "excepto adulterio" in the constitution just mentioned (see the criticism of Longo, *Delictum* 107), it is incredible that *pacisci* was permitted in an adultery case.

[60] Mommsen, *Strafrecht* 700.

[61] See Levy, "Anklägervergehen" (1933/1963) 402.

de crimine).[62] If the agreement led to a collusive prosecution, this was construed as an offense by the same statute, which laid down an identical penalty (loss of the *ius accusandi*):[63]

> Alex. Sev. C. 9.9.10 (a. 225): De crimine adulterii pacisci non licet et par delictum accusatoris praevaricatoris et rei fugientis[64] veritatis inquisitionem est. qui autem pretium pro comperto stupro accepit, poena legis Iuliae de adulteriis tenetur.
>
> Settlements over prosecuting the charge of adultery are prohibited, and liability is the same for the collusive prosecutor and for the defendant evading the inquiry into the truth. Moreover, he who accepts payment for having discovered an act of *stuprum* is liable to the penalty established by the *lex Iulia* on adultery.

The constitution defines liability under no fewer than three statutes. Aside from the ban on *pretium accipere* laid down by the *lex Iulia* and the prohibitions against agreements not to prosecute and collusive prosecutions arising from the Augustan statute governing the criminal courts, the *SC Turpillianum* rounded out earlier enactments making the instigator of the crime, who would usually be the defendant, guilty along with the actual prosecutor.[65] It is worth emphasizing that *pretium accipere* remains a separate offense, punishable in its own right, no matter what the goal or context of the transaction.[66]

The *SC Turpillianum* merits further examination in this context. This statute, passed in A.D. 61, introduced a new series of regulations,[67] punishing those who did not complete a prosecution, once begun, within the period of time prescribed by the presiding magistrate or who gave reason to believe that they would not follow through before the expiration of this time limit *(desistere).*[68] Payment did

---

[62] This is the view of Levy, ''Anklägervergehen'' 401–403, followed by Kaser, *RE* transactio (1937) 2146–2147, against that of Bohacek, who sees a special provision in the adultery statute.

[63] Levy, ''Anklägervergehen'' 408; one should be careful to distinguish the agreement from the actual prosecution, since it was only the latter that was punished as *praevaricatio.* For the repressive treatment at private law of such agreements, see Provera, ''Riflessi'' (1965).

[64] Considerations of style and sense support Cujaz's reading ''rei fugientis'' instead of the manuscript's ''refugientis'': Levy ''Anklägervergehen'' 413 n. 152 (the note is truncated; see *SZ* 53 [1933] 205 n. 1). Other parts of the text have been criticized; for a defense, see Levy, ''Anklägervergehen'' 413 n. 150; Longo, *Delictum* 40–41.

[65] See Fanizza, *Delatori* (1988) 55. Rizzelli, ''*Crimen*'' 476 n. 41, sees *accusator* and *praevaricator* as two different parties.

[66] So Levy, ''Anklägervergehen'' 403, followed by Rizzelli, ''*Crimen*'' 476. To be sure, Levy's criticism of Mommsen's characterization of *pretium* as payment for ''die Abwendung der Adulterienklage'' leads to a somewhat dogmatic result. Cumulative liability must be assumed, since the instigator's liability derives from a paid transaction between him and the prosecutor (see Tac. *Ann.* 14.41, with Levy, ''Anklägervergehen'' 401, 409–410). In the application of the adultery law, cumulative liability aggravated the penalty: Pap. D. 48.5.12(11) pr.

[67] For discussion, see Levy, ''Anklägervergehen'' 417–430; Waldstein, *Begnadigungsrecht* (1964) 112–126; Fanizza, *Delatori.* Besides ''*infamia*'' (understood as the loss of the right to pursue political office and to bring criminal prosecutions), there was a money penalty, the existence of which is denied, wrongly in my view, by Levy and favored, under certain circumstances, by Fanizza (87–89). Cf. Santalucia, *DPR* 122–123.

[68] Levy, ''Anklägervergehen'' 419–422.

not necessarily play a role in such cases, so that the offense did not always fall within the scope of *pretium*.[69] A grant of *abolitio* allowed a prosecuting husband to remarry his wife without fear of committing *lenocinium*.[70]

Alongside of this legislative intervention, the jurists made a number of contributions to the regime for *pretium accipere*. They made a logical extension of the scope of liability to embrace women:[71]

> Pap. (*2 de adult.*) D. 48.5.11(10).1: Mulieres quoque hoc capite legis, quod domum praebuerunt vel pro comperto stupro aliquid acceperunt, tenentur.
>
> Women too are liable under this chapter of the law, if they furnished a venue [for the commission of the crime] or if they accepted payment in connection with discovery of an act of *stuprum*.

As a practical matter, it made perfect sense to hold women responsible for such acts. Again, the law did not limit potential liability to a particular type of individual, as with *quaestum facere* or *deprehensam retinere*, where only the husband could be guilty. Women were eminently capable of providing a venue for the crime, a fact probably recognized from a very early date.[72]

Naturally, women were not able to prosecute under the statute, nor could they exercise the *ius occidendi*. Nevertheless, they were capable, or at least might create the impression that they were capable, of forwarding the information to someone in a position to act. The jurists recognized this as a distinct possibility in their discussions of the role of duress in *pretium*-type transactions (see below). Indeed, roughly the same was true of men who were not husbands or fathers of the female culprit, in the sense that they could not exercise the *ius occidendi* and, though they could prosecute as *extranei*, could not act as privileged accusers and might simply prefer to give information instead.[73] Outsiders of either gender had no responsibility to act, whereas the law defined the acceptance of payment as an offense, without specifying the purpose behind the transaction. Husbands threatening violence or prosecution may have formed the bulk of such cases, but there is no reason to believe that others, including women themselves, were not held liable early on.[74]

The extension of liability to women for commission of accessory offenses perhaps predated the grouping of these crimes under the heading of *lenocinium*, at

---

[69] See Pap. (*lib. sing. de adult.*) D. 48.5.12(11).3, where the jurist criticizes a father-in-law who abandons (*desistere*) a prosecution for adultery, content with seeing the dowry remain within the family. Kaser's misgivings, "Rechtswidrigkeit" (1940) 143, about this text are unfounded in my view. The case seems close to one of constructive *lenocinium*. So Corsanego, *Repressione* (1936) 22, and Beaucamp, *Statut* 1 (1990) 152 n. 83, understand it, though the jurist holds only that the man should be refused an action on the dowry. Fanizza, *Delatori* 72 n. 172, sees a collusive agreement in play.

[70] Val., Gall. C. 9.9.17 (a. 257); see below.

[71] The text also shows that the statute was understood to extend to all forms of compensation, not just money; see above.

[72] So Daube, "Lex Julia" 375.

[73] I depend on Gardner, *Women* (1986) 136 n. 55, who rightly criticizes the notion that men were bribed to forgo prosecution or physical violence, and women alone were bribed to keep their silence.

[74] Contra Daube, "Lex Julia" 375, who regards the circumstance outlandish enough to suggest a postclassical origin for "vel . . . acceperunt."

whatever date this occurred. The analogy of the *leno* operates without difficulty for men not the husband who are guilty of these accessory crimes. A male who accepts money after the fact can be understood as the adulteress's pimp in much the same way as the husband who does so, although the offense may not seem as outrageous. But the identification of women as pimps in the sense envisaged by the law is more difficult, not only because of the typical way in which the *lex Iulia* manipulates gender role but also owing to the sociological assumptions on which this manipulation is founded. The problem is illuminated by the following:

> Marci. (1 *de publ. iud.*) D. 48.5.34(33).2: Si uxor ex adulterio viri praemium acceperit, lege Iulia quasi adultera tenetur.

> If a wife accepts recompense for the adultery of her husband, she is liable under the *lex Iulia* as though she were an adulteress.

Daube identifies this offense as an example of *quaestum facere,* conceding that the discrepancy in language *(praemium)* betrayed a postlegislative extension of the statute.[75] Biondi and Alvarez de Cienfuegos view the culprit as guilty of *lenocinium* under the law.[76]

There can be no doubt that this situation was not contemplated by the statute. It is incredible for the law to have envisaged a case where a wife sold her husband's sexual services to women. The jurist evidently does pattern his construction of this offense on the law's phrasing for *quaestum facere:* "ne quis ex adulterio uxoris suae quaestum facito sciens dolo malo." He is interested in testing the limits of the concept of *lenocinium.* His hypothetical situation stipulates a woman bought off in exchange for her silence after the fact. The language supports this view: Marcian adopts the same verb *(accipere)* used by the statute to define *pretium.*

The wife is punished "quasi adultera," not "quasi leno" or, as the man guilty of *lenocinium* was punished, "quasi adulter."[77] At least by Marcian's day, all penalties for accessory crimes were the same as those inflicted on the principals (for all we know, this was accomplished by the statute itself). There is, however, an important technical distinction. "Pimps" lost one-half their property; adulteresses lost one-third, in addition to one-half of their dowries. No special provision was made, as far as we know, for female offenders under *lenocinium,* with justice, since there was no reason to assume they were married and therefore had a dowry that might be mulcted. In other words, they were punished in the same way as males. The law constructed no separate category of the criminal *lena,* nor did the jurists. At closest, the female offender was treated as a criminal *leno.*

The guilty wife however is punished not as a pimp but as an adulteress.[78] The reason for this may be sought in the value system that determined the law's design and its treatment by jurists who shared its underlying assumptions. A woman could

---

[75] Daube, "Lex Julia" 375; cf. Daube, "Impossible Laws" (1967) 32. See also Esmein, "Délit" (1886) 106, 117; Rizzelli, "*Crimen*" 490–492.

[76] Biondi, "*Leges*" (1946/1965) 208; Alvarez de Cienfuegos, "*Lenocinium*" (1988) 570–571.

[77] On the penalty, see Chapter 5.

[78] *Quasi* often introduces an analogy for the jurists; see Bauman, "*Leges*" (1980) 141, who cites this text. It can also simply mean "as": Daube, "Impossible Laws" 32.

simply not act as her husband's pimp: this was inconceivable.[79] Any woman who accepted payment "pro comperto stupro" in connection with her husband's adultery was defined not as a *lena,* who traded in the honor of another, but as an *adultera,* who forfeited her own honor.[80] To us, her offense seems perfectly analogous to that of the husband who accepts payment in the matter of his wife's adultery and is more or less identical to that of other women who accept payment, but for the Romans such behavior had a different meaning.[81]

Pretium emerges from this discussion as a focal point of juristic and legislative concern. It was, perhaps, the most important type of *lenocinium* in actual practice and was probably identified as a species of such early on.[82] Given the vulnerability of adulterers, what with the (evidently liable to be abused) *ius occidendi* and the harsh penalties laid down by the statute, escape from their predicament would have been worth a good deal to these men. I think it reasonable to suppose that many more husbands were willing to accept compensation afterward than were prepared to sell their wives' services in advance.[83] The generalized phrasing of the statute, along with its broad construction by the jurists, must have encouraged frequent application through prosecution. Once identified as a type of *lenocinium, pretium accipere* seems to have eclipsed *quaestum facere* in importance.

Deprehensam Retinere

The third type of *lenocinium* derives, like the first, directly from the statute. It lies in the failure to divorce a wife and take action against her lover when the pair have been caught in the act of adultery. Of the two duties, that of divorce was the more important and so receives by far the greater share of juristic attention. As noted, the act of divorce occupied a crucial position with respect to the law's operation, since it opened the prescriptive period in which accusations might be launched; more important, as long as the marriage lasted, the husband could not

[79] Bauman, *Women* 125, views Livia's alleged procuring of sexual partners for Augustus as *lenocinium* under the law, but the sources, though they accuse her of procuring (Tac. *Ann.* 5.1.3 ["uxor facilis"]; Suet. *Aug.* 71.1), do not make this point.

[80] This explains the use of *praemium* in place of *pretium.* Compare Lab.-Peg.-Nerva fil.-Ulp. D. 3.2.2.5, where *praemium* is equated to *quaestus.* On its usual meaning in criminal law, see Crook, *Advocacy* (1995) 160.

[81] Alvarez de Cienfuegos, "*Lenocinium*" 571, goes so far as to claim, on the basis of Ulp. D. 48.5.30(29).6, that the *lex Iulia* itself established that women could be guilty of *lenocinium,* but this text proves nothing of the sort.

[82] Perhaps by the end of the first century A.D., to judge from [Quint.] *Decl.* 275.1: "qui pecuniam ob adulterium acceperit, ignominiosus sit. hanc legem adversus eos primum constitutam esse dico, qui pecuniam acceperunt, ut adulterium committeretur, ideoque ignominiam adiunctam quod viderentur rem fecisse lenonis."

[83] Financial compensation had been an accepted manner of healing breaches of sexual honor before the passage of the law. Afterward, there was a marked tendency to assume payment before the fact in situations that might have been more truthfully viewed as *pretium accipere*; see the evidence presented in Chapter 5.

move against the lover,[84] and the wife could not be prosecuted by anyone. This principle remained unaltered throughout the classical period.[85]

The construction of liability for the errant husband was the central focus of discussion under this heading. In other words, who should count as *deprehensi*? One would expect a broad interpretation to be given this by the jurists. No doubt this is consonant with the law's overall design. Several practical constraints were also at work, however. First, the jurists had to avoid a construction that was so broad that it would be incapable of distinguishing cases where the adultery itself was, in fact, only suspected. Second, the limits of this definition were in part set by the other definitions of *lenocinium* that they developed. Finally, the law used very similar language to establish the parameters of the *ius occidendi,* an aspect of the law that for a number of reasons demanded a somewhat restrictive interpretation.

Our first text suggests just how broad a view was possible:[86]

Ulp. (4 *de adult*) D. 48.5.30(29) pr.: Mariti lenocinium lex coercuit, qui deprehensam uxorem in adulterio retinuit adulterumque dimisit: debuit enim uxori quoque irasci, quae matrimonium eius violavit. tunc autem puniendus est maritus, cum excusare ignorantiam suam non potest vel adumbrare patientiam praetextu incredibilitatis: idcirco enim lex ita locuta est "adulterum in domo deprehensum dimiserit," quod voluerit in ipsa turpitudine deprehendentem maritum coercere.

This passage, which has admittedly been shortened by the compilers,[87] is in part supported by another text, which speaks of the man who "adulteram sciens, ut ignorationem simulare non possit, retinet uxorem."[88] The burden of persuasion is shifted to the husband, who must demonstrate his ignorance or, better, provide a plausible rationale for it.[89] Failing this, he must explain away his complaisance on the ground that his wife's infidelity defied belief. The hostile, condemnatory tone of the language is striking: "excusare," "adumbrare," "praetextu"—it almost seems as if the guilt of the putative defendant is assumed. Ulpian, although he mentions the legislative requirement ("adulterum in domo deprehensum"), does not make anything of this in his discussion of the standard of liability, and we may assume that the fact that the husband had come upon the lovers in a place other than in his own home would have been irrelevant to a defense against a charge of *deprehensam retinere*.[90]

---

[84] The ability of *extranei* to move against the lover before divorce may have been a late development; see Chapter 5.

[85] Alex. Sev. C. 9.9.11 (a. 226).

[86] For a translation, see Chapter 5.

[87] See Chapter 5.

[88] Val., Gall. C. 9.9.17.1 (a. 257). Volterra, "Innovazioni" 11, alleges that "sciens ut" and "ignorationem" are "espressioni byzantine" (followed by Goria, *Studi* [1975] 89 n. 5; contra Rizzelli, "*Crimen*" 472 n. 33). The latter, which appears as early as Cicero, is fully classical: *OLD* s.h.v.

[89] Venturini, "Ripudianda" (1988) 273, argues that these texts reflect restrictive interpretation, which is difficult to accept.

[90] For the extensive interpretation of *domus* (not necessarily relevant here), see below.

The jurist evidently uses "in ipsa turpitudine" as a point of departure, in contrast to the regime for the *ius occidendi,* where this idea defines the outermost limit for the application of the privilege. A man could only exercise the "right of slaying" if he caught the pair in the act. To be found liable under *deprehensam retinere,* demonstrable knowledge of the affair was sufficient.

Mere suspicion, on the other hand, was not enough. Here is the other pole of the juristic construction of liability:

> Sev., Ant. C. 9.9.2 (a. 199): Crimen lenocinii contrahunt, qui deprehensam in adulterio uxorem in matrimonio detinuerunt, non qui suspectam adulteram habuerunt.

> They incur a charge of *lenocinium* who remain married to a woman caught in the act of adultery, not if they remain married to a woman who is suspected of being an adulteress.

The mere fact that a husband suspected adultery, that is, had reason to believe that fell short of reasonable certainty, was an insufficient basis on which to convict him of *lenocinium.*[91] The vagueness of the standard created by the construction of these two poles, illustrated by the text of Ulpian discussed just above, gives a very wide discretion to the finder of fact, if it is correct to assume we possess a true sense of the guidelines laid down.

The elaboration of other categories of *lenocinium* (above all, *quaestum facere*) contributed to the construction of a standard of liability for *deprehensam retinere.* An illustration of this occurs in a text already discussed:[92]

> Ulp. (4 *de adult.*) D. 48.5.30(29).4: . . . quod si patiatur uxorem delinquere non ob quaestum, sed neglegentiam vel culpam vel quandam patientiam vel nimiam credulitatem, extra legem positus videtur.

The phrasing is sufficiently general to apply to more than one type of *lenocinium.*[93] All the same, this fragment has a particular relevance for *deprehensam retinere.* With *quaestus* and *pretium* the criterion of payment simplifies the task of defining the crime. One can, with little difficulty, regard almost all behavior not characterized by this criterion as falling beyond the reach of the standard. *Deprehensam retinere* presented a more delicate problem of definition.

In this text, Ulpian uses language that is evidently derived from the standards of care employed in delict and contract law.[94] These are abstract terms that provide a set of objective classifications, to be used in judging cases as they arise. The standard of liability they define is remarkably low, the more so when viewed in

---

[91] The wife herself could not be convicted of adultery on the basis of suspicions alone. This rule applied to all criminal cases through a famous rescript of Trajan: Ulp. D. 48.19.5 pr.

[92] See above, where a translation is given.

[93] The words "si patiatur uxorem delinquere" have a particular affinity with the beginning of Ulp. D. 48.5.2.3 (see below), which pertains to *quaestum facere, pretium accipere,* and *deprehensam retinere.*

[94] The nature and purpose of these standards are the subject of constant debate among scholars, and an attempt to gauge precisely their function in this transferred setting is difficult. For a discussion, see Kaser, *RP* 1[2] (1971) 502–513; Wacke, "Vergehen" (1979) esp. 557 on *nimia neglegentia* and *nimia culpa*; Voci, "Diligentia" (1990); MacCormack, "*Dolus*" (1994).

the light of that given directly for *deprehensam retinere* in the two texts discussed above. The husband is not held to account for failure to exercise ordinary care *(neglegentia)* or even for more serious lapses in the moral oversight of his wife *(culpa)*. He is even exempted from any criminal consequences of displaying "a certain tolerance" and "overcredulousness."

The qualification given *patientia* is of great interest, since the same word appears in the discussion of liability in Ulp. D. 48.5.30(29) pr., where the husband is required to excuse his "tolerance" through a convincing plea of incredulity. The notion of *quaedam patientia* in the principal text is not, I think, inconsistent with this and strikes a note of moral disapproval into the bargain.

The tone of disapproval is even stronger in the following text:

> Ulp. (8 *disp.*) D. 48.5.2.3: Ceterum qui patitur uxorem suam delinquere matrimoniumque suum contemnit quique contaminationi non indignatur, poena adulteri ei[95] non infligitur.

> But he who allows his wife to offend and despises his marriage, and who is not angry at the defilement, is not inflicted with the punishment received by the adulterer.

The fragment that immediately precedes this one is relevant to all three types of *lenocinium* examined thus far: *quaestum facere, pretium accipere,* and *deprehensam retinere.*[96] The new text advances the discussion; although it has been subjected to withering criticism, it is quite classical.

Volterra condemns the entire passage on the basis of the following objections: the use of *delinquere* to describe a criminal offense, *ceterum* positioned at the beginning of a fragment, the verb *indignari,* the rare word *contaminatio,* and "the frequent repetitions in order to express the same concept."[97] In fact, the language seems too highly charged to be an attempt at legislation by the compilers. *Delinquere* and its cognates elsewhere describe offenses against the *lex Iulia.*[98] As for *ceterum,* the classical jurists did not make the breaks between sections in the *Digest.* In any case, the jurists have many instances of *ceterum* beginning a sentence, and a few of these begin individual fragments as well.[99] *Indignari* is not rare in juristic sources.[100]

Contaminatio appears only here in the *Digest,* and the *TLL* shows no secure instances before the early third century. But one of these is contemporary with Ulpian.[101] The meaning of the word in our text is different, since it refers to defilement by sexual intercourse, a meaning amply attested in the classical usage of

[95] Mommsen reads "adulteri ei" instead of the manuscript's "adulterum."
[96] See Chapter 5 and above.
[97] See Volterra, "Innovazioni" 7–8, and Volterra, "Compensazione" (1930) 3–4, whose criticism is accepted by Longo, *Delictum* 29–30.
[98] See above.
[99] *VIR* s.h.v. 4b.
[100] Pomp. D. 1.2.24, Ulp. D. 29.4.4 pr., and Paul. D. 37.6.2.5 are examples. The classical usage is given by *OLD* s.h.v.
[101] This is "locum lustrari . . . ab omni contamination[e]" at *CIL* 6.4.2.32328.23–24 (a. 204), in the record of the celebration of the Ludi Saeculares under Severus and Caracalla.

the verb *contaminare*.[102] The pattern of an action verb developing a meaning that is only later introduced into the language as a noun is a familiar one.[103]

Volterra's criticism of the "repetitions" is subjective and therefore difficult to answer. The contribution made by this text to our understanding of *lenocinium* will I hope emerge with greater clarity from the discussion that follows. I point out, however, that when Volterra wrote, nearly all explanatory material in the juristic texts was liable to be identified as postclassical, a principle of criticism that tends to overlook the fact that the chief task of the compilers was to condense and abbreviate what they found in the classical sources.[104]

In the principal text, Ulpian first addresses the responsibility of the husband with regard to his wife's behavior, next examines what his proper attitude should be to the marriage itself, and then concludes with an emotive phrase invoking the husband's sense of honor. Again he delineates behavior that he considers morally reprehensible but not punishable under the law. Despite the jurist's charged language, the husband who does not accept payment in compensation for tolerating his wife's infidelity or who does not have his betrayal disclosed to him in an open and undeniable manner (and does not divorce his wife) is not liable to the harsh penalties imposed by the law on the husband-pimp.

Viewing the standard of liability for all three of these categories in this manner discloses an effort at synthesis, a pulling together of strands from different definitions that were potentially in conflict. The mutual limits imposed by this procedure led to a sharp differentiation between the legal and social conceptions of proper husbandly behavior. The social expectations of the *maritus* were that he would exercise due care, that he would in fact be alert to any breach of honor, not simply that he would "foresee what a careful person ought to foresee,"[105] but that he would be diligent in such matters.

Tolerance of wifely foibles was out of the question. Society demanded energy be shown, not passive acquiescence. Intelligence was required too, or at least that common sense and awareness about the world and its ways that was the mark of a man. According to the gender-specific roles assigned by the honor-shame syndrome, husbands were responsible for the sexual behavior of their wives. But the law was not prepared to strip someone of half his property and relegate him to an island for being a little too stupid, overcredulous, trusting, or careless.[106] The (potential) conflict among these texts points up the difficulty of translating social expectations into legal norms.[107]

---

[102] *OLD* s.h.v. 5. See Adams, *LSV* (1982) 199, where he links this verb with *corrumpere* and *polluere,* on the basis of Sen. *Contr.* 1.2.7.

[103] As Daube, *Roman Law* (1969) 11–63, has shown.

[104] Later Byzantine law considerably sharpened the rules for the complaisant husband: B. 60.37.4.2-3S, 29.3-4S, with Goria, *Studi* 89–90, 237.

[105] The standard of care for *culpa* under the *lex Aquilia:* Muc.-Pomp. D. 9.2.31.

[106] One notes Augustus's initial reluctance to believe the evidence of his daughter Julia's promiscuity: Dio (in Xiph., *Exc. Val.*) 55.10.12–13.

[107] Beaucamp, *Statut* 1.153 n. 86, offers two possible explanations for the "confusion" of the texts on this issue: controversy among the classical jurists or innovation on the part of the Byzantine compilers. My view all but takes the first alternative for granted, and it must be conceded that both could be correct.

The *lex Iulia,* of course, was a criminal statute, and under it there could be no liability without criminal fault.[108] There are instances in this area of the law where punishment attends behavior that does not qualify as intentional,[109] though this is unusual.[110] Wanton recklessness in this context is treated more harshly than negligence or stupidity.[111]

More directly relevant perhaps is the fact that an *SC* was passed in Tiberius's reign making provincial governors liable for the misdeeds of their wives who acompany them.[112] If this statute did in fact impose a standard of strict liability on the husband,[113] this is extraordinary. The law on adultery required the commission of *adulterium* or *stuprum sciens dolo malo* ("knowingly, with wrongful intent").[114] The same almost certainly held true for *lenocinium.*[115]

A less stringent standard than *dolus* seems utterly inconceivable in all of the other types of developed *lenocinium* apart from *deprehensam retinere.* The jurist, to be sure, writes as if, in the case of *deprehensam retinere,* he would like to punish behavior that did not meet this standard, and perhaps this occurred in egregious cases. But the statute did not enjoin a positive duty on the husband to supervise the behavior of his wife, only to divorce her when he was confronted with unmistakable evidence of her infidelity.

The third influence limiting the range of application for *deprehensam retinere* was the regime established by the law for the *ius occidendi,* the right to kill adulterers when caught in the act. Only husbands and fathers of offending women were entitled to this privilege, which was hedged about with so many qualifications as to make it less likely to be used.[116] An obvious motive was to discourage killing and encourage prosecution. The jurists followed the direction suggested by the statute itself and interpreted this feature narrowly, sometimes even restrictively. This approach informs their answer to the question, which lovers were to be considered *deprehensi?*

Lab.-Pomp.-Ulp. (1 *de adult.*) D. 48.5.24(23) pr.: Quod ait lex "in filia adulterum deprehenderit," non otiosum videtur: voluit enim ita demum hanc potestatem patri competere, si in ipsa turpitudine filiam de adulterio deprehendat. Labeo quoque ita probat, et Pomponius scripsit in ipsis rebus Veneris deprehensum occidi: et hoc est quod Solo et Draco dicunt: *en ergō.*

---

[108] The law did not escape criticism for its "inadequacy" in these terms. Ovid. *Am.* 3.14 presents a bold indictment of the gap between social values and legal standards: Stroh, "Liebeskunst" (1979) 341–343; cf. *Am.* 3.4, *Ars* 1.367–372, 2.589–592.

[109] Ulp. *Coll.* 1.11.1–4, with Daube, "*Cupiditas*" (1956).

[110] *Dolus* is the usual standard of liability: Gaudemet, "Responsabilité" (1962/1979) 475; Gioffredi, *Principi* (1970) ch. 3.

[111] Daube, "*Cupiditas*" 125.

[112] Tac. *Ann.* 4.20.4; Ulp. D. 1.16.4.2. The date and exact content are disputed: Marshall, "Tacitus" (1975) 14; Guarino, "SC fantasma" (1978).

[113] Doubted by Guarino, "SC fantasma."

[114] Ulp. D. 48.5.13(12).

[115] Note "sciens" in Tryph. (3 *disp.*) D. 4.4.37.1. This is given only with the species of *damnatam ducere,* though I think it likely *sciens dolo malo* was the standard for all of the offenses defined by the *lex Iulia.*

[116] See Chapter 5.

The words of the statute "shall have caught the adulterer in his daughter" do not appear to be gratuitous, for the legislative intent was that this privilege should be available to the father if and only if he should catch his daughter in adultery while she was actually engaged in sexual intercourse. Labeo also approves this view, and Pomponius adopted the formula "the man is killed in the very act of love-making," which is also what Solon and Draco say: "in the act."

With regard to *deprehensam retinere,* the jurists interpreted extensively the requirement that the lovers be caught "in domo." As seen, the husband might be held liable in the case of an affair carried on under his nose, without his actually coming upon the pair engaged in intercourse. We should hesitate to conclude that he would be able to escape prosecution for failing to divorce a wife he has discovered *in flagrante* outside the home, though no text in our possession canvasses this relatively unlikely possibility.[117] The unlikelihood of discovery outside the home by the husband made it all the more imperative of course to repress the provision of alternative venues for adultery, through the rules against *domum praebere.*

Another brake on extensive construction of *deprehensam retinere* can be discerned on a broader level. The *lex Iulia* was partly intended to safeguard healthy marriages, a point that may not seem as obvious as it ought. It put a weapon in the hands of meddling outsiders who wished to bring their political or personal enemies into disrepute or ruin. For this very reason, the law and the jurists protected couples whose guilt was not manifest; a woman could not be prosecuted while still married unless her husband had first been convicted of *lenocinium.*

Ultimately, of course, the standard elaborated by the jurists was left to the finder of fact to apply, which should caution us against assuming that the social opprobrium carefully kept separate by Ulpian from the definition of legal liability was of no relevance. The judges had to steer a course between two evils that threatened to subvert the purpose of the law, the Scylla of malicious prosecution and the Charybdis of collusion. The jurists, while putting these men on guard against accepting contrived explanations and turning a blind eye to the husband's lack of responsibility, could not tie their hands too closely. The kind of *patientia* that gave rise to culpability could only be defined by the myriad situations of fact that arose in individual cases, and this, unfortunately, is a chapter in the history of the adultery law that is permanently closed to us.[118]

All the same, a text affords a glimpse of what problems might arise in practice:

Marci. (1 *de iud. publ.*) D. 48.5.34(33).1: . . . quae autem retinetur, punitur.[119] sed[120] si dimissam reduxerit, verbis non tenetur: sed tamen dicendum est, ut teneatur, ne fraus fiat.

[117] The same is true, presumably, of a case where the husband is informed by reliable persons who have themselves caught the lovers outside the marital home.

[118] For treatment of a similar problem in a 1792 English case, see Stone, *Road* (1990) 208–209.

[119] This transition has evidently been butchered by the compilers. It should simply assign liability to the *man* who has failed to divorce the *uxor deprehensa.* For another attempt to make sense of it, see Mommsen ad loc., with the criticism of Rizzelli, "*Crimen*" 492 n. 75. Cf. Kaser (rev. De' Dominicis) (1951) 325.

[120] Mommsen ad loc. proposes inserting "et" here.

If the woman is not divorced, there is liability. But if the husband remarries a woman after divorcing her, he is not liable under the wording of the statute. However, it must be said that he is liable [in accordance with the legislation's intent], so that a fraud is not committed against the law.

Remarrying a *deprehensa* after divorcing her in order to satisfy the legislative requirement is held to be an offense against the spirit, not the letter, of the adultery law.[121] It seems an obvious fraud, and its repression must date to a period long before Marcian wrote.

Other evidence shows that the man who initiated a prosecution for adultery against his wife and remarried her without bringing the prosecution to term, that is, without being granted a formal release *(abolitio)* consistent with the *SC Turpillianum,* was guilty of *lenocinium.*

Is the man who remarries his wife after divorcing her and charging her with adultery guilty of *desistere,* that is, the crime of the *SC Turpillianum,* or *lenocinium facere*?[122] Paul replies that he is indeed guilty of the former and therefore loses his right to prosecute under the adultery statute. The jurist's silence on the question of liability for *lenocinium* is usually understood as a reply in the negative.[123] Surely, however, the answer depends on a showing of the facts (i.e., whether the wife committed adultery). Paul only responds to the question of law.[124]

According to a rescript of Valerian and Gallienus,[125] the husband who has only initiated a prosecution and who can show good reasons for backing away[126] is released from "fear of the *lex Iulia de adulteriis coercendis.*" Since the adultery law did not define *desistere* as a crime, this must be a reference to the (developed) *crimen lenocinii.* The result is consistent with the rule laid down by the texts of Marcian and Paul, if we assume that the compilers have abbreviated the latter.

The evidence of Suetonius is important:[127] Domitian removes from the roll of *iudices* an equestrian who remarried a woman after divorcing her and charging her with adultery. Here too, we do best perhaps to assume that the man did not obtain an *abolitio.*

Neither the offense of *desistere* nor its penalty originated with the *lex Iulia,* but with the *SC Turpillianum.* Was the defendant guilty of *lenocinium* as well?[128] Papinian observes that remarriage is permitted after grant of an *abolitio,* but he appears to speak only to the question of the validity of the union and not to that of criminal liability.[129] A letter of Pliny records a trial for adultery held before

---

[121] On the definition and development of *fraus legis,* see the contrasting opinions registered at McGinn, *"SC"* 284 n. 59.

[122] Paul. D. 48.5.41(40).1. See, e.g., Fanizza, *Delatori* 71–72.

[123] See Levy, "Anklägervergehen" 420, 425 n. 62; Rizzelli, *"Crimen"* 493 n. 77. Because the woman in this text is not said to be a *deprehensa,* I see no conflict with Marcian's position in the principal text (contra Rizzelli, *"Crimen"*).

[124] The *vel* that separates the two alternatives means the choice of one does not necessarily exclude the other: *OLD* s.h.v. 2.

[125] Val., Gall. C. 9.9.17 pr. (a. 257).

[126] The emperors perhaps refer to a request for a formal *abolitio*; see above on the *SC Turpillianum.*

[127] Suet. *Dom.* 8.3.

[128] So Mette-Dittman, *Ehegesetze* (1991) 108–109.

[129] Pap. D. 23.2.34.1.

Trajan and his *consilium*.[130] Upon conviction of his rival, the husband displays reluctance to proceed against his wife, to the point of keeping her in his house. In the end he is persuaded to carry through the prosecution *(peragere)* and so avoids liability under the *SC Turpillianum*. He may have been in danger of liability for *lenocinium* as well.[131]

None of these texts stipulates that the woman was a *deprehensa*, but they suggest that the husband who abused his prosecutorial privileges and compounded his offense by remarrying the defendant might be open to a charge of *lenocinium*. He was treated as if he had caught her in the act of adultery and then failed to divorce her, an argument especially compelling in the last case, where the woman's guilt had been established through the conviction of her lover.[132] If this reading of the evidence is correct, we have a derivative form of *lenocinium*.

We may conclude this section by observing that the scruples that caused the jurists to hesitate to construe *deprehensam retinere* broadly seem to have applied only to the husband's behavior with respect to his wife. Ulpian treats the corresponding element of this species of *lenocinium*, *adulterum dimittere*, in a remarkably extensive fashion, expanding the *right* of restraining the lover to the offended father of the woman, broadening the venue outside the husband's home, and allowing recapture if the man escapes.[133]

Damnatam Ducere

The fourth offense against the *lex Iulia* that came to be viewed by the jurists as a species of *lenocinium* was marrying a woman convicted of adultery. Two texts confirm that this was an original feature of the legislation. In the first, Ulpian extends the rule, which the law had stipulated only for adulteresses, to women convicted of *stuprum*.[134] In the second, Papinian treats a case where a man marries a woman on trial for adultery.[135] The jurist decides that, if she is found guilty, the husband does not suffer from the disadvantages incumbent upon the partner who initiates the divorce,[136] since it is the the law which imposes on him the duty to divorce her.

The rationale for the ban on marrying such women is obvious. Those who had betrayed the marriage tie lost their status as *matres familias* and were considered

---

[130] Plin. *Ep.* 6.31.4–6.

[131] So Mette-Dittmann, *Ehegesetze* 109.

[132] Here *deprehensam retinere* seems more appropriate than *damnatam ducere*, though we are not told outright that the husband failed to divorce her.

[133] Ulp. D. 48.5.26(25) pr.-5; see *PS* 2.26.3.

[134] Ulp. (4 *de adult.*) D. 48.5.30(29).1. Ulpian's language ("quod magis est," "certe") suggests that not every jurist made this extension.

[135] Pap. *(lib. sing. de adult.)* D. 48.5.12(11).13.

[136] The *causa divortii* was relevant to the issue of *retentiones* from the dowry; see Chapter 5. On the text, see Astolfi, *LIP²* (1986) 112–113. On the issue at stake, see also Mod. D. 23.2.26, which permits women merely accused of adultery to remarry. The text is problematic: Venturini, "Divorzio" (1990) 39 n. 43.

unsuitable for marriage.[137] It is less obvious why a violation of this rule came to be defined as *lenocinium*. We know that this occurred as early as Quintilian:

> Quint. *IO* 5.10.47:[138] In such matters, every possible situation regarding both words and deeds is at stake, but in a double sense. For certain things happen because something else is going to happen, and others because something else has already happened. For example, when a man married to a beautiful woman is accused of *lenocinium* because he married[139] her although she had once been convicted of adultery, or a spendthrift is accused of parricide because he said to his father, "you have scolded me for the last time." The former is not a *leno* because he married the woman, but he married her because he was a *leno,* while the latter is not a parricide because he spoke in this manner, but he spoke in this manner because he was about to commit parricide.

Quintilian's remarks provide strong support for a point already argued:[140] the *lex Iulia* itself did not identify this offense as a form of *lenocinium*. Why construct an argument this intricate for a point of black-letter law? On the other hand, it supports the view that by this time the jurists, or at least some of them, had come to regard *damnatam ducere* as a form of *lenocinium*. True, the passage does not enjoy the authority of legal evidence, and the description of the man marrying a *damnata* as a *leno* can be understood as mere courtroom abuse. But, in my view, such skepticism is extreme, and the passage should be taken to show that this offense was defined by some legal authorities as a species of *lenocinium* in Quintilian's day, long before our first certain evidence, a constitution of Alexander Severus dating to A.D. 224.[141]

What did it mean for a man to be guilty of criminal *lenocinium,* that is, to act like a pimp with respect to his own wife simply by marrying a convicted adulteress? The evolution of the juristic treatment of this offense was encouraged by the law's casting of the *damnata* as a prostitute.[142] Once forfeit, her honor was unrecoverable. By marrying such a woman, a man abandoned his honor as surely as if he had kept as wife a woman caught in the act of adultery.

---

[137] Public opinion had always condemned marriage contracted by partners to adultery, whom the law separated by relegation to separate islands: Goria, *Studi* 145–146.

[138] "In his omnis factorum dictorumque ratio versatur, sed dupliciter. nam fiunt quaedam quia aliud postea futurum est, quaedam quia aliud ante factum est: ut cum obicitur reo lenocinii, speciosae marito, quod adulterii damnatam emerit; aut parricidii reo luxurioso, quod dixerit patri, non amplius me obiurgabis. nam et ille non quia emit leno est, sed quia leno erat emit; nec hic, quia sic erat locutus, occidit, sed, quia erat occisurus, sic locutus est."

[139] *Emere* can refer to *coemptio,* one of the ways of acquiring *manus* (Gaius 1.113). Quintilian may be playing on this, but the sense is not entirely innocent. Both prostitutes and adulteresses were considered to be "bought" (*TLL* s.h.v. 514.51–65), and there is, in my view, an unmistakable reference to the relationship between a pimp and a prostitute. For a similar opinion, see Mette-Dittmann, *Ehegesetze* 122.

[140] See Chapter 5.

[141] Alex. Sev. C. 9.9.9 (a. 224): the man knowingly marrying (or remarrying!) a woman convicted of adultery is punished "eadem lege ex causa lenocinii." The language suggests an extension of a statutory provision.

[142] One could then have a *damnata* as a concubine, without fear of prosecution for *stuprum*; see Chapter 5.

The *lex Iulia et Papia* itself appears to have equated the status of the *deprehensa* with that of the woman condemned for adultery in a criminal court *(iudicium publicum)* in its marriage prohibitions, so that all *ingenui* were forbidden to marry such women.[143] The precise nature of the *impedimentum criminis* confronting the adulteress in classical times is controversial.[144] As seen, the adultery law denied adulteresses the right to marry again by punishing their marriage partners.

A later *SC* forbade women convicted in any *iudicium publicum* to marry senators or remain their wives if already married.[145] Perhaps, even later, unions between partners in the offense of adultery were declared void, not, as sometimes claimed, as a direct consequence of or by analogy to the *SC* of Marcus Aurelius and Commodus passed pursuant to the marriage law, but by a separate enactment. This may have been the *SC Turpillianum* or a law that declared mutual bequests by these parties to be forfeit.[146]

Ulpian, in reporting this unnamed *SC,* suggests that the Senate equated *uxorem ducere* with *uxorem retinere.* The jurists drew an analogy between the husband guilty of *damnatam ducere* and *deprehensam retinere.*[147] Thus the type of *lenocinium* identified by the law as not divorcing a *deprehensa* is compared with a new category of offense, that of marrying a *damnata,* in much the same way perhaps that accepting payment after the fact comes to be reckoned alongside accepting payment beforehand.

Domum Praebere

The fifth offense defined as *lenocinium* by the jurists was also an original feature of the *lex Iulia.* The language employed in two key texts betrays a legislative origin.[148] The statute would perhaps have read "ne quis domum suam, ut stuprum adulteriumve mater familias patiatur, praebeto sciens dolo malo."

This offense was not, however, defined by the law itself as a form of *lenocinium.* Ulpian mentions the legislative prescription of five years for *stuprum, adulterium,* and *lenocinium* and then lays down the same rule for the other offenses defined by the law, giving as an example "qui domum suam stupri causa praebuerunt."[149] Ulpian's emphasis on the original dispositions of the legislation ("leg-

[143] See Chapter 3.
[144] Mayer-Maly, "Impedimentum" (1956); Vitali, "Premesse" (1972); Goria, *Studi* esp. ch. 1. I agree in large measure with Astolfi, *LIP*² 103–108.
[145] Ulp. D. 23.2.43.10–13; cf. *Tit.* 13.1–2. This statute was probably early in date; see Chapter 3.
[146] On the former, see above, on the latter, see McGinn, "Concubinage" 354–355 and Chapter 4.
[147] Note how the two offenses are grouped together even in a nonjuristic source such as Val., Gall. C. 9.9.17 (a. 257).
[148] Pap. (2 *de adult.*) D. 48.5.9(8) pr.: "Qui domum suam, ut stuprum adulteriumve cum aliena matre familias vel cum masculo fieret, sciens praebuerit. . . ." Paul. (1 *de adult.*) D. 48.2.3.3: "Sed et si aliud crimen obiciat, veluti quod domum suam praebuit, ut stuprum mater familias pateretur. . . ." See Chapter 5.
[149] Ulp. D. 48.5.30(29).6. Levy's objections to this text as a postclassical gloss are unfounded, insofar as he assumes that *domum praebere* was a form of statutory *lenocinium.* His and Beseler's linguistic objections show at most that the passage has been abbreviated. Flore is right to defend the text: all references are in *Index Itp.* ad loc.

islator voluit'') shows that by *lenocinium* he means statutory *lenocinium*.[150] Besides
the other penalties leveled at the criminal *leno*,[151] the person guilty of *domum
praebere* would be unable to recover the house in question, according to a ruling
of Caracalla.[152]

This prohibition struck at anyone who materially assisted an act of adultery or
stuprum by providing a venue for the act itself. In this way, it sought to discourage
such sexual activity at a secondary level, just as the law established the husband's
liability in *deprehensam retinere* (where his responsibility was not limited to cases
where the adulterous pair were discovered in his house, although this was a likely
setting) and allowed the *ius occidendi* to be exercised in the husband's house (by
the husband) or in either the father's or the husband's house (by the father). The
latter was supposed to discourage use of two of the more obvious venues,[153] and
domum praebere was aimed at preventing a substitute from being provided.

Its extensive interpretation by the jurists shows the importance of this measure.
Early on, as we saw, women were held to be liable, logically enough, since they
were at least as likely as men to serve as go-betweens. Like the words *pretium* and
quaestus, the significance of the central term *domus* is expanded, to include any
type of dwelling space:

Pap. (2 *de adult.*) D. 48.5.9(8).1: Appellatione domus habitationem quoque sig-
nificari palam est.

It is obvious that by the term ''house'' any sort of residence is meant.

This is hardly an extreme step, although it is interesting to see the legislative
concept, which is broadly upper-class and supposes potential defendants to live in
a *domus,* or aristocratic dwelling, run up against the social reality in which the law
was applied. Papinian in fact proceeds further than the line he himself adopted on
the interpretation of *domus* in the context of the *ius occidendi*.[154] The approach
taken by Ulpian is far more radical. He goes beyond the words of the statute, at
times rejecting them outright, in order to broaden the law's field of application. In
one passage he rejects the word ''suam'':

Ulp. (4 *de adult.*) D. 48.5.10(9) pr.: Et si amici quis domum praebuisset, tenetur.

[150] By the same token, the distinction he implicitly draws suggests that he did regard *domum praebere* as a species of this crime himself, which we might describe as ''juristic'' *lenocinium.*
[151] See Chapter 5.
[152] Ant. C. 4.7.2 (a. 215), which does not, to be sure, explicitly give *domum praebere* as the motive
for the loan (''propter turpem causam''): Schwarz, *Condictio* (1952) 175.
[153] The rules on *quaestio servorum* were further deterrent to use of the wife's or the adulterer's
home; see Chapter 5.
[154] Pap. D. 48.5.23(22).2. Here, *domus* is construed as equivalent to *domicilium,* as given by the *lex
Cornelia de iniuriis. Habitatio* implies any dwelling, i.e., more than a dwelling belonging to or inhabited
by one of the principals, which is what *domicilium* means. Cf. Ulp. D. 23.2.43.13, Ulp. D. 48.
5.24(23).2–3. One may compare the *lex Iulia de vi,* in which a prohibition against stockpiling weapons
in a man's *domus,* etc., suggests a broader interpretation: Marci. D. 48.6.1, with Cloud, ''*Lex Iulia* 2''
(1989) 445. On the other hand, the praetorian edict on denying liability for thefts occurring on the
premises of a gambling operation encouraged a narrower approach: Ulp. D. 11.5.1.2.

Even if someone has made available the house of a friend, he is liable.

The jurist understands the law's aim as that of discouraging others from providing trysting places for adulterers. The question of who owns the house is irrelevant.[155] He then takes a further step and discards the word *domus:*

> Ulp. (4 *de adult.*) D. 48.5.10(9).1: Sed et si quis in agro balneove stuprum fieri praebuisset, comprehendi debet.

> And, indeed, if anyone has provided for the commission of *stuprum* out-of-doors or in the baths, he ought to be covered by the statute.

It is immediately obvious how far this analysis proceeds beyond that of Papinian: *balneum* and *ager* are not simply examples of *habitatio*. Ulpian's interpretation fundamentally transforms the nature of the offense; one cannot be said to "provide" a public place[156] such as a bath or an open area as the venue for adultery, but only to arrange that the act take place there.[157] Baths were especially notorious as trysting places.[158] Now that putative offenders are no longer required to "provide" a place, their offense can be construed as any activity facilitating the commission of a crime, in any place. The next fragment enlarges on this point:

> Ulp. (4 *de adult.*) D. 48.5.10(9).2: Sed et si in domum aliquam soliti fuerint convenire ad tractandum de adulterio, etsi eo loci nihil fuerit admissum, verum tamen videtur is domum suam, ut stuprum adulteriumve committeretur, praebuisse, quia sine colloquio illo adulterium non committeretur.

> And if persons have been accustomed to meet at a certain house to plan an act of adultery, even if no such act was committed at that place, nevertheless he [sc., the defendant] seems to have provided his house for the commission of *stuprum* or adultery, since without that particular discussion adultery would not have been committed.

Ulpian returns to the wording of the law; he has altered his interpretative technique from *ex sententia* to *ex verbis*. But his purpose remains unchanged: a highly extensive interpretation. Even persons who permit their houses to be used for meetings and conversations directed toward adultery,[159] rather than as venues for the act itself (which is apparently what the law contemplated), are liable.

---

[155] Corsanego, *Repressione* 25, argues that an administrator (presumably a *vilicus*) might be guilty of *lenocinium* for providing a trysting place *invito domino*.

[156] Of course, there were private *balnea* as well: recognition of this application represented a significant extension of the concept of *domus* by itself. In fact the jurist goes further, insofar as the range of Ulpian's usage cannot be limited to private places: Rizzelli, "*Crimen*" 489 n. 67.

[157] One notes the awkwardness of the expression: Ulpian attempts to retain as much of the statute's language as possible *(praebere)*, but he has essentially rewritten the phrase.

[158] Pimps and prostitutes routinely plied their trade in the baths, a fact explicitly recognized for the former by Ulpian at D. 3.2.4.2. We are dealing here with more than a parallel. Rizzelli, "*Crimen*" 489 n. 67, aptly remarks that the man who arranges trysts with prostitutes in this venue might do the same with matrons. For the regime of the *lex Iulia*, then, this situation presents a neat confluence of legal/ideological symbol with sociological referent in the figure of the *leno*.

[159] The stress on the finality of the action vitiates Bauman's argument, "*Leges*" 132 n. 166, that "motive [was] the dominant factor in *lenocinium*." The last phrase shows that actual *stuprum* or *adulterium* is contemplated in order to give liability. Mere aiding and abetting in the air, so to speak,

In all of the passages under review, Ulpian displays a considerable sensitivity to the nature of the crime. Assistance from third parties, such as the provision of a house or other place for the commission of the deed, would have been necessary above all for members of the upper classes, with their higher visibility. Baths were used often enough for the practice in question, and an isolated field (not to exhaust thereby the implications of *ager*) afforded some degree of security. In the last passage there is a recognition that a certain amount of planning was necessary for the commission of this crime. This was true not simply because adultery was illegal but because of the nature of the undertaking, since adultery is often not strictly a casual sexual relationship but an emotional one as well. The jurist is concerned to strike at every means used to facilitate this crime, since this is how he understands the law's purpose.

This offense is the most difficult to justify in terms of the *lenocinium* rubric, since it presents no apparent analogies with either form of statutory *lenocinium*. But there is persuasive evidence that by the late classical period it was classified as such. *Domum praebere* is frequently linked with the other four types in juristic texts. Aside from Tryph. D. 4.4.37.1, where all five types are found,[160] it is grouped with *adulterum dimittere* (a component of *deprehensam retinere*) and *pretium accipere* in Paul. D. 48.2.3.3, with *quaestum facere* in Pap. D. 48.5.9(8) pr., and with accomplices to *pretium* in Macer D. 48.5.33(32).1. This shows that the late classical jurists were accustomed to treat this offense as another form of *lenocinium*.

The reason for this is not far to seek. The lack of an obvious connection with statutory *lenocinium* was not an insuperable obstacle: the jurists proceeded to draw an analogy directly from social practice. Pimps typically ran brothels and made prostitutes available to customers. Given the manipulation of status and symbol by the adultery regime, it was easy enough to treat as a criminal "pimp" a person who provided a venue for the commission of adultery, an act already punished by the statute. By the Severan period at the latest, almost anyone who acted to facilitate an adulterous liaison might be classified as a *leno* and subject to prosecution for *lenocinium*.

The Uses of Lenocinium

To sum up, the jurists built up the concept of *lenocinium* originally given in the *lex Iulia* from its original two species, *quaestum facere* and *deprehensam retinere*. The other accessory offenses under the law were all added to this rubric: *pretium accipere,* or accepting payment after the fact; *damnatam ducere,* or marrying a woman convicted of adultery; and *domum praebere,* originally conceived as providing a house for the adulterers, later defined as assisting in any way in the commission of the principal crime. For reasons of both language and substance, *quaestum facere* was never given a very extensive interpretation. This legislative provision, modeled on the custom of commercial pimps, seems to have addressed what was more a fear than a real crisis. The jurists exercised considerable freedom

---

will not do. There was no such crime as attempted *lenocinium* or attempted adultery: Corsanego, *Repressione* 24; Genin, *Tentative* (1968) 165–166.

[160] Some of these were perhaps inserted into this text by the compilers; see Chapter 5.

with regard to the other four cases. It is interesting to note that in practical terms, the three new types assumed an importance equal to, if not greater than, the original two forms of *lenocinium*. This is to judge from the number of procedural and substantive issues they generated for the jurists.[161]

Lenocinium eventually developed into an umbrella concept for almost all forms of complicity in the commission of *adulterium* and *stuprum*. The jurists evidently regarded all of these offenses as equally serious, for, once defined as *lenocinium,* they were all visited with the same penalty. We cannot be sure if the statute had stipulated the same penalty for all of these crimes. Some evidence strongly suggests this,[162] but there are passages that show that not all were regulated in precisely the same way. One shows that women convicted under the law for crimes other than adultery were not forbidden to remarry;[163] another, that the five-year prescriptive period was laid down only for *stuprum, adulterium,* and (statutory) *lenocinium.*[164] There is a way to explain these features without supposing a difference in penalty. First, the prescriptive period is, strictly speaking, irrelevant to the question of penalty. Second, the same is true of the remarriage provision taken as a punishment for female offenders, since this defines liability for the male. Moreover, it is argued above that the statute did not contemplate women offenders for the accessory crimes, so that the ban on remarriage (which adulterers, and therefore criminal *lenones,* did not suffer) would have no sense.

The Romans were capable of regarding the liability of accomplices as equal to that of principals, as seen in the law of theft[165] and in the *lex Iulia* itself.[166] An equivalence of penalties would have made it easier and more natural for the jurists to group these offenses under one rubric; however, given the state of our knowledge about the adultery law's penalties, certainty is impossible.

The law punished the husband-pimp "quasi adulter."[167] In the view taken by some jurists of such definitions, this made him a statutory adulterer, as opposed to an adulterer in fact *(natura).* Gaius points out that a statute cannot make an offender who is not an adulterer into an adulterer, any more than it makes a man a thief or a murderer who is neither of these.[168] A law could only punish a man *as if* he had committed a certain crime.[169]

Gaius's analysis appears to overlook the fact that some crimes are entirely the invention of statutes and have no independent existence apart from them. *Lenocinium* is just such a crime—an utterly artificial creation, which did not and could not exist apart from this law. Commercial pimps continued to operate their businesses

---

[161] See, e.g., Scaev. D. 24.3.47; Ulp. D. 48.5.2.6; Macer D. *eod.* 33(32).1.

[162] Val., Gall. C. 9.9.17.1 (a. 257).

[163] Ulp. D. 48.5.30(29).1. The jurist extends the principle to *stuprum.*

[164] Ulp. D. 48.5.30(29).6.

[165] See the discussion in Jolowicz, *Digest 47.2* (1940) lxv–lxviii.

[166] As noted above, accomplices to *pretium* were treated as principals. Ulp. D. 48.5.13(12), in my view, contrasts persuading someone to commit adultery or *stuprum* with someone who uses force: Chapter 5.

[167] See Chapter 5.

[168] Gaius 3.194. I have altered the jurist's emphasis to suit the context.

[169] Gaius 3.194: "at illud sane lex facere potest, ut proinde aliquis poena teneatur atque si furtum vel adulterium vel homicidium admisisset, quamvis nihil eorum admiserit."

without penalty. But the very artificiality of the offense gave the jurists a motive to assimilate the other crimes under this rubric. All of the accessory offenses— even *domum praebere*—resembled statutory pimping in that they assisted law-breaking, namely, the compromise of a respectable woman's honor, a woman in whose sexual integrity society had a recognized interest.

All such persons were definable as "pimps" and all were punishable *quasi adulter*. An apparent exception is the woman who takes payment for her husband's adultery. In strict faithfulness to the gender-based role definitions created by the law, she was punished *quasi adultera*.[170]

The extensions adopted by the jurists can hardly be said to have diluted or weakened the concept of *lenocinium*. The concept was already much stronger, in symbolic terms, than the crimes that were originally identified as *lenocinium*. The limited relevance, in practical terms, of *quaestum facere* hardly diminished its power as an idea. If it remained relatively untested in the crucible of the court system, this perhaps served as a further encouragement to broadening the overall concept of criminal *lenocinium*.

4. The Law on Adultery and the Policymaking Elite

It is clear that I do not share the views of those who argue that the adultery law was unpopular, like the marriage legislation is supposed to have been, and who want to place the Roman jurists on the side of the angels. Venturini finds the jurists working against the law and its purpose.[171] Esmein claims they hated it.[172] Others find it broadly unpopular[173] and ultimately ineffective as well.[174]

The period before the law's passage witnessed lamentations about the sexual disorder of Roman society and calls for reform.[175] The adultery statute itself was

[170] See above. Another anomaly is presented by the *SC* that punished the husband who suborned an adulterer "infamandae uxoris suae causa . . . ut ipse deprehenderet." This was construed to take place not *lenocinii crimine* but *adulterii crimine:* Scaev. D. 48.5.15(14).1. The Senate applied the *sententia legis,* there being no category of *lenocinium* available: Bauman, "*Leges*" 150.

[171] Venturini, "*Accusatio*" (1988) 79–80, who finds "un indirizzo consolidatosi nella giurisprudenza classica come reazione all'allarme sociale suscitato dalla legislazione matrimoniale di Augusto." Venturini expresses similar sentiments at "Ripudianda" 272 and at "Divorzio" 47, which are shared by Guarino, "Lui" (1993) 426.

[172] Esmein, "Délit" 156–160, esp. 90, where he says, apropos of the jurists, ". . . ils ont en haine cette loi de sang."

[173] The most extreme statement of the argument for the unpopularity (and ineffectiveness) of the legislation is put by Raditsa, "Legislation" (1980) esp. 279 (on Raditsa's view of the law, and of the Principate in general, see Spagnuolo Vigorita, *Pernicies* [1984] 121 n. 2). On the related theme of its severity, see Mommsen, *Strafrecht* 691; Bonfante, *Corso* 1 (1925/1963) 348; Biondi, "*Leges*" 197; Raditsa, "Legislation" 305.

[174] On its ineffectiveness, see Schneider, *RE* meretrix (1931) 1021; Foucault, *Care* (1986) 40; Toher, "Augustus" (1990) 142; Fantham, "*Stuprum*" (1991) 290; Treggiari, *RM* 292, 294; Dixon, *TRF* (1992) 88, 121; Evans Grubbs, "Constantine" (1993) 123; and perhaps Cohen, "Augustan Law" 125 ("not entirely successful").

[175] Cic. *Marc.* 23; Sallust. *BC* 12; Varro *Men.* 44 Cèbe; Liv. *Praef.* 9; Hor. *Serm.* 1.2, *Epod.* 7, 16,

well received;[176] complaints were directed at abuses, not toward its fundamental purpose.[177] The law accorded well with popular moral sentiment,[178] with its hatred of unchastity.[179]

The jurists were hardly out of step with this trend. The *lex Iulia de adulteriis coercendis* was the only special criminal *lex* on which the jurists wrote monographs.[180] Three of the Severan greats, Ulpian, Papinian, and Paul, made notable contributions in this area.[181] If these men felt any hostility toward the statute, it is well masked. Their approach to the interpretation of the law, as described in this chapter, is typical of the general juristic position. This in turn may be described as quite favorable, insofar as it aids the policy goals pursued by the statute wherever possible through extensive interpretation.[182]

The jurists were, to an extent, following the lead of the emperors, but it would have been difficult in any case to match the enthusiasm of many of these gentlemen for strict enforcement of the adultery statute. Ulpian interestingly identifies adultery, along with theft, as examples of *probra* that are "base by nature" ("*natura turpia*") as opposed to forms of conduct he deems "base by convention and, so to speak, according to the standard of the community" ("[turpia] civiliter et quasi more civitatis").[183] In a famous passage he refuses to interpret restrictively a provision of the law forbidding a woman divorced by her husband to alienate or manumit slaves, even those quite unlikely to be able to provide evidence of adultery. He comments: "this is indeed very harsh, but such is the way the law is written."[184]

---

[176] Hor. *Carm.* 4.5.21, 15.9–14, *Carm. Saec.* 57–60; Val. Max. 6.1 pr. and Ios. *AI* 18.65–84 (the latter two by implication); Mart. 6.2, 4, 7, 21. On Horace and the Augustan program, see Santirocco, "Horace" (1995). Cf. Ovid. *Fasti* 2.139–144 with *Ars* 3.611–614. Ovid (not to speak of Propertius) merits notice as a signal critic of the regime, above all, on matters of moral reform: see e.g., Syme, *History* (1978) esp. ch. 11; Stroh, "Liebeskunst"; Wallace-Hadrill, "Propaganda" (1985); Nugent, "Ovid" (1990); Feeney and Mackie in Powell, *RPPA* (1992).

Carm. 1.35, 3.6, 3.24. "The ideology . . . was not so much created as exploited by Augustus": Wallace-Hadrill, "Golden Age" (1982) 36.

[177] There is a difference (not to be exaggerated) with the reception accorded the marriage law. Abuses of the repressive mechanism instituted by the adultery law included the cynical manipulation of prosecutions by some emperors who allowed or encouraged the innocent to be persecuted for political reasons, while they themselves flagrantly violated the statute; see Chapters 5, 7.

[178] Well recognized by Humbert, *Remariage* (1972) 64. This is not to deny that adultery may have been tolerated in some sectors among the elite: Treggiari, *RM* 307–309.

[179] See, e.g., Sen. *Ben.* 3.16.2–4; Tac. *Hist.* 1.2.2; Suet. *Iul.* 50–51, *Aug.* 69, 71.1; Dio 60.18.1–3.

[180] Bauman, "*Leges*" 129.

[181] Ulpian: "*ad legem Iuliam de adulteriis coercendis libri V.*" Papinian: "*libri II*" and "*liber singularis.*" Paul: "*libri III*" and "*liber singularis.*" The authenticity of the *libri singulares* has been suspected: Wieacker, *Textstufen* (1959) 419–422; Van de Wouw, "Libri" (1973) 312. For a defense, see Cervenca, "Libri" (1971). For a list of other types of works that comment on the adultery law, see Van de Wouw, "Libri." More generally, see Bauman, "Libri" (1974/1975).

[182] Note, for example, how emperors and jurists cumulate liability for adultery with that for other offenses: Pap. D. 48.5.39(38) pr.-7; cf. Iustinianus C. 9.13.1 (a. 533).

[183] Ulp. (57 *ad ed.*) D. 50.16.42.

[184] Ulp. (4 *de adult.*) D. 40.9.12.1: "quod quidem perquam durum est, sed ita lex scripta est." Cf. Afric.-Ulp. D. *eod.* 12.2.

Zeal most particularly characterizes the Severan emperors, about whom we have good information.[185] Septimius Severus gave open encouragement to adultery prosecutions, which resulted in an explosion of indictments, 3,000 in the docket at one time, according to the famous report of Dio.[186] Significantly, Severus lost interest in pursuing this campaign to completion. Conducting such trials was a nasty business; unpleasant details came to light, and the presiding judge himself was exposed to the risk of embarrassment.[187]

It was usually easier to legislate. Severus and his immediate successors showed little hesitation about using this method. By way of example, a few of the more important innovations may be cited. Severus and Caracalla gave betrothed men the right to prosecute their fiancées for adultery, *iure extranei*.[188] Caracalla increased the range of officials who had jurisdiction over adultery, thus facilitating prosecutions.[189] The same emperor appears to have given complete immunity to husbands who abused the *ius occidendi*.[190] Alexander Severus freed privileged prosecutors from liability for *calumnia*.[191]

In the same way that emperors vaunted the *pax, securitas,* and *libertas* of their reigns, this last ruler adopted as a political slogan *castitas temporum meorum*.[192] Given their approach to the *lex Iulia de adulteriis coercendis,* if imperial legislators and jurists are to be reckoned on the side of the angels, these must have been the avenging kind.

[185] Domitian is the other monarch well known for a revival of the Augustan adultery statute: see Chapter 4.

[186] Dio (in Xiph., *Exc. Val.*) 76.16.4, on which see Kunkel, "Quaestio" (1963/1974) 101–102; Millar, *Dio* (1964) 204–207.

[187] Plin. 6.31.4–6; Ulp. D. 48.5.2.6; Dio 54.16.6.

[188] Ulp. D. 48.5.14(13).3, cf. 8.

[189] Ulp. *Coll.* 14.3.3.

[190] Paul. *Coll.* 4.3.6.

[191] Alex. Sev. C. 9.9.6 (a. 223): only the *ius mariti* is explicitly mentioned, but it is reasonable to suppose that fathers are included too. The constitution appears to extend the privilege to husbands and fathers who prosecute *iure extranei* after the expiration of the favored 60-day period; see Chapter 5.

[192] Alex. Sev. C. 9.9.9 (a. 224); see Beaucamp, *Statut* 1.18 n. 10. For a discussion of this emperor's interventions in the area of "family values," see Liebs, "Alexander Severus" (1980) 130–132; see also Evans Grubbs, "Constantine" 137. For *"pudicitia"* as a slogan advertised on coins, see Wallace-Hadrill, "Virtues" (1981) 312, 322; D'Ambra, "Pudicitia" (1991) 245, with n. 9; Braund, "Juvenal" (1992) 82.

7

The Taxation of Roman Prostitutes

1. Taxing Prostitution

The tax on prostitutes instituted by Caligula in 40[1] provides us with an abundance of evidence on prostitution in the Roman world, especially on its economic importance and the attitude of the imperial administration to it. The scattered and fragmentary nature of this evidence demands close attention if we are to extract from it the true significance of the tax. I begin with the information given by Suetonius and Dio before discussing the motives for its introduction, methods of collection and calculation, later history and eventual abolition, and, finally, the provincial evidence for details of administration. The aim is to assess not only the success of the tax in terms of the original motives for its introduction but also the other effects of the tax, for it has some important implications for Roman public policy toward prostitution in general.

This chapter is a revised version of my paper "The Taxation of Roman Prostitutes," published in *Helios* 16 (1989) 79–110.

[1] The date given by Dio has been questioned because the duration of Caligula's stay in Rome that year was thought to be too short: Willrich, "Caligula" (1903) 425 n. 4. But the Arval records show that Caligula had returned from the north to the suburbs of Rome by the end of May, and his subsequent June–August sojourn in Campania should have been no bar to the drafting of such legislation. For a discussion, see Balsdon, *Gaius* (1934/1964) 96, with n. 1.

2. The Evidence for Caligula's Introduction of the Tax

First there is the notice in Suetonius:

Suet. *Cal.* 40:[2] He [sc., Caligula] levied new and unheard of taxes first through the tax farmers and then, because the revenues were so great, through the centurions and tribunes of the Praetorian Guard. There was no type of commodity or profession upon which he did not impose some kind of levy. For the sort of "fast food" that was sold throughout the city, a fixed, flat rate was set. For lawsuits and legal actions that arose anywhere, a fortieth of the sum under litigation was demanded, and a penalty laid down if anyone was found guilty of settling out of court or simply abandoning his suit. From the daily earnings of porters, one-eighth was required, and from those of prostitutes, the amount each earned for one act of sexual intercourse. And a clause was added to this chapter of the law, providing that even those who had (in the past) practiced prostitution or pimping were liable to the treasury (for the tax) and that married persons were subject to it as well.

The phrase "nullo rerum," etc., is of course hyperbolic, but the details here and in Dio's account indicate that a large number of professions were covered by this legislation. Although introduced together, these levies on different goods and trades formed separate taxes, each calculated by its own rate. Despite the principally Rome-centered viewpoint of Suetonius ("tota urbe"; contrast "ubicumque"),[3] the evidence from the provinces suggests that all of these taxes, but especially the prostitute tax, were collected throughout the empire.

The biographer regards these taxes as quite innovative: "vectigalia nova atque inaudita." This was true only for the Romans themselves. Taxes on trades were already well established in Egypt, and there is evidence (though not always satisfactory) for a tax on prostitutes at Athens, Egypt, Cos, and Syracuse.[4] It has even been argued that Caligula derived his idea for the tax from Egypt.[5] Suetonius is certainly right about the profitability of these taxes. The fact that responsibility for

[2] "Vectigalia nova atque inaudita primum per publicanos, deinde, quia lucrum exuberabat, per centuriones tribunosque praetorianos exercuit, nullo rerum aut hominum genere omisso, cui non tributi aliquid imponeret. pro edulibus, quae tota urbe venirent, certum statumque exigebatur; pro litibus ac iudiciis ubicumque conceptis quadragesima summae, de qua litigaretur, nec sine poena, si quis composuisse vel donasse negotium convinceretur; ex gerulorum diurnis quaestibus pars octava; ex capturis prostitutarum quantum quaeque uno concubitu mereret; additumque ad caput legis, ut tenerentur publico et quae meretricium quive lenocinium fecissent, nec non et matrimonia obnoxia essent."

[3] The phrase "tota urbe" seems to refer to a municipal tax: that this was the original form the tax took seems confirmed by the evidence from Palmyra discussed below. Hurley, *Commentary* (1993) 153, takes the contrast between "tota urbe" and "ubicumque" as a sign that the tax on foodstuffs was collected only at Rome.

[4] For the trade taxes in Egypt see Wallace, *Taxation* (1938) esp. ch. 12. For the prostitute tax at Athens: Aesch. 1.119; Pollux 7.202, 9.29 (cf. Athen. 13.569D for Solon's municipal brothel); see Böckh, *Staatshaushaltung*[3] (1886) 1.404–405. In Cos: *SIG*[3] 1005. (see below for discussion of a possible municipal brothel). In Egypt: Wilcken, *GO* 1 (1899/1970) 217–219; see also below. In Syracuse: Polyaen. 5.2.13 (where the tax does not seem actually to have been implemented). Iustin. 21.5 is not evidence of the tax at Corinth. The evidence does not support the claim of Rostovtsev, "Besatzungen" (1902) 66, that a tax on prostitutes in Tauric Chersonesus predated the Romans.

[5] The evidence is uncertain; see below.

their collection was at some point transferred to the officers of the Praetorian Guard "quia lucrum exuberabat" is supported by the other evidence we have for collection by the military and will be discussed below. The profitability of the prostitute tax can perhaps be inferred from the fact that, unlike other acts of Caligula, it does not seem to have been canceled by Claudius at the start of his reign.[6] In fact, the state eventually became so dependent on the revenue generated by this tax that despite the embarrassment it caused the Christian emperors[7] it was not abolished until 498 (below).

Next we have the passage from Dio:

> Dio (in Xiph., *Exc. Val.*) 59.28.8: This god, then, this Jupiter (for he was, at the end, designated so often in this manner that [these titles] wound up in the official documents) . . . was collecting the most shameful and terrible sorts of revenues. One might omit mention of the goods for sale and the taverns and the prostitutes and the courts and the wage-earning slaves and the other such things (there was nothing that he did not try to profit from). . . .

The details about taxes imposed on prostitutes and lawsuits coincide with Suetonius's information; moreover, the reference to "taverns" ("ta kapēleia") seems roughly to correspond to "edulibus" (this apparently "fast food" of the type sold in taverns).[8] The rest can be subsumed under Suetonius's generalized rubric "nullo rerum," etc. The degree of coincidence between the two sources is interesting; the question of Dio's dependence on the biographer is controversial, and some scholars believe that Dio did not use Suetonius.[9]

3. Caligula's Motives for Introducing the Tax

Dio, like Suetonius,[10] identifies Caligula's greed as his motive for introducing these new taxes. We need not accept this moralizing explanation at face value, given the well-known hostility of the sources and the mere fact that they lump a number of different taxes together. For the prostitute tax, three main explanations have been put forward for Caligula's action. Prostitutes were taxed in connection with their status as disgraced persons or in connection with certain aspects of Caligula's political program or simply to raise as much revenue as possible, which is not precisely the same thing as greed. I argue that the first is unlikely, the second possible, the third virtually certain.

[6] Suet. *Claud.* 11.3, who says that Claudius annulled "Gai . . . omnia acta." Dio 60.4.1 informs us that Claudius abolished gradually, as the opportunity arose, Gaius's taxes and other measures that aroused criticism. But there is no evidence for the interruption or, consequently, resumption of collection of the tax on prostitutes; see the discussion below.

[7] See, e.g., Theod. Nov. 18 (a. 439).

[8] On this tax, see De Laet, *Portorium* (1949/1975) 346–347.

[9] See the discussion in Balsdon, *Gaius* 227–228. Millar, *Dio* (1964) 85–86 (cf. 105), argues however that Dio did use Suetonius as a source and followed him very closely at times.

[10] Suetonius's report is placed in the context of other anecdotes concerning Caligula's greed (*Cal.* 38–42). See Guastella, *Caligola* (1992) 22. Cf. Ios. *AI* 19.28–29.

The introduction of the prostitute tax had this provision: "and a clause was appended to this chapter of the law, providing that even those who had (in the past) practiced prostitution or procuring were liable to the treasury (for the tax), and that married persons were subject to it as well."[11] André Chastagnol argues that prostitutes and pimps are taxed under a different principle from the other professions, both those mentioned specifically by Suetonius and those lumped together in the phrase "nullo rerum," etc.,[12] namely as *infames persones (sic)*. There is, however, no evidence for this.[13]

Another motive is a programmatic one difficult to prove. It consists of two related parts, concerning Egypt and autocracy.

Modern scholars have stressed the importance of Egypt as a source of inspiration for Caligula's political program, especially his claims to personal divinity and autocratic power, laying emphasis on the political legacy of his great-grandfather Antony and/or his father, Germanicus, as well as the fact that he spent much of his youth in the house of his grandmother Antonia.[14] A general influence of Egyptian practice on Caligula's taxation policies has been argued,[15] and some scholars have proposed,[16] on the basis of admittedly thin evidence, that Caligula derived the idea for the prostitute tax from Egypt.

The only piece of pre-Caligulan evidence, an ostracon dating from Tiberius's reign,[17] Wilcken argues to be a receipt for this tax, though the name of the tax is not given. Even if Wilcken's interpretation of this evidence is correct, this does not necessarily mean the prostitute tax was Ptolemaic in origin. One might look more securely for a model for Caligula in the tax on prostitutes established in classical Athens or in the official leases on brothels granted under the Ptolemies, perhaps elaborated by Augustus in his organization of Egypt as a province (see below).

Wilcken has received criticism over the uncertain status of the evidence from Thebes,[18] on the grounds that similar taxes (monthly tax, unspecified) involving men are known and that women did practice other occupations, aside from prostitution, in Roman Egypt.[19] One should add the crucial fact that women who were

---

[11] Suet. *Cal.* 40: "additumque ad caput legis, ut tenerentur publico et quae meretricium quive lenocinium fecissent, nec non et matrimonia obnoxia essent."

[12] Chastagnol, "Zosime" (1966) 50–51.

[13] For example, Chastagnol is wrong to assume that retired pimps and prostitutes were still liable to the tax: the passage refers to an anti-evasion measure. Discussion in McGinn, "Taxation" (1989) 80–83.

[14] Willrich, "Caligula" 90–100; Momigliano, "Personalità" (1932) 210–214 (whose view of Germanicus as pro-senatorial seems flawed); Balsdon, *Gaius* 13, 101, 207–208; Bauman, *Women* (1992) 161–162, 257 nn. 20–21 (with literature). For the heavy influence of Egypt on Caligula's policies in religious and political matters, see Köberlein, *Caligula* (1962); Le Gall, "Successeurs" (1987) 224–226. See now, however, the objections raised by Salvaterra, "Progetto" (1989) 634 and n. 12, and the sharp rebuttal in Barrett, *Caligula* (1989) 218–222.

[15] Garzetti, *Tiberius* (1974) 101.

[16] So Wilcken, *GO* 1.218. Rostovstev, *Diz. Ep. fiscus* (1922) 127–128 (cf. 117), suggests that the tax was initiated under the Ptolemies and continued to be collected as part of the *cheirōnaxia*. Wilcken's argument receives conditional acceptance from Wallace, *Taxation* (1938) 210; cf. Brunt, "Revenues" (1981/1990) 329. See also Bloch, *Prostitution* 1 (1912) 443 (reporting the opinion of Karl Sudhoff).

[17] *O. Wilck.* 1030.

[18] *O. Wilck.* 504 and 1030.

[19] Bagnall, "Trick" (1991) 8.

not prostitutes did pay taxes in Egypt[20] and, most important, trade taxes.[21] Despite this, Wilcken's argument is not impossible, given the structure of gender and work in Roman Egypt and, in particular, the relatively restricted range of professions practiced by women.[22] Lewis even declares that in Roman Egypt "there were two sex-linked occupations: wet-nurses and prostitutes."[23] There is also the long-standing prejudice (held by the Romans, at any rate) that the prostitute was the quintessential working woman.[24] In sum, Wilcken is unlikely to be proved wrong[25] but cannot be assumed to be correct.

If the Egyptian hypothesis remains uncertain, yet another consideration supports the view that Caligula aimed at more than producing revenue. Direct taxes, that is, taxes imposed on income and wealth, were widely regarded as instruments of tyranny in the ancient world[26] and as shameful and appropriate only for members of the lower classes and noncitizens.[27] Despite its peculiar rate, the prostitute tax is essentially an income tax, like those levied on other professions at the same time. The exceptions would be the taxes on "eatables" and lawsuits.[28]

This definition of a direct tax as one imposed on income or wealth, which is typically contrasted with indirect taxes (i.e., taxes imposed on outlays and expenditures, or commodities and services), is that of economists.[29] Ancient historians tend to employ a peculiar, sometimes inconsistent definition of "direct" tax that is misleading, insofar as it is based on incidence.[30] Thus, many historians regard Caligula's tax as indirect.[31]

---

[20] See *BL* 2.1.63 for early criticism of Wilcken on this score.

[21] Bringmann, *Frau* (1939) 72, with n. 22.

[22] See Treggiari, "Urban Labour" (1980), with literature, for conditions in the Roman West. On the evidence from Egypt, see now Drexhage, "Berufsbezeichnungen" (1992). Note also Wilcken's argument for identification of the woman as a prostitute based on lack of a father's name: Wilcken, *GO* 1.218 n. 1. See Calderini, *"Apatores"* (1953) 364.

[23] Lewis, *Life* (1983) 145.

[24] I note in passing that Lewis's remarkable observation, which amounts to an assertion that homosexual prostitution is not attested in Roman Egypt, is contradicted by no certain evidence known to me.

[25] Conceded by Bagnall, "Trick" 8.

[26] See Nicolet, *World* (1980) 151, 156, 185; Finley, *Politics* (1983) 32; and the literature cited by Webber and Wildavsky, *History of Taxation* (1986) 102 n. 20. Such an attitude was not confined to antiquity; see, e.g., Sabine, *History of Income Tax* (1966) esp. chs. 2–3.

[27] Webber and Wildavsky, *History of Taxation* 108; Neesen, *Abgaben* (1980) 4 and 117 n. 2, for direct taxation viewed as a mark of slavery (*nota captivitatis*: Tert. *Apol.* 13.6).

[28] For the latter, compare the analogy of the English stamp taxes of the late eighteenth century: Mathias and O'Brien, "Taxation" (1976) 621. Its incidence would perhaps have fallen upon a higher socioeconomic group than those of the other taxes, making it a relatively rare example of a "socially progressive" indirect tax.

[29] For the definition, see Samuelson and Nordhaus, *Economics*[12] (1985) 730; for an application, see Mathias and O'Brien, "Taxation" 611–633.

[30] Typical examples are the *tributum soli* and *capitis*. See the distinction between indirect and direct taxes adopted by Neesen, *Abgaben* 18 n.5. Neesen, to be sure, does not discuss any of the taxes introduced by Caligula in 40 or, for that matter, any taxes on trades and professions imposed anywhere in the Roman world. Nicolet, *World* 184, regards the *vicesima hereditatum* as the only direct tax levied under the Principate.

[31] Nony, *Caligula* (1986) 362, classifies it as indirect; so also Alpers, *Finanzsystem* (1995) 111. Cf.

Given the widespread identification of direct taxes with tyranny, the levy on prostitutes can be viewed as an instrument of autocracy, the policy of an emperor who aimed at an absolutist regime characterized by ''popular'' tendencies and hostility toward the aristocracy.[32] The status of the tax as a direct tax would then correspond to the evidence for the rate of the tax and Caligula's subsidiary motives (i.e., besides the financial one) for introducing it. The introduction of this tax into Rome and Italy runs counter to a policy of Augustus, whose regime saw the virtual exemption of these areas from direct taxation.[33] The prostitute tax, along with the other taxes on trades,[34] prefigures the harsh fiscal policies adopted toward trades and professions by Diocletian and his successors, especially Constantine.

Despite the negative reaction of the populace, the tax stands as a ''popular'' measure in two distinct ways. First, most obviously, Caligula needed money to support the lavish programs with which he intended to win the approval of the masses.[35] Second, the direct connection between fiscal duty and citizen status was long deemed important by the Romans.[36] Although the taxpayers in this case clearly had no sense of enjoying a privilege, such a motive fits in well with the other evidence for this emperor's ''popular'' ideology.[37]

The question of Caligula's motives for introducing the tax may be raised anew. Suetonius, Dio, and Josephus testify that it was simple greed that induced the emperor to introduce these new taxes. In view of the immense profitability of the prostitute tax in particular, this is in some ways a perfectly sufficient explanation, though it is possible to soften ''greed'' somewhat, in view of the unanimously hostile historical tradition on this emperor[38] (toward which the scholarship of this century has generally adopted a skeptical stance),[39] and the negative social attitudes toward the tax-

---

Auguet, *Caligula* (1975) 146, who views the tax on prostitutes as sumptuary legislation. Barrett, *Caligula* 228, regards all of Caligula's new taxes as direct (despite an implication to the contrary at 226).

[32] All but the most apologetic of modern historians agree broadly on Caligula's absolutism: Momigliano, ''Personalità''; Balsdon, *Gaius* esp. ch. 6; Garzetti, *Tiberius* esp. 86–92 and 580–586. This makes him neither a ''Hellenistic monarch'' nor an ''oriental despot.''

[33] See now Rathbone, ''Taxation'' (1993) 94, 97, 111.

[34] Note that the *cheirōnaxion* is listed among taxes associated with the fiscal system of a satrapy, a type linked with ''oriental despotism'' as described by [Aristot.] *Oecon.* 2.1.4; see Nicolet, *Tributum* (1976) 9.

[35] So Yavetz, *Plebs* (1988) 117–118.

[36] Nicolet, *World* esp. chs. 2 and 6. Of course, a higher tax rating might be imposed as a penalty: Nicolet, *World* 85.

[37] For a discussion, see the works of Momigliano, Balsdon, Garzetti, and Barrett mentioned in the notes above.

[38] On the hostility of the sources, see Balsdon, *Gaius* 222–228, and the discussion below.

[39] The tradition was widely accepted in the nineteenth century, but a sharp reaction is marked by the work of Willrich, ''Caligula.'' Since then, in fact, the scholarship has tended to be critical of the ancient sources: see esp. Balsdon and the discussion of the modern literature in Garzetti, *Tiberius* 580–586; Guastella, *Caligola* 43–50. Barrett's monograph *Caligula* reflects this trend, but an exception, and perhaps the most hostile of all twentieth-century writers on Caligula, is Ferrill, *Caligula* (1991).

ation of certain activities regarded as sordid.[40] Indeed, given the widespread practice of prostitution in the Roman world, coupled with the steep rate for this tax postulated below, the revenues generated by it must have been rather high. Prostitutes (and pimps, for that matter) were vulnerable to exploitation by the state.[41]

Caligula's desire for profit is easily illustrated by reference to his closing of possible loopholes or nullifying anticipated attempts at evasion of the taxes on prostitution and lawsuits. There is also the famous story of the tax inscription written in tiny letters and hung up in a high narrow place, which is the reason the sources allege for the unpopularity of these levies.[42] Caligula appears to have exploited in this way the uncertainty about tax regulations especially characteristic of the first half of the first century A.D.[43]

Profit was without doubt Caligula's primary motive for introducing the tax on prostitutes, and perhaps his only one. Some evidence does, however, suggest other factors were at work, at least on a secondary level. This concerns Caligula's establishment of a brothel on the Palatine.[44] Though at first glance they strain credulity, these reports are, I believe, based on an actual incident,[45] one that reveals that Caligula's motives, while in the main financial, were political as well.

A similar mix of financial and political motives can be argued for the introduction of the tax itself. One mark of *levitas popularis* was a willingness on the part of the *princeps* to share in the popular amusements.[46] So, for example, Nero would visit brothels and similar places.[47] Both Caligula and Nero are said to have patronized prostitutes.[48] Gallienus is alleged to have frequented taverns and eating-houses, where he befriended pimps and drunkards.[49] Commodus and Verus are similarly supposed to have patronized taverns and brothels.[50] Elagabalus is perhaps presented as the best imperial friend to prostitutes and pimps.[51] The information from the *Historia Augusta (HA)* on Gallienus is derivative, that on Commodus and Verus is concocted from the tradition on Nero, that on Elagabalus is sheer fiction.

---

[40] See Titus's reaction against Vespasian's tax on public urinals: Suet. *Vesp.* 23.3; Dio (in Xiph.) 65.14.5. Also relevant is the castigation of the state revenue from gladiatorial shows at *ILS* 5163.1–15, with Mommsen, "SC" (1890/1913) 527; and Oliver and Palmer, "Minutes" (1955) 340. Greed, to be sure, is a common attribute of pimps; see below for its relevance to Caligula's policy.

[41] Compare the explanation for the targeting of property of single women, widows, and orphans in 214 B.C. offered by Kraemer, *Her Share* (1992) 56.

[42] Suet. *Cal.* 41.1; Dio (in Xiph., *Exc. Val.*) 59.28.11. The latter tells us that popular dissatisfaction was expressed in a demonstration at the theater, as does Josephus (*AI* 19.24–27).

[43] See Klingenberg, "Reformedikt" (1979) 63.

[44] Suet. *Cal.* 41.1; Dio (in Xiph., *Exc. Val.*) 59.28.11.

[45] Full discussion of this point is not possible here. See McGinn, "Caligula's Brothel" (forthcoming).

[46] See esp. Yavetz, *Plebs* ch. 5.

[47] Tac. *Ann.* 13.25.1; cf. Suet. *Nero* 26; Dio (in Xiph., *Exc. Val.*) 61.8.1, 9.2–4. Yavetz, *Plebs* 4, 123–124, emphasizes the importance of this point.

[48] Tac. *Ann.* 15.72.2; Suet. *Nero* 27.2, 28.2.

[49] Aur. Vict. *Caes.* 33.6. Cf. *HA Tyr. Trig.* 3.4, 8.9, 9.1.

[50] *HA Comm.* 3.7; *HA Verus* 4.6.

[51] *HA Elag.* 12.4, 25.5, 26.3–5, 27.7 (note the inversion: Elagabalus, instead of deriving state revenues from prostitutes and pimps, is alleged to spend such funds on them), 31.1, 6, 32.5, 9. See also the actions attributed to Carinus at *HA Carin.* 16.7.

The legitimization of prostitution accomplished through the establishment of a tax, not to say a brothel, fits into the context of *levitas popularis*. It is an extreme instance, but not too extreme for Caligula, the only emperor known to have written a reference to sexual intercourse into Roman tax law (see below).

Even on this line of reasoning, however, it is difficult to escape the implications of the profit motive. The idea was, at least in part, to tax the income of the lower classes, or at any rate some relatively better-off elements among them.[52] In this way Caligula's taxes exploited a group heretofore largely unaffected by Roman fiscal policy. To the extent that the burden of these taxes could be passed along to customers, the resources of an even wider group among the lower classes would have been exploited, and these taxes, translated into higher prices for goods and services, were to an extent invisible as such.

As we shall see, for prostitutes, especially lower-priced prostitutes, such a transfer of the burden would not have been possible in large measure, but taxation as an instrument of oppression of a despised social group was not terribly unpopular. It is true that the sources register significant hostility to Caligula's taxes at their introduction. But aside from occasional flare-ups where the prostitute tax was not properly administered, it is not until it becomes a political issue in late antiquity that negative popular reaction to this tax is again recorded.

Caligula's motives with regard to legitimizing prostitution may be debated. Not only does the question of Egyptian influence lie beyond certainty,[53] but the same is true, it must be admitted, of the whole problem of political motives. All the same, the effects of his policy are clear enough. With the opening of a brothel on the Palatine, the legitimizing of prostitution at Rome perhaps reached its apogee. In a subtler way, a similar result was effected through the institution of the tax itself. As a prominent sociologist has pointed out, whenever the proceeds of sexual commerce are utilized for some higher purpose (e.g., state revenues), the result is necessarily a legitimizing of prostitution in some degree.[54]

This fact was widely recognized in antiquity. It was seen perhaps by the unknown biographer who invented the story of Alexander Severus's scruples over such receipts entering the *sacrum aerarium*[55] and by Justin Martyr[56] and most certainly by Emperor Theodosius II, who in 439 ceased collecting the tax from pimps in Constantinople and ejected them from the city. Theodosius deplored the fact that continued collection of the tax had provided the pimps with a justification for carrying on their trade.[57]

---

[52] A comparison of the estimated earnings potential of prostitutes with the scarce data available for other lower-class professions suggests that the income of prostitutes might have been rather high, when this did not go to their exploiters (who themselves were liable to the tax); see below.

[53] I regret that Bagnall, "Trick" 5–9, misses this conclusion, which appears at McGinn "Taxation" 86. It is, I believe, consistent with what he argues.

[54] Davis, "Sociology" (1937) 748. For ancient recognition of the connection between taxation and political legitimacy, see the discussion of Hortensia's famous rebuke of the triumvirs in Peppe, *Posizione* (1984) 17–50.

[55] *HA Alex. Sev.* 24.3; see the discussion below.

[56] Iustin. *Apol.* 1.27, on which see below.

[57] Theod. *Nov.* 18 pr., on which see Chapter 8.

In sum, there are no grounds for believing Caligula taxed prostitutes as *"infames personae."* That the tax had an Egyptian provenance is possible, but unproved. The same might be said regarding the idea that the tax formed part of a larger political program aimed at absolutism. The chief motive for its introduction was to increase the revenues of the Roman state, a motive perhaps accompanied by a secondary one, evidently peculiar to Caligula himself, of granting a degree of legitimacy to the practice of prostitution. It is worth emphasizing once more that Caligula is the only emperor we know to have written a reference to sexual intercourse into Roman tax law.

Given what we can know of Caligula's personality, it seems credible that the statute itself mentioned *unus concubitus* and that this is not just an elaboration supplied by Suetonius. Pimps were known to set the prices prostitutes charged, which typically seem to have been cast *per unum concubitum.*[58] The reference to the rate in the Palmyrene tax document, while substantially unchanged, is "cleaned up."

4. Methods of Collection

As Suetonius indicates, the collection of the prostitute tax, like the other new taxes introduced in 40, was at first entrusted to the *publicani* but later transferred to the officers of the Praetorian Guard "quia lucrum exuberabat." Outside Rome the tax appears to have been collected after this transfer by regular army troops in the military areas, and elsewhere by legionary soldiers serving on detached duty as *beneficiarii* and *curiosi,*[59] where these were available.

It is possible to argue that every locality that has supplied evidence for the tax presents its own method of collection. So we find publicans and then praetorians at Rome, regular army troops at Chersonesus, *beneficiarii/curiosi* at Carthage, liturgical officials (evidently) in Egypt, and local tax farmers at Palmyra. Such diverse practice corresponds well with the overall picture of Roman fiscal administration empirewide. Ockham's razor turns out to be a blunt instrument in attempting to understand the nature of Roman fiscal administration (the same is true for the problem of Caligula's motives in introducing the tax on prostitutes). I argue, however, that the first three instances can be reconciled with a general transfer of responsibility for collection to the military, where this was feasible. Egypt and Palmyra represent exceptions to this trend.

Why should the profitability of the tax cause it to be collected by the soldiers? The answer seems twofold: for the sake of security and to ensure the maximum return. The army was by and large the only source of manpower already available to the state that could be deployed for police and low-level administrative func-

---

[58] See, e.g., Sen. *Contr.* 1.2.1.

[59] Thus in Chersonesus we find regular army units collecting the tax: *CIL* 3.13750 (with Domaszewski's commentary); cf. Rostovtsev, "Besatzungen" 85–86.

tions.[60] For effective and comprehensive collection it was necessary to know precisely who practiced this trade, both pimps and prostitutes alike. While this may have presented no major problem for the public contractors of fourth-century Athens,[61] the surveillance and record-keeping necessary in both the city of Rome and the empire was a much more formidable enterprise, especially given the opportunities for tax fraud in such a business.[62]

Accordingly, the task was entrusted to the soldiers. The greater amount of force at their disposal meant that the task of collection in such hard cases could be combined with the goal of social control (given the types of undesirables liable to the tax and the imperative of constraining prostitution in some way). As patrons, the soldiers would know not only the location of the brothels but the identities of nonbrothel prostitutes and the prices of prostitutes who worked without a *titulus*.[63] Their role in collecting the tax may have helped discourage marginal or part-time prostitutes, since such women would have been compelled to pay at the same tax rate, no matter how little they worked.[64] The revenues went of course to the *fiscus*; there is no evidence for the suggestion that they were earmarked for the maintenance of troops stationed in Rome or in the provinces.[65]

The two most obvious advantages that accrued to the state from farming a tax for a lump-sum payment were that it obviated the need to create a tax-collecting bureaucracy and better assured the income the state could expect to receive.[66] If the government chose instead to lease a tax for a percentage of the take, these advantages were diminished or lost, though any attempt by the farmer to maximize profits benefited the treasury.[67] Collection by the military may have offered the advantages of both systems without the disadvantages of either.

Caligula (and perhaps his successor, following his lead at Rome) may have been persuaded to turn from publicans to soldiers as agents of collection by a pair

---

[60] Millar, "Condemnation" (1984) 126–127. Members of the *familia Caesaris* might fulfill some of the latter: Ott, *Beneficiarier* (1995) 82.

[61] See Aesch. 1.119.

[62] Compare the *matrices* mentioned by Tertullian at *Fuga* 13.3. For (apparently very common) evasion associated with the collection of the *portorium* by the *publicani,* see the discussions in Cagnat, *Étude* (1882) 128–134; De Laet, *Portorium* 437–444. "If the taxpayers' evasions exceeded the government's powers of civil enforcement, then government might resort to the military": MacMullen, "Tax-Pressure" (1987) 752, citing evidence drawn from late antiquity.

[63] It is significant that soldiers' garb was an appropriate disguise for the holy man Abraham on a rescue mission to a brothel: Ward, *Harlots* (1987) 87, 95 (*vita Mariae* 5). For the *titulus*, see below.

[64] For abuses in collection, see the discussion of the Tertullian passage below and of the Chersonesus inscription below; see also Lopuszanski, "Police" 16–17, who documents the corrupt and extortionate practices of the *beneficiarii* and other such soldiers on special duty; and see below for abuses connected with tax collection committed by soldiers in general.

[65] As Rostovtsev, "Besatzungen" 86, maintains; Willrich, "Caligula" 425 n. 4, correctly objects to this view. There is no evidence to support the view of Zubar, "Taurike" (1995) 203, that the provincial authorities shared in the proceeds from the tax.

[66] Brunt, "Publicans" (1990) 378–379; cf. Jones, "Taxation" (1974) 158.

[67] So Brunt, "Publicans" 383, who argues that Augustus's new taxes were leased on a percentage basis and the collection of older taxes was adapted to this method, which in turn helps explain why tax farmers receive increasingly close official supervision ("Publicans" 385–386).

of examples, only one of which involves the use of troops, set in the late Republic and early Empire. In 47 B.C. Julius Caesar made the cities of Asia themselves responsible for collection of *tributum* within their territories and so was able to reduce their tax burden by one-third, through cutting out the publican "middleman."[68] Under Augustus and Tiberius the Frisians had been paying a tax in hides to Roman troops, presumably since the unsettled conditions of the frontier made resort to civilian collectors impractical.[69] It seems quite possible that the Frisians were not the only ones to pay such a tax; however, most, if not all, of the other evidence on soldiers as tax collectors is much later in date.[70]

Tax-collecting officials did rely on assistance from soldiers as early as the mid-first century.[71] Soldiers seem to have provided security for precious metals, whenever extracted, refined, or transported for the direct or indirect benefit of the *fiscus*.[72] The need for security fits the picture drawn by the sources of the tax on prostitutes as a figurative gold mine.

If it is correct to view Caligula as acting under the influence of these practices or others like them, he is once more revealed as no innovator in the strict sense but an administrator quick to grasp the implications of a precedent drawn from another context, which he molds to his own purposes. So having recognized the advantages of cost savings from dropping collection by publicans—now of course the middleman's take went not to the taxpayer but to the state—and of increased security from resort to the military for collection, he combined the two.[73] Where this transfer was impossible or unnecessary, local tax collectors may have stepped in to collect the tax (see below).[74]

One may view the tax on prostitutes in the context of a movement discernible in this period from reliance on tax farmers for the collection of direct taxes to the use of imperial officials for the collection of these taxes,[75] though the employment of the military is an anomaly.[76] Suetonius does not explicitly say when the transfer to the military was made, although he implies that it too took place under Caligula.

---

[68] In other words, Caesar was able to reduce gross liability by eliminating the middleman's (i.e., the publican's) take. Brunt, "Publicans" 355, 380, 389, argues that Caesar's reform extended beyond Asia, "generally and universally." Compare the comments of Hopkins, "Taxes" (1980) 121, with n. 59, on *IG* 5(1) 1432–1433, dated to A.D. 35–44.

[69] Tac. *Ann.* 4.72; with Brunt, "Revenues" 339; Brunt, "Publicans" 390.

[70] MacMullen, *Soldier* (1967) 53, 59–62; Sperber, "Centurion" (1969).

[71] This is to judge from the evidence reviewed by Hanson, "Officials" (1989).

[72] Brunt, "Publicans" 400–401.

[73] I depend on the explanation of Caesar's move offered by Brunt, "Publicans" 380.

[74] On this theory, the prostitute tax was in origin a municipal tax, collected by local publicans. One may postulate a more complex process whereby the *societates publicanorum* first collected the tax, which was later entrusted to soldiers where available and to local, that is, civilian, tax collectors elsewhere.

[75] See Goldsmith, *Systems* (1987) 50. This is the traditional view, which also sees a similar change in the collection of indirect taxes later: Andreotti, "Politica" (1969) 219–220. The process was evidently more protracted than commonly assumed, especially in the latter case: Cimma, *Società* (1981) ch. 3.

[76] Though not to the extent assumed by Ott, *Beneficiarier* 133, who relies on evidence testifying to abuses in the employment of soldiers to collect taxes to argue for their total exclusion from this task as a matter of policy, starting with Tiberius.

Josephus informs us that the responsibility for collection of taxes, overdue because their rate had been doubled, was given by Caligula to Cassius Chaerea, a praetorian tribune.[77] These overdue taxes undoubtedly included the new ones introduced in 40, but it may be incorrect to assume, as Balsdon and Le Gall do, that the primary responsibility for the collection of the new taxes was at this point turned over to the military.[78]

Josephus does not say precisely this.[79] What is more, Licinius Mucianus, in a document dating to the years 68–69, uses the term "tax collector," rather than a reference to the military, with respect to the collection of the prostitute tax.[80] It is possible then that the transfer of the responsibility for collection to the military did not take place for some time, or at the very least that this occurred only for the praetorians, and that the same task outside Rome was still the responsibility of the *publicani* for some time afterward.

At this point contracts with *publicani* were typically (not always) of five years' duration.[81] I do not argue that we should simply assume that Caligula would have respected this term, only that it suggests a lapse of time is possible between the introduction of the tax and the transfer of responsibility for collection to the soldiers. Given what we know of Claudius's administrative reforms, especially in fiscal administration, it seems possible that Caligula's reliance on the military served as a model for his successor. It is conceivable that Claudius acted in stages but took the first decisive steps toward the systematization that our second-and third-century evidence seems to reflect.[82]

This argument is vitiated at first glance by the statement by Suetonius that Claudius annulled all of Caligula's official acts.[83] This generalization is impossible to sustain, however. It is implicitly contradicted by a series of assertions by Dio, which point to a selective, piecemeal abrogation of some elements of Caligula's program by his successor.[84] Dio tells us explicitly that Claudius abolished gradually, as the opportunity arose, Gaius's taxes and other measures of his that aroused criticism.[85]

This of course does not mean that Claudius abolished all of Caligula's taxes.[86] The levy on prostitutes finds attestation afterwards, and may not be alone.[87] I am

---

[77] Ios. *AI* 19.28.

[78] Balsdon, *Gaius* 103; Le Gall, "Habitants" (1979) 120.

[79] It seems possible Suetonius has generalized the specific task attributed to the praetorians of collecting back taxes and somewhat falsified the motive behind this change.

[80] To be sure, this might only show that Mucianus was generalizing, perhaps taking this provision directly from the original tax legislation, which, as Suetonius says, entrusted the *publicani* with the collection of the tax. For his pronouncement, see the discussion of the tax document from Palmyra below.

[81] Cagnat, *Étude* 97; Brunt, "Publicans" 377.

[82] On Claudius's financial policies, see Levick, *Claudius* (1990) ch. 12.

[83] Suet. *Claud.* 11.3: "Gai . . . acta omnia rescidit."

[84] Dio 60.4.1, 5.1, 6.6, 17.2, with Sautel, "Usurpations" (1956) 471 n. 5.

[85] Dio 60.4.1. Bagnall, "Trick" 11, takes this statement as evidence for the abolition of the tax on prostitutes.

[86] See the cautious statement of Barrett, *Caligula* 228: "He [sc., Claudius] gradually abolished most of the taxes. . . ."

[87] Le Gall, "Habitants" 120–121; Harris, "Trade" (1980) 136 n. 44. The evidence of Tertullian (*Fuga* 13.3) is not clear proof of the continuation of any other trade taxes imposed by Caligula. Note

not sure we can take Dio's statement as evidence that Claudius simply reduced the rate of the prostitute tax: the historian writes *kateluse*.[88] Claudius's practice, as Dio describes it, runs counter to that of most emperors, who liked to begin their reigns by lowering taxes in order to show their generosity.[89] The apparent singularity of his approach should put us on guard against casual assumptions about the abolition of the tax on prostitutes. More important is the fact that for reasons of policy en bloc cancellation of an emperor's *acta* was difficult to accomplish[90] and seems uncharacteristic of the early Principate.[91]

Why should Claudius have abolished the tax? The sources, despite their manifest hostility toward Caligula, do not convey the sense that the tax was per se unpopular. Claudius did not face the moral dilemma confronted by his Christian successors in late antiquity. The difficulty they met in ending the tax on prostitutes (see below) is another reason not to assume its abolition by Claudius.

Not surprisingly, the new system of collection by soldiers also led to abuses. Writing at Carthage at the beginning of Caracalla's reign in 212–213, Tertullian complains that Christians are (unfairly) persecuted and are thus classed together with unsavory characters and forced to pay "protection money": "I don't know whether to be sorry or embarrassed when on the registers of the *beneficiarii* and *curiosi,* among the innkeepers, porters, bathhouse thieves, gamblers, and pimps, Christians too are listed as 'liable for payment' "[92] Tertullian inveighs against the practice of extortion, especially by soldiers: "a soldier, perhaps a professional informer, or a personal enemy shakes me down, collecting not a thing for the emperor. . . ."[93]

Tavernkeepers, pimps, and perhaps porters[94] are among those subject to Caligula's tax, and thus they have a place on these military *matrices.* But what of gamblers and bathhouse thieves? It seems more likely that these, like the Christians,

---

the lack of evidence for some important taxes under the Principate: Eck, *Organisation* (1979) 113–114; Brunt, "Princeps" (1983) 47.

[88] The word can refer to a temporary suspension, however: Boegehold, *Lawcourts* (1995) 41 n. 61. If so, this did not last long. Note that the element of the rate of *unus concubitus* is attested again in the Palmyrene document discussed below, suggesting, in my view, continuity with the Caligulan daily rate.

[89] MacMullen, "Tax-Pressure" 737.

[90] Sautel, "Usurpations"; cf. Corcoran, "Licinius" (1993) 100.

[91] Sautel, "Usurpations" 472.

[92] Tert. *Fuga* 13.3: "Nescio dolendum an erubescendum sit, cum in matricibus beneficiariorum et curiosorum inter tabernarios et ianios et fures balnearum et aleones et lenones Christiani quoque vectigales contineantur." On this text see Lopuszanski, "Police" esp. 6–13, who, like Chastagnol, views the *beneficiarii* as acting as a sort of vice squad. This is not to deny that local officials (such as the aediles at Rome) and in some cases municipal police (see Arc. Char. D. 50.4.18.7, with Hirschfeld, "Polizei" [1891/1913] 605) exercised oversight of *mores.* They were not the Roman version of the modern *police des moeurs,* however; see Chapter 5.

[93] Tert. *Fuga* 12.9: "Miles me vel delator vel inimicus concutit, nil Caesari exigens. . . ."

[94] Porters in the ancient sources are often persons starting out at the bottom: Treggiari, "Urban Labour" 49. *Geruli* and *ianii* are not the same; the former were respectable enough to constitute their own *decuria:* Purcell, "*Apparitores*" (1983) 129. The latter might be included in Suetonius's sweeping phrase "nullo rerum," etc., if they were not merely an object of extortion, like Christians.

were simply objects of extortion by virtue of their illegal activities (i.e., they paid up in order to avoid prosecution: so Tertullian's use of the word *delator* with respect to the Christians); of course, the other groups will hardly have been immune to extortion either.[95] Tertullian has simply lumped all of these types together because of their admittedly bad reputations.[96]

Tertullian may even be conflating two different types of lists, though in the case of tavernkeepers and pimps the line between surveillance (i.e., purely police functions) and taxation is hard to draw.[97] Lopuszanski argues that the *beneficiarii* collecting the tax at Carthage were drawn from the urban cohort stationed in that city and acted under the direction of an imperial procurator.[98] The role of this official in collecting taxes in the public provinces remains unclear, however.[99] The important point is that *beneficiarii* and *curiosi* were soldiers.[100] Nor does the fact that Chersonesus was a *civitas libera* make any difference in this respect.[101] It is simply a question of the availability of a standing military force.

So we find praetorians collecting the tax at Rome, regular army troops at the rim of the empire (Tauric Chersonesus), *beneficiarii* and *curiosi* in a provincial capital (Carthage). One might speculate that other soldiers on detached duty, such as *speculatores* and *stationarii,* collected the tax as well. Civilian tax collectors operated in Egypt and Palmyra, though the latter case may be taken to suggest collection by local (i.e., municipal) collectors was the norm where no soldiers were in sight (see below). Egypt is a special case in this respect.

Aside from the depredations of the *beneficiarii* and *curiosi* criticized by Tertullian, there is evidence for similar behavior on the part of regular army troops. An inscription from the town of Chersonesus on the far coast of the Black Sea,[102] dated by Domaszewski to 185 or 186, records, in the form of a decree from a Roman provincial governor, measures taken by the Roman authorities to put an end to the extortion practiced by the local garrison charged with collecting the tax on prostitutes.

[95] Hirschfeld, ''Polizei'' 583, is right about this point but fails to make a necessary distinction between those who must buy off the police because their activity is illegal per se, such as thieves and gamblers, and others, e.g., pimps, whose activity is not outlawed. Christians perhaps form a special category. For a discussion of the nature of their ''illegal'' status, see the famous debate between de Ste. Croix and Sherwin-White in Finley, *SAS* (1974).

[96] At the same time, Tertullian has omitted others from whom the soldiers also collected taxes, notably prostitutes themselves.

[97] For the different (but evidently complementary) activities of *beneficiarii* and *curiosi,* see Hirschfeld, ''Polizei'' 581–586; Lopuszanski, ''Police'' 7–10. On the former, see now the different views of Dise, ''Reassessment'' (1995) and Ott, *Beneficiarier.*

[98] Lopuszanski, ''Police'' 12–13. Ott, *Beneficiarier* 84–85, holds that *beneficiarii* did not serve on the *officia* of governors of senatorial provinces.

[99] See Brunt, ''Publicans'' (1990), who argues that the role of these officials in tax collecting has perhaps been exaggerated. Contrast Burton, ''Procurators'' (1993) esp. 16–20.

[100] See Jones, ''Civil Service'' (1949/1960) 162, on the constitution of the *officium* (Lopuszanski, ''Police'' 45–46, himself emphasizes the status of its members as soldiers).

[101] Contra Rostovtsev, ''Besatzungen'' (1902) 86. Palmyra was most likely a *civitas libera* in the period when civilian tax farmers were collecting the tax; see below.

[102] *CIL* 3.13750 = *IGR* 1.860.

The decree, which is preserved in a fragmentary state, contains seven sections, the first four in Greek, the last three in Latin.[103] The first section is a letter addressed to the townspeople from the provincial governor, apparently of Moesia Inferior,[104] containing an imperial rescript. Both governor and emperor have reviewed the situation and promise a redress of grievances; letters will be sent to the local commanders detailing the proper behavior to be observed by the soldiers with respect to the collection of the tax. The third section contains the petition of the townspeople, complaining of the behavior of the soldiers while collecting the tax. Mention is made of a similar round of disturbances in the past; on that occasion redress had been made by a tribune named Arrius Alcibiades.[105]

The last three sections consist of a series of communications from the emperor to the current local commanders. He orders that "no infraction against military discipline or injury or abuse toward the locals be perpetrated"[106] and forwards a copy of the memo drawn up by Alcibiades in connection with the previous round of disturbances. This memo apparently contained a set of regulations on the responsibilities of the Roman garrison with respect to the collection of the tax. Alcibiades' activities include balancing accounts with the *fiscus*[107] and instituting a series of judicial proceedings (i.e., some form of judicial arbitration) in order to ensure the return of the money that had been unjustly exacted.

This decree illustrates the difficulty of controlling the behavior of troops garrisoned in remote outposts far from their legionary commands.[108] It also has important implications for the collection of the prostitute tax. One notes, for example, that of all the taxes on trades introduced by Caligula and later turned over to the military for collection, only the prostitute tax is mentioned here.[109] Perhaps it was the only tax important enough to be collected by the soldiers in a remote place like Chersonesus, or it was the only one significant enough to inspire extortion.[110]

---

[103] I have followed the accounts given by Domaszewski *(CIL)* and Cagnat *(IGR)*, noting significant differences between the two where they occur. (For the division into sections, see next note.)

[104] See Domaszewski and Cagnat *ad loc.* The troops in Chersonesus at this time will have been under his ultimate authority: Rostovtsev, "Besatzungen" 83–86. In describing the divisions of the inscription I follow Domaszewski, who holds that lines 9–12 of the inscription contain an imperial rescript embedded within that of the governor (thus two sections here instead of one), and that section 4 (immediately following the decree of the town council, lines 32–34) and the three letters written in Latin (sections 5–7) are also from the emperor. Cagnat assigns all the rescripts to the provincial governor. The validity of either view will not affect the interpretation of the document given here.

[105] We learn his name later in the text (36). In this period the local commander of Roman troops at Chersonesus was a military tribune from the Legio I Italica: Rostovtsev, "Besatzungen" 85. His authority extended to other detachments in this area: Zubar, "Taurike."

[106] I follow Cagnat's supplement at 47.

[107] Evidently this was the imperial treasury. See Millar, "Fiscus" (1963) 39, and compare Brunt, "Fiscus" (1966/1990) 138 n. 18, for whom this *fiscus* "*may*" (his emphasis) be a provincial treasury (note, however, his comment [150] on the destination of revenues from direct taxes levied in imperial provinces and see below).

[108] The problem of harassment of civilians by soldiers was of course quite widespread; see Campbell, *Emperor* (1984) 246–254.

[109] It is called the *capitulum lenocinii* at 36 and 45; *vectigal* at 40; and *to telos to pornikon* at 15.

[110] This may not have been true everywhere; see the discussion above concerning Tert. *Fuga* 13.3.

In any case the relative economic importance of the tax and thus indirectly of the business of prostitution is again confirmed, an observation that is further borne out by the direct involvement of the town's leading citizens in this incident.

As Domaszewski points out, no protests are offered against the tax itself but only against the methods employed against leading citizens in its collection. Why were these persons exposed to such rough treatment? The wording of the decree yields no distinction between worthy and unworthy objects of collection: the complaint is that too much money has been collected, and this in a violent manner. Members of the town council have been the target of this violence[111] and they now demand that restitution be made along the lines laid down previously and that the soldiers behave themselves when collecting the tax. No argument is made that they were not liable to the tax, that they owned no brothels, or that they had nothing to do with the practice of prostitution.[112]

Before drawing the most obvious conclusion, we should canvass two other possibilities that would explain why soldiers were evidently collecting the tax from respectable persons. Since soldiers were sometimes used to collect arrears in taxes,[113] we could assume that the tax, though legitimately due from members of the local elite, was not ordinarily collected by soldiers. Another possibility—not entirely unrelated—is that the soldiers were making up a shortfall in the collection of the tax, which had been levied on the entire community, as might happen with the tribute.[114] Nothing in the decree as extant, however, supports either hypothesis, and some of the details, especially at 30–34 (see below), seem to speak against them.

The logical conclusion is that there was no real distinction to draw; that is, worthy citizens were legitimately subject to the tax and thus exposed to the violent and illicit tactics of the soldiers. The security of such taxpayers was of course a concern at the highest levels of the community. If the soldiers had simply been harassing ordinary pimps, it is unlikely that such an uproar would have been raised, with embassies sent to the provincial governor and even the emperor. The conclusion seems justified that the *honesti viri* of Chersonesus invested in the profitable business of prostitution.

This explains why distinguished citizens constituted targets in the first place, why the soldiers are apparently asked to confine their tax gathering to the brothels and behave circumspectly when collecting the tax (30–34), and why the tribune Alcibiades went to the trouble of instituting quasi-judicial proceedings to return the money that had been extorted during the first round of disturbances. But unlike the investors Ulpian mentions who merely own the property concerned,[115] these men

---

[111] This is implied at 16, 18, 22, and elsewhere.

[112] This seems certain, despite the fragmentary state of the inscription. The argument, if not the whole text, of the complaint made in the municipal decree is recoverable. Moreover, we learn from one of the imperial letters that among the issues resolved by Alcibiades was that of the *quantity* of the tax.

[113] Ios. *AI* 19.28; see Brunt, "Revenues" 339.

[114] Brunt, "Revenues" 339–343, 534–540.

[115] Ulp. D. 5.3.27.1.

seem much more closely connected with actual business operations, since like common pimps they are liable to the tax.[116] Domaszewski makes a valid distinction, to be sure, between the homes of the leading citizens who are mentioned at 16 and the places liable to the tax mentioned at 30. No doubt these men had delegates, such as slaves or freedmen, who ran the brothels for them.

As for the Roman authorities, they were interested in more than preserving the internal stability of Chersonesus and maintaining military discipline. The revenues produced by the tax were important and could only be safeguarded by allowing the brothels of the town to operate without fear of terror tactics on the part of the soldiers.[117]

5. The Rate of the Tax

The inscription from Chersonesus, as indeed much of the other evidence, points to the profitability of the tax. This aspect receives further confirmation from the implications of the high rate of taxation imposed on the prostitutes. Suetonius tells us: "ex capturis prostitutarum quantum quaeque uno concubito mereret." This tax rate of the price of one sexual act *(concubitus)* is explicitly confirmed by the wording of the Palmyra inscription, but in neither case are we told outright the interval of time for assessment. It must be either a month or a day, but the former might seem too light and the latter too oppressive.

Though both views have their adherents, the monthly rate is somewhat favored by scholars.[118] The data from Egypt are inconclusive; the amounts given on the very few tax receipts we possess do not seem to support either view,[119] and the evidence for a monthly basis of collection there is not decisive,[120] since the tax,

[116] For a possible analogy from Egypt, where an apparently respectable person is perhaps liable to the tax, see n. 214.

[117] This concern with securing the tax revenues is underscored when the emperor commends the measures taken by Arrius Alcibiades: "omnibus annis fisco pariaverit" (41).

[118] Daily rate: Cagnat, "Remarques" (1884) 137–138; Le Gall, "Habitants" 120; Teixidor, "Tarif" (1983) 250; Chastagnol, "Impôt" (1993) 430. Monthly rate: Wilcken, *GO* 1.217; Dittenberger *OGIS* 2.629 n. 48; Cagnat, *IGR* 3.1056 at 142 (who also suggests a yearly rate); Chabot *CIS* 2.3.3913 at P. 47–51; Février, *Essai* (1931) 63; Herter 2 (1960) 106; Matthews, "Tax Law" (1984) 177 n. 17; Gardner, *Women* (1986) 253; Barrett, *Caligula* 228. Dessau, "Steuertarif" (1884) 517, reserves judgment.

[119] *O. Wilck.* 83; *O. Cair. GPW* 60; *O. Berol.* inv. 25474, the certain evidence; cf. also *O. Wilck.* 504, 1030; *O. Edfou* 1.171. Nelson, "Receipt" (1995) 31, proposes a flat annual rate of 4 drachmas for Upper Egypt. *P. Lond.* inv. 1562 verso, which contains a list of market taxes, including a tax on prostitutes, collected in Oxyrhynchus for a period of the mid–second century A.D., is published and translated in Rea, "Market Taxes" (1982). Unfortunately, the amount recorded for the prostitute levy does not survive (see next note).

[120] *O. Wilck.* 504 and 1030, both conjectural receipts for the tax. In *P. Lond.* inv. 1562 verso, the levy on prostitution is reckoned on a monthly basis and is the only one of the taxes in that document to be so calculated. But here a flat sum appears to have been demanded, instead of an amount tied to the standard of *unus concubitus*; furthermore, these taxes were classed as "hieratic" and thus would have been collected by public officials, not tax farmers: Rea, "Market Taxes" 192–193. All of this

even if calculated on a daily basis, would hardly have been collected every day. The fact that some of the local taxes listed on the Palmyra decree seem to have been collected on a monthly basis is not, as some have thought, compelling evidence for the rate of the tax on prostitutes.

The context of the report in Suetonius provides a clue. Just before the notice on the prostitute tax we have the one on porters: "ex gerulorum diurnis quaestibus pars octava." It seems that the word "diurnis" is meant to be understood also with the immediately following "ex capturis prostitutarum."[121] If we assume an average of four to six sexual contacts per day on the part of the average prostitute (and this figure would probably lie on the lower end of the scale),[122] this tax would represent a significant proportion (17–25%) of the prostitute's income but not impossibly more than the *pars octava* (12.5%) demanded of porters; on the other hand, if the tax were calculated on a monthly basis, it would seem absurdly low.

The evidence for popular hostility toward these taxes (implicit in Suetonius's account and emphasized by Dio and Josephus) is surely better explained by the fact that these very profitable taxes were rather high (as well as more efficiently and forcefully collected) than by the story of the tax inscription written in tiny letters and hung up in a high, narrow place, which is the reason given in the sources for their unpopularity,[123] though this move would no doubt have aggravated matters. The daily rate is more consistent with the best explanation we have of Caligula's motive for introducing the tax. It may also form part of a tendency to tax steeply activities that were not socially approved and thus legitimized, to an extent, the revenues generated for the state.[124] Thus we should prefer the higher, daily rate.

The other element of the rate, *unus concubitus,* also deserves comment. Here Suetonius's report makes the tax seem highly progressive, in that it discriminates against the higher-priced prostitutes. The modern scholarship on sexual commerce has shown that there tends to be an inverse relationship (though not, apparently, one that can be fixed with any precision) between the price a prostitute charges and the frequency of her sexual contacts. A higher-priced prostitute can afford to

---

suggests that this tax at Oxyrhynchus is not to be identified with the prostitute tax as collected elsewhere. Bagnall, "Trick" 9, suggests it may represent payment for lease of a municipal brothel.

[121] Teixidor, "Tarif" 250, makes a similar point. Note that Suetonius appears to indulge in a bit of wordplay here. *Quaestus* can refer to earnings from any profession but has a special resonance for prostitution, especially since it seems to have formed part of the description of a prostitute found in the Augustan legislation; see Chapter 3. This association makes the connection between "diurnis" and "capturis prostitutarum" even tighter.

[122] There are no reliable data from antiquity on this subject. Information drawn from more recent periods can at least suggest certain possibilities. For example, Rosen, *Sisterhood* (1982) 98, gives figures of 4–5 customers per day for high-priced prostitutes in turn-of-the-century America and as many as 13–30 customers for the lowest crib prostitutes. Compare the much higher figures given by Barry, *Slavery* (1979) 3, 59, 65 (cf. 81) for conditions in our own day.

[123] Suet. *Cal.* 41.1; Dio (in Xiph., *Exc. Val.*) 59.28.11.

[124] This is beyond proof and not, I believe, ascribable to Caligula himself. Note, however, the hefty one-third/one-quarter rate imposed on the much maligned gladiatorial shows, a levy abolished in 176/177: *ILS* 5163.5, with Mommsen, "SC" 527.

be selective and tends to work less.[125] There is no reason to assume that this was different in Rome, certainly for free prostitutes; however, since the amount of the tax paid was unaffected by the number of contacts, the rate as it stands in Suetonius would tend to discriminate against those who charged more and worked less. At the same time, the pronouncement of Mucianus discussed below sets an upper limit to the rate: all prostitutes who charge a denarius or more pay a denarius in tax. Although the document dates from 68–69, it seems likely that this provision also formed part of the original legislation.[126]

A word or two about the operation of tax incidence seems appropriate here.[127] Simply because prostitutes or their pimps paid the tax to the government, we should not assume that they were the payers of the tax in an economic sense; an example of this principle can be seen in the operation of the modern sales tax. Who pays the tax in an economic sense is largely a function of the relative elasticity (i.e., price responsiveness) of supply and demand in a given market. It is notoriously difficult to construct elasticities of demand for historical contexts, primarily because of scarcity of data.[128] For supply, at least, it is possible to observe that, given the scarcity of alternative occupations for lower-class women, there would have been relatively less opportunity for prostitutes to avoid the burden of the tax.

In fact, the sources suggest that pimps were often perceived to be the payers of the tax.[129] Many Roman prostitutes were slaves. Even in nonslaveholding societies it is common for prostitutes to be held in virtual bondage by pimps. In professions other than prostitution, independent women, that is, women who were not slaves or subordinate members of family businesses, were relatively rare at Rome.[130] While the question of the extent to which Roman prostitutes found themselves in a condition of slavery or dependency cannot be addressed here, it is certainly true that many prostitutes, whether slave or free, were not allowed to decide how much to charge, how hard to work, or whether or not to remain a prostitute. In such cases, however, these same economic effects would have fallen on their pimps. That is, there was little opportunity for the pimps to move the prostitutes into other equally remunerative professions or to raise prices in order to escape the economic effects of the tax.

The rate of the tax would have discouraged marginal or part-time prostitutes, because the amount paid remained the same no matter how little they worked. The provision of the tax law that was directed against "retired" prostitutes would have discouraged women from working only intermittently as prostitutes, as would the use of soldiers, a more efficient and forceful agency of collection. Marginal pros-

---

[125] Goldman, *Gold Diggers* (1981) 76, 91–99; Rosen, *Sisterhood* 76, 92–97.

[126] It is not surprising, however, to find that the Palmyrene tax document has "cleaned up" the *unus concubitus* standard by eliminating the explicit reference to sexual intercourse; see discussion above and the translations given below.

[127] A discussion of the principles of tax incidence can be found in most elementary economics textbooks. See, e.g., Samuelson and Nordhaus, *Economics*[12] 387–388, 739–740.

[128] Elasticity of supply seems equally difficult to reconstruct: Hawke, *Economics* (1980) 193.

[129] Suet. *Cal.* 40 (in the context of the anti-evasion measure); Tert. *Fuga* 13.3 (who does not even mention prostitutes).

[130] Kampen, *Image* (1981) esp. chs. 4–5.

titutes probably either turned into full-time professionals or left prostitution for good (in the case of slave or dependent prostitutes, the choice was a pimp's), although there perhaps always were women discreet or fortunate enough to escape the tax and its economic effects.

This view of the economic effects of the tax on prostitutes and their pimps is further supported by the following observations. Given the rate ceiling of one denarius, the tax would have had quite different effects on higher-and lower-priced prostitutes. Perhaps the two easiest ways to avoid a tax burden are to cut back on the taxable activity or pass the burden on to others.[131] The higher-priced prostitutes were charging close to a denarius already,[132] and were presumably operating on a selective basis. This means that they (or their pimps) could probably raise their prices to just over a denarius without hurting their business too much, and in this way escape the burden of the tax entirely by passing it along to their customers. Less expensive prostitutes were not so fortunate. If they attempted to shift the incidence of the tax by raising their prices, they risked losing customers. Besides, any price rise up to a denarius was in another sense counterproductive, since it also drove up their tax liability.

Given this particular tax rate, a cutback in taxable activity was counterproductive unless it were total (i.e., the prostitute left the profession). The lower-priced prostitute (or her pimp) was left with only two choices if she were to remain in business: either absorb the cost of the tax herself or seek additional customers at the same (or perhaps even a lower) price. Marginal free prostitutes might have been induced to leave the profession; but the law anticipates this form of "evasion," as the Suetonius passage shows. The majority, influenced above all by lack of alternative employment, probably would have worked more, and slave or dependent prostitutes would have been compelled to do so.[133]

In terms of its economic effects, Caligula's tax is sharply regressive above a denarius, but progressive below that level.[134] For most price levels it would have coincided with the *ad valorem* assessment system that by and large has been thought to characterize the Roman *portorium*.[135] Moreover the *unus concubitus*

---

[131] Musgrave and Musgrave, *Public Finance*[3] (1980) 259.

[132] For example, out of the nearly two dozen prices preserved from Pompeii only one is equal to a denarius, and none are higher; the most common price is two asses. Comparison with contemporary wage and price data suggests that these (and those given in the notes below) are real prices, not insults (like Cicero's *quadrantaria*). For skepticism, see Pomeroy, *Goddesses* (1975) 201; Duncan-Jones, *Economy*[2] (1982) 246; cf. Evans, *War* (1991) 161 n. 124. In this period, 1 denarius = 4 sesterces = 16 asses.

[133] Compare a description of prostitutes' reaction to the repressive measures taken against them in the United States at the time of World War I. "To pay their legal costs, many women had to work longer, rely on intermediaries, or engage in other criminal activity": Rhode, *Justice* (1989) 256.

[134] Given the status of persons most liable to its incidence (whether they are thought to be prostitutes, pimps, or clients), the tax on prostitutes in overall terms fits in with the general description of the Roman system of taxation as regressive: Hopkins, "Taxes" 121; Brunt, "Revenues" 343.

[135] The traditional view: Cagnat, *Étude* 14, 69, 70, 80, 82; De Laet, *Portorium* 47–48, 52–53, 242–245, 368–369; Andreotti, "Politica" 218. Note, however, Foraboschi, "Dogane" (1992) 104. The situation is a bit more complicated with respect to direct taxation. Significant regional differences in tax incidence persisted throughout the first three centuries of the Empire, and some types of direct taxes, such as capitation taxes, were generally not tied to wealth or income. Despite this, an overall

method of calculation itself would have been appealing in an administrative sense, because it would have made collection easier and fraud more difficult.[136]

The prices prostitutes charged often would have been easy to discover. Though they were perhaps open to negotiation and to some extent dependent on the nature of the services rendered,[137] and discovering the prices of those prostitutes who worked in taverns, inns, cookshops, baths, porticoes, or under the arcades of circus or theater might have presented relatively greater difficulty, they were hardly a secret.[138] Epigraphical and literary evidence suggests that they were sometimes even advertised.[139]

In short, the *unus concubitus* standard offered a convenient way to avoid a more complicated assessment tied directly to income, which might have necessitated a sizable administrative bureaucracy if it were to be done accurately: even the army would not have been in a position to measure aggregate traffic or sort out the intricacies incumbent upon charging different prices for different services. Presumably any ambiguity would be interpreted in favor of the enforcing agency. As we have seen, the soldiers needed little incentive to extort money, and the use of this simple standard may have been intended not just to maximize the amount collected but to cut down on the possibilities for extortion, especially since prominent citizens could be targets. This handy yardstick is rationalized even further in the Palmyrene inscription discussed below.

6. Criticism of the Tax

Was the tax collected only from female prostitutes and their pimps? Both Suetonius and Dio emphasize female prostitutes exclusively, as does all the provincial evidence for the tax.[140] At least one source attests to the liability of male homosexual prostitutes, however. This is a passing allusion to the tax in the first *Apology* of Justin Martyr, evidently written in A.D. 152–155.[141] The context is an elaboration of the paradox of the persecution of innocent Christians in a world where pagan

---

preference for *ad valorem* assessment has been argued: Neesen, *Abgaben* 149–179, esp. 172–173. The prostitute tax, as we have seen, is more accurately classed as a direct tax.

[136] One may compare the license fees levied annually on bordellos by the municipality of Buenos Aires beginning in 1875: for purposes of taxation, houses of prostitution were classed as first-class operations regardless of size or location and so were charged a flat rate. The twin goals were social control and profit: Guy, *Sex* (1991) 50–53.

[137] For example, some of the lower prices given at Pompeii refer to *fellatio,* though it is difficult to be certain if this service was provided at a discount: *CIL* 4.1969, 5408, 8160.

[138] Pimps kept *rationes,* according to Sen. *Contr.* 1.2.2.

[139] For the *titulus* and its functions, see Schneider, *RE* meretrix (1931) 1024.

[140] The fact, however, that both authors have male, as well as female, prostitutes in the imperial brothel ("matronae ingenuique") suggests that male prostitutes were subject to the tax from the beginning.

[141] For the date see Barnard, *Justin* (1967) 13–19. The information about male prostitutes is confirmed, perhaps, by the notice on *exsoleti* at *HA Alex. Sev.* 24.4, though this notice is probably false in itself, as the discussion below shows.

vice runs rampant.[142] In this passage, Justin decries the practice of exposing children, claiming that almost all of these are brought up to prostitution:

> Iustinus *Apol.* 1.27: And you receive fees, revenues, taxes from these persons [i.e., from females and effeminates and those who perform unspeakable acts] . . .

While the tricola are obviously designed for rhetorical effect, they inform us that not only female but male prostitutes were liable to the tax and confirm once more that the earnings of prostitutes were a significant source of wealth for investors in the Roman world.[143] It is true that the motives of the author, as well as the rhetorical tone of this passage, caution against accepting what is said here on faith, but all the same the economic significance of prostitution is once again evident.

A few further points about this passage should be stressed. This is our earliest indication of the Christian attitude toward the tax on prostitutes, an attitude very different from that of the pagans and one that ultimately resulted in the abolition of the tax. It is noteworthy that only in a context critical of the tax do male prostitutes receive mention,[144] confirmation, if needed, of the low estimate entertained of male prostitution, not only by Christians. Finally, Justin's combination of the tax receipts *(tele)* with fees paid by clients to practitioners *(misthoi)* suggests a pointed criticism of the Roman state, which is here cast by implication in the role of the pimp.

7. Fictional Criticism and Later History of the Tax

Although we are told that Constantine taxed *tas dustucheis hetairas* ("the unfortunate prostitutes")[145] along with members of other trades and professions in his *collatio lustralis,*[146] it is uncertain whether the tax had previously fallen into abeyance or whether Constantine simply changed the form and circumstances of its collection when he founded the *collatio.*[147] Although the *collatio* was far from being

---

[142] For a discussion of this passage against the background of Justin's criticism of Roman institutions, see De Churruca, "Critique" (1984) 386–387.

[143] "Misthoi kai eisphorai kai tele": "fees, revenues, taxes." The second term *(eisphorai)* seems rather neutral and is perhaps to be regarded as rhetorical filler, if it does not refer to the concession of municipal brothels. (I do not mean, however, to suggest that any of the information contained in this passage is false.) The first term *(misthoi)* refers to the fee paid prostitutes and pimps by clients. Justin may mean that members of the upper classes profited from the proceeds of prostitution just as the state did with the tax.

[144] The same holds for the phony *HA Alex. Sev.* 24.3.

[145] Zos. 2.38. Zosimus is an unfriendly source, a fact that explains the rather indiscriminate sympathy he shows for the payers of the tax, as well as the rhetorical excesses of the passage in general, which is commonly thought to depend on the work of Eunapius: Chastagnol, "Zosime" 43 (on the rhetoric, 48–49; on Zosimus's date, 74–75).

[146] On the *collatio lustralis* or *chrysargyron,* introduced by Constantine (or perhaps by Licinius), see Karayannopulos, *Finanzwesen* (1958) esp. 129–137; Jones, *LRE* (1964) index s.v. *collatio lustralis*; Chastagnol, "Zosime"; Delmaire, *Largesses* (1989) 354–374; Beaucamp, *Statut* 1.126 n. 39; Bagnall, "Periodicity" (1992).

[147] On the calculation of the *collatio* (evidently a flat rate) and its collection every four years, see now Delmaire, *Largesses* 357–360, 368–370; see also Bagnall, "Periodicity."

the most significant source of state revenue, it seems unlikely that it was "a very minor item in the imperial budget,"[148] certainly in its early history.[149] To argue[150] that the emphasis the sources place on the tax on prostitutes as a proportion of the *collatio* is exaggerated and that therefore this proportion was in fact minimal is not logical and is contradicted by the evidence for unsuccessful attempts to abolish the taxation of prostitution (see below).

The only information we have on the tax from the period extending from Tertullian to Constantine is probably false. We are told that two and one-half centuries before the tax on prostitutes was finally abolished by a Christian emperor, Alexander Severus felt misgivings over it: "He [sc., Alexander Severus] forbade the proceeds of the tax levied on pimps, female prostitutes, and male prostitutes to be deposited in the imperial treasury and instead assigned them to the state expenditures for the restoration of theater, circus, amphitheater, and stadium."[151]

Evidently this virtuous prince felt scruples about the proceeds from this tax being mingled with the other imperial moneys and so channeled such income into a special fund. A laudable act perhaps, but one that, given the evidence we have surveyed so far, must raise doubts. Why, after nearly two centuries of uninterrupted and universal collection of this very profitable tax, should a pagan Roman emperor feel so uneasy about it?

Modern scholars have come to view the *Vita Alexandri Severi* as consisting, for the most part, of cunningly wrought fiction.[152] The very context of our passage is suspect, in fact. The subsequent passage[153] has been shown by Chastagnol to be a reworked version of a similar one in Aurelius Victor. It informs us that Alexander Severus contemplated forbidding male prostitution but decided this would be futile and even counterproductive.[154]

Chastagnol goes on to accept, albeit cautiously, the basic truth of the passage about the tax[155] but sees in its fabric intimations of a taxation policy toward prostitutes that was characteristic of a much later time. Chastagnol bases his argument

[148] Jones, "Towns" (1955/1974) 36.

[149] Pleket, "Elites" (1984) 7. Its abolition was a more complex affair than Jones supposes: Karayannopulos, *Finanzwesen* 136–137; Delmaire, *Largesses* 356, 358, 367, 371–374.

[150] Paschoud, "Sources" (1993) 52.

[151] *HA Alex. Sev.* 24.3: "lenonum vectigal et meretricum et exsoletorum in sacrum aerarium inferri vetuit, sed sumptibus publicis ad instaurationem theatri, circi, amphitheatri, stadii deputavit."

[152] Barnes, "Kaisergeschichte" (1970/1984) 33 (with further references); Syme, *Emperors* (1971) 97–100.

[153] *HA Alex. Sev.* 24.4.

[154] The model is Aur. Vict. *Caes.* 28.6–7: Chastagnol, "Zosime" 54–157. For other examples of such "borrowing" from Victor, see Chastagnol, "Utilisation" (1968). Unfortunately, his argument has been widely ignored; see, e.g., Dalla, *Venus* (1987) 176; Cantarella, *SN* (1988) 222; Formigoni Candini, *"Lenones"* (1990) 118; Sicari, *Prostituzione* (1991) 30 (31) n. 10, 128 and n. 6 (Sicari's faith in the reliability of the *HA* is close to inspirational; see 137 n. 23 on the "valore storico" of the *Vita Elagabali* and below).

[155] Chastagnol, "Zosime" 54, 59–61; Chastagnol, "Impôt" (1993) 431; cf. the discussion of his arguments on Caligula's tax above. Barnes, "Kaisergeschichte" 39, in an attempt to salvage fact from fiction in this *vita,* accepts 24.3, because there is evidence from coins for a building program of Alexander Severus; he does not discuss the issue of the tax. For the acceptance of the passage by other scholars, see McGinn, "Taxation" 105 n. 106.

on a series of premises that, in my view, cannot stand.[156] What are we to make of this anecdote?

For a moment, let us consider the nature and purpose of the *HA* as a whole. In recent years, scholars have argued convincingly that the *HA* was written in the last decade of the fourth century, if not later, by a single purveyor of imperial fiction possessed of a keen sense of humor (which is more than once on display in the *Vita Alexandri Severi*).[157] Such is the view of Syme, developed in all three of his books on the *HA*.[158] The late-date, single-author theory was first propounded by Hermann Dessau, who held for c. 395.[159] Some scholars prefer a date as late as 423.[160] Moreover, several scholars have claimed a distinctly pagan perspective for the author, and they have discovered passages where there can be discerned a subtle tone of mockery directed against the Christians and certain articles of their faith.[161]

All of this provides a perfect context for our passage. The Christian emperors were plainly embarrassed by their dependency on the revenues from the prostitute tax: as Theod. Nov. 18 makes clear, they could not live easily with it or without it. The reforms undertaken by Theodosius II in 439 may have seemed at best inadequate: only pimps (nothing is said of prostitutes) are to be expelled from Constantinople,[162] and the tax would continue to be collected from pimps outside the capital[163] and prostitutes inside for another half-century, until 498.[164] To a detached, perhaps cynical observer (as we might imagine our author to be) these policy changes would seem vain, cosmetic, and a frank confession of impotence. Perhaps even less satisfactory measures had been undertaken previously;[165] in any

[156] McGinn, ''Taxation'' 93–94.

[157] For humor in the *HA* see Syme, *Ammianus* (1968) 207–210; Syme, ''Controversy'' (1980/1983) 215; and, particularly in this *vita*; Barnes, ''Kaisergeschichte'' 32.

[158] Syme, *Ammianus*; Syme, *Emperors*; Syme, *Clarity* (1971). See also Syme, ''Controversy.'' *Clarity* is an effective reply to his critics, especially Momigliano.

[159] On the date see Syme, *Clarity* ch. 14; also Chastagnol (rev. Syme) (1969) 271; Honoré, ''Scriptor'' (1987). On the issue of the single author, see Syme, *Clarity* ch. 4; Chastagnol, *Recherches* (1970) 33–37; Marriott, ''Authorship'' (1979), with Sansone, ''Computer'' (1990).

[160] See the summary of views given by Chastagnol, *Recherches* 4–5; also the more recent survey in Dal Covolo, *Severi* (1989) 21 n. 39.

[161] See Chastagnol, *Recherches* 19–26. Several of the passages he discusses are taken from this *vita*. See also Schwarte, ''Christengesetz'' (1963) 207; Syme ''Controversy'' 221; and, with a different emphasis, Honoré, ''Scriptor'' 164. The idea is consistent with a serious purpose: Schwarte, ''Christengesetz'' 201–205; Honoré, ''Lawyers'' (1991) 16.

[162] On laws with limited territorial application in late antiquity, see Harries, ''Background'' (1993) 6.

[163] Chastagnol, ''Impôt'' 432, now would extend the ban to the entire empire (see also Chauvot, *Procope* [1986] 152). In my view both logic and the evidence are against this. The offer by the praetorian prefect Florentius to make up the consequent shortfall impresses Chastagnol by its generosity as well as for its implication of the man's enormous wealth. The extent of these depends of course on the cost to the government of its self-imposed inability to collect from pimps in the capital: in theory the loss of revenue would be minimal, unless many of the pimps expelled took their prostitutes with them.

[164] Similarly, Chastagnol, ''Zosime'' 52–53 (cf. 58–59). For another view, see Sicari, *Prostituzione* 38 n. 20.

[165] It is obviously not necessary to date the unknown author and his work as late as 439. The

case, the embarrassment of the Christian authorities over this tax was apt material for a spoof. Thus the strange scruples and even stranger solution adopted by Alexander Severus can be explained.

Christian sensitivity over the destination of the proceeds of prostitution can be read from the story of the prostitute Pelagia. The bishop Nonnus insists after Pelagia's conversion that none of her earnings remain with the church but all go to widows, orphans, and the poor, "so that whatever evil clings to it may be removed by this good use and the riches of sin become the treasures of righteousness."[166] The question of whether it was appropriate for a prostitute to give alms was debated in late antiquity and in the Middle Ages; in the latter period her liability to the tithe was also a matter of dispute.[167] The period of the Reformation witnessed a crisis of conscience about the destination of proceeds from municipal brothels,[168] a controversy that traces its roots far back in time. The practice of imposing a tax on prostitutes in connection with medical examinations—widespread among nineteenth-century French municipalities—was heavily criticized as immoral, though the proceeds were typically assigned to cover the expenses of the inspection.[169]

The passage's identification of the pre-Alexandrian destination of proceeds from the tax as the *aerarium* strikes a minor false note. In the time of Commodus, at any rate, the revenues from this tax did go to the *fiscus*.[170] The reference to *aerarium* in place of *fiscus* is not anachronistic, however, for the late fourth and early fifth centuries:[171] the *HA* passage refers to the imperial treasury of its own day.[172] After Constantine, like other revenues from the *collatio,* those from the tax on prostitutes went into the treasury of the *comes sacrarum largitionum.*[173]

To be sure, my case against the reliability of this passage can be argued but not proven. One difficulty is that there is more than one possible explanation for its inauthenticity.[174] If there is a grain of truth in this story, it shows perhaps that

---

suppression of homosexual brothels occurred in 390 and may have contributed to an emphasis on *exsoleti* here and in what follows (24.4). The destination of the funds postulated by the author of the *HA* may owe something to the rule laid down in Arc., Hon. CTh. 15.1.36 (a. 397) (cf. Arc., Hon. CTh. 16.10.16, 18 [a. 399]), which directed that stone from demolished temples be employed in public-works projects. For another view see Chastagnol, "Impôt" 434.

[166] Translated by Ward, *Harlots* 73 (*vita Pelagiae* 11).

[167] Ward, *Harlots* 105; Brundage, "Prostitution" (1975/1976) 838–839.

[168] Otis, *Prostitution* (1985) 45 (cf. 55).

[169] Corbin, *Women for Hire* (1990) 89.

[170] *CIL* 3.13750.41.

[171] See Theod. *Nov.* 18 pr. (a. 439) and discussion in Beaucamp, *Statut* 1.126.

[172] See Millar, "Fiscus" 39 n. 144; Kolb, *Untersuchungen* (1987) 93 n. 26; Delmaire, *Largesses* 4; and cf. Brunt, "Fiscus" 151 n. 62. Rostovtsev, "Besatzungen" 128, holds that the tax would now go to an imperial treasury (he suggests there might have been a special one for this purpose) instead of the *aerarium*. Of course, for some time now the *fiscus* and *aerarium* had been completely and indifferently at the disposal of the emperor. See Brunt, "Fiscus" 139, 143, 162, on the confusion in usage of the two terms.

[173] Karayannopulos, *Finanzwesen* 135; Delmaire, *Largesses* 347.

[174] The passage, like others that praise Alexander Severus for his prostitute-*Politik* (see also *HA Alex. Sev.* 24.4, 34.2, 4), is intended to provide a contrast with the deplorable (and equally fictitious,

there was some concern in the early third century over the fact that the collection of the tax by the government granted some measure of legitimacy to the practice of prostitution. That such concerns were in the air is suggested by the criticism of Justin Martyr discussed above and by the presentation of Caligula as a pimp by the sources that describe his introduction of the tax and the brothel.[175] A similar motive of course lies behind not only Theodosius's reforms in 439 and Leo's in 457–468[176] but also the complete abolition of the tax under Anastasius in 498, along with the rest of the *collatio*.[177]

Leo's reform evidently did not accomplish much.[178] On the face of it, he simply extended the Theodosian prohibition of pimping (and collecting the tax from pimps) to the entire empire. Prostitutes themselves may have remained liable to the tax (see below).[179] Jones[180] evidently believes that Leo's edict put an end to both the tax and official toleration of prostitution, but the accounts (which Jones omits to mention) of Anastasius's abolition of the tax make it clear that Leo's decree was ineffectual on both counts.[181] In the absence of evidence it can also be assumed that though Philip's ban on *exsoleti* was acknowledged to be ineffectual (by Aurelius Victor), this does not mean the tax continued to be collected from them.[182]

There is a chance, to be sure, that we do not understand the true scope and purpose of Leo's measure. Two possibilities stand out. One is that Leo's measure did in fact aim only to prohibit the collection of the tax from pimps, as an empire-wide extension of Theodosius' anti-procuring measures. In fact, the sources just given that treat Anastasius' abolition of the *collatio* emphasize prostitutes as payers of the tax, and do not mention pimps. On this theory, the imperial government sought not just to eliminate procuring but to collect the tax directly from prostitutes in the future. One does not have to be a great skeptic to question the feasibility of either project. The other possibility is the traditional version, namely that Leo, while repressing procuring, sought to end all taxation of prostitution, perhaps to

in my opinion) conduct of Elagabalus in this regard. This theme forms part of an overall contrast between the two *vitae*: see Pflaum, "Amours" (1978).

[175] Given the quality of the *Vita Alexandri Severi* as a historical source, however, information about official attitudes toward prostitution in the early third century simply cannot (pace Sicari, *Prostituzione* 128) be read out of this passage, any more than out of the one that immediately follows.

[176] Leo C. 11.41.7 (a. 457–468); cf. C. 1.4.14.

[177] See Jones, *LRE* 1.237 (who omits mention of the tax on prostitutes); Chastagnol, "Zosime" 74–77. Nöldeke, "Aufhebung" (1904) 135, is the first historian to have called attention to the Syriac sources that guarantee the 498 date. Despite repeated demonstrations of the date's validity (Chastagnol, "Zosime"; Delmaire, *Largesses* 371–374), it has too often been ignored. The motives for abolition of the *collatio* were more complex than repugnance at state revenue from prostitution, which receives much attention in the sources: Delmaire, *Largesses* 372.

[178] For another view, see Sicari, *Prostituzione* 42; Gardner (rev. Sicari) (1994).

[179] So Delmaire, *Largesses* 366 who distinguishes between the *collatio* imposed on prostitutes and a separate tax on pimps. There is no evidence for such a separate tax, however.

[180] Jones, *LRE* 2.976.

[181] Evagr. *HE* 3.39–41; Procop. Gaz. *Pan.* 13; Georg. Cedr. p. 626C–627D; Zon. 14.3.11–14; Nic. Call. 16.40. Strangely, Jones does cite much of this evidence without criticism at *LRE* 2.1178 n. 52.

[182] As Bailey, *Homosexuality* (1975) 72, assumes, on the basis of Evagrius. See Chastagnol, "Zosime" 76–77 (cf. 54–60); Chauvot, *Procope* 152.

avoid making it seem that the state was now assuming the role of universal pimp. If so, the abolition of the tax was an utter failure. I infer this from the fact that Anastasius found it necessary to abolish the tax *again* just over a generation later. In other words, this is not just a case of moral legislation that the state enacts and citizens ignore: the state itself was forced to go back on its own reform.[183] The explanation for this must be the compulsion of severe financial necessity. It is no surprise, then, that we have no record of the enabling statute for the reintroduction of the tax: the matter must have been intensely embarrassing for the authorities and might have been accomplished quietly.

To an unsympathetic observer, the situation would have seemed absurd, even risible: I propose above that the unknown author of the *HA* witnessed an unrecorded attempt at reform that was every bit as futile as Leo's. While recognizing that the parallel is inexact, I am reminded by this affair of the morals statutes that a number of American states have kept on their books, which for political reasons can neither be enforced nor repealed: there is ample material for satire here.

Beaucamp doubts that the tax on prostitutes was still collected in the time of Anastasius, an extreme position.[184] I recognize that it is difficult to choose law-skepticism over source-skepticism,[185] but the explicit emphasis of contemporary evidence leaves no other option. One might argue that Leo's measure was originally limited in scope, but, apart from the idea that the pimps alone no longer paid the tax, this is obviously a position of desperation.

In sum, while Leo's statute should be allowed its rightful place in the history of (ineffectual) moral legislation, its importance should not be exaggerated.

8. Two Special Cases: Egypt and Palmyra

Although the details of the method of collection by the military discussed above concern Rome and the greater part of the empire, it should be noted that in certain areas of the Roman world collection was made instead by civilian tax collectors, namely, in Egypt and Palmyra. A brief examination of the evidence for the tax in these two places attempts to explain this detail and perhaps to contribute to our understanding of the tax as it existed elsewhere.

In Egypt, the Romans built on the already existing Ptolemaic structure, while introducing significant changes. The crucial question turns precisely on the balance of continuity and change. In recent years controversy has reigned on this matter, as a challenge has been mounted to the older view, which stressed continuity with

---

[183] Slack enforcement, to be sure, was anticipated by Leo, who threatened officials with physical and financial penalties for failure to comply with his orders: Leo C. 11.41.7 (a. 457–467).

[184] Beaucamp, *Statut* 1.126 n. 42.

[185] The latter option does not seem particularly easy in this case. A number of sources agree that Anastasius ended the taxation of prostitutes (see above). One of these, Procopius of Gaza (*Pan.* 13), makes the claim to the emperor's face and goes on to praise him for succeeding in the exercise of virtue where his well-intentioned predecessors had failed. Chauvot, *Procope* 95–97, dates the *Panegyricus* to 502.

the past and isolation from the other Roman provinces.[186] The new consensus is that Egypt was more "Roman" a province than previously supposed.[187]

At the risk of oversimplifying what is in almost every case a nuanced argument, I summarize the range of views prevailing precisely on the issue of continuity and change in the collection of public revenues.[188] One position holds that the Romans made substantial changes in the fiscal administration of Egypt from the start,[189] while another finds substantial continuity.[190] A third emphasizes both continuity and change.[191] The relevance of this debate for the origins of the tax on prostitutes is clear: if the Romans had utterly overhauled the Ptolemaic system of revenues, this would make a pre-Caligulan Egyptian precedent for the tax less likely, but if they made few changes, the argument for this precedent is stronger.

To be sure, the question of origins cannot be resolved in any definitive sense on the basis of the evidence known to me. It is worth exploring further for two reasons, however: to improve our understanding of the rate of the tax and the manner of collecting it in Egypt.

A fragmentary inscription from Hellenistic Cos[192] lists categories of persons responsible for supporting sacrifices at a religious festival and may provide a clue to later arrangements in Egypt. As it survives, the list begins with a series of types of tax farmers (1–16). Two main categories of tax are farmed out: the collection of direct taxes and that of revenues and rents from public property, sacred and secular.[193] In the first category are farmers of a tax on prostitutes (*hetairai*: 5). In the second are farmers of something described as *to Aphrodeision* (13). This is usually understood to be a sanctuary of Aphrodite,[194] though its exact significance is uncertain.[195] One might suggest it was a municipal or temple brothel on the analogy of the Ptolemaic evidence given below, though the precise connection of

[186] A range of views on the subject may be canvassed in *ANRW* 2.10.1 (see esp. the contributions by Huzar, Geraci, Montevecchi); cf. the survey of modern scholarship in Geraci, "Egitto" (1989), and of some recent approaches in Amelotti, "Egitto" (1989/1990). My treatment of the tax in "Taxation" was influenced by the older view.

[187] Lewis's article "Egypt" (1970) is groundbreaking. See also Bowman, "Papyri" (1976) 160–161; Geraci, *Genesi* (1983); Lewis, "Romanity" (1984); Bowman and Rathbone, "Cities" (1992) 107–108.

[188] For varying treatments of the Roman changes to the Ptolemaic system, see, e.g., Wilcken, *GO* 1.587–601; Wallace, *Taxation* 343–345; Lewis, *Life* ch. 8. One measure of Egypt's administrative and economic isolation after annexation is that it retained its own currency, and imperial currency was not permitted to circulate: West and Johnson, *Currency* (1944/1967) 1, 89; Goldsmith, *Systems* 38.

[189] Geraci, *Genesi* esp. 185–189; Bagnall, "Trick" 9.

[190] Brunt, "Revenues" 328–329; Préaux, "Continuités" (1983); see Fishwick, "Statues Taxes" (1989), for a specific example.

[191] Foraboschi, "Egitto" (1986).

[192] *SIG*³ 1000 = Michel 720. See Reinach, "Inscription" (1891); Reinach, "Impôt" (1892); Toepffer, "Sakralgesetz" (1891/1897); Ziehen, *Leges* 2 (1906) 338–341; Sokolowski, *LSCG* (1969) 292–295; Sherwin-White, *Cos* (1978) esp. 229–235, 304, with literature. The date is controversial, with arguments made for the second and first centuries B.C.: Sherwin-White, *Cos* 230–231.

[193] Reinach, "Inscription" 363; Sherwin-White, *Cos* 231.

[194] Reinach, "Inscription" 370; Sherwin-White, *Cos* 304.

[195] See Toepffer, "Sakralgesetz" 218–219; Dittenberger, *SIG*³ 1000 ad loc.; Sokolowski, *LSCG* 295.

this lease or, for that matter, the tax on prostitutes with a temple is far from clear.[196] The key question is whether either the exploitation of the "brothel" or the securely attested tax on prostitutes (together with these other Coan taxes) was based on a Ptolemaic model, but this too remains uncertain.[197]

It has long been recognized that one of the early changes in the Egyptian fiscal system wrought by the Romans was to assume control of the finances of temples.[198] Exploitation of venal sex was connected with at least one temple in the Ptolemaic period. A decree of Euergetes II, dating from 140–139 B.C.,[199] confirms a series of monopolies practised at an unnamed temple. These include the setting up of *ta aphrodisia,* a phrase commonly taken to mean "brothels."[200] A possible second example exists in the Fayum.[201] This evidence raises the question of whether the Romans adapted this financial exploitation of prostitution to their new fiscal system.

A tax on brothels figures among a list of taxes from Oxyrhynchus levied on a market held in or near the Serapaeum in A.D. 135/136.[202] The historical background of these taxes is far from clear,[203] but the taxes are classed as "hieratic," which appears to mean that originally they were collected by or for the benefit of priests. These details suggest that Caligula's tax was preceded in Egypt by a system under which some revenues from prostitution went to the temples, and were later assumed by the Romans. The exact status of *hiera gē* under the Ptolemies and the Romans is, to be sure, controversial, which complicates understanding of the historical development of fiscal exploitation of prostitution in connection with temples.[204]

Roman confidence in the Ptolemaic system, enhanced by their own recent improvements in the efficiency of collection,[205] might explain why the prostitute tax, instead of being turned over to the military at some point,[206] continued to be

---

[196] See Toepffer, "Sakralgesetz" 209.

[197] Sherwin-White, *Cos* 234–235.

[198] Wallace, *Taxation* 239, with n. 3.

[199] *P. Tebt.* 1.6.

[200] So *LSJ* and Preisigke s.v. *aphrodisios*; see also the discussion in Bissing, "Aphrodision" (1944). On this papyrus, see Lenger *Corpus* (1980) #47 with literature.

[201] Evans, "Temple" (1961) 236–238, conditionally accepts the presence of prostitution at another temple in the Fayum. For the operation of government monopolies in Ptolemaic and Roman times, see the literature in McGinn, "Taxation" 101 n. 38. *PSI* 9.1055a seems to suggest the existence of municipally owned brothels under the Empire: Diethart and Kislinger, "Prostitution" (1991) 20.

[202] Rea, "Market Taxes" 191.

[203] It seems at one time there was a tax concession farmed out to a contractor or group of contractors, whereas at the date of the papyrus the inspectors or supervisors are themselves collecting the taxes: Rea, "Market Taxes" 192–193.

[204] See Rathbone, "Taxation" 83, who notes that despite the fact some of it continues to be administered directly by priests and that revenues from some other *hiera gē* were called *hieratika,* in practice much of it "seems to have been administered as a type of state land subject to the *dioikēsis.*"

[205] This is the element stressed by Lewis, *Life* 160. A major step was the switch from the salaried officials and tax farmers of the Ptolemaic system to liturgic officials drawn from the local communities, according to Rathbone, "Taxation" 111. Certainly the civilian tax collectors were quite unlike Roman *publicani:* Youtie, "Publicans" (1937/1973).

[206] The date of this change is uncertain, at least outside Rome, where it may have been gradual; see above.

handled by civilian tax collectors, though the Romans presumably could have employed soldiers if they chose.[207] Another explanation is that the introduction of the tax in the form known to us was one of the changes wrought by Augustus,[208] and that this is what served as a model for Caligula, who changed the rate and after a brief period—at least in Rome—the method of collection.[209] A third is that the tax was introduced after Caligula, but that its rate and method of collection were adapted to prevailing practice in Egypt.

Reliance on collection by civilians long after Caligula is confirmed by the small number of receipts we possess for this tax on ostraca—a handful at best.[210] Only three of these certainly concern the tax,[211] while the rest are conjectural. Two of the latter group are from Thebes,[212] one from Elephantine,[213] and one from Apollonopolis Magna.[214]

Another possible reason why the collection of the tax in Egypt was not entrusted to the military is that it was not as profitable, because the tax rate was not calculated per diem. The evidence is admittedly too sparse and uncertain to permit an attempt to determine on what basis the tax payments given in these ostraca are assessed.[215] We have no information on prices Egyptian prostitutes

---

[207] Soldiers assisted civilian officials in the collection of taxes as early as the mid–first century B.C.: Hanson, ''Officials'' cf. Lewis, *Life* 161; Alston, *Soldier* (1995) ch. 5. At least one findspot of ostraca recording the prostitute tax seems near enough to known military installations; see Speidel, ''Garrison'' (1988), and Alston, *Soldier* ch. 2, for troops stationed at Syene-Elephantine.

[208] See now Rathbone, ''Taxation'' esp. 87, 89 (cf. 92, 97): the population registers for the (evidently new) poll tax *(laographia)* were also used for the collection of other taxes, such as the trade taxes *(cheirōnaxia)*. One might regard the tax on prostitutes as a new addition to the latter group of taxes or, at any rate, as connected with the Augustan reform.

[209] Caligula's most dramatic departure from precedent would have been his extension of the tax to Italy and Rome, which would explain the emphasis given by Suetonius to collection of the tax in the capital (see above).

[210] For the surprisingly scant evidence for all manner of sexual deviancy in Egypt, see the remarks of Whitehorne, ''Sex'' (1979). For the evidence on prostitution, see Bringmann, *Frau* 120; Biezunska-Malowist, *Esclavage* 2 (1977) 91–93. On the names and status of the prostitutes listed on the tax receipts, see Calderini, ''Apatores'' 364.

[211] *O. Wilck.* 83, from Elephantine, A.D. 111 (1 dr. for balance of year); *O. Cairo GPW* 60, from the Hermonthite nome, A.D. 170 (4 dr. for balance of year); *O. Berol.* inv. 25474, from Memnonia, A.D. 65 (4 dr. for balance of year). There is also a fragment of an account, *O. Elkab* 196, from Elkab, of uncertain date (the editors suggest first or second century); the amount of the tax, evidently given in drachmas, is lost. For ''permissions'' given by tax collectors to prostitutes, see below.

[212] *O. Wilck.* 504 and 1030: in each a woman pays an unspecified tax for certain months; 504 (9 ob.) is dated to A.D. 112, and 1030 (no amount given) to A.D. 31.

[213] *O. Wilb.* 33 (4 dr. for two months): the tax collector had multiple responsibilities, so that we cannot be certain this is a receipt for the prostitute tax, but the male gender of the payer may be explained as a pimp paying on behalf of prostitutes. A male prostitute as payer is unparalleled in Egypt.

[214] *O. Edfou* 1.171 (= *CPJud.* 2.387) A.D. 164 (3 ob. 2 ch.); on this ostracon the reading of the reference to the prostitute tax is uncertain; see Bagnall, ''Trick'' 6–7, who counters Applebaum's proposal that the payer is a pimp with the suggestion of a shortfall in the tax on prostitution apportioned among the entire population. Pimps, however, are known from literary and legal evidence to have been routine payers of the tax (see above).

[215] Bagnall, ''Trick'' 9–10, rightly asserts that the precise time period covered by the amounts given in the certain receipts (see above) cannot be determined; this leaves only the conjectural evidence, which allows no reliable foundation even for speculative estimates.

charged, which makes any attempt to calculate the rate from these receipts essentially circular. We do not know if the women worked as full-time prostitutes, as a sideline, or only occasionally (this is relevant especially to the third option explored below), nor, of course, can we be sure whether these three receipts are representative or anomalous. In the absence of data on prices, we can only test possible alternatives for the tax rate against hypothetical constructions of prices, a speculative procedure, to be sure.

For the rate of the prostitute tax collected in Egypt, three possibilities emerge: (1) the rate is the amount accepted for one *concubitus* per month; (2) the rate is the amount accepted for one *concubitus* per day, as I argue was true for Rome and the rest of the empire; or (3) the rate was assessed like other *cheirōnaxia,* the capitation taxes on trades assessed at a fixed rate.

The first alternative has its attractions. Though, as we have already seen, a monthly system of collections cannot be considered as decisive evidence for a monthly assessment, it might still be taken to indicate this.[216] With an eye on the amounts given in our three certain examples of tax receipts (1 and 4 dr.: there are two examples of the latter), we can postulate a range of monthly payments of 4, 6, and 8 obols, assuming that these reflect the prices charged for sexual intercourse, prices that appear plausible in the light of the data we have from Italy.[217]

A difficulty arises with the notional prices preserved from Palmyra. The sample of prices given by the Palmyrene tax document has 6 asses, 8 asses, 1 denarius. The hypothetical Egyptian prices are, when converted at the customary exchange rate of 1 denarius to the tetradrachm,[218] 9, 12, and 24 obols, all of which are rather high. The difficulties in measuring the relative values of the two currencies should be noted.[219] Diodorus speaks of the low cost of living in Egypt.[220] Although this statement is "not conclusive evidence,"[221] prices and wages were demonstrably lower in Egypt than elsewhere in the empire during the first two centuries.[222]

It is thus reasonable to suppose that Egyptian prostitutes charged less than their counterparts elsewhere. How much less? The uncertainty of the evidence of the receipts permits us to posit even lower prices, for example, 3, 2, or 1 ob. (= 2, 1 1/3, 2/3 asses, respectively). This falls far below the range of prices given in the Palmyrene document but does not seem impossible in light of the Pompeian evidence, where the most commonly attested price is 2 asses. The *lowest* possible monthly payment/price derivable from the 4 dr. (= 24 ob.) offered by *O. Cairo GPW* 60 is 2 ob. (this amount assumes that nothing has been paid previously for the year in question).[223]

[216] This assertion, it must be noted, is based on evidence that is not certain; see above.

[217] On these prices, see above.

[218] For the exchange rate, see Johnson, *ESAR* 2 (1936) 424–445; West and Johnson, *Currency* ch. 9.

[219] Johnson, *ESAR* 2.433–434.

[220] Diod. Sic. 1.80.5–6. For an attempt to reconstruct a standard of living in Roman Egypt, see Drexhage, *Preise* (1991) ch. 9.

[221] So Duncan-Jones, *Economy*² 9 n. 1.

[222] Johnson, *ESAR* 2.434–435; West, "Cost" (1916) esp. 293–297. See Foraboschi and Gara, "Rapporto" (1976), for an attempt to explain this phenomenon.

[223] The same amount is given by *O. Berol.* inv. 25474. See below for the discussion of the hypothesis that this represented an annual rate.

The objection to this alternative is that even at the relatively low average (especially for the inexpensive prostitute) of four sexual contacts a day, this rate would postulate, for a woman charging 6 ob., an annual income of 1,460 dr., far above any figures we have for the wages paid even skilled labor in Egypt in the first two centuries.[224] On the other hand, if (for example) 3 ob. are collected each month on the daily rate, this would yield too low a price: 1/10 ob. Even at the average of 20 sexual contacts a day, this falls far below what the average unskilled laborer earned.[225]

Even with the third alternative there are difficulties. For example, if this was a fixed capitation tax, why do tax collectors give permissions for special occasions? One answer might be that the prostitute tax was handled in a different way from the other taxes on trades.[226] Some distinctions would have been made on the basis of different incomes, and the taxes graded accordingly, as was done with certain classes of handicraftsmen.[227] This might be expected in the case of prostitutes, who would charge different prices in accordance with their youth, beauty, and skills. Furthermore, a basic rate was perhaps set for each group and provision made for additional payments if income exceeded expected levels.[228]

Monthly collection would have facilitated such flexibility, although it was generally inconvenient for the tax collectors to accept the smaller amounts that even this procedure seems sometimes to have entailed (i.e., anything smaller than a tetradrachm).[229] An annual rate, suggested by the best evidence,[230] would perhaps be the most convenient of all. This must be ranked as the leading candidate for the rate, at least in Upper Egypt, in the absence of further evidence.

Evidently there were occasions when prostitutes could anticipate an above-average income, such as festivals.[231] We know of three instances when prostitutes

---

[224] Even if we assume a price of 3 ob. (= 2 asses), a yearly income of 730 dr. is still relatively high. See the information provided by Johnson, *ESAR* 2.306–322; West, "Cost" 304–314; Drexhage, *Preise* ch. 8 (public performers may form an exception, albeit a sporadic one: 409–411). It is worth noting that on the estimate of Bagnall, "Trick" 12, who argues for the monthly rate, payments "would thus amount to perhaps a few drachmas a month." At an average of four customers per day, a 2 dr. charge postulates a yearly income of almost 3,000 dr. If this (unstated but explicitly tied to the Palmyrene rate of *unus concubitus*) assumption about prices is correct, I do not see why the government was reluctant to take a bigger piece of the action.

[225] Johnson *ESAR* 2.306–322; West, "Cost" 304–314; Drexhage, *Preise* ch. 8.

[226] The long-held understanding that there were regional differences in the rates of trade taxes has recently been supplemented by an appreciation of "a great deal of local variation in the name, amount, and method of payment of this assessment": Hobson, "Receipt" (1993) 79 (cf. 82). I believe that this complex state of affairs lends plausibility to the hypothesis I am advancing, but the tax on prostitutes may have been singular all the same.

[227] See Wallace, *Taxation* 191.

[228] See the system of additional payments in *P. Grenf.* 2.41 (tax lease). On this document, once thought to concern the prostitute tax, see Mitteis and Wilcken, *GC* (1912) 2.2 #183. Gardner, *Women* 253, holds to the older view.

[229] Johnson, *ESAR* 2.428; Wallace, *Taxation* 194. Note that of all the trade taxes listed on *P. Lond.* inv. 1562 verso, the prostitute tax is the only one calculated on a monthly basis (see above).

[230] Nelson, "Receipt" 31, argues for an annual rate, at least for Upper Egypt, pointing out that the three certain examples of receipts show this period of time. Two of these receipts have the amount of 4 dr., which he proposes as the flat annual rate for this region.

[231] On prostitutes traveling from festival to festival in Greece, see Dio *Or.* 77.4, with Lane Fox, *Pagans* (1986) 67. See also Strabo 12.8.17.

were given special permission by tax collectors to ply their trade on a single spec-ified day.[232] The suggestion that such receipts were given to out-of-town prostitutes present for a festival (or some other special occasion) is persuasive,[233] and since no amounts are given in any of these cases, it may be that their purpose was simply to register those prostitutes working in the town temporarily; their tax liability would be adjusted later, if necessary. Thus the need for social control is served at the same time that flexibility is maintained in the tax assessment system.

To be explicit, these "permissions" issued by tax collectors may serve a dual function analogous to that of the *matrices,* maintained by *beneficiarii* and *curiosi* at Carthage, mentioned by Tertullian (see above). If so, it suggests that the duties of military and civilian collectors of the prostitute tax were similar and that the preference for one or the other was dictated by considerations of convenience, in accord with the administrative structure of a given province.

To be sure, the function of "control" attested by this Egyptian evidence may have been separate from that of taxation proper, since the "permissions" do not explicitly stipulate additional payments. In other words, they may reflect a require-ment that prostitutes register with local tax authorities whenever they moved about, even temporarily. The fact that they are made out on a daily basis suggests, curi-ously, that the authorities were perfectably capable of collecting the tax on a daily rate, though paradoxically this information is more helpful for our understanding of the rate of the tax outside Egypt.

It is difficult in any case to reconcile these documents with the primary purpose argued for the introduction of the aediles' list at Rome, which was to guarantee an exemption under the adultery law.[234] For example, *O. Wilck.* 1157 grants permis-sion to a woman "to sleep with whomever you wish" on a particular day. Such evidence suggests how the broader functions of this register were taken up by the system of tax collection after the apparent disappearance of the register, which I argue to have followed the discredit it suffered in the wake of the Vistilia incident.

On the theory just advanced, the rate of the tax is not based on the price the prostitute charged for each sexual act but on a flat rate, supplemented perhaps by increments dictated by a rise in her income. Such supplements might vary from month to month, depending on a variety of factors, including her presence at fes-tivals. This hypothesis, one hopes, will be tested against new evidence in the future.

Why should this rate be preferred to either of the others proposed? It seems more realistic, and therefore more profitable for the state, than the monthly rate *per concubitum,* under which prostitutes paid the price of one sexual encounter per

[232] *O. Wilck.* 1157 Syene-Elephantine: A.D. 111); *SB* 6.9545 = Müller, "GO" (1958) 212–213 (#33, A.D. 142/143); *SB* 4.7399 = Plaumann, "Ostraka" (1920) 219–220: (see 220 n. 1 for improvements to *O. Wilck.* 1157) (Syene/Elephantine: A.D. 144/145). Lewis, *Life* 171–172, observes that temporary registration of transient workers was customary in other trades as well. Possibly these women were part-timers; see below.

[233] Plaumann, "Ostraka" 220; Wallace, *Taxation* 210–211; Bagnall, "Trick" 6 n. 5. Müller, "Os-traka" 212–213, points out that not all of the dates we have can be linked with known festivals; there may have been other suitable special occasions. The practice of prostitution associated with festivals, fairs, work projects, carnivals, and conventions is familiar from other cultures, including our own: see e.g., Rossiaud, *Prostitution* (1988) 7, 63; Corbin, *Women for Hire* 81, 151, 152.

[234] See Chapter 5.

month no matter how much they worked. The argument about profitability, however, cannot be made against the daily rate *per concubitum,* which, it seems, would have brought in much more money than either of the other two alternatives.

The "flat rate with supplement" I propose was perhaps more realistic for prostitutes who were not full-time professionals. Further, the Romans had enough confidence in their Egyptian fiscal administration to prefer this flexible means of calculating the tax. If Egyptian prostitutes made significantly less money than prostitutes did elsewhere, this provides a further explanation for the existence of a different rate from the Caligulan, which was sharply regressive above a denarius (see above).

The tax on trades was at least in part an income tax: "the rates on different trades varied, presumably in accordance with the probable incomes to be derived from them."[235] It might seem instructive to compare the tax amounts given for prostitutes with those we possess for other trades.[236] But the paucity of the data on this tax cautions against using the information to draw any conclusions on the relative economic position of prostitutes in Egypt.

We have come close to establishing that the rate of the tax, like the method of collection, was founded on a different principle in Egypt from elsewhere in the empire. More than one explanation is possible for these differences, though none is inconsistent with the idea, which admittedly lies beyond proof, that Caligula found a tax on prostitutes already existing in Egypt and chose to exploit this opportunity throughout the empire.

That the economic status of prostitutes (or their exploiters) might, under certain circumstances, have been rather high is suggested by another document.[237] This inscription does not concern the tax but lists the amounts due from a variety of persons and commodities apparently transported over the roads between Coptos and the Red Sea; these tolls were used for the maintenance of various services, including security from bandits, designed for travelers along this route.[238]

Among the professions and charges listed we find a skipper in the Red Sea trade, 8 dr.; guard, 10 dr.; sailor, 5 dr.; artisan, 8 dr.[239] Given these rates, the entry of 108 dr. each[240] for *gunaikōn pros hetairismon* ("women for prostitution") is astounding.[241] This is followed by *gunaikōn eispleousōn,* 20 dr. each, and *gunaikōn stratiōtōn,* also 20 dr. each. The former may be "sailors' women"; the latter those of soldiers.

There is agreement on the identification of the soldiers' "concubines,"[242] though not on the sailors'.[243] The translation "concubines" is predicated on the

[235] Wallace, *Taxation* 191.

[236] Cf. those given in Wallace, *Taxation* 193–205.

[237] *I. Portes* 67 (= *OGIS* 2.674; *IGR* 1.1183: Coptos A.D. 90).

[238] See Lewis, *Life* 141.

[239] This list is taken from Lewis, *Life* 141.

[240] This is not explicitly given by the inscription but is assumed by commentators for this group and the two that follow.

[241] Presumably, many of these prostitutes would have been kidnapped and shipped by slave dealers. For the Ptolemaic period, see Pomeroy, *Women* (1984) 146–147.

[242] Hogarth, "Inscriptions" (1896) 27–32; Dittenberger, *OGIS* ad loc.

[243] Hogarth, "Inscriptions" 31, interprets *gunaikōn eispleousōn* to refer to women entering Egypt for the purpose of prostitution but who are independent of a pimp. This view, recently preferred

fact that Roman soldiers and sailors could not marry; since many of them did maintain serious, stable relationships that might produce children, Lewis's renderings of "soldiers' women" and "sailors' women" are to be preferred.

These amounts represent what Wallace identifies as the "principal fee" *(apostolion)*. Each traveler was evidently required to pay a smaller amount for a pass *(pittakion):* the uniform rate for all women is given as 4 dr.[244]

Why was the tariff on prostitutes so high? One view holds that the aim was to prevent prostitutes from beyond the Red Sea from coming into Egypt and the rest of the empire; another, that the tariff was simply based on what the traffic would bear.[245] Given the lack of any evidence that the Roman provincial administration ever displayed a paternalistic concern for the protection of public morals, or that Roman imperial taxation policies were ever, as a first order of priority, directed at any higher social purpose than maximizing the amount paid into the treasury,[246] the second view seems correct. One may conclude from the high rate of the tariff that prostitutes in Egypt, or at any rate their exploiters, were very well off indeed.[247]

To sum up, the evidence on the tax in Egypt shows that the means of collecting the tax in this province differed from that employed elsewhere, with civilian tax collectors in place of the military, and suggests that perhaps a different rate obtained as well. While the quality of the evidence permits no firm conclusions, it is possible to state the results summarily. The rate of the price of *unus concubitus* per day is the least likely hypothesis, followed (in order of increasing probability) by that of the price of *unus concubitus* each month, followed by an annual flat rate perhaps supplemented by incidental increments in some cases.

From Palmyra we have a bilingual inscription dating to A.D. 137.[248] This document records an enactment by the town council clarifying the local tax structure (import/export duties and a variety of other local taxes) and setting up a grievance procedure to settle disputes between taxpayers and local tax contractors.[249] The aim

---

by Bernand, *Portes* (1984) 206, was rightly criticized by Lesquier, and Wallace's emendation, *Taxation* 274 n. 102, to *gunaikōn eispleountōn* (i.e., a reference to "the concubines of the marines of the Red Sea fleet") may be the best solution. The possibility that these women were on their way to some (unspecified) professions other than prostitution cannot be discounted entirely but seems less likely.

[244] Wallace, *Taxation* 274 n. 99, rightly criticizes Hogarth's view that this provision is a reference to the practice of polygamy. The "pass-fee" was paid either at the beginning of the journey or at its end, or on both occasions: Bernand, *Portes* 207.

[245] Most scholars accept the second alternative; see the discussion in Wallace, *Taxation* 274–275. See Pomeroy, *Goddesses* 141, who takes the high rate of the tariff for evidence of the high profitability of prostitution in Egypt; and now Lewis, *Life* 141, 145–146.

[246] See, e.g., the discussion in Andreotti, "Politica" 223–224, 230–231.

[247] Pomeroy, *Women* 130, remarks that the highest prices paid for female slaves, as recorded in the archive of Zenon (third century B.C.), were those paid for prostitutes.

[248] *IGR* 3.1056; *OGIS* 2.629; *CIS* 2.3.3913. Matthews, "Tax Law," is the latest full discussion, with translation of the entire Greek text and the Palmyrene where necessary. Full bibliography in Zahrnt, "Fiskalgesetz" (1986). Line references (Palmyrene references preceded by a P) and translation below derive from Matthews.

[249] The local character of the tax is emphasized repeatedly by specialists: e.g., Matthews, "Tax Law" 158. Jones, *Cities*[2] (1971/1983) 458–459 n. 2, and Drexhage, "Handel" (1982) 27, wrongly take it as a frontier customs tariff. One may draw a comparison with the *octroi* levied upon domestically

was to facilitate commerce and avert future disputes between merchants and tax collectors.[250] Scholars recognize a fivefold division of the text but disagree over the significance of the different sections.[251] The best view is that the section immediately following the decree represents the decisions taken by the town council in 137 after a high degree of discretion had been granted to the local authorities in tax matters, probably under Hadrian.[252] The third section is the now-superseded old law, made in the presence of a Roman governor.[253] It is incomplete (owing to damage to the stone) and summary, winding up with a reference to the new law.[254] The next section is an edict on sureties to be given to the tax collectors; there is no equivalent in the Palmyrene version.[255] The last section consists of a series of regulations appended to the old tariff. These represent the pronouncement of a *legatus pro praetore,* evidently of Syria, identified as C. Licinius Mucianus, governor of Syria in 68–69.[256]

Whatever Palmyra's actual status may have been in this period, there are many indications of strong Roman influence in this document,[257] despite the fact that the Palmyrenes themselves seem both to have initiated the new measures and to be collecting the revenues for themselves.[258] Most important for our purposes is the fact that in a part of the regulations promulgated in 137 there is a mention of a tax on prostitutes that confirms the rate given by Suetonius.[259]

---

produced items as they moved into and out of certain towns in the modern period: Mathias and O'Brien, "Taxation" 631.

[250] For the purpose of the law, see Février, *Essai* 39–42; Drijvers, "Hatra" (1977) 842–843; Matthews, "Tax Law" 157. It seems on the whole to be conservative in relation to the previous tariff (see below).

[251] For the divisions and a discussion, see Matthews, "Tax Law" 174, 175 n. 6. The radically different view taken by Zahrnt, "Fiskalgesetz," of the significance and date of the different sections of the inscription is essentially the thesis of Piganiol, somewhat modified. It remains unconvincing but cannot be treated here.

[252] Février, *Essai* 35–36, 38–39. The dominant view sees Palmyra at this time as a *civitas libera* with autonomy in local tax matters: Seyrig, "Statut" (1941) 171; Matthews, "Tax Law" 162. Drijvers, "Hatra" 842–843 argues for status as a client state. Note that the evident status of Chersonesus as a *civitas libera* did not affect the method of collection. More important than status might have been the fact that Palmyra had no standing garrison firmly attested before A.D. 167: Richmond, "Palmyra" (1963) 50; Rey-Coquais, "Syrie" (1978) 51, 68; Millar, *Near East* (1993) 35, 108 (cf. 84). Some have argued for the presence of a Roman garrison in the mid–first century, though on uncertain evidence: Seyrig, "Statut" 159–160, 169–; Jones, *Cities*² 458–(459) n. 52; Teixidor, "Tarif" 241.

[253] This is Marinus or Marianus, the governor (presumably of Syria) mentioned at P.65. For suggestions as to the identity of this man, see Zahrnt, "Fiskalgesetz" 283 n. 17 (with literature).

[254] At P.68 a short list of taxes on commodities breaks off with the reference "as is written above." See the remarks of Matthews, "Tax Law" 178. Presumably the prostitute tax was thus omitted from record in the old tariff; see below.

[255] Matthews, "Tax Law" 178.

[256] So Seyrig, "Statut" 165–167, followed by Matthews, "Tax Law" 179 n. 28. The last section is thus subsequent to the old tariff, though it has come to be merged with it. For Mucianus's career, see *PIR*² L 216.

[257] See 92–93; P.65; 150–151; 181–186; 194–197. The last two refer to letters of Germanicus and Corbulo that may well concern the entire area: Drijvers, "Hatra" 840 n. 154.

[258] The tax on prostitutes is argued to be an exception below.

[259] At 75–79 in the second section (i.e., the new tariff).

284 Prostitution, Sexuality, and the Law in Ancient Rome

The Greek text here is very fragmentary and must be supplemented with the Palmyrene. Matthews translates: "The said tax collector will exact from prostitutes who receive one denarius or more, from each woman, one denarius; from those who receive eight asses [he will exact] eight asses; from those who receive six asses, from each woman, six asses."[260]

It is worth noting that the extant text does not specify whether the tax is collected on a monthly or a daily basis. Matthews supposes a monthly rate since the taxes that follow in the new tariff are collected on this basis.[261] But these taxes are very different and cannot be compared with the prostitute tax. One reason is that these taxes have no grounding in legislation but are collected "according to custom." Moreover, the section of Mucianus's enactment devoted to the prostitute tax does not appear in the context of these other taxes on trades. They should be regarded as completely independent.

A similar rule appears in the fifth section of the inscription, the settlement made by Mucianus.[262] Here the Greek is all but completely lacking,[263] but the Palmyrene is fairly clear. Again Matthews: "As for the tax on slave girls, I have decided as the law declares: the tax collector will exact from slave girls who take one denarius or more, a tax of one denarius for each woman [sic]; and if she receives less, he will exact whatever sum she receives."[264] It is clear that prostitutes are meant.[265] Dessau is correct when he says that the prostitutes meant here are the slaves of a leno,[266] but one should not draw a distinction in terms of tax liability: the tax is collected from both pimps and prostitutes on the same basis, as the passage of Suetonius makes clear.

Thus we see two steps in a process of clarification. Mucianus has explained the regulation in terms of the old tariff, which in turn followed the original legislation.[267] Some years later the Palmyrene town council in essence followed this procedure but outlined two lower price levels, which Mucianus, perhaps in line with the original legislation, had not specified.[268] Problems in collecting the tax

---

[260] Matthews, "Tax Law" 177. Aside from the word "prostitutes" (on the language here see Chabot, *CIS* 2.3.3913 ad loc., and Matthews, "Tax Law" 180 n. 39), the translation does not differ substantially from that of Cooke, *Textbook* (1903) 325; Levick, *Government* (1985) 91. The text at this point is not controversial.

[261] Matthews, "Tax Law" 177 n. 17.

[262] At P.125–128 in the enactment of Mucianus. This item, like five other taxable objects in the same section (on these see Schlumberger, "Réflexions" [1937] 282), refers to "the law" (i.e., the old tariff), which is not otherwise given explicit mention in this part of the document. There is a chance that Mucianus refers to the original legislation of 40, but this seems unlikely.

[263] On the text see Dessau, "Steuertarif" 517 n. 2.

[264] Matthews, "Tax Law" 180, esp. n. 39.

[265] Cooke, *Textbook* 330; Dessau, "Steuertarif" 517–518; Levick, *Government* 93. Cf. Chabot, *CIS* 2.3.3913 at P.125–128, who depends on a reading from a restored Greek text.

[266] Dessau, "Steuertarif" 517–518.

[267] Seyrig, "Statut" 160, supposes that when Mucianus repeats a stipulation of the old tariff, this tax must have fallen into desuetude. It seems more likely that in the case of the tax on prostitutes its collection had given rise to disagreements, if not public disturbances as we witness at Chersonesus, and that this is what motivated Mucianus's intervention.

[268] I understand these amounts to be stated in terms of Roman, not provincial, coinage. See Mat-

may well have arisen before both of these pronouncements were made.[269] The three amounts given by the council do not mean that these were the only taxable rates for prostitutes under a denarius (though they might indicate a typical range of prices at Palmyra); presumably every price under a denarius was taxed and these are meant to serve merely as guidelines.[270]

The tax was established at Palmyra in the original form it had evidently been given at Rome: a municipal tax, with a rate of the price of one *concubitus* per day, collected by civilian tax farmers. It may have been introduced by the Roman governor who approved the first tariff (Marinus or Marianus). At any rate a *terminus ante quem* is afforded by Mucianus's tenure as governor of Syria in 68–69.[271] Note that at this time the tax is collected by civilians, that is, tax farmers.[272] This may indicate that collection by the military had not begun or had not been extended to the provinces or, more likely, that no troops were available to collect it. In any case, the tax and its rate appear to be both confirmed and entrusted to local tax farmers by the local authorities themselves in 137.

Where did the revenue from the tax go? It is generally assumed that all of the revenues mentioned in the inscription benefited the city of Palmyra exclusively.[273] Certainty is impossible, but I would like to suggest making an exception for the tax on prostitutes. First, there is the identity of the rate with the Caligulan *unus concubitus*; second, unlike the mass of taxes in this document, this one is calculated on an *ad valorem* basis.[274] There is also the general point that since Caesar's transfer of responsibility for collecting tribute from the publicans to the Asian cities themselves in 47 B.C., the Romans seem to have relied on *local* tax collectors, supervised by municipalities, to collect direct taxes for them.[275] This would in turn provide an answer to the obvious question of how the tax was collected in areas where troops—praeto-

---

thews, "Tax Law" 177, and the discussion in Melville Jones, "Denarii" (1971), and MacDonald, "Assarion" (1989).

[269] The introductory decree makes this plain for all the taxes: Matthews, "Tax Law" 157.

[270] It is striking that the amounts decrease from the original denarius to eight asses, or half a denarius, and six asses, or ⅜ denarius; perhaps the lower prices are to be understood as more common for Palmyra. There is no evidence for the view of Wilcken, *GO* 1.217 n. 3, that the government set these prices, as in classical Athens (and the evidence there is doubtful: Böckh, *Staatshaushaltung*³ 404).

[271] This evidence is overlooked by Bagnall, "Trick" (1991) 8, who emphasizes that the Egyptian evidence for the tax begins in the second century, as an argument for its abolition after Caligula. He wrote before the publication of *O. Berol.* inv. 25474 (A.D. 65), which shows that the tax was collected in Egypt before Mucianus's term as governor of Syria. It is safe to assume the same is true of Palmyra and elsewhere.

[272] According to Seyrig, "Statut" 164, in this earlier period, Palmyra was not a *civitas libera* but a *civitas stipendiaria*.

[273] See, e.g., Dittenberger, *OGIS* 2.629 at 326 n. 13; Jones, *Cities*² 458 (459) n. 52. To be sure, the assumption that *civitates liberae* did not pay taxes to the Romans has influenced this argument: Seyrig, "Statut" 164. We know, however, that soldiers collected the tax in the *civitas libera* of Chersonesus (see above). Caution is enjoined in generalizing about the tax liability of towns enjoying this status: Jacques and Scheid, *Rome* (1990) 229–230; cf. Sherwin-White, *Citizenship*² (1973) 175–182.

[274] See above and Teixidor, "Tarif" 238.

[275] See above for Caesar's move and its possible significance empirewide. For evidence on local tax collectors, see Jones, "Taxation" 163 n. 71, 165 n. 83, 182.

rians, regular army, *beneficiarii,* et al.—were unavailable. If my argument holds (and it cannot be any more than a hypothesis, since the inscription says nothing about the destination of its revenues), Palmyra is in this sense far from a ''special case.''

If in fact the Palmyrenes collected the tax for themselves, the decision to retain the rate that Caligula had established can be taken as further evidence of the rate's usefulness. Certainly the revenues from such a tax would have been sizable in a flourishing trade center such as Palmyra.[276] The success enjoyed by prostitution in Palmyra is perhaps confirmed by the price levels given as guidelines in this inscription; they tend toward the upper end of the scale of prices attested elsewhere, above all, Pompeii.[277]

Caligula's tax on prostitution was peculiar in several respects. Its rate was reckoned on a daily basis with respect to the price a prostitute charged for sexual intercourse. Another peculiarity resided in the resort to the military as an agency of collection (even if this was not entirely due to Caligula, he at minimum set an example through his use of the praetorians). Special circumstances dictated changes in this setup, so that, for example, Egypt and Palmyra had civilian tax collectors.

The rate may not have been entirely proof against change. The town council at Palmyra was possibly free in 137 to set a monthly rate if it wished, in derogation of the Caligulan model.[278] And, as we have seen, the Egyptian evidence is difficult to reconcile with the rate of one *concubitus* per day.

There is no reason, however, to believe that the Palmyrenes deviated from their Caligulan model with respect to the daily rate. As for the Egyptian sources, they are sufficiently few and uncertain to inspire caution: any theory constructed on the basis of what is now known is just an *ostracon* away from being demolished. But even if we could with absolute certainty put together a rate for the tax in Egypt that differed from the Caligulan, this does not automatically mean that we should extend the implications of this conclusion empirewide. It is quite possible that Egypt was, at least in this aspect of its fiscal system, a ''special case.''[279]

9. Profitability, Legitimacy, and Social Control

The powerful decide what the poor pay.[280]

—Salvian *Gub. Dei* 5.30

Throughout its history the tax on prostitutes had three major implications for the position of this profession within the Roman economic and social system: profit-

---

[276] Février, *Essai* 62–63.

[277] It is also true that the tax collector was perhaps more interested in the more expensive prostitutes.

[278] The Palmyrene rule is hardly a copy of Caligula's law: for example, we have no trace of the anti-evasion provision mentioned by Suetonius. It is perhaps unreasonable to expect all the details of this evidently long and complex document to have been transferred: the rate is the essential feature and is what is conveyed in the regulations of 137 and in the pronouncement of Mucianus. Both (Palmyrene) versions omit the reference to sexual intercourse evidently in the original.

[279] The phrase is Brunt's, ''Revenues'' 327.

[280] ''Decernunt potentes quod solvant pauperes.''

ability, legitimacy, and social control. As we saw at the outset, the primary motive for introducing and maintaining the tax was the enormous revenue it generated; this return moreover serves as indirect testimony to the wide extent and great profitability of prostitution in the Roman world. As with the high rate for prostitutes in the Coptos tariff, this motive fits in well with Roman taxation policies on a broader level: generally the aim was neither to safeguard morality nor even to encourage commerce through adjustments in the tax system but simply to exact as much as possible for the state treasury.[281]

As for legitimacy, whatever Caligula's own motives, it cannot be denied that, as long as the tax was collected, prostitution was officially legitimized to some extent. At the very least there was a trade-off: by conceding a sort of passive official recognition, the authorities obtained (besides the financial benefits) a greater opportunity to exercise control. After Caligula, the transfer of collection to the army made for not only more efficient collection of the tax but closer surveillance of those who paid it.

[281] Cf. Cagnat's statement on the *portorium* (*Étude* 4); similarly, De Laet, *Portorium* 17–18.

8

Ne Serva Prostituatur

Restrictive Covenants in the Sale of Slaves

1. Public Policy and Private Law

Roman law recognized certain restrictive covenants in agreements for the sale of slaves, covenants that directed a certain disposition of the slave on the part of the buyer but that, when violated, did not void the sale.[1] Although they played a relatively minor role in Roman private law, these covenants have important implications for public policy and for the relationship of policy and the private law system. This is especially true of the restrictive covenant that forbade the buyer to prostitute the slave: *ne serva prostituatur.*[2]

An analysis of the content of these covenants and their treatment by both emperors and jurists reaffirms the accuracy of the distinction traditionally drawn in the modern literature between those covenants that were construed to benefit the original vendor and those that were understood to benefit the slave. But while scholars tend, for the most part, to view the legal regimes on these covenants, especially *ne serva,* as fairly static in nature, I argue that a fundamental shift oc-

---

This chapter is a revised version of my paper "*Ne Serva Prostituatur:* Restrictive Covenants in the Sale of Slaves," published in *SZ* 107 (1990): 315–353.

[1] The latest summary is in Kaser, "Beschränkungen" (1977/1986) 185–186. See also Knütel, *Stipulatio* (1976) 357–361; and esp. Kaser, *RP* 1² (1971) 286, 293, 466, 562; 2² (1975) 339, 394; *RZ* (1966) 355, 361, 366.

[2] For discrete treatment, see Sciascia, "Escrava" (1952/1956) and now Sicari, *Prostituzione* (1991). For the sake of completeness, I mention Sokala, "Effectiveness" (1993 [1994]).

curred in the mid–to late second century, when the legal authorities recognized an independent interest of the slave in the fulfillment of the covenant, which might be defended even against the wishes of the person who imposed it but sought to violate it.

Ne serva is also examined in light of the public policy measures taken by the Romans with regard to the practice of prostitution and the treatment of slaves. No connection with (actual as opposed to prospective) prostitution can be shown, and the concern with the condition of slaves provides only a partial explanation. I argue that the covenant is best understood in terms of a value complex known as the honor-shame syndrome. This complex, common to Mediterranean societies, assigns role and status within the household on the basis of gender. In Rome the male members of the family had the responsibility of protecting the sexual integrity of the women, even, in some circumstances, that of slaves about to be alienated.

2. Four Covenants

The classical law recognized essentially four restrictive covenants in the sale of slaves, all of which in some way directed the disposition of the slave after sale:[3] *ut manumittatur, ne manumittatur, ut exportetur, ne serva prostituatur.* The first two provide for and against manumission, respectively, while the third imposes forced migration on the slave.

The covenants, when violated, did not void the sale,[4] but they created more than just an obligation for the buyer. Because they were effected at the time of conveyance as *leges mancipio dictae,*[5] these pacts (which the sources sometimes refer to as *pacta adiecta,* sometimes as *leges*) had ''real'' consequences, becoming in effect liens on the slave. More than one reason can be put forth to account for the references in the sources to *lex venditionis.* The compilers may have altered many references to *mancipatio* in the classical texts. But if it is correct that transfer in sale of *res mancipi* in the late classical period often took place through *traditio,*[6] the focus of the agreement on the covenant would have shifted to the sale contract itself.

Even with the traditional forms of conveyance, the buyer had to be notified of the covenant at the time of sale, given the potential consequences for sale price. The covenants were then given force in both contract and conveyance. Finally,

---

[3] Four is the number usually given by modern scholars: McGinn, ''*NSP*'' (1990) 316. I am not persuaded that *ne servitutem alterius patiatur* is a separate type: Wilinski, ''Alienazione'' (1974/1975) 330 n. 23.

[4] Peters, *Vorbehalte* (1973) 190, with n. 26. Such covenants were also employed for gifts and other transfers, above all testamentary dispositions, but the same rules did not always apply. There is no evidence known to me for nonprostitution clauses for these transfers; at all events, the focus of this chapter is on sale.

[5] Originally, at least, where they provided for *manus iniectio* and liberty, these pacts would have been *leges mancipio dictae (nuncupationes)* and not *leges venditionis*; see the literature at McGinn, ''*NSP*'' 317 n. 6.

[6] So Kaser, ''Beschränkungen'' 186.

there may have been a development where the *lex mancipio dicta* gave way to accessory agreements on the sale.[7] At all events, there is a strong suggestion that the covenants at some point came to be associated with the contract.

These "real" effects were made operative through one of the sanctions frequently invoked in the covenants, the special provision for seizure, *manus iniectio*.[8] This right to *manus iniectio* was typically exercised at the discretion of the original vendor.[9] Seizure led (probably after confirmation by a magistrate) to the reacquisition of ownership over the slave by the original vendor; this right to reacquire ownership was (eventually) valid against third parties, that is, subsequent purchasers who, knowingly or not, violated the terms of the covenant.[10] The "real" effects are also to be seen in the provision granting liberty to the slave if prostituted. Here too enforcement of the covenant typically depended on the original vendor, and the grant of freedom had to be confirmed by a magistrate.

These points have received little attention, but the first two seem guaranteed partly by the fact that the original vendor became patron of the freed slave.[11] This is not to say that the slave was actually freed by the magistrate: he or she became a Junian Latin upon manumission. The need for magisterial confirmation also suggests a role for the original vendor.[12] Logically enough, the sanction of freedom for the slave appears only with the *ne serva* covenant.

The modern consensus that these covenants originated as *leges mancipio dictae* has made a persuasive case but has not resolved all problems associated with this question. The weakness of the evidence for the early history of the covenants and the frequent interventions of the emperors, which often give the impression of creating new law, even where "logical" extensions of real effects are concerned, have encouraged some scholars to seek a legislative basis for one or more of the covenants.[13] It is perhaps true that the covenants had passed through a stage, accompanied by a debate among the jurists, in which they came to be conceived as contractual in nature, and their real effects had to be asserted or perhaps reasserted

---

[7] So Peters, *Vorbehalte* 7 n. 2 and 93, for the agreements on rescission of sale.

[8] Paul. D. 18.1.56, Paul. 18.7.9; Sev., Ant. C. 4.55.1 (a. 200). No source speaks of *manus iniectio* for *ne manumittatur* (Krüger [rev. Frezza] [1935] 391), although it may have played a role earlier in the history of this covenant. Some sources use a less technical phrase, *ius* or *facultas abducendi,* but nothing suggests that there is any difference between this and the right of *manus iniectio*; see Noailles, *Fas* (1948) 166–167, and cf., e.g., the language of Pap. *FV* 6.

[9] There were special circumstances where the state intervened (Sev., Ant. C. 4.55.1, 2 [a. 200]). But in most cases, exercise of *manus iniectio* must have been at the discretion of the original vendor, as suggested by the use of expressions such as *ius* or *facultas abducendi*: Paul. D. 18.1.56, Paul. D. 40.8.7; Sev., Ant. C. 4.55.1; Alex. Sev. C. 4.56.1 (a. 223).

[10] On the reacquisition of ownership, see Peters, *Vorbehalte* 188; Knütel, *Stipulatio* 357–361; Kaser, "Beschränkungen" 185–186. No source directly attests the need for review and approval by a magistrate, but this seems consistent with what is known of the praetor's role with respect to the different forms of *manus iniectio* under the *legis actio* system; on this problem, see the literature at McGinn, "*NSP*" 317 n. 9; add La Rosa, *Repressione* (1990) esp. 190 n. 198; Nicosia, "*Manus iniectio*" (1994). Such magisterial review would have had the practical benefit of discouraging abuses, an important consideration, given the extreme consequence for the buyer of loss of ownership. No evidence suggests reconveyance was necessary.

[11] Ulp. D. 2.4.10.1 (see below); Iustinian. C. 7.6.1.4.

[12] Alex. Sev. C. 4.56.2 (a. 223).

[13] See the discussion at McGinn, "*NSP*" 318 n. 11.

by imperial legislation and court decisions. Equally, the extreme consequences of these effects, which sometimes produced unfair results for blameless subsequent buyers, may have required an authoritative decision even where the law was clear. The state of the evidence does not allow any firm conclusions to be drawn.

Sometimes a monetary penalty was set forth in a separate *stipulatio*.[14] Like the others, this sanction typically depended for its enforcement on the initiative of the original vendor, who retained, to this extent, a legally protected interest in the fulfillment of the covenant.

These covenants operated, then, as effective restrictions on the buyer's rights of ownership over the slave. They figure among the very few restrictions placed on ownership in the classical law, alongside such institutions as servitudes, usufruct, and pledge.[15] They are unusual for the law of sale itself, since they are not found in the sale of other goods, such as land.[16] Even with regard to slave sale, it is striking that the range of covenants was never expanded to include other professions besides prostitution that might be considered dishonorable or even dangerous (e.g., acting on stage or fighting beasts in the arena).

Theoretically, it might be possible to frame any agreement regarding the slave after sale, at least on a contractual basis. The Romans were evidently reluctant to extend the range of covenants with real effects.[17] The potential of such covenants for creating uncertainty both in the marketplace and in the courts militated against any significant extension of their number. All the same, their somewhat extraordinary nature raises a question that may be stated in the form of a paradox: why was the number of recognized covenants so tightly restricted and why did the legal authorities enforce them so aggressively?

3. Migration and Manumission

Part of the answer may be sought in the historical development of these agreements. Late classical jurists made an important analytical distinction between the covenants that were intended in principle to benefit the original seller *(ut exportetur, ne manumittatur)* and those that were intended to benefit the slave *(ut manumittatur, ne serva prostituatur)*.[18] The origins of the restrictive covenants are obscure and controversial.[19] *Ne manumittatur* and *ut exportetur* are attested as early as Augustus but almost certainly predate him. It is reasonably certain that all four covenants

[14] Knütel, *Stipulatio* esp. 357–361. Monetary penalties framed in *pacta adiecta* were also possible, if controversial (Pap. D. 18.7.6 pr.-1, *Pap.* D. 18.7.7).

[15] On the idea of "absolute" ownership at Rome, see Mayer-Maly, "EV" (1984) 149–151; Birks, "Dominium" (1986).

[16] Violations of agreements in sale concerning the disposition of land by the buyer were punished with a monetary penalty arising out of the unfulfilled obligation and did not provide for the voiding of the subsequent (forbidden) alienation, at least in classical law. So Kaser, "Beschränkungen" 177–179, on two important texts, Pomp. D. 2.14.61 and Paul. D. 11.7.11. Similarly, Schlichting, *Beschränkung* (1973) 15–24.

[17] McGinn, "*NSP*" 319 n. 14.

[18] See McGinn, "*NSP*" 320.

[19] What follows is a brief summary of the history of the three covenants concerning migration and manumission. For more detail, see McGinn, "*NSP*" 320–324.

were at first construed to benefit only, or principally, the original vendor. For the two covenants that continued to be understood in this manner by the late classical jurists, this point seems noncontroversial.

If anything, the interest of the original vendor in these two covenants received increasingly favorable treatment. Thus second-century legislation is argued to be responsible at least indirectly for allowing *ne manumittatur* to stand against subsequent owners.[20] Imperial legislation may also have taken the important step of rendering automatically invalid any attempt by the buyer to violate the covenant. For *ut exportetur,* an important development is registered by an imperial constitution that provides for seizure by the *fiscus* (and perhaps sale into perpetual slavery) of any slave whose master has violated the covenant but whose original vendor had not provided for *manus iniectio* at time of sale.[21]

For *ne serva* and *ut manumittatur,* we can infer that they were originally construed to benefit only, or principally, the original vendor from the obvious fact that these were written by him to gratify his wishes in the same way as the other two covenants. Unlike *ut exportetur* and *ne manumittatur,* they also benefited the slave, but this did not automatically and from the first create another locus of interests.

A decisive point in the development of *ut manumittatur* can be traced to a well-known constitution of Marcus Aurelius, dating to late in his reign.[22] This established that breach of the covenant, when the agreed-upon time period had elapsed, provoked manumission by operation of law *(ipso iure),* with the evident result that any agreed-upon penalty or right of seizure was nullified; the latter could be invoked only as an aid to manumission.

4. *Ne Serva Prostituatur:* History

Although the early history of the *ne serva* covenant is largely unrecoverable, it seems clear that the seller usually framed a penalty in case the covenant was violated, such as freedom or right to reclaim the slave, and/or a money payment. Some jurists understood that, even without a stipulated penalty, the seller had incurred a financial loss at the time of sale through the imposition of the covenant and that this amount represented the seller's interest in case of nonfulfillment.[23]

The sources show that juristic interest in *ne serva* went at least as far back as Masurius Sabinus,[24] whereas the earliest instance of imperial intervention is a judicial decision of Vespasian:

> Mod. *(lib. sing. de manumiss.)* D. 37.14.7 pr.: Divus Vespasianus decrevit, ut, si qua hac lege venierit, ne prostitueretur et, si prostituta esset, ut esset libera, si

---

[20] See McGinn, "*NSP*" 321 n. 19. For exceptional treatment through identification of an interest of masters as a class or even that of the individual slave, see Wilinski, "Alienazione" 325–326.

[21] Sev., Ant. C. 4.55.2 (a. 200).

[22] The *constitutio* emanated from both Marcus and Commodus and so dates between 176 and 180: McGinn, "*NSP*" 322 n. 24.

[23] Pap. D. 18.7.6.1 (see below); Scaev. D. 18.7.10; cf. Treb.-Lab.-Iav. 18.1.79.

[24] Pap. D. 18.7.6 pr.

postea ab emptore alii sine condicione veniit, ex lege venditionis liberam esse et libertam prioris venditoris.

The deified Vespasian laid it down in a judicial decision that if a slave woman was sold under the condition that she not be prostituted and that, if she were prostituted, she would be free, and if she has subsequently been sold by the buyer to a third party without the condition (and was in fact prostituted) she should be free in accordance with the condition of sale and should be the freedwoman of the first vendor.

A slave sold previously under a *ne serva* covenant is resold to a third party without the covenant. Vespasian holds the subsequent buyer liable for breach, which means that he loses the slave. Presumably he would have been ignorant of the covenant's existence, since it was not repeated for his benefit, but the question of his knowledge is evidently deemed irrelevant as far as disposition of the slave is concerned.[25]

The text suggests that before Vespasian such covenants were customarily repeated in subsequent sale agreements and were enforced when violated by granting the slave her freedom. Vespasian's decision might seem unfair to a subsequent buyer who had not been warned of the existence of the covenant. Although he presumably would have had recourse against his own vendor,[26] there is no legal relationship between him and the original vendor, and considerable violence is done to the agreement he has made with his own vendor, not to speak of his property rights.[27] Such inconveniences notwithstanding, the interest of the original vendor[28] is upheld to the extent that his terms are enforced and he is permitted the rights of patron over the manumitted slave.

Is Vespasian simply applying settled law? Certainty is impossible, but the passage might be taken to imply that in the period immediately preceding this holding such agreements could not be enforced against subsequent buyers when they were not restated as part of the new transfer of property.[29]

While the turning point in the treatment of *ut manumittatur* occurred under Marcus Aurelius, the decisive change for *ne serva* evidently was produced by a *constitutio* of Hadrian. We owe our knowledge of this ruling to an enactment of Alexander Severus, which "appears to be purely declaratory":[30]

---

[25] The buyer who violates the covenant loses his status as patron (the position in the case of the original vendor is discussed below). The rule goes further than that for *ut manumittatur,* where failure to observe cost the buyer only certain rights as patron, a cost aggravated if the slave had been purchased *suis nummis* (Ulp. D. 2.4.10 pr.): Waldstein, *Operae* (1986) 201–204.

[26] Perhaps through an action *ex empto* (see Iul.-Ulp.-Paul. D. 19.1.43) or one on *dolus*; cf. Buckland, *RLS* (1908/1969) 603 n. 8.

[27] Freedom was only rarely granted against the will of a master. See the rescript of Pius in the notes below and Boulvert and Morabito, "Droit" (1982) 122. Modestinus's text does not show that freedom followed henceforth by operation of law, as claimed by Wagner, "Freiheitserteilung" (1967) 172, after Mitteis, *RP* 1 (1908) 182 n. 62 ("nach Analogie des Statuliber").

[28] On the motives for imposition of the covenant, see below. Pace Sicari, *Prostituzione* 83, there is no mention of *affectio* in this text.

[29] See above. Pace Sicari, *Prostituzione* 79 n. 27, we cannot be absolutely certain Vespasian is making new law.

[30] Buckland, *RLS* 604 (misunderstood by Sicari, *Prostituzione* 125 n. 2). The reference to the *praetor*

Alex. Sev. C. 4.56.1 (a. 223): Praefectus urbis amicus noster eam, quae ita venit, ut, si prostituta fuisset, abducendi potestas esset ei, cui secundum constitutionem divi Hadriani id competit, abducendi faciet facultatem: quod si eum patientiam accommodasse contra legem quam ipse dixerat, ut in turpi quaestu mulier habe-retur, animadverterit, libertate competente secundum interpretationem eiusdem principis perduci eam ad praetorem, cuius de liberali causa iurisdictio est, ut lis ordinetur, iubebit. nec enim tenor legis, quam semel comprehendit, internmittitur, quod dominium per plures emptorum personas ad primum qui prostituit sine lege simili pervenit.

Our good friend, the city prefect, will grant the power of seizure over that slave woman who is sold under the condition that, if she be prostituted, the power of seizure be granted to him who is entitled to it according to the *constitutio* of the deified Hadrian. But if [the prefect] should find that the vendor has held his own moral principles in such contempt[31] as to prejudice the condition that he himself had set, so that the woman be retained in that base profession, since she is entitled to freedom according to the authoritative decision of that same emperor, he will order her to be brought before the praetor with jurisdiction over cases involving liberty so that a proceeding be instituted. The force of the condition, once it has been set, is not broken because ownership has passed, without the condition be-ing stated, through multiple purchasers to the first owner, who has then prosti-tuted her.

Alexander has simply brought the principles enunciated by Hadrian into line with the procedure observed in his own time. *Interpretatio* and its equivalents are used by Hadrian and other emperors to refer to their own lawfinding.[32] The first phrase suggests that the right of seizure was already well established in Hadrian's day, and that this emperor is concerned simply with details of its operation. It is unclear exactly what is meant by "cui . . . competit," but perhaps he prescribes for cases involving the provision of *manus iniectio* what Vespasian had for those concerning the provision of liberty. That is, *manus iniectio* lies where the covenant has been violated by a subsequent buyer, for whose benefit the covenant had not been re-stated by an earlier buyer upon resale.

Again the question arises as to whether the extension may reasonably be re-garded as an imperial innovation. The number of subsequent buyers was evidently immaterial.[33] All the same, the way in which Hadrian applies this modest principle

---

de liberalibus causis cannot be Hadrianic, as this office dates from the Antonine period at the earliest (it is more probably Severan): Nicolau, *Causa* (1933) 67; Franciosi, *Processo* (1961) 126–127.

[31] Or perhaps "adjusted his complaisance." *Patientia* can refer to behavior repressed as *lenocinium* under the Augustan adultery law; see Chapter 5. Here it shows a more direct resonance with commercial pimping.

[32] *FIRA* 1² 78.20–21 (*philanthrōpoteron hermēneuō:* Hadrian); Marcel. D. 28.4.3 pr. (*humanior interpretatio:* Marcus Aurelius); cf. Ulp. D. 38.17.1.6 (*humana interpretatio:* perhaps Commodus; see Meinhart, "Zeugnis" [1965] 254–255). Cf. Sicari, *Prostituzione* 97–103, 123–130, whose speculations on Alexander's innovations of policy find no support in this text.

[33] Paul. (50 *ad edictum*) D. 18.1.56: "Si quis sub hoc pacto vendiderit ancillam, ne prostituatur et, si contra factum esset, uti liceret ei abducere, etsi per plures emptores mancipium cucurrerit, ei qui primo vendidit abducendi potestas fit." ("If someone has sold a slave woman under the condition that she not be prostituted and if this covenant were violated, he has right of seizure; even if the slave has passed through the hands of several buyers, the original vendor preserves the right of seizure.")

is striking: it is invoked not against a buyer, original or subsequent, but against the original seller, who had himself designed the covenant at the time of sale (presumably at a financial penalty reflected in a lower price). Even more, the penalty inflicted on this vendor is loss of the slave, although his covenant allowed for *manus iniectio,* not liberty.

This is logical enough, insofar as it was otherwise impossible to enforce the intent of the covenant (that the slave not be prostituted) and punish its violator. But the result is that the vendor loses his right to revoke the covenant[34] (which he preserved in *ut exportetur* and almost certainly in *ne manumittatur*),[35] and his interest is denied where this conflicts with that of the slave.

However extreme Hadrian's enactment might seem, subsequent emperors and jurists built on it in working out a regime for *ne serva.* Marcellus (followed by Ulpian) laid it down that if the original vendor prostitutes the slave, she is free and he loses some of his rights as patron:

> Marcel.-Ulp. (5 *ad edictum*) D. 2.4.10.1: Prostituta contra legem venditionis venditorem habebit patronum, si hac lege venierat, ut si prostituta esset, fieret libera. at si venditor, qui manus iniectionem excepit, ipse prostituit, quoniam et haec pervenit ad libertatem, sub illo quidem, qui vendidit, libertatem consequitur, sed honorem haberi ei aequum non est, ut et Marcellus libro sexto digestorum existimat.

> The woman who is prostituted in violation of a condition of sale will have the vendor as her patron if she has been sold under the condition that if she were prostituted, she would be free. But if the vendor, who has reserved a right of seizure, himself prostitutes her, since this woman also receives her freedom, she does so, to be sure, with the vendor as her master at the time of manumission, though it is not right that he enjoy the status of patron: this is also the opinion of Marcellus, in the sixth book of his *Digesta.*

If the slave is returned to the original vendor through *manus iniectio* and this man prostitutes her, he loses his rights as patron,[36] a point confirmed by a constitution of Justinian.[37]

Pomponius promoted the interests of the slave at the expense of the buyer (who knowingly violates the covenant) by denying the latter a claim against the vendor when the covenant has been violated:

> Pomp. (27 *ad Sabinum*) D. 21.2.34 pr.: Si mancipium ita emeris, ne prostituatur et, cum prostitutum fuisset, ut liberum esset: si contra legem venditionis faciente

---

[34] For *ut manumittatur,* as noted above, the *constitutio* of Marcus and Commodus eliminated this right and rendered mere refusal to comply on the buyer's part without effect.

[35] For *ut exportetur,* see Pap. *FV* 6, Pap.-Ulp. D. 18.7.1; for *ne manumittatur,* there is no direct evidence regarding remission in the case of sale. Evidence for a right of the vendor to remit is plentiful with respect to the testamentary disposition of slaves, where it was customary and sometimes necessary for the testator to indicate whether the prohibition was intended to be permanent or not: Buckland, *RLS* 585–586. Given the balance of interests present in sale and the presumable influence of *favor libertatis,* it is difficult to see why the framer of this covenant would not be permitted to remit.

[36] Buckland, *RLS* 70 n. 14, 604 n. 5, holds that the man remained patron, "but with limited rights." The thesis of Querzoli, "Prostituzione" (1993) 403–404, that the jurist's position represents a softening of the approach taken under Vespasian and Hadrian rests on a highly uncertain foundation.

[37] Iustinian. C. 7.6.1.4 (a. 531).

te ad libertatem pervenerit, tu videris quasi manumisisse et ideo nullum adversus venditorem habebis regressum.[38]

Suppose you have bought a slave under the condition that you not prostitute [her] and should [she] be prostituted [she] becomes free: if, as a result of your contravention of the term of sale, she attains freedom, you will be deemed to have manumitted [her], in a manner of speaking, and on that account you will have no recourse against the vendor.

Pomponius's remark apropos of the buyer, "tu videris quasi manumisisse," does not contradict those texts that make the original vendor patron when the buyer has breached the covenant. The point is rather to deny the latter a claim against the vendor on eviction (loss of title).[39] The wording might seem to imply *ipso iure* (i.e., by operation of law) manumission. This would represent a further step beyond Hadrian's enactment, while a constitution of Alexander Severus and other texts (see below) hold for manumission upon review by a magistrate.

Severus and Caracalla forbade the original vendor to sell his right of seizure, declaring that there is no real distinction between such an act and the direct violation of the covenant by the original vendor himself, consequent to his exercise of *manus iniectio:*[40]

Paul. *(lib. sing. de libertat. dandis)* D. 40.8.7: Imperator noster cum patre suo constituit in eo, qui, cum possit abducere prostitutam ancillam, pecunia accepta manus iniectionem vendidit, ut libera esset: nihil enim interesse, ipse abducas et prostituas, an patiaris prostitutam esse pretio accepto, cum possis eximere.

Our emperor, together with his father, laid down that the woman be free, in the case of the man who, when he could have seized a slave woman who had been prostituted, sold his right of seizure for cash. "For it makes no difference whether you yourself seize and prostitute her or you allow her, against payment, to be prostituted when you could come to her rescue."

The part of the text following the colon is in indirect discourse and I suggest may quote the rescript. The language *(patiaris, pretio accepto)* is reminiscent of the *crimen lenocinii.*[41]

This and the holding itself are consistent with Hadrian's directive, which has obviously served as a point of departure. Here too, *libertas* has replaced the *manus iniectio* specified in the covenant itself as a sanction, and the two emperors justify their ruling by equating it to the violation punished by Hadrian ("nihil interesse enim . . ."). The result is equally remarkable, as the vendor has accepted a cash payment, which might have been regarded as his material interest in the covenant, the imposition of which had almost certainly lowered the price of the slave in sale.

---

[38] The objections of Gradenwitz to *regressus* are unconvincing: Gradenwitz, *Interpolationen* (1887) 79–80, 82–83.

[39] See Buckland, *RLS* 49. Buckland, 603 n. 7, takes it to exclude recourse to the ordinary aedilician actions on slave sale.

[40] The rescript belongs to Severus and Caracalla, and this text was written by Paul after Severus's death: Fitting, *Alter*[2] (1908) 96.

[41] See Chapter 5.

Two further constitutions, both of Alexander Severus, make minor contributions to the regime on *ne serva*. One provides for a military escort to produce the slave in question before the competent magistrate, in support of the vendor's attempt to enforce his covenant.[42] The second forbids a specific instance of fraudulent violation of the covenant.[43] Alexander's concern reflects the widespread involvement of the staff of *cauponae* and similar establishments in prostitution, an involvement that receives increasing recognition in the law of late antiquity.

Another text illustrates the extent to which the jurists came to uphold the operation of these covenants even to the disadvantage of blameless third parties:[44]

> Marci. *(lib. sing. ad form. hypothec.)* D. 40.8.6: Si quis [obligatum] servum hac lege emerit, ut manumittat, competit libertas ex constitutione divi Marci, licet bona omnia quis obligaverit, quae habet habiturusve esset. tantundem dicendum est et si hac lege emerit, ne prostituatur, et prostituerit.

> If someone buys a [pledged] slave under the condition that he manumit him, the slave is entitled to freedom in accordance with the *constitutio* of the deified Marcus, even if someone has pledged all his goods both present and future. The same holds true even if he bought the slave under the condition that she not be prostituted and he has prostituted her.

The text enters into a modern controversy over whether a debtor whose goods are under a general pledge may manumit slaves. Wagner rightly argues against Schulz that the debtor can manumit, provided of course that his act is not a fraud against creditors in contravention of the *lex Aelia Sentia*.[45] Both accept the text as essentially genuine, although they disagree over the meaning of the *licet* phrase. The concession presents no difficulties to Schulz, for whom the covenant simply presents an exception to the rule that otherwise manumission in such circumstances is impossible. Wagner explains that the situation of a slave freed under a covenant,

[42] Alex. Sev. C. 4.56.2 (a. 223): "Mulierem, quam ita venisse adlegas, ne prostitueretur, aut, si prostituta fuerit, libera esset, per officium militare exhiberi apud tribunale oportet, ut, si controversia referatur pacto (quod tamen si verum est, libertas mulieri existente condicione competit), agatur causa apud eum cuius de ea re notio est. haec autem lex et nisi in tabulas venditionis inserta sit, quamvis epistula vel sine scriptis facta ostenditur, valet." ("The woman, whom you claim to have been sold under the condition that she not be prostituted or that, if she were prostituted, she would be free, ought to be produced under military escort before the magistrate's tribunal, so that if a dispute arises over the sale agreement (all the same, if the facts are as stated, the existence of the condition guarantees the woman her freedom), the case be heard by the magistrate with jurisdiction over it. Moreover, this condition remains valid, even if it has not been included in the bill of sale and can be shown to have been contained in a separate document sent to the buyer or concluded orally.") The phrase "quamvis . . . ostenditur" is criticized by Guarneri-Citati; see *Index Itp.* ad loc.

[43] Alex. Sev. C. 4.56.3 (a. 225): "Eam, quae ita venit, ne corpore quaestum faceret, nec in caupona sub specie ministrandi prostitui, ne fraus legi dictae fiat, oportet." ("She who is sold under the condition that she not work as a prostitute ought not to be prostituted in a tavern under the pretext of working as a barmaid, in order that the condition of sale not be evaded fraudulently.")

[44] The textual objections have tended to be minor, limited to the title of Marcian's work and the word *obligatum,* which cannot stand: Lotmar, "Erlaß" (1912) 344. (Some insert *non*: Buckland, *RLS* 574 n. 5.) Buckland's more serious criticisms have been answered by Schulz (references to literature in *Index Itp.* ad loc.).

[45] Wagner, "Freiheitserteilung." See also Kaser, *Pfandrecht* (1982) 32–33.

where a duty to manumit is imposed on the owner (and according to the constitution the covenant frees the slave without any action on the owner's part), is very different from that of a slave whose master simply decides to manumit.[46] It is even further removed from the rule regarding individually pledged slaves (who could not be freed without permission of the creditor) and so requires the special emphasis afforded by the *licet* phrase.

The text makes two points. The first part concerns the exception of a slave purchased under a covenant *ut manumittatur* from the operation of a general pledge.[47] Few exemptions were permitted to the property placed under such a pledge.[48] Especially important are those texts that support an exception on the basis of *affectio*.[49] The wording suggests the possibility that the slave was sold either by someone whose goods were under a general pledge or to someone in this situation,[50] although the latter seems more probable.[51] The last sentence applies this rule to the *ne serva* covenant.[52]

The compilers, who joined another text on *ne serva*[53] to this one under the title *qui sine manumissione ad libertatem perveniunt,* understood Marcian to extend the principle of manumission *ipso iure* to this covenant too.[54] But such an extension of the constitution seems an extreme step: the buyer is, after all, under no duty to manumit under *ne serva*. The jurist does not specify freedom as a penalty, though it is easy to read this out of the context, as the *Basilica* scholiast has done.[55] Those passages that provide for review of such cases by a magistrate *(praefectus urbi, praetor de liberalibus causis)*[56] show that there was still a need to claim liberty, which was not true of *ut manumittatur* after Marcus's constitution.[57] Finally, slaves freed under *ne serva* became, Junian Latins, while those freed under the *constitutio* acquired full citizenship.[58] All this suggests that the phrase "tantum dicendum est . . ." is better interpreted as applying only the exemption from the general pledge and not the entire regime of *ut manumittatur* to that of *ne serva*.

[46] One notes also that the caveat on fraud and the *lex Aelia Sentia* is irrelevant to the former case: Wagner, "Freiheitserteilung" 175–176. The interest of the pledge creditor is denied.

[47] Details of such pledges are to be found in Wagner, *Generalverpfändung* (1968).

[48] Wagner, *Generalverpfändung* 125–131.

[49] Note above all Ulp. (73 *ad edictum*) D. 20.1.6, where those items "quae ad affectionem eius [sc. the owner] pertineant" are exempted (Wagner defends the text); and Sab.-Pap. D. 18.7.6 pr. (see below). It seems that *affectio* played a role here too (the *affectio* of the original vendor, not the present owner). This principle helps explain how the rule is applied from one covenant to the other.

[50] Lotmar, "Erlaß" 344.

[51] So Wagner, "Freiheitserteilung" 172; cf. Paul. D. 40.1.10.

[52] I note in passing the unpersuasive assertion of Sicari, *Prostituzione* 89–91, that this rule derives directly from the *constitutio*. A glance at the text shows that the first part of the text does not quote the law, so that the phrase "tantum dicendum est . . ." gives the words of Marcian, not of Marcus and Commodus. Similarly, Querzoli, "Prostituzione" 403 n. 25.

[53] Paul. D. 40.8.7.

[54] As does the modern literature, for example, Georgesco, *Essai* (1932) 169; Wagner, "Freiheitserteilung" 172–175; Holthöfer, "Auslegung" (1967) 166, with n. 73.

[55] See Beaucamp, *Statut* 1 (1990) 124 n. 28.

[56] Alex. Sev. C. 4.56.1 and 2; Ulp. D. 1.12.1.8.

[57] See Alex. Sev. C. 4.57.1 (a. 222), with Buckland, *RLS* 636 n. 4.

[58] Buckland, *RLS* 632.

Given the lack of specific information and the import of the rule laid down by Paul in the next text discussed, we may conclude that Marcian excepted slaves from the effects of a general pledge no matter what the penalty prescribed in the covenant. If it were freedom, she was to be free; if the agreement laid down *manus iniectio,* she returned to the ownership of the original vendor.[59]

Paul offers the most extreme consequence of Hadrian's ruling in the context of a discussion of *ut exportetur,* where the slave has been sold more than once since the imposition of the covenant. He introduces *ne serva* to make a point about the operation of *manus iniectio:*[60]

> Paul. (5 *quaest.*) D. 18.7.9: . . . quod si prior ita vendidit, ut prostituta libera esset, posterior, ut manus inicere liceret, potior est libertas quam manus iniectio. plane si prior lex manus habeat iniectionem, posterior libertatem, favorabilius dicetur liberam fore, quoniam utraque condicio pro mancipio additur et sicut manus iniectio, ita libertas eximit eam iniuriam.

> . . . but if the first vendor sold the slave under the condition that if she be prostituted, she should be free, and a later vendor, that she be entitled to *manus iniectio,* the provision for freedom prevails over that for *manus iniectio.* Of course, if the prior condition had *manus iniectio* and the subsequent one had freedom, it will be said, on the ground that freedom in doubtful cases must be preferred, that she will be free, because each term is attached for the benefit of the slave, and like *manus iniectio,* freedom remedies the harm done.

In case of two conflicting arrangements, manumission, as the penalty more favorable to the slave, is upheld. The effect of this is to deny entirely the interest of the original vendor and to strip him of his property even when he is in no way at fault. In support of this drastic solution the principle of *favor libertatis* (implied by *favorabilius* in the text) is invoked,[61] which, according to Buckland, "hardly justifies what is in effect an act of confiscation."[62] Paul observes that the original condition was imposed not simply in order to seize her but for her own interest, which is equally served by giving her freedom. In fact, as already implied with the word *favorabilius,* manumission better serves the interest of the slave.

---

[59] Ulp. D. 13.7.24.3, which extinguishes the pledge (*fiducia,* in the original) of an *ancilla* where the creditor has prostituted the woman, is of doubtful relevance here. Moreover, the phrase in question is widely regarded as nonclassical; see, e.g., Pernice, *Labeo* 2.2² (1900) 115 n. 3.

[60] De Francisci and the editors of the *VIR* (see *Index Itp.*) make passing objections to all or part of the last sentence, but without justification. Buckland, *RLS* 604 n. 6, criticizes "quoniam utraque . . . iniuriam" on the ground that the slave is declared free under the principle of *favor libertatis,* so that the other reasoning given must be interpolated. It is argued here that the two reasons complement each other.

[61] *Favor libertatis* can be defined as an extralegal social policy deployed as an interpretative canon in matters of law. See the literature at McGinn, "*NSP*" 331 n. 57. Add Manning, "Stoicism" (1989) 1533.

[62] Buckland, *RLS* 71. *Favor libertatis* did not go as far when conflicting arrangements were made in testamentary dispositions. A clear expression of the testator's will to the contrary was sufficient to revoke any previous order to manumit, although freedom held where there was any ambiguity: Paul. D. 31.14 pr., Paul. D. 40.4.10.1; Scaev.-Marci. D. 40.5.50.

The two justifications should be taken together in order to understand Paul's decision. The second line of reasoning remains fairly firmly within the ambit of the contract, in that the decision is based upon the now widely recognized distinction between covenants that benefit the slave and those that do not. In fact, the contract has created a new locus of interests in the person of the slave. This much suggests that broader concerns are at work, an inference that is supported by the first rationale given, which introduces the range of social interests represented by the principle of *favor libertatis*.[63]

Another important source sheds light on both the evolution of policy with respect to the *ne serva* covenant and the motivations that lay behind that policy:

Sab.-Pap. (27 *quaest.*) D. 18.7.6 pr.-1: Si venditor ab emptore caverit, ne serva manumitteretur neve prostituatur, et aliquo facto contra quam fuerat exceptum evincatur aut libera iudicetur, et ex stipulatu poena petatur, doli exceptionem quidam obstaturam putant, Sabinus non obstaturam. sed ratio faciet, ut iure non teneat stipulatio, si ne manumitteretur exceptum est: nam incredibile est de actu manumittentis ac non potius de effectu beneficii cogitatum. ceterum si ne prostituatur exceptum est, nulla ratio occurrit, cur poena peti et exigi non debeat, cum et ancillam contumelia adfecerit et venditoris affectionem, forte simul et verecundiam laeserit: etenim alias remota quoque stipulatione placuit ex vendito esse actionem, si quid emptor contra quam lege venditionis cautum est fecisset aut non fecisset.

1. Nobis aliquando placebat non alias ex vendito propter poenam homini irrogatam agi posse, quam si pecuniae ratione venditoris interesset, veluti quod poenam promisisset: ceterum viro bono non convenire credere venditoris interesse, quod animo saevientis satisfactum non fuisset. sed in contrarium me vocat Sabini sententia, qui utiliter agi ideo arbitratus est, quoniam hoc minoris homo venisse videatur.

If a vendor has sold a slave woman to a buyer on condition that she not be manumitted or prostituted, and after the condition has been violated her true owner should recover title to her or she should be declared free, and a penalty is sued for on the basis of the stipulation, certain jurists hold that the *exceptio doli* will defeat the suit, while Sabinus thinks that it will not. But, logically, the stipulation has no basis in law if the condition was designed to prohibit manumission, for it is unthinkable that consideration was taken of the act of the manumitter and not rather of the effect of the benefit on the slave. But if provision were made that she not be prostituted, there is no reason why the penalty ought not to be claimed and exacted, since he [sc., the buyer] has inflicted outrage even on the slave woman and compromised the affection of the vendor and perhaps his sense of modesty as well. The justification is that, otherwise, without the stipulation, it is an accepted principle that there is an action on the sale if the buyer has violated a condition of sale through either positive act or omission.

1. At one time it was my opinion that a suit on the sale could be brought, because of a penalty invoked upon someone, only where the vendor had a mon-

---

[63] Georgesco, in *Essai* 169 and in "*Manus iniectio*" (1944) 384–385 n. 2 explains the development of *ne serva* itself in terms of *favor libertatis*. There is no denying that this played a role where freedom had been laid down as a penalty, but it is a partial explanation at best and does not account for the solicitude over *manus iniectio* and monetary penalties.

etary interest, for example, he had agreed to a penalty, but that it was not appropriate for a good man to hold that there was an interest of the vendor in the nonsatisfaction of the inclinations of a cruel man. But the opinion of Sabinus wins me over to the opposite position: Sabinus thought there was a justification for the suit in the fact that the person is sold at a discount on account of the provision.

Of all the texts under discussion in this chapter, this has been the most heavily criticized, as might be expected, given its complexity and lack of clarity.[64] In recent years, however, the pendulum has turned in favor of accepting it as genuinely classical, at least in principle.[65] Papinian first discusses two variants of a slave sale involving stipulations. A stipulation sets a monetary penalty in order to enforce either a covenant *ne manumittatur* or one forbidding prostitution of the slave. The jurist inquires as to the result if, following a violation of the relevant covenant by the buyer, the slave has been declared to be the property of a third party or not to be a slave.[66] Can the vendor recover the penalty provided for in the stipulation? Papinian reports two divergent opinions. Some believed that, although the stipulation is valid at civil law, it can be met with the *exceptio doli*. Sabinus disagreed. No justification is given for either view.

Sabinus evidently viewed the stipulation as an independent agreement removed from the question of the validity of the sale contract and conveyance, whereas the others held that the stipulation cannot guarantee a covenant that is legally invalid because imposed on someone else's slave (no more possible here than in testamentary dispositions)[67] or a nonslave.

It is clear that Sabinus and his opponents treat the covenants in a uniform manner, without regard to their impact on the slave. This suggests that in the early classical period the fundamental distinction between the two types of covenant had not yet fully developed.

At this juncture, Papinian himself makes a distinction. The stipulation protecting the covenant *ne manumittatur* is invalid according to the *ius civile*, since the manumission is void.[68] In other words, because the covenant cannot be violated

---

[64] What follows is an abbreviated version of the argument at McGinn, "*NSP*" 332–337, which has a detailed discussion of modern views of the passage.

[65] Most objections to the text derive ultimately from Beseler. See the remarks of Wittmann (rev. Wilinski) (1974); Knütel, *Stipulatio* 357–361 (with references to earlier literature); and Kaser, "Beschränkungen" 186 n. 53. (Doubts about *peti et exigi* can be laid to rest through reference to *petitio exactioque* in the *lex Tarentina: FIRA* 1² 18.6.) All serious criticisms have been answered, though some minor editing of the text is conceded. Daube, "Agere" (1960) 94–102, shows that *utiliter agere* means "to sue usefully, successfully, to good purpose." On the textual history of Papinian's *Quaestiones,* see Wieacker, *Textstufen* (1959/1975) 333–340.

[66] This interpretation of the phrase "evincatur aut libera iudicetur" is to be preferred to that offered by Voci, *Obbligazioni* 1.1 (1969) 258, and Knütel, *Stipulatio* 357–361, who take it as sanctioning, respectively, *manus iniectio* or freedom for the slave in case of breach of *ne manumittatur* or *ne serva.* Cf. Wilinski, "Alienazione" 322, who understands the phrase to refer to manumission of the slave in violation of the contract, accomplished not by the buyer himself but with his collusion. "Evincatur" must refer to eviction by a third party, as elsewhere: Kaser, "Beschränkungen" 185 n. 51 (see also Astolfi, "Sabino" [1986] 542).

[67] Ulp. D. 40.4.9.1.

[68] Papinian's holding, when contrasted with those of Sabinus and the others, suggests that in the early first century breach of this covenant was not automatically invalid: see above.

as a matter of law, the penalty cannot be claimed. The jurist measures the parties' intentions in making the stipulation *(cogitatum)* against the actual result.[69] The stipulation safeguarding the second covenant is valid, for it concerns the act of prostituting the slave and its practical consequences, as opposed to an invalid legal status.[70] The emphasis has shifted to a more exclusive focus on the effect of breach on vendor and slave.

Papinian goes on to consider the effects of *pacta* designed to safeguard the same interests protected by the two stipulations.[71] He was once persuaded that a penalty could only be recovered when the vendor had a financial interest in the fulfillment of the covenant, for example, when he was bound by a similar agreement, backed by a stipulation, to his own vendor. An important qualification is introduced: it is inappropriate for the *vir bonus* to reckon the vendor's interest in terms of the nonsatisfaction of the desires of a cruel man. The *saeviens* is the vendor who imposes a covenant punishing the slave.[72] What this means is that an obligation to a previous vendor is required for a sale agreement imposing this type of covenant to give rise to a penalty, whereas a penalty can be sought for breach of a covenant favoring the slave even without a preexisting obligation. Papinian's earlier opinion[73] turns precisely on this distinction, allowing pacts on covenants that protect the slave to stand but rejecting those aimed at punishment where there was no assessable, quantifiable interest, for example, an obligation to a previous vendor.[74]

It is remarkable that the earlier reasoning is consistent with the result that emerges from the discussion of the two stipulations: that which benefits the slave stands; the other fails. Papinian then introduces a new rationale for treating pacts not protected by stipulations. Following Sabinus, he says that the penalty can be justified in terms of a material interest, discoverable in the lower price paid for the slave.

[69] Consideration of intent in the juristic treatment of stipulations is well established by the late classical period: Knütel, "Pacta" (1976) 202.

[70] Under the circumstances, it would be hazardous to apply the jurist's rationale to the other two covenants. In ordinary circumstances (i.e., where title to the slave was not successfully challenged) stipulated penalties held in *ut exportetur* but did not for *ut manumittatur* in Papinian's day (Buckland, *RLS* 69, 71).

[71] There is a transition in the argument at this point that is easily overlooked. Once *pacta* are introduced, the special problem involving loss of title to the slave following the buyer's breach of covenant disappears from view. This transition is aided by Papinian's emphasis on the effects of breach on the slave over the legal claims of buyer and seller and perhaps by the editorial work of the compilers.

[72] As seen, in Papinian's day automatic invalidity of breach of *ne manumittatur* canceled the penalty and thus the vendor's "interest" in nonfulfillment. It remained of course in *ut exportetur*. The jurist's language might seem too strong to refer to the vendor, who had (after all) a widely recognized interest at stake, but is consistent with Papinian's marked hostility to such covenants.

[73] This earlier reasoning is reported in the text that follows in the *Digest*, Pap. D. 18.7.7, from book 10 of the *Quaestiones*. See Wilinski, "*Aestimatio*" (1972) 444–445, with literature.

[74] Note the final phrase of D. 18.7.7: "enimvero poenae non irrogatae indignatio solam duritiam continet." Under the Severans, as Ulpian's commentary on the *epistula ad Fabium Cilonem* (see below) makes clear, the legal system was charged to protect slaves from *duritia* (the word is defended by Wilinski, "*Aestimatio*" 448).

This reasoning would seem to permit a claim in cases where Papinian previously held the penalty invalid because the covenant was imposed for morally objectionable motives.[75] But even if we accept this point, its implications are limited. First, if stipulated penalties in *ne manumittatur,* just as in *ut manumittatur,* could not be collected because these covenants were effected by operation of law, making nonfulfillment impossible (see above), the same must be true of pacts.

This leaves only *ut exportetur* and *ne serva.* The sale price is likely to have been lowered chiefly by those covenants that benefited the slave. All of the covenants infringed upon the buyer's ability to dispose of his property, but the responsibility to manumit or not to prostitute perhaps constituted more of a burden in economic terms than the duty to deny freedom or to compel migration.

Given that this is a sale, the price presumably is understood to reflect the estimation made by both parties of the slave's value. All the same, Sabinus's reasoning suggests he saw the covenant as diminishing the intrinsic value of the slave; that is, it objectively lowered this value. Papinian's earlier view refused to acknowledge this, regarding the effect of the agreement as limited to the interests of the parties to the sale.

If the difference in price were negligible in the two latter cases, a distinction between the two types of covenant would emerge as a practical consequence, although, of course, the reasoning does not turn on this. This argument is supported by the fact that the two rationales are surely not meant to be mutually exclusive: one used to be able to sue (in Papinian's view) only if bound to a previous vendor—unless the covenant benefited the slave; now the difference in price will ground a penalty where there is no preexisting obligation. So the phrases "non alias," "in contrarium," should be understood: Papinian has not rejected the earlier rationale. Instead he admits a second one, rejecting only his previous view that there was only one rationale possible. Of course, there would be a difference in price even in a subsequent sale, but since the vendor presumably himself bought the slave at a lower price, this will not ground an independent *interesse.*

Alternatively, one can simply assume that the point about the difference in price only applied where the covenant benefited the slave. There is no direct support for this in the text, but it may be how the compilers understood D. 18.7.6.1 (together with D. 18.7.7). The result would be that the *pactum* that benefits the slave gives rise to a penalty that otherwise cannot be collected.

There is a visible continuity between the two rationales on the level of language. Papinian's use of the word *homo* to describe vendor and slave seems to place deliberate stress on their common humanity.[76] The appearance of the same word in the phrase describing the rationale for the new opinion suggests that we

[75] So Astolfi, "Sabino" 541.

[76] This is most striking in the famous phrase of D. 18.7.7: "cum beneficio adfici hominem intersit hominis." See also "poenam homini irrogatam" in D. *eod.* 6.1 (the vendor) and the next note. Cf. above all Sen. *Ben.* 3.22.3: "Quid ergo? beneficium dominus a servo accipit? immo homo ab homine" (see also *Clem.* 1.18.2). This passage has relevance also for the question of the responsibility of the urban prefect regarding mistreatment of slaves by their masters; see below. See also Giliberti, "*Beneficium*" (1984) 1847.

should regard this as a means to an end.[77] On this view Sabinus's discovery of the vendor's interest in the difference in price paid for the slave presented Papinian with a more concrete and convincing way of achieving the same goal attempted by his earlier rationale for *pacta.*

In sum, the passage yields a variety of rationales but a uniformity of result. With regard to stipulations, Papinian measures the intentions of the contracting parties against the actual effects of breach. The result, that covenants favoring the slave are privileged, is consonant with that produced by the earlier rationale on pacts. According to this, the vendor who imposed a covenant unfavorable to the slave could only sue in the given circumstances if bound through stipulation to a previous vendor.[78] The result is again a privileging of the covenant that benefits the slave, which is compatible, as we have seen, with the result that emerges from the point about the difference in price.

A single thread regarding *ne serva* runs through the passage. Contravention of this covenant, regardless of whether it is protected by stipulation or *pactum,* produced negative consequences for both the slave and the vendor, consequences that underlie the jurist's reasoning.[79] Two points must be emphasized. First, the coincidence of interest between slave and original vendor is to all appearances decisive in achieving a result favorable for both. Second, the decisions taken are not grounded in "philosophy" or "sentiment" but in considerations of private interest and public policy.[80]

5. *Ne Serva* and Prostitution

It is tempting to explain the regime surrounding *ne serva* in the context of Roman public policy toward prostitution, insofar as this appears to represent the high-water mark in the protective regulation of the profession in classical times. Prostitutes and pimps were otherwise subject to a variety of policy measures negative in intent if limited in their scope, such as the marriage and adultery laws, as well as Caligula's tax.

---

[77] D. 18.7.6.1: "quoniam hoc minoris homo venisse videatur."

[78] The differences between the two rationales should not be exaggerated. Contrast "pecuniae ratione" with "vindictae ratione" (D. 18.7.7); compare "de effectu beneficii" with "beneficio adfici hominem" (D. 18.7.7).

[79] The slave is treated with *contumelia,* and the *affectio* and perhaps even the *verecundia* of the original vendor are slighted. Against the criticisms of Beseler and others, Knütel argues that, although the *Affektionsinteresse* was not universally recognized by the classical jurists, it did play an important role precisely in the area of slave sale: Knütel, *Stipulatio* 360, esp. n. 26 (with literature, above all Raber, "*Pretium*" [1972]. Add Treggiari, "Sentiment" (1979). (Earlier scholars tended to view this recognition as the work of the compilers.)

[80] See the defense of the phrase "affectionis ratione" in D. 18.7.7 offered by Wilinski, "*Aestimatio*" 444. Wilinski rightly objects to the reading of "Christian" or "Byzantine" influences into these texts, seeing more practical considerations at work, but goes too far in excluding all moral concerns; see "*Aestimatio*" 448 and previous note.

The juristic decisions and imperial interventions relating to the *ne serva* covenant stand apart from all of this. This is first because we have no measures designed to benefit actual prostitutes or pimps (as *ne serva* protects women vulnerable to prostitution)[81] and also because, despite the expanding scope of the *ne serva* regime, its practical consequences were limited, affecting what must have been at all times a fairly small number of women compared with those who were actually working as prostitutes.[82] This argument is supported by a text of Callistratus, where he releases a manumitted prostitute from the responsibility of furnishing *operae* in the form of commercial sex.[83] The disqualification of such services as *operae* does not at all imply that the woman was somehow exempted from the practice of prostitution, as the text itself concedes. This holding might in fact have discouraged some owners from manumitting slave prostitutes and potentially depriving themselves of an economic advantage. The measure hardly seems designed to benefit the women who formed its object.

No attempts were made to discourage the practice of female prostitution or to improve the circumstances of its practitioners until the limited and to all appearances ineffectual measures taken by the Christian emperors of late antiquity directed against pimping.[84] It was Justinian who forged a link between this legislation and the regime on the *ne serva* covenant:

Iustinianus C. 7.6.1.4 (a. 531): Similique modo si quis ancillam suam sub hac condicione alienaverit, ne prostituatur, novus autem dominus impia mercatione eam prostituendam esse temptaverit, vel si pristinus dominus manus iniectionem in tali alienatione sibi servaverit et, cum ad eum fuerit reversa, ipse ancillam prostituerit, ilico in libertatem Romanam eripiatur et, qui eam prostituerit, ab omni patronatus iure repellatur. qui enim ita degener et impius constitutus est, ut talem exerceret mercationem, quomodo dignus est vel ancillam vel libertam eam habere?

In like manner, if someone has alienated a slave woman under the condition that she not be prostituted, but the new owner, through a wicked commercial transaction, has attempted to put her to prostitution, or if her former owner has preserved for himself *manus iniectio* in this transfer of ownership, and, after she had returned to him, he himself prostituted the woman, let her be granted full Roman citizenship forthwith and let him who prostituted her be deprived of every privilege of a *patronus*. After all, is there anyone of such degenerate and wicked character

---

[81] This is consistent with Hadrian's measure forbidding the sale of slaves to pimps (as well as to *lanistae*) without justification, reported at *HA Hadr.* 18.8, if this notice can be trusted. For an optimistic assessment, see Bauman, "Resumé, *HA*" (1977). For other sources that appear to support the existence of such a measure, see Marci. D. 18.1.42; Mod. D. 48.8.11.1–2.

[82] Beyond this, the covenants cannot have been easy to enforce: Brunt (rev. Strasburger) (1979) 445; Treggiari, "Women as Property" (1982) 21. For enthusiasm as to their efficacy, see Sicari, *Prostituzione* 134, 136 n. 22, 139.

[83] Call. D. 38.1.38 pr. See Chapter 9.

[84] See Constantius CTh. 15.8.1 (a. 343) (noteworthy as an imperial intervention in slave sale); Theod., Valent. CTh. 15.8.2 (a. 428) (= C. 1.4.12 = C. 11.41.6); Nov. Theod. 18 (a. 439); Leo C. 1.4.14 (a. 457–467) (= [?] C. 11.41.7). Cf. *Tit.* 13.1–2; Constantinus C. 5.27.1 (a. 336).

that he ply a trade of this kind and yet is worthy to have the woman either as his slave or his freedwoman?

The constitution, which abolished Junian Latinity, enumerates those cases where freed slaves formerly eligible for this status are now to be made full citizens.[85] Those slaves who owe their freedom to the contravention of a *ne serva* agreement (this text is our only information that in classical law they became Junian Latins)[86] are grouped with those who, after being abandoned by their masters because they were ill, were granted Latin status by Claudius.[87] The legislator implies that an identical motive inspired change in both cases: a reluctance to see the ex-slave's property pass to the malfeasor at time of death.

It is not easy to take the full measure of the information this text supplies about Junian Latinity. We might conclude that one of Justinian's predecessors had laid down this status for slaves freed upon violation of a *ne serva* covenant. Or perhaps an emperor established this status for *all* ex-slaves who had worked as prostitutes. We can say with certainty that prostitutes do not figure among those types condemned to the status of *dediticii,* as Gaius lists them, which is significant if we can properly assume that this list is complete.[88]

The phrase *impia mercatio* and the entire last sentence stand in evident contrast to the classical texts, which lack the moralizing tone. Such language is not just rhetoric, for Justinian, in the tradition of Christian legislators, viewed prostitution or at least pimping as an activity worthy of condemnation in its own right.[89] This development has its own importance, but aside from the matter of citizen status, the substance of the legal regime regarding such covenants remains unaltered.

6. *Ne Serva* and Slavery

Ne serva can be better understood in the context of the development of Roman public policy in the area of master-slave relations. Recent scholarship on Roman slavery has suggested the need for a redefinition of the traditional explanation of humanitarian tendencies current in the high empire as a motivation for the trend toward better treatment of slaves.[90] One might note that if the political and

---

[85] On Junian status, see Sherwin-White, *Citizenship*[2] (1973) 328–331; Lemosse, "Affranchis" (1994).

[86] The text, while it deals chiefly with the disposition of a slave sold under a penalty of manumission in case of violation, also treats the special case where the original vendor, who has exercised a penalty of *manus iniectio,* himself prostitutes the slave. It is therefore consistent with the holdings of Hadrian and Ulpius Marcellus discussed above.

[87] Suet. *Claud.* 25.2; Mod. D. 40.8.2.

[88] Gaius 1.13–14. On the questions of policy at work in this classification, see Treggiari, *Freedmen* (1969) 237–238; Mette-Dittmann, *Ehegesetze* (1991) 194.

[89] The rule sits uneasily with the measures taken by Theodosius II and Leo I forbidding the prostitution of slaves, which are reproduced in the *Codex Iustinianus.* See also Iustinianus C. 6.4.4.2 (a. 531), which shows a broader, evidently prior rule. For a discussion of the problem, see Beaucamp, *Statut* 1.127.

[90] This is true of scholars with such divergent views as Wilinski, "*Aestimatio*"; Williams, "Indi-

legal authorities really did have at heart the interests of slave women sold under this covenant, it remains difficult to explain why similar protection was not granted to those even less fortunate, for example, to slave prostitutes themselves.

Of course, Roman slave law was designed chiefly for the benefit of the masters,[91] a principle much in evidence in those areas where, as with the *ne serva* covenant, the rules of the private law system intersected with public policy concerns. The interests of the class of masters did not always coincide with those of individual masters, so that limits were placed on the latter. A well-known rescript of Antoninus Pius makes this clear: "It is true that the power of [individual] masters over their slaves ought not to be infringed upon and that no one should be deprived of his rights, but it is in the interest of masters [in general] that relief against cruelty, starvation, or intolerable abuse should not be denied to those who with good grounds seek assistance."[92] The rights of individual masters over their slaves are positively asserted but at the same time subordinated to the interests of the masters as a class or group,[93] in case of conflict. The tension between the two is perhaps nowhere else so strikingly portrayed.[94]

In similar contexts the reference to the interests of the class of masters is replaced by references to the public interest or the interest of the state. Justinian, in introducing Pius's ruling, remarks "it is in the common interest that no one abuse his property."[95] Ulpian declares the grant of a hearing to a slave in cases involving legal recognition of children to be in the interest of both the slave and the public good.[96] Elsewhere the same jurist, apropos of slave testimony under the *SC Silanianum,* holds that slaves acquired in sale under a covenant *ne manumittatur* are to be freed "because it is in the common good."[97] In the matter of *libelli famosi,* he also holds that slaves are to be heard and rewarded for their testimony, since this serves the *publica utilitas.*[98] At times the tension between the interest of

---

viduality" (1976); Bradley, *Slaves and Masters* (1987) [see now *Slavery* [1994]); Watson, *Slave Law* (1987). Representative of the older view is Sciascia, "Escrava" (1952/1956). On *humanitas* and its literature, see Wieacker, "OW" (1977/1983) 177, 192, 196–198; Bauman, "*Leges*" (1980) esp. 173–218; Palma, *HI* (1992).

[91] See Watson, *Slave Law* esp. 1–2, 127–129. For a tendentious criticism of this (rather obvious) point, see Sicari, *Prostituzione* 102–103 n. 6, who seems to believe that Roman slave law was designed chiefly for the benefit of the *slaves.* Note the remarks of Querzoli, "Prostituzione" 404.

[92] Inst. 1.8.2 = Ulp. (8 *de off. procons.*) D. 1.6.2 = Ulp. *Coll.* 3.3.1–3; cf. Gaius 1.53. I have translated only the most pertinent section of the *Collatio* text. Ulp. *Coll.* 3.3.2: "dominorum quidem potestatem in suos servos inlibatam esse oportet nec cuiquam hominum ius suum detrahi: sed dominorum interest, ne auxilium contra saevitiam vel famem vel intolerabilem iniuriam denegetur his qui iuste deprecantur." See Dell'Oro, *Libri* (1960) 172–173.

[93] So Williams, "Individuality" 77; Watson, *Slave Law* 121.

[94] For a general discussion of this issue, see Birks, "Dominium" 24.

[95] Inst. 1.8.2: "expedit enim rei publicae, ne quis re sua male utatur." For a different emphasis, see Gaius 1.53, who refers to Pius's *constitutio* without quoting it; see the discussion in Bonini, *Libro* (1973) 153–160.

[96] Aristo-Ulp. D. 25.4.1.13.

[97] Ulp. (50 *ad edictum*) D. 29.5.3.15: "quod in commune utile est."

[98] Ulp. D. 47.10.5.9–11.

an individual owner and a more general interest is simply implied, as in the passage of Gaius just mentioned.[99]

The seriousness with which this principle was taken is well illustrated by the procedure employed to remedy violations of the *ne serva* covenant. The relevant constitutions of Alexander Severus show that prompt, firm action at the very highest levels could be expected.[100] Another text shows that imperial concern with this covenant went beyond the construction of a legal regime and saw to its enforcement:[101]

> Ulp. *(lib. sing. de off. praef. urbi)* D. 1.12.1.8: Quod autem dictum est, ut servos de dominis querentes praefectus audiat, sic accipiemus non accusantes dominos (hoc enim nequaquam servo permittendum est nisi ex causis receptis), sed si verecunde expostulent, si saevitiam, si duritiam, si famem, qua eos premant, si obscenitatem, in qua eos compulerint vel compellant, apud praefectum urbi exponant. hoc quoque officium praefecto urbi a divo Severo datum est, ut mancipia tueatur ne prostituantur.

> Moreover, the statement that the prefect should grant a hearing to slaves lodging complaints against their masters is one we should accept in this sense: not that the slaves are making accusations against their masters (since this is not at all to be permitted to a slave except in specified cases) but if they should make their appeal with due modesty, if they should set forth before the city prefect a case of cruelty or harshness or starvation whereby their masters were oppressing them, or obscenity—performance of which their masters had compelled or were compelling. This responsibility too was given to the city prefect by the deified Severus, in order that he safeguard chattels from prostitution.

Septimius Severus gave his urban prefect Fabius Cilo a set of detailed instructions that amounted to a charter for the office.[102] Ulpian interprets the part of the charge regarding slaves' complaints against bad treatment by their masters in line with the long-standing practice of the *praefectura urbi*.[103]

---

[99] Gaius 1.53. And in two other imperial rescripts, one of Hadrian, the other of Pius, given at Ulp. *Coll.* 3.3.4–6. Discussion in Marotta, *Sanxit* (1988) 327–330, with literature.

[100] The direct involvement of the *praefectus urbis* and the *praetor de liberalibus causis* is commanded, and a military escort for the woman provided for: Alex. Sev. C. 4.56.1 and 2. Whether these constitutions translated into effective protection for such women is another matter; see above.

[101] Only Beseler (*Index Itp.* ad loc.) has criticized this text, objecting to "hoc . . . receptis" on the ground that the word *nequaquam* is not classical.

[102] Cilo was prefect from as early as 204 to the end of Severus's reign: *PIR*² F 27. On the evolution of the prefect's role as senior imperial appointee, see Millar, *Emperor* (1992) 338–341. On his criminal jurisdiction, see Mantovani, "Competenza" (1988), who takes a very conservative line (for a discussion of the date—perhaps overly cautious—of the *epistula*, see 219–220); cf. De Robertis, "Repressione" (1937/1987) 39–69; Vitucci, *Praefectura* (1956) esp. 61–62, 72–81. On prefects and jurists, see Schiller, "Jurists" (1953) esp. 71–73 and 96–97.

[103] The urban prefect had been hearing slaves' complaints about their masters' *saevitia, libido,* and *in praebendis ad victum necessariis avaritia* at least since Nero's day, to judge from Sen. *Ben.* 3.22.3: Griffin, *Seneca* (1976) 269–270, 460–461; Giliberti, "*Beneficium*" 1857–1858. Pius evidently extended the practice to provincial governors (in the rescript quoted above), and Severus perhaps regularized— or at any rate spelled out in detail—its procedure at Rome, adding repression of the abuse of the *ne serva* covenant to the prefect's charge.

The limited protection afforded slaves under this mandate is consistent with the accepted principle that slaves could bring evidence against their masters only in certain specially defined circumstances.[104] The mid– to late second century witnessed a growing tendency to allow slaves to complain of harsh or unfair treatment by their masters. The rescript of Pius quoted above is one example: officials were to take cognizance of slaves who had fled from their abusive masters and claimed the right of asylum. In some cases actual accusations were allowed. Marcus and Verus permitted slaves bought *suis nummis* but not freed to approach the urban prefect or provincial governor.[105] Marcus and Commodus allowed slaves denied their testamentary freedom because of a suppressed will to make a formal accusation against their masters under the *lex Cornelia de falsis.*[106]

Significant is the qualification given in the principal text that slaves must approach the magistrate *verecunde,* that is, with due respect for the social dignity of their masters and of the prefect and his court. Such behavior no doubt contributed to the credibility of their case.[107] The text is a commentary on a preceding passage, which all but reproduces the words of the *epistula:* "[The urban prefect] is to give a hearing to slaves making complaints about their masters when they have taken refuge at [imperial] statues, for instance, those who have paid with their own money for their manumission."[108]

The last phrase in the principal text must refer to the enforcement of the *ne serva* covenant in sale. I write "must" advisedly. The wording has Severus enjoin an outright ban on the prostitution of slaves, to be enforced by the urban prefect.[109] Not surprisingly, this is the way moderns typically understand the rule.[110] But this view is not plausible. The great number of contemporary and subsequent legal sources that discuss prostitution neither mention such a ban nor presuppose its existence. This includes most of the evidence for the *ne serva* covenant given in this chapter. It is hard to see the need for a covenant if the urban prefect was supposed to discourage the prostitution of slaves outright. Two scholars have noticed the difficulty and attempted to overcome it. Robinson proposes that the ban concerns only slaves who were unwilling.[111] Sicari suggests that the prefect was instructed, not to prohibit the prostitution of slaves, but to exercise "a deliberate 'watchfulness' in protecting slaves from being prosti-

---

[104] On these restrictions, see Liebs, "Schutz" (1980); Schumacher, *Servus Index* (1982).

[105] Marci. D. 40.1.5 pr.

[106] An unusual move: Liebs, "Schutz" 180; Schumacher, *Servus Index* 210.

[107] Mayer-Maly, "*Verecundia*" (1988) 383, understands the word as "glaubwürdig." On the Stoic content of the passage, see Mayer-Maly, "*Verecundia*" (a comparison with Sen. *Ben.* 3.22.3).

[108] Ulp. *(lib. sing. de off. praef. urbi)* D. 1.12.1.1: "Servos qui ad statuas confugerint, vel sua pecunia emptos ut manumittantur, de dominis querentes audiet." See Mantovani, "Competenza" 203 n. 90. Compare Ulpian's introduction to the rescript of Antoninus Pius, which is translated above in the text.

[109] Given the state of the text, it is hazardous to affirm with Mantovani, "Competenza" 208 n. 97, that this provision derives from a source other than the *epistula ad Fabium Cilonem.* Similarly now, and at great length, Sicari, *Prostituzione* 141–149.

[110] See Mommsen, *Staatsrecht* 2.2³ (1887/1969) 1064 n. 5; Sturm, "Quod datur" (1986) 281 n. 2; Dalla, *Venus* (1987) 2.

[111] Robinson, "Slaves" (1981) 221–222, 242.

tuted.''[112] Neither solution is consistent with the Latin of the principal text—hardly an absolute objection, in my view, since the same is true of my own hypothesis. But neither theory will stand against the difficulties that each encounters in the legal and literary evidence for this period. One cannot suppose that the ban was never enforced or was valid for only a short time: why should Ulpian mention it in either case?[113]

A particularly interesting piece of evidence suggests that Severus had no interest in forbidding the prostitution of all slaves or even just unwilling ones. In 197 Tertullian complains that in the context of an outbreak of persecution, a Christian woman has been compelled to prostitution.[114] This is the first certain recorded instance of a practice that recurs repeatedly over the third and early fourth centuries.[115]

This persecution of 197 was a local one,[116] and there is no evidence to link Severus directly with the enforced prostitution of Christians. This hardly signifies, however, that the measure contradicted the emperor's wishes or offended his sense of propriety.[117] We are not informed of the status of the woman condemned ''ad lenonem'' at Carthage, but this hardly matters.

The incident at Carthage has a larger significance for *ne serva*. If some slave women might be rewarded for their loyal service through exemption from forced prostitution through imposition of the covenant, others might be punished for their failings through installation in a brothel. We have a glimmer of what might be described as the covenant's ''evil twin'': a practice perhaps more widespread as a private form of punishment than the sources allow us to see.[118]

The principal text implies that slaves by themselves could appeal for redress against the violation of the covenant, which may have been true, particularly where the original vendor himself was at fault; otherwise, he would be the logical choice to enforce the covenant and the only one entitled to *manus iniectio*.

There is perhaps an irony in the fact that in the case of the *ne serva* covenant, the interest of the class of masters or, conceivably, of the state is identified with the interest of the female slave, a figure very low in terms of status. The real concern was that the system operate as safely and efficiently as possible. Certain benefits conferred on slaves, or what might be described better as the manipulation of such benefits by their masters, served this purpose. Owners used the rewards of family life and manumission, as well as the allocation of slave *peculia,* as a means of control.[119] Gratuitous interference in this system of rewards, like the administration of gratuitous punishment by individual owners, spelled trouble for the sys-

[112] Sicari, *Prostituzione* 137–158. (149–[150] n. 36: ''una tendenziale ''attenzione'' per la tutela degli schiavi dalla prostituzione'').

[113] The *liber singularis de officio praefecti urbi* was written during the sole reign of Caracalla at the earliest: Fitting, *Alter*² 120.

[114] Tert. *Apol.* 50.12.

[115] See the literature given at McGinn, ''*SC*'' (1992) 277 n. 20.

[116] Schwarte, ''Christengesetz'' (1963) 195 (cf. 199).

[117] It is reasonable to suppose that Tertullian, who is interested in separating Severus from the brutal actions of his persecuting governors, might have made something of this were it true. To be sure, Severus himself is likely to have persecuted Christians: Dal Covolo, *Severi* (1989) 42–43.

[118] *HA Hadr.* 18.8; Ulp. D. 13.7.24.3.

[119] Bradley, *Slaves and Masters* esp. chs. 2, 3; Watson, *Slave Law* 95.

tem itself. There is plenty of evidence that the legal and political authorities were, by the early second century at any rate, not slow to intervene.

For the *ne serva* covenant on sale, this meant that a private agreement designed to benefit a figure low in the social and legal hierarchy received protection at the highest levels. The jurists, as well as the emperors who legislated on this issue, were willing to step beyond the immediate context of the contract and its makers and address questions of policy concerning the treatment of slaves. In so doing they recognized, and attempted to balance, the claims of competing sets of interests on different levels, not only between buyer and seller but between the personal interests of these parties and the public interest, which is here, I argue, identified with the slave.[120]

Broadly similar considerations can be seen at work with the other three covenants. The covenant that forced migration upon the slave, *ut exportetur,* was intended to protect individual masters from their slaves (the jurists give this explicitly as a motive for imposing the covenant)[121] and should also be understood as a relatively mild form of punishment.[122] The same was true for *ne manumittatur.*[123] In both covenants the interests of individual masters are easily reconcilable with those of the class of masters, since both groups had an interest in the correction of slaves.[124]

On this analysis, it is the covenant that provided for manumission after sale that most closely resembles *ne serva,* since here too the interests of master and slave, when in conflict, are weighed in the balance. The slave and class of masters are favored over the individual master. In the case of *ut manumittatur,* the tendency is a familiar one; indeed, the regime for this covenant can largely be explained as an aspect of *favor libertatis,* with regard to both policy and ideology.

7. Honor and Shame

Ne serva is not so easily understood. Here there is no general policy background, no ideological framework, that can serve as a ready frame of reference, as with *ut*

---

[120] The extraordinary quality of the regime developed for the covenant *ne serva prostituatur* may be measured against the fact that it was not until late antiquity that the authority of "recognized" exploiters—parents, masters, and ultimately all pimps—comes to be challenged. Compare Dioclet., Maxim. C. 8.50(51).7 (a. 291), which adheres to the general classical tendency, visible beyond the scope of *ne serva,* that represses only, and under certain circumstances, those persons not authorized to exploit the sexual commerce of others.

[121] Pap. *FV* 6; Pap.-Ulp. D. 18.7.1.

[122] That is, as opposed to beating, branding, maiming, killing. But the anguish felt by the slave over forced separation from familiar places and persons should not be underestimated. Economic assets or a profession might be left behind as well. The reluctance of American slaves to submit to forced migration (often a condition of full manumission) is poignant testimony: Howington, *What Sayeth the Law* (1986) 41–54.

[123] In the sense that this covenant provided for the safety of the master (through physical separation after sale) and punishment for the slave. The two covenants are sometimes treated together: Ulp. D. 40.1.4.9; Mod. D. 40.7.25; cf. Suet. *Aug.* 21.2.

[124] Note, however, that a slave alienated *ne manumittatur* could be freed if he or she gave information under the *SC Silanianum:* Ulp. D. 29.5.3.15. The exception proves the rule; see also Ulp. D. 40.1.4.7.

manumittatur and *favor libertatis*. Although a partial explanation has been sought in the norms aimed at encouraging better treatment of slaves,[125] this is not completely satisfactory, particularly if we restate a question raised above. Why were covenants forbidding the prostitution of slaves granted such recognition while there is no evidence of covenants designed to safeguard them from other professions that were dishonorable or even dangerous, such as acting or fighting as a gladiator?[126]

One firm argument against expanding the number of recognized covenants is protection of the market in slaves. Although such covenants could bring certain advantages to buyers, greater risk and uncertainty seem equally likely.[127] The Roman law of slave sale was "buyer-friendly" as a rule;[128] moreover, the slave market itself has been argued to have suffered from uncertainty and periodic shortages in supply under the Principate.[129] But while this may help explain why other covenants were not introduced, it does not shed any direct light on the anomaly of *ne serva*.

The concerns underlying this covenant go to the heart of the Roman sense of social ethics. The point was to safeguard the sexual integrity of the household, which rested more or less exclusively with the female members but which it was the responsibility of the males to defend. We see this concern manifested in the *lex Iulia de adulteriis coercendis,* especially in the special privileges granted to the husband and father of the offending woman in regard to prosecution and self-help.[130] Of course the sexual behavior of slaves was not regulated by the *lex Iulia,*[131] and this raises the question of why this should have been an issue, especially where the slave was to be alienated.

The work of Mediterraneanist anthropologists on the honor-shame syndrome is relevant.[132] Research in traditional societies of the Mediterranean basin has shown that the honor of the family pertains to everyone; it is collective in nature. Any individual may compromise this honor, but women are regarded as especially vulnerable because of certain assumptions about their sexual nature. The respon-

---

[125] Sicari's (*Prostituzione* 117 n. 27) imputation to me of a monocausal explanation is founded on an acute misunderstanding (and contradicts what she writes at 153 n. 42).

[126] The latter might seem particularly surprising in view of the *lex Petronia,* which prohibited masters from sending slaves into the amphitheater to face beasts without a prior court judgment (where this was done through sale, both buyer and seller were penalized): Watson, *Slave Law* 121–122. An enactment of Hadrian (if the *HA* can be trusted) forbade sale of slaves to *lanistae* (as well as to pimps) without justification: *HA Hadr.* 18.8 (pace Sicari, *Prostituzione* 94 n. 7, this text provides no evidence for the existence of a covenant prohibiting slaves from being used as gladiators). Such measures may have reduced the overall need for other forms of legal protection, but they were no substitute for a covenant.

[127] Advantages might have included a lower price than market value, without an "opportunity cost" imposed by the restriction on use of the slave; see below. The fact situation addressed by the ruling of Vespasian quoted above (Mod. D. 37.14.7 pr.) illustrates the point about risk and uncertainty.

[128] Compare the warranties on defects under this system with the most extreme prevailing in the antebellum American South: Fede, "Protection" (1987).

[129] On the slave supply, see Harris, "Trade" (1980); for a more optimistic view, see Whittaker, "Circe's Pigs" (1987) 97–99; Bradley, "Supply" (1987).

[130] See Chapter 5.

[131] The sources are given by Buckland, *RLS* 76. See esp. Pap. D. 48.5.6 pr.

[132] See Chapter 1. The phenomena associated with the syndrome are not unique in all respects to traditional Mediterranean cultures, though they may cohere in a peculiar manner there; see below.

sibility for defending the women's honor or for avenging any breaches or affronts devolves upon the male members of the group.

Of course, the cultures under study do not have slavery, and most seem to define those women whose sexual honor must be protected primarily in terms of kinship ties.[133] But even on this principle there is a broad range. The female relatives whose sexual honor the male is obliged to defend may include—besides wives, daughters, and sisters—sisters-in-law, wife's aunts, and even wife's aunt's daughters.[134] A man's honor might be at stake even with nonrelatives. Pitt-Rivers has shown that the risk to honor extends, at least for upper-class males, to all women in whom an investment of masculine pride has been made (e.g., mistresses).[135] Other evidence suggests the same is true for household servants, or any person with whom the socially superior male enjoys a permanent relationship.[136]

More important, a similar phenomenon has been observed in slaveholding societies. In fact, its implications reach beyond the notion of sexual honor. In his comparative study, Patterson concludes that the master's acquisition of honor through his slaves forms one of the three "constituent elements" of slavery.[137] He shows how, in many such societies, sexual offenses against slaves came to be defined as offenses against the master's honor; the master's sexual involvement with a slave might increase his risk.[138]

The antebellum American South can serve as an illustration of this point.[139] Here too, we find a gender-specific sexual division of labor, where men acted as the guardians of a feminine virtue that was assumed to be highly vulnerable and easily lost. The sense of collective honor went beyond the master's female relatives to encompass the household slaves, whose sexual integrity, when violated by predators from without the household, was avenged at law or, when this was to no avail, through self-help.

It is well known that the Romans provided legal means for a master to redress sexual affronts to his slaves. Most of these involved the law of delict.[140] Liability

---

[133] The distinction between slavery and kinship maintained here is to some extent artificial. Many Roman slaves were blood relatives of their masters; see below. One can find in non-Mediterranean societies a concern with the sexual honor of domestic servants: Hobson, *Virtue* (1990) 60, 127–128 (cf. 65). Of course, they were easier to dismiss than slaves.

[134] Davis, *Pisticci* (1973) 62–64.

[135] Pitt-Rivers, *Shechem* (1977) 38.

[136] See Cutileiro, *Society* (1971) ch. 25.

[137] Patterson, *Slavery* (1982) ch. 3: the slave himself or herself is without honor but the master acquires honor through the slave.

[138] Patterson, *Slavery* 82, 85 (cf. 93). The concern is typically with the master's honor, not the welfare of the slave.

[139] See Wyatt-Brown, *Honor* (1982) ch. 12, whose picture of a rigidly patriarchal society is in some respects overdrawn according to Ely and Bodenhammer, "Regionalism" (1986) 562.

[140] It would surely count as *iniuria*: Ulp. D. 47.10.25; cf. Pap. D. 48.5.6 pr., which must itself be a case of consensual intercourse. *PS* 2.26.16 raises problems that cannot be addressed here. Under the appropriate circumstances rape could give rise to charges of kidnapping and theft; see next note. The position on liability for *vis publica* in the classical law is less clear: *PS* 2.26.12; Dioclet., Maxim. C. 9.9.24(25) (a. 291); cf. Ant. C. 9.20.1 (a. 213), with Mommsen, *Strafrecht* (1899) 664. Ulp. D. 48.5.30(29).9 is inconclusive.

would often cumulate.[141] Mere attempts on the chastity of slaves might be punished through the action on *iniuria*.[142]

The diverse instances of liability under the actions for theft, under the *lex Aquilia*, for corruption of a slave, and especially for *iniuria*, all show that it was the master's interest in the sexual integrity of the slave, not the injury to the slave, that was taken into account.[143] The master might even decide to relinquish all claims to the chastity of the slave, for example by prostituting her. This would tend to extinguish liability for those who engaged in unauthorized sex or related activity with the slave.[144]

But if the master wanted to protect the sexual integrity of his slave, the law system was prepared to recognize his interest in the matter. He might not only refrain from prostituting the slave himself but forbid a subsequent owner to do so by means of the *ne serva* covenant on sale. The vigor with which offenses against that sense of honor are confronted by the legal authorities mirrors the interest displayed in discouraging or punishing unauthorized sex with slaves. One text already examined speaks to this point:

> Sab.-Pap. (27 *quaest.*) D. 18.7.6 pr.: . . . ceterum si ne prostituatur exceptum est, nulla ratio occurit, cur poena peti et exigi non debeat, cum et ancillam contumelia adfecerit [sc. emptor] et venditoris affectionem, forte simul et verecundiam laeserit. . . .

The *affectio*, no matter how interpreted,[145] should occasion no surprise. *Verecundia* requires more explanation. The jurist allows that the buyer has perhaps violated the vendor's sense of sexual shame by prostituting the slave,[146] direct evidence that cultural values associated with the honor-shame syndrome influenced the development of the *ne serva* covenant.

In fact, Papinian goes further. The language he uses with respect to the slave, "ancillam contumelia adfecerit," refers not just to another locus of interests, as

---

[141] Paul. D. 47.2.83(82).2 (= *PS* 2.31.31; *PS* 2.31.12 is not classical as it stands); Ulp. 47.2.39, Ulp. D. 47.10.25. Pap. D. 48.5.6 pr. emphasizes the point.

[142] Ulp. D. 47.10.9.4 (male and female slaves). Cf. Ulp. D. *eod.* 15.15.

[143] So Buckland, *RLS* 76: "the injured woman does not seem to have been considered." For an American parallel, see Getman, "Control" (1984) 146: ". . . the legal system treated the rape of a slave woman by a white man as a property crime against her master, not a personal crime against the woman."

[144] Thus there was no liability for certain offenses if the slave was a *meretrix* (Ulp. D. 47.2.39) or if she was already *impudica* (to be inferred from Ulp. D. 47.10.9.4, with Paul. D. *eod.* 10). The same point is implied by the aggravated liability for sex with a *virgo immatura* (Ulp. D. *eod.* 25) and perhaps by the recognition of liability where the slaves become *deteriores* after sex (*PS* 2.26.16).

[145] *Affectio* is a juristic term of art, used in an objective sense "to describe subjective feelings as neutrally as possible": Treggiari, "Sentiment" 76. It is argued below that the imposition of such a covenant does not predicate the existence of a sexual relationship between master and slave. On the classical status of the *Affektionsinteresse*, see above.

[146] For *verecundia* with the meaning "sense of (sexual) shame," see the standard dictionary entries: *L & S* s.h.v. II.2 and *OLD* s.h.v. 3, 4. Mayer-Maly, "*Verecundia*" examines the uses of this word—traditionally suspect—in the legal sources. It seems to have entered the Roman legal vocabulary under Marcus Aurelius and is favored above all by Papinian. Its range of meaning is not reducible to a single, precise usage, nor does its appearance guarantee the classical status of a text (Mayer-Maly accepts this passage as classical).

defined above, but to a second locus of sexual honor.[147] The point is made explicit by a text of Paul, quoted above, that actually speaks of recompense for *"iniuria"* committed against the slave:

> Paul. (5 *quaest.*) D. 18.7.9: ... quoniam utraque condicio pro mancipio additur et sicut manus iniectio, ita libertas eximit eam iniuriam.

The language is extraordinary, even if one keeps in mind that in both this passage and the previous one the jurist does not speak of delict proper. In cases of true *iniuria,* the slave had no standing, no honor to be offended, and might be virtually ignored.[148] Generally speaking, a slave had no honor of his or her own,[149] and the *ne serva* covenant stands out as one of the rare exceptions to this rule.

It is an important question, but we simply do not know if any Roman slave owner who sold a slave under a *ne serva* agreement had maintained a sexual relationship with that slave before the sale.[150] Such relationships were common, and the comparative evidence suggests that such a tie would have increased the master's investment of honor in the sexual integrity of the slave. Situations would surely have arisen where a master was compelled (or perhaps simply chose) to sell a slave lover.[151]

There is no need to suppose, however, that this was a routine motive for the imposition of the covenant. The protected slave may have been a blood relative[152] or enjoyed a position in the household of the vendor that brought her into close contact with him and his family, perhaps as an attendant for one or more of the women of the house.[153]

The sorts of slaves, otherwise ineligible, who could be freed *iusta causa* under the *lex Aelia Sentia* included relatives and attendants.[154] Someone who received an estate containing his natural father, mother, or brothers did not have to hand them

[147] Since Labeo, *contumelia* was central to the classical definition of *iniuria:* Kaser, *RP* 1² 623–624, 2² 605; Lübtow, "Injurienrecht" (1969) 162–167; Wittmann, *Körperverletzung* (1972) 23–25. Here it must refer to an offense against the *slave's* sexual honor.

[148] Only the master's interest mattered. See Buckland's observation, quoted above. There was, to be sure, the *actio iniuriarum servi nomine.* But this was a late creation, of limited application, and was in fact designed to protect the master's interest: Buckland, *RLS* 81–82.

[149] Patterson, *Slavery* ch. 3, elevates this into a general principle for all slave societies. This does not mean that all Roman slaves were sexually promiscuous: Martin, "Vie" (1978) 122–123. But they were regarded as such routine objects of sexual exploitation that their behavior lay beyond the sort of criticism the freeborn could expect: Martin, "Vie" 123–124; Garrido-Hory, *Martial* (1981) 163–168; Kolendo, "Esclavage" (1981).

[150] Note for purposes of contrast that Ulp. D. 40.2.16 pr. excludes from grounds for exemption under the *lex Aelia Sentia luxuria* and *deliciae;* cf. Ulp. D. 7.7.6.2, which excludes, in an action for slave's *operae,* any reckoning based on *voluptas* or *affectio.*

[151] See Mart. 6.71, 11.70, for what I take to be a pair of fictional elaborations of a practice more mundane and rather common in reality.

[152] For slave relations, see Mart. 1.84; and the sources in Niziolek, "Phrase" (1975) 318–321, 334.

[153] Treggiari, *RM* (1991) 375: "Since women slaves were of little use to him in normal work roles, he [sc., a Roman husband] might lend her [sc., his wife] his own women and their female offspring" (cf. Treggiari, "Jobs" [1976] 84; Treggiari, "Women as Property" 13). On the preference of women owners for female slaves, especially young ones, see Sigismund Nielsen, "Examen" (1991) 236.

[154] Gaius 1.19, 39; Ulp. D. 40.2.13; Paul. D. *eod.* 15.1; Marcel., Ulp. D. *eod.* 20.3. Ulpian ([2 *ad legem Aeliam et Sentiam*] D. *eod.* 16 pr.) defines the *iusta causa* as arising "ex affectu."

over as legacies but might substitute a monetary equivalent.[155] Exceptions from forced sale of property upon bankruptcy included concubines and natural children.[156] Similar exceptions from the operation of a general pledge embraced persons *necessarii* or bound to the owner by sentiment (the latter category comprising concubines, natural children, and *alumni*).[157] Purchase of a slave brother or son *ut manumittatur* is given as an example in the discussion of exceptions to the rules for mandate.[158]

The honor-shame syndrome, the anthropologists note, is closely linked to the question of gender role, especially to the ways in which ideas about gender role define the range of acceptable economic pursuits for both men and women. In Roman society too there were only limited opportunities for female employment,[159] a phenomenon that had, as one of its effects, a gender imbalance in upper-class slave households, with men far outnumbering the women.[160] Another aspect of this is brought into relief by the *ne serva* covenant. "Economically" (to take our sense of the word), it made sense to prostitute female slaves: breeding and wool-working had their limits.[161] Masters with a delicate sense of honor did not, however, have this option available to them, an opportunity cost magnified by the diminution in sale price they tolerated when they chose—or were forced—to sell their female slaves and then attempted to preserve their honor through the imposition of a *ne serva* covenant.[162] Of course, not all masters were possessed of such a sensibility; to judge from the legal texts, the covenants were sometimes ignored, even by the very people who framed them. One presumes that in such cases "economic" concerns outweighed sensitivities about honor.

8. *Humanitas* and Policy

This analysis has stressed the unusual features of the four restrictive covenants on sale and the strong interest taken by the legal and political authorities in their enforcement. An examination of the juristic treatment of these agreements has

---

[155] Ulp. D. 30.71.3.

[156] Paul. D. 42.5.38 pr.

[157] See Ulp. D. 20.1.6, 8.

[158] See Pap. (27 *quaest.*) D. 17.1.54 pr. *(affectus ratio);* cf. Paul. D. 19.5.5 pr.; Pap. D. 40.1.19. For a *fideicommissum ut manumittatur* benefiting a slave nephew, see Scaev. D. 36.1.80(78).2.

[159] See Kampen, *Image* (1981), esp. chs. 4–5.

[160] The work of Susan Treggiari is especially important on this point. See the literature given at McGinn "*NSP*" 351 n. 134. Similarly, Harris, "Trade" 119; contra Bradley, "Supply" 50, 52 (cf. 58). It is acknowledged that an imbalance in the number of job titles does not always and of itself predict an imbalance in sheer numbers, despite Sigismund Nielsen, "Examen" 224.

[161] "Breeding" signifies slave reproduction both for estate uses and for sale to other owners. I mean neither to underestimate the importance of either practice (see, e.g., Treggiari, "Jobs" 94, and "Women as Property" 10, on the role of female *contubernales*) nor to imply that other uses were impossible (see "Women as Property" 12 for wet nurses and midwives). Of course, women slaves, like their male counterparts, might fulfill more than one function: Bradley, *Slaves and Masters* 62 n. 54 (cf. 72).

[162] Given the diminution in price, this opportunity cost would not have fallen on the buyer of the slave. Moreover, the buyer who intended to use the slave for an "honorable" purpose, such as domestic or personal attendant, would lose nothing through such a purchase.

confirmed the position taken by most scholars that a crucial analytical distinction was made in the classical period between those agreements that benefited the slave and those that did not. Over time this distinction became even more marked and was given considerable weight both by the interventions of the emperors and by the interpretative work of the jurists.

The frequency and force of imperial legislation suggest that important issues of policy were at stake, an impression tested by an examination of these issues. Above all, the interests of masters in protecting themselves and punishing slaves and the interests of the slaveholding society in manumission and proper treatment of slaves had to be safeguarded. Both types of covenants served as instruments of social control, but in notably different ways. *Ne manumittatur* and *ut exportetur* were designed to punish and deter wrongdoing, and the others rewarded the well-deserving slave.

Even so, *ne serva* emerges as something of an anomaly, given the lack of covenants sheltering slaves from other dangerous or dishonorable professions. This covenant is to be understood not just in terms of a weighing of the interests of masters, slaves, and the slaveholding society but from a moral/ideological perspective as well. Founded upon deep-rooted notions of gender role and sexual shame, it protected the original vendor's sense of honor and went on to create an independent locus of honor for the slave. As with *ut manumittatur,* we have an illustration of how a legal system can translate ideology into action while channeling the effects of this transformation within very narrow limits. The covenants were few in number. The dependency on an initiative taken by a master—the original vendor—was absolute. No slave was ever freed or sheltered from prostitution unless his or her master at some point determined that it be so.[163] It is unrealistic to think that enforcement was easy or frequent, despite the procedural safeguards provided. On the other hand, the legal regimes established for these covenants helped to open an avenue for claims on the system by the slaves themselves[164] and to create a means for criticizing the operation of the system without challenging its underlying premises.[165]

Through the legal system, the state promoted social conformity by educating all of society in the norms and values favored by the elite and creating a new type and level of civil society.[166] Stoicism, which operated through the legal system itself by the late classical period, played a similar role in simultaneously criticizing and preserving the social order.[167] A law system that openly and uniformly protected the interests of the powerful would serve as a crude and unwieldy instrument for those same interests.[168]

[163] For an analogy taken from a Justinianic rule on concubines and their children, see Beaucamp, *Statut* 1.304.

[164] See Genovese, *Roll, Jordan, Roll* (1974) 25–49.

[165] Finley (rev. Davis) (1973) 397.

[166] Gramsci, *Quaderni* 3 (1975) 1570–1571: "in quanto [sc. lo Stato] tende appunto a creare un nuovo tipo e livello di civiltà" (see also 2.756–758, 773–774); and cf. Cic. *Leg.* 1.58 and Sen. *Ep.* 94.37).

[167] Shaw, "Economy" (1985).

[168] See the remarks of Wacke, "*Potentiores*" (1980) 588.

The two overall approaches adopted here to explain *ne serva* are perfectly compatible, especially when the "material" aspects of honor are given proper emphasis. This emphasis is more easily accomplished where breaches of honor— that is, violations of the covenant—could be remedied through the payment of monetary damages. Such compensation is characteristic, moreover, of the ways in which sexual affronts to slaves were redressed. Honor emerges, in a sense, as another "interest," whose satisfaction or nonsatisfaction depended upon the weighing of the exigencies of individual cases by the competent legal authority. This is also true for the locus of honor created for the slave. Within its narrow scope of application, honor appears as a criterion for decision making, near kin in this function to *favor libertatis,* with which, as we have seen, it is often closely associated in practice.[169]

All the same, the material element of honor should not be overrated. The four covenants served quite specific ends in the areas of policy and ideology. They helped make the system more efficient, safer, and more respectable in the eyes of those who mattered most: the upper-class slaveholders.[170] The authorities were able to perform their duties in a more acceptable, and so more powerful, manner, because compassionate.[171] This is not at all to deny the role of *humanitas* in such policymaking[172] but to attempt to define what this meant.[173] It is important not to view *humanitas* in terms of mere altruism or by reference to its presumed antinomy, a cynical, even hypocritical pursuit of self-interest.[174]

Humanitas represents an extralegal element at times decisive in the formation of policy. Perhaps easier understood at the level of individual motivation, for example, in the imposition or enforcement of the *ne serva* covenant, *humanitas* becomes rather more complex as one moves from the perspective of the individual to that of the policymaker.[175] Even on the level of the individual slaveholder, motives influencing the treatment of slaves were potentially complex, or at least varied: this factor was likely to have an impact on policy.[176] The tension between utilitarianism and charity in the practical application of *humanitas* has been usefully explored, albeit with somewhat inharmonious results, by students of Seneca's views on slavery.[177] For an understanding of what was at stake, one can do worse than to consult the content and context of the statement by Marcellus: "in circumstances

---

[169] See above. One may usefully compare the role of *benigna interpretatio* in policymaking: Wolff, "Benigniora" (1951); Wubbe, "Benignus" (1968); Wubbe, "Interpretatio" (1972) esp. 372; cf. Wieacker, "OW" 177, 192, 196–198.

[170] See Wiedemann, "Regularity" (1985) 164, 175; Manning, "Stoicism" 1539–1540.

[171] See Perry, "Insiders" (1985) 149.

[172] In this sense, I do not follow Bradley, *Slaves and Masters* 21–23, 127–129, *Slavery* chs. 7–8, whose fundamental skepticism about the meaning of *humanitas* I share.

[173] On the difficulty of defining *humanitas* in light of its complex role in lawfinding, see Wubbe, "Humanitas" (1990) 262.

[174] Or, like *aequitas,* to define it simply as an ethics-influenced tendency that offers an alternative to strict adherence to the law: see Fuhrmann, "Alleinherrschaft" (1963) esp. 486–487.

[175] This difficulty informs approaches taken not only to slavery generally but also to gladiatorial games: Wiedemann, *Emperors* (1992) 128.

[176] Manning, "Stoicism" 1540–1541.

[177] Griffin, *Seneca* ch. 8; Giliberti, *"Beneficium"*; Bradley, "Seneca" (1986); Manning, "Stoicism."

of uncertainty, it is every bit as just as it is safe to follow the milder interpreta-tion."[178] The regime for the *ne serva* covenant, operating on a narrow front, was easy to pursue in an aggressive manner. Marcellus's reasoning, with its implicit limitations, helps explain why the regimes for these covenants were treated with such energy and seriousness of purpose and at the same time why the range of covenants was never expanded.

[178] Marcel. (29 *digest.*) D. 28.4.3 pr. (= [in this part] D. 50.17.192.1: ". . . in re dubia benigniorem interpretationem sequi non minus iustius est quam tutius.''

9

Prostitution and the Law of the Jurists

1. Private Law and Prostitution

The chapters that precede may suffice to give an idea of the rich variety of Roman approaches to the making of policy regarding prostitution. One more very important area of the law remains to be introduced: the private law of the jurists. A scattering of some dozen or so juristic texts enables us to take the examination of lawfinding about prostitution a crucial step further.

Because of the complex, often highly technical, questions surrounding the exegesis of almost every single one of these texts, and because they represent such a broad range of legal issues, it is not possible to offer a detailed examination in this place. I present a brief summary of my work in what follows, reserving detailed discussion for a more appropriate venue.[1]

Roman private law never developed a comprehensive approach toward prostitution and its practitioners. The absence of such an approach is not merely a product of its casuistry but reveals its basic orientation as a law system designed by and for members of the upper classes. This fact, to be sure, suggests that for many purposes private law could ignore prostitution. All the same, problems related to the practice of prostitution did arise from time to time in widely scattered areas of the law. The classical juristic texts preserved by Justinian's compilers, supplemented in one case by a pair of texts taken from another postclassical collection,

---

[1] For this reason, I keep citations of secondary literature to the barest minimum. A small mountain of this stands behind virtually every text in this chapter.

allow us to take up the threads of policies fashioned for the procedural law and positive enactments studied in earlier chapters. Two fundamental concerns emerge, which can be identified in general terms as the conservation of patrimony and the safeguarding of honor. I refer to these principles in a shorthand manner as "economics" and "honor," though it should be recognized from the start that for the Romans "economics" could have a strong moral component. The tension between these two concerns is broadly speaking the theme of what follows.

2. Damaged Goods: *Fiducia*/Pledge

In his commentary on the edict, Ulpian raises the possibility of a slavewoman being prostituted in the context of a discussion of debtor's rights where an object given as security has been mistreated by the creditor.[2]

> Ulp. (30 *ad edictum*) D. 13.7.24.3: In [pigneraticio] <fiduciae> iudicio venit et si res [pignori] <fiduciae> datas male tractavit creditor vel servos debilitavit. plane si pro maleficiis suis coercuit vel vinxit vel optulit praefecturae vel praesidi, dicendum est, [pigneraticia] <fiduciae> creditorem non teneri. quare si prostituit ancillam vel aliud improbatum facere coegit, ilico [pignus] <fiducia> ancillae solvitur.

> One may also bring suit with the action on *fiducia* if the creditor mistreats property given as security or weakens slaves. To be sure, if it is on account of their own wrongdoings that he punishes them, binds them, or hands them over to prefect or governor, it must be said that the creditor is not liable in the action on *fiducia*. If, therefore, he puts a slave woman to prostitution or compels her to behave disreputably in some other manner, the *fiducia* of her is immediately discharged.

Like the regime for the restrictive covenant *ne serva prostituatur,* the rule does not pertain to all masters (or only to unwilling slaves) but to those under a special obligation. In *fiducia* there is a duty of the creditor to return the item he held as collateral when the debt is paid. If he damages the item through deliberate action or negligent behavior so as to reduce its value, he must pay the difference,[3] as with pledge.

The "damage" done to the slave is to her sexual honor. The jurist is more interested in the economic consequences of this than in the fact itself. A prostituted slave might be a valuable asset to a low-status owner, but her value was circumstantial at best: when sold she was next to worthless, a drug on the market. She had been rendered unfit by this one profession for employment in every other one. Most upper-class slave owners were not, of course, pimps, and so by their standards the slave had been rendered unfit for return by the creditor.

---

[2] Lenel, *EP*[3] (1923/1974) 291–295, observed that the compilers, as elsewhere in book 30, replaced the text's references to *fiducia* (a form of real security in which ownership and possession of the object were transferred to the creditor against repayment of the debt) with "pledge."

[3] The principle is certain; positive applications are difficult to identify. *FV* 18 perhaps dealt with this problem, but the state of the text permits no firm conclusions. Alex. Sev. C. 4.24.3 (a. 222) may originally have dealt with *fiducia*: Kaser, *RP* 1[2] (1971) 462 n. 31.

3. Good Money after Bad: Inheritance, Mandate, and *Usucapio* in Sale

Because the acquisition of property to any significant degree by prostitutes and pimps was a sensitive matter, it is not surprising to find discussions of this problem under the law of inheritance. According to Paconius and Paul, a *parens manumissor* had the right to *bonorum possessio contra tabulas* when his emancipated son made a prostitute heir.[4]

> Pac.-Paul. (8 *ad Plautium*) D. 37.12.3 pr.: Paconius ait, si turpes personas, veluti meretricem, a parente emancipatus et manumissus heredes fecisset, totorum bonorum contra tabulas possessio parenti datur; aut [constitutae] partis, si non turpis heres institutus.

The limits implied by this holding are worth noting. There is no reason to believe the jurist would have extended this privilege to the other heirs on intestacy.[5] The *parens manumissor* had a special claim to one-half the estate, while the others might only ask for one-quarter of what they would have been entitled to without a will. His father dead, an *emancipatus* might satisfy his close relatives and still leave the bulk of his estate to a prostitute or to any other person.

Although it is unrealistic to suppose, given what we know of the behavior of magistrates in some cases,[6] that a prostitute or pimp would have been preferred to any deserving heir on intestacy, the rules themselves[7] protected bequests to prostitutes, up to a point. Where it was a matter of leaving property within the family, the courts perhaps respected such wishes. A prostitute might be trusted to pass on her property to her children, and the jurists, at any rate, were prepared to recognize her right to do so.[8]

In general, prostitutes were widely believed to be a threat to the conservation of patrimony, especially that of young men.[9] This concern is reflected elsewhere in the writings of the jurists. For example, Ulpian denies an action on mandate to someone who stands surety for a prostitute *(meretrix)*, in full knowledge of the facts, at the behest of a dissolute young man *(adulescens luxuriosus):*

> Ulp. (31 *ad edictum*) D. 17.1.12.11: Si adulescens luxuriosus mandet tibi, ut pro meretrice fideiubeas, idque tu sciens mandatum susceperis, non habebis mandati actionem, quia simile est, quasi perdituro pecuniam sciens credideris. sed et si ulterius directo mandaverit tibi, ut meretrici pecuniam credas, non obligabitur mandati, quasi adversus bonam fidem mandatum sit.
>
> If a dissolute young man gives you a mandate to stand surety on behalf of a prostitute and you undertake this commission in full knowledge of the facts, you

---

[4] This text is also discussed in Chapter 4, where a translation is given.

[5] The father who had emancipated a child enjoyed the right, protected by the praetor with the *querela inofficiosi testamenti,* to one-half the estate of the decedent: Kaser, *RP* 1² 701, 709–713.

[6] See Val. Max. 7.7.6, 7, which concern denial of testamentary bequests.

[7] Maec. D. 36.1.5, see Chapter 4.

[8] See Ulp. D. 38.17.2.4 and Chapter 4.

[9] There is an abundance of evidence. See, e.g., Plaut. *Merc.* 42–43; more evidence at Herter 1 (1957) 1164–1165, 2 (1960) 82–83.

will not have an action on mandate. The reason is that this case is like that of knowingly lending money to someone about to squander it. Indeed, further, if he gives you a mandate to lend money to the prostitute, he will not be liable to you on an action for mandate, on the ground that the mandate was contracted contrary to good faith.

Ulpian compares such behavior to the act of someone who knowingly lends money to a person about to squander it and adds that if a mandate is aimed at having you lend money to a prostitute, there is no action on mandate. There is nothing to suggest that the prostitute's *turpitudo,* so important for questions regarding her social status, played any explicit role in prejudicing the contract. We might instead look for *turpitudo* in the agreement itself, but there is again no evidence that this was intended for any purpose defined as *turpis* in itself or that taking money for the reason stated was considered *turpis.* Just as with the imperial measures taken for the protection of slaves from abuse,[10] the motive is a concern for the community's interest in the conservation of privately held resources. Young men who threw away money on prostitutes were particularly liable to be branded as *luxuriosi,* a term that in this text and the next suggests persons not technically labeled as *prodigi* but who, in their waste of resources, behave like them.[11]

The result is that in some circumstances, an additional burden was placed on one of the parties to a contract: if he knew that his partner was about to squander the money received in the deal, and he went ahead with it anyway, he lost his claim in case of nonfulfillment. The jurist introduces another hypothetical to illustrate his argument. If the *adulescens luxuriosus* mandates you to loan money *(mandatum crediti)* to a prostitute, he is not liable to you on the contract. Knowledge on the part of the mandatary that the prospective debtor is a prostitute is to be inferred from the previous case, and there is again the necessary assumption that the prostitute will prove incapable of repaying the loan.

Broadly similar concerns are raised in a fragment of Julian, who reports, with approval, the majority juristic view that if a buyer knows a seller is going to squander the sale price, the sale is valid:

> Iul. (2 *ex Minicio*) D. 41.4.8: Si quis, cum sciret venditorem pecuniam statim consumpturum, servos ab eo emisset, plerique responderunt eum nihilo minus bona fide emptorem esse, idque verius est: quomodo enim mala fide emisse videtur qui a domino emit? nisi forte et is, qui a luxurioso et protinus scorto daturo pecuniam servos emit, non usucapiet.

> If someone, although he knew that the seller was immediately going to squander the sale price, bought slaves from him, most jurists have held that he is nonetheless a buyer in good faith, and this is the better view, for how can someone be considered to have bought in bad faith if he has purchased [the object] from its owner? Unless, to be sure, the buyer happens to purchase slaves from a dissolute young man about to hand over the money to a whore: he will not usucapt.

Julian makes an exception to this rule in the case that the seller is a dissolute person *(luxuriosus)* about to hand over the money to a whore *(scortum).* The issue

---

[10] See Chapter 8.
[11] [Quint.] *Decl.* 356 (for the theme, Calp. Fl. 37); Calp. Fl. 30.

again is not sexual turpitude but waste of patrimony. The jurists, in contrast to their stance on loan and surety, were not so concerned about agreements on sale made with such persons, since, from an objective perspective, the balance of risk was more favorable and the potential for gratuitous waste of material resources less. It is therefore not surprising to find a controversy among them on this subject, as Julian holds with the majority that the buyer has acted in good faith in most situations. The minority believed otherwise, which meant that the man had, in their view, no claim on his wastrel partner if the object of sale had not been handed over, and no power to usucapt if it had been.

4. An Honest Day's Wage: *Condictio*

The themes of "honor" and "economics" intersect again in a famous text of Ulpian, which denies a remedy known as the *condictio*[12] to recover money paid a prostitute *(meretrix),* citing Labeo and Marcellus as authorities:

> Lab.-Marcel.-Ulp. (26 *ad edictum*) D. 12.5.4.3: Sed quod meretrici datur, repeti non potest, ut Labeo et Marcellus scribunt, sed nova ratione, non ea, quod utriusque turpitudo versatur, sed solius dantis: illam enim turpiter facere, quod sit meretrix, non turpiter accipere, cum sit meretrix.

> On the other hand, what is given to a prostitute cannot be recovered, as Labeo and Marcellus write, but under a new rationale, not that which imputes disgrace to both parties, but one which attributes disgrace to the giver alone, for [they say] she does behave disgracefully, since she is a prostitute, while she does not accept money disgracefully, being a prostitute.

The holding turns on a "new" justification, not that which excludes recovery on the ground of the *turpitudo* of both parties to the transaction (evidently the older rationale), but that which recognizes only the *turpitudo* of the giver, that is, the prostitute's client. I argue that it is easier to explain this as originating with Labeo than two centuries later with Ulpian. Labeo works out a distinction that is fundamental to the definition of "prostitute" under the *lex Iulia et Papia.* He emphasizes promiscuity over payment and sets apart what a prostitute does from what a prostitute is. Marcellus and Ulpian follow suit.[13]

Labeo writes before the introduction of the tax on prostitutes, but this development only strengthened the argument. The prostitute could not pay the tax if she were not paid her fee. This was not a windfall, an incursion on someone's patrimony, or an amount of money that threatened to raise the socioeconomic status of the prostitute above a tolerable level. The fee was typically a small amount of money, often freely negotiated with the customer.[14] Like any sum turned over to a prostitute, it would be regarded as difficult, if not impossible, to recover, another possible influence on the jurists' thinking.

[12] See Kaser, *RP* 1² esp. 597–598, on the *condictio ob turpem rem/causam.*

[13] As did the canon law: Brundage, "Prostitution" (1975/1976) 837; Ward, *Harlots* (1987) 105.

[14] On the amounts and negotiations, see Chapter 7.

This is not to deny a doctrinal influence on the jurists' position: the *nova ratio* gives a more complex account of *turpitudo*. One important factor may have been the definition developed by the jurists with respect to the marriage law.[15] Without waxing metaphysical, it can be said that the marriage law definition reveals promiscuity, not the individual act, as the basis for the prostitute's *turpitudo*. It is the repeated action that matters: a pattern of behavior becomes a quality that adheres to the person and that does not disappear even after she ceases to perform the individual act(s). Beyond this, the jurists' holding against the customer may be influenced by a consideration that, from an elite perspective, sex with a prostitute, like visiting a brothel (see below), could be a somewhat discreditable enterprise. The authority, and ultimately the legitimacy, of the court system might also be better safeguarded by discouraging such plaintiffs from bringing suit.

All things considered, we should not be too impressed, I think, by this juristic concession to prostitutes. More remarkable than the holding and its justification perhaps is the fact that the question was even put in the first place. The following texts suggest that prostitutes and their owners could not count on the willingness of the legal authorities to safeguard their interests.

5. Coveting Thy Neighbor's Harlot: Theft and Wrongful Appropriation of Slave Prostitutes

Honor again plays a decisive role in determining a question of legal liability, this time under the regimes for theft and *plagium,* as reported in a text of Ulpian and two from the postclassical *Pauli Sententiae:*

> Ulp. (41 *ad Sabinum*) D. 47.2.39: Verum est, si meretricem alienam ancillam rapuit quis vel celavit, furtum non esse: nec enim factum quaeritur, sed causa faciendi: causa autem faciendi libido fuit, non furtum. et ideo etiam eum, qui fores meretricis effregit libidinis causa, et fures non ab eo inducti, sed alias ingressi meretricis res egesserunt, furti non teneri. an tamen vel Fabia teneatur, qui suppressit scortum libidinis causa? et non puto teneri, et ita etiam ex facto, cum incidisset, dixi: hic enim turpius facit, quam qui subripit, sed secum facti ignominiam compensat, certe fur non est.

> It holds true that, if someone abduct or conceal the prostitute slave woman of another, this is not theft; for one must look not to the behavior but to the motive thereof, and the motive for the act is lust, not theft. And on that account [it is true] that even he is not liable for theft who has broken down a prostitute's doors out of lust, and thereafter thieves, not introduced by him but entering on their own, have removed the woman's goods. All the same, is it perhaps the case that the man who has appropriated to himself a whore out of lust will be liable under the *lex Fabia*? Again, I do not think he is liable, and this is the opinion I did indeed give when a case was presented on these facts: for he behaves more dis-

[15] See Chapter 4.

gracefully than a man who has acted like a thief, but he offsets the shame of his action with himself; at any rate he is not a thief.

Paul. (*2 sent.*) D. 47.2.83(82).2 (= *PS* 2.31.31): Qui ancillam non meretricem libidinis causa subripuit, furti actione tenebitur et, si subpressit, poena legis Fabiae coercetur.

One who out of lust abducts a slave woman who is not a prostitute will be liable on the action for theft and, if he appropriates her to himself, is punished with the penalty of the *lex Fabia*.

PS 2.31.12: Qui meretricem libidinis causa rapuit et celavit, eum quoque furti actione <non> teneri placuit.

It is generally accepted that one who has abducted and concealed a [slave] prostitute out of lust is also not liable on an action for theft.

All three texts can be reconciled in the sense that they give liability for theft for abducting or concealing someone else's slave woman and liability under the *lex Fabia* for wrongfully appropriating the woman (*plagium*) only if she is not a prostitute (*meretrix, scortum*). If she is a prostitute, the motive, writes Ulpian, is lust, not theft. He compares such behavior to the situation where someone breaks down the doors of a prostitute out of lust ("'libidinis causa''') and thieves not acting out of complicity with him enter and steal property belonging to the prostitute:[16] there is no liability here as a constructive accomplice.

Liability for theft and/or wrongful appropriation of a slave might lie independently of whether the actor had sexual relations with the slave. With regard to slave prostitutes, however, liability for unauthorized sex is difficult to construe under the law of delict. There can be no liability for outrage, none for corrupting a slave; as for *damnum iniuria datum*, it is difficult to justify this on the basis of the juristic evidence. The position on liability for *vis* in the case of rape of prostitutes, free or slave, is unclear.

Cato seems to refer to an authoritative pronouncement that exempted free prostitutes from protection against *vis*, which may be understood to include forcible rape at this date: "but except for the person who has been making money openly with his body or who has hired himself out to a pimp, even if he had been infamous and suspect, they judged [or "voted"] that it was not right that force be visited upon the body of a free person.''[17] Cicero asserts that the gang rape of a *mimula* was condoned by usage.[18] If we can trust this evidence, it might be argued that prostitutes were a fortiori outside the protection of the law.

---

[16] The holding applies whether the prostitute is free or slave (in the latter case her owner's property is at issue), whereas she must be a slave in Ulpian's first and third hypotheticals, where she is the notional object of theft and *plagium*.

[17] Gell. 9.12.7 (Cato M. fr. 212M): "sed nisi qui palam corpore pecuniam quaereret aut se lenoni locavisset, etsi famosus et suspiciosus fuisset, vim in corpus liberum non aecum censuere adferri.''

[18] Cic. *Plan.* 30, with MacMullen, "Difference" (1986/1990) 145. In medieval France, gang rape committed by bands of young men was claimed as a privilege of masculinity: Rossiaud, *Prostitution* (1988) chs. 2–3 (esp. 21); for the argument that rape of a debauched woman was not a crime, see 152.

The outcome of the fracas that took place between the curule aedile A. Hostilius Mancinus and the prostitute Manilia in the middle of the second century B.C. offers a contrast, however.[19] Mancinus brought suit against Manilia (whose name suggests free status), alleging he was struck by a rock thrown from her dwelling at night. Manilia appealed to the tribunes, protesting that Mancinus had approached her establishment in the guise of a reveler, and when she refused him access, he attempted entry by force, only to be repulsed by a shower of stones. The tribunes decided in her favor and quashed Mancinus's suit.[20]

This incident, which turns upon the violent approach by a reveller to a prostitute's dwelling, is relevant to the principal case from Ulpian, which stipulates smashing of a prostitute's doors, *libidinis causa,* with the aim of abducting the prostitute. This is a behavior of comasts familiar in literature, especially Comedy.[21]

The heft of this incident is apparently supported by the assumption in a *controversia* of Seneca that a prostitute who killed a rapist might effectively claim self-defense.[22] A passage of Ausonius may be understood to refer to the existence of legal penalties for raping a prostitute but is far from conclusive.[23] A declamation and a (late) poem are at any rate a poor foundation for an understanding of the law. One might be tempted to argue from this evidence that although rape of prostitutes might not be prosecuted in the courts, victims might be allowed to practice self-help in their own defense, but no firm conclusions are possible.[24]

The *PS* and, in other contexts, Ulpian give liability for theft when sex was the motive and/or result of interference with another's slave.[25] The *PS* names *libido* as the motive for the theft, whereas Ulpian simply mentions the sexual act (*flagitare*) in connection with abduction of the slave.

How are we to justify the holdings regarding slave prostitutes in the principal texts? The answer is that the situation of the slave prostitute stolen or wrongfully appropriated is "somehow different" from virtually any imaginable instance where a slave has been stolen or wrongfully appropriated with an eye to exploitation of the slave's profession. Unlike other slave owners, the pimp has betrayed the honor of his female slaves; indeed, he profits from their sexual disgrace. For this reason he is denied a host of legal remedies available to owners of slaves: actions on outrage, corruption of a slave, the *lex Aquilia,* and so on. The rationale for the

[19] Gell. 4.14 (reporting Capito 8 *coniect.*). See Chapter 2.
[20] The language Gellius uses in reporting their decision suggests that it was appropriate for aediles to visit brothels in the course of duty; see Chapter 5.
[21] Plaut. *Persa* 569–573; Ter. *Ad.* 88–92. On the latter, see Don. *Ad.* 1.2.9, who says of the fulminating Demea's complaint about the violent break-in by the youthful protagonist "et bene "alienas" [sc. aedes] dicit quia "lenonis" si diceret, parva res erat" (for other examples of such circumlocution: 9, 10, 12). Cf. the pimp's lamentations at Herodas *Mim.* 2.
[22] Sen. *Contr.* 1.2, esp. 1.2.6, where the words of the pimp defending the prostitute's actions are reported (with irony, given the source) in language suggestive of a recognized legal defense: "merito occisum militem."
[23] Auson. *Epigr.* 23.8.
[24] The position was unclear in the medieval canon law until it was decided that rape—or attempted rape, at any rate—of a prostitute was not punishable: Brundage, "Prostitution" 840; cf. Rossiaud, *Prostitution* 151–152.
[25] Ulp. D. 47.1.2.5, Ulp. D. 47.10.25.

exclusion of an action on theft is similar. It supports the goal of keeping pimps, prostitutes, and their legal problems, above all squabbles generated by the *comissatio,* out of court.[26] But the main point is that women without honor, and their masters if they are slaves, lose the legal protection to which they would otherwise be entitled in situations that are provoked by a third party's *libido.* The advantage sought by the thief is not defined in economic terms but as an offense to honor, which will not hold up in court for a pimp under the circumstances defined by the jurists, that is, when *libido* is the motive for the act.

This is not to say that there were not strong policy arguments in favor of finding liability in such cases. The regime for theft is well known for its qualities of punishment and deterrence. But ultimately it was the pimp's interest in his property and the prostitute's in her belongings that were denied. Acts that prejudiced these interests were not excused; they were simply not construable as theft. A theory of justification prevailed.

Wrongful appropriation (*plagium*) is not so easily reconciled to this line of reasoning. Like the regime for *vis,* it catered to another matrix of social interests, which are not so closely identified with those of the lower-status owner and object. Above all, the concern was with the maintenance of public order, especially problems caused by slaves beyond their masters' control. For Ulpian and the author of the *PS,* at any rate, these interests were outweighed in the balance by those associated with the honor-shame syndrome, and this is the canon of interpretation on which they chose to rely. With regard to both theft and wrongful appropriation, the prostitute or her owner could not claim elementary legal protection available in theory to other Romans. This situation is not, it might be noted, unique to ancient Rome.

6. All Honorable Men: The *Petitio Hereditatis, Compromissum,* and *Operae*

Recognition of a right to the fee exacted in return for services might seem a meager compensation when measured against the vulnerability of prostitutes' owners to theft and *plagium* (and prostitutes to theft) when motivated by *libido.* We find in the next set of texts that the jurists could show a greater sensitivity when the interests of members of the elite devoted to the pursuit of profit were at stake. At the same time, they might respect, or even insist upon, the need for social distance in this field.

The first source suggests that when it was a question of making money from, rather than losing money to, prostitution, the juristic perspective might shift dramatically in its favor. Ulpian, in his commentary on the edict, allows rents received from urban property, even property that houses brothels, to come under a claim on an inheritance, that is, the *petitio hereditatis:*

---

[26] The *comissatio* appears distinctly in Ulpian's second hypothetical but is implied by the others as well.

Ulp. (15 *ad edictum*) D. 5.3.27.1: Sed et pensiones, quae ex locationibus prae-
diorum urbanorum perceptae sunt, venient, licet a lupanario perceptae sint: nam
et in multorum honestorum virorum praediis lupanaria exercentur.

Again, rents received from the letting of urban property will come under the claim
[sc., the *petitio hereditatis*] even if they have derived from a brothel. For brothels
are operated even on the property of many respectable and socially prominent
men.

Relevant to the holding are the economic interests of the heirs, presumably of the
same station and respectability as those who bequeathed such establishments. It is
noteworthy that the brothels themselves pass into the inheritance without comment.
    We cannot suppose that the principals themselves were directly involved in
the management of such businesses: they would have risked being branded as
pimps and might even have found visiting their property inconvenient, to judge
from the following text. Middlemen—slaves, freedmen, and outside entrepre-
neurs—would have collected the rents and perhaps even operated the brothels on
their behalf. We have no satisfactory direct evidence on profitability, but that this
was high may be inferred from evidence drawn from other societies in which the
practice of prostitution was itself despised.[27]
    It was, of course, a different matter for a gentleman of rank to set foot in a
brothel. Such behavior was tolerated of young men, provided the freedom was not
carried to excess.[28] In general, however, persons of high status were dishonored
simply by entering such a place of business. So again Ulpian, in his commentary
on the edict, holds that the arbitrator (*arbiter*) appointed by private agreement to
settle a legal dispute (*compromissum*) cannot compel the litigants to appear in a
disreputable place, such as a fast-food restaurant (*popina*) or a brothel (*lupanar-
ium*):

> Viv.-Cels.-Ulp. (13 *ad edictum*) D. 4.8.21.11: Sed si in aliquem locum inhonestum
> adesse iusserit, puta in popinam vel in lupanarium, ut Vivianus ait, sine dubio
> impune ei non parebitur: quam sententiam et Celsus libro secundo digestorum
> probat. unde eleganter tractat, si is sit locus, in quem alter ex litigatoribus honeste
> venire non possit, alter possit, et is non venerit, qui sine sua turpitudine eo venire
> possit, is venerit, qui inhoneste venerat, an committatur poena compromissi quasi
> opera non praebita. et recte putat non committi: absurdum enim esse iussum in
> alterius persona ratum esse, in alterius non.

But if he [sc., the *arbiter*] ordered them [sc., the litigants] to appear in some
disreputable place, for example, a fast-food restaurant or a brothel, as Vivianus
says, there is no doubt that he may be disobeyed with impunity. Celsus too, in
book 2 of his *Digesta,* approves this view. He goes on to provide a rather nice
justification for it: if the place is one to which one of the parties could not honorably come, but the other could, and the one who could come there without
dishonor fails to do so, and the one for whom it was a dishonor to come has done

---

[27] For example, nineteenth-century France: Corbin, *Women for Hire* (1990) 53, 65, 66, 344, 346.
[28] See the argument in Cic. *Cael.* and Hor. *Serm.* 1.2.

so, is the penalty on the *compromissum* incurred on the ground that the act promised has not been performed? And Celsus rightly holds that the penalty is not incurred, for it is absurd, he says, that the order be valid for one party to the suit but not for the other.

The jurist cites Vivianus and Celsus as authorities and repeats with approval the latter's justification, which holds, in highly simplifed form, that even if it is dishonorable only for one of the parties to the suit to appear in the brothel, neither incurs the penalty for noncompliance with the arbitrator's instructions.

The equation of the two venues of *popina* and brothel in this context is of interest. Superficially, this might be explained by the fact that prostitutes were known to have solicited customers in *popinae,* as in all places of public entertainment.[29] This is certainly true, but the ancient descriptions of the *popina* do not always stress this.[30] Its dishonorable status is rather more social than "sexual" in origin, which may in fact be thought true of the brothel itself. In other words, what chiefly distressed upper-class Romans about such places was the close physical contact between persons of different rank that they encouraged.

Honor and economics emerge as clashing interests in a third passage. Callistratus denies owners who prostituted slaves their rights to sexual *operae* after the slaves' manumission:

Call. (3 *ed. mon.*) D. 38.1.38 pr.: Hae demum impositae operae intelleguntur, quae sine turpitudine praestari possunt et sine periculo vitae. nec enim si meretrix manumissa fuerit, easdem operas patrono praestare debet, quamvis adhuc corpore quaestum faciat: nec harenarius manumissus tales operas, quia istae sine periculo vitae praestari non possunt.

Only those services are understood to have been imposed that can be performed without disgrace and without endangering life. For if a prostitute has been manumitted, she is not held to performing the same services for her patron, although she still earns a living with her body. Nor should a gladiator be held to such services after manumission, because they cannot be performed without endangering life.

One observes first that this ruling does not have broad implications. The fact that commercial sex did not qualify as *operae* would not exclude the *patronus* from any and all interest in such activity. He might still benefit directly or indirectly if he acted as the woman's pimp or had someone else carry on in this capacity. As master of the slave he must have profited from her earnings as a prostitute. In other words, he, or someone in his stead, has been acting as her pimp. Nothing prevents the former master or his representative from continuing in this role, except that the sexual commerce of the freedwoman is not recognized as *operae*. The former owner may be both *patronus* and pimp, but the jurist insists on a separation of these roles.

Indeed, the disqualification of such services as *operae* does not at all imply that the woman was somehow exempted from the practice of prostitution, as the

[29] Herter 2.73–75, 85–88.
[30] See, e.g., Iuv. 8.171–178; cf. Paul. D. 47.10.26.

text itself concedes. This holding might in fact have discouraged some owners from manumitting slave prostitutes and potentially depriving themselves of an economic advantage. The measure hardly seems designed to benefit the women who formed its object.

One aim of the rule may have been to discourage the grant of freedom (with concomitant citizenship) to prostitutes. Dionysius of Halicarnassus complained two centuries earlier that it was easy for slave prostitutes to earn the price of their manumission and that too many of them were taking advantage of this.[31] It is possible that Augustus laid down, in the *lex Aelia Sentia,* that such slaves became Junian Latins, and not full citizens, upon manumission. The principle that slaves freed under a *ne serva* covenant[32] became Junian Latins perhaps makes better sense if this was the rule in ordinary circumstances. Several of the other types of slaves whose manumission Dionysius criticizes (those guilty of brigandage, housebreaking, murder, and other crimes) were evidently rendered *dediticii* upon manumission under the Augustan statute.[33] They were, after all, criminals, whereas a milder regime makes sense for prostitutes, who therefore enjoyed the same chance (often difficult, to be sure) at full citizenship as other Junian Latins.[34]

Another goal may have been to avoid embroiling the courts in this ill-beseeming aspect of *operae libertorum,* a legal institution that by Roman standards was rather heavily regulated. For example, raising the issue of whether other sorts of sexual services counted as *operae* was perhaps undesirable.[35] Further, the regime for *operae* itself was not a morally neutral legal institution. The relationship between *patronus* and freedman was ideally based on trust, on close personal acquaintance, and on a sense of mutual responsibility.[36]

7. Sexual Harassment: *Iniuria*

Another important text dealing with the social insulation of respectable persons from prostitution and its practitioners is a text of Ulpian that denies liability for outrage (*iniuria*) if someone accosts (*appellare*) or abducts the attendant (*comitem abducere*) of respectable young girls who were clothed, not in a manner appropriate to their rank, that is, in the garb of a *matrona/mater familias,* but in clothing appropriate to a prostitute (*meretricia vestis*):

[31] Dion. Hal. 4.24.4–6; cf. *Priapea* 40.

[32] See Chapter 8.

[33] This law classified as such those who had been bound as a punishment, branded, tortured for an offense and found guilty, handed over to fight in the arena with men or beasts, or consigned to a *ludus* or *custodia.* All of these can be construed as investigative procedure or punishment for criminal activity of the sort described by Dionysius. See Suet. *Aug.* 40.4; Gaius 1.13, 15, 25–27, 3.74–76; *Tit.* 1.11, 20.14, 22.2

[34] Sherwin-White, *Citizenship*[2] (1973) 328–330.

[35] Sen. *Contr.* 4 *praef.* 10: "impudicitia in ingenuo crimen est, in servo necessitas, in liberto officium." Of course they did not: Waldstein, *Operae* (1986) 84 n. 226, 245 n. 30; cf. Dalla, *Venus* (1987) 48–49. Seneca reports that the *sententia* immediately became the object of ridicule.

[36] Waldstein, *Operae*; Wacke, "Manumissio" (1989) esp. 426.

Ulp. ([77] <57>[37] *ad edictum*) D. 47.10.15.15: Si quis virgines appellasset, si tamen ancillari veste vestitas, minus peccare videtur: multo minus, si meretricia veste feminae, non matrum familiarum vestitae fuissent. si igitur non matronali habitu femina fuerit et quis eam appellavit vel ei comitem abduxit, iniuriarum <non> tenetur.

If someone accosts respectable young girls, even though they are in slaves' clothing, he is understood to commit a lesser offense: a much lesser offense, if the women were dressed as prostitutes and not as respectable women. Therefore, if a woman has not been wearing respectable clothing and someone has accosted her or abducted her companion, he is not liable to the action on outrage.

The text derives from Ulpian's commentary on a subrubric of the delict of *iniuria* known as *de adtemptata pudicitia*.[38] Under this subrubric, the praetor granted redress for three well-defined instances of harassment, two of which are mentioned in the principal text; along with accosting and abducting an attendant, there is persistent pursuit (*adsectari*, see below). The text raises three initial questions.

First, who were the women protected under the edict? Ulpian mentions *virgines* and refers to the clothing of respectable women as that of the *mater familias* and *matrona. Virgines* are socially respectable,[39] young, unmarried women, the junior version of *matres familias*. I argue that the edict had, in addition to *praetextatus*, these terms, *mater familias* and *virgo* (and not *praetextata* in place of the latter, as has been assumed).[40]

Next, what sorts of clothing are given in the principal text? Ulpian is vague on all three counts. Prostitutes are known to have worn a variety of garments, including togas, clothing characteristic of the lower orders, and (presumably only upmarket prostitutes) sexually revealing garments made from Coan silk.[41] As for slaves, they shared clothing types with lower-status Romans in general; slaves in fact had no distinctive dress.[42] Ulpian assumes that the garb of respectable women is readily distinguishable from that of nonrespectable women, but the distinction between prostitutes' clothing and slaves' clothing is cloudy, both in this passage and elsewhere. On the other hand, there is no ambiguity, outside the principal text, about the type of clothing worn by respectable women themselves.[43] Ulpian's vagueness on this point is at first sight puzzling, the more so since elsewhere he

[37] Lenel, *Pal.* (1889/1960) 2 cols. 771–772, following an earlier suggestion of Schulting, corrects the *inscriptio*. See Raber, *Grundlagen* (1969) 24 n. 14.

[38] See Lenel, *EP*³ 400; Kaser, *RP* 1² 624.

[39] The edict may be assumed to apply even to lower-status women who were prepared to comport themselves like upper-class women in public, at least in matters other than clothing.

[40] The edict would then read: "Qui matrifamilias aut praetextato aut virgini comitem abduxisse quive eum eamve adversus bonos mores appellasse adsectatusve esse dicetur, in eum iudicium dabo." Cf. Lenel, *EP*³ 400.

[41] See Chapter 5.

[42] App. *BC* 2.120; Sen. *Clem.* 1.24.1; *HA Alex. Sev.* 27.1–4 (the latter source is suspect as to its literal truth).

[43] This consists principally of stola, palla, and tunic. Bieber, *RE* stola (1931) 58–60; Wilson, *Clothing* (1938) ch. 12.

is quite explicit and detailed in his description of articles of clothing appropriate for the *mater familias*.[44] At minimum, he must mean the stola.

Third, what were the typical forms of behavior that created liability for the male subject? *Appellare* is understood as a verbal attempt to seduce,[45] qualified as *blanda oratio* in contrast with *turpia verba*.[46] *Adsectari* is the silent, close, persistent pursuit of someone in an attempt to seduce him or her.[47] *Comitem abducere* is fairly self-explanatory,[48] but it is worth noting that the jurists interpreted this offense extensively. Any *comes,* free or slave, male or female, counted: Labeo gives the word a broad definition.[49] The act of abduction does not have to be characterized by the use of force; mere persuasion is enough.[50] Not to abduct, but *appellare* or *adsectari* an attendant, gives liability, an obvious extension.[51] The only limitation recognized by Ulpian is Labeo's stipulation that the act of abduction must be carried through to completion, not simply initiated, in order to constitute *comitem abducere* under the subrubric.[52]

Two of these acts, *appellare* and *adsectari,* were explicitly required to be performed "contrary to sound morals." One important result of the application of the notion of *boni mores* is that the same conduct that would create liability if exhibited toward a respectable woman has no such consequences if the woman is a prostitute. The principle is an obvious one. It was impossible to compromise such a woman's chastity, whether by accosting her, pursuing her, or abducting her attendant. Paul states the principle in general terms: "An attempt is said to be made on chastity when this is done so that a chaste person becomes unchaste."[53] The *meretrix* was *impudica* by definition.[54]

We want to know then if the wearing of slaves' or prostitutes' clothing by respectable women constitutes an offense against the common standard of decent behavior implied by *boni mores*. The answer must be in the affirmative, if full credit is given to the fact that it was the respectable males of the community, the custodians of women's honor, who defined this standard, molded it into a legal regime, and enforced its rules. Three arguments demonstrate the truth of this as-

[44] Ulp. D. 34.2.23.2. Tertullian, again in the context of a discussion of the problem of respectable women wearing prostitutes' garb in public, is more detailed than the principal text. There is an oblique but unmistakable reference to the stola at *Cultu Fem.* 2.12.1. At *Pallio* 4.9, he is more explicit, mentioning the stola, *supparum, crepidulum,* and *caliendrum.*

[45] Sen. *Contr.* 2.7 *thema;* Quint. *IO* 4.2.98; cf. [Quint.] 363.

[46] Ulp. D. 47.10.15.20, 21.

[47] Ulp. D. 47.10.15.22. Raber, *Grundlagen* 52–54, understands *frequenter* and *frequentia* in this text to mean "repeatedly" and "more than once." I take these terms to signify physical proximity; so also the Philadelphia *Digest.*

[48] Naev. *Danae* fr. 12W; Plaut. *Amph.* 929–930, *Merc.* 402–411; Sen. *Contr.* 2.7.3.

[49] Lab.-Ulp. D. 47.10.15.16.

[50] Ulp. D. 47.10.15.18.

[51] Ulp. D. 47.10.15.19.

[52] Lab.-Ulp. D. 47.10.15.17.

[53] Paul. (55 *ad edictum*) D. 47.10.10.

[54] Sen. *Contr.* 2.7.5; Quint. *IO* 8.4.2.; Tac. *Ann.* 2.85.2, with Adams, "Words" (1983) 342. At Athens, prostitution might be described as hiring oneself out "for *hybris*": Halperin, *Hundred Years* (1990) 96.

sertion: the fact that no intent to outrage is attributed to the subject, that consent was construed on the part of the object, and that no harm was inflicted, in other words, that the situations of fact as reported did not constitute the Roman delict of outrage.

Respectable women were expected to be unapproachable in public.[55] A woman had to be careful as to her dress, walk, speech, appearance: Valerius Maximus cites the example of a man who divorced his wife for having appeared in public with her head uncovered.[56] Even her *comites* had to be carefully chosen; for example, they had to be of an age that would discourage seducers.[57] It was evidently common for women to bring slave attendants into a marriage as part of the dowry,[58] though there is evidence a husband might contribute them as well.[59]

More than merely the guardians and guarantors of virtue, attendants were fashion accessories for elite women: even here, one sees traces of aristocratic competition, so that, for example, Plotina is praised for moderation in their use, a quality especially valued, to be sure, in the wife of an emperor.[60] Prominent women would also be escorted by women of status, at least on special occasions.[61] One might, in times of hardship, travel in the guise of a slave, but a handful of attendants was a rock-bottom necessity.[62] To be alone in the street was the mark of a prostitute.[63]

It will be clear that the question of proper dress formed just one aspect of the many-sided problem of women's behavior in public. As early as the time of the two Senecas, the wearing of certain types of clothing in public might brand a woman as an adulteress.[64] The opinions of moralists and trial lawyers are hardly irrelevant to our understanding of the application of the juristic standard of *boni mores*. Women who declassed themselves—sexually and socially—by openly adopting the dress of the class of exploited women were not, in the sense of the edict, chaste.

This does not deny the fact that the jurist attributes a certain responsibility to the male predator, especially when the woman was clothed in the ambiguous dress of a slave.[65] In ordinary circumstances he would have been punished, and future wrongdoers deterred, through the mechanism of compensation awarded to the injured party. But in the hypothetical situations of fact described in the principal text,

---

[55] Hor. *Serm.* 1.2.98.

[56] Val. Max. 6.3.10.

[57] Sen. *Contr.* 2.7.3–4; cf. Plaut. *Merc.* 402–411.

[58] Plin. *Ep.* 6.32.1. See Treggiari, "Women as Property" (1982) 11–12; Saller, "Slavery" (1987) 78.

[59] Plaut. *Amph.* 929–930.

[60] Plin. *Pan.* 83.7–8.

[61] Treggiari, *RM* (1991) 424.

[62] Val. Max. 6.7.3 (with App. *BC* 4.39).

[63] Plaut. *Cist.* 331; cf. Naev. *Danae* fr. 12W: attendants were a convention no doubt beyond the ability of many poor women to afford.

[64] Sen. *Contr.* 2.5.7, 2.7 exc.; Sen. *Ben.* 7.9.5, *Helv.* 16.4, *Ep.* 90.20.

[65] In my treatment of the principal text, I follow the line adopted by all scholars who have written about this in that I take Ulpian's tone to be earnest. It is possible that he is sarcastic when he speaks of *minus peccare* and *multo minus (peccare)*. We would perhaps be more willing to accept this if Julian or Celsus were speaking, but I do not think the possibility can be ruled out entirely.

he is guilty only in the moral sense, as suggested by the use of *peccare,* which Ulpian uses in its broad moral sense, with specific reference to sexual wrongdoing. He evaluates the subject's conduct in light of commonly accepted standards (as expected under the doctrine of *boni mores*) and finds it wanting, but not so much under the circumstances as to give rise to liability for *iniuria.* Not every *peccatum* is a delict.

The real villain of the piece is the woman, a fact that the liberal temper of modern scholarship can do little to alter. For the Romans, who punished this offense *pro stupro* under the criminal law, a respectable woman who wore nonrespectable clothing in public was not a contradiction in terms: she was a whore. To deny her protection under the edict was a way of fulfilling its goal of repressing certain unacceptable types of sexual behavior. The true miscreant was punished, and future wrongdoers (it was hoped) were deterred. As for compensation, there was no question of this for a woman who had abandoned her own honor. On a broader level, the holding fits in well with a series of legal regulations and complaints by moralists on Roman public dress that go back two hundred years.

The parameters of the issue are given outright or implied by Ulpian in his conclusion. The woman, insofar as she is not a *virgo* or *mater familias* in the sense of the edict, cannot claim for sexual harassment. There are no gradations made, no distinctions drawn between types of clothing or types of behavior: either one wears the dress of respectable women, the stola, palla, etc., or one wears the dress of nonrespectable women. The stark dualism of the conclusion shows just how easily broad social assumptions about female sexuality influenced the juridical conception of prostitute. The implications, however, are limited to the delict of outrage. In strict logic, the *virgo* in prostitutes' clothing would have been relegated, in public and private law, to the class of adulteresses and/or prostitutes. But here the jurist and the moralist parted ways, perhaps at the cost of some tension in the realm of Roman sexual politics.[66]

The pragmatic consideration that the regime for *de adtemptata pudicitia* may be read as a reflection of the relative freedom of movement of Roman women does not diminish this conclusion. "Women still bore the brunt of the penalties against illicit sexuality."[67]

8. Diamonds Are Forever: *Donatio*

It is impossible to predict the exact balance that the jurists will strike in applying a given legal regime to prostitutes. Since they lacked a comprehensive approach, each individual solution was bound to be somewhat ad hoc, determined by the exact circumstances at hand. All the same, it has been possible to trace the two principal themes of "honor" and "economics" as a twin current running throughout the juristic reasoning underlying these texts. We now come to a passage where

---

[66] It is obvious that the rules operated to constrain the behavior of women in public: Beaucamp, *Statut* 1 (1990) 138.

[67] Hobson, *Virtue* (1990) 70, in the context of a discussion of nineteenth-century efforts in the United States to protect women by statute from abduction and seduction.

honor is paramount. In fact, the social and sexual status of prostitutes is compared implicitly with that of respectable women. Ulpian holds that gifts given out of affection (''affectionis gratia'') are valid, without regard to their status as honorable or dishonorable: honorable gifts are those made to deserving friends and relations; dishonorable ones, to prostitutes.

> Ulp. (32 *ad Sabinum*) D. 39.5.5: Affectionis gratia neque honestae neque inhonestae donationes sunt prohibitae, honestae erga bene merentes amicos vel necessarios, inhonestae circa meretrices.

> When they are made out of affection, neither honorable nor dishonorable gifts are prohibited. Honorable gifts are those made to deserving friends and relations; dishonorable ones are those made to prostitutes.

The reference to *affectio* as a motive for gift giving shows that the text falls under the regime of gifts made between spouses.[68] Such transactions were void under a rule that originated in *mores* under the Republic and was perhaps associated with the early *ius civile*.[69] The two main rationales for the prohibition were a desire to protect the patrimony of each spouse and the moral principle that marriage is ideally founded on considerations of a nonmaterial nature. The idea of *affectio* linked both rationales: true *affectio* could be compromised through greed or might bankrupt the more generous partner in marriage.[70]

There is something paradoxical about the concession of validity to gifts bestowed upon prostitutes. Like those exchanged between spouses, they were motivated by an emotion that risked impoverishing the giver. What is more, this particular emotion was regarded as blameworthy in itself: *libido,* not *amor honestus*.[71] Social deprecation of such gifts is reflected in Ulpian's description of them as *donationes inhonestae*.

The explanation is simply that prostitutes, like concubines, did not enjoy the same social and sexual status as wives. The difference in *dignitas* justified, in general, different treatment.[72] The ideological underpinnings of the regime for gifts between spouses, with the emphasis it laid on marriage as a moral ideal, was decisive for the role accorded honor in formulating the rule for prostitutes.

More to the point, perhaps, there is a paternalist purpose behind this prohibition, which was intended to protect spouses from the deleterious effects of their own generosity. Those persons who preferred to be lavish with prostitutes and concubines, instead of contracting a respectable marriage, did not merit the same

---

[68] Moreover, this is the only subject treated in Ulpian's *Liber* 32 *ad Sabinum:* Lenel, *Pal.* 2 cols. 1137–1144.

[69] See Kaser, *RP* 1² 331, who himself inclines to an Augustan date.

[70] Ulp. D. 24.1.1, Ulp. D. *eod.* 3 pr.; Paul. D. *eod.* 28.2; Proc.-Pomp. D. *eod.* 31.7; cf. Plut. *Quaest. Rom.* 7, 8.

[71] On *libido* felt for prostitutes, see the discussion on theft above; on *amor honestus* in marriage, see Ulp. D. 24.1.3 pr. (quoting a rescript of Severus and Caracalla that regulated gifts between spouses); Lenel, *Pal.* 2 Ulp. #2760.

[72] Cf. Ulp. D. 32.49.4, where the distinction in rank has no bearing on the effect of legacies to wives and concubines: McGinn, ''Concubinage'' (1991) 349. Under the *lex Iulia et Papia,* prostitutes enjoyed a special status; see Chapter 3.

protection. It is as if they had been deprived of an economic and legal privilege because they failed to act honorably.

The pragmatic reflection that such gifts, once given, were bound to be difficult to recover in most cases did not perhaps play much of a role here. The fact that stolen property is often difficult to recover does not after all tend to discourage the development of a regime repressing theft. What is remarkable is that the concern with waste of resources in the hands of prostitutes, a theme common to several of the passages examined in this chapter, is eclipsed by considerations of honor, that is, the promotion of the wife's dignity in contrast to the prostitute's disgrace. One might compare the result here to the case discussed above regarding the *condictio*. The economic dimensions are potentially far greater here of course, and the decision is handed down without a trace of the justifications offered or posited for the prostitute's right to keep the price of a trick.

10

Conclusion

Diversity and Unity in Roman Legal Perspectives on Prostitution

1. Summary of Findings

For all of the variety of legal approach evidenced in the juristic texts set forth in Chapter 9, it is possible to trace a fundamental similarity with the classical law explored in previous chapters. The "policy" developed in this period remains essentially ad hoc. Initiatives are undertaken in scattered areas of the law that fail to display an overall coherency. No progressive linear development can be discerned.

For the sake of clarity, I will set forth an analytical summary of the findings contained in the preceding chapters before proceeding to a synthetic conclusion. Chapter 1 set forth basic principles concerning the relationship of society and law and went on to address two issues of prime importance for the formation of social policy on prostitution: the honor-shame syndrome at Rome and the marginal status of prostitutes.

Chapter 2 mapped the position of practitioners as Roman citizens. An exploration of the consequences of gender for citizen status argues that Roman women were not marginalized or noncitizens and in fact are poor candidates even for status as second-class citizens, unless one adopts a male-oriented definition of citizenship. Gender was not a unitary category at Rome. Thus, female prostitutes did not enjoy the same status as respectable women, as the articulation of their role in cult, separate and inferior, shows. Given the exclusion of women from office-holding and public life, a full account of political disabilities shifts the focus to male prostitutes and pimps. They were routinely and categorically excluded from all participation in political office under both Republic and Empire, as well as from service in the army. I argue that the censorial oversight of lower-class Romans was more consistent and negative in effect than is usually held to be true, regularly placing prostitutes and pimps in the least favorable position possible in the Roman socio-political hierarchy.

Practitioners of both genders were disadvantaged in the role they were permitted to play in the civil and criminal courts. In principle, they were not permitted to make pleas on others' behalf (or represent others) in the praetor's court, to bring criminal accusations, or to act as witnesses. In a final section of the second chapter I seek to establish the precise position of prostitutes and pimps in the nexus between legal disability and social prejudice, concluding that they were placed in a core category of disgrace, along with a few other types.

Chapter 3, after a summary of the content and aims of the *lex Iulia et Papia,* examined the sparse evidence for the marriage status of prostitutes before the passage of the law and concluded that a severe social sanction, backed by the censorial *nota,* awaited freeborn Romans who married prostitutes. This sanction was transformed into a legal rule by the Augustan marriage law, which named prostitutes and pimps among a small group of types forbidden to marry freeborn Romans.

The statute, which intended to encourage not only selection of appropriate marriage partners but the very practice of marrying and raising children, took care not to punish prostitutes overmuch, since, though notionally eligible for marriage with freedmen, they were not well placed to comply with the law's strictures, and it may have been thought desirable to discourage them from trying. The law allowed unmarried prostitutes to receive up to one-fourth of a decedent's estate through testamentary bequest. The chapter ended with an examination of the law's possible relation to social practice, concluding that the prohibition of marriage with practitioners had little direct practical effect for the upper orders, who were not, to all appearances, disposed to contemplate marriage with prostitutes and pimps. Evidence for the marriage practices of the vast bulk of Roman citizens, though inadequate, suggests caution in generalizing from the experience of the elite.

The first part of Chapter 4 made a negative contribution in that I argued that Domitian's punishment of the *feminae probrosae* concerned adulteresses, not prostitutes. It emerged that the status of prostitutes under the *lex Iulia et Papia* remained essentially unchanged during the classical period, as they continued to be eligible for the testamentary *quarta.* The second half of the chapter, dealing with juristic interpretation of relevant aspects of the marriage law, began with an analysis of a text of Paul that suggests that marriages between members of the senatorial order and prostitutes were not only rare but strictly hypothetical. There followed an exegesis of the definitions of ''prostitute'' and ''procuress'' developed by the jurists in connection with the statute.

Chapter 5 introduced the evidence concerning practitioners of prostitution for the *lex Iulia de adulteriis coercendis.* A review of the statute's contents and goals preceded analysis of the social and sexual statuses it created. Liability for the new criminal offenses of adultery and criminal fornication was defined in terms of the woman's status. If she qualified as a *mater familias,* or respectable woman, liability for nonmarital sexual relations resulted for both parties. A woman disgraced through conviction under the law was cast as a prostitute, most visibly through imposition of the label of the toga, the prostitute's badge of shame. The exclusive focus of the *lex Iulia* on the female partner in constructing a basis for liability meant that there was no reason to invent a respectable status for Roman males to mirror that of the *mater familias*. The law, however, did set forth a disgraced equivalent for the adulteress-prostitute. This was the *maritus-leno,* the man who had failed to live up to his responsibility as a husband and guardian of his wife's sexual behavior. The law, for all its apparent severity, was not as demanding on this score as the prevailing social mores. At the same time, it responded to a concern that, from what we can tell, was not well grounded in reality.

The logical corollary of defining liability for respectable women was to exempt sexual relations with nonrespectable women. Close attention to the evidence suggests that the statute did not place many types in the latter category. Only prostitutes (and perhaps procuresses) qualified expressly, plus slaves and peregrines by implication, and convicted adulteresses by juristic extension. This fact brings into sharper relief the role of prostitutes in the design of this law as a symbol of sexual shame. The adultery statute had another use for pimps and (perhaps) prostitutes, one that suggests the power of this symbol. This was their liability to be slain in the outraged husband's exercise of the *ius occidendi.* A concluding section viewed the implications of the statute in light of Roman social policy.

Chapter 6 examined a single relevant piece of legislation passed pursuant to the *lex Iulia de adulteriis coercendis:* the *senatus consultum* enacted in A.D. 19 in the wake of the Vistilia incident. This episode witnessed a female member of the senatorial order attempting to escape liability for adultery by claiming exempt status through her registration as a prostitute with the aediles. This was an exceptional case, despite modern assumptions to the contrary. The *SC* made it illegal for members of the senatorial and equestrian orders to practice prostitution and closed the loophole in the law Vistilia had attempted to exploit.

Evidence for juristic interpretation of this statute deals with the offense of *lenocinium* (an exception is a constitution of Diocletian that I argue to speak for the jurists' definition of "prostitute" under this law). The discussion showed how jurists and emperors elaborated the statute's conception of criminal pimping, as it grew from its two statutory species to embrace three other accessory offenses set forth by the law.

Chapter 7 reviewed the evidence for the taxation of prostitutes. Caligula's motive for introducing the tax was at minimum a desire for revenue. This goal was evidently realized in abundance, a fact that encouraged responsibility for its collection to be transferred from publicans to the military. The rate was set at the price of one sexual act per day (a different rate prevailed in Egypt, where civilian collectors continued to operate, as they did in Palmyra). In late antiquity the tax was collected as part of the *collatio lustralis* until its abolition in 498.

Chapter 8 showed that an extraordinary protection existed in private law for a master who did not want a slave he sold to be prostituted by a new owner. A restrictive covenant on sale, "that a slave woman not be prostituted," buttressed by penalties of reacquisition through *manus iniectio* or freedom for the slave, created a "real" effect, becoming in a sense a lien upon the slave. As the regime developed over time, the covenant was upheld against subsequent buyers for whom it had not been restated at time of purchase and even against the original owner himself if he reacquired the slave and violated his own covenant. This regime was the joint creation of juristic and imperial lawfinding. Its rationale is to be discovered, not in the areas of policy developed for prostitution or even slavery per se, but in the context of the honor-shame syndrome, which explains how an owner might retain an interest in the sexual integrity of a slave even after alienation.

The theme of honor-shame was explored further in the context of a text dealing with "real" security in Chapter 9, which treated in summary fashion the approaches to prostitution taken by the jurists in private law. A series of texts was then presented that displayed concern with wasteful expenditure on prostitutes with regard to inheritance, mandate, and *usucapio* on sale. The concern with extravagance did not extend to a denial of her fee to the prostitute. In the fields of theft and wrongful appropriation *(plagium),* however, the rights of prostitutes and (if slaves) their owners underwent a curious derogation under circumstances where the actor's motives were characterized by *libido.*

The themes of honor and economic exploitation of prostitution intersect in a series of texts relating to the *petitio hereditatis, compromissum,* and *operae.* The behavior of respectable women and the clothing appropriate to their station are issues that arise in a passage of Ulpian dealing with *iniuria,* where, I argue, liability for outrage is denied in case of otherwise inappropriate behavior directed at "respectable" women dressed as prostitutes. A final text grants validity of gifts made to prostitutes, while the validity of gifts made to wives was denied, an interesting and not entirely predictable result in light of the other evidence discussed in this chapter.

2. Prostitution and the Law

Nowhere is it possible to discover a "law of prostitution." The law situated prostitutes and pimps at the margin of society through the imposition of a series of civic and legal disabilities whose function was to place practitioners outside the pale of the community of honor, which alone enjoyed a claim to rank and its privileges. Prostitutes and pimps were two of a very small set of marginal types who found themselves in this penumbra of Roman citizen status. They fell just barely inside the line separating the Roman community and true outsiders, who might as *peregrini* have had a better claim to recognition to honor than these "deviant insiders."[1]

This ambiguous status at the margin of Roman society was lent emphasis by a statute, the *lex Iulia et Papia,* which denied prostitutes and pimps marriage partners outside the ranks of ex-slaves. Another Augustan law, the *lex Iulia de adulteriis coercendis,* articulated their dishonored status by exempting them from the penalties it laid down for illicit sexual relations, setting them aside formally as a category of persons without honor. The law punished men and women from the

---

[1] For this phrase used to describe the position of prostitutes in early modern Seville, see Perry, "Insiders" (1985) 143.

community of honor who violated its precepts by relegating them to the margin of society, that space occupied by the dishonored. It isolated, excluded, and defined the latter through use of three devices: special clothing for matrons and prostitutes, the registration of the latter with the aediles, and the descriptive terminology of the law itself.

Their despised situation did not prevent the state from profiting from the activity of prostitutes and pimps. In fact, the state acted in a manner similar to that of many respectable private persons who invested in the sale of sex, for example, through ownership of urban real estate where brothels operated. Taxation also gave increased scope for control, though it also had the consequence of legitimizing the practice of prostitution. The adultery statute, as well as other areas of the law, had a similar consequence.

The symbolic importance of the social classification into the honorable and the dishonored makes it unsurprising to find its full articulation even in a narrow field of private law, the restrictive covenant on the sale of slaves forbidding their prostitution. Nevertheless, the energy with which the policymaking establishment pursued this subject, to the point of recognizing an independent interest in the slave whose covenant is violated, is striking.

Paradoxically, the ideological import of the regime for this covenant is strengthened, not weakened, by what I argue to be its relative insignificance in practice. The law system was willing to go to great lengths in its role as the guarantor of virtue and was equally interested in advertising the same. This was easier to do when the actual stakes were low.

Prostitution, on an individual level—that is, the level of the individual upper-class male—presented a double threat to patrimony and honor, or *damnum* and *dedecus,* as Horace puts it.[2] A dozen texts from private law allow us to trace the curious impact that prostitution had on well-established rules in the private law. For example, Julian denies ability to usucapt to a buyer who knows his seller is a dissolute person about to hand over the sale price to a prostitute, while Ulpian (and, perhaps, Paul) holds the person who steals a slave prostitute out of lust not to be a thief. Owning property containing a brothel was a legitimate enterprise for a respectable member of the elite, whereas setting foot in such an institution was not.

One text, dealing with the delict of outrage, speaks to the issue of appropriate conduct for respectable females. Its holding resonates in an interesting way with the import of the Augustan adultery law. Significant differences, it is true, exist in the degree of fault (and so its consequences) and in the complicity of the male in each case. But both correlate clothing with status, and both identify behavior with status. The underlying point is that women who behave in a manner associated with prostitutes can expect to be treated as such. Once again the law defines the dividing line between honor and shame.

There is then a broad diversity in the legal approaches taken toward prostitution. In the same way, the status of prostitutes shows interesting complexity. Of course, the status of an individual prostitute (or pimp) depended first on her (or

---

[2] Hor. *Serm.* 1.2.52–53.

his) assignment to one of the fundamental classifications of peregrine, slave, freed, or freeborn. But even qua prostitutes and pimps they do not appear to have possessed a single unified status before the law, that is, a coherent ensemble of rights and duties that are enumerated with clarity and precision in the legal texts.[3] All the same, the overwhelming direction of policy is so prejudicial that one cannot seriously speak of a "status dissonance" in their case, as one might assert for actors.[4]

3. Public Policy

Generalizations about Roman public policy toward prostitution may more safely proceed from a comparative historical perspective.[5] The three policies most commonly adopted toward prostitution have been repression, regulation, and toleration.

Toleration, which, for example, broadly characterizes much of present-day Europe, may be identified ideally as the absence of the other two forms. While in theory encouragement of prostitution might characterize a tolerationist approach, indifference is more likely to be its hallmark. This indifference may be qualified by regulation or repression of some aspects of prostitution, such as procuring or public solicitation, that society finds objectionable.

Regulation, which has typically meant official registration of prostitutes, medical examination, and the licensing of brothels, accepts prostitution as inevitable, because regulationists assume male desire to be an uncontrollable natural force that is at best capable of being diverted away from respectable women toward prostitutes. Regulation therefore attempts to control prostitution, with the aim of maintaining order, defending morality, and/or preventing disease. This policy was widespread in continental Europe of the nineteenth century and was particularly associated with France.

Repression often leads to the criminalization of prostitution and the activities associated with it, such as public solicitation, procuring, and keeping a brothel. Repression was popular in Europe at the time of the Reformation and has been the leading American response to prostitution, above all since the Progressive era.

Rarely if ever do any of these policies appear in their pure forms. Classical Rome is a good example of this fact. Romans were profoundly unconcerned to regulate or repress prostitution in the truest sense of these terms. At the same time, they kept a register of prostitutes (for a time), entrusted junior magistrates with the oversight of brothels, and imposed a tax on prostitution, measures more consonant with a policy of regulation or even repression. Late antiquity saw a different mix of policy, with measures aimed at suppressing procuring and the eventual repeal of the tax.

It is not clear, however, that the overall thrust of classical Roman policy should be described as "toleration" simply because it cannot be labeled as a policy of

[3] For the similar situation of actors, see Ducos, "Acteurs" (1990).
[4] See Leppin, *Histrionen* (1992) 160–168, for a discussion.
[5] See McGinn, *ESH* Prostitution (1994) 589–590, for more detail.

either "repression" or "regulation." Is this an accurate classification, after all, when the Romans were so careful to discriminate against the practitioners of prostitution in so many ways?

One way to answer this question is to distinguish between the definition of practitioners' rights or status under law, a subject in which the Romans show a keen interest, and the operation of the business itself, where the principle of non-interference was the rule. Comparison with policy regimes in other historical cultures makes tolerance easier to identify with Rome, as suggested above. But a strong argument can be made that the Romans simply did not have a policy toward prostitution, choosing only to deal with some of its manifestations in an ad hoc and sometimes indirect manner. These measures tended to address the practitioners of prostitution, not the institution itself. The approach may be contrasted with that adopted for slavery, which is vastly more comprehensive and, one may say, "institutional" in nature.

More interesting perhaps is the degree to which Roman policymakers actually legitimized prostitution, in some ways fairly directly, in others almost by default, in part as a consequence of declining to develop a general approach. Some features of this trend have already been discussed. Others are obvious enough. All Romans were notionally free to prostitute themselves or others, in particular their slaves (unless the owner had purchased the slave under a *ne serva* covenant). Upper-class investment in prostitution or at least in property where it was practiced, seems to have been both common and well tolerated. This is paralleled by the state's exploitation of prostitution through receipt of tax revenues.

Beyond this, the law recognized the prostitute's right to retain her fee and allowed her a modest claim to property left as bequests to her. This is remarkable in the face of the threat to patrimony that the prostitute was perceived to pose. As to her personal inviolability, the evidence is sparse and ambiguous, but the Manilia incident at minimum suggests that her rights might be respected at the highest levels of the political order. Prostitutes were allowed their own role in cult, separate and unequal, to be sure, but a role that guaranteed their status as insiders.

The Romans were not concerned to outlaw prostitution, because, like marriage, it represented for them a form of licit sexuality. This held true as long as they were able to identify it, control it, and distinguish it carefully from its counterpart, the respectable institution of marriage. Prostitution might thus serve its recognized function of protecting marriage, whereas illicit forms of sexuality such as adultery threatened to connect and confuse the two.[6] The consequences of trying to eliminate prostitution might be paradoxically to blur the distinction between licit and illicit.[7] Prostitution might be well tolerated by making prostitutes accessible and respectable women inaccessible.[8]

For the same reason, just as it elevated the status of respectable women, the law placed prostitutes and pimps in a category of the most degraded citizens. There is no contradiction here with the legitimizing of prostitution: it suggests that the

[6] See Villa, "Prostituzione" (1981) 312.
[7] See Roper, "Discipline" (1985) 18–21.
[8] Roper, "Discipline" 6.

overall thrust of policy was double-edged. Prostitutes were tolerated at the margin of society and left to practice their profession under the condition that they remain "marginal."

A good illustration of this double-edged tendency is found in the Augustan adultery law. It remands prostitutes and procuresses to a degraded category of "exempt" women. Like sex with slaves, here is a tolerated field of nonmarital sexual activity. In identifying these women as permissible sexual outlets, the statute implicitly legitimizes the function society prescribes for them as sexual "lightning rods," or distractions for male predators away from respectable women. This does not mean that prostitutes themselves are in any significant sense "legitimized." Instead, the law marks them as officially disgraced, and they are joined in this category of the dishonored by convicted adulteresses. The statute's very design reveals that adultery and *stuprum* were conceived, not simply as sexual, but as social offenses—especially, but not uniquely, when the status of the male lover was inferior to that of his partner. This double-edged strategy was not without its ambiguities and risks. This fact was revealed the day the senatorial Vistilia chose to register with the aediles as a claim of exemption under the adultery law.

4. Society and Law

The attempt to strike a balance between tolerance and degradation explains much detail in those areas of the Roman law that deal with prostitution and its practitioners. The issues that drive lawfinding on this subject are fairly constant and not simply the residue of long-term social trends moving in a single direction. The evolutionary hypothesis to my mind cannot explain the development of law regarding prostitution.

I hope to have shown in this book that the relationship between life and law was not as straightforward as the evolutionary hypothesis assumes. The progress of neither law nor society was a linear development whereby changes in social values and practices were followed, often at a distance of decades, by corresponding adjustments in legal rules. Instead, the law changed, but not always in one direction, and it arose from the balancing of ever-present interests more than as a reflection of steady-state historical trends, which in turn we must be careful not to read out of a perceived change in law.

This pattern holds true despite the fact that the issues at stake are sufficiently pressing to pose a challenge to the concept of autonomy of law. Time and again, we have seen prostitution interject an element that appears to shape lawfinding in a direct manner, apparently unmediated by doctrine and tradition, so that social norms are readily transformed into law. One may view this as a general tendency where the elemental social values in the field of sexuality intersect with the legal order.[9]

One piece of evidence I would advance in support of this argument is the fact that for all of their complexity and sophistication, the statutes we have examined

[9] This is not true exclusively for matters sexual; see Wacke, *"Potentiores"* (1980) 568–569, and Dixon, "Breaking" (1985) 533–534, for apposite examples.

are in some respects poorly designed. Important reform of the Augustan marriage law was deemed necessary very early on, both during and immediately after the reign of Augustus.[10] The jurists complain of inadequate statutory language.[11] Some problems in the regulation of morals are not easily managed, even in the face of a fury of legal skill.[12] When the Romans attempted to regulate sexual conduct, the results were often inadequate, self-contradictory, or just bad law. A strain of Roman moral criticism appears to recognize this difficulty when it condemns resort to law in this field as itself a confession of desperation.[13]

It is not surprising of course to find a society under stress, as Rome was in its transition from Republic to Principate, attempting to restore order through imposition of a rigid code of moral conduct.[14] Larger-scale and more complex societies tend to require the intervention of the state in private disputes between citizens, and there is no reason to exclude this tendency in the field of sexual honor.

In the final analysis, however, the principle of autonomy of the legal order reasserts itself. One finds this principle accepted chiefly with respect to the private law of the jurists,[15] but I mean it to apply more broadly, for two reasons. One has to do with the fact that it is in practice impossible to separate the work of the jurists from almost all of the positive enactments I have studied, whether comitial statutes, enactments of the Senate, or imperial decisions. The second depends on the fact that the few juristic texts that deal exclusively with prostitution and private law by and large show no obvious difference with respect to the principle of autonomy of law.

The Roman legal response to prostitution does not hold up a mirror to this social institution. Instead, it transforms its image, at times almost beyond recognition. Not that law consistently provides a less useful reading of actual social conditions, which our literary and other nonlegal sources barely permit us to glimpse. A good example is the problem of *lenocinium,* whose legal regime may help provide a useful correction to the exaggerations of moralists. It is useful to compare the Augustan marriage prohibitions, at any rate those designed for the senatorial order. The existence of such rules does not by itself support the inference that a barrier had been successfully challenged.[16]

---

[10]For the legislative history, see Chapter 3. Note the perceived need for Tiberius's reform commission of A.D. 20: Tac. *Ann.* 3.25–28, with Bauman, *LPRE* (1989) 56–59.

[11]Gaius 3.47: ". . . quamvis parum diligenter ea pars legis scripta sit"; Mette-Dittmann, *Ehegesetze* (1991) 154–155. Compare Lab.-Ulp. D. 24.3.64.9 and the observations of the jurists regarding the usage of *adulterium* and *stuprum* in the Augustan adultery law, see Chapter 5.

[12]The jurists were not able to discover an adequate solution to the challenge of concubinage: McGinn, "Concubinage" (1991). In a similar way tensions and contradictions were at work in the application of the Augustan marriage law: Wacke, "Manumissio" (1989) 424–425.

[13]Hor. *Carm.* 3.24.35–36: "quid leges sine moribus vanae proficiunt?" Tac. *Germ.* 19.5: "Plusque ibi boni mores valent quam alibi bonae leges." On a more general level, Roman caution toward reliance on positive law was grounded in their deep moral conservatism: Honsell, "Gesetzesverständnis" (1982) esp. 134, 148.

[14]See Stone, *Road* (1990) 278.

[15]For a recent statement, see Crook, *Advocacy* (1995) 178–179.

[16]For a similar point, see Marshall, "Civil Courts" (1989) 39.

5. Unity in Diversity

In the field of prostitution, Roman law effects this distortion through what one may argue to be an adequate management, understood on Roman terms, and even then only in a qualified sense, of the two trends in policy identified above: toleration and degradation. As evidence of this accommodation I cite the truest instance of the unity of Roman policy toward prostitution. This is the remarkable manner in which lawfinders describe prostitutes. This is nearly perfectly monochrome, in the sense that it occurs in three nearly indistinguishable shades. The statutes have the technojuridical ''qui quaeve palam quaestum facit fecerit.'' The jurists, when not commenting on legislation, prefer the bland *meretrix* or an equally colorless verb such as *prostituere*. On two occasions they use the expression *scortum,* less neutral than the others, perhaps, but no one's model of sociological precision.

Comparative evidence suggests that in most societies, at least complex ones, prostitution exists in a multiplicity of forms.[17] Were there no higher-status prostitutes at Rome, no near equivalents to the familiar Greek *hetaira*? What about part-time prostitutes, temporary prostitutes, prostitutes who worked primarily (or not) in other professions, as dancers, musicians, waitresses, bath attendants, and so on? The question scarcely interests the jurists, except in a few instances when they trouble to insist that a certain legal rule designed for prostitutes applies to some or (to generalize) all of the above.

The ultimate aim of Roman law regarding prostitution was to draw a line, perhaps better understood as two parallel lines, that would ideally keep prostitutes and pimps frozen in place on the periphery of Roman society. On the one hand, the highly prejudiced legal position of practitioners seems contradicted by the éclat that a small number of them, for example, Volumnia Cytheris, were able to enjoy.[18] On the other hand, some results seem broadly satisfactory, at least from a Roman perspective. The tax brought in a big return. The restrictive covenant on slave sale, which had nothing to do with most prostitutes, made a low-cost statement about society's readiness to safeguard sexual honor. The adultery law, which helped guarantee the sexual availability of a degraded class of women, made a similar statement, though surely at a greater cost. Practitioners were effectively barred from the upper reaches of society, though one may question to what extent this was the direct effect of civic disabilities and the Augustan marriage prohibitions.

On a strictly practical level, these latter measures appear almost unnecessary or irrelevant. To judge their true utility for the Romans, it is convenient to resort to a Foucauldian analysis, which is able to locate in the law a discourse, generated by the confluence of power and knowledge, that aims to shape practices in a society. In this area, Foucauldians have shown greater perspicacity than Foucault himself, who in my view prematurely excluded law from his examination of ancient discourses on sexuality.[19]

---

[17] See, e.g., Villa, ''Prostituzione'' 306.

[18] A similar contradiction existed for actors: Leppin, *Histrionen* (1992) 20 (cf. 23). Few succeeded in overcoming the legal impediments: Leppin, *Histrionen* esp. 77, 107.

[19] See Foucault, *HS* 1 (1978) esp. 90–91, whose conception of law seems peculiarly inappropriate

The principle of the autonomy of law does not mean that legal norms regarding sexuality are an aspect of culture that cannot be related to a society's discursive practices overall.[20] The repeated assertions of ineligibility for various privileges of citizenship help produce the desired effect by themselves, which is to say that discourse breeds disability.[21] To put the matter in a more general way, law qualifies as a constitutive rhetoric, in the sense that it constitutes reality.[22] This reality is a "culture of argument, perpetually remade by its participants."[23]

Prostitutes, although marginal to Roman society, are central to this discourse on sexuality. The crucial role they play in the cultural iconography of the Augustan laws on marriage and adultery—whose categories of social and sexual disgrace show greater economy than once assumed—may serve as an illustration of this point. To adapt a concept familiar from anthropology, Roman makers of social policy found prostitutes convenient to think with.

Another fundamental aim of Roman policy was to prevent members of the upper classes from behaving, in effect, like prostitutes and pimps. Pessimism remains the trend among moderns in the evaluation of the adultery law's success, as we have seen. Whether this is justified or not, it is impossible to say, though it is important to remember that the Romans had a standard of measurement higher, I argue, than our own. There may only have been one Vistilia, but only one Vistilia was necessary to reveal to Roman eyes the contradictions and inadequacies shown by their social policy in this area.

The Romans' own measure of adequacy is not the only one available to us, of course. On any estimate of social justice we might prefer, a rather huge failure begins to emerge in Roman policy toward prostitution. This difference in perspective I am inclined to attribute to the legacy left by the Christians. Whatever the internal contradictions, accommodations to practice, and continuities with the pagan world one finds in Christian moral discourse on prostitution, there is at least one important new development. This is the idea that the prostitute may be redeemed. In its extreme form, the idea represents the prostitute as an allegory of the human soul, in its fallen state, able to be saved nevertheless through the gift of divine grace. Humanity finds itself alone in the desert, in the person of the harlot Thais, facing the East and begging the mercy of the Creator, whose name she deems herself unworthy to utter.[24] We have come as far as we possibly can from Ulpian and his colleagues laying down the law in the center of power, Rome.

---

for Rome. I take as significant the fact that in *HS* 3 (1986), which purports to be a history of Roman discourse on sexuality, one finds only scattered mention of Roman law.

[20] For the general point regarding Rome, see Edwards, *Politics* (1993) 75, 89.

[21] See Swarney, "Status" (1993) 142, 146, 154–155.

[22] Crook, *Advocacy* 26.

[23] White, *Heracles' Bow* (1985) 35 (cf. 39, 41–42, 46, 48).

[24] See Ward, *Harlots* (1987) esp. 84 (*vita Thaisis* 3).

Bibliography

Abbreviations for philological and historical works generally follow those given by *L'année philologique*; for Roman legal literature, those given by Kaser, *RP* 1²; Guarino, *DPR*⁹. Citations in the notes give the abbreviations listed below, plus (at first appearance in each chapter) date of publication.

Abramenko, "Liberti" = A. Abramenko, "Liberti als Dekurionen: Einige Überlegungen zur lex Malacitana," *Laverna* 3 (1992) 94–103.

Adams, *LSV* = J. N. Adams, *The Latin Sexual Vocabulary* (Baltimore 1982).

Adams, "Words" = J. N. Adams, "Words for 'Prostitute' in Latin," *RhM* 126 (1983) 321–358.

Aigner, "Stellung" = H. Aigner, "Zur gesellschaftlichen Stellung von Henkern, Gladiatoren, und Berufsathleten," in Weiler, *SRAA* (1988) 201–220.

Albanese, *Persone* = B. Albanese, *Le persone nel diritto privato romano* (Palermo 1979).

Alföldy, "Stellung" = G. Alföldy, "Die Stellung der Ritter in der Führungsschicht des Imperium Romanum," *Chiron* 11 (1981) 169–215.

Alföldy, *Social History* = G. Alföldy, *The Social History of Rome* (Baltimore rev. ed. 1988).

Allen, "Theodora" = P. Allen, "Contemporary Portrayals of the Empress Theodora (A.D. 527–548)," in B. Garlick et al. eds., *Stereotypes of Women in Power: Historical Perspectives and Revisionist Views* (New York 1992) 93–103.

Alpers, *Finanzsystem* = M. Alpers, *Das nachrepublikanische Finanzsystem: Fiscus und Fisci in der frühen Kaiserzeit* (Berlin 1995).

Alston, *Soldier* = R. Alston, *Soldier and Society in Roman Egypt: A Social History* (New York 1995).

Alvarez de Cienfuegos, "*Lenocinium*" = F. J. Alvarez de Cienfuegos, "Algunas observaciones a proposito de la represion del *lenocinium* en la *lex Iulia de adulteriis,"* in *Estudios en homenaje al Profesor J. Iglesias* 2 (Madrid 1988) 565–577.

Amelotti, "Egitto" = M. Amelotti, "L'Egitto augusteo tra novità e continuità," *JJP* 20 (1990) 19–24 (= Criscuolo and Geraci, *ESA* [1989] 243–249).

Anagnostou-Cañas, "Femme" = B. Anagnostou-Cañas, "La femme devant la justice provinciale dans l'Égypte romaine," *RHD* 62 (1984) 337–360.

André, "Statut" = J. M. André, "Les élégiaques romains et la statut de la femme," in *L'élégie romaine* (Paris 1980) 51–61.

André, "Zuschauerschaft" = J. M. André, "Die Zuschauerschaft als sozialpolitischer Mikrokosmos zur Zeit des Hochprinzipats," in Blänsdorf, *TGIR* (1990) 165–173.

Andreau and Bruhns, *Parenté* = J. Andreau and H. Bruhns eds., *Parenté et stratégies familiales dans l'antiquité romaine* (Coll. Éc. Franç. Rome 129) (Rome 1990).

Andréev, "Divorce" = M. Andréev, "Divorce et adultère dans le droit romain classique," *RHD*⁴ 35 (1957) 1–32.

Andréev, "Lex Iulia" = M. Andréev, "La lex Iulia de adulteriis coercendis," *Stud. Clas.* 5 (1963) 165–180.

Andreotti, "Politica" = R. Andreotti, "Su alcuni problemi del rapporto fra politica di sicurezza e controllo del commercio nell'impero romano," *RIDA*³ 16 (1969) 215–257.

Angelini, *Procurator* = P. Angelini, *Il Procurator* (Milan 1971).

Ankum, "*Captiva*" = H. Ankum, "La *captiva adultera*: Problèmes concernant l'*accusatio adulterii* en droit romain classique," *RIDA*³ 32 (1985) 153–205.

Ankum, "*Sponsa*" = H. A. Ankum, "La *sponsa adultera*: Problèmes concernant l'*accusatio adulterii* en droit romain classique," in *Estudios de derecho romano en honor de A. D'Ors* 1 (Pamplona 1987) 161–198.

Arangio-Ruiz, "Legislazione" = V. Arangio-Ruiz, "La legislazione," *Scritti di diritto romano* 3 (Naples 1977) 249–294 (= *Augustus: Studi in occasione del bimillenario augusteo* [1938] 101–146).

Astin, "*RM*" = A. E. Astin, "*Regimen Morum*," *JRS* 78 (1988) 14–34.

Astolfi, "Aspetti" = R. Astolfi, "Aspetti del diritto matrimoniale in età arcaica," *SDHI* 58 (1992) 230–261.

Astolfi, "Endogamia" = R. Astolfi, "L'endogamia della clientela gentilizia," *SDHI* 60 (1994) 75–81.

Astolfi, *LIP*² = R. Astolfi, *La Lex Iulia et Papia*² (Padua 1986) [cf. *LIP*³ (Padua 1995): all references are to the second ed.].

Astolfi, "Sabino" = R. Astolfi, "Sabino e la vendita degli schiavi," *SDHI* 52 (1986) 537–542.

Auguet, *Caligula* = R. Auguet, *Caligula, ou le pouvoir à vingt ans* (Paris 1975).

Austin, *Caelio*³ = R. G. Austin, *M. Tulli Ciceronis Pro M. Caelio Oratio*³ (Oxford 1960).

Badian, "Marriage Law" = E. Badian, "A Phantom Marriage Law," *Philologus* 129 (1985) 82–98.

Badian, "*Scribae*" = E. Badian, "The *Scribae* of the Roman Republic," *Klio* 71 (1989) 582–603.

Bagnall, "Divorce" = R. Bagnall, "Church, State, and Divorce in Late Roman Egypt," in K.-L. Selig and R. Somerville eds., *Essays in Honor of Paul Oskar Kristeller* (New York 1987) 41–61.

Bagnall, *Egypt* = R. Bagnall, *Egypt in Late Antiquity* (Princeton 1993).

Bagnall, "Periodicity" = R. Bagnall, "The Periodicity and Collection of the Chrysargyron," *Tyche* 7 (1992) 15–17.

Bagnall (rev. Beaucamp) = R. Bagnall (review of Beaucamp, *Statut*), *BASP* 32 (1995) 65–86.

Bagnall, "Trick" = R. Bagnall, "A Trick a Day to Keep the Tax Man at Bay? The Prostitute Tax in Roman Egypt," *BASP* 28 (1991) 5–12.

Bailey, *Homosexuality* = D. S. Bailey, *Homosexuality and the Western Christian Tradition* (London 1975).

Balsdon, *Gaius* = J. P. V. D. Balsdon, *The Emperor Gaius* (Oxford 1964 repr. of 1934 Oxford ed.).

Baltrusch, *RM* = E. Baltrusch, *Regimen Morum: Die Reglementierung des Privatlebens der Senatoren und Ritter in der römischen Republik und frühen Kaiserzeit* (Vestigia 41) (Munich 1989).

Balzarini, *Iniuria* = M. Balzarini, *De iniuria extra ordinem statui: Contributo allo studio del diritto penale romano dell'età classica* (Padua 1983).

Balzarini, *"Lex Cornelia"* = M. Balzarini, "Ancora sulla *lex Cornelia de iniuriis* e sulla repressione di talune modalità di diffamazione," in *Estudios en homenaje al Profesor J. Iglesias* 2 (Madrid 1988) 579–603.

Barnard, *Justin* = L. W. Barnard, *Justin Martyr: His Life and Thought* (Cambridge 1967).

Barnes, "Kaisergeschichte" = T. D. Barnes, "The Lost Kaisergeschichte and the Latin Historical Tradition," in *Early Christianity and the Roman Empire* (London 1984) IV 13–43 (= *BHAC 1968/1969* [Bonn 1970] 13–43).

Barrett, *Caligula* = A. A. Barrett, *Caligula: The Corruption of Power* (New Haven 1989).

Barry, *Slavery* = K. Barry, *Female Sexual Slavery* (Englewood Cliffs 1979).

Bassanelli Sommariva, "Considerazioni" = G. Bassanelli Sommariva, "Brevi considerazioni su CTh. 9.7.1," *AAC* 7 (Naples 1988) 309–323.

Bauman, "Aediles" = R. A. Bauman, "Criminal Prosecutions by the Aediles," *Latomus* 33 (1974) 245–264.

Bauman, *Impietas* = R. A. Bauman, *Impietas in Principem: A Study of Treason against the Roman Emperor with Special Reference to the First Century* A.D. (Munich 1974).

Bauman, "*Leges*" = R. A. Bauman, "The *Leges Iudiciorum Publicorum* and Their Interpretation in the Republic, Principate, and Later Empire," *ANRW* 2.13 (Berlin 1980) 103–233.

Bauman, "Libri" = R. A. Bauman, "I libri *de iudiciis publicis*," *Index* 5 (1974/1975 [1979]) 39–48.

Bauman, *LPRE* = R. A. Bauman, *Lawyers and Politics in the Early Roman Empire* (Munich 1989).

Bauman, "*Metus*" = R. A. Bauman, "The Rape of Lucretia, *Quod metus causa,* and the Criminal Law," *Latomus* 52 (1993) 550–566.

Bauman, "Quaestio" = R. A. Bauman, "Some Remarks on the Structure and Survival of the *Quaestio de Adulteriis*," *Antichthon* 2 (1968) 68–93.

Bauman, "Resumé, *HA*" = R. A. Bauman, "The Resumé of Legislation in the Early Vitae of the Historia Augusta," *SZ* 94 (1977) 43–75.

Bauman, "Resumé, Suetonius" = R. A. Bauman, "The Resumé of Legislation in Suetonius," *SZ* 99 (1982) 81–127.

Bauman, *Women* = R. A. Bauman, *Women and Politics in Ancient Rome* (London 1992).

Beard, "Re-reading" = M. Beard, "Re-reading Vestal Virginity," in Hawley and Levick, *Women* (1995) 166–177.

Beard, "Status" = M. Beard, "The Sexual Status of Vestal Virgins," *JRS* 70 (1980) 12–27.

Beaucamp, *Statut* = J. Beaucamp, *Le statut de la femme à Byzance (4e–7e siècle)* 1: *Le droit impérial* (Paris 1990), 2: *Les pratiques sociales* (Paris 1992).

Becker, *Gallus*² = W. A. Becker (F. Metcalfe trans.), *Gallus or Roman Scenes from the Time of Augustus*² (London and New York 1920).

Behrends, "Eheverbot" = O. Behrends, "Die Rechtsregelungen der Militärdiplome und das die Soldaten des Prinzipats treffende Eheverbot," in W. Eck and H. Wolff eds., *Heer und Integrationspolitik: Die römischen Militärdiplome als historische Quelle* (Cologne and Vienna 1986) 116–166.

Behrends, "Prokuratur" = O. Behrends, "Die Prokuratur des klassischen römischen Zivilrechts," *SZ* 88 (1971) 215–299.

Bellebaum, "Randgruppen" = A. Bellebaum, "Randgruppen: Ein Beitrag zur Soziologie sozialer Probleme und sozialer Kontrolle," in Weiler, *SRAA* (1988) 47–57.

Bellen, *Sklavenflucht* = H. Bellen, *Studien zur Sklavenflucht im römischen Kaiserreich* (Forsch. zur ant. Sklaverei 4) (Wiesbaden 1971).

Bellen, "Sklaverei" = H. Bellen, "Die antike Sklaverei als moderne Herausforderung: Zur Situation der internationalen Sklavenforschung," *Ak. Wiss. Lit. Mainz 1949–1989* (Wiesbaden 1989) 195–208.

Bellen, "Status" = H. Bellen, "Novus Status—Novae Leges: Kaiser Augustus als Gesetzgeber," in G. Binder ed., *Saeculum Augustum* 1: *Herrschaft und Gesellschaft* (Darmstadt 1987) 308–348.

Bénabou, "Pratique" = M. Bénabou, "Pratique matrimoniale et représentation philosophique: Le crépuscule des stratégies?" in Andreau and Bruhns, *Parenté* (1990) 123–137.

Berger, *Dictionary* = A. Berger, *An Encyclopedic Dictionary of Roman Law* (Philadelphia 1953).

Berger, *RE* Paconius (2) = A. Berger, s.v. Paconius (2), *RE* 36.1 (1942) 2124–2125.

Bernand, *Portes* = A. Bernand, *Les portes du désert: Recueil des inscriptions grecques d'Antinooupolis, Tentyris, Koptos, Apollonopolis Parva et Apollonopolis Magna* (Paris 1984).

Besnier, "Lois" = R. Besnier, "L'application des lois caducaires d'Auguste d'après le Gnomon de l'Idiologue," *RIDA* 2 (1949) 93–118.

Besnier, "Pline" = R. Besnier, "Pline le Jeune et l'application des lois démographiques," in *Mélanges Dauvillier* (Toulouse 1979) 89–98.

Bieber, *RE* stola = Bieber, s.v. stola, *RE* 13 (1931) 56–62.

Biezunska-Malowist, *Esclavage* 2 = I. Biezunska-Malowist, *L'esclavage dans l'Égypte gréco-romaine* 2: *Période romaine* (Warsaw, Cracow, Gdansk 1977).

Biondi, "*Leges*" = B. Biondi, "*Leges Populi Romani,*" *Scritti giuridici* 2 (Milan 1965) 189–306 (= S. Riccobono ed., *Acta Divi Augusti* 1 [Rome 1946] 103–223).

Biondi, "Legislazione" = B. Biondi, "La legislazione di Augusto," *Scritti giuridici* 2 (Milan 1965) 77–188 (= *Conferenze augustee nel bimillenario della nascita* [Milan 1939] 141–262).

Biondi, "Poena" = B. Biondi, "La poena adulterii da Augusto a Giustiniano," *Scritti giuridici* 2 (Milan 1965) 47–74 (= *Studi Sassaresi* 16 [1938] 63–96) (= *Scritti di diritto e di economia in onore di F. Mancaleoni*).

Biondi, "SCC" = B. Biondi, "Senatusconsulta," *Scritti giuridici* 2 (Milan 1965) 307–354 (= S. Riccobono ed., *Acta Divi Augusti* 1 [Rome 1946] 227–274).

Birks, "Dominium" = P. Birks, "The Roman Law Concept of Dominium and the Idea of Absolute Ownership," *AJ 1985* (1986) 1–37.

Birks, "New Light" = P. Birks, "New Light on the Roman Legal System: The Appointment of Judges," *Cambridge L.J.* 47 (1988) 36–60.

Birley, "Notes" = A. R. Birley, "Some Notes on HA Severus 1–4," *BHAC 1968/1969* (Bonn 1970) 59–77.

Bissing, "Aphrodision" = F. W. von Bissing, "Aphrodision," *RhM* n.F. 92 (1944) 375–381.

Blänsdorf, *TGIR* = J. Blänsdorf ed., *Theater und Gesellschaft im Imperium Romanum* (Tübingen 1990).

Bloch, *Prostitution* = I. Bloch, *Die Prostitution* 1 (Berlin 1912), 2 (Berlin 1925).

Boatwright, *Hadrian* = M. T. Boatwright, *Hadrian and the City of Rome* (Princeton 1987).

Boatwright, "Imperial Women" = M. T. Boatwright, "The Imperial Women of the Early Second Century A.D.," *AJP* 112 (1991) 513–540.

Böckh, *Staatshaushaltung*³ = A. Böckh (M. Fränkel ed.), *Die Staatshaushaltung der Athener*³ (Berlin 1886).

Boegehold, *Lawcourts* = A. L. Boegehold, *The Lawcourts at Athens* (Princeton 1995) (= *The Athenian Agora* 28).

Bollinger, *TL* = T. Bollinger, *Theatralis Licentia: Die Publikumsdemonstrationen an den öffentlichen Spielen im Rom der früheren Kaiserzeit und ihre Bedeutung im politischen Leben* (Winterthur 1969).

Bömer, *Fasten* = F. Bömer, *P. Ovidius Naso, Die Fasten: Herausgegeben, übersetzt und kommentiert* 1 (Heidelberg 1957), 2 (Heidelberg 1958).

Bonfante, *Corso* 1 = P. Bonfante, *Corso di diritto romano* 1: *Diritto di famiglia* (Milan 1963 repr. of Rome 1925 ed.).

Bonfante, *Corso* 6 = P. Bonfante, *Corso di diritto romano* 6: *Le Successioni* (Rome 1930).

Bonifacio, *NNDI* compromesso = F. Bonifacio, s.v. compromesso (diritto romano), *NNDI* 3 (1959) 784–786.

Bonini, "Libro" = R. Bonini, "Note sul primo libro delle Istituzioni giustinianee (I. 1.6.7 e 1.8.2)," in *Studi in memoria di G. Donatuti* 1 (Milan 1973) 143–160.

Bonini, *RDG*² = R. Bonini, *Ricerche di diritto giustinianeo*² (Milan 1990).

Bonner, *Declamation* = S. F. Bonner, *Roman Declamation in the Late Republic and Early Empire* (Liverpool 1949).

Bonner, *Education* = S. F. Bonner, *Education in Ancient Rome, from the Elder Cato to the Younger Pliny* (Berkeley and Los Angeles 1977).

Boswell, *Kindness* = J. Boswell, *The Kindness of Strangers: The Abandonment of Children in Western Europe from Late Antiquity to the Renaissance* (New York 1988).

Bouché-Leclercq, "Lois" = A. Bouché-Leclercq, "Les lois démographiques d'Auguste," *RH* 57 (1895) 241–292.

Boulvert and Morabito, "Droit" = G. Boulvert and M. Morabito, "Le droit de l'esclavage sous le Haut-Empire," *ANRW* 2.14 (Berlin 1982) 98–182.

Bowersock, "Pontificate" = G. W. Bowersock, "The Pontificate of Augustus," in Raaflaub and Toher, *BRE* (1990) 380–394.

Bowman, "Papyri" = A. K. Bowman, "Papyri and Roman Imperial History," *JRS* 66 (1976) 153–173.

Bowman and Rathbone, "Cities" = A. K. Bowman and D. Rathbone, "Cities and Administration in Roman Egypt," *JRS* 82 (1992) 107–127.

Bradley, "Ideals" = K. R. Bradley, "Ideals of Marriage in Suetonius' *Caesares*," *RSA* 15 (1985) 77–95.

Bradley, *Slavery* = K. R. Bradley, *Slavery and Society at Rome* (Cambridge 1994).

Bradley, "Seneca" = K. R. Bradley, "Seneca and Slavery," *C & M* 37 (1986) 161–172.

Bradley (rev. Evans) = K. R. Bradley (review of Evans, *War*), *CP* 88 (1993) 237–250.

Bradley, *Slaves and Masters* = K. R. Bradley, *Slaves and Masters in the Roman Empire: A Study in Social Control* (New York and Oxford rev. ed. 1987).

Bradley, "Supply" = K. R. Bradley, "On the Roman Slave Supply and Slave Breeding," *Slavery & Abolition* 8 (1987) 42–64 (= M. I. Finley ed., *Classical Slavery* [London 1987]).

Branca, *ED* adulterio = G. Branca, s.v. adulterio (diritto romano), *ED* 1 (1958) 620–662.

Brasiello, "Desuetudine" = U. Brasiello, "Sulla desuetudine dei *iudicia publica,*" in *Studi in onore di E. Betti* 4 (Milan 1962) 551–570 (= *Riv. trim.* 17 [1963] 220–234).

Brasiello, *Repressione* = U. Brasiello, *La repressione penale in diritto romano* (Naples 1937).

Braund, "Juvenal" = S. H. Braund, "Juvenal—Misogynist or Misogamist?" *JRS* 82 (1992) 71–86.

Bringmann, "Reform" = K. Bringmann, "Zur Gerichtsreform des Kaiser Augustus," *Chiron* 3 (1973) 235–244.

Bringmann, *Frau* = L. Bringmann, *Die Frau im ptolemäisch-kaiserlichen Aegypten* (Diss. Bonn 1939).

Broughton, *MRR* = T. R. S. Broughton, *The Magistrates of the Roman Republic* 1 (Atlanta 1986 repr. of New York 1951 ed.), 2 (New York 1952/Atlanta 1984), 3 (Atlanta 1986).

Brown, *Body* = P. Brown, *The Body and Society: Men, Women, and Sexual Renunciation in Early Christianity* (New York 1988).

Bruhns, "Kompromiß" = H. Bruhns, "Ein politischer Kompromiß im Jahr 70 v. Chr.: Die *Lex Aurelia iudiciaria,*" *Chiron* 10 (1980) 263–272.

Brundage, "Prostitution" = J. A. Brundage, "Prostitution and the Medieval Canon Law," *Signs* 1 (1975/6) 825–845.

Brunt, "Equites" = P. A. Brunt, "The Equites in the Late Republic," in *The Fall of the Roman Republic and Related Essays* (Oxford 1988) 144–193.

Brunt, "Fiscus" = P. A. Brunt, "The 'Fiscus' and Its Development," in *Roman Imperial Themes* (Oxford 1990) 134–162 (= *JRS* 56 [1966] 75–91).

Brunt, *IM* = P. A. Brunt, *Italian Manpower: 225 B.C.–A.D. 14* (Oxford rev. ed. 1987).

Brunt, "Judiciary Rights" = P. A. Brunt, "Judiciary Rights in the Republic," in *The Fall of the Roman Republic and Related Essays* (Oxford 1988) 194–239.

Brunt, "Lex" = P. A. Brunt, "The Lex Valeria Cornelia," *JRS* 51 (1961) 71–83.

Brunt, "Princeps" = P. A. Brunt, "Princeps and Equites," *JRS* 73 (1983) 42–75.

Brunt, "Publicans" = P. A. Brunt, "Publicans in the Principate," in *Roman Imperial Themes* (Oxford 1990) 354–432.

Brunt, "Remarks" = P. A. Brunt, "Remarks on the Imperial *Fiscus,*" in *Roman Imperial Themes* (Oxford 1990) 347–353 (= *LCM* 9/1 [1984] 2–4).

Brunt, "Revenues" = P. A. Brunt, "The Revenues of Rome," in *Roman Imperial Themes* (Oxford 1990) 324–346 (with 531–540) (= *JRS* 71 [1981] 161–172).

Brunt, (rev. Strasburger) = P. A. Brunt (review of H. Strasburger, *Zum antiken Gesellschaftsideal* [Heidelberg 1976]), *Gnomon* 51 (1979) 443–448.

Buckland, *RLS* = W. W. Buckland, *The Roman Law of Slavery: The Roman Law of Slavery from Augustus to Justinian* (New York 1969 repr. of Cambridge 1908 ed.)

Burdese (rev. Angelini) = A. Burdese (review of Angelini, *Procurator*), *SDHI* 37 (1971) 307–328.

Burton, "Procurators" = G. P. Burton, "Provincial Procurators and the Public Provinces," *Chiron* 23 (1993) 13–28.

Buti, "*Cognitio*" = I. Buti, "La *cognitio extra ordinem* da Augusto a Diocleziano," *ANRW* 2.14 (Berlin 1982) 29–59.

Buttrey, *Chronology* = T. V. Buttrey, *Documentary Evidence for the Chronology of the Flavian Titulature* (Meisenheim am Glan 1980).

Cagnat, *Étude* = R. Cagnat, *Étude historique sur les impôts indirects chez les Romains jusqu'aux invasions des Barbares, d'après les documents litteraires et épigraphiques* (Paris 1882).

Cagnat, "Remarques" = R. Cagnat, "Remarques sur un tarif récemment découvert à Palmyre," *RPh*² 8 (1884) 135–144.

Calderini, *"Apatores"* = A. Calderini, *"Apatores,"* *Aegyptus* 33 (1953) 358–369.

Calderini, "Riforme" = A. Calderini, "Le riforme sociali di Augusto," *Conferenze augustee nel bimillenario della nascita* (Milan 1939) 119–138.

Cameron, "Women" = A. Cameron, "Women in Ancient Culture and Society," *AU* 32.2 (1989) 6–17.

Campbell, "Marriage" = B. Campbell, "The Marriage of Soldiers under the Empire," *JRS* 68 (1978) 152–166.

Campbell, *Emperor* = J. B. Campbell, *The Emperor and the Roman Army: 31* B.C.–A.D. *235* (Oxford 1984).

Cantarella, "Famiglia" = E. Cantarella, "Famiglia romana e demografia sociale: Spunti di riflessione critica e metodologica," *Iura* 43 (1992) 99–111.

Cantarella, "Homicides" = E. Cantarella, "Homicides of Honor: The Development of Italian Adultery Law over Two Millennia," in D. I. Kertzer and R. P. Saller eds., *The Family in Italy from Antiquity to the Present* (New Haven and London 1991) 229–244.

Cantarella, *SN* = E. Cantarella, *Secondo natura: La bisessualità nel mondo antico* (Rome 1988).

Carcaterra, *"Mater Familias"* = A. Carcaterra, *"Mater familias,"* *AG* 123 (1940) 113–164.

Carvarzere, *"Fufio"* = A. Carvarzere, *"De teste Fufio* (Cicerone e il trattamento dei testimoni nella *Pro Caelio*)," in A. Burdese ed., *Idee vecchie e nuove sul diritto criminale romano* (Padua 1988) 117–136.

Casavola, *Azioni* = F. Casavola, *Studi sulle azioni populari romane: Le actiones populares* (Naples 1958).

Castelli, "Concubinato" = G. Castelli, "Il concubinato e la legislazione augustea," in *Scritti giuridici* (Milan 1923) 143–163 (= *BIDR* 27 [1914] 55–71).

Castello, *Matrimonio* = C. Castello, *In tema di matrimonio e concubinato nel mondo romano* (Milan 1940).

Castello, "Soldati" = C. Castello, "Sul matrimonio dei soldati," *RISG* 15 (1940) 27–119.

Cervenca, "Libri" = G. Cervenca, "Appunti sui *libri singulares de adulteriis* di Papiniano e di Paolo," *Studi in onore di E. Volterra* 3 (Milan 1971) 395–416.

Champlin, *FJ* = E. Champlin, *Final Judgements: Duty and Emotion in Roman Wills, 200* B.C.–A.D. *250* (Berkeley, Los Angeles, Oxford 1991).

Chaniotis (rev. Baltrusch) = A. Chaniotis (review of Baltrusch, *RM), Gött. gel. Anz.* 243 (1991) 68–86.

Chastagnol, "Clarissimat" = A. Chastagnol, "La législation du clarissimat féminin de Sévère Alexandre à la fin du IVe siècle," *AAC* 5 (1983) 255–262.

Chastagnol, "Dioclétien" = A. Chastagnol, "Dioclétien et les *clarissimae feminae*," *Studi Biscardi* 2 (Milan 1982) 65–67.

Chastagnol, "Femmes" = A. Chastagnol, "Les femmes dans l'ordre sénatorial: Titulature et rang social à Rome," *RH* 262 (1979) 3–28.

Chastagnol, "Impôt" = A. Chastagnol, "L'impôt des proxénètes," *AAC* 9 (Naples 1993) 429–437.

Chastagnol, *"Latus Clavus"* = A. Chastagnol, *"Latus Clavus* et *Adlectio:* L'accès des hommes nouveaux au sénat romain sous le haut-empire," in C. Nicolet ed., *Des ordres à Rome* (Paris 1984) 199–216 (= *RHD* 53 [1975] 375–394).

Chastagnol, *"Ordo"* = A. Chastagnol, "La naissance de l'*ordo senatorius*," in C. Nicolet ed., *Des ordres à Rome* (Paris 1984) 175–198 (= *MEFRA* 85 [1973] 581–607).

Chastagnol, *Préfecture* = A. Chastagnol, *La préfecture urbaine à Rome sous le bas-empire* (Paris 1960).

Chastagnol, *Recherches* = A. Chastagnol, *Recherches sur l'Histoire Auguste avec un rap-*

port sur les progrès de la Histoire Auguste–Forschung depuis 1963 (Bonn 1970) (= BHAC 6).

Chastagnol (rev. Syme) = A. Chastagnol (review of Syme, *Ammianus*), *RPh*³ 43 (1969) 268–274.

Chastagnol, *Sénat* = A. Chastagnol, *Le sénat romain à l'époque impériale* (Paris 1992).

Chastagnol, "Utilisation" = A. Chastagnol, "L'utilisation d'Aurelius Victor dans l'Histoire Auguste," *BHAC 1966/1967* (Bonn 1968) 53–65.

Chastagnol, "Zosime" = A. Chastagnol, "Zosime II, 38 et l'Histoire Auguste," *BHAC 1964/1965* (Bonn 1966) 43–78.

Chauvot, *Procope* = A. Chauvot, *Procope de Gaza, Priscien de Césarée: Panégyriques de l'empereur Anastase I*ᵉʳ (Antiquitas 1.35) (Bonn 1986).

Cherry, "Recruitment" = D. Cherry, "Soldiers' Marriages, and Recruitment in Upper Germany and Numidia," *AHB* 3 (1989) 128–130.

Cimma, *Società* = M. R. Cimma, *Ricerche sulle società di publicani* (Milan 1981).

Clark, *Women* = G. Clark, *Women in Late Antiquity: Pagan and Christian Life-Styles* (Oxford 1993).

Cloud, "Constitution" = D. Cloud, "The Constitution and Public Criminal Law," in *CAH*² 9 (Cambridge 1994) 491–530.

Cloud, "*Lex Iulia* 1" = D. Cloud, "*Lex Iulia de vi:* Part I," *Athenaeum* n.s. 66 (1988) 581–595.

Cloud, "*Lex Iulia* 2" = D. Cloud, "*Lex Iulia de vi:* Part II," *Athenaeum* n.s. 67 (1989) 427–465.

Cloud, "Satirists" = D. Cloud, "Satirists and the Law," in S. H. Braund ed., *Satire and Society in Ancient Rome* (Exeter 1989) 49–67.

Cohen, "*Ordines*" = B. Cohen, "Some Neglected *Ordines:* The Apparitorial Status Groups," in Nicolet, *Ordres* (1984) 23–60.

Cohen, "*Ordo*" = B. Cohen, "La notion d'*ordo* dans la Rome antique," *Bull. Ass. Budé*⁴ 2 (1975) 259–282.

Cohen, "Augustan Law" = D. Cohen, "The Augustan Law on Adultery: The Social and Cultural Context," in D. I. Kertzer and R. P. Saller eds., *The Family in Italy from Antiquity to the Present* (New Haven and London 1991) 109–126.

Cohen, "Greek Law" = D. Cohen, "Greek Law: Problems and Methods," *SZ* 106 (1989) 81–105.

Connelly, *Response* = M. T. Connelly, *The Response to Prostitution in the Progressive Era* (Chapel Hill 1980).

Conte, *LL* = G. B. Conte (J. B. Solodow trans.), *Latin Literature: A History* (Baltimore 1994).

Cooke, *Textbook* = G. A. Cooke, *A Textbook of North Semitic Inscriptions* (Oxford 1903).

Corbett, *Marriage* = P. E. Corbett, *The Roman Law of Marriage* (Oxford 1930).

Corbier, "Divorce" = M. Corbier, "Divorce and Adoption as Roman Familial Strategies (Le divorce et l'adoption en plus)," in Rawson, *Marriage* (1991) 47–78.

Corbin, *Women for Hire* = A. Corbin, *Women for Hire: Prostitution and Sexuality in France after 1850* (Cambridge 1990).

Corcoran, "Licinius" = S. Corcoran, "Hidden from History: The Legislation of Licinius," in Harries and Wood, *TC* (1993) 97–119.

Coroï, *Violence* = J. Coroï, *La violence en droit criminel romain* (Paris 1915).

Corsanego, *Repressione* = C. Corsanego, *La repressione romana dell'adulterio* (Rome 1936).

Cotterrell, *SOL*² = R. Cotterrell, *The Sociology of Law: An Introduction*² (London 1992).

Courtney, *Juvenal* = E. Courtney, *A Commentary on the Satires of Juvenal* (London 1980).

Craig, *Form* = C. P. Craig, *Form as Argument in Cicero's Speeches* (Atlanta 1993).

Cremades and Paricio, *Dos et Virtus* = I. Cremades and J. Paricio, *Dos et Virtus: Devolución de la dote y sanción a la mujer romana por sus malas costumbres* (Barcelona 1983).

Criscuolo and Geraci, *ESA* = L. Criscuolo and G. Geraci eds., *Egitto e storia antica dall'ellenismo all'età araba: Bilancio di un confronto* (Bologna 1989).

Crook, *Advocacy* = J. A. Crook, *Legal Advocacy in the Roman World* (Ithaca 1995).

Csillag, *Augustan Laws* = P. Csillag, *The Augustan Laws on Family Relations* (Budapest 1976).

Culham, "Colour" = P. Culham, "Again What Meaning Lies in Colour!" *ZPE* 64 (1986) 235–245.

Cumont, *Égypt* = F. Cumont, *L''Égypt des astrologues* (Brussels 1937).

Cutileiro, *Society* = J. Cutileiro, *A Portuguese Rural Society* (Oxford 1971).

Dal Covolo, *Severi* = E. Dal Covolo, *I Severi e il cristianesimo: Ricerche sull'ambiente storico-istituzionale delle origini cristiane tra il secondo e il terzo secolo* (Rome 1989).

Dalla, *Incapacità* = D. Dalla, *L'incapacità sessuale in diritto romano* (Milan 1978).

Dalla, *Venus* = D. Dalla, *Ubi Venus mutatur: Omosessualità e diritto nel mondo romano* (Milan 1987).

D'Ambra, "Pudicitia" = E. D'Ambra, "Pudicitia in the Frieze of the Forum Transitorium," *MDAI* 98 (1991) 243–248.

Daube, "Accuser" = D. Daube, "The Accuser under the *Lex Julia de Adulteriis,*" *Congrès int. études byz.* (= *Pepr. 9. Dieth. Byz. Syn.*) 2 (Athens 1956) 8–21 (= *CS* 1 [1991] 561–574).

Daube, "Agere" = D. Daube, "Utiliter Agere," *Iura* 11 (1960) 69–148 (= *CS* 2 [1991] 923–994).

Daube, *CS* = D. Daube, (D. Cohen and D. Simon eds.), *Collected Studies in Roman Law* (2 vols.) (Frankfurt am Main 1991).

Daube, "Cupiditas" = D. Daube, "A Meaning of *Cupiditas,*" in *Studi in onore di P. De Francisci* 1 (Milan 1956) 121–126 (= *CS* 1 [1991] 545–549).

Daube, *Duty* = D. Daube, *The Duty of Procreation* (Edinburgh 1977).

Daube, *Forms* = D. Daube, *Forms of Roman Legislation* (Oxford 1956).

Daube, "Fraud" = D. Daube, "Fraud No. 3," in N. Maccormick and P. Birks eds., *The Legal Mind: Essays for Tony Honoré* (Oxford 1986) 1–17 (= *CS* 2 [1991] 1409–1428).

Daube, "Impossible Laws" = D. Daube, "Greek and Roman Reflections on Impossible Laws," *Natural Law Forum* 12 (1967) 1–84 (= *CS* 2 [1991] 1129–1222).

Daube, "Lex Julia" = D. Daube, "The Lex Julia concerning Adultery," *Irish Jurist* 7 (1972) 373–380 (= *CS* 2 [1991] 1267–1276).

Daube, "Marriage" = D. Daube, "The Marriage of Justinian and Theodora: Legal and Theological Reflections," *Catholic Univ. L.R.* 16 (1967) 380–399 (= *CS* 2 [1991] 1223–1244).

Daube, "Martial" = D. Daube, "Martial, Father of Three," *AJAH* 1 (1976) 145–147 (= *CS* 2 [1991] 1321–1324).

Daube, *Roman Law* = D. Daube, *Roman Law: Linguistic, Social and Philosophical Aspects* (Edinburgh 1969).

Daviault, *Comoedia* = A. Daviault, *Comoedia Togata: Fragments* (Paris 1981).

Davis, *Pisticci* = J. Davis, *Land and Family in Pisticci* (London 1973).

Davis, "Sociology" = K. Davis, "The Sociology of Prostitution," *Amer. Sociol. Rev.* 2 (1937) 744–755.

De Churruca, "Critique" = J. De Churruca, "Critique chrétienne aux institutions de l'empire chez Justin (vers 150)," in *Sodalitas: Scritti in onore di A. Guarino* 1 (Naples 1984) 367–389.

De Churruca, "Rescrit" = J. De Churruca, "Un rescrit de Caracalla utilisé par Ulpien et interprété par Saint Augustine," in *Collatio Iuris Romani: Études dédiées à H. Ankum* 1 (Amsterdam 1995) 71–79.

De' Dominicis, "Origini" = M. A. De' Dominicis, "Sulle origini romano-cristiane del diritto del marito ad accusare *constante matrimonio* la moglie adultera (a proposito di Dig. 48.5.27[26] pr.)," *SDHI* 16 (1950) 221–253.

De Laet, *Portorium* = S. J. De Laet, *Portorium: Étude sur l'organisation douanière chez les Romains, surtout à l'époque du haut-empire* (New York 1975 repr. of Bruges 1949 ed.).

Del Castillo, "*Conubium*" = A. Del Castillo, "Reflexiones en torno a la concesión del *conubium* entre libres de nacimento y libertos," *RIDA*³ 41 (1994) 179–205.

Del Castillo, "Fecha" = A. Del Castillo, "Problemas en torno a la fecha de la legislación matrimonial de Augusto," *Hispania antiqua* 4 (1974) 179–189.

Dell'Oro, *Libri* = A. Dell'Oro, *I libri de officio della giurisprudenza romana* (Milan 1960).

Delmaire, *Largesses* = R. Delmaire, *Largesses sacrées et res privata: L'aerarium impérial et son administration du IVᵉ au VIᵉ siècle* (Rome 1989).

De Martino, "Nota" = F. De Martino, "Nota sulla *Lex Julia Municipalis*," in *Studi in onore di U. E. Paoli* (Florence 1956) 225–238.

Demougin, "Juges" = S. Demougin, "Les juges des cinq décuries originaires de l'Italie," *Anc. Soc.* 6 (1975) 143–202.

Demougin, "Notables" = S. Demougin, "Notables municipaux et ordre équestre à l'époque des dernières guerres civiles," *Les "bourgeoisies" municipales italiennes aux IIᵉ et Iᵉʳ siècles av. J.-C.* (Paris 1983) 279–298.

Demougin, *Ordre* = S. Demougin, *L'ordre équestre sous les Julio-Claudiens* (Coll. Éc. Franç. Rome 108) (Rome 1988).

De Pascale, "Divieto" = M. De Pascale, "Sul divieto per il *miles* di fungere da *cognitor* o *procurator* in giudizio," *Index* 15 (1987) 399–404.

De Robertis, "Condizione" = F. M. De Robertis, "La condizione sociale e gli impedimenti al matrimonio nel basso impero," *Scritti vari di diritto romano* 1 (Bari 1987) 177–203 (= *ABari* n.s. 2 [1939] 45–69).

De Robertis, "Repressione" = F. M. De Robertis, "La repressione penale nella circoscrizione dell'urbe (il praefectus urbi e le autorità concorrenti)," *Scritti vari di diritto romano* 3 (Bari 1987) 35–104 (= *Repressione* [Bari 1937]).

des Bouvrie, "Legislation" = S. des Bouvrie, "Augustus' Legislation on Morals—Which Morals and What Aims?" *SO* 59 (1984) 93–113.

Dessau, "Steuertarif" = H. Dessau, "Der Steuertarif von Palmyra," *Hermes* 19 (1884) 486–533.

Deutsch, *Nerves* = K. W. Deutsch, *The Nerves of Government: Models of Political Communication and Control* (New York and London rev. ed. 1966).

Diethart and Kislinger, "Prostitution" = J. Diethart and E. Kislinger, "Papyrologisches zur Prostitution im byzantinischen Ägypten," *JÖB* 41 (1991) 15–23.

Dignös, *Aedilen* = G. Dignös, *Die Stellung der Aedilen im römischen Strafrecht* (Diss. Munich 1962).

Di Salvo, *Lex Laetoria* = S. Di Salvo, *Lex Laetoria: Minore età e crisi sociale tra il III e il II a.C.* (Naples 1979).

Dise, "Reassessment" = R. L. Dise, "A Reassessment of the Functions of *beneficiarii consularis*," *AHB* 9.2 (1995) 72–85.

Dixon, "Breaking" = S. Dixon, "Breaking the Law to Do the Right Thing: The Gradual Erosion of the Voconian Law in Ancient Rome," *Adelaide L.R.* 9 (1985) 519–534.

Dixon, "Finances" = S. Dixon, "Family Finances: Terentia and Tullia," in Rawson, *FAR* (1986) 93–120.

Dixon, "*Infirmitas*" = S. Dixon, "*Infirmitas Sexus:* Womanly Weakness in Roman Law," *TR* 52 (1984) 343–371.

Dixon, *Mother* = S. Dixon, *The Roman Mother* (Norman 1988).

Dixon, *TRF* = S. Dixon, *The Roman Family* (Baltimore 1992).

Dobson, "Centurionate" = B. Dobson, "The Centurionate and Social Mobility during the Principate," in *Recherches sur les structures sociales dans l'antiquité classique* (Paris 1970) 99–116.

Dorey, "Adultery" = T. A. Dorey, "Adultery and Propaganda in the Early Roman Empire," *Univ. Birmingham Historical Journal* 8 (1961) 1–6.

D'Ors, *Ley* = A. D'Ors, *La Ley Flavia municipal (texto y comentario)* (Rome 1986).

D'Ors, "Lista" = A. D'Ors, "Una nueva lista de acciones infamantes," in *Sodalitas: Scritti in onore di A. Guarino* 6 (Naples 1984) 2575–2590.

Drexhage, "Berufsbezeichnungen" = H.-J. Drexhage, "Feminine Berufsbezeichnungen im hellenistischen Ägypten," *MBAH* 11 (1992) 70–79.

Drexhage, *Preise* = H.-J. Drexhage, *Preise, Mieten/Pachten, Kosten und Löhne im römischen Ägypten bis zum Regierungsantritt Diokletians* (St. Katherinen 1991).

Drexhage, "Handel" = R. Drexhage, "Der Handel Palmyras in römischer Zeit," *MBAH* 1 (1982) 17–34.

Drijvers, "Hatra" = H. J. W. Drijvers, "Hatra, Palmyra und Edessa: Die Städte der syrisch-mesopotamischer Wüste in politischer, kulturgeschichtlicher und religionsgeschichtlicher Beleuchtung," *ANRW* 2.8 (Berlin 1977) 799–906.

Ducos, "Acteurs" = M. Ducos, "La condition des acteurs à Rome: Données juridiques et sociales," in Bländsdorf, *TGIR* (1990) 19–33.

Duncan-Jones, *Economy*^{2} = R. Duncan-Jones, *The Economy of the Roman Empire: Quantitative Studies*^{2} (Cambridge 1982).

Duncan-Jones, "Rank" = R. Duncan-Jones, "Equestrian Rank in the Cities of the African Provinces under the Principate: An Epigraphic Survey," *PBSR* 35 (1967) 147–186.

Dyson, "Rotary Club" = S. L. Dyson, "Age, Sex, and Status: The View from the Roman Rotary Club," *EMC* n.s. 11 (1992) 369–385.

Earl, *Tradition* = D. Earl, *The Moral and Political Tradition of Rome* (Ithaca 1967).

Eck, *Organisation* = W. Eck, *Die staatliche Organisation Italiens in der höhen Kaiserzeit* (Vestigia 28) (Munich 1979).

Eck, "Sozialstruktur" = W. Eck, "Sozialstruktur des römischen Senatorenstandes der höhen Kaiserzeit und statistische Methode," *Chiron* 3 (1973) 375–394.

Edwards, *Politics* = C. Edwards, *The Politics of Immorality in Ancient Rome* (Cambridge 1993).

Eisele, "Beiträge" = F. Eisele, "Beiträge zur Erkenntniss der Digesteninterpolationen," *SZ* 11 (1890) 1–30.

Eisenhut, *RE* Vinalia = W. Eisenhut, s.v. Vinalia, *RE* Suppl. 10 (1965) 1172–1176.

Ely and Bodenhammer, "Regionalism" = J. W. Ely and D. J. Bodenhammer, "Regionalism and American Legal History: The Southern Legal Experience," *Vand. L.J.* 39 (1986) 539–567.

Eppers and Heinen, "*Servi Venerii*" = M. Eppers and H. Heinen, "Zu den *Servi Venerii* in Ciceros Verrinen," in *Sodalitas: Scritti in onore di A. Guarino* 1 (Naples 1984) 219–232.

Esmein, "Délit" = A. Esmein, "Le délit d'adultère à Rome et la loi *Julia de adulteriis,*" in *Mélanges d'histoire du droit et de critique: Droit romain* (Paris 1886) 71–169.

Evans, "Temple" = J. A. S. Evans, "A Social and Economic History of an Egyptian Temple in the Greco-Roman Period," *YCS* 17 (1961) 149–283.

Evans, *War* = J. K. Evans, *War, Women and Children in Ancient Rome* (London and New York 1991).

Evans, "Prostitution" = R. J. Evans, "Prostitution, State and Society in Imperial Germany," *P & P* 70 (1976) 106–129.

Evans Grubbs, "Constantine" = J. Evans Grubbs, "Constantine and Imperial Legislation on the Family," in Harries and Wood, *TC* (1993) 120–142.

Evans Grubbs, *Law* = J. Evans Grubbs, *Law and the Family in Late Antiquity: The Emperor Constantine's Legislation on Marriage and the Family* (Oxford 1995).

Falcão, *Prohibiciones* = M. Falcão, *Las prohibiciones matrimoniales de caracter social en el Imperio Romano* (Pamplona 1973).

Fanizza, *Delatori* = L. Fanizza, *Delatori e accusatori: L'iniziativa dei processi di età imperiale* (1988).

Fantham, "Censorship" = E. Fantham, "Censorship, Roman Style," *EMC* 21 (1977) 41–53.

Fantham, "*Stuprum*" = E. Fantham, "*Stuprum:* Public Attitudes and Penalties for Sexual Offences in Republican Rome," *EMC* n.s. 10 (1991) 267–291.

Fede, "Protection" = A. Fede, "Legal Protection for Slave Buyers in the U.S. South: A Caveat concerning *Caveat Emptor*," *Amer. Journal of Legal Hist.* 31 (1987) 322–358.

Fehrle, "Ehegesetze" = R. Fehrle, "Augusteische Ehegesetze—Bevölkerungspolitik in der Antike," *Journal für Geschichte* 1 (1984) 18–23.

Fernández Gómez and del Amo y de la Hera, *Lex* = F. Fernández Gómez and M. del Amo y de la Hera, *La Lex Irnitana y su contexto arqueologico* (Seville 1990).

Ferrero, *Grandezza* = G. Ferrero, *Grandezza e decadenza di Roma* 4 (Milan 1906 [1914]).

Ferrill, "Augustus" = A. Ferrill, "Augustus and His Daughter: A Modern Myth," in C. Deroux ed., *Studies in Latin Literature and Roman History* 2 (Brussels 1980) 332–346.

Ferrill, *Caligula* = A. Ferrill, *Caligula, Emperor of Rome* (London 1991).

Février, *Essai* = J. G. Février, *Essai sur l'histoire politique et économique de Palmyre* (Paris 1931).

Field, "Purpose" = J. A. Field, "The Purpose of the *Lex Iulia et Papia Poppaea*," *CJ* 40 (1945) 398–416.

Finley, *Politics* = M. I. Finley, *Politics in the Ancient World* (Cambridge 1983).

Finley (rev. Davis) = M. I. Finley (review of D. B. Davis, *The Problem of Slavery in Western Culture* [Ithaca 1966]), in A. Weinstein and F. O. Gatell eds., *American Negro Slavery: A Modern Reader²* (New York 1973) 394–400.

Finley, *SAS* = M. I. Finley ed., *Studies in Ancient Society* (London 1974).

Finley, *Slavery* = M. I. Finley, *Ancient Slavery and Modern Ideology* (London 1980).

Fisher, "Theodora" = E. A. Fisher, "Theodora and Antonina in the Historia Arcana: History and/or Fiction?" in J. Peradotto and J. P. Sullivan eds., *Women in the Ancient World: The Arethusa Papers* (Albany 1984) 287–313 (= *Arethusa* 11 [1978] 253–279).

Fishwick, "Statues Taxes" = D. Fishwick, "Statues Taxes in Roman Egypt," *Historia* 38 (1989) 335–347.

Fitting, *Alter²* = H. Fitting, *Alter und Folge der Schriften römischen Juristen von Hadrian bis Alexander²* (Halle 1908).

Flexner, *Prostitution* = A. Flexner, *Prostitution in Europe* (New York 1914).

Flore, "*Vis*" = G. Flore, "Di alcuni casi di *vis publica*," *Studi Bonfante* 4 (Milan 1930) 336–352.

Flory, "Exempla" = M. B. Flory, "Sic exempla parantur: Livia's Shrine to Concordia and the Porticus Liviae," *Historia* 33 (1984) 309–330.

Foraboschi, "Dogane" = D. Foraboschi, "Dogane e dazi: *Ad valorem* e a quota fissa," *ZPE* 94 (1992) 104.

Foraboschi, "Egitto" = D. Foraboschi, "L'Egitto," in M. H. Crawford ed., *L'impero romano e le strutture economiche e sociali delle province* (Biblioteca di Athenaeum 4) (Como 1986) 109–125.

Foraboschi and Gara, "Rapporto" = D. Foraboschi and A. Gara, "Il rapporto dracma-argento nell'Egitto romano," *Chronique d'Égypte* 51 (1976) 169–177.

Formigoni Candini, "*Lenones*" = W. Formigoni Candini, "*Ne lenones sint in ullo loco reipublicae Romanae,*" *Annali Ferrara: Sez. Giur.* n.s. 4 (1990) 97–127.

Foucault, *HS* = M. Foucault (R. Hurley trans.), *The History of Sexuality* 1: *An Introduction* (New York 1978), 2: *The Use of Pleasure* (New York 1985), 3: *The Care of the Self* (New York 1986).

Franciosi, *Clan*[4] = G. Franciosi, *Clan gentilizio e strutture monogamiche: Contributo alla storia della famiglia romana*[4] (Naples 1989).

Franciosi, *Processo* = G. Franciosi, *Il processo di libertà in diritto romano* (Naples 1961).

Frank, "Legislation" = R. I. Frank, "Augustus' Legislation on Marriage and Children," *CSCA* 8 (1975) 41–52.

Frederiksen, "Municipal Laws" = M. W. Frederiksen, "The Republican Municipal Laws: Errors and Drafts," *JRS* 55 (1965) 183–198.

Friedländer, *Sittengeschichte* = L. Friedländer (G. Wissowa ed.), *Darstellungen aus der Sittengeschichte Roms in der Zeit von August bis zum Ausgang der Antoninen* 1[10] (Leipzig 1919), 2[10] (Leipzig 1920), 3[10] (Leipzig 1920), 4[9,10] (Leipzig 1921).

Friedman, *System* = L. M. Friedman, *The Legal System: A Social Science Perspective* (New York 1975).

Frier, "Bees 1" = B. W. Frier, "Bees and Lawyers," *CJ* 78 (1982/1983) 105–114.

Frier, "Bees 2" = B. W. Frier, "Why Did the Jurists Change Roman Law? Bees and Lawyers Revisited," *Index* 22 (1994) 135–149.

Frier, *Rise* = B. W. Frier, *The Rise of the Roman Jurists: Studies in Cicero's Pro Caecina* (Princeton 1985).

Fuchs, "Frau" = J. G. Fuchs, "Die rechtliche Stellung der Frau im alten Rom," in *Festgabe zum siebzigsten Geburtstag von M. Gerwig* (Basel 1960) 31–54.

Fuhrmann, "Alleinherrschaft" = M. Fuhrmann, "Die Alleinherrschaft und das Problem der Gerechtigkeit (Sen. De Clementia)," *Gymnasium* 70 (1963) 481–514.

Gabba, "Senati" = E. Gabba, "Sui senati delle città siciliane nell'età di Verre," *Athenaeum* n.s. 37 (1959) 304–320.

Gabba, "Strutture" = E. Gabba, "Strutture sociali e politica romana in Italia nel II sec. a.C.," in *Les "bourgeoisies" municipales italiennes aux IIe et Ier siècles av. J.-C.* (Paris 1983) 41–45.

Gagé, *Jeux* = J. Gagé, *Recherches sur les jeux séculaires* (Paris 1934).

Gagé, *Matronalia* = J. Gagé, *Matronalia: Essai sur les dévotions et les organisations cultuelles des femmes dans l'ancienne Rome* (Collection Latomus 60) (Brussels 1963).

Galinsky, *Augustan Culture* = K. Galinsky, *Augustan Culture, An Interpretive Introduction* (Princeton 1996).

Galinsky, "Legislation" = K. Galinsky, "Augustus' Legislation on Morals and Marriage," *Philologus* 125 (1981) 126–144.

Galsterer, "Loi" = H. Galsterer, "La loi municipale des Romaines: Chimère ou réalité?" *RHD* 65 (1987) 181–203.

Galsterer, "Municipium" = H. Galsterer, "Municipium Flavium Irnitanum: A Latin Town in Spain," *JRS* 78 (1988) 78–90.

Garcia Garrido, *Ius uxorium* = M. Garcia Garrido, *Ius uxorium: El régimen patrimonial de la mujer casada en derecho romano* (Rome and Madrid 1958).

Gardner, *Being* = J. F. Gardner, *Being a Roman Citizen* (New York 1993).

Gardner, "Purpose" = J. F. Gardner, "The Purpose of the Lex Fufia Caninia," *EMC* n.s. 10 (1991) 21–39.

Gardner (rev. Sicari) = J. F. Gardner (review of Sicari, *Prostituzione), Gnomon* 66 (1994) 181–183.

Gardner, *Women* = J. F. Gardner, *Women in Roman Law and Roman Society* (London and Sydney 1986).

Gardthausen, *Augustus* = V. E. Gardthausen, *Augustus und seiner Zeit* (Aalen 1964 repr. of Leipzig 1896 ed.).

Garland, *Eye* = R. Garland, *The Eye of the Beholder: Deformity and Disability in the Graeco-Roman World* (Ithaca 1995).

Garnsey, "Adultery Trials" = P. Garnsey, "Adultery Trials and the Survival of the *Quaestiones* in the Severan Age," *JRS* 57 (1967) 56–60.

Garnsey, "Descendants" = P. Garnsey, "Descendants of Freedmen in Local Politics: Some Criteria," in B. Levick ed., *The Ancient Historian and His Materials: Essays in Honour of C. E. Stevens on His Seventieth Birthday* (Salisbury 1975) 167–180.

Garnsey, "Severus" = P. Garnsey, "Septimius Severus and the Marriage of Soldiers," *CSCA* 3 (1970) 45–53.

Garnsey, *Status* = P. Garnsey, *Social Status and Legal Privilege in the Roman Empire* (Oxford 1970).

Garofalo, "Competenza" = L. Garofalo, "La competenza a promuovere *iudicia populi* avverso donne," *SDHI* 52 (1986) 451–476.

Garofalo, *Processo* = L. Garofalo, *Il processo edilizio: Contributo allo studio dei iudicia populi* (Padua 1989).

Garrido-Hory, *Martial* = M. Garrido-Hory, *Martial et l'esclavage* (Ann. Litt. Besançon 255) (Paris 1981).

Garzetti, *Tiberius* = A. Garzetti (J. R. Foster trans.), *From Tiberius to the Antonines: A History of the Roman Empire, A.D. 14–192* (London rev. ed. 1974).

Gaudemet, "*Matrimonium*" = J. Gaudemet, "*Justum Matrimonium,*" *Études de droit romain* 3 (Camerino 1979) 103–162 (= *RIDA* 3 [1950] 309–366).

Gaudemet, "Responsabilité" = J. Gaudemet, "Le problème de la responsabilité penale dans l'antiquité," *Études de droit romain* 3 (Camerino 1979) 457–484 (= *Studi in onore di E. Betti* 2 [Milan 1962] 481–508).

Gaudemet, "Tendances" = J. Gaudemet, "Tendances nouvelles de la législation familiale au IVe siècle," in *Transformations et conflits au IVᵉ siècle ap. J.-C.* (Antiquitas 1.29) (Bonn 1978) 187–207.

Geffcken, *Comedy* = K. Geffcken, *Comedy in the Pro Caelio* (Leiden 1973).

Gehrich, *Kognitur* = W.-D. Gehrich, *Kognitur und Prokuratur in rem suam als Zessionsformen des klassischen römischen Rechts* (Göttingen 1963).

Geiger, "Tiberius" = J. Geiger, "Tiberius and the *Lex Papia Poppaea,*" *Scr. Class. Isr.* 2 (1975) 150–156.

Genin, *Tentative* = J.-C. Genin, *La répression des actes de tentative en droit criminel romain (contribution à l'étude de la subjectivité répressive à Rome)* (Diss. Lyons 1968).

Genovese, *Roll, Jordan, Roll* = E. D. Genovese, *Roll, Jordan, Roll: The World the Slaves Made* (New York 1974).

Georgesco, *Essai* = V.-A. Georgesco, *Essai d'une théorie générale des leges privatae* (Diss. Paris 1932).

Georgescu, "*Manus iniectio*" = V.-A. Georgescu, "La *manus iniectio* en matière de vente d'esclaves," *SZ* 64 (1944) 376–388.

Geraci, "Egitto" = G. Geraci, "L'Egitto romano nella storiografia moderna," in Criscuolo and Geraci, *ESA* (1989) 55–88.

Geraci, *Genesi* = G. Geraci, *Genesi della provincia romana d'Egitto* (Bologna 1983).

Geremek, *Margins* = B. Geremek (J. Birrell trans.), *The Margins of Society in Late Medieval Paris* (Cambridge 1987).

Germani, *Marginality* = G. Germani, *Marginality* (New Brunswick 1980).

Getman, "Control" = K. A. Getman, "Sexual Control in the Slaveholding South: The Implementation and Maintenance of a Caste System," *Harvard Women's L.J.* 7 (1984) 115–152.

Gibson, *Prostitution* = M. Gibson, *Prostitution and the State in Italy, 1860–1915* (New Brunswick and London 1986).

Giddens, *Constitution* = A. Giddens, *The Constitution of Society: Outline of the Theory of Structuration* (Berkeley and Los Angeles 1984).

Giliberti, "*Beneficium*" = G. Giliberti, "*Beneficium e iniuria* nei rapporti col servo: Etica e prassi giuridica in Seneca," in *Sodalitas: Scritti in onore di A. Guarino* 4 (Naples 1984) 1843–1860.

Gilmore, *Honor and Shame* = D. D. Gilmore ed., *Honor and Shame and the Unity of the Mediterranean* (Washington 1987).

Gioffredi, *Principi* = C. Gioffredi, *I Principi di diritto penale romano* (Turin 1970).

Girard and Senn, *Lois*[7] = P. F. Girard and F. Senn, *Les lois des Romains*[7] (Naples 1977).

Giunti, *Adulterio* = P. Giunti, *Adulterio e leggi regie: Un reato fra storia e propaganda* (Milan 1990).

Gizewski, "Mores" = C. Gizewski, "Mores maiorum, regimen morum, licentia: Zur Koexistenz catonischer und plautinischer Sittlichkeitsvorstellungen," in *Festschrift R. Werner* (Konstanz 1989) 81–105.

Gleason, "Semiotics" = M. W. Gleason, "The Semiotics of Gender: Physiognomy and Self-Fashioning in the Second Century C.E.," in D. M. Halperin et al. eds., *Before Sexuality: The Construction of Erotic Experience in the Ancient Greek World* (Princeton 1990) 389–415.

Goethert, *RE* toga = F. W. Goethert, s.v. toga (2), *RE* 6.2 (1937) 1651–1660.

Goette, *Toga* = H. R. Goette, *Studien zu römischen Togadarstellungen* (Mainz am Rhein 1990).

Golden (rev. Rawson) = M. Golden (review of Rawson, *FAR*), *EMC* n.s. 7 (1988) 78–83.

Golden, "Uses" = M. Golden, "The Uses of Cross-Cultural Comparison in Ancient Social History," *EMC* n.s. 11 (1992) 309–331.

Goldman, *Gold Diggers* = M. S. Goldman, *Gold Diggers and Silver Miners: Prostitution and Social Life on the Comstock Lode* (Ann Arbor 1981).

Goldman, "Clothing" = N. Goldman, "Reconstructing Roman Clothing," in J. L. Sebesta and L. Bonfante eds., *The World of Roman Costume* (Madison 1994) 213–237.

Goldsmith, *Systems* = R. W. Goldsmith, *Premodern Financial Systems: A Historical Comparative Study* (Cambridge 1987).

Gomez Ruiz, *Divorcio* = C. Gomez Ruiz, *El divorcio y las leyes augusteas* (Seville 1987).

González, "*Lex Irnitana*" = J. González, "The *Lex Irnitana*: A New Copy of the Flavian Municipal Law," *JRS* 76 (1986) 147–243.

Goodyear, *Annals* = F. R. D. Goodyear, *The Annals of Tacitus* 1 (Cambridge 1972), 2 (Cambridge 1981).

Goria, "Abito" = F. Goria, "La Nov. 134.10, 12 di Giustiniano e l'assunzione coattiva dell'abito monastico," in *Studi in onore di G. Grosso* 6 (Turin 1974) 55–76.

Goria, "Dibattito" = F. Goria, "Il dibattito sull'abrogazione della lex Oppia e la condizione giuridica della donna romana," in R. Uglione ed., *Atti del convegno nazionale sulla donna nel mondo antico, Torino 21–23 aprile 1986* (Turin 1987) 265–303.

Goria, *ED* ratto = F. Goria, s.v. ratto (diritto romano), *ED* 38 (1987) 707–724.

Goria, *Studi* = F. Goria, *Studi sul matrimonio dell'adultera nel diritto giustinianeo e bizantino* (Turin 1975).

Gradenwitz, *Interpolationen* = O. Gradenwitz, *Interpolationen in den Pandekten: Kritische Studien* (Berlin 1887).

Gradenwitz, "Tafel" = O. Gradenwitz, "Die Gemeindeordonnanzen der Tafel von Heraclea," *SB Heidelberger Akad. der Wiss.; phil.-hist. Kl.*, 14 (1916) 1–54.

Gramsci, *Quaderni* = A. Gramsci, *Quaderni del carcere* (4 vols.) (Turin 1975).

Graβl, "Grundsätzliches" = H. Graβl, "Grundsätzliches und Methodisches zur historischen Randgruppenforschung," in Weiler, *SRAA* (1988) 41–46.

Greenidge, *Infamia* = A. H. J. Greenidge, *Infamia: Its Place in Roman Public and Private Law* (Oxford 1894).

Grelle, "*Correctio morum*" = F. Grelle, "La *correctio morum* nella legislazione flavia," *ANRW* 2.13 (1980) 340–65.

Grieve, "TC" = L. J. Grieve, "*Tabulae Caeritum,*" in C. Deroux ed., *Studies in Latin Literature and Roman History* 3 (Brussels 1983) 26–43.

Griffin, *Latin Poets* = J. Griffin, *Latin Poets and Roman Life* (Chapel Hill 1986).

Griffin, "Tribune" = M. T. Griffin, "The Tribune C. Cornelius," *JRS* 63 (1973) 196–213.

Griffin, *Seneca* = M. T. Griffin, *Seneca: A Philosopher in Politics* (Oxford 1976).

Grimal, *Love* = P. Grimal (A. Train trans.), *Love in Ancient Rome* (Norman and London 1986).

Grimal, "Matrona" = P. Grimal, "Matrona (les lois, les moeurs et la langage)," in *Hommage à J. Granarolo* (Nice 1985) 195–203.

Groag, *RE* Caecina (24) = E. Groag, s.v. Caecina (24), *RE* 3.1 (1897) 1241–1243.

Groag, *RE* Cornelius (181) = E. Groag, s.v. Cornelius (181), *RE* 4.1 (1900) 1363–1364.

Grodzynski, "Tortures" = D. Grodzynski, "Tortures mortelles et catégories sociales: Les *summa supplicia* dans le droit romain aux IIIe et IVe siècles," in *Du châtiment dans la cité: Supplices corporels et peine de mort dans le monde antique* (Rome 1984) 361–403.

Guareschi, "Note" = A. Guareschi, "Le note di Marciano ai *de adulteriis libri duo* di Papiniano," *Index* 21 (1993) 453–488.

Guarino, *DPR*⁹ = A. Guarino, *Diritto privato romano*⁹ (Naples 1992).

Guarino, "*Incestum*" = A. Guarino, "Studi sull'*incestum,*" *SZ* 63 (1943) 175–267.

Guarino, "Lui" = A. Guarino, "Lui, lei e l'altro nel matrimonio romano," *Index* 21 (1993) 411–431.

Guarino, "Messalina" = A. Guarino, "In difesa di Messalina," *Labeo* 20 (1974) 12–26 (= *PDR* 2 [Naples 1993] 267–281).

Guarino, "SC fantasma" = A. Guarino, "Il senatoconsulto fantasma," in *Estudios juridicos en homenaje al profesor U. Alvarez Suarez* (Madrid 1978) 201–211.

Guastella, *Caligola* = G. Guastella, *Gaio Suetonio Tranquillo: La vita di Caligola* (Roman 1992).

Guy, *Sex* = D. J. Guy, *Sex and Danger in Buenos Aires: Prostitution, Family, and Nation* (Lincoln and London 1991).

Guyot, *Eunuchen* = P. Guyot, *Eunuchen als Sklaven und Freigelassene in der griechisch-römischen Antike* (Stuttgart 1980).

Hackl, "Eques" = U. Hackl, "Eques Romanus equo publico: Ein Beitrag zur Definition des römischen Ritterstandes während der Zeit der Republik," *Xenia* 22 (1989) 107–115 (= W. Dahlheim et al. eds., *Festschrift R. Werner* [Konstanz 1989]).

Hallebeek, "Responsum" = J. J. Hallebeek, "Si ob stuprum datum sit, cessat repetitio: The Palingenesis of an Early Responsum," *SZ* 112 (1995) 400–410.

Hallett, *Fathers and Daughters* = J. P. Hallett, *Fathers and Daughters in Roman Society: Women and the Elite Family* (Princeton 1984).

Halperin, *Hundred Years* = D. M. Halperin, *One Hundred Years of Homosexuality and Other Essays on Greek Love* (New York and London 1990).

Hanson, "Officials" = A. E. Hanson, "Village Officials at Philadelphia: A Model of Romanization in the Julio-Claudian Period," in Criscuolo and Geraci, *ESA* (1989) 429–440.

Hardy, *Laws* = E. G. Hardy, *Roman Laws and Charters* (Aalen 1977 repr. of Oxford 1911–1912 ed.).

Hardy, *Problems* = E. G. Hardy, *Some Problems in Roman History* (Oxford 1924).

Harries, "Background" = J. Harries, "Introduction: Background to the Code," in Harries and Wood, *TC* (1993) 1–17.

Harries and Wood, *TC* = J. Harries and I. Wood eds., *The Theodosian Code* (Ithaca 1993).

Harris, "Trade" = W. V. Harris, "Towards a Study of the Roman Slave Trade," *MAAR* 36 (1980) 117–140 (= J. H. D'Arms and E. C. Kopff eds., *The Seaborne Commerce of Ancient Rome: Studies in Archaeology and History* [Rome 1980]).

Hartkamp, *Zwang* = A. S. Hartkamp, *Der Zwang im römischen Privatrecht* (Amsterdam 1971).

Hartmann, "Incapacität" = G. Hartmann, "Über die Voraussetzungen und Grenzen der Incapacität nach der lex Iulia et Papia," *ZRG* 5 (1866) 219–255.

Hawke, *Economics* = G. R. Hawke, *Economics for Historians* (Cambridge 1980).

Hawley and Levick, *Women* = R. Hawley and B. Levick eds., *Women in Antiquity: New Assessments* (London and New York 1995).

Heinecke, *Commentarius*³ = J. G. Heinecke, *Commentarius ad legem Iuliam et Papiam Poppaeam*³ (Opera 7) (Geneva 1747/1749).

Henderson, "Ordo" = M. I. Henderson, "The Establishment of the *Equester Ordo*," *JRS* 53 (1963) 61–72.

Hermansen, "Inns" = G. Hermansen, "The Roman Inns and the Law: The Inns of Ostia," in J. A. S. Evans ed., *Polis and Imperium: Studies in Honour of E. T. Salmon* (Toronto 1974) 167–181.

Hermansen, *Ostia* = G. Hermansen, *Ostia: Aspects of Roman City Life* (Edmonton 1981).

Herrin, "Search" = J. Herrin, "In Search of Byzantine Women: Three Avenues of Approach," in A. Cameron and A. Kuhrt eds., *Images of Women in Antiquity* (Detroit rev. ed. 1993) 167–189.

Herter 1 = H. Herter, s.v. Dirne, *RAC* 3 (1957) 1149–1213.

Herter 2 = H. Herter, "Die Soziologie der antiken Prostitution im Lichte des heidnischen und christlichen Schrifttums," *JbAC* 3 (1960) 70–111.

Hillard, "Stage" = T. Hillard, "On the Stage, behind the Curtain: Images of Politically Active Women in the Late Republic," in P. Allen et al. eds., *Stereotypes of Women in Power: Historical Perspectives and Revisionist Views* (New York 1992) 37–64.

Hinard, "*Praecones*" = F. Hinard, "Remarques sur les *praecones* et le *praeconium* dans la Rome de la fin de la République," *Latomus* 35 (1976) 730–746.

Hirschfeld, "Polizei" = O. Hirschfeld, "Die Sicherheitspolizei im römischen Kaiserreich," in *Kleine Schriften* (New York 1975 repr. of Berlin 1913 ed.) 576–612 (= *SB Berlin* [1891] 845–877).

Hobson, *Virtue* = B. M Hobson, *Uneasy Virtue: The Politics of Prostitution and the American Reform Tradition* (Chicago rev. ed. 1990).

Hobson, "Context" = D. Hobson, "Towards a Broader Context of the Study of Greco-Roman Egypt," *EMC* n.s. 7 (1988) 353–363.

Hobson, "Receipt" = D. Hobson, "Receipt for cheirōnaxion," *JJP* 23 (1993) 75–92.

Hogarth, "Inscriptions" = D. G. Hogarth, "The Classical Inscriptions," in W. M. Flinders Petrie ed., *Koptos* (London 1896) 26–35.

Holtheide, "Matrona" = B. Holtheide, "Matrona stolata—Femina stolata," *ZPE* 38 (1980) 127–131.

Holthöfer, "Auslegung" = E. Holthöfer, "Ein Beitrag zur Auslegung und Interpretationsgeschichte des Fragments D. 18.7.7," *Ius Commune* 1 (1967) 150–180.

Honoré, "Lawyers" = T. Honoré, "Lawyers and Government in the *Historia Augusta,*" *Iura* 42 (1991) 13–41.

Honoré, "Scriptor" = T. Honoré, "Scriptor Historiae Augustae," *JRS* 77 (1987) 156–176.

Honoré, *Ulpian* = T. Honoré, *Ulpian* (Oxford 1982).

Honsell, "Gesetzesverständnis" = H. Honsell, "Gesetzesverständnis in der römischen Antike," in *Europäisches Rechtsdenken in Geschichte und Gegenwart: Festschrift für H. Coing zum 70. Geburtstag* (Munich 1982) 129–148.

Hopkins, *Death* = K. Hopkins (with G. Burton in chs. 2 and 3), *Death and Renewal* (Cambridge 1983).

Hopkins, "Taxes" = K. Hopkins, "Taxes and Trade in the Roman Empire (200 B.C.–A.D. 400)," *JRS* 70 (1980) 101–125.

Horak, *RD* = F. Horak, *Rationes Decidendi* 1 (Innsbruck 1969).

Howington, *What Sayeth the Law* = A. E. Howington, *What Sayeth the Law: The Treatment of Slaves and Free Blacks in the State and Local Courts of Tennessee* (New York and London 1986).

Humbert, "Hispala" = M. Humbert, "Hispala Faecenia et l'endogamie des affranchis sous la République," *Index* 15 (1987) 131–140.

Humbert, "Individu" = M. Humbert, "L'individu, l'état: Quelle stratégie pour le mariage classique?" in Andreau and Bruhns, *Parenté* (1990) 173–198.

Humbert, *Remariage* = M. Humbert, *Le remariage à Rome: Étude d'histoire juridique et sociale* (Milan 1972).

Humphreys, "Law as Discourse" = S. Humphreys, "Law as Discourse," *History and Anthropology* 1 (1985) 241–264.

Hurley, *Commentary* = D. Hurley, *An Historical and Historiographical Commentary on Suetonius' Life of C. Caligula* (Atlanta 1993).

Jacques, *Privilège* = F. Jacques, *Le privilège de liberté: Politique impériale et autonomie municipale dans les cités de l'Occident romain (161–244)* (Coll. Éc. Franç. Rome 76) (Rome 1984).

Jacques, "Sénat" = F. Jacques, "L'éthique et la statistique: A propos du renouvellement du sénat romain (Ier-IIIe siècle de l'empire)," in Andreau and Bruhns eds., *Parenté* (1990) 415–438.

Jacques and Scheid, *Rome* = F. Jacques and F. Scheid, *Rome et l'integration de l'empire, 44 av. J.C.–260 ap. J.C.* 1 (Paris 1990).

Janssen, *Vita* = J. Janssen, *C. Suetonii Tranquilli Vita Domitiani* (Groningen 1919).

Johnson, *ESAR* 2 = A. C. Johnson, *An Economic Survey of Ancient Rome 2: Roman Egypt to the Reign of Diocletian* (Baltimore 1936).

Johnston, "Three Thoughts" = D. Johnston, "Three Thoughts on Roman Private Law and the Lex Irnitana," *JRS* 77 (1987) 62–77.

Johnston, *Trusts* = D. Johnston, *The Roman Law of Trusts* (Oxford 1989).

Jolowicz, *Digest 47.2* = H. F. Jolowicz, *Digest XLVII.2: De Furtis* (Cambridge 1940).

Jones, *Cities*² = A. H. M. Jones, *Cities of the Eastern Roman Provinces*² (Amsterdam 1983 repr. of Oxford 1971 ed.).

Jones, "Civil Service" = A. H. M. Jones, "The Roman Civil Service (Clerical and Sub-clerical Grades),'' in *Studies in Roman Government and Law* (Oxford 1960) 151–175 (= *JRS* 39 [1949] 38–55).

Jones, *Courts* = A. H. M. Jones, *The Criminal Courts of the Roman Republic and Principate* (Totowa 1972).

Jones, ''Elections'' = A. H. M. Jones, ''The Elections under Augustus,'' *Studies in Roman Government and Law* (Oxford 1960) 27–50 (= *JRS* 45 [1955] 9–21).

Jones, *LRE* = A. H. M. Jones, *The Later Roman Empire, 284–602: A Social, Economic and Administrative Survey* (2 vols.) (Oxford and Norman 1964).

Jones, ''Rome'' = A. H. M. Jones, ''Rome and the Provincial Cities,'' *TR* 39 (1971) 513–551.

Jones, ''Taxation'' = A. H. M. Jones, ''Taxation in Antiquity,'' in P. A. Brunt ed., *The Roman Economy: Studies in Roman Economic and Administrative History* (Oxford and Totowa 1974) 151–185.

Jones, ''Towns'' = A. H. M. Jones, ''The Economic Life of the Towns of the Roman Empire,'' in P. A. Brunt ed., *The Roman Economy: Studies in Roman Economic and Administrative History* (Oxford and Totowa 1974) 35–60 (= *Rec. Soc. J. Bodin* 7 [1955] 161–192).

Jones, *Domitian* = B. W. Jones, *The Emperor Domitian* (London 1992).

Jones, *DSO* = B. W. Jones, *Domitian and the Senatorial Order: A Prosopographical Study of Domitian's Relationship with the Senate, A.D. 81–96* (MAPS 132) (Philadelphia 1979).

Jones, ''Stigma'' = C. P. Jones, ''*Stigma:* Tattooing and Branding in Graeco-Roman Antiquity,'' *JRS* 77 (1987) 139–155.

Jonkers, ''Reflections'' = E. J. Jonkers, ''A Few Reflections on the Background of Augustus's Laws to Increase the Birth Rate,'' *Symbolae ad jus et historiam antiquitatis pertinentes Julio Christiano van Oven dedicatae* (Leiden 1946) 285–296.

Jörs, *E.* = P. Jörs, *Die Ehegesetze des Augustus* (Marburg 1894) (orig. in *Fs. Mommsen* [Marburg, 1893] now repr. in T. Spagnuolo Vigorita, *Iuliae Rogationes* [Naples 1985]).

Jörs, *V.* = P. Jörs, *Über das Verhältnis der Lex Iulia de Maritandis Ordinibus zur Lex Papia Poppaea* (Diss. Bonn 1882) (now repr. in T. Spagnuolo Vigorita, *Iuliae Rogationes* [Naples 1985]).

Jory, ''Syrus'' = E. J. Jory, ''Publilius Syrus and the Element of Competition in the Theatre of the Republic,'' in N. Horsfall ed., *Vir Bonus Discendi Peritus: Studies in Celebration of Otto Skutsch's Eightieth Birthday* (London 1988) (= *BICS Supplement* 51).

Jung, ''Eherecht'' = J. H. Jung, ''Das Eherecht der römischen Soldaten,'' *ANRW* 2.14 (Berlin 1982) 302–346.

Jusek, ''Morality'' = S. Jusek, ''Sexual Morality and the Meaning of Prostitution in Fin-de-Siècle Vienna,'' in J. Bremmer ed., *From Sappho to De Sade: Moments in the History of Sexuality* (London 1989) 123–142.

Kampen, *Image* = N. Kampen, *Image and Status: Roman Working Women in Ostia* (Berlin 1981).

Karayannopulos, *Finanzwesen* = J. Karayannopulos, *Das Finanzwesen des frühbyzantinischen Staates* (Südosteuropäische Arbeiten 52) (Munich 1958).

Karlowa, ''Geschichte'' = O. Karlowa, ''Zur Geschichte der *Infamia*,'' *ZRG* 9 (1870) 204–238.

Karlowa, *RR* = O. Karlowa, *Römische Rechtsgeschichte* 2 (Leipzig 1901).

Karras, ''Brothels'' = R. M. Karras, ''The Regulation of Brothels in Later Medieval England,'' *Signs* 14 (1989) 399–433.

Kaser, ''Beschränkungen'' = M. Kaser, ''Rechtsgeschäftliche Verfügungsbeschränkungen im römischen Recht,'' *Römische Rechtsquellen und angewandte Juristenmethode* (Vienna, Cologne, Graz 1986) 173–196 (= F. Baur et al. eds., *Festgabe für J. Sontis* ([Munich 1977] 11–31).

Kaser, "Infamia" = M. Kaser, "Infamia und ignominia in den römischen Rechtsquellen,'' *SZ* 73 (1956) 220–278.

Kaser, "Jahrhundert" = M. Kaser, "Ein Jahrhundert Interpolationenforschung an den römischen Rechtsquellen,'' *Römische Rechtsquellen und angewandte Juristenmethode* (Vienna, Cologne, Graz 1986) 112–154 (= *Anz. Öst. Ak. Wiss., phil.-hist. Kl.*, 116 [1979] 83–113).

Kaser, *Pfandrecht* = M. Kaser, *Studien zum römischen Pfandrecht* (Antiqua 16) (Naples 1982) [repr. of three articles with indices and notes].

Kaser, "Praesumptio" = M. Kaser, "*Praesumptio Muciana,*'' in *Studi in onore di P. De Francisci* 1 (Milan 1956) 213–227.

Kaser, "Rechtswidrigkeit" = M. Kaser, "Rechtswidrigkeit und Sittenwidrigkeit im klassischen römischen Recht,'' *SZ* 60 (1940) 95–150.

Kaser, "Restitutio" = M. Kaser, "Zur in integrum restitutio, besonders wegen metus und dolus,'' *SZ* 95 (1978) 101–183.

Kaser, *RE* transactio = M. Kaser, s.v. transactio, *RE* 6A (1937) 2139–2147.

Kaser (rev. De' Dominicis) = M. Kaser (review of De' Dominicis, "Origini''), *Iura* 2 (1951) 324–325.

Kaser, *RP* = M. Kaser, *Das römische Privatrecht* 1^2 (Munich 1971) 2^2 (Munich 1975).

Kaser, *RZ* = M. Kaser, *Das römische Zivilprozessrecht* (Munich 1966).

Kaser, *Verbotsgesetze* = M. Kaser, *Über Verbotsgesetze und verbotswidrige Geschäfte im römischen Recht* (*SB Österr. Ak. Wiss., phil.-hist. Kl.,* 312) (Vienna 1977).

Kehoe, "Mime" = P. H. Kehoe, "The Adultery Mime Reconsidered,'' in D. F. Bright and E. S. Rampage eds., *Classical Texts and Their Traditions: Studies in Honor of C. R. Trahman* (Chico 1984) 89–106.

Kelly, "Edict" = J. M. Kelly, "The Growth-Pattern of the Praetor's Edict,'' *IJ* 1 (1966) 341–355.

Kelly, *Judicature* = J. M. Kelly, *Studies in the Civil Judicature of the Roman Republic* (Oxford 1976).

Kelly, *Litigation* = J. M. Kelly, *Roman Litigation* (Oxford 1966).

Kienast, *Augustus* = D. Kienast, *Augustus: Prinzeps und Monarch* (Darmstadt 1982).

Kienast, "Rechtsordnung" = D. Kienast, "Der augusteische Prinzipat als Rechtsordnung,'' *SZ* 101 (1984) 115–141.

Klingenberg, "Reformedikt" = G. Klingenberg, "Das abgabenrechtliche Reformedikt des Jahres 58 n. Chr.,'' in *Reformen des Rechts: Festschrift zur 200-Jahr-Feier der rechtswissenschaftlichen Fakultät Graz* (Graz 1979) 57–74.

Knütel, "Pacta" = R. Knütel, "Stipulatio und Pacta,'' in D. Medicus and H. H. Seiler eds., *Festschrift für M. Kaser* (Munich 1976) 201–228.

Knütel, *Stipulatio* = R. Knütel, *Stipulatio Poenae: Studien zum römischen Vertragsstrafe* (Forsch. zum röm. Recht 34) (Cologne and Vienna 1976).

Köberlein, *Caligula* = E. Köberlein, *Caligula und die ägyptischen Kulte* (Beitr. zur klass. Phil. 3) (Meisenheim am Glan 1962).

Koestermann, *Annalen* = E. Koestermann, *Cornelius Tacitus: Annalen* (4 vols.) (Heidelberg 1963–1968).

Kolb, "Symbolik" = F. Kolb, "Zur Statussymbolik im antiken Rom,'' *Chiron* 7 (1977) 239–259.

Kolb, *Untersuchungen* = F. Kolb, *Untersuchungen zur Historia Augusta* (Antiquitas 4.20) (Bonn 1987).

Kolendo, "Esclavage" = J. Kolendo, "L'esclavage et la vie sexuelle des hommes libres à Rome," *Index* 10 (1981) 288–297.

Kraemer, *Her Share* = R. S. Kraemer, *Her Share of the Blessings: Women's Religions among Pagans, Jews, and Christians in the Greco-Roman World* (Oxford 1992).

Krause, *Witwen* 1, 2, 3, 4 = J.-U. Krause, *Witwen und Waisen im römischen Reich* 1: *Verwitwung und Wiederverheiratung* (Stuttgart 1994), 2: *Wirtschaftliche und gesellschaftliche Stellung von Witwen* (Stuttgart 1994), 3: *Rechtliche und soziale Stellung von Waisen* (Stuttgart 1995), 4: *Witwen und Waisen im frühen Christentum* (Stuttgart 1995).

Krenkel, "Familienplanung" = W. A. Krenkel, "Familienplanung und Familienpolitik in der Antike," in A. K. Siems ed., *Sexualität und Erotik in der Antike* (Darmstadt 1988) 375–384 (= *Würzburger Jb.* n.F. 4 [1978] 197–203).

Krenkel, "Pueri" = W. A. Krenkel, "Pueri Meritorii," *WZ Rostock* 28 (1979) 179–189.

Krüger, "Bemerkungen" = H. Krüger, "Bemerkungen über den Sprachgebrauch der Kaiserkonstitutionen im Codex Justinianus," *Archiv für lateinische Lexikographie und Grammatik* 11 (1900) 453–467.

Krüger (rev. Frezza) = H. Krüger (review of P. Frezza, "Osservazioni sopra il sistema di Sabino," *Riv. it.* 8 [1933] 412–471), *SZ* 55 (1935) 388–395.

Krüger, "Verweisungsedikte" = H. Krüger, "Verweisungsedikte im prätorischen Album," *SZ* 37 (1916) 230–316.

Krüger and Kaser, "Fraus" = H. Krüger and M. Kaser, "Fraus," *SZ* 63 (1943) 117–174.

Krüger, *Collectio* = P. Krüger ed., *Collectio librorum iuris anteiustiniani* 2 (Berlin 1878).

Kübler, "Ius 1, 2" = B. Kübler, "Über das Ius liberorum der Frauen und die Vormundschaft der Mutter: Ein Beitrag zur Geschichte der Rezeption des römischen Rechts in Ägypten," *SZ* 30 (1909) 154–183; 31 (1910) 176–195.

Kübler (rev. Legras) = B. Kübler (review of Legras, *Table*), *SZ* 28 (1907) 409–415.

Kübler (rev. Pommeray) = B. Kübler (review of Pommeray, *Infamie*), *SZ* 58 (1938) 298–307.

Kunkel, *Herkunft*² = W. Kunkel, *Herkunft und soziale Stellung der römischen Juristen*² (Forsch. zum röm. Recht 4) (Graz, Vienna, Cologne 1967).

Kunkel, "Quaestio" = W. Kunkel, "Quaestio," in *Kleine Schriften* (Weimar 1974) 33–110 (= *RE* s.h.v. [1] 24 [1963] 720–763).

Kunkel, *RE* mater familias = W. Kunkel, s.v. mater familias, *RE* 28 (1930) 2183–2184.

Kunkel, *Untersuchungen* = W. Kunkel, *Untersuchungen zur Entwicklung des römischen Kriminalverfahrens in vorsullanischer Zeit* (Abh. Bay. Ak. Wiss., phil.-hist. Kl., n.F. 56) (Munich 1962).

Laffi, "Senati" = U. Laffi, "I senati locali nell'" Italia repubblicana," in *Les "bourgeoisies" municipales italiennes aux IIᵉ et Iᵉʳ siècles av. J.-C.* (Paris 1983) 59–74.

Lamberti, *Tabulae* = F. Lamberti, *Tabulae Irnitanae: Municipalità e Ius Romanorum* (Naples 1993).

Lambertini, "Ancora" = R. Lambertini, "Ancora sui legittimati a uccidere *iure patris ex lege Iulia de adulteriis* (a proposito di un recente saggio)," *SDHI* 58 (1992) 362–375.

Lambertini, *DUO* = R. Lambertini, *Dum utrumque occidat: Lex Iulia e uccisione in continenti degli adulteri iure patris* (Bologna 1992).

Lambertini, *Plagium* = R. Lambertini, *Plagium* (Milan 1980).

Lane Fox, *Pagans* = R. Lane Fox, *Pagans and Christians* (San Francisco 1986).

Lanfranchi, *Retori* = F. Lanfranchi, *Il diritto nei retori romani: Contributo alla storia dello sviluppo del diritto romano* (Milan 1938).

Langum, *Crossing* = D. J. Langum, *Crossing over the Line: Legislating Morality and the Mann Act* (Chicago 1994).

Lanza, "Impedimenti" = C. Lanza, "Impedimenti del giudice: Alcuni modelli di "diritto classico"," *BIDR*³ 29 (1987) 467–541.

La Rosa, *Repressione* = R. La Rosa, *La repressione del furtum in età arcaica: Manus iniectio e duplione damnum decidere* (Naples 1990).

Last, "Social Policy" = H. Last, "The Social Policy of Augustus," *CAH* 10 (1934) 425–464.

Latte, *RR* = K. Latte, *Römische Religionsgeschichte* (Munich 1960).

Lebek, "Curien" = W. D. Lebek, "Die municipalen Curien oder Domitian als Republikaner: Lex Lati (Tab. Irn.) Paragraph 50(?) und 51," *ZPE* 107 (1995) 135–194.

Lebek, "Duumvirn" = W. D. Lebek, "Domitians *Lex Lati* und die Duumvirn, Aedilen und Quaestoren in Tab. Irn. Paragraph 18–20," *ZPE* 103 (1994) 253–292.

Lebek, "*Lex Lati*" = W. D. Lebek, "La *Lex Lati* di Domiziano (Lex Irnitana): Le strutture giuridiche dei capitoli 84 e 86," *ZPE* 97 (1993) 159–178.

Lebek, "SC" = W. D. Lebek, "Standeswürde und Berufsverbot unter Tiberius: Das SC der Tabula Larinas," *ZPE* 81 (1990) 37–96.

Le Gall, "Femme" = J. Le Gall, "Un critère de différenciation sociale: La situation de la femme," in *Recherches sur les structures sociales dans l'antiquité classique* (Paris 1970) 275–286.

Le Gall, "Habitants" = J. Le Gall, "Les habitants de Rome et la fiscalité sous le Haut-Empire," in H. van Effenterre ed., *Points de vue sur la fiscalité antique* (Paris 1979) 113–126.

Le Gall, "Successeurs" = J. Le Gall, "Successeurs d'Auguste mais descendants d'Antoine," *Bull. Soc. Ant.* (1987) 223–229.

Legras, *Table* = H. Legras, *La table latine d'Héraclée (la prétendue Lex Julia Municipalis)* (Paris 1907).

Leifer, *RE* postulatio = Leifer, s.v. postulatio, *RE* 21.1 (1953) 874–889.

Lemosse, "Affranchis" = M. Lemosse, "Les affranchis Latins," *TR* 62 (1994) 309–316.

Lenel, "Edictcommentaren" = O. Lenel, "Quellenforschung in den Edictcommentaren," *SZ* 3 (1882) 104–120.

Lenel, *EP*³ = O. Lenel, *Das Edictum Perpetuum: Ein Versuch zu seiner Weiderherstellung*³ (Aalen 1974 repr. of Leipzig 1923 ed.).

Lenel, "Kunde" = O. Lenel, "Beiträge zur Kunde des Edicts und der Edictcommentare," *SZ* 2 (1881) 14–83.

Lenel, *Pal.* = O. Lenel, *Palingenesia Iuris Civilis* (Graz 1960 repr. of Leipzig 1889 ed. with suppl. by L. E. Sierl).

Lenger, *Corpus* = M.-T. Lenger, *Corpus des ordonnances des Ptolémées* (Brussels rev. ed. 1980).

Leontsini, *Prostitution* = S. Leontsini, *Die Prostitution im frühen Byzanz* (Diss. Vienna 1989).

Leppin, *Histrionen* = H. Leppin, *Histrionen: Untersuchungen zur sozialen Stellung von Bühnenkunstlern im Westen des römischen Reiches zur Zeit der Republik und des Principats* (Bonn 1992).

Levi, *Introduction* = E. H. Levi, *An Introduction to Legal Reasoning* (Chicago and London 1949).

Levick, *Claudius* = B. Levick, *Claudius* (New Haven 1990).

Levick, *Government* = B. Levick, *The Government of the Roman Empire: A Sourcebook* (London and Sydney 1985).

Levick, "Rhodes" = B. Levick, "Tiberius' Retirement to Rhodes in 6 B.C.," *Latomus* 31 (1972) 779–813.

Levick, "*SC*" = B. Levick, "The *Senatus Consultum* from Larinum," *JRS* 73 (1983) 97–115.

Levick, *Tiberius* = B. Levick, *Tiberius the Politician* (London 1976).

Levy, "Anklägervergehen" = E. Levy, "Von den römischen Anklägervergehen," in *Gesammelte Schriften* 2 (Cologne 1963) 379–432 (= *SZ* 53 [1933] 151–233).

Levy, *Hergang* = E. Levy, *Der Hergang der römischen Ehescheidung* (Weimar 1925).

Levy, "Infamie" = E. Levy, "Zur Infamie im römischen Strafrecht," *Gesammelte Schriften* 2 (Cologne 1963) 509–526 (= *Studi Riccobono* 2 [1932] 79–100).

Levy, *PS* = E. Levy, *Pauli Sententiae: A Palingenesia of the Opening Titles as a Specimen of Research in West Roman Vulgar Law* (New York 1969 repr. of Ithaca 1945 ed.).

Lévy, "*Dignitas*" = J. P. Lévy, "*Dignitas, gravitas, auctoritas testium,*" in *Studi in onore di B. Biondi* 2 (Milan 1965) 27–94.

Lewis, "Egypt" = N. Lewis, " 'Greco-Roman Egypt': Fact or Fiction?" in *Proceedings of the Twelfth International Congress of Papyrology* (Toronto 1970) 3–14.

Lewis, *Life* = N. Lewis, *Life in Egypt under Roman Rule* (Oxford 1983).

Lewis, "Romanity" = N. Lewis, "The Romanity of Roman Egypt: A Growing Consensus," *Atti XVII cong. int. pap.* 3 (Naples 1984) 1077–1084.

Liebs, "Alexander Severus" = D. Liebs, "Alexander Severus und das Strafrecht," *BHAC 1977/1978* (Bonn 1980) 115–147.

Liebs, *Jurisprudenz* = D. Liebs, *Römische Jurisprudenz in Africa: Mit Studien zu den pseudopaulinischen Sentenzen* (Berlin 1993).

Liebs, "Provinzialjurisprudenz" = D. Liebs, "Römische Provinzialjurisprudenz," *ANRW* 2.15 (Berlin 1976) 288–362.

Liebs, "Schutz" = D. Liebs, "Der Schutz der Privatsfäre in einer Sklavengesellschaft: Aussagen von Sklaven gegen ihre Herren nach römischen Recht," *BIDR*[3] 22 (1980) 147–189.

Linderski, "Pontia" = J. Linderski, "The Death of Pontia," *RhM* n.F. 133 (1990) 86–93.

Link, "Bürgerrecht" = S. Link, ". . . *ut optimo iure optimaque lege cives Romani sint:* Bürgerrecht, Liturgie-und Steuerfreiheit im Übergang von der Republik zum Prinzipat," *SZ* 112 (1995) 370–384.

Lintott, *Reform* = A. W. Lintott, *Judicial Reform and Land Reform in the Roman Republic: A New Edition, with Translation and Commentary, of the Laws from Urbino* (Cambridge 1992).

Lintott, *Violence* = A. W. Lintott, *Violence in Republican Rome* (Oxford 1968).

Lo Cascio, "*Praeconium*" = E. Lo Cascio, "*Praeconium* e *dissignatio* nella *Tabula Heracleensis,*" *Helikon* 15/16 (1975/1976) 351–371.

Lokin, "End" = J. H. A. Lokin, "The End of an Epoch: Epilegomena to a Century of Interpolation Criticism," in *Collatio Iuris Romani: Études dediées à H. Ankum* 1 (Amsterdam 1995) 261–273.

Longo, *Delictum* = G. Longo, *Delictum e crimen* (Milan 1976).

Longo, "Riflessioni" = G. Longo, "Riflessioni critiche in tema di matrimonio," in *Sodalitas: Scritti in onore di A. Guarino* 5 (Naples 1984) 2357–2383.

López Barja de Quiroga, "Mobility" = P. López Barja de Quiroga, "Freedmen Social Mobility in Roman Italy," *Historia* 44.3 (1995) 326–348.

Lopuszanski, "Police" = G. Lopuszanski, "La police romaine et les Chrétiens," *AC* 20 (1951) 5–46.

Lorenzi, "Figlia" = C. Lorenzi, "Pap. Coll. 4.8.1: La figlia adultera e il *ius occidendi iure patris,*" *SDHI* 57 (1991) 158–180.

Lotmar, "Erlaβ" = P. Lotmar, "Marc Aurels Erlaβ über die Freilassungsauflage," *SZ* 33 (1912) 304–382.

Lotmar, "Incestum" = P. Lotmar, "Lex Julia de adulteriis und incestum," in *Mélanges P. F. Girard* 2 (Paris 1912) 119–143.

Lübtow, "Injurienrecht" = U. von Lübtow, "Zum römischen Injurienrecht," *Labeo* 15 (1969) 131–167.

Luce, *Livy* = T. J. Luce, *Livy: The Composition of His History* (Princeton 1977).

Luhmann, *Rechtssystem* = N. Luhmann, *Rechtssystem und Rechtsdogmatik* (Berlin, Cologne, Mainz 1974).

Luhmann, *Theory* = N. Luhmann (E. King and M. Albrow trans.), *A Sociological Theory of Law* (London 1985).

MacCormack, "*Dolus*" = G. M. MacCormack, "*Dolus, Culpa, Custodia* and *Diligentia:* Criteria of Liability or Content of Obligation," *Index* 22 (1994) 189–209.

MacCormack, "Ope" = G. M. MacCormack, "Ope consilium furtum factum," *TR* 51 (1983) 271–293.

MacCormack, "*Sciens*" = G. M. MacCormack, "*Sciens dolo malo,*" in *Sodalitas: Scritti in onore di A. Guarino* 3 (Naples 1984) 1445–1453.

MacDonald, "Assarion" = D. MacDonald, "The Worth of the Assarion," *Historia* 38 (1989) 120–123.

MacMullen, "Difference" = R. MacMullen, "What Difference Did Christianity Make?" in *Changes in the Roman Empire: Essays in the Ordinary* (Princeton 1990) 142–155 (= *Historia* 35 [1986] 322–343).

MacMullen, "Habit" = R. MacMullen, "The Epigraphic Habit in the Roman Empire," *AJP* 103 (1982) 233–246.

MacMullen, "Love" = R. MacMullen, "Roman Attitudes to Greek Love," in *Changes in the Roman Empire: Essays in the Ordinary* (Princeton 1990) 177–189 (= *Historia* 31 [1982] 484–502).

MacMullen, *Soldier* = R. MacMullen, *Soldier and Civilian in the Later Roman Empire* (Cambridge 1967).

MacMullen, "Tax-Pressure" = R. MacMullen, "Tax-Pressure in the Roman Empire," *Latomus* 46 (1987) 737–754.

Manfredini, "Costantino" = A. D. Manfredini, "Costantino la tabernaria il vino," *AAC* 7 (Naples 1988) 325–341.

Manfredini, "Vestem" = A. D. Manfredini, "Qui commutant cum feminis vestem," *RIDA*³ 32 (1985) 257–271.

Manning, "Stoicism" = C. E. Manning, "Stoicism and Slavery in the Roman Empire," *ANRW* 2.36.3 (Berlin 1989) 1518–1543.

Manthe, *SC* = U. Manthe, *Das Senatus Consultum Pegasianum* (Berlin 1988).

Mantovani, "Competenza" = D. Mantovani, "Sulla competenza penale del *praefectus urbi* attraverso il *liber singularis* di Ulpiano," in A. Burdese ed., *Idee vecchie e nuove sul diritto criminale romano* (Padua 1988) 171–223.

Marotta, *Sanxit* = V. Marotta, *Multa de iure sanxit: Aspetti della politica del diritto di Antonino Pio* (Milan 1988).

Marquardt, *Privatleben*² = J. Marquardt (A. Mau ed.), *Das Privatleben der Römer*² (2 vols.) (Darmstadt 1990 repr. of Leipzig 1886 ed.).

Marriott, "Authorship" = I. Marriott, "The Authorship of the *Historia Augusta:* Two Computer Studies," *JRS* 69 (1979) 65–77.

Marshall, "Civil Courts" = A. J. Marshall, "Ladies at Law: The Role of Women in the Roman Civil Courts," in C. Deroux ed., *Studies in Latin Literature and Roman History* 5 (Brussels 1989) 35–54.

Marshall, "Maesia" = A. J. Marshall, "Roman Ladies on Trial: The Case of Maesia of Sentinum," *Phoenix* 44 (1990) 46–57.

Marshall, "Provinces" = A. J. Marshall, "Roman Women and the Provinces," *Anc. Soc.* 6 (1975) 109–127.

Marshall, "Tacitus" = A. J. Marshall, "Tacitus and the Governor's Lady: A Note on Annals iii.33–4," *G & R*² 22 (1975) 11–18.

Marshall, "Women on Trial" = A. J. Marshall, "Women on Trial before the Roman Senate," *ECM* n.s. 9 (1990) 333–366.

Martin, "Vie" = R. Martin, "La vie sexuelle des esclaves d'après les *Dialogues Rustiques* de Varron," in *Varron: Grammaire antique et stylistique latine* (Paris 1978) 113–126.

Masi Doria, "Bürgerrecht" = C. Masi Doria, "Zum Bürgerrecht der Freigelassenen," in M. J. Schermaier and Z. Végh eds., *Ars Boni et Aequi: Festschrift für W. Waldstein zum 65. Geburtstag* (Stuttgart 1993) 231–260.

Mathias and O'Brien, "Taxation" = P. Mathias and P. O'Brien, "Taxation in Britain and France, 1715–1810: A Comparison of the Social and Economic Incidence of Taxes Collected for the Central Governments," *Journ. Europ. Econ. Hist.* 5 (1976) 601–650.

Matthews, "Tax Law" = J. F. Matthews, "The Tax Law of Palmyra: Evidence for Economic History in a City of the Roman East," *JRS* 74 (1984) 156–180.

Mattingly, "Naevius" = H. B. Mattingly, "Naevius and the Metelli," *Historia* 9 (1960) 414–439.

Mau, *RE* comissatio = A. Mau, s.v. comissatio, *RE* 4 (1901) 610–619.

May, *Trials* = J. M. May, *Trials of Character: The Eloquence of Ciceronian Ethos* (Chapel Hill and London 1988).

Mayer-Maly, "*CBM*" = T. Mayer-Maly, "*Contra bonos mores,*" in *Iuris Professio: Festgabe Max Kaser* (Vienna 1986) 151–167.

Mayer Maly, "EV" = T. Mayer-Maly, "Das Eigentumsverständnis der Gegenwart und die Rechtsgeschichte," *Festschrift für H. Hübner zum 70. Geburtstag* (Berlin 1984) 145–158.

Mayer-Maly, "Impedimentum" = T. Mayer-Maly, "Impedimentum criminis und römisches Recht," *SZ (Kan. Abt.)* 42 (1956) 382–388.

Mayer-Maly, *RE* vidua = T. Mayer-Maly, s.v. vidua (viduus), *RE* 2.8.2 (1958) 2098–2107.

Mayer-Maly, "*Verecundia*" = T. Mayer-Maly, "*Verecundia* in der Rechtssprache," in *Estudios en homenaje al Profesor J. Iglesias* (Madrid 1988) 375–389.

Mazzacane, *ED* infamia = A. Mazzacane, s.v. infamia (diritto romano e intermedio), *ED* 21 (1971) 382–387.

McGinn, "Caligula's Brothel" = T. A. J. McGinn, "Caligula's Brothel on the Palatine," *EMC/CV* (forthcoming).

McGinn, "Concubinage" = T. A. J. McGinn, "Concubinage and the *Lex Iulia* on Adultery," *TAPA* 121 (1991) 335–375.

McGinn, "Definition" = T. A. J. McGinn, "The Legal Definition of 'Prostitute' in Late Antiquity," *MAAR* (forthcoming).

McGinn, *ESH* Prostitution = T. A. J. McGinn, s.v. Prostitution, *Encyclopedia of Social History* (New York and London 1994) 588–591.

McGinn, "*Feminae Probrosae*" = T. A. J. McGinn, "*Feminae Probrosae* and the Litter," *CJ* 93 (1997/1998) 241–250.

McGinn, "*NSP*" = T. A. J. McGinn, "*Ne Serva Prostituatur:* Restrictive Covenants in the Sale of Slaves," *SZ* 107 (1990) 315–353.

McGinn, *PRS* = T. A. J. McGinn, *Prostitution and Roman Society* (Univ. Michigan Press, forthcoming).

McGinn, "*SC*" = T. A. J. McGinn, "The *SC* from Larinum and the Repression of Adultery at Rome," *ZPE* 93 (1992) 273–295.

McGinn, *Social Policy* = T. A. J. McGinn, *Prostitution and Julio-Claudian Legislation: The Formation of Social Policy in Early Imperial Rome* (Diss. Michigan 1986).

McGinn, "Taxation" = T. A. J. McGinn, "The Taxation of Roman Prostitutes," *Helios* 16 (1989) 79–110.

McKeown, "Elegy" = J. C. McKeown, "Augustan Elegy and Mime," *PCPS* n.s. 25 (1979) 71–84.

Meinhart, "Datierung" = M. Meinhart, "Die Datierung des SC Tertullianum, mit einem Beitrag zur Gaiusforschung," *SZ* 83 (1966) 100–141.

Meinhart, *SCC* = M. Meinhart, *Die Senatusconsulta Tertullianum und Orfitianum in ihrer Bedeutung für das klassische römische Erbrecht* (Graz 1967).

Meinhart, "Zeugnis" = M. Meinhart, "Ulp. D. 38.17.1.6: Ein Zeugnis für Humana Interpretatio," *TR* 33 (1965) 230–265.

Melville Jones, "Denarii" = J. R. Melville Jones, "Denarii, Asses and Assaria in the Early Roman Empire," *BICS* 18 (1971) 99–105.

Mercogliano, "*Tituli*" = F. Mercogliano, "Un'ipotesi sulla formazione dei *Tituli ex corpore Ulpiani,*" *Index* 18 (1990) 185–207.

Mette-Dittmann, *Ehegesetze* = A. Mette-Dittmann, *Die Ehegesetze des Augustus: Eine Untersuchung im Rahmen der Gesellschaftspolitik des Princeps* (Historia Einzelschr. 67) (Stuttgart 1991).

Meyer, *Konkubinat* = P. M. Meyer, *Der römische Konkubinat nach den Rechtsquellen und den Inschriften* (Leipzig 1895).

Meyer, "P. Cattaoui" = P. M. Meyer, "Papyrus Cattaoui II: Kommentar," *APF* 3 (1906) 67–105.

Millar, "Condemnation" = Millar, "Condemnation to Hard Labour in the Roman Empire, from the Julio-Claudians to Constantine," *PBSR* 39 (1984) 124–147.

Millar, *Dio* = F. Millar, *A Study of Cassius Dio* (Oxford 1964).

Millar, *Emperor* = F. Millar, *The Emperor in the Roman World (31 B.C.–A.D. 337)* (Ithaca rev. ed. 1992).

Millar, "Empire" = F. Millar, "Empire and City, Augustus to Julian: Obligations, Excuses and Status", *JRS* 73 (1983) 76–96.

Millar, "Fiscus" = F. Millar, "The Fiscus in the First Two Centuries," *JRS* 53 (1963) 29–42.

Millar, *Near East* = F. Millar, *The Roman East, 31 B.C.–A.D. 337* (Cambridge and London 1993).

Mirkovic, "Soldatenehe" = M. Mirkovic, "Die römische Soldatenehe und der Soldatenstand," *ZPE* 40 (1980) 259–271.

Mitteis, "Papyrusstudien" = L. Mitteis, "Romanistische Papyrusstudien," *SZ* 23 (1902) 274–314.

Mitteis, *RP* = L. Mitteis, *Römisches Privatrecht bis auf die Zeit Diokletians* 1 (Leipzig 1908).

Mitteis and Wilcken, *GC* = L. Mitteis and U. Wilcken, *Grundzüge und Chrestomathie der Papyruskunde* (2 vols.) (Leipzig and Berlin 1912).

Molé, *NNDI* stuprum = M. Molé, s.v. stuprum, *NNDI* 18 (1971) 582–587.

Moles, "Livy's Preface" = J. Moles, "Livy's Preface," *PCPS* 39 (1993) 141–168.

Momigliano, "Personalità" = A. Momigliano, "La personalità di Caligola," *ASNP*[2] 1 (1932) 205–228.

Momigliano (rev. Syme) = A. Momigliano (review of Syme, *RR*), *JRS* 30 (1940) 75–80.

Mommsen, "Commentaria" = T. Mommsen, "Commentaria ludorum saecularium quintorum et septimorum," in *Gesammelte Schriften* 8[2] (Berlin 1913) 567–626 (= [rev.] *Eph. Ep.* 8 [1891] 225–301).

Mommsen, "*SC*" = T. Mommsen, "Senatus consultum de sumptibus ludorum gladiatoriorum minuendis factum a.p.c. 176/7," in *Gesammelte Schriften* 8[2] (Berlin 1913) 499–531 (= [rev.] *Eph. Ep.* 7 [1890] 388–428).

Mommsen, *Staatsrecht³* = T. Mommsen, *Römisches Staatsrecht³* (3 vols.) (Graz 1969 repr. of Leipzig 1887 ed.).

Mommsen, "Stadtrechte" = T. Mommsen, "Die Stadtrechte der latinische Gemeinden Salpensa und Malaca in der Provinz Baetica," *Gesammelte Schriften* 1 (Berlin 1905) 265–382 (= *Abh. Sächs. Ges. Wiss.* 3 [1855] 361–507).

Mommsen, *Strafrecht* = T. Mommsen, *Römisches Strafrecht* (Leipzig 1899).

Mooney, *Vita* = G. W. Mooney, *C. Suetonii Tranquilli de Vita Caesarum: Libri VII–VIII* (London 1930).

Moreau, *Clodiana Religio* = P. Moreau, *Clodiana Religio: Un procès politique en 61 av. J.-C.* (Paris 1982).

Mrozek, "Randgruppen" = S. Mrozek, "Die epigraphisch belegte sozialen Randgruppen in den Städten Italiens (Prinzipatszeit)," in Weiler, *SRAA* (1988) 243–255.

Müller, "GO" = W. Müller, "Griechische Ostraka," *APF* 16 (1958) 190–213.

Musgrave and Musgrave, *Public Finance³* = R. M. Musgrave and P. B. Musgrave, *Public Finance in Theory and Practice³* (New York 1980).

Nardi, "Divieti" = E. Nardi, "Sui divieti matrimoniali delle leggi augustee," *SDHI* 7 (1941) 112–146.

Nardi, "Incapacitas" = E. Nardi, "La incapacitas delle feminae probrosae," *Studi Sassaresi* 17 (1938) 151–178.

Nardi, *Posizione* = E. Nardi, *La reciproca posizione successoria dei coniugi privi di conubium* (Milan 1938).

Neesen, *Abgaben* = L. Neesen, *Untersuchungen zu den direkten Staatsabgaben der römischen Kaiserzeit (27 v. Chr.–284 n. Chr.)* (Antiquitas 1.32) (Bonn 1980).

Nelson, "Receipt" = C. A. Nelson, "Receipt for Tax on Prostitutes," *BASP* 32 (1995) 23–33.

Newbold, "Social Tension" = R. F. Newbold, "Social Tension at Rome in the Early Years of Tiberius' Reign," *Athenaeum* n.s. 52 (1974) 110–143.

Nicolau, *Causa* = M. Nicolau, *Causa liberalis: Étude historique et comparative du procès de liberté dans les législations anciennes* (Paris 1933).

Nicolet, "Augustus" = C. Nicolet, "Augustus, Government, and the Propertied Classes," in F. Millar and E. Segal eds., *Caesar Augustus: Seven Aspects* (Oxford 1984) 89–128.

Nicolet, "Cens" = C. Nicolet, "Le cens sénatorial sous la République et sous Auguste," in *Ordres* (1984) 143–174 (= *JRS* 66 [1976] 20–38).

Nicolet, "Classes" = C. Nicolet, "Les classes dirigeantes romaines sous la République: Ordre sénatorial et ordre équestre," *Annales ESC* 32 (1977) 726–755.

Nicolet, "*Finitores*" = C. Nicolet, "Les *finitores ex equestri loco* de la loi Servilia de 63 av. J.-C.," *Latomus* 29 (1970) 72–103.

Nicolet, *Ordre* 1 = C. Nicolet, *L'ordre équestre à l'époque républicaine (312–43 av. J.-C.)* 1 (Paris 1966).

Nicolet, *Ordres* = C. Nicolet ed., *Des ordres à Rome* (Paris 1984).

Nicolet, *Tributum* = C. Nicolet, *Tributum: Recherches sur la fiscalité directe sous la République romaine* (Antiquitas 1.24) (Bonn 1976).

Nicolet, *World* = C. Nicolet (P. S. Falla trans.), *The World of the Citizen in Republican Rome* (Berkeley 1980).

Nicols, "Patrona" = J. Nicols, "*Patrona Civitatis:* Gender and Civic Patronage," in C. Deroux ed., *Studies in Latin Literature and Roman History* 5 (Brussels 1989) 117–142.

Nicols, "Size" = J. Nicols, "On the Standard Size of the Ordo Decurionum," *SZ* 105 (1988) 712–719.

Nicosia, "*Manus iniectio*" = G. Nicosia, "La *manus iniectio:* Dal regime originario a quello della *manus iniectio pura*", in *Praesidia Libertatis: Garantismo e sistemi processuali nell'esperienza di Roma repubblicana* (Naples 1994) 163–183 (= *ACOP* 6).

Nippel, *Order* = W. Nippel, *Public Order in Ancient Rome* (Cambridge 1995).

Niziolek, "Phrase" = M. Niziolek, "Meaning of the Phrase *Liberi Naturales* in Roman Law Sources Up to Constantine's Reign," *RIDA*³ 22 (1975) 317–344.

Noailles, *Fas* = P. Noailles, *Fas et Jus: Études de droit romain* (Paris 1948).

Nöldeke, "Aufhebung" = T. Nöldeke, "Die Aufhebung des Chrysargyrums durch Anastasius," *Byz. Zeitschr.* 13 (1904) 135.

Nony, *Caligula* = D. Nony, *Caligula* (Paris 1986).

Nörr, "Ethik" = D. Nörr, "Ethik von Jurisprudenz in Sachen Schatzfund," *BIDR*³ 14 (1972) 11–40.

Nörr, "Legislation" = D. Nörr, "The Matrimonial Legislation of Augustus: An Early Instance of Social Engineering," *IJ* n.s. 16 (1981) 350–364 (= [in substantially revised form] "Planung in der Antike: Über die Ehegesetze des Augustus," in *Freiheit und Sachszwang: Beiträge zu Ehren Helmut Schelskys* [Opladen 1977] 309–334).

Nörr, *Rechtskritik* = D. Nörr, *Rechtskritik in der römischen Antike* (*Abh. Bay. Ak. Wiss., phil.-hist. Kl.*, n.F. 77) (Munich 1974).

Nowak, *Censoren* = M. Nowak, *Die Strafverhängungen der Censoren* (Diss. Breslau 1909).

Noy, "*SC*" = D. Noy, "The *Senatus Consultum Gaetulicianum: Manus* and Inheritance" *TR* 56 (1988) 299–304.

Nugent, "Ovid" = S. G. Nugent, "*Tristia* 2: Ovid and Augustus," in Raaflaub and Toher, *BRE* (1990) 239–257.

Oliver and Palmer, "Minutes" = J. H. Oliver and R. E. A. Palmer, "Minutes of an Act of the Roman Senate," *Hesperia* 24 (1955) 320–349.

Oppermann, "Bevölkerungspolitik" = H. Oppermann, "Die Bevölkerungspolitik des Augustus," *Neue Jahrbücher für Wissenschaft und Jugendbildung* 12 (1936) 116–133.

Ostrow, "*Augustales*" = S. E. Ostrow, "The *Augustales* in the Augustan Scheme," in Raaflaub and Toher, *BRE* (1990) 364–379.

Otis, "Prostitution" = L. L. Otis, "Prostitution and Repentance in Late Medieval Perpignan," in J. Kirshner and S. F. Wemple eds., *Women of the Medieval World: Essays in Honor of J. H. Mundy* (Oxford and New York 1985) 137–160.

Otis, *Prostitution* = L. L. Otis, *Prostitution in Medieval Society: The History of an Urban Institution in Languedoc* (Chicago 1985).

Ott, *Beneficiarier* = J. Ott, *Die Beneficiarier: Untersuchungen zu ihrer Stellung innerhalb der Rangordnung des römischen Heeres und zu ihrer Funktion* (Historia Einzelschr. 92) (Stuttgart 1995).

Pailler, *Bacchanalia* = J.-M. Pailler, *Bacchanalia, la répression de 186 av. J.-C. à Rome et en Italie: Vestiges, images, tradition* (Rome 1988).

Palma, *HI* = A. Palma, *Humanior Interpretatio: Humanitas nell'interpretazione e nella normazione da Adriano ai Severi* (Turin 1992).

Palmer, "Shrines" = R. E. A. Palmer, "Roman Shrines of Female Chastity from the Caste Struggle to the Papacy of Innocent I," *RSA* 4 (1974) 113–159.

Palmer and Humphrey, *Deviant Behavior* = S. Palmer and J. A. Humphrey, *Deviant Behavior: Patterns, Sources, and Control* (New York 1990).

Parker, "Body" = H. N. Parker, "Love's Body Anatomized: The Ancient Erotic Handbooks and the Rhetoric of Sexuality," in A. Richlin ed., *Pornography and Representation in Greece and Rome* (Oxford 1992) 90–111.

Parkin, *Demography* = T. G. Parkin, *Demography and Roman Society* (Baltimore 1992).

Parks, *Schools* = E. P. Parks, *The Roman Rhetorical Schools as a Preparation for the Courts under the Early Empire* (Diss. Johns Hopkins 1945).

Parsi-Magdelain, "Cura" = B. Parsi-Magdelain, "La cura legum et morum," *RHD* 42 (1964) 373–412.

Paschoud, "Sources" = F. Paschoud, "Sources littéraires comme témoines de la transformation de la propriété dans l'antiquité tardive," *AAC* 9 (Naples 1993) 39–66.

Patlagean, "Moine" = E. Patlagean, "L'histoire de la femme déguisée en moine et l'évolution de la sainteté féminine à Byzance," in *Structure sociale, famille, chrétienté à Byzance, IVe–XIe siècle* (London 1981) XI 597–623 (= *Studi medievali*³ 17 [1976] 597–623).

Patterson "*Attikai*" = C. Patterson, "*Hai Attikai:* The Other Athenians," *Helios* 13.2 (1987) 49–67 (= M. Skinner ed., *Rescuing Creusa: New Methodological Approaches to Women in Antiquity* [Lubbock 1987]).

Patterson, *Family* = C. Patterson, *The Family in Greek History* (forthcoming Cambridge 1998).

Patterson, *Slavery* = O. Patterson, *Slavery as Social Death* (Cambridge 1982).

Paul, "Sempronia" = G. M. Paul, "Sallust's Sempronia: The Portrait of a Lady," *PLLS* 5 (1985) 9–22.

Pavan, "Police" = E. Pavan, "Police des moeurs, société et politique à Venise à la fin du Moyen Age," *RH* 536 (1980) 241–288.

Pennitz, "Athleten" = M. Pennitz, "Zur Postulationsfähigkeit der Athleten im klassischen römischen Recht," *SZ* 112 (1995) 91–108.

Penta, "Viduitas" = M. Penta, "La viduitas nella condizione della donna romana," *ANap.* 91 (1980) 341–351.

Peppe, *Posizione* = L. Peppe, *Posizione giuridica e ruolo sociale della donna romana in età repubblicana* (Milan 1984).

Pernice, *Labeo* = A. Pernice, *Labeo: Römisches Privatrecht im ersten Jahrhundert der Kaiserzeit* 1 (Halle 1873), 2.1² (Halle 1895), 2.2² (Halle 1900), 3.1 (Halle 1892).

Perry, "Insiders" = M. E. Perry, "Deviant Insiders: Legalized Prostitution and a Consciousness of Women in Early Modern Seville," *Comp. Stud. Soc. Hist.* 27 (1985) 138–158.

Perry, "Lost Women" = M. E. Perry, " 'Lost Women' in Early Modern Seville: The Politics of Prostitution," *Feminist Studies* 4 (1978) 195–214.

Peters, *Vorbehalte* = F. Peters, *Die Rücktrittsvorbehalte des römischen Kaufrechts* (Cologne and Vienna 1973).

Pfaff, *RE* stuprum = Pfaff, s.v. stuprum, *RE* 4.1 (1931) 423–424.

Pflaum, "Amours" = H.-G. Pflaum, "Les amours des empereurs dans l'Histoire Auguste," *BHAC 1975/1976* (Bonn 1978) 157–166.

Picard, *Auguste et Néron* = G. C. Picard, *Auguste et Néron: Le secret de l'empire* (Paris 1962).

Pieri, *Cens* = G. Pieri, *L'histoire du cens jusqu'à la fin de la République romaine* (Paris 1968).

Pighi, *Ludis*² = J. B. Pighi, *De Ludis Saecularibus Populi Romani Quiritium*² (Amsterdam 1965).

Pitt-Rivers, "Honour" = J. Pitt-Rivers, "Honour and Social Status," in J. G. Peristiany ed., *Honour and Shame: The Values of Mediterranean Society* (Chicago 1966) 19–77.

Pitt-Rivers, *Shechem* = J. Pitt-Rivers, *The Fate of Shechem, or The Politics of Sex: Essays in the Anthropology of the Mediterranean* (Cambridge 1977).

Plaumann, "Ostraka" = G. Plaumann, "Einige Ostraka der Berliner Papyrussammlung," *APF* 6 (1920) 218–221.

Pleket, "Elites" = H. W. Pleket, "Urban Elites and the Economy in the Greek Cities of the Roman Empire," *MBAH* 3.1 (1984) 3–36.

Pleket, "Labor" = H. W. Pleket, "Labor and Unemployment in the Roman Empire: Some Preliminary Remarks," in Weiler, *SRAA* (1988) 267–276.

Pólay, *"RM"* = E. Pólay, "Das *Regimen Morum* des Zensors und die sogenannte Hausgerichtsbarkeit," in *Studi in onore di E. Volterra* 3 (Milan 1971) 263–317.

Pomeroy, *Goddesses* = S. B. Pomeroy, *Goddesses, Whores, Wives, and Slaves* (New York 1975).

Pomeroy, *Women* = S. B. Pomeroy, *Women in Hellenistic Egypt from Alexander to Cleopatra* (New York 1984).

Pommeray, *Infamie* = L. Pommeray, *Études sur l'infamie en droit romain* (Paris 1937).

Powell, *RPPA* = A. Powell ed., *Roman Poetry and Propaganda in the Age of Augustus* (London 1992).

Préaux, "Continuités" = C. Préaux, "L'attache à la terre: Continuités de l'Égypte ptolémaïque à l'Égypte romaine," in *Das römisch-byzantinische Ägypten: Akten des internationalen Symposions 26.–30. September 1978 in Trier* (Mainz am Rhein 1983) 1–5.

Premerstein, "Tafel" = A. von Premerstein, "Die Tafel von Heraclea und die Acta Caesaris," *SZ* 43 (1922) 45–152.

Provera, "Riflessi" = G. Provera, "Riflessi privatistici dei pacta de crimine," in *Studi in onore di B. Biondi* 2 (Milan 1965) 541–569.

Pugliese, "Linee" = G. Pugliese, "Linee generali dell'evoluzione del diritto penale pubblico durante il principato," *ANRW* 2.14 (Berlin 1982) 722–789.

Pugliese, "Pretori" = G. Pugliese, "I pretori fra trasformazione e conservazione," in *Roma tra oligarchia e democrazia: Classi sociali e formazione del diritto in epoca mediorepubblicana* (Naples 1989) 189–198 (= *ACOP* 3).

Pugliese, *Processo* = G. Pugliese, *Il processo civile romano 2: Il processo formulare* 1 (Milan 1963).

Purcell, *"Apparitores"* = N. Purcell, "The *Apparitores:* A Study in Social Mobility," *PBSR* 51 (1983) 125–173.

Purcell, "Livia" = N. Purcell, "Livia and the Womanhood of Rome," *PCPS* 32 (1986) 78–105.

Querzoli, "Prostituzione" = S. Querzoli, "La prostituzione della schiava nel diritto fra Augusto e gli Antonini," *Ostraka* 2 (1993) 399–404.

Raaflaub and Samons, "Opposition" = K. Raaflaub and L. J. Samons II, "Opposition to Augustus," in Raaflaub and Toher, *BRE* (1990) 417–454.

Raaflaub and Toher, *BRE* = K. Raaflaub and M. Toher eds., *Between Republic and Empire: Interpretations of Augustus and His Principate* (Berkeley and Los Angeles 1990).

Rabello, *"Ius occidendi"* = A. M. Rabello, "Il *ius occidendi iure patris* della *Lex Iulia de adulteriis coercendis* e la *vitae necisque potestas* del *paterfamilias,"* *Atti Sem. Rom. Int.* (Perugia 1972) 228–242.

Raber, *Grundlagen* = F. Raber, *Grundlagen klassischer Injurienansprüche* (Forsch. zum röm. Recht 28) (Vienna, Cologne, Graz 1969).

Raber, *"Pretium"* = F. Raber, "Zum *Pretium Affectionis,"* in F. Horak and W. Waldstein eds., *Festschrift für A. Herdlitczka* (Munich and Salzburg 1972) 197–213.

Raditsa, "Legislation" = L. F. Raditsa, "Augustus' Legislation concerning Marriage, Procreation, Love Affairs, and Adultery," *ANRW* 2.13 (Berlin 1980) 278–339.

Raepsaet-Charlier, *"Clarissima femina"* = M.-T. Raepsaet-Charlier, *"Clarissima femina,"* *RIDA*[3] 28 (1981) 189–212.

Raepsaet-Charlier, "Egalité" = M.-T. Raepsaet-Charlier, "Égalité et inégalité dans les couches supérieurs de la société romaine sous le Haut-Empire," *L'égalité* 8 (1982) 452–477.

Raepsaet-Charlier, "Ordre" = M.-T. Raepsaet-Charlier, "Ordre sénatorial et divorce sous le haut-empire: Un chapitre de l'histoire des mentalités," *Acta Classica Univ. Scient. Debrecen.* 17/18 (1981/1982) 161–173.

Raepsaet-Charlier, "Vie" = M.-T. Raepsaet-Charlier, "La vie familiale des élites dans la Rome impériale: Le droit et la pratique," *CCG* 5 (1994) 165–197.

Rantz, "Avocates" = B. Rantz, "Valère Maxime VIII, iii: Des avocates à Rome?" *RIDA*³ 33 (1986) 179–183.

Rasi, *NNDI* avvocati = P. Rasi, s.v. avvocati e procuratori (diritto romano), *NNDI* 1² (1957) 1662–1663.

Rath, "Prostitution" = B. Rath, "Prostitution und spätmittelalterliche Gesellschaft im österreichischen-süddeutschen Raum," in *Frau und spätmittelalterlicher Alltag* (*SB Österr. Ak. Wiss., phil.-hist. Kl.,* 473) (Vienna 1986) 553–571.

Rathbone, "Taxation" = D. W. Rathbone, "Egypt, Augustus and Roman Taxation," *CCG* 4 (1993) 81–112.

Rauh, "Auctioneers" = N. Rauh, "Auctioneers and the Roman Economy," *Historia* 38 (1989) 451–471.

Rawson, *FAR* = B. Rawson, *The Family in Ancient Rome: New Perspectives* (Ithaca 1986).

Rawson, "Relationships" = B. Rawson, "Adult-Child Relationships in Roman Society," in Rawson ed., *Marriage, 7–30.*

Rawson, *Marriage* = B. Rawson ed., *Marriage, Divorce and Children in Ancient Rome* (Oxford 1991).

Rawson, "*Spurii*" = B. Rawson, "*Spurii* and the Roman View of Illegitimacy," *Antichthon* 23 (1989) 10–41.

Rawson, "*Discrimina*" = E. Rawson, "*Discrimina Ordinum:* The *Lex Julia Theatralis,*" in *Roman Culture and Society: Collected Papers* (Oxford 1991) 508–545 (= *PBSR* 55 [1987] 83–114).

Rea, "Market Taxes" = J. R. Rea, "P. Lond inv. 1562 *verso:* Market Taxes in Oxyrhynchus," *ZPE* 46 (1982) 191–209.

Reinach, "Code 1, 2" = T. Reinach, "Un code fiscal de l'Égypte romaine: Le Gnomon de l'Idiologue," *NRH* 43 (1919) 583–636; 44 (1920) 5–134.

Reinach, "Impôt" = T. Reinach, "L'impôt sur les courtisanes à Cos," *REG* 5 (1892) 100–102, 253.

Reinach, "Inscription" = T. Reinach, "Inscription de l'ile de Cos," *REG* 4 (1891) 357–376.

Reinhold, "Usurpation" = M. Reinhold, "Usurpation of Status and Status Symbols in the Roman Empire," *Historia* 20 (1971) 275–302.

Rey-Coquais, "Syrie" = J.-P. Rey-Coquais, "Syrie romaine, de Pompée à Dioclétien," *JRS* 68 (1978) 44–73.

Reynolds, "Mime" = R. W. Reynolds, "The Adultery Mime," *CQ* 39 (1945) 77–84.

Rhode, *Justice* = D. L. Rhode, *Justice and Gender* (Cambridge 1989).

Riccobono, "Politica" = S. Riccobono, "La politica demografica di Augusto," *Capitolium* 12 (1937) 573–580.

Riccobono, *Gnomon* = S. Riccobono, *Il Gnomon dell'Idios Logos* (Palermo 1950).

Riccobono, "Opera" = S. Riccobono, "L'opera di Augusto e lo sviluppo del diritto imperiale," *AUPA* 18 (1939).

Rice Holmes, *Architect* = T. Rice Holmes, *The Architect of the Roman Empire, 27 B.C.–A.D. 14* 2 (Oxford 1931).

Richlin, "Approaches" = A. Richlin, "Approaches to the Sources on Adultery at Rome," in H. P. Foley ed. *Reflections of Women in Antiquity* (New York 1981) 379–404.

Richlin, *Garden* = A. Richlin, *The Garden of Priapus: Sexuality and Aggression in Roman Humor* (Oxford rev. ed. 1992).

Richlin, "*Irrumare*" = A. Richlin, "The Meaning of *Irrumare* in Catullus and Martial," *CP* 76 (1981) 40–46.

Richlin, *Pornography* = A. Richlin ed., *Pornography and Representation in Greece and Rome* (Oxford 1992).

Richmond, "Palmyra" = I. A. Richmond, "Palmyra under the Aegis of Rome," *JRS* 53 (1963) 43–54.

Riesenberg, *Citizenship* = P. Riesenberg, *Citizenship in the Western Tradition: Plato to Rousseau* (Chapel Hill 1992).

Riggsby, "Lenocinium" = A. Riggsby, "Lenocinium: Scope and Consequences," *SZ* 112 (1995) 423–427.

Rilinger, *Humiliores* = R. Rilinger, *Humiliores-Honestiores: Zu einer sozialen Dichotomie im Strafrecht der römischen Kaiserzeit* (Munich 1988).

Rizzelli, "Accusa" = G. Rizzelli, "Alcuni aspetti dell'accusa privilegiata in materia di adulterio," *BIDR*³ 28 (1986) 411–441.

Rizzelli, "*Crimen*" = G. Rizzelli, "Il *crimen lenocinii*," *AG* 210 (1990) 457–495.

Rizzelli, "*Stuprum*" = G. Rizzelli, "*Stuprum* e *adulterium* nella cultura augustea e nella *lex Iulia de adulteriis* (Pap. 1 *adult*. D. 48.5.6.1 e Mod. 9 *diff.* D. 50.16.101 pr.)," *BIDR*³ 29 (1987) 355–388.

Robinson, *AR* = O. F. Robinson, *Ancient Rome: City Planning and Administration* (London and New York 1992).

Robinson, *CLAR* = O. F. Robinson, *The Criminal Law of Ancient Rome* (Baltimore 1995).

Robinson, "Slaves" = O. F. Robinson, "Slaves and the Criminal Law," *SZ* 98 (1981) 213–254.

Robinson, "Status" = O. F. Robinson, "The Status of Women in Roman Private Law," *JR* pt. 2 (1987) 143–162.

Roper, "Discipline" = L. Roper, "Discipline and Responsibility: Prostitution and the Reformation in Augsburg," *History Workshop* 19 (1985) 3–28.

Rosen, *Sisterhood* = R. Rosen, *The Lost Sisterhood: Prostitution in America, 1900–1918* (Baltimore and London 1982).

Rossiaud, *Prostitution* = J. Rossiaud (L. G. Cochrane trans.), *Medieval Prostitution* (Oxford 1988).

Rostovtsev, "Besatzungen" = M. I. Rostovtsev (as M. Rostowzew), "Römische Besatzungen in der Krim und das Kastell Charax," *Klio* 2 (1902) 80–95.

Rostovtsev, *Diz. Ep. fiscus* = M. I. Rostovtsev (as M. Rostowsew), s.v. *fiscus,* in E. De Ruggiero ed., *Diz. Ep.* 3 (1922) 96–139.

Rotondi, *Leges* = G. Rotondi, *Leges Publicae Populi Romani: Elenco cronologico con una introduzione sull'attività legislativa dei comizi romani* (Hildesheim 1962 repr. of Milan 1912 ed.).

Rousselle, *Persecution* = R. J. Rousselle, *The Roman Persecution of the Bacchic Cult, 186–180 B.C.* (Diss. SUNY Binghampton 1982).

Royo, "Palais" = M. Royo, "Le palais dans la ville: Formes et structures topographiques du pouvoir impérial d'Auguste à Néron," *MEFRA* 106 (1994) 219–245.

Rudd, *Themes* = N. Rudd, *Themes in Roman Satire* (Norman and London 1986).

Ruggiero, *Eros* = G. Ruggiero, *The Boundaries of Eros: Sex, Crime and Sexuality in Renaissance Venice* (Oxford 1985).

Russo Ruggeri, "*Ius occidendi*" = C. Russo Ruggeri, "Qualche osservazione in tema di *ius occidendi ex lege Iulia de adulteriis coercendis,*" *BIDR*³ 31/32 (1989–1990) 93–120.

Ryan, "*Lex Scantinia*" = F. X. Ryan, "The *Lex Scantinia* and the Prosecution of Censors and Aediles," *CP* 89 (1994) 159–162.

Sabbatucci, "Edilità" = D. Sabbatucci, "L'edilità romana: Magistratura e sacerdozio," *Mem. Acc. Lincei, Cl. sc. mor. stor. e fil.*, 6.3 (1954) 255–334.

Sabine, *History of Income Tax* = B. E. V. Sabine, *A History of Income Tax* (London 1966).

Saller, "Punishment" = R. P. Saller, "Corporal Punishment, Authority, and Obedience in the Roman Household," in Rawson, *Marriage* (1991) 144–165.

Saller, "Slavery" = R. P. Saller, "Slavery and the Roman Family," *Slavery and Abolition* 8 (1987) 65–87 (= M. I. Finley ed., *Classical Slavery* [London 1987]).

Saller and Shaw, "Tombstones" = R. P. Saller and B. D. Shaw, "Tombstones and Roman Family Relations in the Principate: Civilians, Soldiers, and Slaves," *JRS* 74 (1984) 124–156.

Salvaterra, "Progetto" = C. Salvaterra, "Considerazioni sul progetto di Caligola di visitare Alessandria," in Criscuolo and Geraci, *ESA* (1989) 531–656.

Samuelson and Nordhaus, *Economics*[12] = P. A. Samuelson and W. D. Nordhaus, *Economics*[12] (New York 1985).

Sander, "Recht" = E. Sander, "Das Recht des römischen Soldaten," *RhM* n.F. 101 (1958) 152–191, 193–234.

Sansone, "Computer" = D. Sansone, "The Computer and the *Historia Augusta:* A Note on Marriott," *JRS* 80 (1990) 174–177.

Santalucia, *DPR* = B. Santalucia, *Diritto e processo penale nell'antica Roma* (Milan 1989).

Santalucia, "Edili" = B. Santalucia, "Edili e processi populari," in *Studi di diritto penale romano* (Rome 1994) 65–76 (= *Iura* 40 [1989] 75–84).

Santalucia, "Repressione" = B. Santalucia, "La repressione dei reati communi in età repubblicana," in *Studi di diritto penale romano* (Rome 1994) 129–143 (= A. Burdese ed., *Idee vecchie e e nuove sul diritto criminale romano* [Padua 1988] 5–21).

Santirocco, "Horace" = M. Santirocco, "Horace and Augustan Ideology," *Arethusa* 28 (1995) 225–243.

Sattler, "Julia" = P. Sattler, "Julia und Tiberius: Beiträge zur römischen Innenpolitik zwischen den Jahren 12 v. und 2 n. Chr.," in W. Schmitthenner ed., *Augustus* (Darmstadt 1969) 486–530 (= *Studien aus dem Gebiet der Alten Geschichte* [Wiesbaden 1962] 1–36).

Sautel, "Usurpations" = G. Sautel, "Usurpations du pouvoir impérial dans le monde romain et *rescissio actorum*," in *Studi in onore di P. De Francisci* 3 (Milan 1956) 461–491.

Savigny, *System* = F. C. von Savigny, *System des heutigen römischen Rechts* (8 vols.) (Berlin 1840–1849).

Sawer, *Law* = G. Sawer, *Law in Society* (Oxford 1965).

Scamuzzi, "*Lex Roscia*" = U. Scamuzzi, "Studio sulla *lex Roscia theatralis* (con una appendice sulla *gens Roscia*)," *RSC* 17 (1969) 133–165, 259–315, 18 (1970) 5–57, 374–447.

Scheidel, "*Ius*" = W. Scheidel, "Columellas privates *Ius liberorum*: Literatur, Recht, Demographie, Einige Probleme," *Latomus* 53 (1994) 513–527.

Schiemann, "Soldatenkinder," = G. Schiemann, "Zur Rechtsstellung der Soldatenkinder in vor-severischer Zeit," in H.-P. Benöhr et al. eds., *Iuris Professio: Festgabe für M. Kaser zum 80. Geburtstag* (Vienna 1986) 232–244.

Schiller, "Jurists" = A. A. Schiller, "Jurists and Prefects of Rome," *BIDR*[2] 16/17 (1953) 60–97.

Schiller, *Roman Law* = A. A. Schiller, *Roman Law: Mechanisms of Development* (The Hague 1978).

Schilling, *RR* = R. Schilling, *La religion romaine de Vénus depuis les origines jusqu'au temps d'Auguste* (Paris rev. ed. 1982).

Schilling, "*Vénus*" = R. Schilling, "Le sanctuaire de Vénus près de Casinum," in *Perennitas: Studi in onore di A. Brelich* (Rome 1980) 445–451.

Schlichting, *Beschränkung* = G. Schlichting, *Die Verfügungsbeschränkung des Verpfänders im klassischen römischen Recht* (Karlsruhe 1973).

Schlumberger, "Réflexions" = D. Schlumberger, "Réflexions sur la loi fiscale de Palmyre," *Syria* 18 (1937) 271–297.

Schmähling, *Censoren* = E. Schmähling, *Die Sittenaufsicht der Censoren: Ein Beitrag zur Sittengeschichte der römischen Republik* (Stuttgart 1938).

Schmitz, *Zeugen* = D. Schmitz, *Zeugen des Prozeßgegners in Gerichtsreden Ciceros* (Frankfurt am Main 1985).

Schneider, *RE* meretrix = K. Schneider, s.v. meretrix, *RE* 15 (1931) 1018–1027.

Schnurr, "*Lex Julia*" = C. Schnurr, "The *Lex Julia Theatralis* of Augustus: Some Remarks on Seating Problems in Theatre, Amphitheatre, and Circus," *LCM* 17.10 (1992) 145–160.

Schrage, "Infamie" = E. J. H. Schrage, "Symon Vicentinus und die Infamie," *RIDA*³ 37 (1990) 385–417.

Schroff, *RE* matrona = Schroff, s.v. matrona, *RE* 28 (1930) 2300–2305.

Schuhmann, "Charakteristik" = E. Schuhmann, "Zur unterschiedlichen Charakteristik von *uxores* und *meretrices* in den Komödien des Plautus," in *Actes du VIIᵉ Congrès de la FIEL* 1 (Budapest 1983) 453–456.

Schulz, *Epitome* = F. Schulz, *Die Epitome Ulpiani des Codex Vaticanus Reginae 1128* (Bonn 1926).

Schulz, *Studium* = F. Schulz, *Einführung in das Studium der Digesten* (Tübingen 1916).

Schulze, *Eigennamen* = W. Schulze, *Geschichte der lateinischer Eigennamen* (Berlin 1966 repr. of Göttingen 1964 ed.).

Schumacher, *Servus Index* = L. Schumacher, *Servus Index: Sklavenverhör und Sklavenanzeige im republikanischen und kaiserzeitlichen Rom* (Wiesbaden 1982).

Schwarte, "Christengesetz" = K. H. Schwarte, "Das angebliche Christengesetz des Septimius Severus," *Historia* 12 (1963) 185–208.

Schwarz, *Condictio* = F. Schwarz, *Die Grundlage der Condictio im klassischen römischen Recht* (Münster and Cologne 1952).

Sciascia, "Escrava" = G. Sciascia, "A alienaçao da escrava com clausula *ne prostituatur* no direito romano," in *Varietà giuridiche* (Milan 1956) 103–109 (= *Investig.* 4.45 [1952] 57–64).

Scullard, *Festivals* = H. H. Scullard, *Festivals and Ceremonies of the Roman Republic* (Ithaca 1981).

Seckel/Meyer, "Gnomon" = E. Seckel (P. M. Meyer ed.), "Zum sog. Gnomon des Idioslogos," *SB Preuss. Ak. Wiss., phil.-hist. Kl.*, 26 (1928) 424–456.

Sehling, "Strafsystem" = E. Sehling, "Das Strafsystem der lex Julia de adulteriis," *SZ* 4 (1883) 160–163.

Seiler, "Ehe" = H. H. Seiler, "Römische Ehe und augusteische Ehegesetzgebung," in G. Seifert ed., *Ehestabilisierende Faktoren* (Göttingen 1990) 75–86.

Selb, "Edikt" = W. Selb, "Das prätorische Edikt: Vom rechtspolitischen Programm zur Norm," in H.-P. Benöhr ed., *Iuris Professio: Festgabe für M. Kaser zum 80. Geburtstag* (Vienna, Cologne, Graz 1986) 259–272.

Sensi, "Ornatus" = L. Sensi, "Ornatus e status sociale delle donne romane," *APer.* n.s. 18 (1980/1981) 53–102.

Seyrig, "Statut" = H. Seyrig, "Le statut de Palmyre," *Syria* 22 (1941) 155–175 (= *Ant. Syr.*³ 36 [1946] 142–161).

Shaw, "Believers" = B. D. Shaw, "Among the Believers," *EMC* 28 (1984) 453–479.

Shaw, "Economy" = B. D. Shaw, "The Divine Economy: Stoicism as Ideology," *Latomus* 44 (1985) 16–54.

Shaw, "Epigraphy" = B. D. Shaw, "Latin Funerary Epigraphy and Family Relations in the Later Empire," *Historia* 33 (1984) 457–497.

Shaw, "Family" = B. D. Shaw, "The Family in Late Antiquity: The Experience of Augustine," *P & P* 15 (1987) 3–51.

Shaw, "Meaning" = B. D. Shaw, "The Cultural Meaning of Death: Age and Gender in the Roman Family," in D. I. Kertzer and R. P. Saller eds., *The Family in Italy from Antiquity to the Present* (New Haven 1991) 66–90.

Sherwin-White, *Citizenship*² = A. N. Sherwin-White, *The Roman Citizenship*² (Oxford 1973).

Sherwin-White, *Pliny* = A. N. Sherwin-White, *The Letters of Pliny: A Historical and Social Commentary* (Oxford rev. ed. 1985).

Sherwin-White (rev. Bleicken) = A. N. Sherwin-White, (review of J. Bleicken, *Senatsgericht und Kaisergericht* [Göttingen 1962]), *JRS* 53 (1963) 203–205.

Sherwin-White, *Cos* = S. M. Sherwin-White, *Ancient Cos: An Historical Study from the Dorian Settlement to the Imperial Period* (Göttingen 1978).

Siber, "Ehegesetzgebung" = H. Siber, "Die Ehegesetzgebung des Augustus: Inhalt, Ziel und Auswirkung," *Deutsche Rechtswissenschaft* 4 (1939) 156–167.

Siber, *RV* = H. Siber, *Römisches Verfassungsrecht in geschichtlicher Entwicklung* (Lahr 1952).

Sicari, *Prostituzione* = A. Sicari, *Prostituzione e tutela giuridica della schiava: Un problema di politica legislativa nell'impero romano* (Bari 1991).

Sigismund Nielsen, "Examen" = H. Sigismund Nielsen, "Ditis Examen Domus? On the Use of the Term *Verna* in the Roman Epigraphical and Literary Sources," *C & M* 42 (1991) 221–240.

Sijpesteijn, "Papyri" = P. J. Sijpesteijn, "Die chōris kyriou chrēmatizousai dikaiō teknōn in den Papyri," *Aegyptus* 45 (1965) 171–189.

Simshäuser, "Juridiction" = W. Simshäuser, "La juridiction municipale à la lumière de la *lex Irnitana*," *RHD* 67 (1989) 619–650.

Sirks, "Favour" = A. J. B. Sirks, "A Favour to Rich Freedwomen *(Libertinae)* in 51 A.D.: On Suet. *Claud.* 19 and the *Lex Papia*," *RIDA*³ 27 (1980) 282–294.

Sirks, "*Munera*" = A. J. B. Sirks, "*Munera Publica* and Exemptions (*Vacatio, Excusatio, and Immunitas*)," in J. Sobrequés and M. T. Peláez eds., *Studies in Roman Law and Legal History in Honour of R. Abadel I Vinyals on the Occasion of the Centenary* (Barcelona 1989) 79–111.

Smith, "Reforms" = R. E. Smith, "The Army Reforms of Septimius Severus," *Historia* 21 (1972) 481–500.

Smith, "Husband" = W. S. Smith, "Husband vs. Wife in Juvenal's Sixth Satire," *CW* 73 (1980) 323–332.

Sokala, "Effectiveness" = A. Sokala, "The Effectiveness of the ''Ne Prostituatur'' Clauses in Roman Law," *Eos* 81 (1993) 97–100.

Sokolowski, *LSCG* = F. Sokolowski, *Lois sacrées des cités grecques* (Paris 1969).

Solazzi, "*Caduca*" = S. Solazzi, "Attorno ai *Caduca*," *Scritti di diritto romano* 4 (Naples 1963) 265–379 (= *ANap*. 61 [1942] 71–225).

Solazzi, "Definizione" = S. Solazzi, "La definizione del procuratore," *Scritti di diritto romano* 2 (Naples 1957) 557–67 (= *RIL* 56 [1923] 142–156).

Solazzi, "Divieti" = S. Solazzi, "Sui divieti matrimoniali delle leggi augustee," *Scritti di diritto romano* 4 (Naples 1963) 81–98 (= *ANap*. 59 [1939] 269–290).

Solazzi, "Glosse" = S. Solazzi, "Glosse a Gaio I," *Scritti di diritto romano* 6 (Naples 1972) 153–267 (= *Studi Riccobono* 1 [1936] 73–191).

Solazzi, "Glossemi" = S. Solazzi, "Glossemi nelle fonti giuridiche romane," *Scritti di diritto romano* 4 (Naples 1963) 181–195 (= *BIDR* 46 [1939] 49–67).

Solazzi, "Manumissio" = S. Solazzi, "Manumissio ex mancipatione," *Scritti di diritto romano* 3 (Naples 1960) 199–218 (= *Athenaeum* 15 [1927] 101–32).

Solazzi, "Note" = S. Solazzi, "Note di Diritto Romano," *Scritti di diritto romano* 3 (Naples 1960) 587–672 (= *ANap.* 55 [1937] 1–110).

Solazzi, "Procurator ad litem" = S. Solazzi, "Il procurator ad litem," *Scritti di diritto romano* 5 (Naples 1972) 115–135 (= *ANap.* 62 [1949] 162–186).

Solazzi, "Storia" = S. Solazzi, "Per la storia della giurisprudenza romana," *Scritti di diritto romano* 4 (Naples 1963) 517–526 (= *AG* 133 [1946] 3–14).

Spagnuolo Vigorita, "Bona Caduca" = T. Spagnuolo Vigorita, "Bona Caduca e giurisdizione procuratoria agli inizi del terzo secolo d.C.," *Labeo* 24 (1978) 131–168.

Spagnuolo Vigorita, "Nota" = T. Spagnuolo Vigorita ed., *Paul Jörs: Iuliae Rogationes: due studi sulla legislazione matrimoniale augustea* (Antiqua 36) (Naples 1985).

Spagnuolo Vigorita, *Pernicies* = T. Spagnuolo Vigorita, *Exsecranda Pernicies: Delatori e fisco nell'età di Costantino* (Naples 1984).

Speidel, "Garrison" = M. P. Speidel, "Nubia's Roman Garrison," *ANRW* 2.10.1 (Berlin 1988) 767–798.

Sperber, "Centurion" = D. Sperber, "The Centurion as a Tax-Collector," *Latomus* 38 (1969) 186–188.

Stavely, "Iudex" = E. S. Stavely, "Iudex Selectus," *RhM* n.F. 96 (1953) 201–213.

Stead, "Model" = M. Stead, "A Model to Facilitate the Study of Temple Administration in Graeco-Roman Egypt," *Atti XVII cong. int. pap.* 3 (Naples 1984) 1045–1052.

Stein, *RR* = A. Stein, *Der römische Ritterstand: Ein Beitrag zur Personengeschichte des römischen Reiches* (Münch. Beitr. 10) (Munich 1927).

Steinwenter, *RE ius* = A. Steinwenter, s.v. ius liberorum, *RE* 10.2 (1919) 1281–1285.

Stone, *Road* = L. Stone, *The Road to Divorce: England, 1530–1987* (Oxford 1990).

Stroh, "Liebeskunst" = W. Stroh, "Ovids Liebeskunst und die Ehegesetze des Augustus," *Gymnasium* 86 (1979) 323–352.

Stroh, *Taxis* = W. Stroh, *Taxis und Taktik: Die advokatische Dispositionskunst in Ciceros Gerichtsreden* (Stuttgart 1975).

Sturm, "Quod datur" = F. Sturm, "Quod meretrici datur repeti non potest," *Iuris Professio: Festgabe für M. Kaser zum 80. Geburtstag* (Vienna, Cologne, Graz 1986) 281–288.

Sturm, "Weib" = F. Sturm, "Gesellschafterausgaben für Weib und Würfel," *Iura* 30 (1979) 78–83.

Sullivan, *Martial* = J. P. Sullivan, *Martial: The Unexpected Classic* (Cambridge 1991).

Sullivan, *Satyricon* = J. P. Sullivan, *The Satyricon of Petronius: A Literary Study* (Bloomington and London 1968).

Summers, *Instrumentalism* = R. S. Summers, *Instrumentalism and American Legal Theory* (Ithaca 1982).

Suolahti, *Censors* = J. Suolahti, *The Roman Censors: A Study on Roman Structure* (Helsinki 1963).

Swarney, "Status" = P. Swarney, "Social Status and Social Behavior as Criteria in Judicial Proceedings in the Late Republic," in B. Halpern and D. Hobson eds., *Law, Politics and Society in the Ancient Mediterranean World* (Sheffield 1993) 137–155.

Syme, *Ammianus* = R. Syme, *Ammianus and the Historia Augusta* (Oxford 1968).

Syme, *Clarity* = R. Syme, *The Historia Augusta: A Call of Clarity* (BHAF 8) (Bonn 1971).

Syme, "Controversy" = R. Syme, "Controversy Abating and Credulity Curbed?" in *Historia Augusta Papers* (Oxford 1983) 209–233 (= *London Rev. Books* [Sept. 4–17, 1980] 15ff.).

Syme, *Emperors* = R. Syme, *Emperors and Biography: Studies in the Historia Augusta* (Oxford 1971).

Syme, *History* = R. Syme, *History in Ovid* (Oxford 1978).

Syme, *RR* = R. Syme, *The Roman Revolution* (Oxford 1939).

Syme, *Tacitus* = R. Syme, *Tacitus* (2 vols.) (Oxford 1958).

Talamanca, *Compromissum* = M. Talamanca, *Ricerche in tema di compromissum* (Milan 1958).

Talamanca, *Schema* = M. Talamanca, *Lo schema genus-species nelle sistematiche dei giuristi romani* (*Accad. Naz. Lincei, Quad.* 221) (Rome 1977).

Talbert, *Senate* = R. J. A. Talbert, *The Senate of Imperial Rome* (Princeton 1984).

Teixidor, "Tarif" = J. Teixidor, "Le Tarif de Palmyre I: Un commentaire de la version palmyrénienne," *Aula Orientalis* 1 (1983) 235–252.

Thomas, "Accusatio" = J. A. C. Thomas, "Accusatio adulterii," *Iura* 12 (1961) 65–80.

Thomas, "Lex Julia" = J. A. C. Thomas, "Lex Julia de adulteriis coercendis," in *Études offertes à J. Macqueron* (Aix-en-Provence 1970) 637–644.

Thomas, "Prescription" = J. A. C. Thomas, "Prescription of Crimes in Roman Law," *RIDA*³ 9 (1962) 417–430.

Thomas, "Double Standard" = K. Thomas, "The Double Standard," *Journal of the History of Ideas* 20 (1959) 195–216.

Thomas, "Mariages" = Y. Thomas, "Mariages endogamiques à Rome: Patrimoine, pouvoir et parenté depuis l'époque archaïque," *RHD* 58 (1980) 345–382.

Thomasson, *Laterculi* = B. E. Thomasson, *Laterculi Praesidum* 1 (Göteborg 1984).

Tibiletti, "Tertulliano" = C. Tibiletti, "La donna in Tertulliano," in *Misoginia e maschilismo in Grecia e Roma* (Ist. fil. class. med. 71) (Genoa 1981) 69–85.

Toepffer, "Sakralgesetz" = J. Toepffer, "Koisches Sakralgesetz," in *Beiträge zur griechischen Altertumswissenschaft* (Berlin 1897) 204–229 (= *MDAIA* 16 [1891] 411–432 and *BCH* 16 [1892] 161–165).

Toher, "Augustus" = M. Toher, "Augustus and the Evolution of Roman Historiography," in Raaflaub and Toher, *BRE* (1990) 139–154.

Tomulescu, "Justinien" = C. S. Tomulescu, "Justinien et le concubinat," in *Studi in onore di G. Scherillo* 1 (Milan 1972) 299–326.

Torelli, *Lavinio* = M. Torelli, *Lavinio e Roma: Riti iniziatrici e matrimonio tra archeologia e storia* (Rome 1984).

Townend, *Poets* = G. Townend, *The Augustan Poets and the Permissive Society* (The Fifth Jackson Knight Memorial Lecture) (Abingdon-on-Thames 1972).

Tracy, "Leno" = V. A. Tracy, "The Leno-Maritus," *CJ* 72 (1976/1977) 62–64.

Treggiari, "*Concubinae*" = S. Treggiari, "*Concubinae,*" *PBSR* 49 (1981) 59–81.

Treggiari, "Divorce" = S. Treggiari, "Divorce Roman Style: How Easy and How Frequent Was it?" in Rawson, *Marriage* (1991) 31–46.

Treggiari, *Freedmen* = S. Treggiari, *Roman Freedmen during the Late Republic* (Oxford 1969).

Treggiari, "Jobs" = S. Treggiari, "Jobs for Women," *AJAH* 1 (1976) 76–104.

Treggiari, "Ladies" = S. Treggiari, "Libertine Ladies," *CW* 64 (1970/1971) 196–198.

Treggiari, *RM* = S. Treggiari, *Roman Marriage: Iusti Coniuges from the Time of Cicero to the Time of Ulpian* (Oxford 1991).

Treggiari, "Sentiment" = S. Treggiari, "Sentiment and Property: Some Roman Attitudes," in A. Parel and T. Flanagan eds., *Theories of Property: Aristotle to the Present* (Waterloo 1979) 53–85.

Treggiari, "Urban Labour" = S. Treggiari, "Urban Labour in Rome: *Mercennarii* and *Tabernarii*," in P. Garnsey ed., *Non-slave Labour in the Greco-Roman World* (1980) 48–64.

Treggiari, "Women as Property" = S. Treggiari, "Women as Property in the Early Roman Empire," in D. K. Weisberg, *Women and the Law: A Social Historical Perspective* 2 (Cambridge 1982) 7–33.

Trexler, "Prostitution" = R. C. Trexler, "La prostitution florentine au XVᵉ siècle," *Annales ESC* 36 (1981) 983–1015.

Turcan, *Tertullien* = M. Turcan ed., *Tertullien: Les spectacles* (Paris 1986).

Van Bremen, *Limits* = R. Van Bremen, *The Limits of Participation: Women and Civic Life in the Greek East in the Hellenistic and Roman Periods* (Amsterdam 1996).

Van de Wouw, "Libri" = J. A. C. J. Van de Wouw, "Papinians Libri Duo de Adulteriis: Versuch einer kritischen Palingenesie," *TR* 41 (1973) 311–324.

Van Effenterre, *Points de vue* = H. Van Effenterre ed., *Points de vue sur la fiscalité antique* (Paris 1979).

Vatin, *Mariage* = C. Vatin, *Recherches sur le mariage et la condition de la femme mariée à l'époque hellénistique* (Paris 1970).

Venturini, "*Accusatio*" = C. Venturini, "*Accusatio adulterii* e politica costantiniana (per un riesame di *CTh.* 9.7.2)," *SDHI* (1988) 65–109.

Venturini, *Crimen* = C. Venturini, *Studi sul crimen repetundarum nell'età repubblicana* (Milan 1979).

Venturini, "Divorzio" = C. Venturini, "Divorzio informale e *crimen adulterii* (per una riconsiderazione di D. 48.5.44[43])," *Iura* 41 (1990) 25–51.

Venturini, "*Manumissiones*" = C. Venturini, "Sulla legislazione augustea in materia di *manumissiones*," in *Sodalitas: Scritti in onore di A. Guarino* 5 (Naples 1984) 2455–2476.

Venturini, "Matrimonio" = C. Venturini, "Matrimonio, divorzio, ripudio: Premesse romanistiche ad una problematica attuale," *Nova Tellus* 6 (1988) 167–186.

Venturini, "Ripudianda" = C. Venturini, "La ripudianda (in margine a *CTh.* 3.16.1)," *BIDR*³ 30 (1988) 253–276.

Verdière, "Plaidoyer" = R. Verdière, "Plaidoyer pour Messaline," *Paideia* 44 (1989) 3–15.

Vigneron, "Loi" = R. Vigneron, "L'antifeministe loi Voconia et les *Schleichwege des Lebens*," *Labeo* 29 (1983) 140–153.

Villa, "Prostituzione" = R. Villa, "La prostituzione come problema storiografico," *Studi storici* 22 (1981) 305–314.

Villers, "Droit" = R. Villers, "Le droit romain, droit d'inégalite," *REL* 47 (1969) 462–481.

Villers, "Mariage" = R. Villers, "Le mariage envisagé comme institution d'État dans le droit classique de Rome," *ANRW* 2.14 (Berlin 1982) 285–301.

Vincenti, "Aspetti" = U. Vincenti, "Aspetti procedurali della *cognitio senatus*," *BIDR*³ 24 (1982) 101–126.

Vincenti, *Genera* = U. Vincenti, *Duo genera sunt testium: Contributo allo studio della prova testimoniale* (Padua 1989).

Vitali, "Premesse" = E. Vitali, "Premesse romanistiche a uno studio sull'*impedimentum criminis* (adulterio e divieti matrimoniali)," in *Studi in onore di G. Scherillo* 1 (Milan 1972) 275–298.

Vitucci, *Praefectura* = G. Vitucci, *Ricerche sulla praefectura urbi in età imperiale (sec. I–III)* (Rome 1956).

Voci, *DER* = P. Voci, *Diritto ereditario romano* 1² (Milan 1967), 2² (Milan 1963).

Voci, "*Diligentia*" = P. Voci, "*Diligentia, custodia, culpa:* I dati fondamentali," *SDHI* 56 (1990) 29–143.

Voci, *Obbligazioni* = P. Voci, *Le obbligazioni romane* 1.1 (Milan 1969).

Voci (rev. Longo) = P. Voci (review of Longo, *Delictum*), *Iura* 28 (1977) 216–219.

Volkmann, *Augustus*² = H. Volkmann, *Zur Rechtsprechung im Principat des Augustus: Historische Beiträge*² (Munich 1969).

Volterra, "*Accusatio*" = E. Volterra, "Per la storia dell'*accusatio iure mariti vel patris,*" *Studi economici e giuridici della Università di Cagliari* 17 (1928) 1–63 (= *SG* 1 [1991] 219–278).

Volterra, "*Compensazione*" = E. Volterra, "Sulla compensazione dei reati in diritto romano," *Temi Emiliani* 7.2 (1930) 1–11.

Volterra, "*Conventio*" = E. Volterra, "Nuove ricerche sulla *conventio in manum,*" *Mem. Acc. Lincei, Cl. sc. mor. stor. e fil.*, (ser. 8) 12.4 (1966) 251–355 (= *SG* 3 [1991] 3–107).

Volterra, "*D.* 48.5.44(43)" = E. Volterra, "Intorno a D. 48.5.44(43)," in *Studi in onore di B. Biondi* 2 (Milan 1965) 125–140 (= *SG* 2 [1991] 521–536).

Volterra, "*IM*" = E. Volterra, "*Iniustum matrimonium,*" in *Studi in onore di G. Scherillo* 2 (Milan 1972) 441–470 (= *SG* 3 [1991] 177–206).

Volterra, "*Innovazioni*" = E. Volterra, "Alcune innovazioni giustinianee al sistema classico di ripressione dell'adulterio," *Rendiconti del Reale Istituto Lombardo di Scienze e Lettere* 63 (1930) 3–11 (= *SG* 1 [1991] 329–337).

Volterra, *NNDI* SCC = E. Volterra, s.v. senatusconsulta, *NNDI* 16 (1969) 1047–1078.

Volterra, *SG* = E. Volterra (M. Talamanca ed.), *Scritti giuridici* 1–3 (Naples 1991), 4–5 (Naples 1993).

Vonglis, *Loi* = B. Vonglis, *La lettre et l'esprit de la loi dans la jurisprudence classique et la rhétorique* (Paris 1968).

Vööbus, *SRL* = A. Vööbus, *The Syro-Roman Lawbook* 1: *The Syriac Text with an Introduction* (Stockholm 1982), 2: *A Translation with Annotations* (Stockholm 1983).

Wacke, "*Potentiores*" = A. Wacke, "Die *Potentiores* in den Rechtsquellen: Einfluß und Abwehr gesellschaftlicher Übermacht in der Rechtspflege der Römer," *ANRW* 2.13 (Berlin 1980) 562–607.

Wacke, "*Manumissio*" = A. Wacke, "Manumissio matrimonii causa: Le mariage d'affranchies d'après les lois d'Auguste," *RHD* 67 (1989) 413–428.

Wacke, "*Vergehen*" = A. Wacke, Fahrlässige Vergehen im römischen Strafrecht," *RIDA*³ 26 (1979) 505–566.

Wagner, "*Freiheitserteilung*" = H. Wagner, "Zur Freiheitserteilung in den einem Generalpfandnexus unterliegenden Sklaven," *SDHI* 33 (1967) 163–188.

Wagner, *Generalverpfändung* = H. Wagner, *Voraussetzungen, Vorstufen und Anfänge der römischen Generalverpfändung* (Marburg 1968).

Waldstein, *Begnadigungsrecht* = W. Waldstein, *Untersuchungen zur römischen Begnadigungsrecht: Abolitio—Indulgentia—Venia* (Innsbruck 1964).

Waldstein, *Operae* = W. Waldstein, *Operae Libertorum: Untersuchungen zur Dienstpflicht freigelassener Sklaven* (Forsch. zur ant. Sklaverei 19) (Stuttgart 1986).

Waldstein, "*Stellung*" = W. Waldstein, "Zur Stellung der Frau im römischen Recht," in P. Handel and W. Meid eds., *Festschrift für R. Muth zum 65. Geburtstag* (Innsbruck 1983) 559–571.

Walkowitz, *Prostitution* = J. R. Walkowitz, *Prostitution and Victorian Society: Women, Class, and the State* (Cambridge 1980).

Wallace, *Taxation* = S. L. Wallace, *Taxation in Egypt from Augustus to Diocletian* (Princeton and London 1938).

Wallace-Hadrill, "Civilis Princeps" = A. Wallace-Hadrill, "Civilis Princeps: Between Emperor and King," *JRS* 72 (1982) 32–48.

Wallace-Hadrill, "Elites" = A. Wallace-Hadrill, "Elites and Trade in the Roman Town," in J. Rich and A. Wallace-Hadrill eds., *City and Country in the Ancient World* (London 1991) 241–272.

Wallace-Hadrill, "Family and Inheritance" = A. Wallace-Hadrill, "Family and Inheritance in the Augustan Marriage Laws," *PCPS* n.s. 27 (1981) 58–80.

Wallace-Hadrill, "Golden Age" = A. Wallace-Hadrill, "The Golden Age and Sin in Augustan Ideology," *P & P* 95 (1982) 19–36.

Wallace-Hadrill, *Houses* = A. Wallace-Hadrill, *Houses and Society in Pompeii and Herculaneum* (Princeton 1994).

Wallace-Hadrill, *Patronage* = A. Wallace-Hadrill ed., *Patronage in Ancient Society* (London 1989).

Wallace-Hadrill, "Propaganda" = A. Wallace-Hadrill, "Propaganda and Dissent? Augustan Moral Legislation and the Love Poets," *Klio* 67 (1985) 180–184.

Wallace-Hadrill, *Suetonius* = A. Wallace-Hadrill, *Suetonius: The Scholar and His Caesars* (New Haven 1983).

Wallace-Hadrill, "Virtues" = A. Wallace-Hadrill, "The Emperor and His Virtues," *Historia* 30 (1981) 298–323.

Ward, *Harlots* = B. Ward, *Harlots of the Desert: A Study of Repentance in Early Monastic Sources* (Oxford 1987).

Watson, *"Enuptio"* = A. Watson, *"Enuptio gentis,"* in A. Watson ed., *Daube Noster: Essays in Legal History for David Daube* (Edinburgh and London 1974) 331–341.

Watson, *LM* = A. Watson, *Law Making in the Later Roman Republic* (Oxford 1974).

Watson, *Obligations* = A. Watson, *The Law of Obligations in the Later Roman Republic* (Oxford 1965).

Watson, *Persons* = A. Watson, *The Law of Persons in the Later Roman Republic* (Oxford 1967).

Watson, *Slave Law* = A. Watson, *Roman Slave Law* (Baltimore 1987).

Watson, *Soldier* = G. R. Watson, *The Roman Soldier* (Ithaca 1969).

Weaver, "Children" = P. R. C. Weaver, "Children of Freedmen (and Freedwomen)," in B. Rawson ed., *Marriage, Divorce and Children in Ancient Rome* (Oxford 1991) 166–190.

Weaver, *FC* = P. R. C. Weaver, *Familia Caesaris: A Social Study of the Emperor's Freedmen and Slaves* (Cambridge 1972).

Webber and Wildavsky, *History of Taxation* = C. Webber and A. Wildavsky, *A History of Taxation and Expenditure in the Western World* (New York 1986).

Weber, "Freigelassene" = E. Weber, "Freigelassene—eine diskriminierte Randgruppe?" in Weiler, *SRAA* (1988) 257–265.

Weiler, "Randgruppen" = I. Weiler, "Soziale Randgruppen in der antiken Welt: Einführung und wissenschaftsgeschichtliche Aspekte," in Weiler, *SRAA* (1988) 11–40.

Weiler, *SRAA* = I. Weiler ed., *Soziale Randgruppen und Außenseiter in Altertum: Referate vom Symposion "Soziale Randgruppe und antike Sozialpolitik" in Graz (21 bis 23 September 1987)* (Graz 1988).

Weiler, "Verhalten" = I. Weiler, "Abweichendes Verhalten von Außenseitern und soziale Randgruppen: Ansätze zu einer Theoriebildung im Altertum, dargestellt vor allem am Beispiel der Kyniker," in Weiler, *SRAA* (1988) 177–189.

Wesel, *Statuslehre* = U. Wesel, *Rhetorische Statuslehre und Gesetzesauslegung der römischen Juristen* (Cologne 1967).

Wessner, *RE* Acron = Wessner, s.v. Helenius Acron, *RE* 7.2 (1912) 2840–2844.

West, "Cost" = L. C. West, "The Cost of Living in Roman Egypt," *CP* 11 (1916) 293–314.

West and Johnson, *Currency* = L. C. West and A. C. Johnson, *Currency in Roman and Byzantine Egypt* (Amsterdam 1967 repr. of Princeton 1944 ed.).

White, *Heracles' Bow* = J. B. White, *Heracles' Bow: Essays on the Rhetoric and Poetics of the Law* (Madison 1985).

Whitehorne, "Ovid" = J. E. G. Whitehorne, "Ovid *AA* 1.101–132, and Soldiers' Marriages," *LCM* 4.8 (1979) 157–158.

Whitehorne, "Sex" = J. E. G. Whitehorne, "Sex and Society in Greco-Roman Egypt," *Actes du XVᵉ Congrès International de Papyrologie* 4 (1979) 240–246.

Whittaker, "Circe's Pigs" = C. R. Whittaker, "Circe's Pigs: From Slavery to Serfdom in the Later Roman World," *Slavery & Abolition* 8 (1987) 88–122 (= M. I. Finley ed., *Classical Slavery* [London 1987]).

Wieacker, "OW" = F. Wieacker, "Offene Wertungen bei den römischen Juristen," *Ausgewählte Schriften* 1 (Frankfurt am Main 1983) 174–204 (= *SZ* 94 [1977] 1–42).

Wieacker, *RRG* = F. Wieacker, *Römische Rechtsgeschichte 1: Quellenkunde, Rechtsbildung, Jurisprudenz und Rechtsliteratur* (Munich 1988).

Wieacker, *Textstufen* = F. Wieacker, *Textstufen klassischer Juristen* (Göttingen 1975 repr. of Göttingen 1959 ed.).

Wiedemann, *Emperors* = T. E. J. Wiedemann, *Emperors and Gladiators* (London 1992).

Wiedemann, "Regularity" = T. E. J. Wiedemann, "The Regularity of Manumission at Rome," *CQ* n.s. 35 (1985) 162–175.

Wilcken, *GO* = U. Wilcken, *Griechische Ostraka aus Aegypten und Nubien: Ein Beitrag zur antiken Wirtschaftsgeschichte* (2 vols.) (Amsterdam 1970 repr. of Berlin and Leipzig 1899 ed.).

Wilinski, "Aestimatio" = A. Wilinski, "Zur *litis aestimatio* in den *bonae fidei iudicia,*" *Index* 3 (1972) 443–453.

Wilinski, "Alienazione" = A. Wilinski, "Ricerche sull'alienazione degli schiavi nel diritto romano: Vendita dello schiavo con la clausola ne manumittatur," *Index* 5 (1974/1975) 321–330 (= [in summary] "Aliénation" = "Études sur l'aliénation d'esclaves en droit romain privé: Vente d'esclaves avec la clause prohibant l'affranchissement," *Annales Univ. Lublin* 19.2 sectio G [1972] 29–52 [in Polish; summaries in Russian (49–50) and French (50–52)]).

Williams, "Maecenas" = G. Williams, "Did Maecenas 'Fall From Favor'? Augustan Literary Patronage," in Raaflaub and Toher, *BRE* (1990) 258–275.

Williams, "Individuality" = W. Williams, "Individuality in the Imperial Constitutions: Hadrian and the Antonines," *JRS* 66 (1976) 67–83.

Willrich, "Caligula" = H. Willrich, "Caligula," *Klio* 3 (1903) 85–118, 288–317, 397–470.

Wilson, *Clothing* = L. M. Wilson, *The Clothing of the Ancient Romans* (Baltimore 1938).

Wilson, *Toga* = L. M. Wilson, *The Roman Toga* (Baltimore 1924).

Wiseman, "Definition" = T. P. Wiseman, "The Definition of "Eques Romanus" in the Late Republic and Early Empire," *Historia* 19 (1970) 67–83 (= *Roman Studies: Literary and Historical* [Liverpool 1987] 57–73).

Wiseman, *New Men* = T. P. Wiseman, *New Men in the Roman Senate, 139 B.C.–A.D. 14* (Oxford 1971).

Wissowa, *RE* Floralia = G. Wissowa, s.v. Floralia, *RE* 6.2 (1909) 2749–2752.

Wissowa, *Religion*² = G. Wissowa, *Religion und Kultus der Römer*² (Munich 1912).

Witke, *Latin Satire* = C. Witke, *Latin Satire: The Structure of Persuasion* (Leiden 1970).

Wittmann, *Körperverletzung* = R. Wittmann, *Die Körperverletzung an Freien im klassischen römischen Recht* (Munich 1972).

Wittmann (rev. Wilinski) = R. Wittmann (review of Wilinski, "Aliénation"), *SZ* 91 (1974) 539–540.

Wlosok, "Scham" = A. Wlosok, "Nihil nisi ruborem: Über die Rolle der Scham in der römischen Rechtskultur," *GB* 9 (1980) 155–172.

Wolff, "Benigniora" = H. J. Wolff, "In dubiis benigniora (D. 50.17.16)," *Seminar* 9 (1951) 36–49.

Wolff, "Wirksamkeit" = H. J. Wolff, "Zur Wirksamkeit des Eheverbots für römische Soldaten," in A. Biscardi et al. eds., *Mnēmē G. A. Petropoulos* (Athens 1984) 79–84.

Wolodkiewicz, "*Mater familias*" = W. Wolodkiewicz, "Attorno al significato della nozione di *mater familias*," in *Studi in onore di C. Sanfilippo* 3 (Milan 1983) 735–756.

Wubbe, "Benignus" = F. B. J. Wubbe, "Benignus Redivivus," in J. A. Ankum et al. eds., *Symbolae Iuridicae et Historicae M. David Dedicatae* 1 (Leiden 1968) 238–262.

Wubbe, "Humanitas" = F. B. J. Wubbe, "L'*humanitas* de Justinien," *TR* 58 (1990) 249–262.

Wubbe, "Interpretatio" = F. B. J. Wubbe, "Benigna Interpretatio als Entscheidungskriterium," in F. Horak and W. Waldstein eds., *Festgabe für A. Herdlitczka* (Munich and Salzburg 1972) 295–315.

Wyatt-Brown, *Honor* = B. Wyatt-Brown, *Southern Honor: Ethics and Behavior in the Old South* (New York and Oxford 1982) (= [in abridged form] *Honor and Violence in the Old South* [New York and Oxford 1986]).

Yavetz, *Plebs* = Z. Yavetz, *Plebs and Princeps* (New Brunswick rev. ed. 1988).

Youtie, "*Apatores*" = H. C. Youtie, "*Apatores*: Law vs. Custom in Roman Egypt," *Scriptiunculae Posteriores* 1 (Bonn 1981) 17–34 (= *Le monde grec: Hommages à C. Préaux* [Brussels 1975] 723–740).

Youtie, "Publicans" = H. C. Youtie, "Publicans and Sinners," *Scriptiunculae* 1 (Amsterdam 1973) 554–578 (= [with notes] *Michigan Alumnus* 43 [1937] 650–662; *ZPE* 1 [1967] 1–20).

Zablocka, "Costituzione" = M. Zablocka, "La costituzione del *cognitor* nel processo romano classico," *Index* 12 (1984/1985) 140–156.

Zablocka, "*Ius*" = M. Zablocka, "Il *ius trium liberorum* nel diritto romano," *BIDR*³ 30 (1988) 361–390.

Zablocka, "Modifiche" = M. Zablocka, "Le modifiche introdotte nelle leggi matrimoniali augustee sotto la dinastia giulio-claudia," *BIDR*³ 28 (1986) 379–410.

Zahrnt, "Fiskalgesetz" = M. Zahrnt, "Zum Fiskalgesetz von Palmyra und zur Geschichte der Stadt in hadrianischer Zeit," *ZPE* 62 (1986) 279–283.

Zanker, *Power of Images* = P. Zanker (A. Shapiro trans.), *The Power of Images in the Age of Augustus* (Ann Arbor 1988).

Ziegler, *Augustus* = H.-D. Ziegler, *Untersuchungen zur Strafrechtsgesetzgebung des Augustus* (Diss. Munich 1964).

Ziehen, *Leges* = L. Ziehen, *Leges Graecorum Sacrae e Titulis Collectae* 2 (Leipzig 1906).

Zilletti, "Note" = U. Zilletti, "Note sulla *restitutio in integrum damnatorum*," in *Studi in onore di G. Grosso* 2 (Turin 1968) 33–93.

Zubar, "Taurike" = V. M. Zubar, "Zur römischen Militärorganisation auf der Taurike in der zweiten Hälfte des 2. und am Anfang des 3. Jahrhunderts," *Historia* 44.2 (1995) 192–203.

Zucca, "Venus" = R. Zucca, "*Venus Erycina* tra Sicilia, Africa e Sardegna," in A. Mastino ed., *L'Africa romana* 6 (Sassari 1989) 771–779.

Index of Sources

Literary Sources

Epigraphical and Papyrological Sources

118　47	138–139　33	7–9　66, 67
122–123　33, 100	139–141　37	11–15　66
123　33, 100, 102	144　37	14–15　66
133–134　33	*Tabula Larinas*	16　93
135–142　37	6–9　218	

Legal Sources

Gai Institutiones	15.3–4　73	323　49
1.13–14　306	15.3　73	*Collatio*
1.13　331	16.1　74	1.11.1–4　235
1.15　331	16.1a　73	3.3.1–3　307
1.18–19　86	16.2　94, 112	3.3.2　307
1.19　315	16.3　74	3.3.4–6　308
1.25–27　331	16.4　73	4.2.2　142
1.29–30　81	17.1　74, 101	4.3.1–4　204
1.39　315	17.2　74	4.3.2　204
1.53　307, 308	17.3–4　74	4.3.4　204
1.71–72　81	20.14　331	4.3.6　205, 247
1.80　81	22.2　331	4.4.1–2　59, 60, 207
1.113　239	26.8　109, 110	4.4.2　58, 59
1.145　77	29.2–3　80	4.5　59, 60, 207
2.111　73, 77	29.3　76	4.12.3　99, 204
2.144　74	29.6–7　75	4.12.7　170
2.206–208　73	29.7　80	5.2.2　142
2.286　74	*Pauli Sententiae*	9.2.2　47, 61
2.286a　73, 74	1.2.1　49	9.2.3　62
3.39–54　77	2.26.3　178, 238	14.3.3　247
3.42　75	2.26.4　99, 204	*Codex Theodosianus*
3.47　76, 346	2.26.8　179	4.6.3　78
3.49–54　75	2.26.11　198	8.16.1　78, 91
3.74–76　331	2.26.12　313, 236	8.17.1　78
3.194　244	2.26.14　142, 143	8.17.2　78
4.182　47	2.26.16　196, 313, 314	8.17.3　78
Frag. de iure fisci	2.31.31　314	9.7.1　150, 198
3　74	2.26.31　314, 326	9.7.2　145
Tituli ex corpore Ulpiani	4.9　110	11.36.4　143
1.11　331	4.9.1　77	15.1.36　272
1.12–13a　86	4.9.7　77	15.7.12　171
1.21　73, 74	5.4.14　185	15.8.1　305
6.12　142	*Fragmenta Vaticana*	15.8.2　305
6.13　145	6　290, 295, 311	16.10.16　272
11.20　81, 94	18　321	16.10.18　272
13.1–2　72, 91, 240, 305	168　72, 75	*Novellae Posttheod.*
13.1　86, 99	197　75, 76	Theod. 18　136, 250, 251,
13.2　72, 92, 123, 143	198　75, 76	305
14　74	247　75	18 pr.　255, 272
15.1　73, 95	320　50	SYRO-ROMAN LAWBOOK
15.2　73	322　49	L. 9, P. 4　120

Corpus Iuris Civilis

Institutiones	1.10 pr.　81	4.10 pr.　49
1.8.2 (= D. 1.6.2 = *Coll.*	2.10.6　63	4.13.11(10)　52
3.3.1–3)　307	3.3　110	4.18.4　143, 181

Index of Persons

Includes characters in literature and mythology.

Cornelius Scipio Aemilianus, P., 28, 40, 43
Cornelius Scipio Asiagenus, L., 35
Cornelius Sulla, L. (dictator), 35, 89, 141
Creticus (in Juvenal), 164

Demea (in Terence's *Adelphoe*), 327
Dio Cassius (historian), 86
Dio Chrysostom (writer), 135
Diocletian (emperor), 136, 219–220, 226,
  253, 311, 313
Dionysius of Halicarnassus (historian), 28,
  331
Domitian (emperor)
  and his *correctio morum,* 5, 32, 42, 106–
    120
  promulgates *lex Lati,* 35
  punishes *feminae probrosae,* 96, 106–120,
    126, 184, 339
  removes equestrian from roll of *iudices,*
    106–107, 237
  revives adultery law, 106–120, 247
Domitius Ahenobarbus, Cn. (censor in 115
  B.C.), 41
Domitius Corbulo, Cn., 283
Draco, 235–236

Elagabalus (emperor), 254, 273
Euergetes II (of Egypt), 276
Eunapius (historian), 269

Fabius Cilo (L. Fabius Cilo, urban prefect),
  302, 308–309
Fabius Gurges (Q. Fabius Maximus Gurges),
  170
Fabulla, 164
Fadia (wife of Antony), 85
Faecenia Hispala (prostitute), 86–89
Flora (prostitute), 88
Florentius (Flavius Florentius, praetorian
  prefect), 271
Fortuna Virilis, 25
Fulvia (Catilinarian), 58

Gabba, 182–183
Galerius Trachalus, P. (cos. in A.D. 68), 95
Gallienus (emperor), 254. *See also* Valerian
Gellius Poplicola, L., 85
Germanicus Caesar, 251, 283
Gracchi (brothers), 79
Gracchus. *See* Sempronius

Hadrian (emperor)
  denies adulteresses *capacitas* with regard to
    military wills, 116–120
  grants Palmyra discretion in taxation, 283
  legislates (perhaps) against abuse of slaves,
    305, 312

legislates on interest of class of slave
  owners, 308
legislates through *interpretatio,* 294
legislates on *ne serva prostituatur,* 293–
  295, 299
Herennius Rufinus, 187–189
Horace (Q. Horatius Flaccus, poet), 165, 246,
  342
Hortensia, 255
Hortensius Hortalus, M., 84, 111
Hostilius Mancinus, A., 60, 201, 327

Isidore of Seville (writer), 167–168
Isis, 24
Iunius Brutus, M. (praetor in 44 B.C.), 51
Iunius Q. Vibius Crispus, L. (cos. I suff.
  before A.D. 60), 95

Julia (Iulia, daughter of Augustus), 168–170,
  234
Julian (Salvius Iulianus, jurist), 111, 188, 332
Julius Caesar (C. Iulius Caesar, dictator)
  assigns remainder of *ager Campanus,* 79
  changes tax-collection for cities of Asia,
    258, 285
  divorces Pompeia, 13, 192
  drops third decury of jurors, 31
  legislates (perhaps) on *vis,* 62
  makes generous gifts to mistresses, 185
  regulates membership in order of
    decurions, 32, 35
  supervises morals, 79
Juno Lucina, 25
Justin Martyr, 255, 268–269, 273
Justinian (emperor)
  assumes that mothers leave property to
    their children, 110
  and his compilers, 7, 53, 124–125, 177,
    222, 234, 237, 298, 304, 320
  legislates against abuse of slaves, 307
  legislates on adultery, 171, 179, 246
  legislates on concubines and children, 317
  legislates on *ne serva prostituatur,* 290,
    295, 305–306
  and the redemption of prostitutes, 132
  and Theodora, 193
Juvenal (D. Iunius Iuvenalis, satirist), 169

Labeo (M. Antistius Labeo, jurist), 50, 134,
  151, 324, 333
Laberius, D., 29, 42
Leo I (emperor), 273–274, 306
Licinii Luculli, M. et L. (brothers), 193
Licinius (emperor), 269
Licinius Mucianus, C. (governor of Syria,
  A.D. 68–69), 259, 266, 283–286
Livia (wife of Augustus), 82, 77, 192, 230

Index of Subjects

abolitio, 90, 228, 237
acting, 291, 312
actio de eo quod metus causa factum erit,
    190, 205
actio de servo corrupto, 196, 314,
    326–327
actio iniuriarum, 315
actors
    admitted as honorary decurions, 36
    and citizen status, 16
    declassed by censors, 41–43, 52
    excluded from criminal accusations, 59
    excluded from decurionate, 33–34, 37
    excluded by the *lex Roscia,* 29
    excluded from *postulare,* 46
    ineligible for benefits under the *lex Iulia et*
        Papia, 76, 80
    liable to the *ius occidendi,* 203
    punished by Augustus, 210
actors, actresses
    difficult to study, 9
    and earnings, 279
    expelled (?) from Rome, 41–42
    forbidden (perhaps) to perform at Rome, 41–
        42
    as a marginal type, 14, 16, 23, 347
    and their children prohibited by *lex Iulia et*
        Papia from marrying senatorials, 91–94,
        99–100

actresses
    alleged to be raped with impunity, 326
    forbidden to wear the habit of nuns, 171
    ranked (in error) among *feminae probrosae,*
        5, 96, 107, 116
    ranked (in error) among women exempted
        under *lex Iulia* on adultery, 195, 198
adlectio, 30
adoption, 122
adsectari, 331–335
adulterae, 106–120, 156–171, 334–335
adulteri, 174, 176–179, 183
adulterium, 106–120, 344–346
adultery. *See adulterium*
advocatus, 45, 48
aediles
    and criminal prosecutions, 141, 201–202
    enforce regulations on clothing, 161, 201–
        202
    oversee brothels, 60, 201–202, 327, 343
    register prostitutes, 201–202, 217–218, 280,
        340, 342, 345
aequitas, 318
aerarii, 40–41, 44
aerarium, 73, 255, 272
affectio, 293, 298, 304, 314–316, 336
Agrigentum, 35
Alexandria, 201
alimenta, 83, 111